D0246660

THE ATLAS OF BREEDING BIRDS
IN BRITAIN AND IRELAND

The Atlas of Breeding Birds
in Britain and Ireland

Compiled by

J. T. R. SHARROCK

British Trust for Ornithology
Irish Wildbird Conservancy

PUBLISHED BY

T. & A. D. Poyser

ATLAS WORKING GROUP

I. J. Ferguson-Lees (chairman) (1967–76)
Dr J. J. M. Flegg (1969–75)
R. A. O. Hickling (1973–76)
The late D. J. Munns (1967–73)
Dr F. H. Perring (1967–76)
Trevor Poyser (1974–76)
Dr J. T. R. Sharrock (1969–76)
Dr D. W. Snow (1967–69)
Robert Spencer (1975–76)
Kenneth Williamson (1967–76)

ORGANISER OF SURVEY

Dr J. T. R. Sharrock

TEXTS

Dr J. T. R. Sharrock, L. A. Batten, Dr J. J. M. Flegg, H. B. Ginn,
D. E. Glue, Robert Hudson, C. J. Mead, R. A. Morgan, A. J. Prater,
Robert Spencer and Kenneth Williamson

EDITING

Kenneth Williamson (principal editor), I. J. Ferguson-Lees and
Dr J. T. R. Sharrock, assisted by Robert Hudson, G. R. Humphreys,
C. J. Mead, Major R. F. Ruttledge, David Scott and Robert Spencer

MAP PRODUCTION

Biological Records Centre, Institute of Terrestrial Ecology,
Monks Wood Experimental Station

ADDITIONAL MAPS AND FIGURES

Brenda Hudson and L. A. Batten

ILLUSTRATIONS

Robert Gillmor, Leslie Baker, Hilary Burn, C. J. F. Coombs,
Crispin Fisher, P. J. Grant, R. A. Richardson, D. A. Thelwell,
Donald Watson and Ian Willis

PRODUCTION AND DESIGN

Trevor Poyser

Contents

Foreword

by JAMES FERGUSON-LEES

This book represents a giant step forward in our knowledge of the distributions of British and Irish birds. It is by far the biggest co-operative effort ever undertaken by field ornithologists in these islands, indeed probably anywhere in the world, which will stand for many years as a tribute to the enthusiasm and industry of a large number of people. It is the outcome of fieldwork by an estimated 10,000 to 15,000 observers, organised regionally by a dedicated band of around 150 ornithologists who have lived with the project in all its stages for nine exhausting but exciting years of encouragement, recording, checking and double-checking. The scheme has been administered centrally by national organisers in both countries, backed by a small working group whose job it has been to plan, guide and take policy decisions. At a much later stage, the book itself has been the result of intensive work by some 30 people who are credited on page 5. The British Trust for Ornithology and the Irish Wildbird Conservancy have every reason to be proud of what has been achieved.

Before 1950, there were few attempts at mapping bird distributions, except locally or for individual species. *Birds of the Soviet Union* edited by G. P. Dementiev and N. A. Gladkov (1951–54), *A Field Guide to the Birds of Britain and Europe* by Roger Peterson, Guy Mountfort and P. A. D. Hollom (1954) and *Atlas of European Birds* by K. H. Voous (1960) were the first extensive attempts at such maps for Europe, though inevitably based on incomplete data with scales so small that much of Britain and Ireland were filled in even where species were very local. Then, after researches by J. L. F. Parslow and others for the British Ornithologists' Union's *The Status of Birds in Britain and Ireland* (1971), that author was able to draw more comprehensive and larger-scale maps of these islands for the Reader's Digest *Book of British Birds* (1969) and *The Birds of Britain with North Africa and the Middle East*, by Hermann Heinzel, Richard Fitter and John Parslow (1972). About the same time, amended versions of the same maps, many of them altered and some completely revised in the light of preliminary information from the fieldwork for the present *Atlas*, were used by Bruce Campbell and myself in *A Field Guide to Birds' Nests* (1972) and, with further updating, by John Parslow in *Breeding Birds of Britain and Ireland* (1973). All these works, however, relied largely on the method of joining known localities on the limits of ranges and were able to take little account of gaps or isolated pockets of distribution; more significantly, they were also based mainly on subjective assessments rather than objective surveys.

Nevertheless, the first steps had already been taken in a quite different technique for recording bird distribution. In 1960, C. A. Norris, later president of the BTO, published a paper entitled 'The breeding dis-

tributions of thirty bird species in 1952' (*Bird Study* 7: 129–184). This was based on a survey carried out in 1952, following a pilot scheme in the W Midlands on 100 species in 1950; it plotted the British and Irish ranges of 30 species selected to illustrate different types of distribution and, while the pilot study had been based on rural district council areas, it used what was a new standard in ornithology, at least at the national level—the 25-km squares of the National Grid. The distributions shown were somewhat patchy and were still the result of subjective opinion, not objective fieldwork, but this was undoubtedly the seed from which the present *Atlas* developed. The following sentence in that paper is worth quoting: 'No survey of this kind can hope to cover every corner of the British Isles and the absence of competent and willing observers and organisers must for many a year continue to detract from the value of field work of this kind.' How quickly that statement has been confounded. Then, in 1966, a paper by Ian Prestt, now director of the Royal Society for the Protection of Birds, and A. A. Bell appeared under the title 'An objective method of recording breeding distributions of common birds of prey in Britain' (*Bird Study* 13: 277–283); this was the first ornithological publication based on the now familiar 10-km squares.

Although the 1950 pilot survey in the W Midlands 'had used, probably for the first time, a new technique which relied on the opinion of selected observers with special knowledge of their districts', the concept of dividing a country into units, and mapping on presence or absence, was by no means without precedent in the botanical field. As far back as 1860–80, a German—Hermann Hoffmann—invented his own grid reference system for central Europe and mapped certain plants. Even in Britain, R. D'O. Good showed the distribution of the lizard orchid on a grid basis as long ago as 1936, and some of the 'New Naturalist' volumes included such maps from 1945 onwards. Other authors used vice-counties and, in 1932, G. B. Blaker had surveyed Barn Owls *Tyto alba* by 10-mile squares (see pages 250, 460).

Then, in 1962, came the publication by the Botanical Society of the British Isles of the *Atlas of the British Flora*, by F. H. Perring and S. M. Walters. This mapped plant distributions by presence or absence within each 10-km square of the National Grid. It pointed the way for a similarly comprehensive and equally objective mapping of distributions of breeding birds, but several years of doubts and worries were to pass before the plunge was taken. Although 1,500 botanists had managed to plot the distributions of some 2,000 plant species over ten years, this seemed much too long a period for birds, whose ranges are constantly changing; it was also felt that ornithologists, despite being far more numerous, would

9

have great difficulty in coping with a mere 200 or so species because of the mobility of birds, their diversity of distribution and, above all, the problem of proving breeding.

For over two years, the possibility of an *Atlas of Breeding Birds* was discussed regularly by both the Council and the Scientific Advisory Committee of the BTO. There was a seemingly irreconcilable division of opinion between the optimists and enthusiasts on the one hand and the pessimists and diffidents on the other, the latter believing that such a project was doomed to failure through inadequate coverage. Individual ornithologists consulted were equally divided. Even the optimists said that, because of the uneven spread of observers and their scarcity or absence in remoter areas, the best coverage that could be expected was 90% in England, 50% in Wales and a mere 25% in Scotland; the pessimists were putting these estimates much lower. Furthermore, nearly everyone thought that the coverage would be so thin in Ireland that nothing should be attempted in that country. How wrong we all were.

Some ornithologists also considered that the whole concept lacked sufficient scientific merit to justify its being undertaken at all, but in this direction the majority were agreed in regarding it as a potentially invaluable tool for conservation and of considerable importance as a permanent record, for future comparison, of bird distributions at a time of great environmental change. Eventually, after sample fieldwork in 1966 and 1967, the Council of the BTO decided to proceed and on 30th September 1967 appointed an Atlas Working Group to supervise the organisation. As one of the Council members who had strongly advocated making the attempt, I was asked to be its chairman. It was a daunting task, but an exciting one, and I feel privileged to have been so closely involved with the project from beginning to end. The members of the Atlas Working Group are listed on page 5, but I must make mention here of the late D. J. Munns, then also a Council member, whose help and advice were invaluable until his sad death in 1973. He was able to speak from personal experience during the planning stages because a survey of the breeding birds of Staffordshire, Warwickshire and Worcestershire by 10-km squares had already been started by the West Midland Bird Club. This resulted in the publication in 1970 of the *Atlas of Breeding Birds of the West Midlands*, by J. Lord and D. J. Munns. Once again, following the example of C. A. Norris in 1950–60, the W Midlands had shown the way.

It was decided that five years was the shortest period in which a worthwhile picture could be obtained and, contrary to the general feeling about the practicability of including Ireland, it was agreed that the IWC must be encouraged to take part. After being launched by R. C. Homes, then president of the BTO, in *BTO News* in February 1968, the scheme was co-ordinated for that year by members of the Trust's regular staff, first Dr D. W. Snow and then Mr and Mrs C. J. Mead. At the end of 1968, thanks to a substantial grant from the Leverhulme Trust, later supplemented by another, it became possible to appoint Dr J. T. R. Sharrock as full-time national

organiser. In March 1972, a sizeable grant was also made by the Republic of Ireland's Department of Lands and the project became officially, as it already had been informally, under the joint sponsorship of the BTO and the IWC. Let there be no misunderstanding, however, about the size of the BTO's own financial contribution. The central running of the scheme has cost at least £30,000 which, thanks to rampant inflation, was only partly met by the various grants; and this takes no account of the time spent on it by the Trust's staff (particularly in revising and editing texts) or by the Biological Records Centre at Monks Wood (map production), let alone by the regional organisers and so many others. Certain IWC members have also put in countless hours at the various stages.

Acknowledgements are made elsewhere in the book, but I must express here my personal gratitude to Tim Sharrock and also to David Scott who acted, unpaid, as his counterpart in the Republic of Ireland throughout the duration of the project. Without their drive and energy, their tireless attention to detail and, not least, their constant encouragement and sometimes coercion of all concerned, this *Atlas* could not have been anything like the huge success that we are sure it both has been in completeness and will be in popularity. They would be the first to admit, however, that they could have achieved little without the vast army of fieldworkers, the network of regional organisers, and the enormous amount of time given to the project by various other individuals. Also, it has meant a great deal to Tim, through eight long and difficult years, to have the constant understanding and practical assistance of his wife, Erika.

We must beware of losing sight of those who put in so much effort during the actual survey, particularly the regional organisers listed on pages 14–16; in some cases, the work they did amounted to far more than the contributions of the team responsible for the actual production of the book, who are set out on page 5. In the latter category, however, I cannot let pass this opportunity of thanking the BTO staff in its entirety and the IWC personnel for the way in which they rose to the occasion in writing, rewriting, commenting on and editing the texts against the maps. In particular, Kenneth Williamson, Robert Hudson, C. J. Mead and Robert Spencer at Beech Grove and David Scott, Major R. F. Ruttledge and G. R. Humphreys in Ireland all achieved prodigious deeds on an extremely tight schedule. At the same time, bearing in mind that there are over a quarter of a million dots in this book, the map production would have been a tedious process without the staff of the Biological Records Centre at Monks Wood, especially Dr F. H. Perring, Henry Arnold, John Heath and Miss Diana Scott. Equally, the BTO's decision to undertake the actual publication itself would have seemed far more daunting if it had not been possible to draw on the expertise of Trevor Poyser in the fields of design and production.

When I think back to the estimates of coverage forecast in 1966–67—as low, it will be remembered, as 25% in Scotland and even worse in Ireland—it is clear that thousands of people deserve a pat on the back. In the event, every single one of the 3,862 10-

km squares in Britain and Ireland was surveyed for this *Atlas*, a remarkable achievement. Obviously, the depth of the survey varied quite considerably. In some cases, a whole square had to be worked in a single day while, at the other end of the scale, Tim Sharrock and I spent over 200 hours in TL14 in 1968 and 1969, assessing the problems and trying out different techniques. Where distant squares could be visited only briefly, it meant inevitably that confirmation of breeding was much more difficult to obtain and that some secretive or local birds were missed. For most species, however, coverage has been nearly complete throughout the two countries; for the rest, it is more than adequate to show the pattern of distribution. The end-product exceeds our wildest dreams of ten years ago.

Nor is this really the end, but rather the beginning of an era. It has long been envisaged that, if successful, the present *Atlas* should be the first of a series at intervals of, say, 25 years so that changes in bird distribution in Britain and Ireland can be periodically monitored. A lot may happen in 25 years: in 1951, few ornithologists would have forecast the spread of Hen Harriers *Circus cyaneus* or Bearded Tits *Panurus biarmicus*; the near-extinction of Wrynecks *Jynx torquilla* and Red-backed Shrikes *Lanius collurio*; the return of Ospreys *Pandion haliaetus*, Black-tailed Godwits *Limosa limosa*, Ruffs *Philomachus pugnax* and Savi's Warblers *Locustella luscinioides*; or the colonisation by Wood Sandpipers *Tringa glareola*, Snowy Owls *Nyctea scandiaca*, Fieldfares *Turdus pilaris*, Redwings *T. iliacus*, Cetti's Warblers *Cettia cetti* and Firecrests *Regulus ignicapillus*; the Little Ringed Plover *Charadrius dubius* was still very rare and, as there were no field guides, most British and. Irish birdwatchers had not even heard of the Collared Dove *Streptopelia decaocto*.

It is obviously difficult to forecast what major new factors will affect British and Irish birds in the next 25 years, as pesticides have in the last, but climatic recession is a palpable example and the pressures from oil, both as a direct contaminant of the sea and in its associated land-based developments, are likely to grow; so, too, is human disturbance of remoter areas. Terns and auks are always at risk, the former from interference and the latter from oil, but so are Red-throated *Gavia stellata* and Black-throated Divers *G. arctica* from predation following disturbance. Corncrakes *Crex crex* continue to decline, and what will happen to the Red-necked Phalarope *Phalaropus lobatus* and the Stone Curlew *Burhinus oedicnemus*? Are modern agricultural methods going to militate more and more against the Barn Owl *Tyto alba* and the Little Owl *Athene noctua*? Who knows, in another 25 years or less, we may have all but lost our Nightjars *Caprimulgus europaeus*, Woodlarks *Lullula arborea* and Cirl Buntings *Emberiza cirlus*.

On the credit side, continued spread by Siskins *Carduelis spinus* and Redpolls *Acanthis flammea* looks likely and the Serin *Serinus serinus* may well have gained a firm foothold after more than a decade with a toe in the door. Dotterels *Eudromias morinellus* may conceivably colonise parts of East Anglia, as they have done the polders of the Netherlands. Goshawks *Accipiter gentilis* and Ruddy Ducks *Oxyura jamaicensis*, the former probably from introduced stock and the latter certainly so, are likely to become more widespread, while the Ring-necked Parakeet *Psittacula krameri* seems destined to establish a thriving feral population, though its ability to withstand the rigours of a really hard winter will be the acid test.

There are also a number of species which could colonise or, in some cases, recolonise these islands. In 1971 (*BTO News* 44: 6), I stuck my neck out and forecast 14: Purple Heron *Ardea purpurea*, Spoonbill *Platalea leucorodia* and Turnstone *Arenaria interpres*, which I still regard as highly probable; Broad-billed Sandpiper *Limicola falcinellus*, Jack Snipe *Lymnocryptes minimus* and Long-tailed Skua *Stercorarius longicaudus*, which are perhaps no more or less likely than some other species to follow the recent trend of colonisation by Scandinavian birds; Little Gull *Larus minutus* and Shore Lark *Eremophila alpestris*, which have both now made nesting attempts; Cetti's Warbler, which has now colonised southern England; Great Reed Warbler *Acrocephalus arundinaceus* and Bonelli's Warbler *Phylloscopus bonelli*, which are still strong contenders; Great Grey Shrike *Lanius excubitor* and Ortolan Bunting *Emberiza hortulana*, which are widespread on the Continent, but perhaps most likely to come from Scandinavian stock; and Scarlet Rosefinch *Carpodacus erythrinus*, which may still seem a longer shot. To these, I would now add Little Bittern *Ixobrychus minutus*, Penduline Tit *Remiz pendulinus* and, above all, Fan-tailed Warbler *Cisticola juncidis*, which has been emulating Cetti's Warbler in its spread into northern France. But it is all a guessing game and, following the nesting of a pair of American Spotted Sandpipers *Tringa macularia* in Scotland in 1975, it is possible even that one or two transatlantic vagrants, doomed to migrate north and south in the Old World, may build up viable populations.

Already, following the example of Britain and Ireland, similar bird atlas projects have been started in 16 other European countries. At the special working conference on European ornithology, held at Green Park, Aston Clinton (Buckinghamshire), in 1971, under the joint auspices of the BTO and Vogelwarte Radolfzell of Germany, a European Ornithological Atlas Committee was set up, with Tim Sharrock and Tommy Dybbro, organiser of the Danish atlas scheme, as conveners. One of the committee's important functions is to co-ordinate projects leading up to the ambitious concept of a European atlas of breeding birds. This will be mapped on a 50-km square basis, but individual countries will be encouraged to use, where possible, finer grids which can be converted for this wider scheme. It is hoped to begin fieldwork for such a European atlas in 1985, which would be only 17 years from the launching of the present *Atlas*, but clearly, as leaders in this field, we must be prepared to support such a venture.

Thus, it may be that the survivors of the present network will, in under nine years' time, be asked to start again. I am sure that ornithologists everywhere, and the readers of this remarkable book, will agree that it is all very worthwhile.

Roxton, Bedford, 31st May 1976

Introduction

The historical background to the British Trust for Ornithology/Irish Wildbird Conservancy *Atlas* project is set out in his foreword by James Ferguson-Lees.

Using the BSBI *Atlas of the British Flora* (1962) as its model, the Atlas Working Group co-ordinated ideas and plans in the early stages and then advised and supervised the project throughout the five years of fieldwork and subsequent stages up to publication. This introduction is intended to serve as a permanent record of the methods used and decisions taken, whether they proved in the event to be right or wrong.

PLANNING

The aim of the project, to determine accurate distributions of all bird species breeding in Britain and Ireland during as short a period as possible, was agreed at an early stage. While some species' ranges were believed to have changed little over many years, others were known to have altered considerably and at least a few of these, such as the Collared Dove *Streptopelia decaocto* and the Woodlark *Lullula arborea*, both quickly and dramatically. Thus there was no question of combining past records with observations from fieldwork. The vast literature, especially the information scattered through the annual county bird reports, presented such daunting collation problems that preparation of separate maps of past distributions (or the combination of past and present records on the same maps with different symbols) was considered impracticable. Therefore, the aim was to carry out the survey in as short a time as was consistent with satisfactorily complete coverage. This decision depended upon others, especially the methods to be employed, but five years was selected in view of the uneven distribution of observers in Britain and Ireland (most in SE England, many fewer in Scotland and hardly any in Ireland). This was felt to be a short enough time to freeze distributions, but long enough to ensure an adequate sample of remote areas.

Our model, the BSBI atlas, had used 10-km squares as the recording unit. There were several advantages in adopting the same system, but with two modifications. First, the botanical atlas, in the absence of an alternative at that time (1954), had used an artificial extension of the British National Grid for Ireland, preparing special field maps for the purpose. The Irish grid, however, is now shown on readily available maps and, with strong representations from Irish biologists, this grid was adopted (and has now been accepted for all biological, including botanical, recording in Ireland). Secondly, in botanical recording, coastal squares containing only tiny portions of land had been amalgamated with those adjacent. Since, in ornithological recording, this would have led to long-established seabird colonies being shown incorrectly and often inland, the decision was taken to treat each square as a separate unit, regardless of the amount of land it contained. This decision resulted in a 6% increase over the botanical atlas in the number of units to be surveyed, from 3,630 to 3,862. There were only two exceptions to this rule: Fair Isle (Shetland), falling in four squares, and Jersey (Channel Islands), falling in six squares, were each treated as one unit square, the latter at the specific request of local observers. It should be noted that dots are always plotted in the centre of the 10-km square and this sometimes results in coastal ones appearing in the sea.

The possibility of using different sizes of recording unit in different parts of our area (eg 2-km squares in SE England, 10-km squares over most of Britain and 50-km squares in N Scotland and Ireland) was considered but discarded, since the advantages of a uniform system were obvious. Even though only a small sample of 10-km squares might be covered in the remote areas with few observers, the results could be directly compared with (a) those elsewhere and (b) the same areas at a later date, should a repeat survey be undertaken. Once a coarser grid was adopted for some areas, such comparisons could not be made, especially since the anticipated growth in interest in ornithology was likely to result in an observer-force increasingly capable of dealing with a relatively fine grid over the whole area.

The botanical survey had been confined to strict presence or absence data. If a species was found in a square, whether one plant or many over large areas, it was represented by a single dot; if the species was not found, the square remained blank. There was strong feeling among some ornithologists that any survey of breeding birds should attempt to obtain a quantitative measure. This would certainly have been possible for certain species which are easily counted (eg Great Crested Grebe *Podiceps cristatus*) but would have been most difficult for others which are very common over most of Britain and Ireland (eg Dunnock *Prunella modularis*). One method tested was coverage by 2-km squares (tetrads) and then rating each species as a score out of 25 (the number of tetrads in a 10-km square). It became clear, however, that tetrad coverage could be achieved only in the areas such as SE England where observers were most numerous. Further, where observers were thin on the ground (eg Ireland) or the terrain was difficult with few or no access roads (eg the Scottish Highlands), even the simplest subjective quantitative assessments would be so time-consuming that the basic requirements of the survey would be adversely affected. The firm decision was taken, therefore, that uniform coverage by the simplest possible method should be the aim. These three basic decisions of (1) a five-year survey, (2) the adherence to 10-km squares and (3) the avoidance of quantitative assessments and counts have proved, in the event, to have been absolutely correct, as will be shown later.

One essential modification of presence or absence recording was made. While the finding of a growing plant in a native habitat is sufficient evidence for inclusion on a distribution map, birds are mobile and migrants frequently occur in areas where the species does not nest. Thus, it was necessary, in a survey of breeding birds, to define evidence of nesting. It was acknowledged that this might often be difficult to obtain, even where the species was common and obviously breeding. To ensure uniform treatment, therefore, categories of evidence were defined and then grouped into grades of 'possible breeding', 'probable breeding' and 'confirmed breeding'. These categories are listed on page 17.

Finally, in the planning stages it was clear that the setting up of a sizeable observer-force, distribution of recording documents, collection of data and, especially, the verification of reports from observers were best carried out on a regional basis. Such regional representation had long been established by the BTO and had been a great help in smaller enquiries. With additional recruits (especially in the larger areas), the Trust's regional representatives formed the basis for a network of Regional Atlas Organisers covering the whole of Britain and Ireland. The existence of this network was a great asset, but there remained the problem of relating county boundaries to 10-km squares and more than two years elapsed before the responsibility for every square was allocated, with no duplication or gaps. Regional organisers form a nearly essential element in any atlas scheme and minor problems like this would not arise if such a network were established from scratch.

The areas for which each organiser was responsible are shown in fig. 1. As can be seen, these varied from one to several hundred squares, the average being 34.

Regional Atlas Organisers

SCOTLAND

1 R. J. Tulloch
2 R. H. Dennis 1968–70, R. A. Broad 1971–73
3 E. Balfour
4 W. A. J. Cunningham
5 C. G. Headlam 1968–70, Dr I. D. Pennie 1971–73
6 D. M. Stark 1968–71, Mrs P. M. Collett 1972–73
7 C. G. Headlam
8 C. G. Headlam 1968–70, Dr J. J. M. Flegg 1971–73
9 Dr R. Richter
10 J. Edelsten
11 N. Picozzi assisted by M. A. Macdonald and Dr W. R. P. Bourne
12 Dr M. Rusk assisted by M. I. Harvey
13 Hon. Douglas Weir assisted by H. Burton
14 C. M. Morrison
15 C. G. Headlam 1968–70, M. J. P. Gregory 1971–73
16 Miss V. M. Thom
17 D. W. Oliver
18 J. Mitchell assisted in Renfrewshire by W. Wild
19 H. Robb
20 C. G. Headlam 1968–70, C. G. Booth 1971–73
21 J. H. Swan 1968–71, Mrs B. Grey 1972–73
22 Miss N. J. Gordon
23 Professor T. C. Smout
24 K. S. Macgregor
25 R. W. J. Smith
26 C. G. Headlam 1968–70, Dr J. A. Gibson 1971–73
27 D. Grant 1968–69, C. G. Headlam 1970, Dr J. I. Meikle 1971–73
28 Dr M. E. Castle
29 C. G. Headlam 1968–70, D. L. Clugston 1971–73
30 J. Maxwell 1968–73, J. G. Young 1968–71
31 A. D. Watson
    Co-ordinator for Scotland: C. G. Headlam 1968–70

ENGLAND

32 C. C. E. Douglas 1968, L. G. Macfarlane 1969–73
33 R. Stokoe
34 Dr J. D. Summers-Smith 1968–69, Dr R. Norman 1970–73
35 Dr J. D. Summers-Smith
36 J. A. G. Barnes assisted by J. Parkin
37 A. J. Wallis
38 Dr G. L. Watson 1968–69, J. A. G. Barnes assisted by L. A. Cowcill 1970–73
39 E. S. Skinner assisted by C. W. Armitstead, M. V. Bell and F. A. Wardman
40 E. Chambers 1968, D. Taylor 1969–73
41 D. B. Cutts
42 A. F. G. Walker
43 K. G. Spencer 1968–69, R. A. Cadman 1970–73
44 K. G. Spencer
45 M. Densley
46 R. P. Cockbain
47 R. G. Hawley 1968–71, D. Herringshaw 1972–73
48 P. Wilson
49 L. A. Pownall 1968–70, J. R. Mullins 1971–73
50 D. L. Clugston 1968–69, J. R. Mullins 1970–73
51 A. B. Wassell
52 J. M. McMeeking assisted by A. Dobbs
53 D. J. Munns 1968–70, F. C. Gribble 1971–73
54 A. L. Bull
55 J. G. Goldsmith
56 C. E. Wright
57 R. A. O. Hickling
58 A. E. Vine
59 D. J. Munns
60 N. C. Moore 1968–69, C. J. Coe 1970–73
61 B. S. Milne
62 G. B. G. Benson
63 R. H. Baillie 1968, A. J. Smith 1969–73
64 J. N. Dymond 1968–71, P. F. Bonham 1972–73
65 D. J. Steventon 1968–70, A. E. Vine 1971–73
66 C. M. Reynolds
67 J. Bevan assisted by E. Byrne and Mrs S. Cowdy 1968–73, R. E. Youngman 1972–73
68 P. Dymott
69 C. J. Mead
70 Mrs P. V. Upton
71 D. J. Montier 1970–73, P. J. Sellar 1968–73
72 Mrs E. Barnes assisted by Miss B. Gillam
73 Miss C. Graham
74 P. E. Standley
75 Major G. F. A. Munns
76 D. E. Ladhams
77 M. J. Rayner 1968–69, R. H. B. Forster 1970–73
78 H. P. Sitters
79 J. H. Taverner

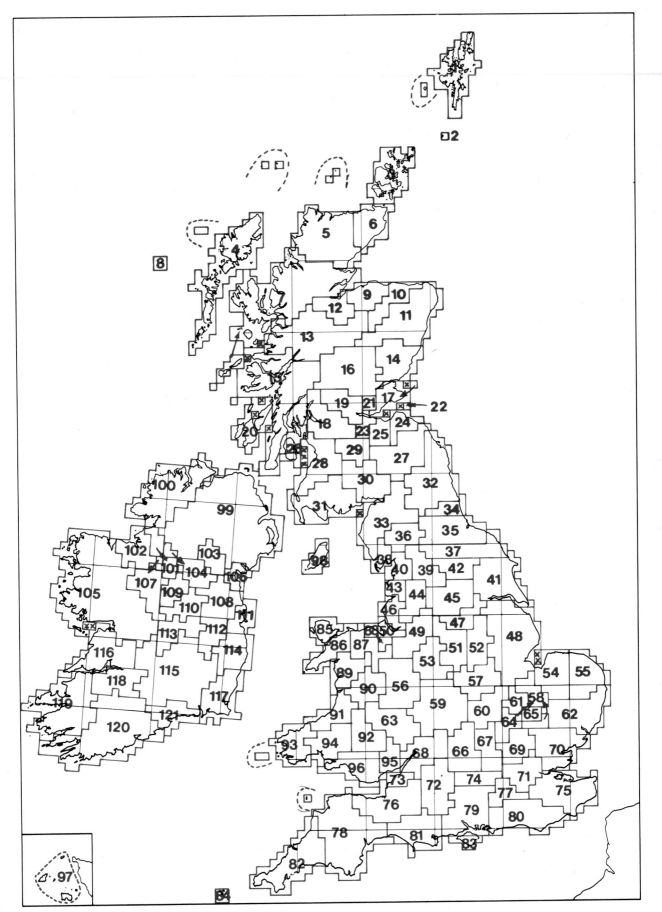

Fig. 1. Regional Atlas Organisers' areas

80 Dr A. B. Watson
81 D. P. Hutchins 1968–69, J. V. Boys 1970–73
82 D. F. Musson 1968–69, R. D. Penhallurick 1970–73
83 J. Stafford
84 D. F. Musson 1968–69, Miss H. M. Quick 1970–73

WALES

85 A. J. Mercer
86 A. J. Mercer 1968, Dr R. G. Gibbs 1969–71, Dr P. J. Dare 1971–73
87 J. M. Harrop
88 E. J. Stokes
89 P. Hope Jones
90 R. R. Lovegrove
91 P. E. Davis
92 M. V. Preece
93 J. H. Barrett assisted by J. W. Donovan 1968–70, D. R. Saunders 1971–73
94 Colonel H. Morrey Salmon 1968, D. H. V. Roberts 1969–73
95 H. W. Hamar 1968–69, W. G. Lewis 1970–73
96 Colonel H. Morrey Salmon 1968–69, Mrs A. Heathcote 1970–73

CHANNEL ISLANDS

97 Mrs A. Le Sueur assisted by A. Bisson and F. R. G. Rountree

ISLE OF MAN

98 Dr L. S. Garrad

NORTHERN IRELAND

99 F. D. Hamilton 1968–70, J. S. Furphy assisted by Mrs N. D. Blamire 1968–73

REPUBLIC OF IRELAND

100 D. Scott and T. Wood
101 D. Scott
102 N. Murphy and D. Scott
103 D. Scott 1968–71, J. K. Lovatt 1972
104 D. Scott 1968–71, J. K. Lovatt 1972
105 D. Scott
106 D. Scott
107 P. McDermot and D. Scott
108 D. Scott 1968–71, J. K. Lovatt and K. Finch 1972
109 D. Scott
110 D. Scott 1968–71, B. D. Carrick 1972
111 D. Scott 1968–71, J. M. Keys 1972
112 D. Scott 1968–71, J. M. Keys 1972
113 D. E. Batchen and D. Scott
114 D. Scott 1968–71, J. M. Keys 1972
115 D. Scott
116 L. Stapleton and D. Scott
117 O. J. Merne and P. J. Roche
118 D. Scott 1968–70, Lt Col The O'Grady 1971, R. W. S. Forster 1972
119 F. King
120 K. Preston
121 M. O'Meara

Co-ordinator for the Republic of Ireland: D. Scott

RECORDING METHODS

Two years of field trials in 1966 and 1967 ironed out most of the problems involved in recording the three grades of breeding evidence (possible, probable and confirmed) and led to 14 categories being applied uniformly. These are shown opposite. The integration of the BTO/IWC scheme into a European atlas project during the formation of a European Ornithological Atlas Committee (see page 23) necessitated some compromises. This *Atlas* uses the BTO/IWC system but, for comparison, the EOAC categories are also shown. Future schemes in Britain and Ireland will adopt the EOAC system.

It will be noted that, in the BTO/IWC codes, possible breeding is indicated by a tick, all codes for probable breeding by a single, easily remembered initial letter and all codes for confirmed breeding by a pair of no less easily remembered initial letters. This made recording easy. Indeed, by the middle of the project, the codes had entered observers' normal vocabulary: 'There's an FL' or 'I found a UN'. It was also of great assistance in checking, since the record cards (fig. 2) had three columns (one for each degree of breeding evidence) and an entry in the wrong column was easily detected. The EOAC numbers (0 to 16) are intended only to signify sequence, each country using its own single or double initial letters appropriate to the language concerned.

The 10-km squares of Britain and Ireland are designated by two systems, one with four numerals and one with two letters (one for Irish squares) and two

BRITISH TRUST FOR ORNITHOLOGY
ATLAS PROJECT
(10 km. sq. Breeding Bird Survey)

Observer I. J. FERGUSON-LEES & J. T. R. SHARROCK
Address B.T.O.
Year 1968-72
Square TL14

Bl-th Diver	001				Com Scoter	026				R-l Prtrdge	051			NY	Avocet	076			
Rd-th Diver	002				Eider	027				Partridge	052			NY	R-n Phal	077			
Gt Cr Grebe	003			NY	Rd-br Merg	028				Quail	053				Stne Curlew	078			
Slavn Grebe	004				Goosander	029				Pheasant	054			NY	Arctic Skua	079			
Bl-nd Grebe	005				Shelduck	030				Water Rail	055		S		Great Skua	080			
Little Grebe	006			NE	Gr Lg Goose	031	✓			Spot Crake	056				G B-b Gull	081			
Lch's Petrl	007				Canada Gse	032				Corncrake	057				L B-b Gull	082			
Storm Petrl	008				Mute Swan	033			NY	Moorhen	058			NY	Herring Gull	083			
Manx Shwtr	009				Gldn Eagle	034				Coot	059			NY	Comm Gull	084			
Fulmar	010				Buzzard	035				Oysterctchr	060				Blk-hd Gull	085			
Gannet	011				Sparrowhwk	036	✓			Lapwing	061			NY	Kittiwake	086			
Cormorant	012				Kite	037				Ringed Plov	062				Comm Tern	087			
Shag	013				Honey Bzzd	038				L R Plover	063			NE	Arctic Tern	088			
Heron	014			NY	Msh Harrier	039				Gldn Plover	064				Roseate T	089			
Bittern	015				Hen Harrier	040				Dotterel	065				Little Tern	090			
Mallard	016			NY	Montagu's H	041				Snipe	066			NY	Sandwich T	091			
Teal	017	✓			Osprey	042				Woodcock	067			NY	Razorbill	092			
Garganey	018				Hobby	043			NY	Curlew	068				Guillemot	093			
Gadwall	019				Peregrine	044				Whimbrel	069				Bl Guille	094			
Wigeon	020				Merlin	045				Bl-t Godwit	070				Puffin	095			
Pintail	021				Kestrel	046			FY	Wood Sand	071				Stock Dove	096			ON
Shoveler	022	✓			Red Grouse	047				Com Sand	072				Rock Dove	097			
Scaup	023				Ptarmigan	048				Redshank	073			NE	Woodpigeon	098			NY
Tufted Duck	024		T		Blck Grse	049				Greenshank	074				Turtle Dove	099			NY
Pochard	025			NY	Capercaillie	050				Dunlin	075				Colld Dove	100			NY

Cuckoo	101			NE	Crested Tit	129				Whitethroat	157			NY	Chaffinch	185			NY
Barn Owl	102		T		Marsh Tit	130			NY	L Whiteth	158			FL	Yllhammer	186			NY
Little Owl	103			NY	Willow Tit	131			FY	Dartfd Wblr	159				Cn Bunting	187			FL
Tawny Owl	104			FL	Long-t Tit	132			NY	Willow Wblr	160			NY	Cirl Bunting	188			
L-e Owl	105			NY	Nuthatch	133			NY	Chiffchaff	161			NY	Reed Bunt	189			NY
S-e Owl	106				Treecreeper	134			NY	Wood Wblr	162				Snow Bunt	190			
Nightjar	107		T		Wren	135			NY	Goldcrest	163			NY	Hse Sparrow	191			NY
Swift	108			ON	Dipper	136				Firecrest	164				Tree Sprrw	192			NY
Kingfisher	109	✓			Bearded Tit	137				Spot Flyc	165			NY	Grey Wagt	193			
Grn Wdpkr	110			NY	M Thrush	138			NY	Pied Flyc	166				Feral Pigeon	209			NY
Gt S Wdpkr	111			FY	Song Thrush	139			NY	Dunnock	167			NY	LADY A'S PH.				NY
Lr S Wdpkr	112			ON	Redwing	140				Mead Pipit	168				GOLDEN PH.		✓		
Wryneck	113				Ring Ouzel	141				Tree Pipit	169			NE					
Woodlark	114				Blackbird	142			NY	Rock Pipit	170								
Skylark	115			NE	Wheatear	143				Pied Wagt	171			NY					
Swallow	116			NE	Stonechat	144				Yellow Wgt	172			NY					
Hse Martin	117			NY	Whinchat	145			NE	R-bd Shrike	173								
Sand Martin	118			NY	Redstart	146			NY	Starling	174			NY					
Raven	119				Bl Redstart	147				Hawfinch	175			FL					
Carr/~~Hd~~ Cr	120			ON	Nightingale	148		S		Greenfinch	176			NY					
Rook	121			NY	Robin	149			NY	Goldfinch	177			NE					
Jackdaw	122			NY	Grassh Wblr	150			NE	Siskin	178		S						
Magpie	123			FY	Savi's Wblr	151				Linnet	179			NY					
Jay	124			NE	Reed Wblr	152			NY	Twite	180								
Chough	125				Marsh Wblr	153				Redpoll	181			NE					
Great Tit	126			NY	Sedge Wblr	154			NY	Serin	182								
Blue Tit	127			NY	Blackcap	155			NE	Bullfinch	183			NY					
Coal Tit	128			NY	Gdn Wblr	156			FL	Crossbill	184	✓							

Largest town or village in the square: TL14 BIGGLESWADE / SANDY

Before filling in, please read accompanying 'Instructions for completing record cards'.

Return *by 31 August* to your local organiser.
If you have no local organiser, return to:

B.T.O. ATLAS PROJECT,
59 CURLEW CRESCENT,
BEDFORD

Fig. 2. Front and back of a standard 15 cm × 10 cm recording card

BTO/IWC CODES	EOAC CODES
	Grade A
	0 Species observed in breeding season
Possible breeding	**Grade B**
✓ Bird recorded in breeding season in possible nesting habitat, but no other indication of breeding noted	1 Species observed in breeding season in possible nesting habitat
	2 Singing male(s) present (or breeding calls heard) in breeding season
Probable breeding	**Grade C**
S Singing male present (or breeding calls heard) on more than one date in same place	3 Pair observed in suitable nesting habitat in breeding season
T Bird (or pair) apparently holding territory	4 Permanent territory presumed through registration of territorial behaviour (song, etc) on at least two different days a week or more apart at same place
D Courtship and display; or agitated behaviour or anxiety calls from adults, suggesting probable presence of nest or young nearby; or brood-patch on trapped female	5 Courtship and display
N Visiting probable nest-site	6 Visiting probable nest-site
	7 Agitated behaviour or anxiety calls from adults
	8 Brood patch on adult examined in the hand
B Nest-building (including excavating nest-hole)★	9 Nest-building or excavating of nest-hole
Confirmed breeding	**Grade D**
DD Distraction-display or injury-feigning	10 Distraction-display or injury-feigning
UN Used nest found	11 Used nest or eggshells found (occupied or laid within period of survey)
FL Recently fledged young	12 Recently fledged young (nidicolous species) or downy young (nidifugous species)
	13 Adults entering or leaving nest-site in circumstances indicating occupied nest (including high nests or nest-holes, the contents of which cannot be seen) or adult seen incubating
FS Adult carrying faecal sac	14 Adult carrying faecal sac or food for young
FY Adult(s) with food for young	
ON Adult(s) entering or leaving nest-site in circumstances indicating occupied nest (including colonies)	
NE Nest and eggs, or bird sitting and not disturbed, or eggshells found away from nest	15 Nest containing eggs
NY Nest with young or *downy* young of ducks, gamebirds, waders, etc.	16 Nest with young seen or heard

★ For many species, nest-building was regarded as confirmed breeding, and these records were upgraded at the end of the project (B being converted to BB). The birds for which this was not done were shearwaters and petrels (Procellariiformes), Gannet *Sula bassana*, raptors (Falconiformes), waders (Charadrii), Cuckoo *Cuculus canorus*, owls (Strigiformes), Raven *Corvus corax*, Carrion/Hooded Crow *C. corone*, Rook *C. frugilegus*, Jackdaw *C. monedula*, Wren *Troglodytes troglodytes* and the *Acrocephalus* and *Sylvia* warblers.

numerals. Although the four-numeral system was used for data processing, observers were instructed to use the letter-and-numeral system, since this reduces potential error (due to inadvertent transposition of digits) to one-twelfth. To serve as a check that correct square numbers were given, the cards had a space for the naming of an identifying feature of the square, such as the largest town.

The recording cards had printed on them the names, sometimes abbreviated, of all the birds on the British and Irish list known to be breeding regularly when the survey started. This included some introduced species with established feral populations; others (*eg* Lady Amherst's Pheasant *Chrysolophus amherstiae*) were not at that time accepted on the official list and were omitted, which was undoubtedly a misjudgment. Although there were spaces on the cards for adding species, and appeals were made to observers to do so, it is likely that some records of introduced birds were ignored by observers. The Feral Pigeon *Columba livia* was similarly omitted from early cards (though added from 1970 onwards) and, likewise, there is little doubt that records are incomplete as a result. Any future scheme should certainly include all such species on the cards from the start.

While the majority of records were submitted on the cards (95,000 of which were used during the five years), duplicated casual record sheets (fig. 3) were also supplied on demand to observers travelling through numerous squares on long journeys. The processing of data received in this way was very time-consuming, however, and these sheets were discontinued in the final year. The use of a record card for a single observation may appear to be a waste of money, but the cost of handling sheets with records from many squares (particularly distribution for verification by several regional organisers) is even more costly.

Instructions for completing cards, the background to the project and various forms of advice on recording were provided annually as a special supplement to *BTO News*. These were distributed free to all members of the Trust and spare copies were supplied to all regional organisers for distribution to the observers in their regions. The number printed annually rose from 10,500 in 1968 to over 21,000 in both 1971 and 1972. These instructions also proved useful as handouts to landowners and others, in explanation of the purpose of the fieldwork, and provided an essential means of feed-back to participating observers. By this method, together with short articles in *BTO News* and occasionally in *British Birds*, observers were informed how the project was progressing and, after the end of the 1968 season, provisional species maps were produced. At first, these species maps highlighted the gaps where further work was needed, but their most important role was to show that the project was producing useful results. In that way, the initial pessimism of many potential participants was converted to enthusiasm. A project of this nature can succeed only if those taking part believe that it will reach a successful conclusion. The other essential feature is that amateur participants should enjoy doing the work. To emphasise this aspect of the project, winter lectures were given to many local bird societies.

The determination of the limits of a 10-km square and the coverage of all the habitats within it were aided by the 1 inch to 1 mile and, particularly, the $2\frac{1}{2}$ inch to 1 mile Ordnance Survey maps. The former were available for the whole of the UK and the latter (each covering exactly one or exactly two 10-km squares) for most of Britain except for parts of Scotland; both had the relevant grid lines clearly indicated. The only maps available for the Republic of Ireland were $\frac{1}{2}$ inch to 1 mile, but these, too, had the Irish grid lines clearly marked.

It was realised in the planning stages that rarities and extralimital records would create problems, since observers might well wish these to remain confidential for the protection of the birds. Therefore, fieldworkers were asked to submit such records on separate cards, marked 'secret', and they were given the undertaking that these would be seen only by the national organiser (and relevant regional organiser if originally submitted through him) until those concerned gave permission for the security to be lifted. Over 1,800 such records were received and, though only 0.5% of the total, their collation and the associ-

B. T. O. ORNITHOLOGICAL ATLAS

Form for submitting casual records only.

(This form is for use when away from your usual area. Please use a CARD if there is more than a handful of records for any one square)

Year 19 .69

Name .. D. L. CLUGSTON

Address .. 32 EDINBURGH ROAD WALLASEY CHESHIRE

10 km. square	County; and largest town or village in the square		Species	Breeding evidence code (see Instructions) Col. 1	Col. 2	Col. 3
EXAMPLE: SP 91	Herts.	Tring	Lssr. Spot. Wd.			ON
"	"	"	Hawfinch		N	
TL 14	Beds.	Sandy	Wood Warbler	✓		
NN06	ARGYLL	BALLACHULISH	MALLARD			NY
"	"	"	EIDER			NY
"	"	"	COMMON GULL			NE
"	"	"	MUTE SWAN			NY
"	"	"	GREY WAGTAIL			FY
NC 86	S'LAND	STRATHY POINT	BLACK GUILLEMOT			NE
"	"	"	FULMAR			NE
"	"	"	SHAG			NE
"	"	"	ROCK DOVE			ON
NC 50	"	LAIRG	BUZZARD			NY
"	"	"	SISKIN		T	
NH 73	INVERNESS	LOCH MOY	COMMON TERN			NE
HU 41	SHETLAND	SUMBURGH	ARCTIC TERN			NE
"	"	"	COMMON TERN			NE
"	"	"	COMMON GULL			NE
"	"	"	GREAT SKUA			NY
HY31	ORKNEY	FINSTOWN	HEN HARRIER			NY
"	"	"	MERLIN			NY
"	"	"	LAPWING			NY
"	"	"	CURLEW			NY
NH 52	INVERNESS	LOCH MHOR	RED-THROATED DIVER		T	
"	"	"	WIGEON		T	
"	"	"	RED-BREASTED MERGAN.		T	
"	"	"	DUNLIN		D	
"	"	"	OYSTERCATCHER			DD

If all the records on this form relate to one county, return by 31st August to the county organiser.
If the records relate to several counties, return by 31st August to Dr. J.T.R. Sharrock, 59 Curlew Crescent, Bedford.

Fig. 3. Casual record sheet

ated correspondence became a major element in the final stages of preparation (see page 22).

DATA COLLECTION

Initially, most fieldwork was carried out by observers surveying their local 10-km squares, in which they either lived or traditionally carried out much of their home birdwatching. When offers of help were made to regional organisers, they allocated squares, thus attempting to ensure minimal duplication of effort. Nevertheless, the distribution of observers was such that, in the first couple of years, some squares were surveyed by a dozen or more different people while many others remained uninvestigated. This situation greatly improved over the five years; in particular, the good results in areas where field-workers were particularly active convinced those in other areas that the project was viable.

The aim in covering a square was to record every species breeding in it during 1968–72 and, if possible, to prove breeding for each one. To this end, the main guidance given to observers was that they should visit samples of every different habitat in the square during the main breeding season of April to July, to make visits outside this period for certain species (eg in February or March for owls) and to make dusk and night visits for crepuscular and nocturnal species. No set times were given, since it was appreciated that highly skilled observers would achieve the aims quicker than less experienced observers, and that squares with a great variety of habitats or difficult terrain would take far longer to cover adequately than those that were relatively uniform or had easy access. It was found, in the event, that experienced observers working in typical lowland squares with easy access could find about 50% of the breeding species in just over two hours, 75% in less than 10 hours and 87% in 16 hours, but that 100% were not found even after over 200 hours (Ferguson-Lees and Sharrock 1971, Sharrock 1973). Satisfactory distribution maps resulted, however, provided 70–80% of the species were found in each square, since this would include all the common species and a proportion of the scarcer ones.

Experience showed that, with the obvious exception of early breeders, it was far easier to obtain evidence of breeding for most species late in the season—by observing adults carrying food, or recently fledged young—than early in the season. In one example, the proportion of proved breeding records obtained in a day's fieldwork increased from 35% in late April and early May to over 70% in July (Sharrock 1971). The actual finding of nests was therefore a relatively minor part of Atlas fieldwork, which was lucky since this is an aspect of ornithology at which few birdwatchers are proficient and one which can cause excessive disturbance. It was possible to state truthfully in the annual instructions: 'In most cases, breeding can be proved without ever approaching the nest.' This served to encourage those who were not gifted in this direction, and also to allay the fears of potential critics of the project.

Observers were instructed always to obtain permission before entering private property. Although in a few cases access was limited to one or two named people, I know of no instance where permission was refused. We owe a great debt of gratitude to the many landowners who not only gave permission for their land to be visited, but who often provided facilities, advice and hospitality.

After the first year's fieldwork had shown the areas where coverage was likely to be thin (fig. 4), attempts were made to fill the gaps by short, intensive visits. On a small scale this was achieved by day trips into out-of-the-way squares, but elsewhere, particularly in Ireland and Scotland, local observers were too few for this to suffice. As shown already, ornithologists experienced in Atlas techniques could adequately sample the habitats in most squares in the course of a single day at the right time of year. The national organiser spent eight months during 1969–72, with a caravan as a mobile base, carrying out such square-a-day surveys, mostly in Scotland and Ireland. Large areas of Ireland were also covered in this way by a small group of dedicated Irish observers led by David Scott. Such expeditions became more frequent in the closing years of the project, as the gaps left by 'normal' coverage became apparent. Expert Atlas fieldworkers were recruited for this purpose and funds supplied by the BTO, the Scottish Ornithologists' Club and the British Ornithologists' Union were used to assist these groups with travelling expenses to reach remote areas or offshore islands.

By the end of the penultimate season's work (fig. 7), it was clear that it would be possible to achieve coverage of every one of the 3,862 squares. To make the best use of manpower in the fifth and final year, regional organisers were asked to peruse their 1968–71 records and study maps of their regions to estimate the probable number of breeding species in each square. From these estimates (acknowledged to be very approximate in some large regions where remote parts were not well known), the coverage achieved in each square to date was calculated as a percentage of the number of species estimated. Then, in the last year, each of the 400 squares with less than 75% of the estimated species already found was allocated at least two independent observers. To ensure that illness or other factors would not cause last-minute gaps, these observers were asked to submit preliminary cards at the beginning of June, in the absence of which squares were given emergency coverage by a flying squad of special experts. This procedure was directed by Mrs Gwen Bonham.

We were fortunate that two other national breeding bird surveys coincided or overlapped with the BTO/IWC Atlas project. First, the Wildfowl Trust's survey of breeding and summering wildfowl in Britain, covering 1965–70, was also based on 10-km squares and, fortunately, each year's records had been kept separate. Both projects benefited, therefore, from an exchange of 1968–70 data on ducks, geese and swans (see Yarker and Atkinson-Willes 1971). Secondly, the Seabird Group's 'Operation Seafarer', the aim of which was to obtain counts and estimates of all seabirds breeding in Britain and Ireland, was carried out mainly in 1969–70. Although this was not based on 10-km squares, each section of coast surveyed was precisely defined and the Seafarer national organiser, D. R. Saunders, was able to allocate most records to the appropriate squares. Again, an exchange of data made both projects more complete. Additional wildfowl and seabird records obtained in this way were passed to the regional *Atlas* organisers before incorporation into the files, to maintain the checking system which was applied to all records.

Organisers of national surveys and those studying particular species co-operated fully. Exchanges of information, except for secret records, were made for Grey Heron *Ardea cinerea* (C. M. Reynolds), Golden Eagle *Aquila chrysaetos* (M. J. Everett), Red Kite *Milvus milvus* (Kite Committee), Peregrine *Falco peregrinus* and Dotterel *Eudromias morinellus* (Dr D. A. Ratcliffe), Woodcock *Scolopax rusticola* (Mrs Monica Vizosa), Red-necked Phalarope *Phalaropus lobatus* (M. J. Everett), Stone Curlew *Burhinus oedicnemus* (P. A. Wright), Marsh Warbler *Acrocephalus palustris* (Marsh Warbler Panel) and Red-backed Shrike *Lanius collurio* (C. J. Bibby).

The BTO's files of ringing records included many thousands of records of nestlings and unfledged young ringed during 1968–72. These would have provided confirmed breeding records of use to the *Atlas*, but they were scattered through the ringing schedules with localities defined by geographical co-ordinates rather than 10-km squares, so that the task of extracting them would have been immense. It was considered that the relatively small number of new records expected did not justify the work that this would have involved. All ringers were, therefore, specially asked to ensure that they submitted their records of nestlings and unfledged young during 1968–72 for use in the *Atlas*, and they were supplied with casual record sheets on which to do this.

There were also over 120,000 relevant nest record cards in the BTO's files, each one concerning an instance of confirmed breeding in 1968–72. Although in the last two years of the *Atlas* project the nest record cards had spaces for entering the 10-km square number and indicating whether or not the record had already been submitted for the *Atlas*, most cards did not include these details. The likely return on time expended in full extraction of the records was estimated on samples of Whinchat *Saxicola rubetra*, Sedge Warbler *Acrocephalus schoenobaenus*, Pied Flycatcher *Ficedula hypoleuca* and the owls (Strigiformes), and it was concluded that only in the case of the scarcer species was extraction justified; for the commoner birds, breeding had already been confirmed in most squares during the *Atlas* fieldwork, and determination of 10-km square numbers for nest record cards was largely wasted effort. It was considered that the manpower, time and money involved could be better used by putting fieldworkers into undercovered squares. It was also found that such extraction was so tedious that even the most careful workers made a large number of transcription errors. For the scarcer species, therefore, the extraction had to be repeated and the data double-checked. The decision to limit the extent of this extraction was undoubtedly correct. These data, like all others, were submitted to the relevant regional organisers for vetting, before incorporation into the *Atlas* files.

Towards the end of the project, it was suspected that certain species were being under-recorded. Each regional organiser was asked to list such species for his area and the results of these enquiries were analysed. The birds considered to be under-recorded throughout Britain and Ireland were then mapped, and special articles, including advice on finding them, were published in *BTO News*. The most distinctive and unmistakable of these species were also mentioned in appeals on BBC radio and, as a result, several hundred records of Quails *Coturnix coturnix*, Barn Owls *Tyto alba* and Kingfishers *Alcedo atthis* were received from the general public. Those that included substantiating details (such as the snoring noises of young Barn Owls) were passed to the regional organisers and incorporated into the *Atlas* files. Similar appeals were made in *The Farmers' Weekly* (Quail, Corncrake *Crex crex* and Barn Owl), *The Gamekeepers' Gazette* (Sparrowhawk *Accipiter nisus*, Merlin *Falco columbarius*, Ptarmigan *Lagopus mutus*, Black Grouse *Lyrurus tetrix*, Capercaillie *Tetrao urogallus*, Quail, Bob-white Quail *Colinus virginianus*, Golden Pheasant *Chrysolophus pictus*, Lady Amherst's Pheasant *C. amherstiae*, Reeves's Pheasant *Syrmaticus reevesi*, Woodcock, Barn Owl, Little Owl *Athene noctua*, Tawny Owl *Strix aluco*, Long-eared Owl *Asio otus* and Short-eared Owl *A. flammeus*), and *The Climber* (Ptarmigan, Golden Plover *Pluvialis apricaria* and Dotterel *Eudromias morinellus*). These appeals resulted in many valuable records, their inclusion or exclusion from the *Atlas* files being decided by the relevant regional organisers on the basis of the evidence supplied by the informants. In some cases, such information was personally checked by a visit from the local organiser: it should be put on record that the reports were almost invariably found to be correct. Appeals of this sort to the general public are time-consuming (each record has to be assigned to its 10-km square), but the exercise proved to be very worthwhile.

The number of observers supplying records to the *Atlas* is not exactly known. In many cases cards were submitted with just one person's name, but with 'and others' appended; some cards gave the name of only the local bird club or society; and no count was made of the many single records received in letters. Contributors certainly numbered over 10,000, however, and probably under 15,000. These numbers may seem large in relation to the 3,862 10-km squares involved, but, without denying the value of many small contributions, it must be stated that the bulk of the work was carried out by about 1,500 dedicated observers, whose enthusiasm ensured the final satisfactory result. Those who took on responsibility for a square, and especially those who then went on to tackle other more distant squares as well, provided most of the data and deserve most of the credit.

DATA CHECKING

All records went through four checking processes and the majority five. Each regional organiser checked the cards submitted to him and queried any unlikely records to eliminate identification and transcription errors. After this first check, the cards were passed to the national organiser who, in the course of compiling a master card for each square, again looked for possible errors. Most regional organisers maintained their own sets of master cards (or a master record sheet) and, as well as submitting original field cards, from 1969 onwards also supplied a combined master card each year, summarising records to date. Comparison of these with the national organiser's master cards provided the third check. Thus, by the end of the five years, there was one set of original cards and two master cards for each square in most regions. In 1973, the national organiser's set of master cards was photocopied twice (free of charge, by Rank Xerox Ltd) and these photocopies were sent to the regional organisers and also to the county or regional report editors. The former compared them with their own master cards and the latter checked them for unusual records which required verification. In this way, the master cards, with over a quarter of a million separate records, were thoroughly checked for errors. The last check was made, after data processing, by supplying each regional organiser with a complete set of provisional maps.

The master cards were the same as the ordinary field cards, but only one was used for each square, and amended each year, with the highest category of evidence being entered for each species. The process would have been simplified if transparent master cards had been used, so that records could have been traced directly from the field cards: this is recommended for future projects.

The checking and verification of records depended largely upon the network of regional organisers. The efforts of this band of volunteers cannot be too highly praised. As the success of the project exceeded expectations, so did the amount of work they were called upon to do. Being amateurs, working for the *Atlas* in their spare time, some found it increasingly difficult to keep pace with the incoming records, and the resulting delays must be regarded as inevitable in a project of this sort. Some also found that their personal sets of master cards had an increasing number of errors and omissions, due to their giving priority to speed of submission over accuracy. The rather complicated checking procedures already explained became necessary because of this. Additional use of photocopying, to provide each regional organiser with an up-to-date duplicate set of master cards annually, should be seriously considered in any future project: the additional expense would probably be fully justified by the saving in the national organiser's time.

The check of the Xeroxed 1968–72 master cards by regional organisers in 1973 included not only elimination of copying errors, but also a reassessment of early records in the light of later ones. A three-page instruction sheet was issued to ensure uniform checking and editing. Certain parts of this summarise the editing attitude which the Atlas Working Group wished regional organisers to adopt, and these sections are, therefore, reproduced below:

'If there is doubt about the identification you should be ruthless in rejecting the record. In this case, and also with the correction of copying slips, please make sure to mark all columns where deletion is required. Remember that, even if a NE record is incorrect, there may be, say, a perfectly valid T (which may need to be inserted as a new record).

The only records which may need editing out on the grounds that breeding definitely did not take place during 1968–72 are first column ticks and second column S. To obtain uniform treatment throughout the 3,862 squares, the following rule must be applied rigidly: *A tick or S should be edited out only if it is known for certain that breeding could not have taken place during 1968–72.*

There can be only two ways of knowing this: (1) because there is no suitable breeding habitat in the square, or (2) because the only birds of the species seen in the five years were in a well-watched area and did not stay long enough to breed.

The fact that a species has not been known to breed in your county before is *not* a valid reason for deleting a tick or S. Summering non-breeding birds should be included, provided there is suitable breeding habitat. Below are some examples to act as guidelines:

(A) Odd Grey Herons seen in a wooded square but where no heronry is known; even if there is a known heronry in a nearby square, *retain tick*.
(B) Water Rails heard in marsh on a visit in early April but not on subsequent visits; *retain tick* (because this is an elusive species).
(C) Gulls frequenting rubbish-tips throughout the summer, in unsuitable breeding habitat; *omit*.
(D) Adult Cormorants spending whole summer on a lake with wooded islands or other suitable breeding habitat; *retain tick*.
(E) Whimbrel calling on moorland for three weeks but then no futher signs; *retain S*.
(F) Single Lesser Whitethroat seen and heard singing and nest found (but no second bird ever seen) in northern Scotland; *retain B*.
(G) Ducks spending the whole summer on a lake but no display or broods seen; *retain tick*.

You will see from these examples that, whereas we are asking you to be ruthless in deleting records where there is doubt about the identification, we are asking you to make the minimum number of editorial deletions. The *Atlas* must, so far as possible, contain facts and not opinions.

Please do not apply your own rules for your region. We must try to be consistent. Bedfordshire is far better known ornithologically than, say, Argyllshire; most of the *Atlas* work in Hampshire has been done by local observers yet most of that in, say, western Inverness-shire has been done by visitors from elsewhere, mostly on short trips. The only way to obtain uniformity is to make minimal editing in all areas. We do *not* want the cards for your area to be edited 'better' than those for any other area. If you have any doubts about whether a tick or S should be retained or deleted, please retain it. Deletion means you are *sure* that the species did not breed in 1968–72. One valid entry in just one of the five years is all that is required.'

DATA PROCESSING
The checked and edited master cards were passed to a commercial firm, which transferred the data to punched paper-tape and guaranteed an error rate not exceeding 1 in 10,000 characters. With nearly two million characters, however, this was expected to introduce some 200 errors, and subsequent experience showed that this level was approached or possibly exceeded: a sad state of affairs after the care taken in data preparation.

The paper-tapes were passed to the Biological Records Centre at Monks Wood Experimental Station. After transposition of the data (from grades for each species in each square to grades in each square for each species) by Atlas computer at Cambridge, maps were prepared by the BRC standard mapping machinery (basically an adapted electric typewriter printing symbols on to base maps).

The first set of maps contained a number of obvious errors, resulting from inaccurate tape-punching, which were eliminated before production of the final versions. It is probable, however, that the maps in this *Atlas* still contain 50–100 minor errors out of over 285,000 dots. A complete manual check would have been very time-consuming and the Atlas Working Group considered that this possible error rate of less than 0.035% was scientifically unimportant.

Nevertheless, it is hoped that anyone spotting an error or omission in the maps will write to the Atlas Correction Editor, BTO, Beech Grove, Tring, Herts, HP23 5NR. Please bear in mind, however, that for maps with secret records it cannot be stated whether a dot is misplaced or omitted, since this could reveal data which are being intentionally concealed.

DATA PRESENTATION

The three grades of evidence of breeding—possible, probable and confirmed—are shown on the maps as three increasing sizes of dots. The absence of a dot indicates that the species was not *reported* in suitable breeding habitat during the breeding seasons of 1968–72. Such blank areas will often accurately reflect the species' absence, but this cannot be assumed, as it is only in certain cases that truly negative records can be obtained. It is usually safe to assume, however, that the species is not common in such blank squares.

In the few cases where past distribution surveys have been made and maps for earlier periods are available, these are shown in an appendix on pages 454–465.

Changes in many county boundaries and names came into effect in England and Wales on 1st April 1974 and in Scotland on 16th May 1975. Since the *Atlas* survey covered the period 1968–72, and much of the organisation was based on the county units, the names and boundaries used at that time are retained throughout this book. Both the old and the new county boundaries are shown on an overlay. On all the main maps, the Channel Islands are shown in an inset block at the bottom left hand corner.

The texts accompanying the maps are sometimes speculative and are intended primarily to provide an interesting and interpretive background to the maps, which contain the hard facts obtained by the *Atlas* project. Many of the texts have been checked by specialist referees, usually ornithologists who have studied the species concerned. More detailed analyses of distributions will doubtless be the subject of future scientific papers and are considered to be out of place in this book.

The factors affecting bird distributions are complex and usually not fully understood. A number of relevant factors have been mapped as transparent overlays, obtainable separately from the BTO, and the reader may care to compare these with the species maps. The reasons for range changes are similarly frequently obscure. Parslow (1973) has documented our knowledge up to 1967 and Williamson (1975) has reviewed the general situation with respect to climatic change. This *Atlas* is the first stage in the

precise documentation which may aid interpretation of distribution changes.

As already noted (page 18), over 1,800 British records of rare or locally rare birds were submitted on secret cards. At the end of 1972, the observers submitting these were asked whether they should still be regarded as confidential. In many cases, usually because the species had been found to be commoner than expected or the birds had not reappeared in subsequent years, all restrictions were lifted. Where secrecy was still considered to be justified, however, observers were asked to allow the Rare Breeding Birds Panel (and sometimes also a specialist consultant) to see the *Atlas* map and recommend a method of treatment which was safe for the species. Permission for this was refused by only eleven observers (35 records). In many cases, those concerned agreed that the Rare Breeding Birds Panel's recommended treatment be implemented without further consultation.

In the botanical atlas, dots of a few rare species were displaced by one 10-km in any direction without the fact that this had been done being indicated. The methods of treatment recommended by the Rare Breeding Birds Panel varied according to the species, but were aimed at providing full protection for vulnerable birds or sites, while distorting the distribution maps as little as possible. The usual methods were (1) moving dots by one or two 10-km squares in any direction; (2) placing dots centrally in shaded 50-km or 100-km squares; or (3) omitting dots entirely. Secret records in the Republic of Ireland have been treated in the same way, except that here Major R. F. Ruttledge and David Scott were the advisors. *These protective devices have in no case been used without the fact being clearly stated alongside the map.* Where a specialist consultant gave advice on treatment, this is also stated.

With this background, it can be understood that a dot for a rare species may refer to one pair which nested in 1968 and has never returned. Alternately, where a dot has been moved by one or two squares, it may refer to any of the eight or 24 neighbouring squares. Thus, while the maps truly reflect each species' total distribution during 1968–72, the major direct threats to rare birds, from egg-collectors, falconers and over-enthusiastic birdwatchers and photographers, will not be increased by the publication of this *Atlas*.

Analyses of the records appear at the end of each text. These give the number of squares in which the species was reported in 1968–72, and the percentage of all the squares in Britain and Ireland that this represented; and the number of these squares in which possible, probable and confirmed breeding was reported, with each expressed as a percentage of the number of squares in which the species was found. Since they are rounded to the nearest whole number, the sum of these percentages is, of course, often 99% or 101%, rather than 100%.

For some species, usually the scarcer ones, accurate censuses have been made. Where such figures are available, they have been quoted. For the majority of species, however, it is possible only to guess at the total numbers breeding in Britain and Ireland. Though the scientific validity of such guesses is open to question, the *Atlas* survey has placed us in a better position than ever before to make rough estimates, since we now know for the first time the precise extent of each species' range. With a knowledge of densities in different parts of the British and Irish range, from small-scale census work or field experience in a variety of areas during the *Atlas* survey, rough assessments can be made of the average number of pairs per 10-km square. These are inevitably personal judgments, open to amendment in the light of future census work. From these figures, an approximate assessment of the total British and Irish population in 1972 has been made, and this is frequently compared with the most recent previous estimate, that of Parslow (1973). Such speculative use of the *Atlas* data is open to criticism, but we hope that the figures will be treated as a helpful guide to those of our readers who are unfamiliar with the relative abundance of species here.

The vernacular names, scientific names and sequence follow *A Species List of British and Irish Birds*, BTO Guide 13, edited by Robert Hudson (1971). In the few instances where a scarce species is relegated to the end of the list, this fact is boldly noted in the species' correct position.

COMMON BIRDS CENSUS

The CBC is mentioned in many of the texts in this book, and graphs derived from it are shown for 20 species. This scheme, which started in 1962 and has been carried out annually since then, is designed to detect and measure population changes of certain common species, using sample census areas. Defined areas are visited on eight to a dozen or more occasions during March–July and registrations of all birds seen or heard are plotted on to maps. Standard methods, both of recording and of analysis, are rigidly adhered to, and clusters of registrations are taken to indicate the birds' territories. Since the same observers visit the same areas each year, counts of the number of territories provide an index of population change.

The census areas are scattered over the UK, but most are in England. In 1972, there were 86 areas on farmland, totalling 6,154 ha (average 72 ha), and 62 in woodland, totalling 1,591 ha (average 26 ha).

By 1966, many resident species had fully recovered from the depletions of the severe winter of 1962/63. The graphs show population levels in relation to that of 1966, which is assigned the value of 100 (shown by the horizontal dotted line).

FINAL RESULTS AND BIAS

The number of species which had been found in each 10-km square by the end of each year of fieldwork is shown by ranges in figs 4–8. These display visually the progress of the survey. Although certain squares were undoubtedly more thoroughly surveyed than others, coverage was relatively uniform within Britain and Ireland as a whole. In the opinion of the regional organisers, at least 75% of the expected species were found in every square. It must be admitted, however, that the estimates of expected species were very approximate in some areas; they were made after examination of the 1968–71 results, but there were many instances where the total number of species found in a square eventually exceeded the estimate made six months earlier. It is safe to say, however, that no square was badly under-surveyed and that the degree of coverage was comparable in all areas of Britain and Ireland. It is obvious that the smaller number of species which nest in some parts of our area (*eg* Ireland, Outer Hebrides) make it impossible directly to relate number of species to coverage.

Severe winter weather can cause serious declines in the numbers of resident species, thereby making it far more difficult to find them in the breeding season, and can even significantly alter breeding distributions. With no really hard winter since that of 1962/63, populations were high and distributions extensive when the *Atlas* project started in 1968. We were very lucky that the following four winters were also mild. The fieldwork was, therefore, easier than it might have been, bias did not occur (as it would have if some squares had been surveyed before and others after a hard winter) and the distributions of resident species are probably close to their maxima. Two problem species also 'co-operated' by timing their invasions to suit the *Atlas* project. Quail *Coturnix coturnix* have a restricted breeding distribution except in those years when more than usual arrive on spring migration: 1970 was such a year. On the other hand, no irruption of Crossbills *Loxia curvirostra* occurred until June/July 1972, and most records of such migrants could be separated from breeding birds, so the *Atlas* map shows a minimum for that species— those isolated pockets which survive even between irruptions. A Crossbill irruption in 1970 or 1971 would have created coverage problems and probably resulted in a patchy and misleading map. The Whitethroat *Sylvia communis*, and to a lesser extent some other species associated with the Sahel zone of Africa in winter, suffered a population crash, however, whilst others, such as the Redpoll *Acanthis flammea*, extended their ranges during 1968–72. Comment on such events is made under the individual species, but we were lucky that, on the whole, the period of the *Atlas* survey was for most species fairly representative of any five years between the mid-1960s and mid-1970s.

THE FUTURE

Other breeding bird atlas projects, using the same techniques as here, were started in France in 1970 and Denmark in 1971. Interest in distribution mapping was so great at the 'Study Conference on the Co-ordination and Encouragement of Amateur Ornithology in Europe', held at Green Park, Aston Clinton (Buckinghamshire) during 6th–10th December 1971, that a European Ornithological Atlas Committee was formed to co-ordinate all European projects. By 1976, 18 European nations were undertaking atlas projects under the aegis of the EOAC, and it is planned that the whole of Europe, including Britain and Ireland, will be covered by new or repeat surveys, starting in 1985. National projects usually use 10-km squares (or convenient alternatives) but Europe-wide mapping is by 50-km squares on the Universal Transverse Mercator grid.

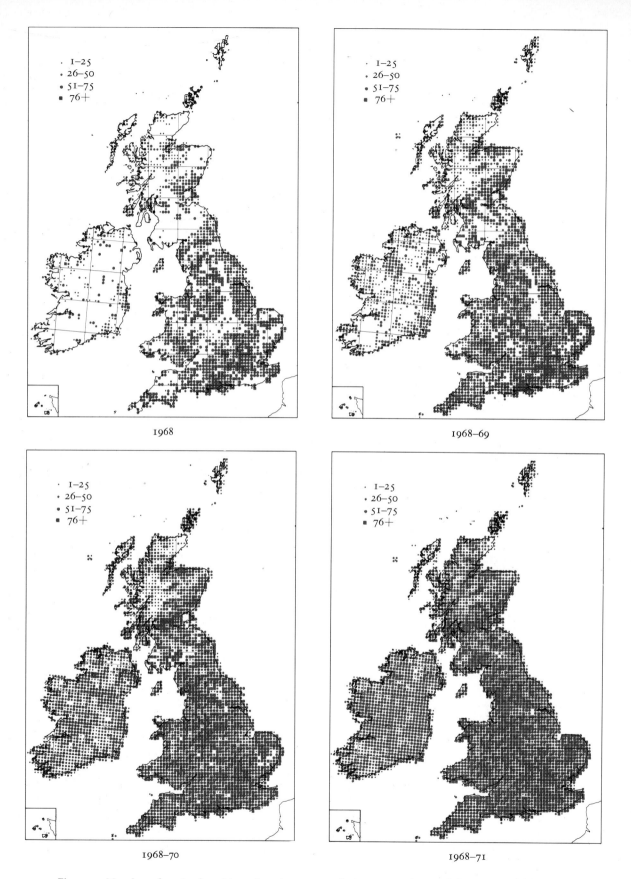

Figs. 4–7. Number of species found in each 10-km square after one, two, three and four years of fieldwork

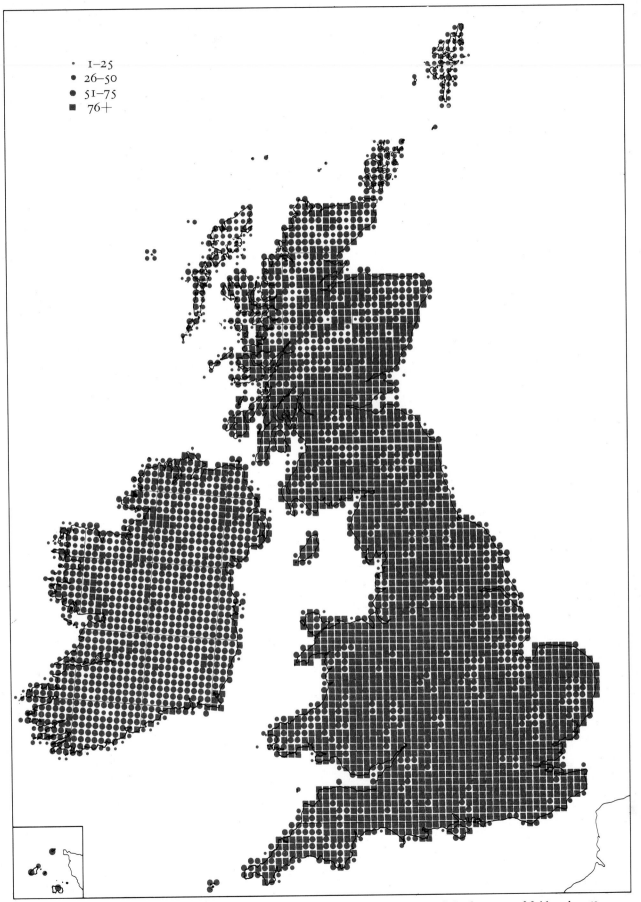

Fig. 8. Number of species which had been found in each 10-km square by the end of the five years of fieldwork 1968–72

England, Wales and Scotland

The basic principle of the Protection of Birds Act, 1954–67, is that all wild birds and their nests and eggs are protected at all times by law. There are certain specified exceptions to allow for the taking or killing by authorised persons, such as landowners and their agents, of pest species (listed in the Second Schedule) and of certain species of wildfowl and waders which, though protected during their breeding seasons, may be shot as sporting quarry during September to January inclusive (Third Schedule). About 60 of the rarer British breeding species are listed separately in the First Schedule and are accorded special protection. The remaining unscheduled species, numbering about 370, receive ordinary protection.

Except as permitted by licence under the Act, it is an offence to take or kill, or to take or destroy the nest, eggs or nestlings of, any protected wild bird, or to take for ringing any wild bird. In the cases of specially protected (First Schedule) species, which are individually noted at the ends of the appropriate *Atlas* texts, it is also an offence wilfully or knowingly to disturb the birds on or near a nest containing eggs or unflown young. Offences involving specially protected species carry a special penalty.

The Secretaries of State are empowered to alter the protection status of any species, either by revising the Schedules or by making local orders. For example, a formerly common species which becomes rare may be placed on the First Schedule; a protected species which becomes a pest may be transferred to the Second Schedule, either nationally or in specified districts.

Northern Ireland

The Wild Birds Protection Acts, 1931–68, allow for the complete protection of all species, with the exceptions of (1) a small list of pest species, (2) a much smaller list of pests of fruit trees and (3) the sporting species. In addition, the Conservation Branch of the Department of the Environment (Northern Ireland) also administers the Game Acts, which allow for various protection measures; currently the Partridge *Perdix perdix* is completely protected. The same branch also administers the Amenity Lands Act, under which the National Nature Reserves are declared.

Republic of Ireland

Comprehensive new legislation on wildlife and habitat now (May 1976) going through the legislature will give full protection throughout the year to all birds and their nests and eggs, except certain excessively numerous species, such as the House Sparrow *Passer domesticus* and the Woodpigeon *Columba palumbus*. It provides for open seasons for gamebirds, accidental destruction in the course of farming, and other specific exceptions. Disturbance of the nests of certain species will also be illegal. There are potentially important powers to create nature reserves. Ringing may be carried out only under licence, and the taking of birds of prey for falconry is regulated.

MAP PRODUCTION

It may be found that the dots on some maps are not wholly within the appropriate 10-km squares. This is not a printing fault, but is caused by varying degrees of inaccuracy inherent in the original print-out process from the punched cards. All the more evident misplacements have been adjusted, but total accuracy throughout would have added unreasonably to the cost and the minor degrees of error remaining are unlikely to be misleading.

In preparing the maps for printing, not only was it necessary to reorientate each print-out to conform with the approved Irish grid, but all dots for Orkney and Shetland had to be repositioned by hand, since the computer print-out followed the common practice of placing these islands in a box off the Scottish east coast.

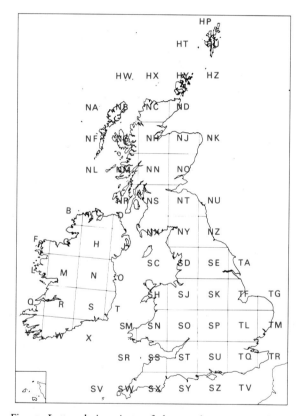

Fig. 9. Letter designations of the 100-km squares of the British and Irish grids

LITERATURE

Text references are limited to those where a book or paper deals exclusively or nearly exclusively with the species being discussed, or contains data specifically mentioned in the text.

The most recent county bird book and/or county bird report has been referred to whenever specific counties are mentioned, and these detailed references are not all listed.

Certain standard works have been frequently consulted in the writing of this book. The reader would find it tedious if these were mentioned on each occasion in the text, so they are listed here. These invaluable sources of reference have been consulted for every relevant species and much is owed to their authors:

BAXTER, E. V. and L. J. RINTOUL. 1953. *The Birds of Scotland*. Edinburgh and London. 2 vols.

CAMPBELL, B. and I. J. FERGUSON-LEES. 1972. *A Field Guide to Birds' Nests*. London.

CRAMP, S., W. R. P. BOURNE and D. SAUNDERS. 1974. *The Seabirds of Britain and Ireland*. London.

DOBINSON, H. M. and A. J. RICHARDS. 1964. The effects of the severe winter of 1962/63 on birds in Britain. *Brit. Birds* 57: 373–434.

HUDSON, R. 1973. *Early and Late Dates for Summer Migrants*. BTO Guide 15. Tring.

KENNEDY, P. G., R. F. RUTTLEDGE and C. F. SCROOPE. 1954. *The Birds of Ireland*. Edinburgh and London.

PARSLOW, J. 1973. *Breeding Birds of Britain and Ireland*. Berkhamsted. (This is mainly a reprint of a series of papers which appeared in *British Birds* in 1967–68; when the time scale is important it may be referred to in the text as 'Parslow (1967)', but otherwise merely as 'Parslow'.)

RUTTLEDGE, R. F. 1966. *Ireland's Birds*. London.

VOOUS, K. H. 1960. *Atlas of European Birds*. Amsterdam and London.

WITHERBY, H. F., F. C. R. JOURDAIN, N. F. TICEHURST and B. W. TUCKER. 1938–41. *The Handbook of British Birds*. London. 5 vols.

References cited in the Introduction or related to methodology:

FERGUSON-LEES, I. J. and J. T. R. SHARROCK. 1971. A comparison between basic Atlas and tetrad techniques. *Bird Study* 18: 227–228.

LORD, J. and D. J. MUNNS. 1970. *Atlas of Breeding Birds in the West Midlands*. London.

NORRIS, C. A. 1960. The breeding distribution of thirty bird species in 1952. *Bird Study* 7: 129–184.

PARSLOW, J. 1973. *Breeding Birds of Britain and Ireland*. Berkhamsted.

PERRING, F. H. and S. M. WALTERS. 1962. *Atlas of the British Flora*. London and Edinburgh.

PRESTT, I. and A. A. BELL. 1966. An objective method of recording breeding distribution of common birds of prey in Britain. *Bird Study* 13: 277–283.

SHARROCK, J. T. R. 1971. Seasonal changes in ease of proving breeding. *Bird Study* 18: 38.

— 1973a. Rate of species-registration in Atlas work. *Bird Study* 20: 88–90.

— 1973b. Ornithological Atlases. *Auspicium* 5, suppl.: 13–15.

— 1974a. Minutes of the second meeting of the European Ornithological Atlas Committee. *Acta Orn.* 14: 404–411.

— 1974b. The ornithological Atlas project in Britain and Ireland. Methods and preliminary results. *Acta Orn.* 14: 412–428.

— 1974c. Le projet d'Atlas en Grande-Bretagne et en Irelande. *Aves* 11: 137–142.

— 1974d. The changing status of breeding birds in Britain and Ireland. pp 203–220 in HAWKSWORTH, D. L. (ed), *The Changing Flora and Fauna of Britain*. London and New York.

— 1975. Dot-distribution mapping of breeding birds in Europe. *Ardeola* 21: 797–810.

WILLIAMSON, K. 1975. Birds and climatic change. *Bird Study* 22: 143–164.

YARKER, B. and G. L. ATKINSON-WILLES. 1971. The numerical distribution of some British breeding ducks. *Wildfowl* 22: 63–70.

ABBREVIATIONS
The following abbreviations are used in the text:

BBC	British Broadcasting Corporation
BRC	Biological Records Centre
BSBI	Botanical Society of the British Isles
BTO	British Trust for Ornithology
CBC	BTO Common Birds Census
cm	centimetre
E	east
ha	hectare
IWC	Irish Wildbird Conservancy
km	kilometre
km²	square kilometre
LNR	Local Nature Reserve
m	metre
N	North
NCC	Nature Conservancy Council
NNR	National Nature Reserve
OS	Ordnance Survey
RSPB	Royal Society for the Protection of Birds
S	South
UK	United Kingdom
W	West
WAGBI	Wildfowlers' Association of Great Britain and Ireland
10-km square	10 km × 10 km square of the British or Irish National Grids

Black-throated Diver

Gavia arctica

Black-throated Divers are summer visitors to their freshwater breeding haunts, spending the winter at sea or in estuaries, or sometimes on lakes or man-made waters near the coast. In summer they require large lochs, since their food is usually obtained close at hand, and they need a long take-off before becoming airborne (*cf* Red-throated Diver *G. stellata*). They are vulnerable to disturbance and, for this reason, the nest is usually on an islet, which also serves as a protection from land-based predators, especially Foxes. Although perfectly adapted for swimming and diving, all divers move awkwardly on land; the nest is usually sited within a metre or so of the water's edge, only slightly above water level and, in consequence, lochs subject to large fluctuations are unsuitable. This objection applies to those with an inadequate outlet, and also to lakes harnessed for hydro-electric schemes, where control of the water level may be erratic.

In Britain and Ireland, the species' requirements are seemingly met only in Scotland, with the majority of sites in the most desolate areas of the west. Some breeding lochs are close to public roads, however, and the birds can be observed from a parked car without disturbance. They usually nest earlier than the Red-throated: the two chicks often hatch before the end of May, and can be watched as they follow their parents, dipping their heads below the surface in imitation of the adults (Watson 1972). The Black-throated is one of our scarcest birds and, with increasing tourism in its breeding range, care must be taken if this attractive species is to maintain its numbers.

There were signs of a decline earlier in this century, but recently numbers have remained fairly constant (though those actually nesting vary from year to year, depending upon the effects of rainfall on water levels). The range has spread to Arran and SW Scotland since 1951 and 1956 respectively, and a pair with chicks in Galloway in 1974 represented the first successful hatch in that region. This may be part of a continuing spread in the west, for Harvie-Brown (1895) showed that Skye, Mull, Jura, Islay and Kin-

tyre were all outside the breeding range (see map on page 454). On the other hand, there seems to have been a contraction in the east, with poor breeding success and disappearance from some long-established sites. The absence from Orkney and Shetland is strange; breeding has been reported in both island groups in the past, but has never been regular. The species is relatively rare in Ireland, even as a migrant, and there are no nesting records. The possibility should be borne in mind, however, for the nearest Scottish site is only some 40 km from the coast of Northern Ireland.

The problem of low breeding success has troubled Scottish ornithologists in recent years, and there is now a regular RSPB monitoring scheme for sample sites throughout the Highlands. In 1972, 58–59 pairs were checked, of which 10 pairs reared 13 young and the rest failed; in 1973, 35 pairs produced only 8–10 young and breeding success was no better in 1974. In all three years, summer flooding was rated as more harmful than human disturbance.

Confirmed or probable breeding was recorded in 145 10-km squares during 1968–72. There is seldom more than one pair on a loch and only one to three pairs are likely to have bred in any square, while it is probable that the same pair will sometimes have been recorded on different lochs (and in other squares). It seems likely that the Scottish population exceeds the estimate of 'under 100 pairs' made by Campbell and Ferguson-Lees (1972), but it is certainly less than 200 and likely to be close to Parslow's estimate of 150.

This species is afforded special protection in Great Britain under Schedule I of the Protection of Birds Act, 1954–67.

Number of 10-km squares in which recorded:
212 (5%)
Possible breeding   67 (32%)
Probable breeding   49 (23%)
Confirmed breeding   96 (45%)

Six dots have been moved by up to two 10-km squares (as recommended by the Rare Breeding Birds Panel)

References

HARVIE-BROWN, J. A. 1895. In *Atlas of Scotland*. Edinburgh.
RANKIN, N. 1947. *Haunts of British Divers*. London.
WATSON, D. 1972. *Birds of Moor and Mountain*. Edinburgh.

Great Northern Diver *Gavia immer,* **see page 446**

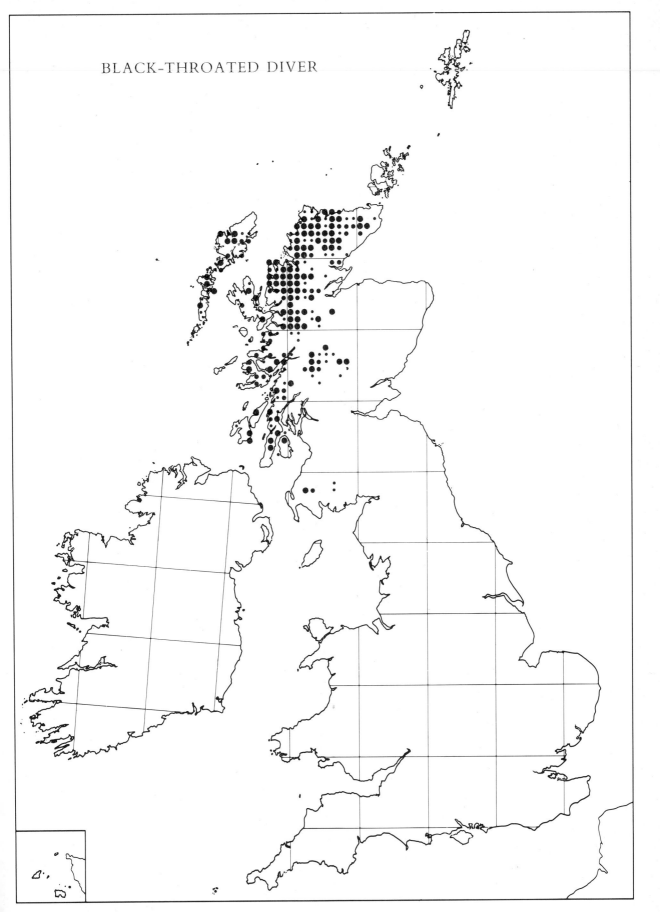

BLACK-THROATED DIVER

29

Red-throated Diver

Gavia stellata

Like the Black-throated *G. arctica*, the Red-throated Diver is found mostly in coastal waters in winter, returning to its breeding grounds in April or May. The main difference between the two species' habitat requirements hinges on the Red-throated's ability to take off in a shorter space, allowing it to utilise smaller waters such as remote hill lochans. Most of its food is obtained at some distance from the nest site, either on the sea or on large sea-lochs. With its habit of flying to the sea for food, one would anticipate a more coastal distribution than that of the Black-throated Diver; this is so, but the difference is less marked than might be expected.

The peat pools or *dubh-lochans* where most Red-throated Divers nest may be tiny, some so small that they are not even marked on the 2½ inches to 1 mile (1:25,000) maps. Watson (1972) remarked that on one Inner Hebridean island there was a pair on each of over a dozen lochs in a single tract of moorland. The pools may be situated in vast areas of blanket-bog and moor where the casual visitor is unlikely to come across them; although their water level is only slightly below the surrounding land, they are often invisible to an observer only 50 m away. The birds are often vocal, their resonant, quacking 'kok-ok-ok' being used when flying down to the sea, or as a greeting and communication call when arriving at the loch. Initial location of breeding pairs, except those on the larger lochs, is more difficult than for Black-throated Divers, but, once found, they are easier to prove breeding (as shown by 60% confirmed records for the Red-throated, compared with 45% for the Black-throated).

As with the Black-throated Diver, the breeding range is mostly in N and W Scotland, but there are three striking differences between the two species. First, Red-throated Divers breed commonly in Shetland and Orkney, Black-throated Divers being absent; this partly reflects the profusion of small waters and lack of larger lochs. Secondly, although pairs nested in Ayrshire and probably in Kircudbright-shire in the 1950s, and a single pair bred in Galloway in 1973, none was located in SW Scotland during 1968–72, though Black-throated Divers were present. Thirdly, there is a small population in NW Ireland: despite growing disturbance, these have held on and increased since one pair was discovered in 1884.

Comparing the species' present distribution with that given by Harvie-Brown (1895) (see map on page 454), it is clear that Kintyre, Islay, Jura and Perthshire represent major extensions of range in the last 80 years. The greatest increase, however, has probably occurred in the Northern and Western Isles, perhaps because of reduced persecution. A drop in numbers on the mainland during the early 1940s has been attributed to predation by Foxes, which increased as a result of the fewer gamekeepers during the 1939–45 war years.

Human disturbance is probably the greatest threat to the Red-throated Diver, for the birds fly from the loch when put off the nest and may not return for half an hour or so, during which time predators such as gulls or crows are likely to eat the eggs. Extreme care should be exercised, therefore, when in Red-throated Diver country. Of 62 pairs monitored in the Highlands in 1972, only 28–29 pairs bred successfully, rearing 42 young, though this was much better than the corresponding figure for the Black-throated.

Since the location of nest sites is far less easy than for the Black-throated Diver, it is more difficult to deduce approximate breeding numbers from *Atlas* data. Presence in suitable habitat in the breeding season is, however, more indicative of nesting, and many squares hold more than one pair, so it is probable that the number of pairs is well in excess of the 319 squares in which they were found. Parslow classed the Red-throated Diver as 'scarce' (100–1,000 pairs). Bundy (1976) found 41 pairs on the Shetland island of Unst in 1974, when there were at least 60 pairs elsewhere in Shetland and some 40 in Orkney. In the absence of a wider census, an intelligent guess would place the present British and Irish population at over 750 pairs.

This species is afforded special protection in Great Britain under Schedule I of the Protection of Birds Act, 1954–67.

Number of 10-km squares in which recorded:
319 (8%)
Possible breeding   70 (22%)
Probable breeding   57 (18%)
Confirmed breeding   192 (60%)

Within the shaded square, dots are conventionally placed centrally (as recommended by Major R. F. Ruttledge and D. Scott)

References

BUNDY, G. 1976. Aspects of breeding biology of the Red-throated Diver. *Bird Study* 23:

HARVIE-BROWN, J. A. 1895. In *Atlas of Scotland*. Edinburgh.

RANKIN, N. 1947. *Haunts of British Divers*. London.

WATSON, D. 1972. *Birds of Moor and Mountain*. Edinburgh and London.

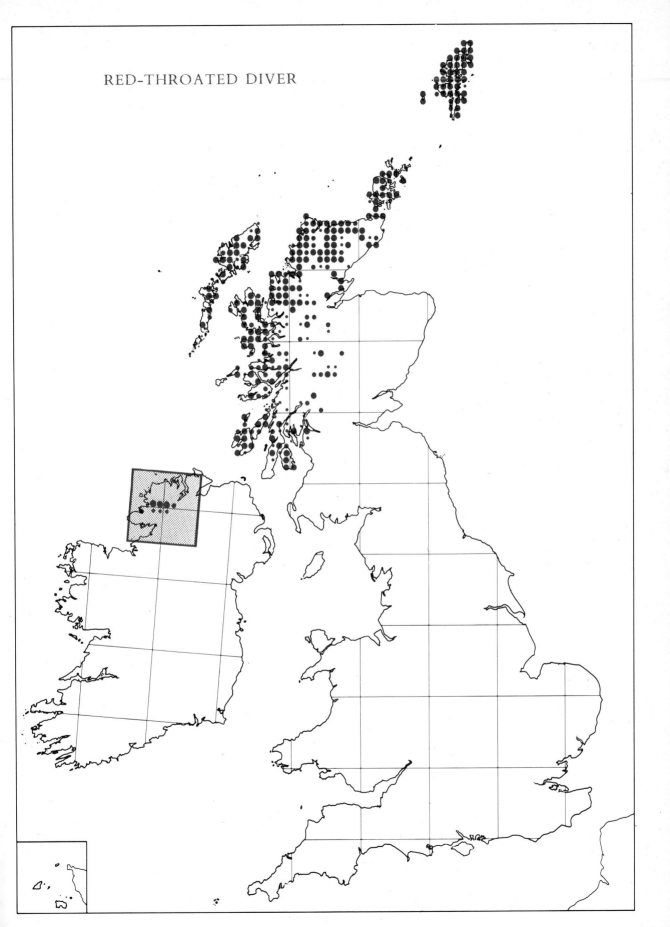

RED-THROATED DIVER

Great Crested Grebe

Podiceps cristatus

The history of this very attractive species provides a classic success story, the population showing a good recovery from impending disaster at the end of the last century.

Great Crested Grebes breed almost exclusively on shallow lakes, usually with a depth not exceeding 3–4 m. The deep lochs of highland Scotland are unsuitable. Small ponds are seldom occupied since the species has a long take-off run; each pair usually requires 2–3 ha of open water. Though most of the shallow lakes are in the lowlands, breeding sometimes occurs at altitudes of over 200 m.

Up to about 1850, Great Crested Grebes were well distributed in small numbers in about 13 counties, and over a score of lakes are known to have had breeding grebes since at least 1840. About the middle of the 19th century, however, the under-pelts became fashionable as 'grebe furs'. Initially these were imported from the Continent, but from 1857 a massacre of the British stock continued until, by 1860, possibly only 32 pairs were left. Three-quarters of these were in Cheshire and Norfolk, whilst Staffordshire, Suffolk, Lancashire and Yorkshire harboured the rest. Some remained on the Cheshire meres and Norfolk Broads, but privately owned lakes on large estates where shooting was restricted may have served as the main refuge at this time of crisis.

Bird Protection Acts in 1870, 1873 and 1877 helped the grebes, but full protection in the breeding season (March to July) did not come until 1880. Before this, however, fresh colonisation had occurred. Some influx from the Continent was expected, since this and other wetland species were spreading northwest as a result of the drying-up of lakes in SE Europe and SW Asia (Kalela 1949). The first nesting in Scotland was in 1877 and, from a single pair at Tring Reservoirs (Hertfordshire) in 1867, there was within less than 20 years a breeding stock of 75 pairs, which acted as a nucleus for the colonisation of S England.

The first detailed census in 1931 recorded 1,154–1,161 pairs in England and Wales and about 80 pairs

in Scotland. Further sample surveys were made during 1935 and 1946–55, but it became clear that partial counts must be treated with caution, for changes in numbers, even in adjoining areas, need not show any correlation. By 1965, when another full census was carried out, numbers had further increased to about 4,132–4,737 birds (see maps on page 454). This growth probably took place mostly after the 1940s. The species has a marked ability to colonise new sites as soon as these become available. Some new reservoirs afford suitable haunts, but one of the main habitats now, at least in S England and the Midlands, is flooded gravel-pits. Disused sections soon have a luxuriant vegetation, and the pits usually have an ideal depth of water.

In Ireland a great increase occurred during this century and is continuing. Co Wexford was colonised in 1946 and Co Limerick then or the following year. Man-made waters are fewer, but some of the range expansion (*eg* in Co Cork since 1967) is linked with artificial sites.

The 1968–72 map probably reflects accurately the distribution in those years, since the habitat is clear-cut and the birds are easy to spot on open water. The high proportion (nearly four-fifths) of records relating to confirmed breeding and, particularly, the very low proportion of probable records reflect the ease with which breeding can be proved. The nests are frequently conspicuous mounds of vegetation, and young grebes can be readily observed since they often ride on the adults' backs rather than hide in the reed-beds, thus gaining protection from predators such as Pike.

Despite high residues of organochlorine pesticides in some Great Crested Grebes, the main threat to the species now is probably the leisure activities of affluent man: water-skiing and small boat recreation on the grebes' lakes cause unacceptable disturbance, and the wave-action from motor-boats can swamp the nests. A suitable compromise, leaving some waters for man's aquatic pastimes, and others free from such disturbance, should ensure the birds' continued presence.

Number of 10-km squares in which recorded:
987 (26%)

Possible breeding   128 (13%)
Probable breeding   77 (8%)
Confirmed breeding   782 (79%)

References

HARRISSON, T. H. and P. A. D. HOLLOM. 1932. The Great Crested Grebe enquiry, 1931. *Brit. Birds* 26: 62–92, 102–131, 142–155, 174–195.

HOLLOM, P. A. D. 1936. Report on Great Crested Grebe sample count 1935. *Brit. Birds* 30: 138–158.

HOLLOM, P. A. D. 1959. The Great Crested Grebe sample census, 1946–55. *Bird Study* 6: 1–7.

KALELA, O. 1949. Changes in geographic ranges in the avifauna of northern and central Europe in relation to recent changes in climate. *Bird Banding* 20: 77–103.

PRESTT, I. and D. H. MILLS. 1966. A census of the Great Crested Grebe in Britain, 1965. *Bird Study* 13: 163–203.

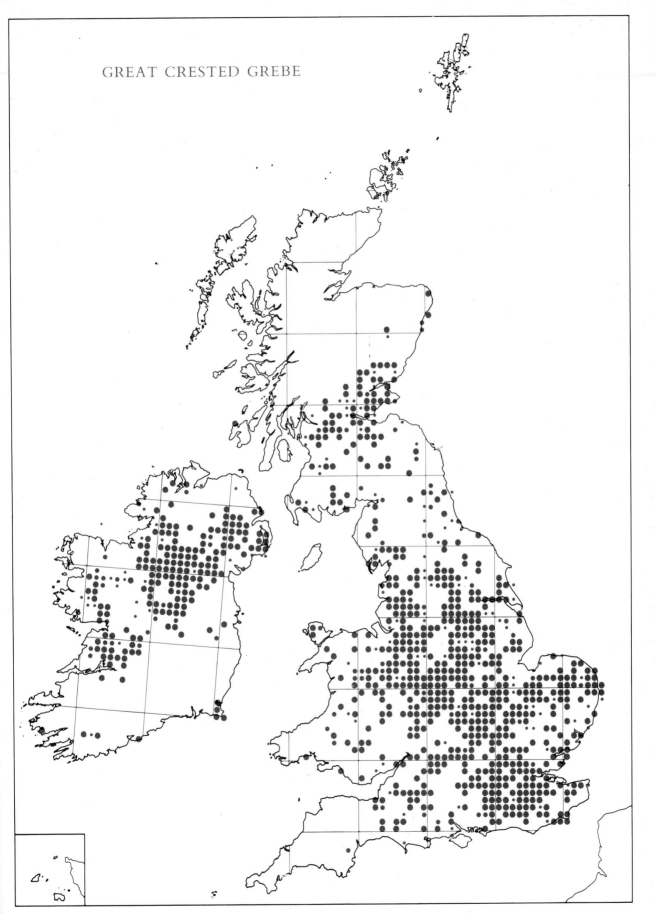

GREAT CRESTED GREBE

Slavonian Grebe

Podiceps auritus

Slavonian Grebes in the Scottish Highlands are very much birds of still, shallow, freshwater lochs, usually remote from regular human disturbance, although the breeding pairs themselves are quite confiding. They are not found so much on small lochans as are Black-necked Grebes *P. nigricollis*, seeming to prefer sites with less densely vegetated margins and more extensive areas of open water; nevertheless, they like some emergent vegetation in which to anchor their nests. Such lochs are likely to be surrounded by rocks and acidic heather moor, and there are no breeding records from similar waters on the alkaline sands of the Hebridean machair.

Slavonian Grebes winter on tidal waters and return to their lochs between mid-March and early April. Most in Scotland are colonial and, despite the strong territorial interactions and chases that are provoked—initiating displays which have been fully described by Fjeldså (1973b)—the nests may be within a few feet of one another, or in equally close proximity to those of Black-headed Gulls *Larus ridibundus*. There are Scottish records of seven nests in one patch of reeds measuring about 40 m² and, on another loch, of 11 nests in one bay and four in another (Bannerman 1959). 'A colony is a scene of scurrying activity punctuated with trilling call-notes, softer in pitch than the equivalent sound made by Little Grebes *Tachybaptus ruficollis*' (Watson 1972). The nest is a typical grebe's floating platform of dead and decaying vegetation with the cup only slightly above water level; although built 2–3 m from the shore in a bed of aquatic plants, it is sometimes very exposed and so easier to find than those of other grebes.

The small Scottish population has been building up slowly since the first nest was found in Inverness-shire in 1908, and this initial site is today the nucleus of the range. Though Sutherland was colonised in 1929, the grebes did not prosper there and none has nested for some years; but definite gains are Caithness (from 1929), Morayshire (since the 1950s) and Perthshire (from 1973). Breeding has also occurred occasionally in Aberdeenshire since 1960, while in 1972 there was an extraordinary record of a Slavonian

apparently interbreeding with a Black-necked Grebe on a loch in the central lowlands (Dennis 1973). Since 1971 there have been annual censuses, and these are summarised below in tabular form. Although a decline is apparent in Caithness, this has been amply compensated for by increases in Inverness-shire, where there were said to be only about 15 pairs in 1958 (Bannerman 1959), but 47–51 pairs dispersed over 19 lochs in 1974.

Scottish Slavonian Grebes suffer from disturbance and illegal egg-collecting; their breeding is impaired if water levels are too low, or rise too quickly after rain, while the young are preyed upon by Pike and gulls. Breeding success is low in most years: in Inverness-shire about 40 pairs reared 16–17 young in 1971 and 23–26 young in 1972. Despite this, the slow growth continues and, unless Slavonian Grebes have a very high mean adult survival rate, some immigration must still be taking place.

This species is afforded special protection in Great Britain under Schedule I of the Protection of Birds Act, 1954–67.

Scottish breeding Slavonian Grebes (pairs)

County	1971	1972	1973	1974
CAITHNESS	6–10	2–3	2	2
INVERNESS				
N of Great Glen	11	12–13	18–19	18–20
S of Great Glen	27–29	27–28	23–24	28–30
Strathspey	1	1	1	1
MORAY	7	6	5–6	5–6
ABERDEEN	—	—	—	1
PERTH	—	—	2	2
Totals	52–58	48–51	51–54	57–62

Number of 10-km squares in which recorded:
20 (0.5%)
Possible breeding   7 (35%)
Probable breeding   1 (5%)
Confirmed breeding   12 (60%)

Within the shaded areas, the dots are conventionally placed centrally (as recommended by the Rare Breeding Birds Panel)

References

DENNIS, R. H. 1973. Possible interbreeding of Slavonian Grebe and Black-necked Grebe in Scotland. *Scott. Birds* 7: 307–308.

FJELDSÅ, J. 1973a. Distribution and geographical variation of the Horned Grebe *Podiceps auritus* (Linn. 1758). *Orn. Scand.* 4: 55–86.

FJELDSÅ, J. 1973b. Antagonistic and heterosexual behaviour of the Horned Grebe *Podiceps auritus*. *Sterna* 12: 161–217.

WATSON, D. 1972. *Birds of Moor and Mountain*. Edinburgh.

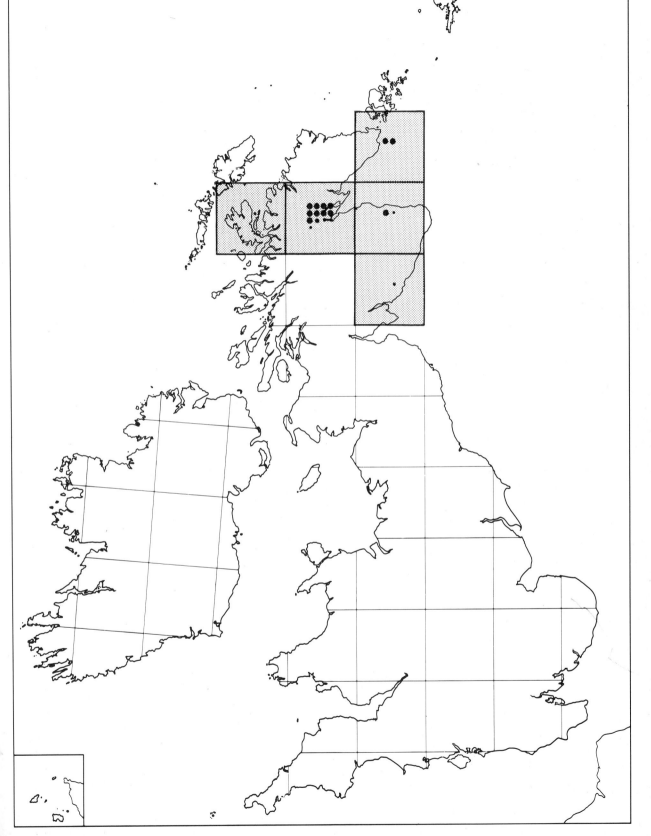

SLAVONIAN GREBE

Black-necked Grebe

Podiceps nigricollis

Black-necked Grebes are commoner as winter visitors to our coasts and inland waters than as breeding birds. They usually arrive at their nesting haunts in April and depart in August, frequenting eutrophic pools with a luxuriant growth of shore plants and submerged and floating aquatic vegetation, often with very little open water. Though not uncommon in Ireland, particularly in limestone areas, this type of pool is relatively rare in Britain, which is doubtless one of the reasons for the species' scarcity; there are far fewer suitable sites for Black-necked than for the other grebes, including the Slavonian *P. auritus*. Sporadic nesting may occur almost anywhere, however; for instance, a pair nested successfully in 1971 at a temporary pond formed by water pumped from a coal mine. On the Continent there is frequently a loose association with breeding terns or Black-headed Gulls *Larus ridibundus*, which provide a protective 'umbrella' against avian predators, so marshy pools with tussocks are often favoured.

Black-necked Grebes were unknown as breeding birds in Britain and Ireland until early in this century. Breeding first occurred in Wales in 1904 (perhaps earlier), Ireland in 1915 (perhaps 1906), England in 1918 and Scotland in 1930. The main periods of colonisation, however, were in 1918–20 and 1929–32, during a general northwesterly range expansion across Europe, attributed by Kalela (1949) to the desiccation of the lakes in the steppes of the Caspian region. A northwards range extension has also occurred in N America.

This species provided what was perhaps the most exciting piece of detective work involving breeding birds in Britain and Ireland this century. A pair and three downy young were obtained at a western lake in Ireland by J. ffolliott Darling on 17th June 1918, but Darling died without disclosing the locality. In 1929, after many years of diligent searching, C. V. Stoney and G. R. Humphreys discovered a large colony at what was almost certainly the same site, Lough Funshinagh in Co Roscommon. In 1930, they estimated some 250 breeding pairs; in 1932, 155 nests

were examined and there may have been as many again. Unfortunately the tale ends sadly. Although the site was subject to periodic drying up, like many turloughs in W Ireland, the nearby Shannon hydro-electric scheme resulted in more permanent drainage in 1934; a few pairs bred in subsequent years, but none has nested there since 1959.

Short-term colonisations are reported from time to time, and these delightful birds may well be under-recorded. Their favoured haunt is such that in some circumstances they may not be visible from the shore, and investigation by boat may be necessary to locate them or find their nests. It is difficult to justify such investigation, which is bound to cause disturbance. In at least one recent instance, observers laudably preferred to leave the birds in peace, forgoing the opportunity to confirm breeding.

Occasional pairs, sometimes up to 15, have nested spasmodically at various places, but these groups have seldom lasted for more than a few years, and there are now only three or four regular sites in Britain and Ireland. Even at these, the annual totals of late have not exceeded about 50 adults, including less than 20 breeding pairs, and Black-necked Grebes retain only a precarious foothold here.

This species is afforded special protection in Great Britain under Schedule I of the Protection of Birds Act, 1954–67.

Number of 10-km squares in which recorded:
  12 (0.3%)
Possible breeding   5 (42%)
Probable breeding   2 (16%)
Confirmed breeding   5 (42%)

Within the shaded areas, the dots are conventionally placed centrally (as recommended by the Rare Breeding Birds Panel, Major R. F. Ruttledge and D. Scott)

References

KALELA, O. 1949. Changes in geographic ranges in the avifauna of northern and central Europe in relation to recent changes in climate. *Bird Banding* 20: 77–103.

NOWAK, E. 1971. *O. Rozurzestragenlaniu sis Zweirsat I. Jego.* Warsaw.

SHARROCK, J. T. R. *et al.* 1975. Rare breeding birds in the United Kingdom in 1973 and 1974. *Brit. Birds* 68: 5–23, 489–506.

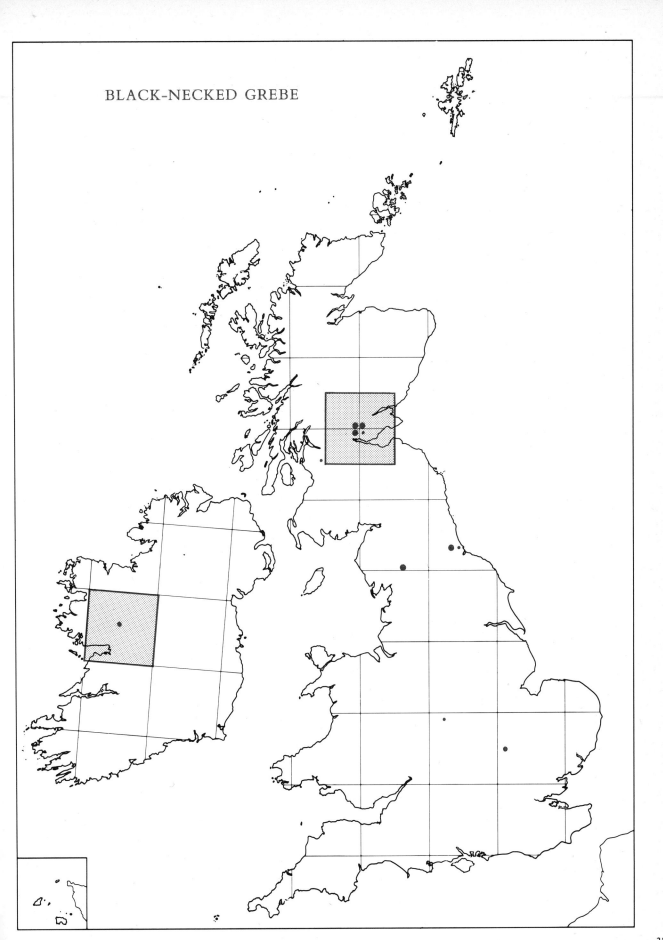

BLACK-NECKED GREBE

Little Grebe

Tachybaptus ruficollis

This species' requirements are far less restricted than those of the other grebes in Britain and Ireland. This is reflected in the world distribution, for in Eurasia, Africa and Australasia the Little Grebe or Dabchick is both more widespread and usually more numerous than are the other members of the family. The only controlling factor seems to be the presence of luxuriant vegetation, both on the bottom of the lake and as a dense growth of emergent plants. Whilst Little Grebes may be found on the larger lakes and gravel pits frequented by Great Crested Grebes *P. cristatus*, they also occupy quite small pools, such as farm ponds only 20 m or so in diameter, and urban park lakes (even at the hearts of cities as large as London, where Buckingham Palace lake is a regular breeding site). Other haunts include marshes, slow-flowing streams and canals, and even moorland *dubh-lochans*, sometimes at altitudes exceeding 100 m, and up to 350 m in Perthshire.

The Little Grebe's diet of fish smaller than those which will satisfy the Great Crested Grebe permits the occupation of shallower, as well as smaller, waters and accounts for the greater range of habitats and more widespread distribution in Britain and Ireland (49% of squares compared with 26%). Even so, it is mainly a lowland bird, with the chief concentrations in the same general areas as the Great Crested Grebe. It is, therefore, somewhat surprising to find that there were over 100 squares where the larger species but not the Little Grebe was found. These were mainly in Montgomeryshire, Sussex, W Kent and Lincolnshire. Interestingly in this context, it is suspected that the growing human population pressure in the Netherlands is forcing Great Crested Grebes on to smaller waters, previously the province of Little Grebes which are then tending to disappear, presumably because they cannot compete successfully with the larger species.

The nest is often more concealed than the Great Crested Grebe's and, where there is extensive cover, the birds may remain hidden for long periods, their presence revealed only by loud, whinnying trills.

This doubtless explains the lower proportion of confirmed breeding records. Possibly because they spend so much time concealed in marshland vegetation, Little Grebes lack the highly developed breeding season adornments of other members of the family; but they are the most distinctively vocal of European grebes, and Huxley (1919) suggested that the visual stimulation of display (developed to such an elaborate extent in the others) had been replaced by auditory stimuli. Often the high-pitched, whinnying peal of 'laughter' is carried out as a duet by both members of the pair. Where several territories fringe an area of weed-free, open water, this may be regarded as neutral ground by all pairs (Hartley 1933, 1937).

The breeding season is long, from late March to July, and though not so extended as the Great Crested Grebe, it allows most pairs to be double brooded and some occasionally to have a third. Normally the eggs are covered with weed by the departing adult, in the fashion of other grebes. Losses during incubation are growing as disturbance due to man's recreational activities increases. Eggs may be washed off the platform, or the whole nest swamped, by a passing boat.

There is evidence of a general increase, attributed to climatic amelioration, since the late 19th century, and a temporary decline following the hard winter of 1962/63. Since many Little Grebes appear to remain on their breeding sites throughout the year (though some move to estuaries), it is likely that severe winters are the main factor influencing numbers in Britain and Ireland. The Swedish population is sometimes nearly exterminated by particularly severe winters (Voous 1960). With the *Atlas* survey following and embracing a succession of mild winters, it is probable that this map displays a near maximum for the species' status in Britain.

On some waters, Little Grebes may reach a high density, so that nesting is almost colonial. This situation may be a reflection of their relatively sedentary habits, particularly as it seems to be most frequent in Ireland, where winters are seldom severe. For this reason, since a dot on the map may represent a single pair or scores of pairs, it is difficult to estimate the total population. A very rough guess, however, based on the assumption that each dot represents an average of 5–10 pairs, would put the figure at 9,000–18,000 pairs, and thus certainly near or above the higher limit of Parslow's category of 1,000–10,000 pairs.

Number of 10-km squares in which recorded:
  1,882 (49%)
Possible breeding   260 (14%)
Probable breeding   233 (12%)
Confirmed breeding   1,389 (74%)

References
HARTLEY, P. H. T. 1933. Field notes on the Little Grebe. *Brit. Birds* 27: 82–86.
HARTLEY, P. H. T. 1937. The sexual display of the Little Grebe. *Brit. Birds* 30: 266–275.
HUXLEY, J. 1919. Some points in the sexual habits of the Little Grebe, with a note on the occurrence of vocal duets in birds. *Brit. Birds* 13: 155–158.

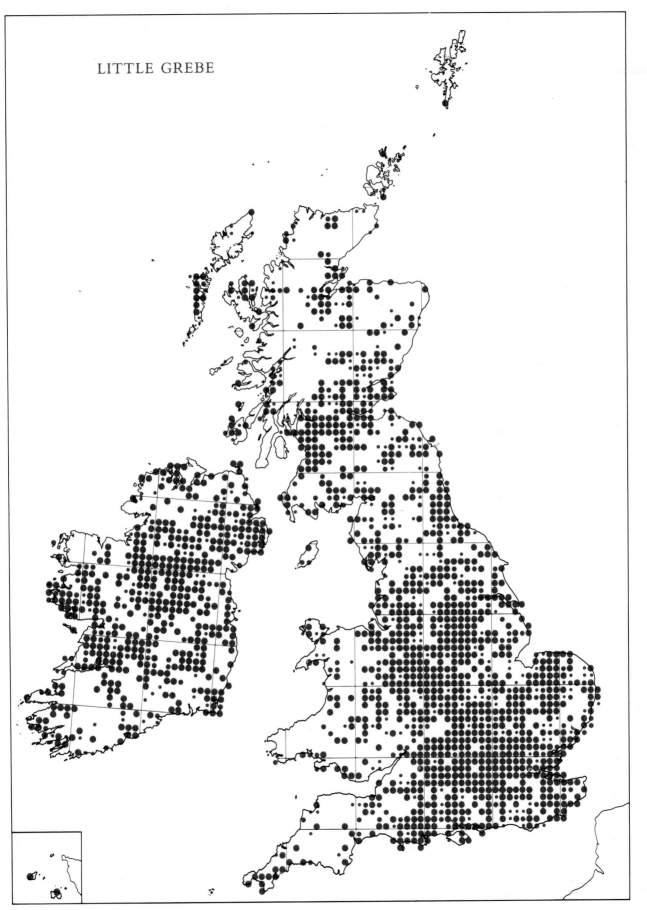

LITTLE GREBE

39

Fulmar

Fulmarus glacialis

This now familiar bird of British and Irish coasts has proved a source of fascination to many ornithologists because of its remarkable history, its interesting breeding habits, and not least its great individual appeal. The fantastic range expansion and growth in Fulmar numbers during the past 200 years have been the subject of numerous papers, and the history of its colonisation of Britain and Ireland has been traced in detail by Fisher (1952, 1966) and discussed by Cramp *et al* (1974).

Fulmars are known to have inhabited St Kilda, 80 km west of the Outer Hebrides, for at least eight or nine centuries, and Fisher thought that this and Grímsey—just inside the arctic circle north of Iceland—were the only NE Atlantic colonies in the Middle Ages. In about 1750 an increase was noticed in Iceland; birds had begun to settle the Faeroe Islands by 1820; and 12 pairs were found on Foula (Shetland) in 1878. Almost all the suitable cliffs of Britain and Ireland, especially on Atlantic-facing coasts, have now been settled. The colonisation was rapid at first, but has slowed down in recent years, though Cramp *et al* (1974) believed that it was still proceeding at a rate of 7% a year.

Fisher (1952) held the view that this rapid expansion was due to a population explosion in Iceland, and not to St Kildan birds; independent support came from Wynne-Edwards (1952), who showed that there was a slight differentiation in bill structure between the two groups. There is also a behavioural difference, for while the colonists of Shetland and other northern areas are attracted to deserted villages, ruined crofts and other buildings, and will nest at the feet of dry-stone walls, the St Kildan Fulmars show no interest in the old village or the hundreds of other stoneworks on the islands (Williamson and Boyd 1960).

Diverse views have been expressed concerning the reasons for this amazing spread, and the cause remains a matter for conjecture. Fisher (1952) linked the expansion with the growth of, first, the whaling and, later, the trawling industries, the processing at sea

making large amounts of offal available. Wynne-Edwards (1962) argued that a special genotype must have arisen in Iceland, enabling the population to break away from the constriction of nesting in huge, dense, but widely separated colonies, like those in the high arctic. Salomonsen (1965) sought an oceanographical explanation, pointing out that much of the expansion occurred during the warming up of the NE Atlantic in the late 19th and 20th centuries: its early stages, however, coincided with colder periods, such as the 1820s–1840s and 1860s–1890s, when conditions were severe around Iceland.

It is probable that the St Kilda stock has stayed fairly stable throughout, at around 40,000 pairs (about 20,000 on the main island of Hirta). Large numbers were taken for food, feathers and oil by the islanders. The average annual catch during 1829–43 was about 12,000 Fulmars for the support of 100 people, or half the estimated annual output of the colony. The fowling per person had changed little by 1929, when 32 islanders are said to have required 4,000 Fulmars.

Proof of breeding, with so many non-breeders settling and displaying on ledges, and the egg remaining covered for very long periods, is never easy. From mid-August into September, however, the young are recognisable by their pure white plumage (as opposed to 'old ivory' of the adults), their flesh-coloured rather than grey legs and the mats of preened-off down lying on the ledges. They beg, and accept food, with a loud rasping noise. Almost from hatching they can forcibly eject a stream of reddish-amber stomach oil at intruders—an efficient defence mechanism which has emancipated the Fulmar from the need to seek the protection of burrows or rock-cavities as nest sites.

Operation Seafarer estimated about 305,600 occupied sites in Britain and Ireland in 1969–70, of which 268,000—nearly 90%—were in Shetland, Orkney, the Outer Hebrides, St Kilda and NW Scotland. Only on the coasts of E, SE and SW England and S Wales were they sparse, however, these areas accounting for about 1% of the population.

Number of 10-km squares in which recorded:
725 (19%)
Possible breeding   63 (9%)
Probable breeding   61 (8%)
Confirmed breeding   601 (83%)

References

FISHER, J. 1952. *The Fulmar*. London.

FISHER, J. 1966. The Fulmar population of Britain and Ireland, 1959. *Bird Study* 13: 5–76.

SALOMONSEN, F. 1965. The geographical variation of the Fulmar (*Fulmarus glacialis*) and the zones of marine environment in the North Atlantic. *Auk* 82: 327–355.

WILLIAMSON, K. and J. M. BOYD. 1960. *St Kilda Summer*. London.

WYNNE-EDWARDS, V. C. 1952. Geographical variation in the bill of the Fulmar. *Scott. Nat.* 64: 84–101.

WYNNE-EDWARDS, V. C. 1962. *Animal Dispersion in Relation to Social Behaviour*. Edinburgh.

FULMAR

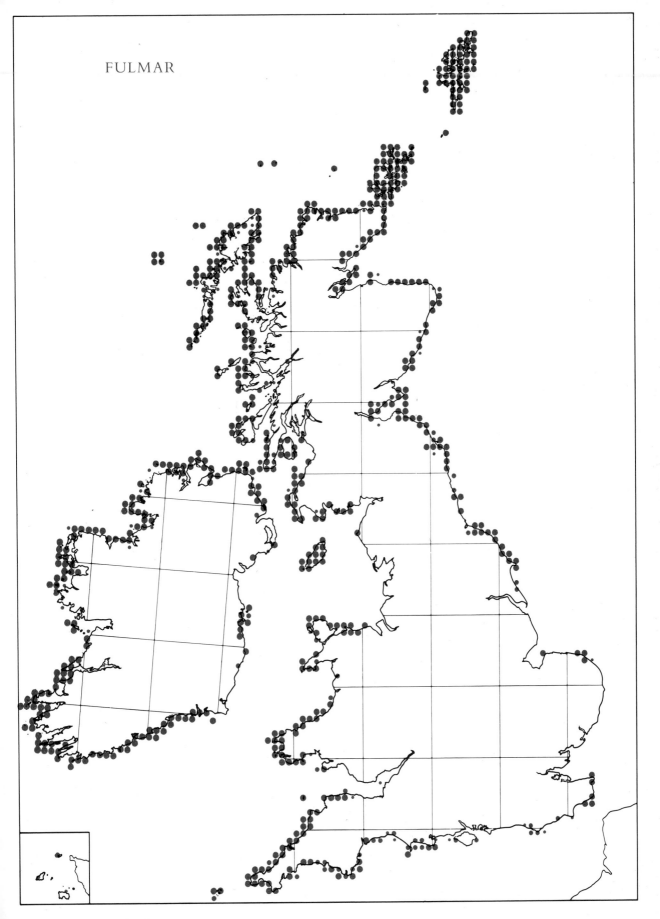

Manx Shearwater

Puffinus puffinus

Manx Shearwaters, like the smaller petrels, are sea-birds which nest underground, mostly on remote islands, and which visit their breeding areas only at night, often after gathering in huge 'rafts' offshore late in the day. Though most colonies are on islands, some smaller ones exist on the mainland. The majority of colonies are fairly close to the shore, but on Rhum (Inverness-shire) there is a huge one which reaches more than 3 km inland, at an altitude of 500–800 m.

While the burrows at large colonies are easily located, those in small ones (especially on cliffs) may be overlooked. There is also the problem of access and, despite Operation Seafarer, some established island colonies (including several off Ireland) went unvisited during 1968–72. By day, colonies can be found by searching for occupied burrows, but the best method is to pay nocturnal visits to likely areas, when the eerie cacophony of the adults' caterwauling as they fly overhead, particularly on dark nights, advertises their presence. Change-over at the nest is made only at night (to escape the predatory attentions of Great Black-backed Gulls *Larus marinus*) and the incubating bird may have been waiting for some days for the return of its mate from a fishing trip. The one underground in the nest responds eagerly to its mate's crowing, cooing call and, when it does so, occupied nest chambers can be located quickly.

Adults (mostly five or more years of age) visit their breeding grounds from February to September. Immatures also visit the colonies, but not until June and July of their second year; they return progressively earlier in the season as they grow older. The nest is usually in soft earth, the birds excavating their own burrows, but it may also be in a hole or crevice in the cliff or under rocks.

In the past, reduction in numbers at a few places occurred through human consumption of the fat young shearwaters as delicacies; and the final disappearance of some colonies followed the accidental introduction of rats from shipwrecks (Williamson 1940). Though the larger colonies appear to be thriving, some smaller ones seem to have declined in this century. This may be true of the Isles of Scilly, and another English site, on Lundy (Devon), now has very few pairs. It is, however, much more difficult to determine changes which may be occurring in large colonies, and census problems make it impossible to ascertain current trends.

It is very pleasing that the distribution map during 1968–72 includes a big dot for a classic site, the Calf of Man at the southern extremity of the Isle of Man. After a gap of about 150 years, breeding (suspected for several years) was proved there again in 1967 (Brun 1961, Alexander 1968). A vivid description of what can only have been the cacophony of a huge Manx Shearwater colony appears in the Icelandic *Njal's Saga*, showing that the Calf was occupied as long ago as 1014 (Williamson 1973).

Censusing a large colony is extremely difficult. Ringing and retrapping, mapping, and sample counts of birds gathering offshore in rafts have been attempted, but all are very time-consuming and inapplicable to colonies on remote islands visited by observers for only short spells. Operation Seafarer estimated that the total population was 'almost certainly over 175,000 pairs and may well have been over 300,000 pairs'. Recent estimates at three sites alone—35,000 pairs on Skokholm (Perrins 1967), 95,000 on Skomer (Corkhill 1973) and well over 100,000 on Rhum (Wormell 1976)—together approach the latter figure, and there are big colonies on Rhum's neighbouring islands Canna and Eigg, as well as on Middleholm (Pembrokeshire), Puffin Island (Co Kerry) and elsewhere.

Number of 10-km squares in which recorded:
86 (2%)
Possible breeding   38 (44%)
Probable breeding   11 (13%)
Confirmed breeding   37 (43%)

References

ALEXANDER, M. 1968. Breeding birds, 1967. *Calf of Man Bird Obs. Rep.*, 1966–1967 3–9.

BRUN, E. 1961. The return of the Manx Shearwater. *J. Manx Mus.* 6 (77): 103–104.

CORKHILL, P. 1973. Manx Shearwaters on Skomer: population and mortality due to gull predation. *Brit. Birds* 66: 136–143.

LOCKLEY, R. M. 1942. *Shearwaters*. London.

LOCKLEY, R. M. 1953. On the movements of Manx Shearwaters at sea during the breeding season. *Brit. Birds*, 46, suppl.: 1–48.

PERRINS, C. M. 1967. The numbers of Manx Shearwaters on Skokholm. *Skokholm Bird Obs. Rep.*, 1967: 23–25.

WILLIAMSON, K. 1940. The 'Puffins' of the Calf Isle. *J. Manx Mus.* 4: 178–180, 203–205.

WILLIAMSON, K. 1973. The antiquity of the Calf of Man Manx Shearwater colony. *Bird Study* 20: 310–311.

WORMELL, P. 1976. The Manx Shearwaters of Rhum. *Scott. Birds* 9: 103–118.

MANX SHEARWATER

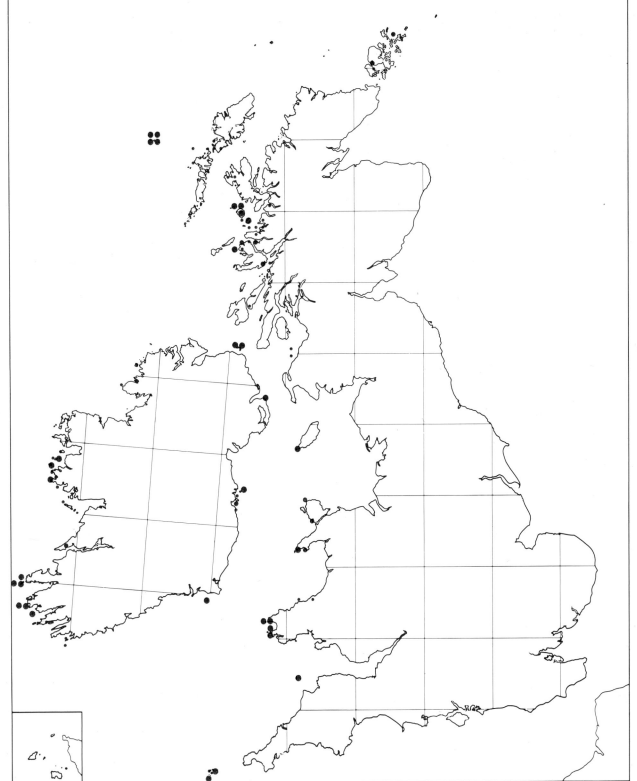

Storm Petrel

Hydrobates pelagicus

Storm Petrels are ·far commoner breeding birds in Britain and Ireland than are Leach's Petrels *Oceanodroma leucorhoa*. Both occupy the same sorts of habitat, mainly on remote islands, and come ashore only at night (though the Storm Petrel arrives earlier where both are found). Because of the species' abundance, Storm Petrel colonies are easier to locate, though counting presents an insoluble problem. Away from its main strongholds, looking for a Leach's Petrel is like searching for a needle in a haystack; at least with the present species there are often thousands of needles.

Most colonies in Britain and Ireland are on off-shore islands, but there may be more mainland ones than are at present known, since these are always in relatively inaccessible places, away from human disturbance. Unlike that of Leach's Petrel, the nest site is usually in a crevice or hole, although nest burrows are often excavated by the birds themselves. Burrows dug by Rabbits or Puffins *Fratercula arctica* may be utilised, side chambers being excavated by the petrels if the hole is already occupied, and the nest may be a metre or more down amongst small boulders. As well as natural sites, man-made constructions such as dry-stone walls, old buildings, and even occupied dwellings may be used. Perhaps the most famous examples are the large colony in the great broch on Mousa (Shetland), and the nests in the walls of the bird observatory on Skokholm (Pembrokeshire), where the species was studied intensively by Lockley (1932) and Davis (1957).

The dots on the map do not reflect its numerical distribution. The huge colonies of over 20,000 pairs on Inishtearaght, and over 10,000 pairs on Inishvickillane (both Co Kerry)—probably the largest in our area—are shown as single dots, just as are the single pair that nested under the floor of a building on the Fastnet Rock (Co Cork) in 1972 (the first birds ever known to have nested there) and the six pairs at Gulland Rock (Cornwall). Large colonies can hardly be missed if an area is visited at night or the distinctive musky smell is detected at burrows (but the smell of Leach's Petrel seems identical to us). Small colonies may well have been overlooked, however, even though the results obtained by the fieldworkers for Operation Seafarer and the *Atlas* were completely exchanged. To take just one example, it is not known if Storm Petrels now nest on Cape Clear Island (Co Cork), even though this has been the site of a bird observatory for over 15 years (Sharrock 1973). Some well-known Irish sites were not visited during 1968–72 and the inset map probably gives a truer picture than does the *Atlas* map.

The total number of Storm Petrels breeding in Britain and Ireland is impossible to calculate, but the Co Kerry colonies probably have the bulk of the world population and the results of Operation Seafarer show that there are certainly well over 50,000 pairs in Britain and Ireland as a whole and perhaps at least double or even treble that number, even though breeding was proved in only 54 10-km squares during the *Atlas* project.

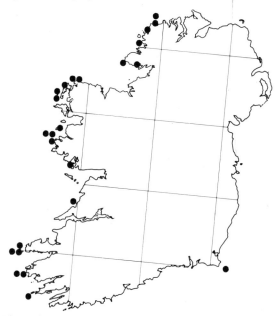

The *Atlas* map is believed to be incomplete for Ireland. This map shows the colonies documented by Ruttledge (1966)

Number of 10-km squares in which recorded:
  79 (2%)
Possible breeding   18 (23%)
Probable breeding   7 (9%)
Confirmed breeding   54 (68%)

References
DAVIS, P. E. 1957. The breeding of the Storm Petrel. *Brit. Birds* 50: 85–101, 371–384.
FISHER, J. and R. M. LOCKLEY. 1954. *Sea-Birds*. London.
GORDON, S. 1931. Some breeding habits of the Storm Petrel. *Brit. Birds* 24: 245–248.
LOCKLEY, R. M. 1932. On the breeding habits of the Storm Petrel, with special reference to its incubation and fledging-periods. *Brit. Birds* 25: 206–211.
SHARROCK, J. T. R. (ed.) 1973. *The Natural History of Cape Clear Island*. Berkhamsted.

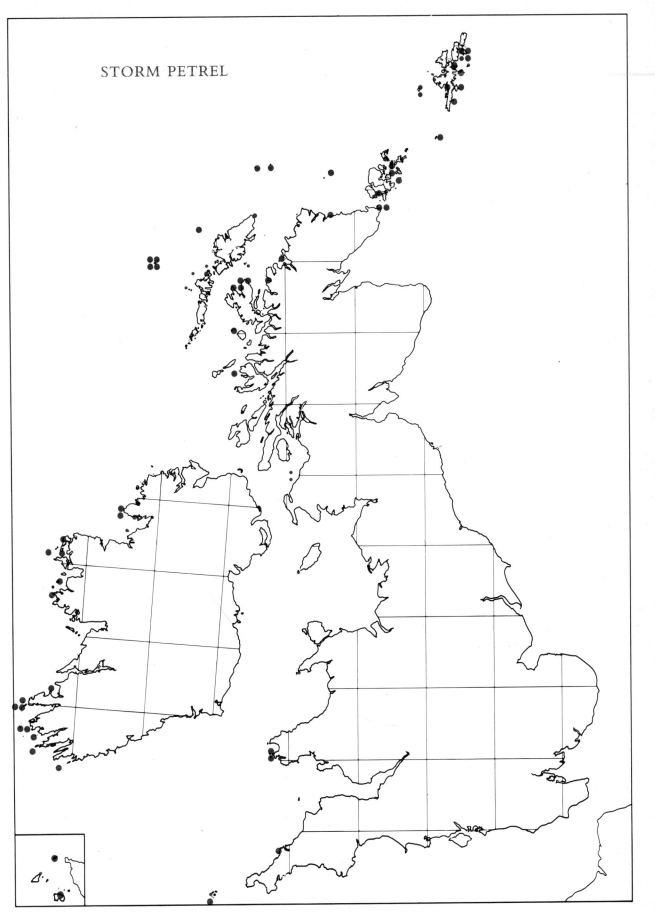

STORM PETREL

Leach's Petrel

Oceanodroma leucorhoa

This is one of our most elusive breeding birds, nesting on remote islands on both sides of the N Atlantic, and usually in rough terrain, so that colonies are difficult to reach, let alone study. To these problems must be added the fact that Leach's Petrels are nocturnal while ashore, visiting their colonies only from an hour or more after sunset until an hour or so before dawn, and that their nests are subterranean. Location is not an easy matter, therefore, and censusing is even more difficult; Operation Seafarer was unable to shed any light on the sizes or trends of the Scottish breeding groups.

The habitat includes gently sloping cliff-brows, scree slopes, peaty banks and inaccessible cliff faces; and returning birds announce their arrival with clear, staccato calls which have been likened to 'demoniacal laughter', the growing chorus creating an eerie atmosphere in the gathering gloom. When in their burrows, the species has a vibrant reeling or crooning 'song' similar to that uttered by the Storm Petrel *Hydrobates pelagicus*. Leach's Petrels prefer to excavate their own burrows, which usually have a flattened oval entrance, in soil or peat banks; but where this is impossible the single white egg will be laid under a boulder, in a stone cairn, or in the crumbling walls of an abandoned stone building. Thus, on the exposed island of North Rona the main colony is in the old village area, where the petrels burrow into the turf overlying the walls and ruins.

Britain has four principal breeding stations all long established, and these were the only confirmed ones during the *Atlas* period. In the St Kilda group there are large colonies on Hirta, Dun and Boreray and smaller ones on Stac Levenish and Soay (Williamson and Boyd 1960). On the Flannan Islands the main colonies are on Eilean Mor; breeding has also been established on Eilean Tighe, Roareim, Eilean a' Ghobha, Soray and Sgeir Toman, though not on any of the smaller stacks (Anderson *et al* 1961). The other two principal breeding stations are North Rona (where there are large numbers) and Sula Sgeir (which probably has the least of the four). There are

no reliable estimates of Scottish breeding numbers, but these four main stations together undoubtedly hold several thousand pairs.

It is possible that small numbers nest at other sites in W Ireland, such as Inishtearaght and Inishnabro (Kerry), Blackrock and Duvillaun Beg (Mayo), where breeding was recorded before the 1914–18 war, and the Stags of Broadhaven (Mayo) and Great Skellig (Kerry), where birds were seen or heard in 1946–47 and 1965. Similarly in Scotland, breeding was confirmed in 1974 on Foula (Shetland), having been suspected for some years. Other likely sites are Bearasay, off Lewis (Outer Hebrides), where two were found in burrows in 1955 and some were heard calling at night in 1962 (Cramp *et al* 1974); and on the seldom visited Sule Skerry (Orkney), where a nest was found in 1933 and no less than 28 birds were mist-netted in July 1975. Leach's Petrels have appeared in mist-nets set for Storm Petrels on a number of islands, however, and probably most of these were merely visitors, since during the long period of immaturity wandering birds turn up in midsummer on islands remote from the few known breeding stations. If there are more sites such as Foula, where a few pairs of Leach's Petrels are present amidst large numbers of Storm Petrels, breeding will be difficult to prove; nocturnal calling provides the best hope of initial location, though it is seldom practicable for observers to spend nights ashore.

Away from Scotland, the only other known colonies of Leach's Petrels in the NE Atlantic are on Mykinesholmur in the Faeroe Islands, on Heimay in the Vestmann Islands (Iceland) and on Røst in the Lofoten Islands (Norway).

Number of 10-km squares in which recorded:
  10 (0.3%)
Possible breeding   1 (10%)
Probable breeding   2 (20%)
Confirmed breeding   7 (70%)

References

AINSLIE, J. A. and R. ATKINSON. 1937. On the breeding habits of Leach's Fork-tailed Petrel. *Brit. Birds* 30: 234–248.

AINSLIE, J. A. and R. ATKINSON. 1938. *Island Going.* London.

ANDERSON, A., T. B. BAGENAL, D. E. BAIRD and W. J. EGGELING. 1961. A description of the Flannan Isles and their birds. *Bird Study* 8: 71–88.

FISHER, J. and R. M. LOCKLEY. 1954. *Seabirds.* London.

WILLIAMSON, K. and J. M. BOYD. 1960. *St Kilda Summer.* Edinburgh.

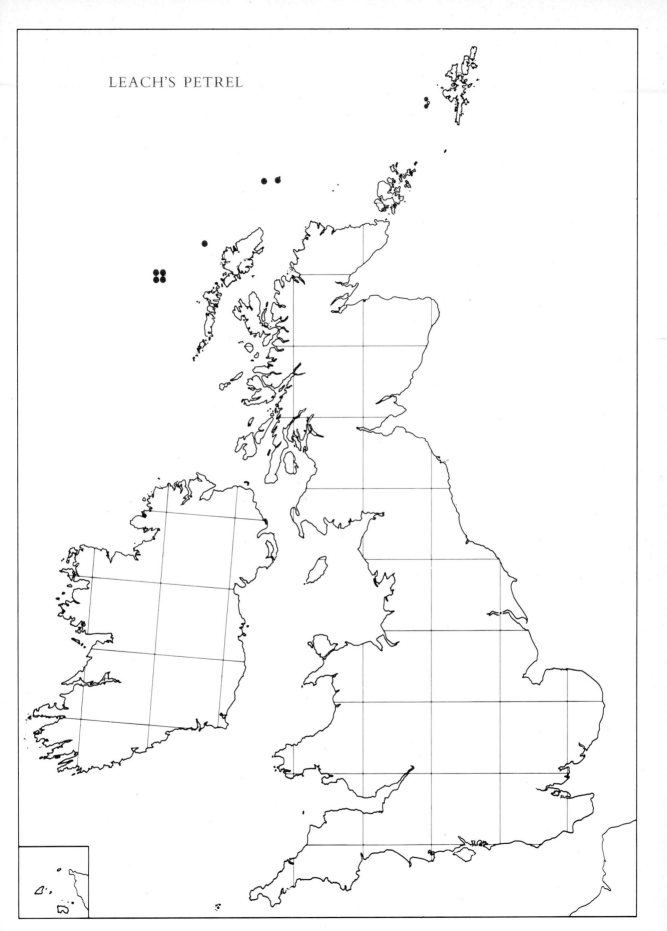

LEACH'S PETREL

Gannet

Sula bassana

Nesting on cliff-ledges, or sometimes on flat-topped islets, the traditional large colonies of this conspicuous bird are well-known and could not be overlooked. New or transient small colonies on outlying islands or remote cliffs might, however, escape detection for a few years. One such colony of 16 pairs on Roareim, in the Flannan Islands, was found in 1969 and another was established on Dronger Stack, Fair Isle, in 1974–75.

The mapping method used, presence or absence in 10-km squares, is unsatisfactory for this species. Two colonies in the Channel Islands happen to fall in one square, so both are shown by a single dot, while each of the colonies on Ailsa Craig, Hermaness and Noss happens to fall in two squares and each, therefore, is represented by two dots. For the sake of consistency this mapping method is retained, but the 16 colonies then known are listed below with the totals assessed by Operation Seafarer in 1968–70 and more recent counts supplied by Dr J. B. Nelson.

These totals represent over 70% of the world population, St Kilda alone holding more than 40% on Boreray and its great rocks, Stac an Armin and Stac Lee. The 17 occupied gannetries (all these with the later addition of Fair Isle) represent the highest number since ornithological recording began, and only three other definite former sites are known— Gulland Rock (Cornwall), Isle of May (Fife), and Lundy (Devon). These became extinct after 1468, about 1850, and in 1909 respectively.

Gannets were probably declining during the last century on both sides of the N Atlantic, due partly to persecution by man, but since early in the present century there has been a general increase. Cropping was greater on the American side than in Britain and Ireland, but since it ended the growth has been nearly threefold and figures for the world population (pairs) are: 1909, 67,000; 1939, 82,500; 1969, 196,500; and 1974, 197,000. This represents an increase of about 3% per annum, which is almost exactly the rate to be expected on known mortality and reproductive rates on both sides of the Atlantic (Dr J. B. Nelson *in litt*).

Although persecution may have played a part in the earlier decline, it seems likely that present increases are not due solely to its relaxation, and a climatic factor affecting the abundance and distribution of surface-shoaling fish, such as Mackerel and Saithe, may be involved. There is no shortage of breeding sites on the islands of the west and north of Britain and Ireland and, if the current growth-rate continues, we may see new colonies established in the next few years, as has happened recently in Norway and Iceland.

Gannetries in Britain and Ireland

	Earliest known year of occupation	Number of pairs 1968–70	1971–74
Hermaness, Unst (Shetland)	1917	5,894	5,894
Noss (Shetland)	1914	4,300	4,300
Sula Sgeir	by 1549	8,964	9,000
Sule Stack	by 1710	4,018	4,018
Flannan Islands (O Hebrides)	1969	16	16
St Kilda (O Hebrides)	by 800–900	52,000	59,000
Bass Rock (E Lothian)	by 1521	8,977	10,500
Ailsa Craig (Ayrshire)	by 1526	13,054	9,500
Scar Rocks (Wigtownshire)	1939	450	482
Bempton Cliffs (Yorkshire)	1937	18	100
Great Saltee (Wexford)	1929	155	225
Little Skellig (Kerry)	by 1700	20,000	18,000
Bull Rock (Cork)	1850s	1,500	1,500
Grassholm (Pembrokeshire)	1820–60	16,128	15,100
Ortac, Alderney (CI)	1940	1,000	1,000
Les Etacs, Alderney (CI)	about 1940	2,000	2,000
Totals		138,474	140,635

Number of 10-km squares in which recorded:
 19 (0.5%)
Possible breeding   0
Probable breeding   1 (5%)
Confirmed breeding   18 (95%)

References

GURNEY, J. H. 1913. *The Gannet: a Bird with a History.* London.

FISHER, J. and H. G. VEVERS. 1943, 1944. The breeding distribution, history and population of the North Atlantic Gannet (*Sula bassana*). *J. Anim. Ecol.* 12: 173–213; 13: 49–62.

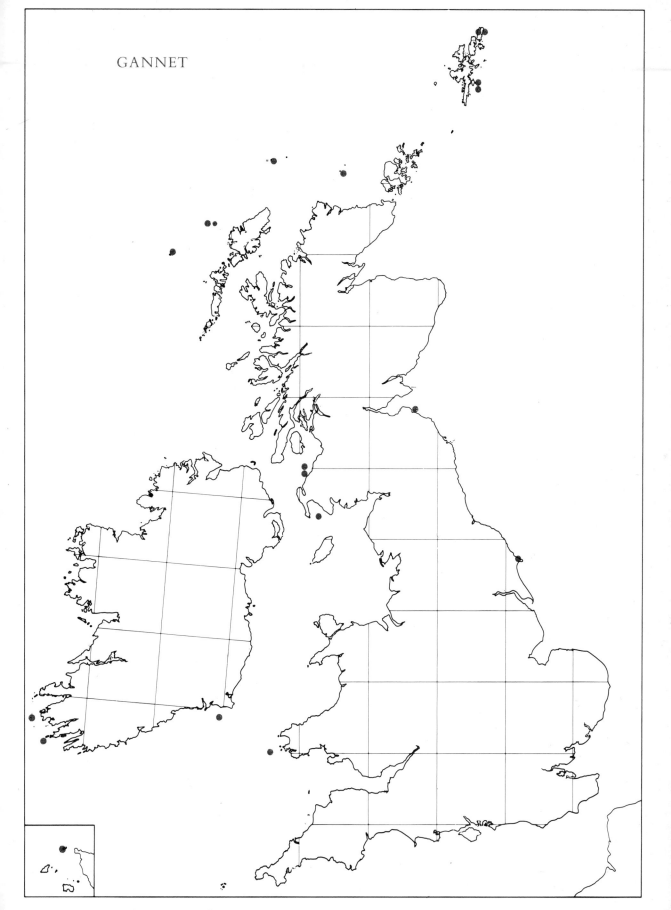

GANNET

49

Cormorant

Phalacrocorax carbo

Cormorants are large and conspicuous birds which build prominent nests. The sites are usually in the open on broad cliff ledges, or on flat ground on stacks or islets (*cf* the Shag *P. aristotelis*) and the birds breed gregariously, the white guano making their colonies noticeable from a distance. Most breeding places are therefore likely to be found during a survey, and the large number of records in the 'possible breeding' category probably represent non-breeding or feeding birds away from colonies, rather than undetected nesting haunts. Census counts are also likely to be fairly reliable. Cormorants can be found on their breeding ledges at any time from late March to mid-September, but eggs are not laid until late April or early May, even later in N Scotland, so that proof of breeding is easiest to obtain from late June to mid-August.

The British and Irish distribution is mainly on western coasts, where the most suitable cliffs and islets are found. On the Continent tree-nesting at inland sites is fairly frequent, but this is no longer so in Britain, due to extirpation of the species in the few areas (*eg* East Anglia) where such nesting formerly occurred. Some tree colonies still exist in Ireland, however. Regarding inland records, it should be noted that the summering of what are probably non-breeders on Irish loughs is more widespread than the map suggests, for the standard set for the inclusion of such records was more severe than in the case of the Scottish lochs.

Cormorants are persecuted by man because of the adverse effect they are thought to have on fish stocks. They usually feed in shallow coastal waters (particularly bays and estuaries) and mainly on flat-fish and other bottom feeders, so that this species and the Shag have relatively few of the more numerous fishes common to their diets (Pearson 1968). Cormorants may also be found inland on lakes and rivers, where the usual prey seems to be Brown Trout, Perch, young Salmon and Eels. Predation by Cormorants is unlikely to affect coastal fish stocks significantly, and it has been claimed that on inland waters they may even be beneficial in reducing numbers of coarse fish which prey on young Salmon. Cormorants may well be detrimental in trout waters, however, since they eat fish large enough to be of value to man, but a report of the Department of Agriculture and Fisheries for Scotland (Mills 1965) concluded that no good purpose would be served by bounty payments. Persecution of Cormorants has probably decreased with increasing knowledge of their diet, and in future it may be limited to special instances where Brown Trout are at risk.

No general trend is noticeable in the numbers since, while some isolated colonies have disappeared, there have been corresponding increases elsewhere, and with a rather mobile population the changes may merely reflect movement from one area to another. Smith (1969) estimated that the Cormorants nesting in Scotland in the mid-1960s numbered about 3,000 pairs, whereas the counts of Operation Seafarer in 1969–70 revealed 3,671 pairs. In view of the great similarity between the two surveys in location of colonies it seems that there has been a real increase in Scotland during the last few years. Indeed, the *Atlas* distribution indicates that Cormorants may have increased and spread since Operation Seafarer. For example, the colony on the Lamb (Firth of Forth) had increased from five pairs in 1957, when breeding was first recorded, to 177 pairs by 1965 and to 240 pairs by 1968. In addition to the 3,671 pairs in Scotland during Operation Seafarer, there were 1,865 in Ireland, 1,420 in Wales, 1,116 in England and 62 in the Channel Islands, making a grand total of 8,134 pairs. With Operation Seafarer as a basis, it may be possible to monitor changes in the numbers of this conspicuous species fairly easily in the future.

Number of 10-km squares in which recorded:
575 (15%)
Possible breeding   259 (45%)
Probable breeding   29 (5%)
Confirmed breeding   287 (50%)

References

LACK, D. 1945. The ecology of closely related species with special reference to Cormorant (*Phalacrocorax carbo*) and Shag (*P. aristotelis*). *J. Anim. Ecol.* 14: 12–16.

MILLS, D. H. 1965. The distribution and food of the Cormorant in Scottish inland waters. *Freshwater and Salmon Fisheries Research* no. 35. HMSO.

PEARSON, T. H. 1968. The feeding biology of sea-bird species breeding on the Farne Islands, Northumberland. *J. Anim. Ecol.* 37: 521–552.

SMITH, R. W. J. 1969. Scottish Cormorant colonies. *Scott. Birds* 5: 363–378.

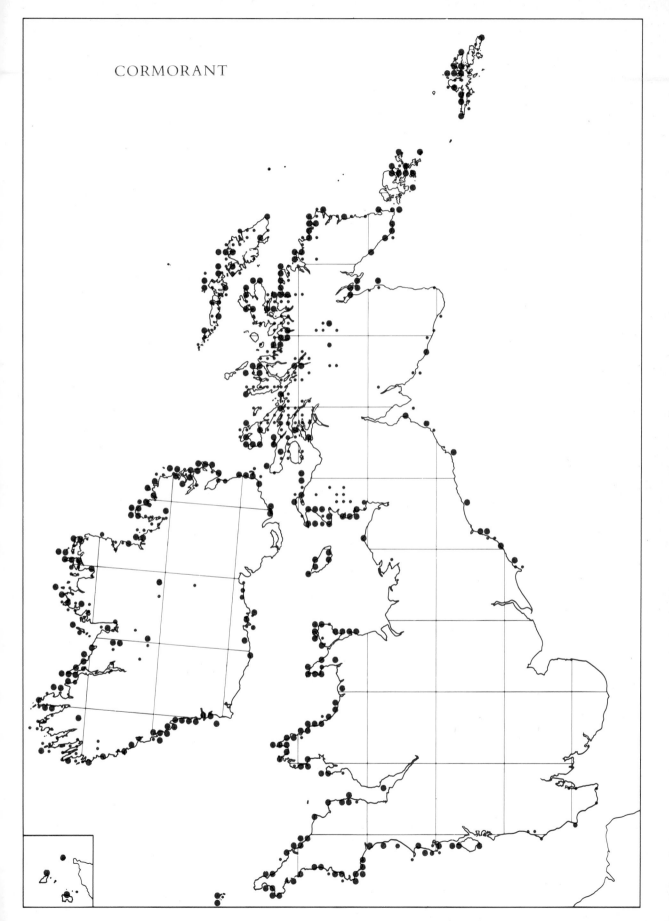

CORMORANT

Shag

Phalacrocorax aristotelis

Though resembling the Cormorant *P. carbo* in appearance, the Shag is far more strictly coastal, seldom feeding and never nesting inland. The British and Irish distributions of both species reflect the presence of rocky cliffs and islands, which form the nesting habitat. The actual nest sites differ, however, for Shags tend to occupy narrower ledges than Cormorants, and also favour concealed sites on rock shelves in sea caves and in crevices among boulders.

Detailed studies in Northumberland, where open sites are mainly used, have shown that the favoured, higher and more sheltered situations are occupied by the older and more experienced adults, which are the first to return to the colony in spring. Young Shags breeding for the first or second time, arrive later and may be forced to use sites that are exposed to wave action in rough seas, with the resulting risks of nests being washed away or unattended chicks being chilled by spray. Those which arrive late in the season may occupy a site without building a nest, perhaps even without pairing, while established breeders which arrive early lay the largest eggs or clutches, and rear most young. Egg-volume increases with the age of the adults and probably results in larger and stronger chicks: a difference of up to 13% has been shown to exist between the eggs of two- and eight-year-old birds (Coulson *et al* 1969).

Despite the difficulty of locating Shag nests in cave and boulder sites, Operation Seafarer found four times as many Shags as Cormorants, involving twice as many 10-km squares. The 150 10-km squares of possible or probable nesting are, thus, more suggestive of undetected breeding than in the case of the Cormorant, though in some places Shags use traditional perches on apparently suitable cliffs without nesting there (Campbell and Ferguson-Lees 1972). Comparing only the confirmed breeding records, the average number of pairs of Shags in occupied squares was 59, more than double the comparable figure for Cormorants.

Shags feed mainly in deeper water than Cormorants, catching free-swimming rather than bottom-feeding fish. The chief prey seems to be sand-eels, while fish of prime commercial value, such as flatfish, are seldom taken. Thus, unlike the Cormorant, there is no need for nest sites (or, indeed, wintering areas) to be near shallow bays or estuaries and, as the *Atlas* map shows, almost any piece of rocky coast provides suitable breeding places. The long lengths of coastline which lack Shag colonies are for the most part low or otherwise unsuitable, as in NW and SE England and most of E Ireland; nevertheless, the Shag's scarcity on the Yorkshire cliffs and absence from Cumberland are a little surprising.

Since the 1920s there has been a striking upward trend in the numbers of Shags at various colonies, especially in NE England and SE Scotland, and there have been coincident increases of a number of other seabirds. It has been suggested that environmental or climatic changes may have led to an improved food supply. It is not known, however, whether such hypothetical changes, or simply recovery from low population levels occasioned by excessive persecution in the last century, account for the recent growth. Natural factors have occasionally caused temporary and local reversals. For example, an outbreak of paralytic shellfish-poisoning (caused by a 'red tide' superabundance of a toxic dinoflagellate of the genus *Gonyaulax*) killed about 80% of the Shags on the Farne Islands (Northumberland) in 1968.

Operation Seafarer located about 31,600 nesting pairs of Shags in 1969–70, of which by far the largest numbers (25,200 pairs) were in Scotland, including a concentration of 8,600 in Shetland. Ireland had 2,600 pairs, England 2,700 pairs, and Wales and the Channel Islands 570 pairs each. Decreases have been reported since the 1950s in S Devon (a marginal area), the Firth of Clyde and the northern Inner Hebrides, but Shags appear to have increased in all other areas for which previous figures are available (Cramp *et al* 1974). Since 1970, a continuing increase has been most apparent in the Firth of Forth, with the colonisation of Fidra in 1971 and Inchkeith in 1974, while the Isle of May breeding population rose from 880 pairs in 1969 to 1,130 by 1973.

Number of 10-km squares in which recorded:
682 (18%)
Possible breeding   128 (19%)
Probable breeding   22 (3%)
Confirmed breeding   532 (78%)

References

COULSON, J. C., G. R. POTTS, I. R. DEANS and S. M. FRASER. 1968. Exceptional mortality of Shags and other seabirds caused by paralytic shellfish poison. *Brit. Birds* 61: 381–404.

COULSON, J. C., G. R. POTTS and J. HOROBIN. 1969. Variation in the eggs of the Shag (*Phalacrocorax aristotelis*). *Auk* 86: 232–245.

LACK, D. 1945. The ecology of closely related species with special reference to Cormorant (*Phalacrocorax carbo*) and Shag (*P. aristotelis*). *J. Anim. Ecol.* 14: 12–16.

POTTS, G. R. 1969. The influence of eruptive movements, age, population size and other factors on the survival of the Shag. *J. Anim. Ecol.* 38: 53–102.

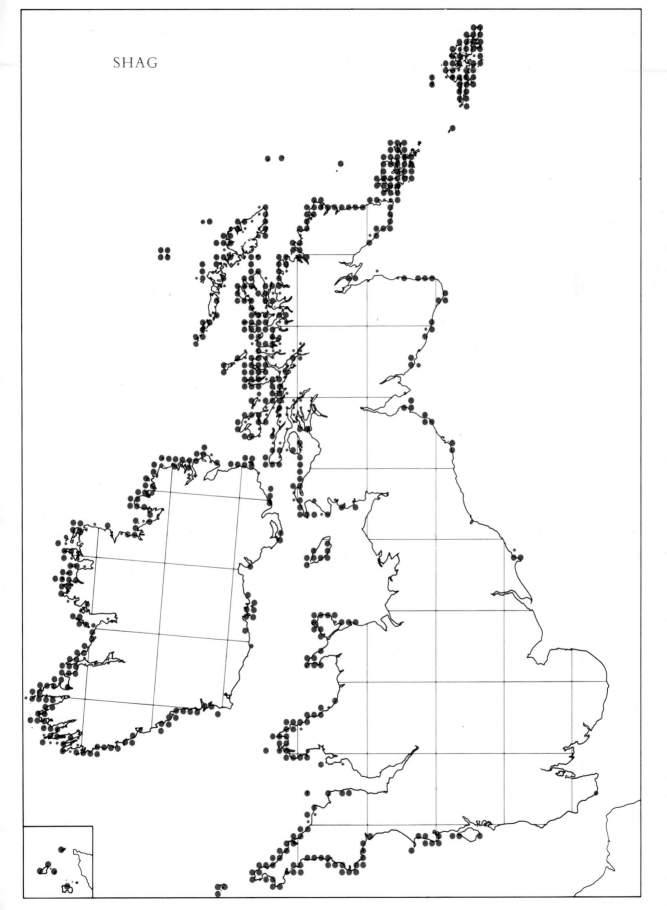

SHAG

Grey Heron

Ardea cinerea

Heronries in Britain and Ireland are usually situated in trees, but a few are known in reed-beds and on cliffs. Where trees are absent, as in parts of Connemara (Galway) and N Scotland, nests may be in low bushes and deep heather. Only 1% of nests in England, Wales and Ireland is not in a tree, but in Scotland 16% are in some other site, 7% being on cliffs. Heronries in such atypical situations are less likely to be found than those in trees, so these figures may well be underestimates.

In view of the large size of the birds and their nests, it might be thought that heronries are easy to locate, but this is not always so. Isolated pairs and groups of two or three nests, and also those built in conifers, can be often overlooked; and even large heronries in deciduous woods have been missed during summer visits. The small dots on the map may represent undetected heronries in some cases, though a proportion certainly reflects the presence of non-breeding or feeding birds from nearby colonies.

The BTO's Census of Heronries has been carried out annually since 1928. The population indices are calculated from about 200 English and Welsh heronries which are counted in each of two successive years; in any five-year period, however, only about 50 heronries are counted in all the years. The totals have fluctuated between approximately 2,250 and 4,925 pairs in England and Wales, with the lowest numbers following severe winters (see below). The estimated population increased progressively from 3,725 pairs in 1968 to 4,625 pairs in 1972, the annual growth varying from 1% to 11%. Heronries found during *Atlas* fieldwork included about 100 in England and Wales, 384 in Ireland and 286 in Scotland which had never been included in the national census. The average colony size is smaller in Ireland and Scotland than in England and Wales (1954 figures were Scotland 6, Northern Ireland 8, Wales 12 and England 21). The newly discovered ones in England and Wales were probably mostly smaller than average, and many may have been single nests, some perhaps used in only one year.

The map clearly shows a higher density of heronries in Ireland than in Britain: in England, Wales and Scotland there is roughly one to every four 10-km squares, whereas in Ireland the proportion is one to 2.7 squares. As the average colony size is smaller in Scotland and Ireland, however, England and Wales have a denser population. The figures suggest that each 10-km square may support up to 1.6 pairs in Scotland, 3.0 pairs in Ireland and 4.5 pairs in England and Wales. The factors which cause Irish Grey Herons to nest in many small heronries, while those in England and Wales nest in fewer and larger colonies deserve investigation: one is doubtless the felling of mature timber, which followed the breaking up of large estates in Ireland.

The total number of breeding Grey Herons in Britain and Ireland during the *Atlas* period clearly exceeds the maximum figure produced by the annual sample census. With about 770 newly discovered nesting sites, it may be estimated that the population in 1972 was certainly over 6,500, but less than 11,500 pairs, rather higher than Parslow's 3,000–8,000 pairs.

Number of 10-km squares in which recorded:
2,461 (64%)
Possible breeding 1,197 (49%)
Probable breeding 153 (6%)
Confirmed breeding 1,111 (45%)

References

BURTON, J. F. 1956. Report on the national census of heronries, 1954. *Bird Study* 3: 42–73.

GARDEN, E. 1958. The national census of heronries in Scotland 1954 with a summary of the 1928/29 census. *Bird Study* 5: 90–109.

LOWE, F. A. 1954. *The Heron*. London.

REYNOLDS, C. M. 1974. The census of heronries 1969–73. *Bird Study* 21: 129–134.

STAFFORD, J. 1969. The census of heronries 1962–63. *Bird Study* 16: 83–88.

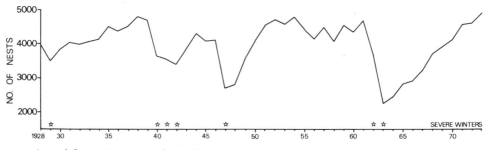

Annual fluctuations in numbers of nests of Grey Heron, from BTO Census of Heronries

Purple Heron *Ardea purpurea*, **Night Heron** *Nycticorax nycticorax* **and Little Bittern** *Ixobrychus minutus*, **see page 446**

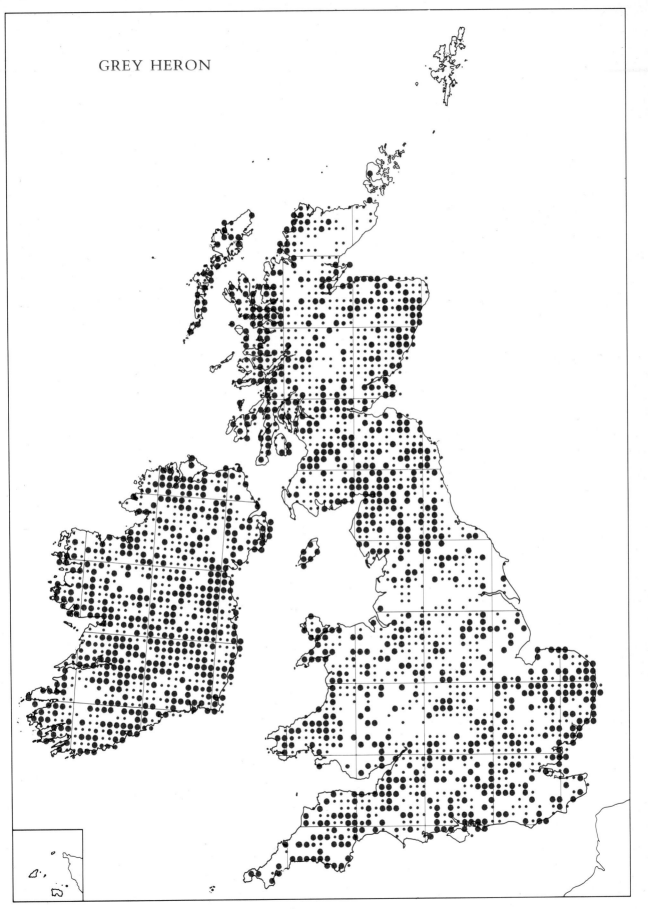

GREY HERON

Bittern

Botaurus stellaris

Breeding in large, dense reed-beds of marshes, fens and sluggish rivers, this secretive bird would be very difficult to locate if it were not for the deep resonant 'booming' voice of the male. This 'song' is used to proclaim territory from mid-February to late June, although in the milder western parts of its range booming often starts in January. The sound may be heard throughout the day and night with a definite peak of activity at dawn and dusk. In favourable conditions it is audible for up to 5 km, so that presence even in large reed-beds is easily established. The nest is usually built deep in the reeds, so confirmation of breeding can be difficult, as disturbance must be kept to a minimum. The young, however, usually leave the nest some time before they can fly, and in well-watched localities they can occasionally be seen being fed by their parents at the edge of the reeds.

The map largely reflects the distribution of wetlands with extensive *Phragmites* beds, though there are several apparently suitable areas which have not yet been colonised. Breeding density appears to be the highest in wet freshwater reed-beds, while tidal or very dry beds are only rarely used.

Bitterns bred formerly in many parts of England, Wales and S Scotland, and even in Ireland up to about 1840. At the beginning of the 19th century they were still common in the fens and broads of E England, and roast Bittern was a regular item of country fare. With the drainage of the fens and many other wetlands to increase agricultural production, the numbers declined rapidly. Shooting and egg-collecting also had an important adverse effect, and by 1850 the species was virtually extinct as a breeding bird, the last nest and eggs being found in Norfolk in 1868.

After a gap of more than 30 years, booming was once again heard in Norfolk in 1900 and recolonisation by Continental birds took place, though breeding was not proved until 1911. By 1923 the estimated population was 16–17 pairs, increasing to 23–25 pairs by 1928. Nesting was first reported in Suffolk in 1926, but otherwise they were confined to the Norfolk Broads. The slow, gradual spread continued with the most northerly site, Leighton Moss (Lancashire), being colonised in the early 1940s, and other western localities in the next decade. Close protection by the Norfolk Naturalists' Trust and RSPB has been an important factor, while the creation of a number of new reed-beds such as Minsmere (Suffolk) and Leighton Moss, together with the predominance of mild winters in this century, has helped to foster the recovery. The current breeding range is probably more extensive than at any time in the past 140 years.

The only practical way to census Bitterns is by a count of booming males, and recent censuses suggest that the British population reached a peak in the 1950s. Since then there has been a decline in some areas, especially Norfolk where a census in 1954 gave a total of 58–60 booming males, declining to 28–30 by 1970. Similar decreases have been reported from Kent and Somerset. Reed cutting, water pollution and disturbance by Coypus have all been suggested as possible causes of the decline; certainly severe winters, such as those of 1946/47 and 1962/63, have caused short-term losses, especially in E England. The current population in England and Wales is probably in the region of about 80 pairs: Norfolk and Suffolk are the main centres with about 50 pairs, while Leighton Moss has nine.

This species is afforded special protection in Great Britain under Schedule I of the Protection of Birds Act, 1954–67.

Number of 10-km squares in which recorded:
  36 (0.9%)
Possible breeding   9 (25%)
Probable breeding   13 (36%)
Confirmed breeding   14 (39%)

Two dots (both of confirmed breeding in W Britain) have been omitted (as recommended by the Rare Breeding Birds Panel)

References
DUTT, W. A. 1906. *Wild Life in East Anglia*. London.
RIVIERE, B. B. 1930. *History of the Birds of Norfolk*. London.

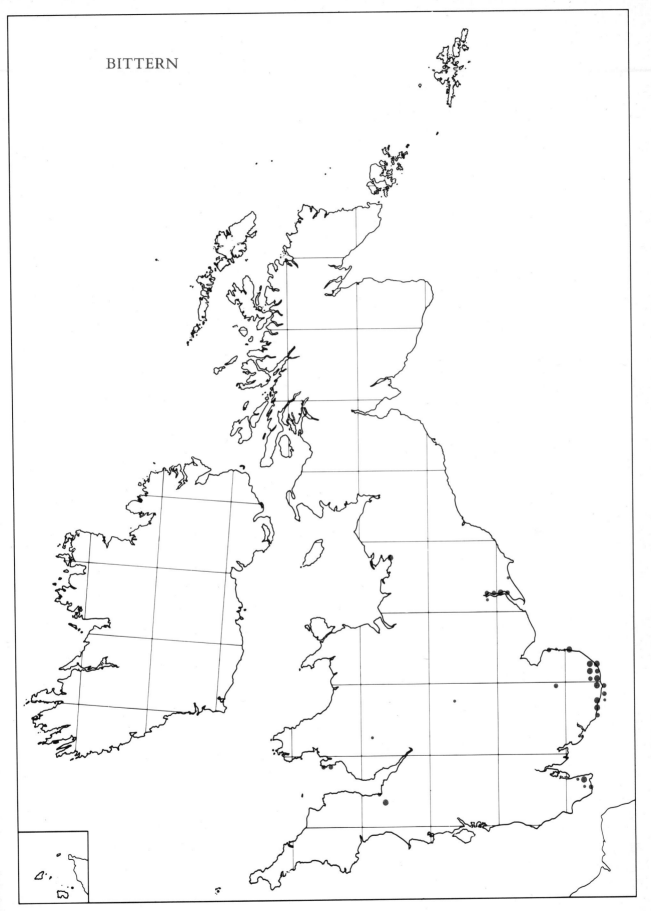

BITTERN

Mallard

Anas platyrhynchos

The Mallard is the most numerous and widely distributed of our resident waterfowl. Nesting occurs in a great variety of freshwater and brackish habitats, from small ponds to the largest lakes and reservoirs, as well as in the vicinity of rivers, streams and floods. Moreover, semi-tame birds are a regular feature of urban and suburban parks, village ponds, rivers and canals in places where they are fed regularly by the public. Part of the Mallard's success has been its ability to live alongside man when not directly molested, and no doubt the development of this trait has been helped by interbreeding with captive stock.

Mallards use a bewildering variety of nest-sites (Campbell and Ferguson-Lees 1972). Typically, the nest is on the ground in thick undergrowth such as grass, nettles, brambles, bracken and heather; islands are preferred where available, but nests can be on hillsides 2 km or more from the nearest water. Some on the ground are fairly exposed; others are at the feet of fences, inside tree stumps, on the crowns of pollarded willows and in tree holes up to 10 m high. Unusual sites in built-up areas have included roof gardens, flower boxes, static water tanks, bridge supports, and moored barges. Breeding may begin only a week after ground temperatures have risen above freezing point, and in S England this can be during the second half of February if the winter has been mild (Ogilvie 1964). Early nests are prone to heavy predation, however, due to the scarcity of cover, and ducklings appear mainly from mid-April to July. When first attempts fail, Mallards readily lay replacement clutches, though these are on average somewhat smaller. Eggs and small ducklings have been found in October and November; it is known that some of these belong to young females reared earlier the same year, breeding when only six months old (Boyd 1957).

Wildfowlers are actively involved in releasing hand-reared birds in order to augment wild stocks. The practice of turning down artificially reared birds is an old one, but originally had short-term objectives, so that 90% or more were shot during their first winter. WAGBI has been liberating Mallards since 1954, specifically to increase wild populations and so eventually to improve sport; this is done by liberating birds in protected areas where first-year survival will be high (Harrison and Wardell 1970). Large numbers are now turned down annually: a total of nearly 84,000 during 1968–72. Such local restocking is thought to have been partly responsible for an increase on the N Kent marshes from 250 pairs in 1964 to 440 pairs by 1969 (Harrison 1972). Similar releases are now being carried out in Ireland under the auspices of the Department of Lands.

As the *Atlas* map shows, the Mallard is one of the most widely distributed of our breeding birds; but densities vary considerably. There are 400–450 pairs on the 42 ha St Serf's Island in Loch Leven (Kinross), and an even higher density of about 70–80 pairs in the 2 ha decoy wood at Slimbridge (Gloucestershire). Yet such concentrations around reserves and major wetlands are exceptional. The Common Birds Census index showed a steady increase on farmland during the seven years following the severe winters of the early 1960s, reaching more than $3\frac{1}{2}$ times the 1963 level by 1970. In 1972 the average density on farmland was 2.4 pairs per km^2. On the other hand, Boyd and King (1960) reported that in N Somerset there was an average of only one pair per 500 ha, despite a concentration of over 100 pairs around Chew Valley Reservoir. If this density (about 20 pairs per 10-km square) is representative, then Britain and Ireland hold some 70,000 pairs; but if the average is only one-fifth of that suggested by the CBC, the population could exceed 150,000 pairs. These speculations may be compared with Atkinson-Willes's (1970) estimate of 40,000 pairs in Britain alone.

Number of 10-km squares in which recorded:
3,549 (92%)
Possible breeding   199 (6%)
Probable breeding   88 (2%)
Confirmed breeding   3,262 (92%)

References

ATKINSON-WILLES, G. L. 1970. Wildfowl situation in England, Scotland and Wales. *Proc. Int. Reg. Meet. Conserv. Wildfowl Res., Leningrad 1968*: 101–107.

BOYD, H. 1957. Early sexual maturity of a female Mallard. *Brit. Birds* 50: 302–303.

BOYD, H. and B. KING. 1960. A breeding population of the Mallard. *Wildfowl Trust Ann. Rep.* 11: 137–143.

HARRISON, J. 1972. *Wildfowl of the North Kent Marshes*. WAGBI, Chester.

HARRISON, J. and J. WARDELL. 1970. WAGBI duck to supplement wild populations. pp. 91–209 in SEDGWICK, N. M., P. WHITAKER and J. HARRISON (eds), *The New Wildfowler in the 1970s*. London.

HOMES, R. C. *et al.* 1957. *The Birds of the London Area since 1900*. London.

OGILVIE, M. A. 1964. A nesting study of the Mallard in Berkeley New Decoy, Slimbridge. *Wildfowl Trust Ann. Rep.* 15: 84–88.

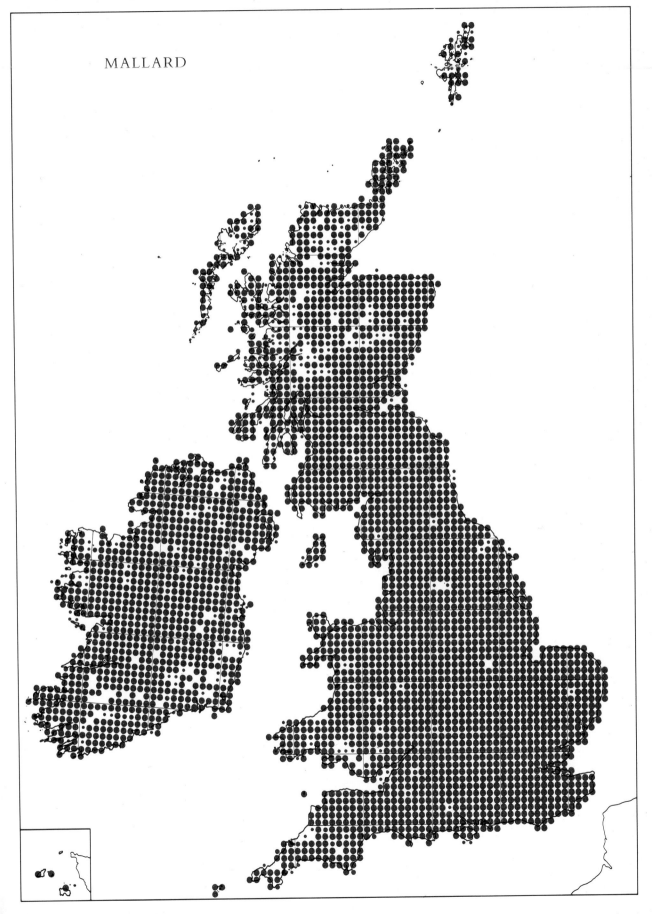

MALLARD

Teal

Anas crecca

In the breeding season, Teal favour rushy moorland and heath pools, bogs and peat mosses, and the typical habitat in Britain and Ireland embraces such small upland waters as the *dubh-lochans* of Scottish moors and flows, the bog-holes of Ireland, and the pools on the mosses of N England. The species also nests in lowland areas, where lakes, rivers, streams and marshes (freshwater and brackish) are frequented, but less often and only if there is plenty of cover provided by emergent or other peripheral vegetation. Breeding is sporadic in many parts of England and Wales, with pairs nesting at some sites in perhaps only one or two years in each decade.

The nest is almost always in thick cover, and is more closely associated with water than is the case with the Mallard *A. platyrhynchos*. Even so, nests may be up to 150 m from the nearest pool or stream and longer distances from water have been recorded, with nests built among heather or gorse on dry ground or in bracken-covered glades in woods. Breeding is less easy to prove than for the Mallard, since broods seldom swim in open water, where they would be readily visible; rather, females and young usually remain well hidden in reed-beds or other emergent vegetation, or under overhanging banks. Most of the *Atlas* records of confirmed breeding resulted from observations of adults performing injury feigning or distraction displays. Many of the records of possible breeding, especially in central England, may refer to summering or late passage birds. In late June and July it is necessary to be cautious about drakes, which (as is usual among *Anas* species) desert their mates while the latter are incubating, and disperse before moulting. Moult migrations of grand proportions occur on the Continent, though it seems that many British Teal drakes moult singly or in small groups near the nesting grounds.

The scarcity of breeding Teal in W Scotland north of mid-Argyll is a distributional feature shared by other species, notably Wigeon *A. penelope*, Tufted Duck *Aythya fuligula* and Black-headed Gull *Larus ridibundus*. It may be that the wetter summer weather adversely affects brood survival; or a limit may be imposed by the vegetation, which is generally poor except on the fertile limestone outcrops at such places as Elphin/Knochan, Durness and Islay, all of which have good numbers of these birds.

With a species so thinly distributed as the Teal, it is not easy to detect population trends, but the available information suggests a slight decrease. Atkinson-Willes (1963) noted that parts of Aberdeenshire, Perthshire and Fifeshire, formerly regarded as breeding strongholds, had been almost abandoned during the previous 30 years, though elsewhere no major changes had been detected; and Parslow reported an apparent decrease in parts of Galloway. South of a line from the Humber to Carmarthen, the Teal has always had a scattered breeding distribution; possibly breeding has become even more sporadic in such counties as Dorset and Cornwall over the last 30 years, while during this period there may have been a decline in East Anglia, where a few pairs still breed fairly regularly. Unlike the Mallard, the Teal has received little attention under the introduction and restocking programmes of wildfowling organisations, largely because it will not breed at all freely in captivity. Some wild-caught Teal were turned down, feather-cut, in 1969 on the Medway marshes (Kent), where no wild Teal had nested for several years; four broods were seen that summer and there were still two breeding pairs in 1972 (Mouland *et al* 1970, Harrison *et al* 1973). This may be a pointer to future management.

The Teal is an extremely difficult bird to study or census during the nesting season; nowhere in its vast Palearctic breeding range does it occur at high densities, and there are wide peripheral areas where nesting is only spasmodic. Atkinson-Willes (1970) suggested that the British breeding population was in the order of 1,000–1,500 pairs. Even though it excluded Ireland, this estimate is clearly too low from *Atlas* experience. Fieldwork during 1968–72 in central and N Scotland, Ireland and E England suggests that the average number per occupied 10-km square is probably three to five pairs; and this guess leads to a rough estimate of some 3,500–6,000 pairs.

Number of 10-km squares in which recorded:
    1,766 (46%)
Possible breeding   565 (32%)
Probable breeding   294 (17%)
Confirmed breeding   907 (51%)

References

ATKINSON-WILLES, G. L. 1963. *Wildfowl in Great Britain*. Nature Conserv. Monograph no. 3, London.

ATKINSON-WILLES, G. L. 1970. Wildfowl situation in England, Scotland and Wales. *Proc. Int. Reg. Meet. Conserv. Wildfowl Res., Leningrad 1968*: 101–107.

HARRISON, J., J. N. HUMPHREYS and G. GRAVES. 1973. *Breeding birds of the Medway estuary*. WAGBI, Chester.

MOULAND, B., H. MOULAND and J. HARRISON. 1970. The 'Netherby experiment' repeated with Teal. *WAGBI Rep. and Year Book* 1969–70: 55.

OGILVIE, M. A. 1975. *Ducks of Britain and Europe*. Berkhamsted.

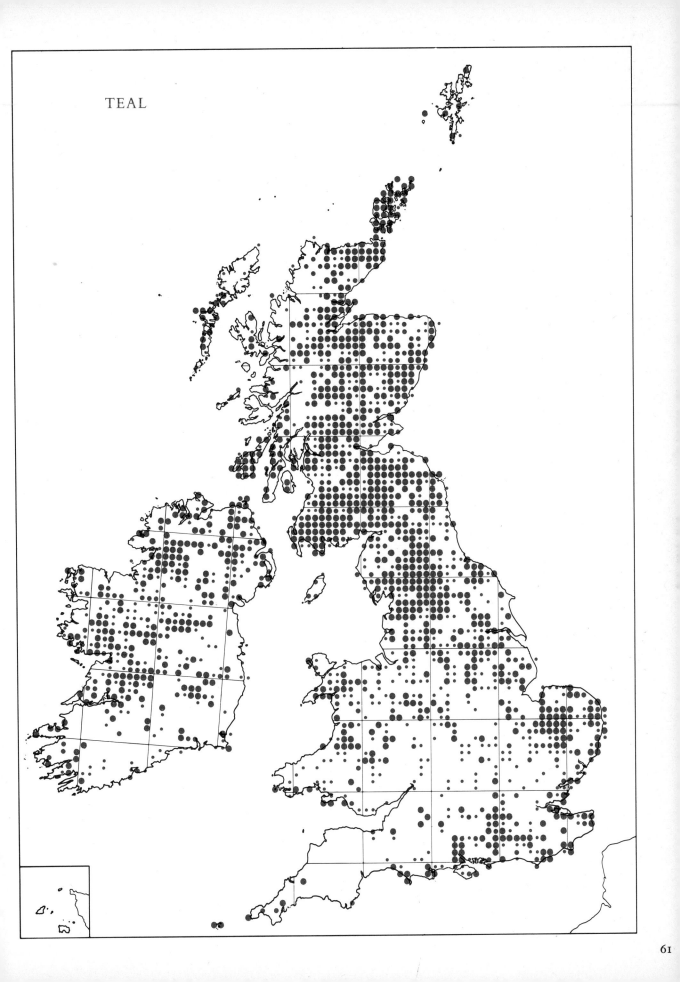

TEAL

Garganey

Anas querquedula

The Garganey is unique among British waterfowl in being exclusively a summer migrant, arriving in late March and April and departing during September.

The Garganey requires shallow fresh or brackish pools for feeding and breeding, and the nest is usually located within 50 m of water, well concealed amidst tall grass. These are difficult birds to find, remaining hidden away in vegetation for much of the nesting season, the drakes often leading their mates off the nests during darkness (Harrison 1972). Immigration may continue until May or early June, and return movements sometimes start as early as mid-June (Harrison and Harrison 1970). Thus, summer occurrences are not necessarily indicative of breeding. Late summer flocks may reflect local breeding success, but the difficulty of proving this is shown by the fact that only 33% of *Atlas* registrations related to confirmed breeding.

Britain is on the periphery of the Garganey's range, and the numbers reaching these islands vary from year to year, the biggest arrivals being in warm springs in anticyclonic conditions. The British breeding population is largest in years when a strong immigration follows a period of wet weather, so that plenty of shallow pools have formed on water-meadows and coastal freshwater marshes. There are relatively few areas where Garganeys breed annually, and even at these the numbers fluctuate markedly. The fens of E England form the British headquarters; in 1952 there were 40–50 pairs in this region, including 25–35 pairs on the Ouse Washes. Although the Welland and Nene Washes have since declined in importance, there were still 23–24 pairs on the Ouse in 1968 and 1969, though only 12–15 in 1970 and seven in 1972. This slump coincided with winters of below-average rainfall and, in consequence, less flooding, and with generally cold springs.

Parslow reported a gradual increase and spread which began about 1900 and continued to the early 1950s; this coincided with the period of climatic amelioration which probably caused the observed northwestwards extension of the European breeding range. The trends in Britain are shown in the table.

Breeding was confirmed in 18 counties during 1968–72, and the map shows a combination of a few regular sites, occupied almost annually, and others used in only one or two of the five *Atlas* years. It therefore exaggerates the picture for any one year.

This opportunistic breeding at sites which may be only temporarily suitable helps to explain the very scattered distribution, though it is also clear that there has been some contraction since the 1950s. There may be a connection with drainage of some of the areas previously occupied in years of strong immigration: Sussex, Kent and the fenland have certainly been affected in this way, and the drainage of the Welland Washes in about 1962 marked the end of regular nesting by Garganeys in Lincolnshire. It is also likely that fewer have reached Britain in the cooler springs of recent years; the great influx of 1959 has had no subsequent counterpart. In the past, nesting has been confirmed only very rarely in Ireland, Scotland and Wales; none was proved in either Ireland or Scotland in 1968–72, though a pair summered in Ayrshire in 1970, and the three Welsh breeding records on the map were all isolated instances.

The requirements of the *Atlas* survey, that breeding need be confirmed once only in each 10-km square, makes it impossible to determine the number of sites used each year; but with such a localised species an independent check can be made with county bird reports. These suggest that the British breeding population was about 65–70 pairs in 1968 and 1969, when the Ouse Washes total was high, but probably barely 50 pairs during 1970–72. Atkinson-Willes (1970) estimated a national total of 50–100 pairs, and it is unlikely that the higher figure is exceeded even in the best years.

This species is afforded special protection in Great Britain under Schedule I of the Protection of Birds Act, 1954–67.

Numbers of English counties with breeding Garganey

| | Breeding | | |
	regularly	irregularly	Totals
Pre-1900	2–3	5	7–8
1900–19	5	4	9
1920–39	9	4	13
1940–52	10	13	23
1953–65	8	12	20

Number of 10-km squares in which recorded: 138 (4%)
Possible breeding   60 (43%)
Probable breeding   32 (23%)
Confirmed breeding   46 (33%)

References

ATKINSON-WILLES, G. L. 1970. Wildfowl situation in England, Scotland and Wales. *Proc. Int. Reg. Meet. Conserv. Wildfowl Res., Leningrad 1968*: 101–107.

HARRISON, J. 1972. *Wildfowl of the North Kent Marshes*. WAGBI, Chester.

HARRISON, J. M. and J. G. HARRISON. 1970. Mid-summer movements of duck in south-east England. *WAGBI Rep. and Year Book 1969–70*: 64–68.

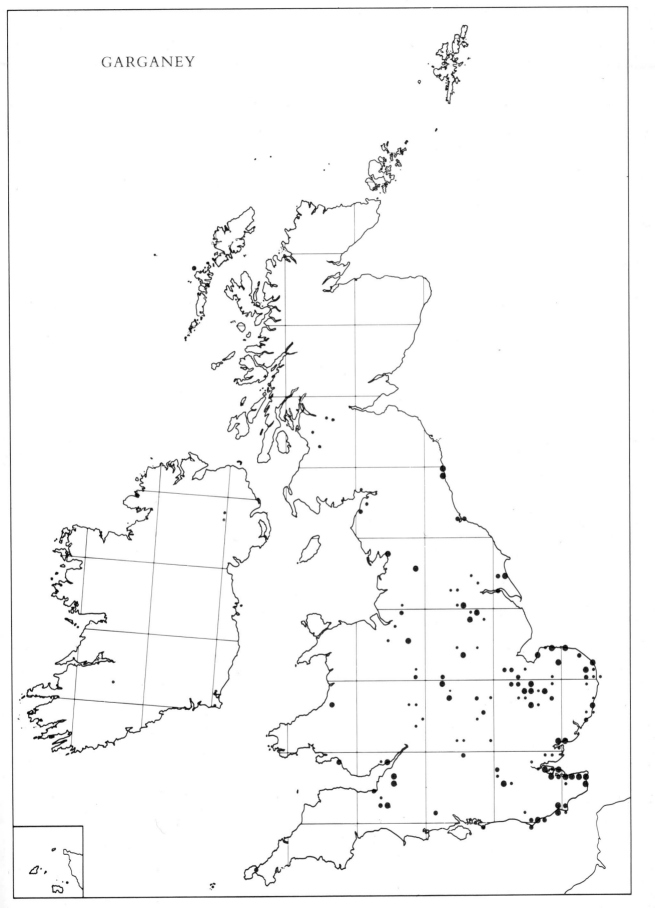

GARGANEY

Gadwall

Anas strepera

The main breeding range of the Gadwall lies well to the south of those of most European dabbling ducks, and the species is largely absent from Scandinavia, Finland and the forested taiga of the USSR. As a breeder it is otherwise patchily distributed everywhere to the west of Russia; there are an estimated 163,000 nesting pairs in the western USSR, compared with only a few hundred in mainland Europe outside Russia (Isakov 1970). Nevertheless, the Gadwall increased in Iceland (colonised in 1862) and became more firmly established in S Sweden during the period of climatic amelioration earlier in this century; yet it is uncertain whether recent increases elsewhere in W Europe are natural or artificially aided, both having applied in Britain and Ireland.

As dabbling ducks, feeding on insects, seeds and water plants, Gadwalls favour shallow, lowland sheets of freshwater surrounded by luxuriant vegetation. In Britain the breeding habitat consists of lakes, meres, reservoirs, freshwater marshes and slow-flowing streams; nests are situated in the intermediate zone between open water and dry land, or on islands, and are always well hidden in rank vegetation. Since they are seldom over 15–20 m from water, they are rather easier to find than those of most ducks; even so, most *Atlas* records of proved breeding came from seeing ducklings.

The Gadwall did not breed in Britain or Ireland before about 1850. Then a pair of migrants decoyed at Dersingham (Norfolk) were wing-clipped and turned down at Narford in the Brecks, where they bred. A substantial population had arisen from this source by 1875; by 1897 they had crossed into the Suffolk side of Breckland, and ten years later were breeding in the valley of the River Lark and in marshes at the source of the River Waveney. Stevenson and Southwell (1890) thought it probable that this increase was aided by Continental winter visitors being induced by the feral stock to settle and breed. By 1906 some 1,400–1,500 were said to frequent one Breckland water alone; such numbers must have been artificially maintained by winter feeding, and no flocks of over 500 have been seen there in modern times. Nevertheless, this is still the British headquarters of the species. Subsequent spread from Breckland was slow: E Suffolk was colonised in the 1930s, and breeding became regular in the Norfolk

Broads in the 1950s, when the Ouse Washes and E Essex were also settled.

In London, over 60 full-winged young flew away from St James's Park during the 1930s and breeding was proved at Barn Elms Reservoir in 1935. There is now an established feral population in the Greater London area, though Gadwalls breeding in W Kent are believed to stem from post-1965 releases by WAGBI. Other feral breeding centres include the Isles of Scilly, where the species was turned down in the 1930s; Somerset (mainly Chew Valley Reservoir), resulting from escapes from the Wildfowl Trust at Slimbridge (Gloucestershire); and the Lake District and N Lancashire, derived from releases by wildfowlers. In fact, all English and Welsh breeding records are believed to stem from these or similar liberations.

In Scotland, Gadwalls have nested on Loch Leven since 1909, and have spread to Perthshire and Fife; elsewhere, breeding has tended to be spasmodic, but may now be regular on North Uist (Outer Hebrides). Breeding was first confirmed in Ireland in 1933 and since then the species has nested in six or seven counties, but is known to do so regularly only in Co Wexford (1–3 pairs). Unlike those in England, which are thought to be almost all of feral origin, it is probable that the Scottish and Irish breeders are largely natural colonists. Whether these came from W Europe or Iceland, or both, is unknown; but Icelandic breeders overwinter in Ireland and presumably visit W Scotland also. The number wintering in Ireland has increased in recent years.

Parslow estimated the British and Irish population at 260 pairs, which seems of the right order. *Atlas* fieldwork produced confirmed or probable breeding in 110 squares. Nesting in some of these is doubtless irregular, but others contain concentrations, notably 25–30 pairs on Loch Leven, 20–25 pairs on Chew Valley Reservoir, about 40 pairs at Minsmere (Suffolk), and up to 24 pairs on the Ouse Washes. No estimates are available for the big Breckland population, though 16 broods were counted along an 8 km stretch of the River Lark in 1972.

Number of 10-km squares in which recorded:
171 (4%)
Possible breeding   61 (36%)
Probable breeding   22 (13%)
Confirmed breeding   88 (51%)

Though some records were originally submitted in confidence, all dots are now shown accurately (as recommended by the Rare Breeding Birds Panel)

References

HARRISON, J. M., J. G. HARRISON and D. HARRISON. 1969. Some preliminary results from the release of hand-reared Gadwall. *WAGBI Rep. and Year Book 1968–69*: 37–40.

ISAKOV, Y. A. 1970. Distribution and numbers of waterfowl populations on their breeding grounds in Europe and West Asia. *Proc. Int. Reg. Meet. Conserv. Wildfowl Res., Leningrad 1968*: 19–23.

STEVENSON, H. and T. SOUTHWELL. 1890. *The Birds of Norfolk*. Vol. 3. London.

GADWALL

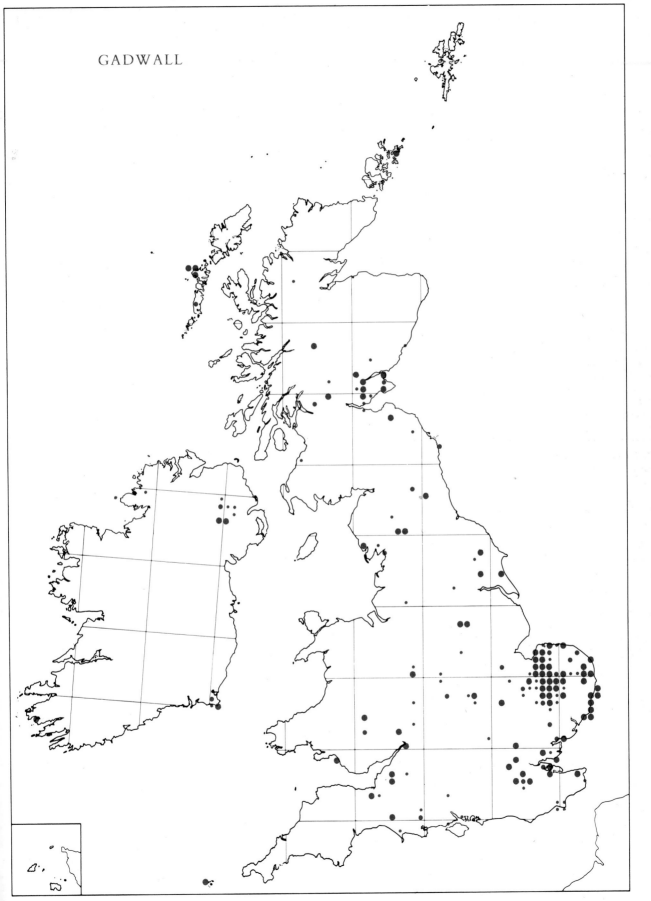

Wigeon

Anas penelope

Despite the fact that the largest single nesting concentration in these islands is on low-lying Loch Leven (Kinross), British breeding Wigeon appear to prefer moorland tarns, lochs and streams; horseshoe lakes along meandering rivers provide ideal sites. Boggy and even wooded country is also frequented, and pairs nesting irregularly in S England will use brackish coastal marshes and inland pools with adjacent rough ground. Islands seem to be favoured where they exist, for they have the benefit of reducing, or even eliminating, mammalian predation. Pairs will nest socially in optimum habitat and especially on loch islands: on St Serf's Island in Loch Leven, Wigeon's nests are 15–40 m from those of their neighbours, a more generous spacing than is tolerated by other duck species on this crowded 42 ha site. As with other dabbling ducks, the nest is a ground hollow lined with dead vegetation and down, and is well concealed among long heather, bracken, rushes or tussocky grass. Like the nests of most ducks, it is difficult to find; it may be fairly close to water (especially on islands) or 150 m or more away on a bracken-clad hillside overlooking a tarn or loch. Proof of breeding is best obtained later in the year by watching for ducklings.

The Wigeon is one of several subarctic ducks which appear to have colonised Britain during the cooler climatic phase of the 19th century. The first nest was found in Sutherland in 1834, and subsequently breeding birds spread southwards down the middle of Scotland; lateral expansion was slower, but the Tweed region was reached in the 1890s, Galloway in 1906, and the Outer Hebrides in the 1920s (Berry 1939). Baxter and Rintoul (1953) reported that it nested fairly commonly north of the Firths of Clyde and Forth, and had earlier been described as the commonest breeding duck in Caithness and central Ross-shire, though there were fewer in the Lowlands, W Scotland and the Hebrides. This phase of rapid increase and expansion appears to have ended by 1950; and since then there have even been local reversals, with fewer breeding instances reported from the marginal areas of S and W Scotland.

In England, the first breeding records came from Yorkshire in 1897, Cumberland in 1903, and Northumberland in 1913. Farther south, and in Wales, nesting attempts have always been irregular, and in some cases are thought to have involved birds which had escaped from waterfowl collections, possibly also wild ones which had not migrated as a result of being slightly injured during the preceding shooting season. This species has not been the subject of any serious release experiments by wildfowling clubs. There have been only two reports of nesting in Ireland, in 1933 and 1953.

At the present time, the overwhelming majority of nesting pairs are to be found along the upland spine of England and Scotland, from Yorkshire and Westmorland to the Pentland Firth, with main centres on the N Pennine moors, the Ettrick Forest (Selkirkshire), in central and E Perthshire (extending into Kinross), upper Speyside, central and E Sutherland, Caithness and Orkney. The current pattern of distribution is basically the same as 50 years ago, except that there is some suggestion of a shift to the east in the central Scottish Highlands. Former centres on Rannoch Moor and the lochs of Black Mount (N Perthshire) have been almost deserted, though breeding has increased in eastern areas as far apart as Kinross and Aberdeenshire (Yarker and Atkinson-Willes 1971). These authors deduced that the British Wigeon population is holding its own, but is probably not increasing to any marked extent. Since the species is still largely confined to areas occupied 50 years ago, it seems likely that some unidentified ecological factor is restricting further expansion, in which case the possibility of increased disturbance through tourism might lead to a decline in the long term.

Atlas fieldwork produced confirmed or probable breeding in 157 squares, of which those south of a line from Morecambe Bay (Lancashire) to Flamborough Head (Yorkshire) undoubtedly represent irregular nesting. Rather little information is available on densities farther north. The Yorkshire Pennines (eight squares) had 18–20 pairs in 1970–71, and there are known to be 25–30 pairs on Loch Leven. At several localities in Sutherland and Caithness a dozen or more attendant drakes have been seen, and similarly on Speyside and in Perthshire counts of adults are well in excess of proven nesting instances (Yarker and Atkinson-Willes 1971). A conservative average of two or three pairs per 10-km square with probable or confirmed breeding would give a total population of 300–500 pairs, which may be compared with the estimate of 350 pairs given by Yarker and Atkinson-Willes.

Number of 10-km squares in which recorded:
283 (7%)
Possible breeding   126 (45%)
Probable breeding   40 (14%)
Confirmed breeding   117 (41%)

References

BERRY, J. 1939. The status and distribution of wild geese and wild duck in Scotland. *Internat. Wildfowl Inquiry*. Vol. 2. Cambridge.

NEWTON, I. and C. R. G. CAMPBELL. 1975. Breeding of ducks at Loch Leven, Kinross. *Wildfowl* 26: 83–102.

YARKER, B. and G. L. ATKINSON-WILLES. 1971. The numerical distribution of some British breeding ducks. *Wildfowl* 22: 63–70.

WIGEON

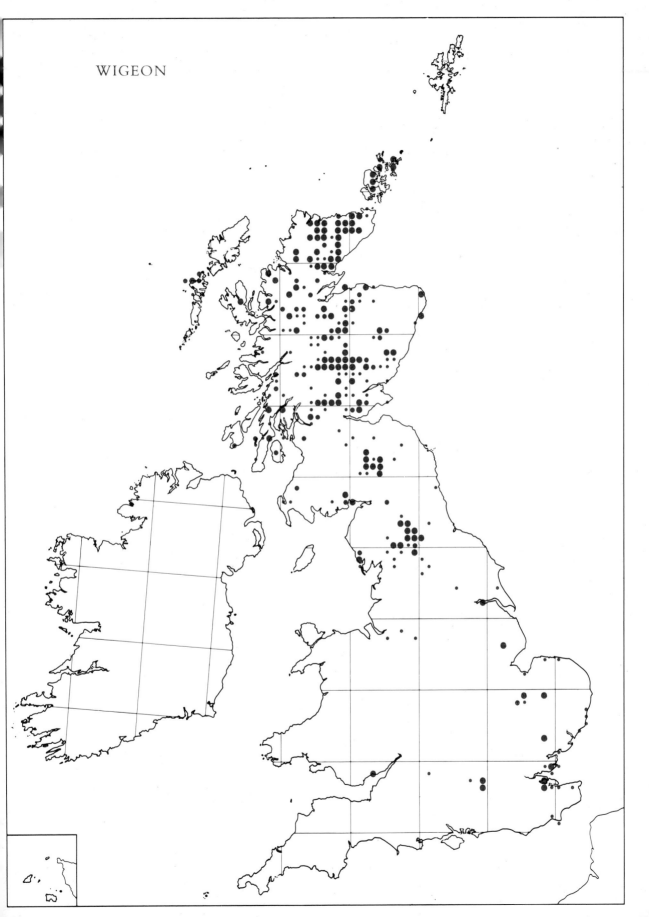

Pintail

Anas acuta

The Pintail's diverse breeding habitats include moorland pools and lochs, and lowland lakes and freshwater marshes. In Scotland the species has been found breeding at upland lochs in the Highlands as well as at low-lying ones on large outer islands; and in England the two regular centres consist of sea-level fen and marsh where rough grazing land is intersected by numerous drainage dykes. As the Pintail is a dabbling duck, waters frequented have to be fairly shallow, at least at their margins. Nests tend to be more exposed than those of other ducks (apart from Eiders *Somateria mollissima*), often being on open ground in short grass, though concealed sites among heather, rushes and long grass are also used, and they may be 50–200 m from water. Exceptionally, nests have been found in marram grass on coastal dunes. No dabbling duck's nest is easy to find, but in the case of the Pintail the tendencies to use exposed sites, and for the drakes to remain nearby, are of assistance (Campbell and Ferguson-Lees 1972). Most *Atlas* records of confirmed breeding rested on distraction display or a sight of the brood; the proportion of possible breeding is high, and presumably this category includes many that were actually late migrants or summering non-breeders.

A 19th century colonist of these islands, the Pintail was first proved breeding in Scotland in 1869 (Inverness-shire), England in 1910 (Kent), and Ireland in 1917 (Co Roscommon). It maintained a slow expansion into the 1950s, but remained curiously scattered, with few sites occupied for more than a few years at a time.

In Scotland, Berry (1939) reported more or less consistent breeding in the Northern Isles and the Moray, Dee and Forth Basins. Loch Leven (Kinross) was the main centre: the Pintail bred there in varying numbers from 1898 to 1939, but had gone by 1946, and has nested only once since. Baxter and Rintoul (1953) said that it still bred in fair numbers in Orkney and Shetland; it is now rare in the former, with one to three pairs nesting in five of the seven years 1968–74, but has not nested in Shetland for some years. Parslow considered that the only three Scottish counties where Pintails nested regularly were Caithness, Inverness-shire and Aberdeenshire; breeding was registered in all three during the *Atlas* years, but was not annual.

England's first nesting records came from Romney Marsh (Kent), where one or two pairs seem to have bred irregularly during 1910–36. In 1947 a brood was seen on the N Kent marshes, and this remains one of only two more or less regular English breeding areas. During the 28 years 1947–74, Pintails are known to have been present there in 22 summers, with peaks of six pairs in 1952 and five in 1962; the Thames and Swale have been more favoured than the Medway. The other occupied area is the fen country on the Cambridgeshire/Norfolk boundary, where Pintails were first found breeding in 1929; 20 pairs nested on the Ouse Washes in 1969–70, though the normal population is between three and six pairs. Otherwise, instances of nesting in England have been few and far between, apart from a small feral population in the northwest: since 1964, pinioned birds have been kept on a WAGBI reserve at Millom (Cumberland), and their young have been allowed to fly away; several feral pairs now nest around this reserve (Swift 1974). This is a possible origin for the several scattered *Atlas* breeding records between the Solway and the Mersey. Pintails have nested in six Irish counties since 1917, but have never become established; the only breeding records in 1968–72 were of single pairs at Lough Beg (Northern Ireland) and in Co Roscommon.

It is possible that breeding Pintails have declined since the 1950s, but it is difficult to be sure in view of their irregularity at individual sites; the desertion of a known locality might mean no more than settlement elsewhere. Atkinson-Willes (1970) estimated the British breeding total at 50 pairs, while Parslow believed it to be a fluctuating population with over 100 pairs in some years. The *Atlas* produced confirmed or probable breeding in only 46 squares during five years' fieldwork. Since not all squares were occupied annually, the map exaggerates the picture for any one season; and, as densities are normally low everywhere, the total population may be under 50 pairs in most years, which would make this our rarest breeding dabbling duck.

Number of 10-km squares in which recorded:
94 (2%)
Possible breeding   48 (51%)
Probable breeding   11 (12%)
Confirmed breeding   35 (37%)

References

ATKINSON-WILLES, G. L. 1970. Wildfowl situation in England, Scotland and Wales. *Proc. Int. Reg. Meet. Conserv. Wildfowl Res., Leningrad 1968*: 101–107.

BERRY, J. 1939. The status and distribution of wild geese and wild duck in Scotland. *Internat. Wildfowl Inquiry*. Vol. 2. Cambridge.

SWIFT, J. 1974. Pintail; a project assessing the release of hand-reared birds. *WAGBI Rep. and Year Book 1973–74*: 55–58.

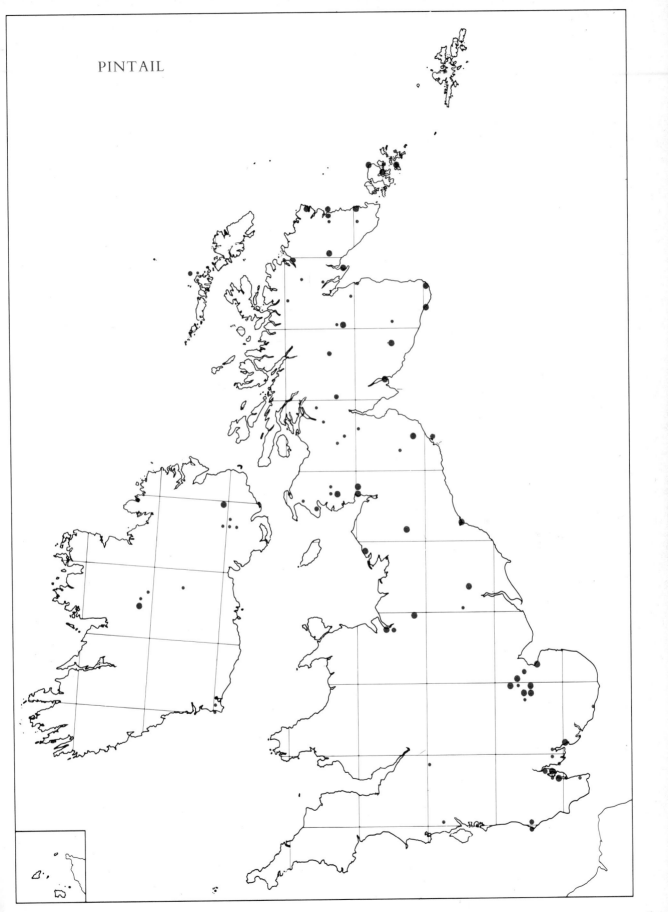

PINTAIL

Shoveler

Anas clypeata

The drake Shoveler is one of our most striking ducks. The most unusual feature is the broad, spatulate bill, both mandibles edged with fine, intermeshing lamellae which superficially resemble the teeth of a small comb; these distinguish the species as one adapted for filter-feeding.

This method of feeding necessitates shallow, eutrophic waters, and it is therefore no surprise that Shovelers are found almost exclusively on brackish and fresh water at all seasons. For breeding they require marshy pools and dykes, or lakes and reservoirs with shallow margins and plenty of water-weeds; a regular haunt in SE England consists of low-lying grazing marshes drained by reed-fringed fleets and ditches. As denizens of shallow, muddy waters, Shovelers are necessarily restricted to the lowlands; nowhere do they breed above the 400 m contour.

The nest is a lined hollow on the ground, usually well hidden within the thick cover of tall grass, nettles, heather or gorse, or even in a reed-bed clearing; but Shovelers also nest in fairly open situations, among tufts of short grass in meadows or grazed marshland, and up to 40 m from water or water-logged ground. Nests in salt-marsh vegetation have been found in N Kent. Breeding is not easy to prove unless ducklings are seen; nevertheless, it seems likely that most *Atlas* records of presence only were actually non-breeders, for it is by no means unusual for this species to occur in early summer on marginal waters away from regular breeding centres.

The Shoveler is a British breeding bird of long standing, formerly rare, but no longer so as a consequence of a major increase and spread, mainly during 1900–50. This was matched by similar expansion in W Europe, and may have been linked with climatic amelioration. Nevertheless, as the map shows, breeding Shovelers are still localised, as are the shallow, marshy areas on which they depend. The largest numbers are in the low-lying southeast, between the Wash and the Thames Estuary; and elsewhere in England there is a tendency for sites to be grouped, as in Northumberland, E Yorkshire, the Lancashire mosses, and the meres of the W Midlands. Southwest of a line from Wirral to the Isle of Wight, large areas are devoid of nesting Shovelers, and breeding may be regular only in Anglesey and the counties of the lower Severn.

Scotland was colonised from the 1840s onwards, but, even 60 years later, breeding localities were few; here too the real impetus of spread occurred after 1900. The main centres are now in the southeast lowlands, which may hold as many pairs as all the rest of Scotland, even though nesting takes place as far north and west as the lochs of Caithness and Orkney and the machair of the Outer Hebrides. A shortage of suitable lowland marshes, especially north of the Clyde and the Tay, doubtless accounts for the Shoveler's fragmented range in Scotland.

It is not clear whether there has been any general change in breeding status in Britain since 1950. Local increases have been reported, but are probably balanced by equally local declines elsewhere; and, in any case, annual fluctuations at the species' strongholds in Fenland and East Anglia make it difficult to assess trends. The favoured marshy habitats are undoubtedly being slowly despoiled through drainage and other developments, as for example in the Trent Valley (Nottinghamshire) where, following reclamation, Shovelers slumped from 40 pairs in 1947 to the present 5–6 pairs.

At the end of the 19th century, Shovelers were thought to be breeding in 18 Irish counties, though only sparsely in some; and five further counties had been added by 1950 (Ruttledge 1966). They may never have been numerous as nesting birds in Ireland, but *Atlas* fieldwork revealed them to be even scarcer than had hitherto been thought, and with a curiously local and disjointed distribution. It seems clear that there has been a significant contraction in Ireland, but also an over-optimistic interpretation of the scattered records in the past.

A few notable concentrations of breeding Shovelers were reported during 1968–72, including up to 200 pairs on the Ouse Washes (Cambridgeshire), up to 100 pairs in the N Kent marshes, and about 30 pairs at Minsmere (Suffolk); there are also important numbers in Norfolk, though no recent figures are available. Elsewhere, this species tends to be sparsely distributed in the nesting season, and it is irregular on some small waters. Yarker and Atkinson-Willes (1971) considered that the British breeding population was probably under 500 pairs. During 1968–72, however, the Fens, East Anglia and Kent together are thought to have held about that number. Further, these areas accounted for less than 100 of the 10-km squares with confirmed or probable breeding records and, allowing only the conservative figure of two pairs for each of the remainder, a British and Irish total of about 1,000 pairs is indicated.

Number of 10-km squares in which recorded:
  571 (15%)
Possible breeding   197 (35%)
Probable breeding   99 (17%)
Confirmed breeding   275 (48%)

Reference
YARKER, B. and G. L. ATKINSON-WILLES. 1971. The numerical distribution of some British breeding ducks. *Wildfowl* 22: 63–70.

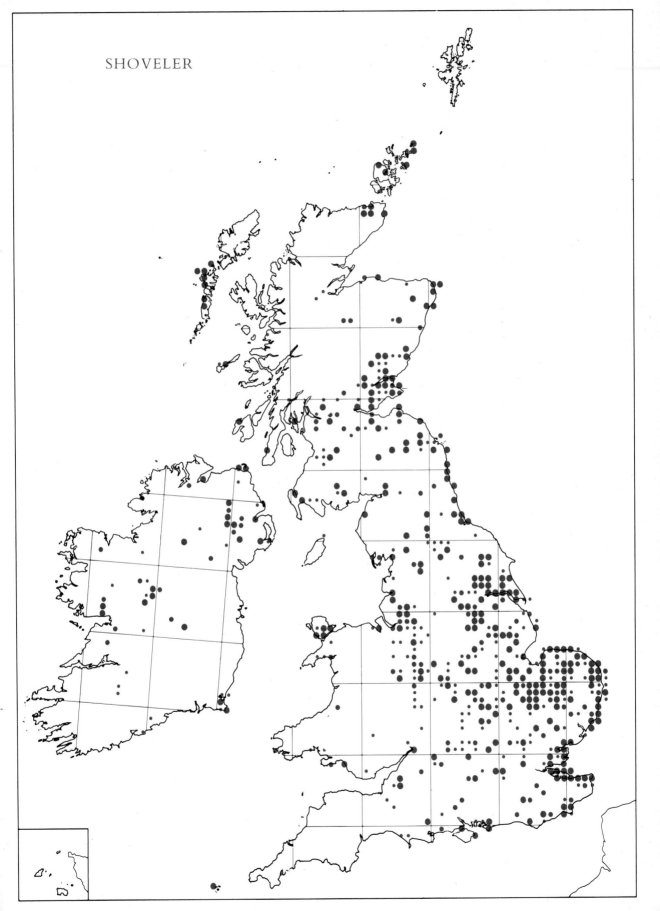

SHOVELER

Mandarin Duck

Aix galericulata

The natural home of the Mandarin Duck is in E Asia—Japan, E China (including Manchuria) and adjacent parts of the USSR (Ussuriland and Sakhalin). The species was imported into Britain as early as 1747, and was first bred in captivity in 1834, but it was not until the 20th century that a feral population became established, and not until 1971 that it gained official admission to the British and Irish list.

The Mandarin differs from our native breeding ducks in being more arboreal, often perching on branches or in shrubs, and invariably nesting in holes in trees. In Britain the preferred habitat is typified by Windsor Great Park, the Mandarin's headquarters here: mature, open deciduous woodland containing secluded streams or ponds. The most important trees are oak, sweet chestnut and beech, which provide the acorns, nuts and mast which are the staple winter foods. Secondary cover for shelter is also needed, and rhododendron thickets are especially favoured.

Having a high wing-to-weight ratio, and a proportionately long tail, Mandarins have great aerial manoeuvrability, and are adept at weaving through trees; they seldom fly higher than canopy level. Nest-holes are usually in old trees, with the entrance holes commonly 7–8 m or more above ground level. Open country is sometimes frequented, though old trees containing suitable nesting cavities remain essential; pollarded willows are used at one marginal site. This species would benefit from the provision of artificial nest-boxes in areas where woodland management has reduced the amount of old standing timber. Despite the height at which they are hatched, the ducklings have no problem in descending to the ground. With their small but needle-sharp claws they scramble up the sides of their nest cavity to the entrance, and their thick down and light weight enable them to parachute safely to the ground. It has been shown experimentally that *Aix* ducklings have no fear of height, unlike the young of ground-nesting ducks.

Nests are very difficult to find in woodland, and are usually discovered purely by chance. If the cavity is shallow, the presence of white down at the entrance may reveal the site, but occupied holes are usually deep, and the parents are particularly secretive when approaching or leaving the nest. In the event, most confirmed breeding records in 1968–72 came from observations of broods after they had left the nest and had been led to water: discovery was facilitated by the Mandarin being a resident species with most of its regular haunts already known.

By far the most important feral population is in Surrey and E Berkshire, stemming, at least in part, from Foxwarren Park (between Byfleet and Cobham), where six full-winged pairs were turned down in 1928, bred freely, and soon spread. It is likely that other sources have also contributed, such as a release in London parks in 1930 of 99 birds, all of which promptly dispersed. By 1932, Mandarins were established in small numbers in Windsor Great Park and nearby Virginia Water. Since then the range has expanded, and they now occur west to Swallowfield (Berkshire), east to Esher and Leatherhead (Surrey), north to Maidenhead and Wraysbury (Buckinghamshire), and south to the Surrey/Sussex boundary. By the winter of 1950/51, there were estimated to be 400 birds between Windsor and Bagshot, and 150 around Cobham (Fitter 1959). The increase evidently continues, and in 1969 there were 55–60 pairs along the River Mole between Mickleham and Esher alone.

As the map shows, there are scattered groups of Mandarin Ducks elsewhere in Britain, and all can be associated with, or are dependent upon, nearby waterfowl collections or bird farms such as those at Leckford (Hampshire), Leeds Castle (Kent), Monken Hadley (Hertfordshire)—which is known to be responsible for feral breeding in N Middlesex—Salhouse (Norfolk), Eaton Hall (Cheshire) and Holmwood (near Perth). Mandarins from the Perth collection are known to feed regularly along the River Tay up to 20 km away. This flock increased to 60–70 birds by late 1974, most of which breed in garden nest-boxes at Holmwood; one or two pairs nest ferally, usually within 5 km, though they and their young rejoin the main flock in October for the winter feeding (*per* Sir Christopher Lever). A once-thriving colony at Woburn (Bedfordshire) has dwindled in recent years, and none was reported outside this park during 1968–72, although breeding was proved at Old Linslade 8 km to the south in 1973.

Campbell and Ferguson-Lees (1972) considered that the British feral population numbered over 250 pairs. The River Mole figure quoted above shows densities reaching 15 pairs per occupied 10-km square, and on this basis the total population is perhaps about 300–400 pairs.

Number of 10-km squares in which recorded:
   41 (1%)
Possible breeding   12 (29%)
Probable breeding   3 (7%)
Confirmed breeding   26 (63%)

References
FITTER, R. S. R. 1959. *The Ark in our Midst*. London.
SAVAGE, C. 1952. *The Mandarin Duck*. London.

Red-crested Pochard *Netta rufina*, **see page 446**

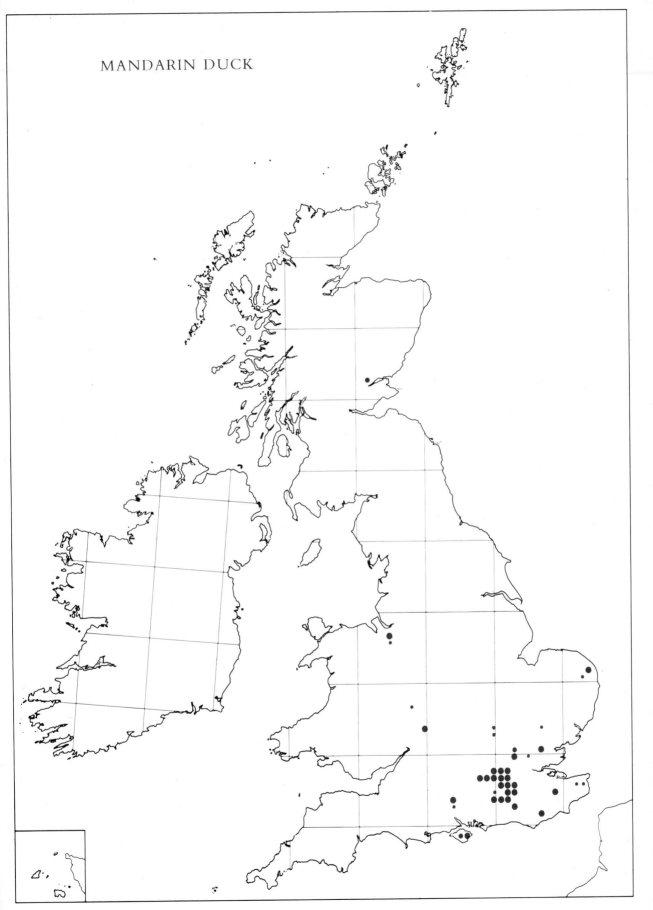

MANDARIN DUCK

Wood Duck

Aix sponsa

Attempts to naturalise the Wood Duck, a N American species sometimes known as the Carolina Duck, were being made in Britain as long ago as the 1870s. Bicton House, near Exeter (Devon), then possessed one of the largest ornamental waterfowl collections in the country, and its full-winged Wood Ducks ranged as far afield as Slapton and Plymouth. Before the 1939–45 war, unpinioned flocks were also kept at various times at Woburn (Bedfordshire), Falloden (Northumberland) and Foxwarren Park (Surrey). Today a number of private collections have free-flying birds. It is not clear, however, whether a self-maintaining feral population has yet been established, and the species is not fully accepted on the British and Irish list.

The *Atlas* map represents a five years' accumulation of isolated nesting records, and must be read accordingly. The small group in Surrey was discussed by Wheatley (1973): free-flying Wood Ducks were released on a private estate at Puttenham (SW of Guildford) in the late 1960s, nested successfully, and had increased to ten pairs by 1972; but only once (in 1969) has breeding been proved away from the protection of the home estate, though adults often visit nearby waters. Elsewhere in Surrey, there was an unsuccessful nesting attempt in 1968 on Vann Lake, near Ockley, an area where there are known to be several waterfowl breeders; and a brood of unknown origin was seen on Guildford sewage farm in 1970. Wood Ducks have also been seen intermittently on Virginia Water (Surrey/Berkshire), a major haunt of the closely related Mandarin Duck *A. galericulata*; breeding is known to have occurred there in 1969, but the origins of these birds are likewise uncertain.

Isolated *Atlas* breeding records elsewhere are also believed to be due to the propinquity of local collections. There is a full-winged flock based on the Tropical Bird Gardens at Rode (Somerset), and at least one pair breeds outside its confines, on the nearby River Frome, though adults and young rejoin the main flock later (Risdon 1973). During 1972–74, adults with ducklings were seen at Bishops Offley, near Eccleshall (Staffordshire), and it is suspected that breeding takes place on a private estate upstream

(*per* Sir Christopher Lever). Similar circumstances are assumed to account for the *Atlas* records from central Sussex and NW Norfolk; and a further such instance from Broughton (N Lancashire) can probably be associated with a WAGBI reserve on the Duddon Estuary.

Since *Atlas* fieldwork ended, isolated breeding records have continued to accrue and an attempt is being made to introduce the species to Grizedale Forest in the Lake District. The only further instance of nesting in Surrey was on Virginia Water in 1973, and the following year a brood was seen nearby, in Windsor Great Park (Berkshire). Also in 1974, a nest was found in Cranbury Park, near Winchester (Hampshire) (W. C. James *in litt*).

One has the impression that most nesting records in recent years have related to pairs which bred outside collections to which they afterwards returned, perhaps for supplementary winter feeding; if this was so, they were not truly feral. Why the Wood Duck has so far failed to become established is unknown, for it is a hardy species. It has a longer fledging period than the Mandarin Duck, and Savage (1952) suggested that this would extend the period of vulnerability to predators and lead to lower comparative breeding success. It seems equally likely, however, that ecological factors may be involved. Like the Mandarin, its natural habitat consists of old, deciduous woodland near water, and it nests in holes in decaying trees. Most breeding records have come from Surrey and adjacent parts of Berkshire, where the birds may be in direct competition for food and nest sites with Mandarin Ducks already firmly established there; while the very local distribution of the Mandarin elsewhere suggests that areas of suitable habitat are limited, it being against modern forestry practice to leave old trees to rot.

The Wood Duck takes readily to nest boxes, a habit to which it probably owes its survival in its Nearctic home. Drainage and logging eliminated many woodland swamps in N America in the late 19th and early 20th centuries, and this, coupled with excessive shooting, had brought the species to the brink of disaster by 1918. Protective legislation, captive breeding programmes, and large-scale provision of nest boxes in woodland saved the species and enabled it to increase, and it is now common again over much of its former range (Ripley 1965).

Number of 10-km squares in which recorded:
11 (0.3%)
Possible breeding 2 (18%)
Probable breeding 0
Confirmed breeding 9 (82%)

References
RIPLEY, S. D. 1965. Surface-feeding ducks and tree ducks. pp 154–171 in WETMORE, A. (ed), *Water, Prey, and Game Birds of North America*. Washington.
RISDON, H. S. 1973. Report of the Tropical Bird Gardens at Rode, 1972. *Avic. Mag.* 79: 52–55.
SAVAGE, C. 1952. *The Mandarin Duck*. London.
WHEATLEY, J. J. 1973. Recent Carolina Duck breeding records in Surrey. *Surrey Bird Rep.* 20: 64–65.

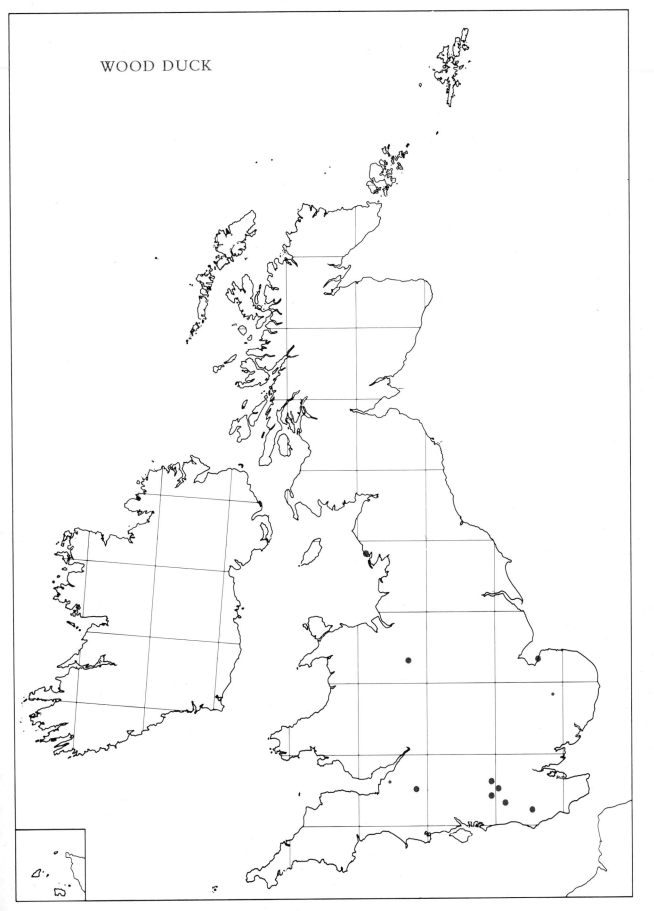

WOOD DUCK

Scaup

Aythya marila

This duck is primarily a winter visitor here, having been recorded nesting only infrequently in Britain and never in Ireland. There is no evidence that it has been more regular, not even during the colder climatic phase of the 19th century, when the species bred farther south in N Europe and was more numerous in Iceland. Indeed, the first confirmed British breeding record came as late as 1897, from South Uist (Outer Hebrides), where the Scaup then seems to have nested annually until 1902 (three pairs in 1900) and at intervals to 1913, but not since. The only other acceptable report for that era concerns a nest found in Sutherland in 1899.

Subsequently, the following instances have been published. In Orkney, breeding occurred on Papa Westray during 1954–59, with three pairs present in 1955 and two nests found in both 1956 and 1959; there was also isolated nesting on North Ronaldsay in 1965 (where birds were also present in 1966), on W Mainland in 1969, and at Loch of Isbister in 1973. On the other hand, one pair at Balranald (North Uist) in 1969 was the only confirmed modern record in the Outer Hebrides, which is perhaps surprising since this group of islands provided all but one of Scotland's breeding records before the 1914–18 war. The mainland of Scotland has produced records from three counties: a brood at an unspecified locality in Caithness in 1939; a pair on a coastal island in Wester Ross in 1946; and three nests at one site in Perthshire in 1970. The only proved breeding record in England involved a female and half-grown brood, presumed to be locally bred, at Tetney (Lincolnshire) in 1944, but an unmated female laid infertile clutches on Havergate Island (Suffolk) for five consecutive years during 1967–71.

It may be significant that, of the 21 years in which Scaup have nested in Scotland, only one fell in the period between the 1914–18 and 1939–45 wars, when the climatic amelioration was most marked; apart from the series on South Uist, however, most are since 1945, during which time there has been a great increase in the number of birdwatchers.

Compared with its close relative the Tufted Duck *A. fuligula*, this species has a more northern breeding distribution, of which the normal southwestern limit passes to the north of Britain. Voous (1960) gave the July isotherm extremes for the breeding range as 6°–17°C for the Scaup and 8°–24°C for the Tufted Duck, which shows the latter's greater temperature tolerance. Scotland has July means of 12°–14°C and so might seem suitable for the Scaup, but other factors —such as rainfall and humidity—may be involved.

Typically, the Scaup breeds on fairly extensive sheets of open water, ranging from bleak moorland and tundra pools to lakes and rivers in the boreal region. Nests are situated on the ground, sometimes exposed, but more often hidden among herbage such as heather; they are frequently on islets, and far enough back from the water-line to avoid flooding. Few details are available from Scottish breeding sites, which have included lochs on upland moors (as in Perthshire) and low-lying parts of outer islands (as in Orkney); nests have been in rank vegetation, tufts of long grass or rushes, and on small islets in lochs. In the main breeding range, it is normal for pairs to nest socially, and this tendency has been noticed even in Scotland (South Uist, Orkney and Perthshire).

As happens with other northern ducks, one or two Scaup may linger after the others have migrated and such birds occasionally spend the summer on freshwater lochs. Inevitably, nesting has been suspected on a number of occasions, but it is unlikely that it takes place anywhere in Britain on a regular basis. None of the authenticated instances in the last 40 years has led to sustained breeding, the longest span being the six consecutive years in the 1950s, during which one to three pairs nested on Papa Westray in Orkney. Atkinson-Willes (1970) was surely optimistic when he published a notional value of ten pairs for a reputed British breeding population.

This species is afforded special protection in Great Britain under Schedule I of the Protection of Birds Act, 1954–67.

Number of 10-km squares in which recorded:
8 (0.2%)
Possible breeding   4 (50%)
Probable breeding   0
Confirmed breeding   4 (50%)

One dot has been moved by up to two 10-km squares (the Rare Breeding Birds Panel's recommendation was accurate plotting)

References

ANDREW, D. G. 1968. Scaup breeding in Orkney. *Scott. Birds* 5: 23–24.

ATKINSON-WILLES, G. L. 1970. Wildfowl situation in England, Scotland and Wales. *Proc. Int. Reg. Meet. Conserv. Wildfowl Res., Leningrad 1968*: 101–107.

BROWN, P. E. 1945. Observations on a Scaup-Duck and brood on the Lincolnshire coast. *Brit. Birds* 38: 192–193.

WALKER, K. G. 1967. Scaup breeding in Orkney. *Scott. Birds* 4: 503–504.

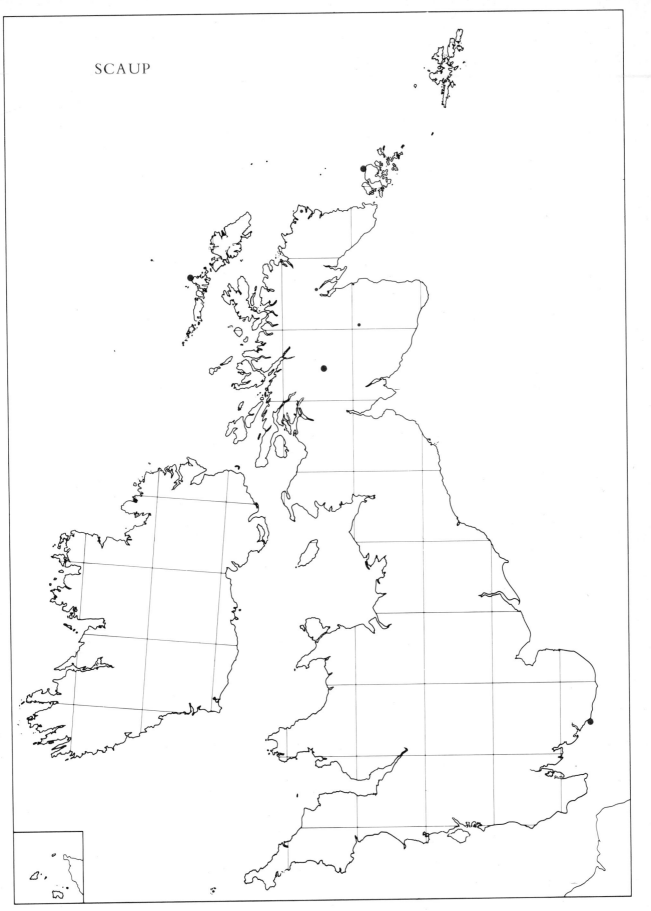

SCAUP

Tufted Duck

Aythya fuligula

Tufted Ducks breed on lakes, lochs and reservoirs, especially those with islands. They tended to favour larger freshwater bodies than did Pochards *A. ferina*, but this distinction is breaking down, due to the Tufted's population expansion. This species has now taken to nesting on lakes in urban parks, where waterfowl are protected and often become quite tame; moreover, it has also benefited from the recent great increase in the number of gravel pits, which are adopted for breeding when they are flooded and sufficient rank herbage has grown around them. In some areas, too, it now nests successfully on sluggish reaches of river. Whereas the Pochard is primarily vegetarian, the Tufted Duck's diet is predominantly animal. A staple food in England is the introduced zebra mussel, which was found in the London docks in 1824, spread rapidly, and by 1950 was present in 42 vice-counties; these mussels multiply in reservoirs and gravel pits, and Olney (1963) suggested that they represent an important factor in the spread of the Tufted Duck.

While nests are occasionally over water, on reed platforms or old nests of Coots *Fulica atra* among emergent vegetation, they are usually on dry ground within 10 m of the water's edge, and well concealed in rank herbage. Social breeding on islands is by no means unusual, and on St Serf's Island in Loch Leven (Kinross) some 500–600 pairs nest close together, interspersed with pairs of five other duck species. At that site, Tufted Ducks' nests are only 5–11 m from those of their neighbours, and hatching success is better for the pairs nesting inside a large colony of Black-headed Gulls *Larus ridibundus*, probably because the gulls keep out the more serious predators. Tufted Ducks nest considerably later than the majority of waterfowl: most do not lay until mid-May or later, and broods are seldom seen much before July. Thus, several visits may be needed to establish breeding and, because of the difficulties of finding single nests, proof usually comes from the sight of ducklings.

Breeding in Britain was unknown until the first cases in Yorkshire (1849), Nottinghamshire (1851) and Sussex (1853). In Scotland, the first known breeding occurred in Perthshire in 1872 and Kinross in 1875; but only five years later over 100 broods were seen in the latter area. Ireland was colonised in 1877, major expansion following after 1900; on Lough Neagh, there were only a few pairs in 1920, but 20 years later over 100 nests were found on a single island. By the 1930s Tufted Ducks had occupied most of the suitable waters available in Britain, and subsequent increases, which are still occurring, can be attributed largely to prompt exploitation of the many new reservoirs and flooded gravel pits. In recent years a number of natural sites in Scotland have been colonised, and there has been an increase in the small Shetland population; while in Ireland Co Wexford was settled as recently as 1970 and Waterford in 1974. The only restrictions to breeding seem to be physical ones: Tufted Ducks require waters at least 1 ha in extent and they do not normally breed above 400 m, while it is apparent from the scattered occurrences in NW Scotland and elsewhere that they are dependent upon the proximity of limestone or other non-acid formations (Yarker and Atkinson-Willes 1971). As with other wildfowl, the initial expansion was probably stimulated by the climatic amelioration, but there can be little doubt that the species has been opportunistic in taking advantage of the new range of artificial freshwater sites, and that this has enabled the breeding population to maintain the impetus of expansion for much longer than would otherwise have been possible.

The largest breeding concentrations are 800–1,000 pairs on Loughs Beg and Neagh (Northern Ireland), 500–600 pairs on Loch Leven and 200 pairs on Lower Lough Erne (Co Fermanagh). Also, there are 50–60 pairs each on Chew Valley Reservoir (Somerset), Grafham Water (Huntingdonshire) and Hanningfield Reservoir (Essex), while a number of other waters hold colonies of 20–30 pairs. From a perusal of county bird reports, it seems reasonable to assume average densities of three or four pairs in each occupied 10-km square. On this basis, excluding records of only possible breeding but adding in the major colonies already named, there may be as many as 4,000–5,000 pairs in Britain and about 2,000 in Ireland. The estimate of 1,500–2,000 pairs in Britain alone, by Yarker and Atkinson-Willes (1971), was clearly too low. The Tufted Duck undoubtedly ranks as one of our most successful breeding wildfowl.

Number of 10-km squares in which recorded:
  1,622 (42%)
Possible breeding 386 (24%)
Probable breeding 213 (13%)
Confirmed breeding 1,023 (63%)

References
NEWTON, I. and C. R. G. CAMPBELL. 1975. Breeding of ducks at Loch Leven, Kinross. *Wildfowl* 26: 83–102.
OLNEY, P. J. S. 1963. The food and feeding habits of Tufted Duck *Aythya fuligula*. *Ibis* 105: 55–62.
YARKER, B. and G. L. ATKINSON-WILLES. 1971. The numerical distribution of some British breeding ducks. *Wildfowl* 22: 63–70.

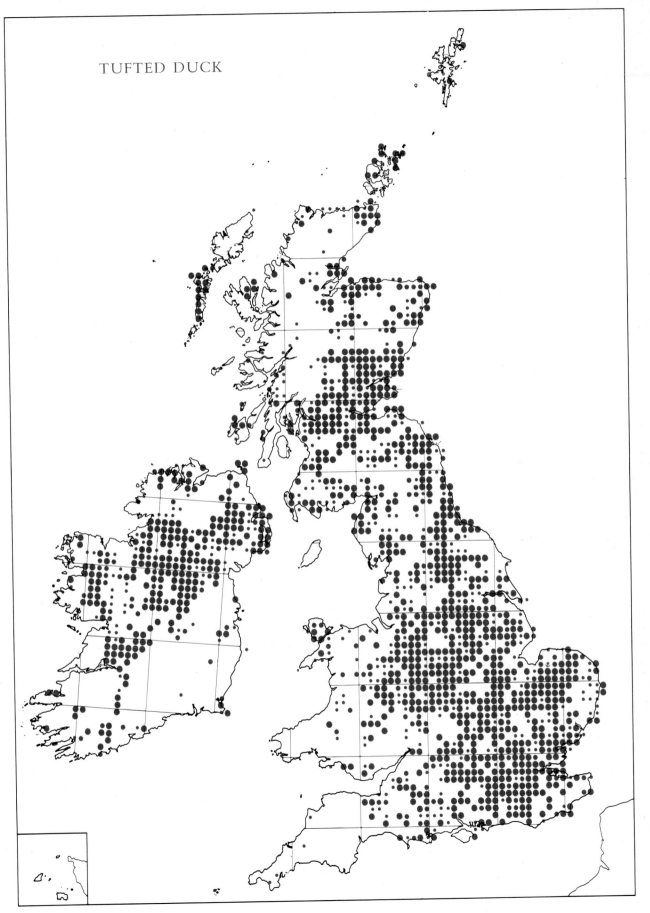

TUFTED DUCK

Pochard

Aythya ferina

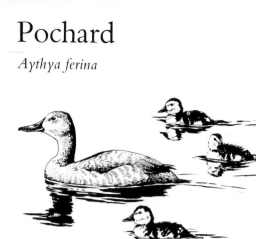

The Pochard is scarce and local as a breeding bird. It does not nest at altitudes over 300 m, and seeks large pools, lakes, marsh fleets and slow-flowing streams edged with dense, though not necessarily broad, beds of emergent vegetation. Unlike the Tufted Duck *A. fuligula*, it does not yet breed commonly on the expanding, man-made habitats of gravel pits, and hardly more on reservoirs, but it frequents both in winter.

The nest may be a lined hollow up to 10 m from water, well hidden in sedges, gorse (particularly in Ireland) or other rank growth, but more often it is a substantial platform of aquatic vegetation over water or waterlogged ground within a reed-bed, built up to keep the eggs dry. The presence of a pair does not necessarily mean they are nesting, for they will not do so if plant growth is inadequate. Breeding is most easily proved by watching for broods. In N Kent there are favoured nursery areas to which broods hatched in surrounding marshland travel via the interconnecting network of fleets and ditches (Hori 1966).

In Europe, the Pochard belongs to boreal and temperate climate zones and its main population centres lie to the south of those of many other waterfowl. Unlike several basically subarctic ducks which colonised Britain within the last 100 years or so, this species has been breeding here for a long time, though it seems that until the 1840s it was rare and perhaps restricted to East Anglia. Breeding occurred in Yorkshire in 1844 and on the Tring Reservoirs (Hertfordshire) in about 1850, these events signalling the start of a phase of slow increase and expansion. Advancing mainly up the eastern half of the country, the Pochard first bred in Scotland in 1871 and reached Caithness by 1921. Nevertheless, nesting localities remain scattered, with large areas unoccupied, due to the species' restricted breeding habitat requirements. This situation is reflected in the *Atlas* map, which indicates how sparsely distributed it still is in Ireland and W Britain.

During the last 30 years or so, the general picture has been one of a continued slow increase in England, with several instances of new colonies being formed, especially in East Anglia and the Thames Basin, but of a marked decline in Scotland. Colonisation of the London area, mainly since 1953, has doubtless been aided by the full-winged progeny of pairs breeding in the inner parks. The N Kent marshes were colonised about 1946 and numbers attained a peak of about 50 pairs in 1960, but have since stabilised at around 20–30 pairs. A similar expansion has occurred in Hampshire since breeding was first proved in 1961: the Pochard is now well established in the lower Test Valley, and is spreading eastwards into the Itchen Valley. There, as around London, breeding may perhaps have been started by feral stock (Yarker and Atkinson-Willes 1971). Taking England as a whole, the species nested regularly in 16 counties in 1964 compared with ten in 1938; but in Scotland, where it has declined seriously, especially in the Highlands, it was breeding regularly in only six counties in 1964, compared with 17 in 1938.

The Pochard first bred in Ireland in 1907, but it is still no more than a sporadic nester there, mainly in the low-lying midlands. Though the *Atlas* fieldwork produced confirmed and probable breeding in nine and 11 squares respectively, these were spread over five years and probably give a false impression of the numbers in any one.

During 1968–72, there was confirmed breeding in 192 squares in Britain and Ireland and probable breeding in a further 65. Doubtless a fair number of these represent single pairs and sites used only occasionally, but densities are certainly higher in some areas. Yarker and Atkinson-Willes (1971) estimated the British breeding population at about 200 pairs. From local bird reports, it is evident that the coastal counties from Lincolnshire to Kent together hold 100–120 pairs, while there are up to 30 pairs in Greater London, up to 20 in Hampshire, and several other counties hold 5–10 pairs each. The British and Irish total is certainly over 200 pairs now, and may be as high as 400; this would represent an average of just over two pairs in each 10-km square for which breeding was proved.

Number of 10-km squares in which recorded:
563 (15%)
Possible breeding   306 (54%)
Probable breeding   65 (12%)
Confirmed breeding   192 (34%)

References

HARRISON, J. 1972. *Wildfowl on the North Kent Marshes.* WAGBI, Chester.

HORI, J. 1966. Observations on Pochard and Tufted Duck breeding biology with particular reference to colonisation of a home range. *Bird Study* 13: 297–305.

YARKER, B. and G. L. ATKINSON-WILLES. 1971. The numerical distribution of some British breeding ducks. *Wildfowl* 22: 63–70.

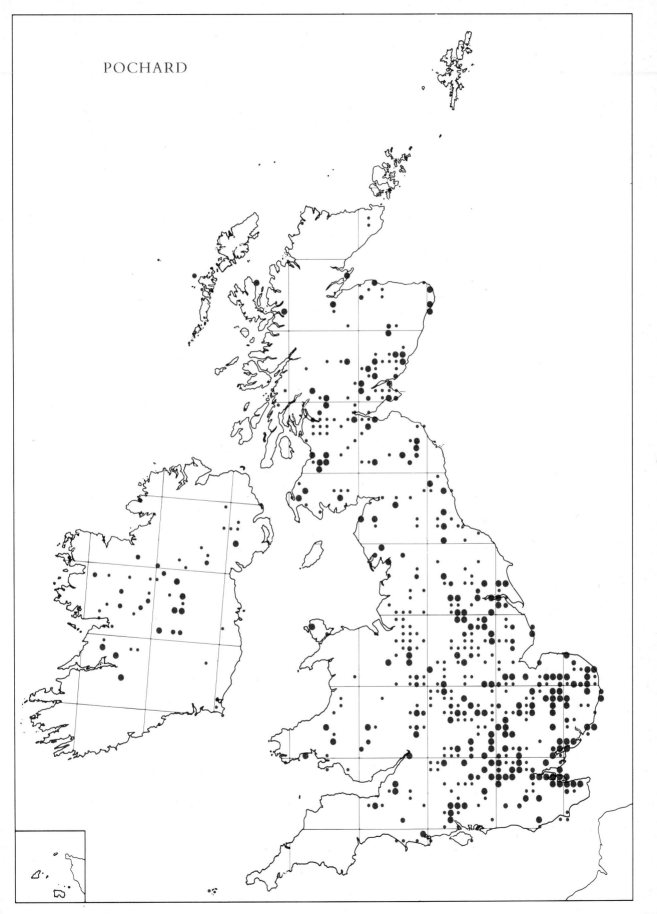

POCHARD

Goldeneye

Bucephala clangula

The usual habitats of the Goldeneye are the lakes and rivers of the forested taiga zone, which extends across N Eurasia and N America. The nest is almost invariably placed in a deep hole in a tree, and only occasionally in a cavity under logs or boulders. The large holes drilled by Black Woodpeckers *Dryocopus martius* (or by the Pileated Woodpecker *D. pileatus* in Canada), commonly at heights of 10–15 m, are often used. Some of the Scottish Highland lochs, surrounded by trees, seem to be ideal in all respects save for a scarcity of nest sites. Fortunately, the species will take readily to nest boxes.

Although a freshwater duck in the breeding season, and frequently seen on reservoirs and lakes in winter, the vast majority of European Goldeneyes—assessed at about 150,000 birds—spend the winter on the sea, perhaps 10,000–12,000 visiting British and Irish coasts. The summer diet comprises insects and larvae, leeches, tadpoles and freshwater shrimps, obtained by probing with the strong bill among stones on the bed of lakes or rivers. The peculiarly domed head accommodates large air sinuses above the skull, carrying a reserve supply of air which, it has been suggested, may enable the bird to prolong its dives (Ogilvie 1975).

Late wintering birds stay on inland waters into May, and pairs may be seen displaying even earlier in the spring. Up to 30 regularly summer on Lough Neagh (Northern Ireland). The species is, therefore, more likely to be dismissed as non-breeding, rather than overlooked completely. This was especially true in Scotland before 1970, for birds had often remained far into June without any evidence that they were nesting. Proving breeding by finding the nest is likely to be difficult and, as with most ducks, the best chance is to watch for the downy young accompanying the female at a later stage.

The normal clutch is 8–11 eggs and incubation occupies 27–32 days. The fledging period lasts for 57–66 days, but the ducklings become independent after about 50. They do not breed until their second year. The nest site may be as much as 3 km from the water where the duck intends to rear her brood, and she will lead them there on the day they leave the nest. In the case of one of the Scottish pairs, Ogilvie (1975) wrote: 'They breed in a nest box put up beside what was thought to be a perfectly suitable water. The female Goldeneye, however, has other ideas and each year leads her brood safely over a railway line, a main road and a river, to another loch more than a kilometre away.'

Single pairs, possibly pricked birds, are reported to have nested in 1931 and 1932 in Rabbit burrows adjacent to saltmarsh at Burton, on the Dee estuary (Cheshire); one clutch with down was taken and identification was accepted, despite the improbable site (Taylor 1938, Hardy 1941). There was no further breeding record until 1970, when a duck with four well-grown young was seen on a lochan in E Inverness-shire; and breeding in this region has been confirmed annually since then. In 1971 a nest with broken shells and two addled eggs was found, but no ducklings were seen; and on 28th May 1972 a female was seen with nine ducklings, of which six or seven were eventually reared. After the *Atlas* period, three pairs nested in both 1973 and 1974, and the species now appears to be becoming firmly established as a Scottish breeder. This is at least partly a result of the extensive erection of nest boxes in the breeding area, five of the six nests in 1973–74 being in such artificial sites.

This species is afforded special protection in Great Britain under Schedule I of the Protection of Birds Act, 1954–67.

Number of 10-km squares in which recorded:
19 (0.5%)
Possible breeding   14 (74%)
Probable breeding   3 (16%)
Confirmed breeding   2 (11%)

Four dots have been moved by up to two 10-km squares (as recommended by the Rare Breeding Birds Panel)

References
HARDY, E. 1941. *The Birds of the Liverpool Area.* Arbroath.
MACMILLAN, A. T. 1970. Goldeneye breeding in East Inverness-shire. *Scott. Birds* 6: 197–198.
OGILVIE, M. A. 1975. *Ducks of Britain and Europe.* Berkhamsted.
TAYLOR, F. 1938. Untitled note on Goldeneye nesting in Cheshire. *Bull. Brit. Ool. Assoc.* 5 (59): 108–110.

Long-tailed Duck *Clangula hyemalis*, **see page 447**

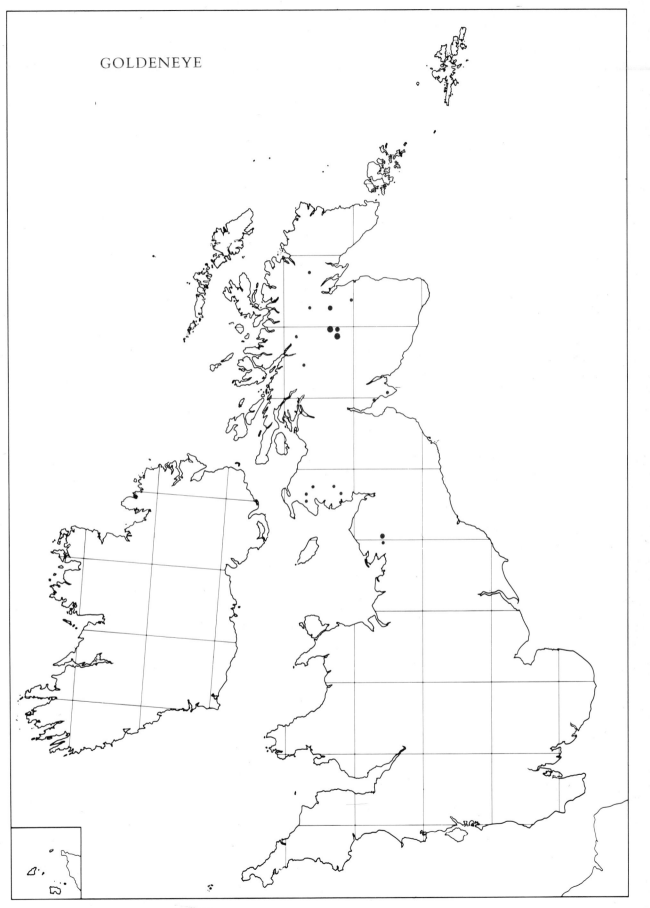

GOLDENEYE

Common Scoter

Melanitta nigra

In Scotland, the nesting habitat consists of small lochs set in moorland, such as the *dubh-lochans* of flow country in Caithness and Sutherland, the high mountain lochs of the central Highlands and the freshwater lochs of larger islands. Nests tend to be among heather within 20 m of the loch shore; in Caithness, where nests are often a considerable distance from water, they are usually reached via overgrown drainage ditches (Berry 1939). In Ireland the habitat is completely different, breeding occurring on large lakes, including some of the largest in the country. There, Common Scoters occupy heathery and tree-clad islands and, to a lesser extent, peninsulas, wherever these are large enough to allow the nest to be at least 10 m from the water's edge.

Scoters start returning to their breeding lakes in March or April, and all are back by early May; eggs are laid in late May and June. On the Continent there are spectacular summer moult migrations by drakes, which leave northern countries and pass through the Baltic into the North Sea (some flocks moulting off Britain's east coast), but Scottish drakes probably move only to adjacent coasts and Irish ones have been located moulting in Donegal Bay in July (Ferguson 1971). Meanwhile, the females tend the young, which go to sea when they have learned to fly, usually in August.

The first authentic British breeding record came from Sutherland in 1855, and ten years later the species was described as breeding annually in several parts of the Caithness moors. It is not now possible to say whether the Common Scoter colonised N Scotland at that time, or whether this was a small but long established population only then discovered: few ornithologists visited that remote area until the second half of the 19th century, when egg-collecting became a popular pursuit. What is undoubtedly genuine is the slow spread since. Nesting had occurred in Inverness-shire and Argyllshire by the 1880s, and was first proved in Shetland in 1911, Ross-shire in 1913, and Perthshire in 1921; but breeding was only sporadic until about the 1930s (Berry 1939). Counts have been made recently at the known sites. In Shetland, about eight pairs summered on Main-

land and Yell in 1972 and 1973, though few were proved nesting; in Caithness, ten to 13 pairs were scattered over several lochs in 1972; in Sutherland, Ross-shire and Perthshire, only single pairs have been located in recent years; in Inverness-shire, there were about 15 pairs (six nests found) on one loch in 1974; in Argyllshire, there were five pairs in 1970 and seven in 1973 on Islay, and one mainland pair in 1973; in Dumbartonshire/Stirlingshire, breeding was first proved on Loch Lomond in 1971 and three pairs were present in 1972. A female and three half grown young were seen on the sea off Wigtownshire in 1970. On the above figures, it seems likely that the Scottish population is about 30–50 pairs, but it is known to fluctuate from year to year.

The Common Scoter was first found nesting in Ireland, on Lower Lough Erne in Co Fermanagh, in 1905. Thereafter numbers increased steadily: there were seven pairs in 1917, about 50 pairs by 1950 and 140–150 pairs during 1967–69, but this increase has now halted, and there are even signs of a reversal— 122 pairs in 1973 and only 110 pairs in 1974. In both years, few young were reared, though it is not clear whether climatic or environmental factors were responsible. Smaller numbers breed in Co Mayo: this community was established in 1948 on Lough Conn, where there were 20–30 pairs in 1958 and 28–31 in 1968, numbers having been maintained despite a drop in water level. One or two additional pairs were present on Lough Carra during 1968–70, a nest being found in 1969, but there is no evidence that breeding became regular there. The Irish breeding population is now probably 130–140 pairs, making a total of 160–190 pairs for Britain and Ireland together.

This species is afforded special protection in Great Britain under Schedule I of the Protection of Birds Act, 1954–67.

Number of 10-km squares in which recorded:
  57 (1%)
Possible breeding   29 (51%)
Probable breeding   5 (9%)
Confirmed breeding   23 (40%)

Though some records were originally submitted in confidence, all dots are now shown accurately (as recommended by the Rare Breeding Birds Panel)

References
BERRY, R. 1939. The status and distribution of wild geese and wild duck in Scotland. *Internat. Wildfowl Inquiry*. Vol. 2. Cambridge.
FERGUSON, A. 1968. The breeding of the Common Scoter on Lower Lough Erne, Co Fermanagh. *Irish Bird Rep*. 15 (1967): 8–11.
FERGUSON, A. 1971. Notes on the breeding of the Common Scoter, *Melanitta nigra* L., in Ireland. *Irish Nat. J*. 17: 29–31.
SHARROCK, J. T. R. *et al*. 1975. Rare breeding birds in the United Kingdom in 1973 and 1974. *Brit. Birds* 68: 5–23, 489–506.

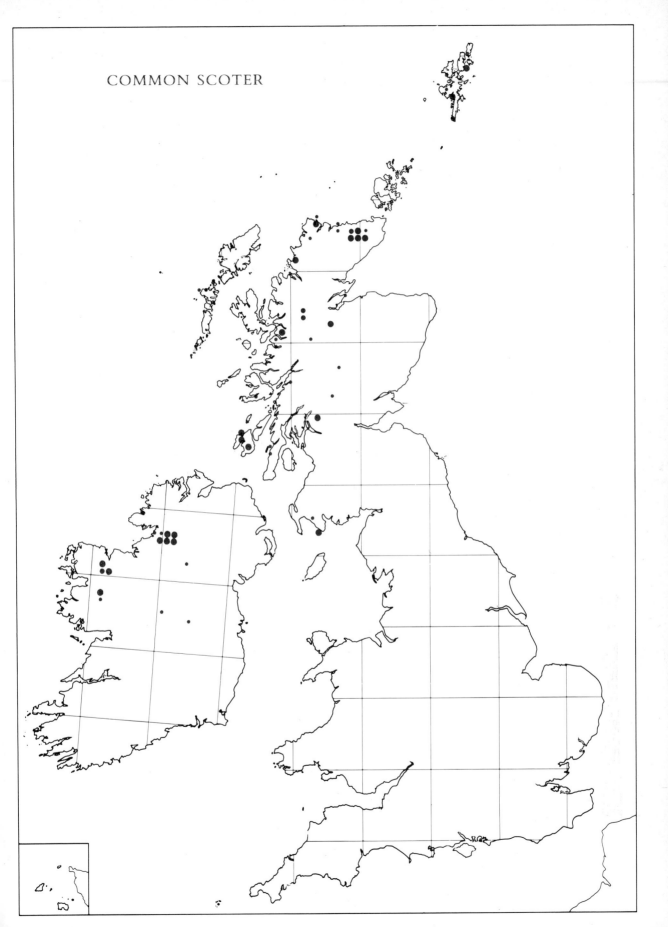

COMMON SCOTER

Eider

Somateria mollissima

The Eider is one of the most numerous ducks in the world. The population wintering in Europe alone probably exceeds 2,000,000, and there are also large numbers on the W Atlantic and Pacific coasts. Although there are a few records of breeding more than 10 km inland, virtually all are coastal nesters. In Britain and Ireland the Eider has a northern distribution, being common in places in W Scotland, Orkney and Shetland, though most of the really big breeding groups belong to E Scotland—*eg* 2,000 pairs at the Sands of Forvie (Aberdeenshire) in 1970 (Milne 1974); 3,000 pairs between Fife Ness (Fifeshire) and Gourdon (Kincardineshire) (Pounder 1974). The Eider breeds in a few places in Northumberland, including over 1,000 pairs on the Farne Islands, and on Walney Island (Lancashire). The most southerly breeding area in W Europe is the Dutch Waddensee.

Rafts of Eiders gathering inshore in late March and early April provide good clues to breeding sites, and in most cases the birds will have wintered nearby. Prospecting for nest sites is carried out in mid-April, mainly by the females, though sometimes attended by drakes. Egg-laying is started shortly afterwards, most clutches at the Sands of Forvie, for instance, being laid between 20th April and 10th May. Many ducks sit in exposed situations among the rocks or in the heather, relying for safety on their stillness and cryptic plumage; nevertheless, there is a high predation rate, due mainly to crows and gulls. On Tentsmuir Point (Fifeshire), Eiders nest well within the forestry plantations (Pounder 1974). Jenkins (1971) noted that at Aberlady Bay (East Lothian) those nesting up to 4 km inland enjoyed better success than those on the coast, which suffered greater disturbance. After an incubation period lasting 26 days, the ducklings are led to the sea, one or more other ducks sometimes joining the brood to give it further protection. It has been stated that 55% of the ducklings fail to survive the first week of life, but after the remainder are half-grown—at about four weeks—the survival rate is high until fledging at seven to eight weeks old. The majority are able to fly in the first part of August.

Eider numbers have been steadily increasing and the range expanding since the middle of the 19th century, before which the species' main home was in the northern and western isles, with some on the east coast. Ireland was colonised in 1912, Walney Island in 1949 and, on the Continent, the Netherlands in 1906 (Taverner 1959). The Walney colony had grown from a single pair to over 300 by 1972, and the Sands of Forvie colony from about 1,200 in the early 1960s to 2,000 pairs by 1970. In England and Ireland there has been little recent spread, although several places on the Northumberland coast have been occupied in the last decade, and Co Sligo was settled in 1961. Protection measures have greatly assisted the species. The Farne Islands colony, which declined sharply as a result of persecution during the 1939–45 war, so that only 130 pairs remained in 1946, has increased under protection to a total of over 1,000 pairs.

The colonisation of new areas has sometimes been preceded by the presence of summering birds in inshore waters, mostly immatures, with drakes predominating. Such rafts, seen in E England from Yorkshire south to Sussex, may originate from the large Dutch population. One of the largest concentrations is off Whitford Point in the Burry Inlet (Glamorgan), but this has been in existence for at least 30 years without any signs of settlement (Taverner 1959). It is an intriguing circumstance that there has been a growing tendency in recent years for adult King Eiders *S. spectabilis* to join such groups in Scotland, and interbreeding of the two species, which occurs regularly in Iceland (Palmer 1973), is a possibility.

The total number of pairs breeding on European coasts from Iceland to the White Sea and south to Britain has been estimated as 600,000–650,000 (Alerstam *et al* 1974). Our own British and Irish population of 15,000–25,000 pairs, almost half of which are on the coasts of E Scotland and NE England, is but a small percentage of this. Nevertheless, the Eider is our second most numerous breeding wildfowl species, being outnumbered only by the Mallard *Anas platyrhynchos*.

Number of 10-km squares in which recorded:
498 (13%)
Possible breeding   51 (10%)
Probable breeding   14 (3%)
Confirmed breeding   433 (87%)

References

ALERSTAM, T., C. BAUER and G. ROOS. 1974. Spring migration of Eiders *Somateria mollissima* in southern Scandinavia. *Ibis* 116: 194–210.

JENKINS, D. 1971. Eiders nesting inland in East Lothian. *Scott. Birds* 6: 251–255.

MILNE, H. 1974. Breeding numbers and reproductive rate of Eiders at the Sands of Forvie National Nature Reserve, Scotland. *Ibis* 116: 135–154.

PALMER, R. S. 1973. Icelandic eiders—a few observations. *Wildfowl* 24: 154–157.

POUNDER, B. 1974. Breeding and moulting Eiders in the Tay region. *Scott. Birds* 8: 159–176.

TAVERNER, J. H. 1959. The spread of the Eider in Great Britain. *Brit. Birds* 52: 245–258.

EIDER

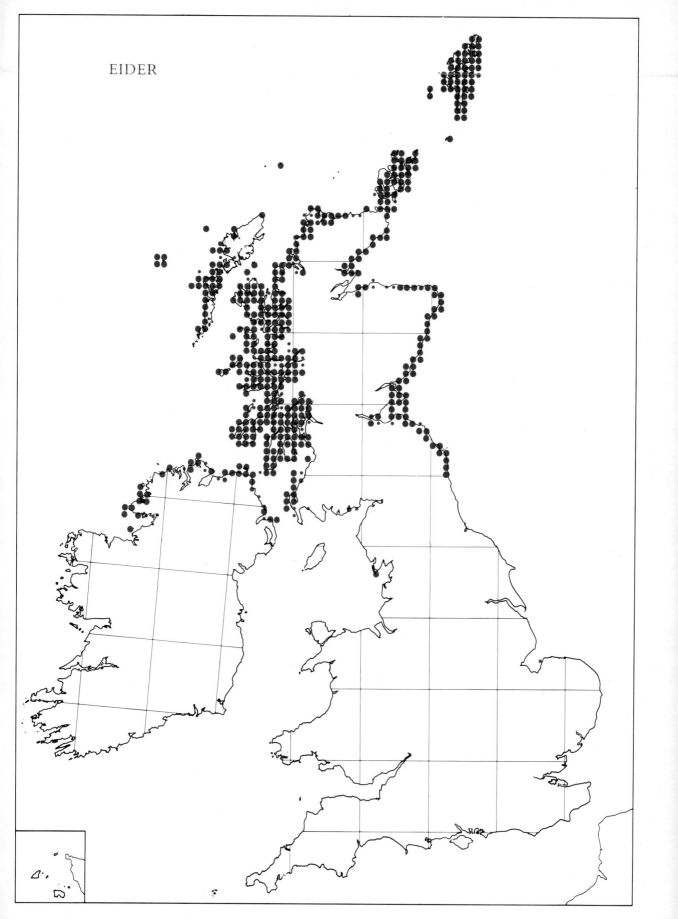

Ruddy Duck

Oxyura jamaicensis

The Ruddy Duck is a N American species which has been introduced to Britain, and was admitted to the official British and Irish list as recently as 1971. In contrast to most introductions, this one came about entirely accidentally. The Wildfowl Trust imported three pairs in 1948, and they began breeding in the Slimbridge (Gloucestershire) collection the following year, but the ducklings proved difficult to rear by the artificial techniques then in use. It was soon found that better results could be obtained by allowing parents to rear their own young, and in consequence some young avoided pinioning. It is thought that about 70 juveniles have flown away from Slimbridge over the years, mainly during 1956–63, and it is from these that the present feral population has arisen.

Ruddy Ducks are essentially aquatic birds, flying only when moving from one water to another. Their legs are set well back like a grebe's, so that they walk awkwardly on land. For this reason the nest is usually a floating structure anchored to stems in a reed-bed. It follows, therefore, that a breeding water must have adequate peripheral growth of emergent vegetation dominated by reed, bulrush or club-rush. Another requirement is that the water must not be too deep, or alternatively have shallow bays or margins, since Ruddy Ducks feed on insect larvae and the seeds of aquatic plants obtained during underwater dives. Flowing waters such as rivers are avoided, the preference being for sheltered freshwater pools, meres, lakes, reservoirs and, sometimes, flooded gravel pits.

Having striking chestnut plumage, contrasting with white cheeks and a blue bill, the drakes are conspicuous, and so occupied waters are unlikely to be overlooked. Proof of breeding is less readily obtained, however, for the nests are not easy to find, and the species tends to breed late, the broods remaining within the protective cover of reeds. It is not unusual for ducklings to appear as late as August or early September. Nevertheless, most *Atlas* records of confirmed breeding were made from seeing young, and the map, being a composite of five years' fieldwork, is believed to give an accurate picture of the distribution by 1972.

The first records of feral breeding came as recently as 1960 (one pair in Somerset) and 1961 (two broods in Staffordshire and one in Somerset); but in the following year six pairs were known, including one in an additional county, Gloucestershire. The severe winter of 1962/63 caused a temporary setback, but in 1965 the national total was again six pairs (Somerset, Gloucestershire, Staffordshire, Shropshire and Hertfordshire), and there has been a steady increase since. During the first *Atlas* year, 1968, there were at least ten feral pairs, but by 1972 the total had risen to at least 25 pairs. This increase continues, at a rate of around 25% per year: there were about 35 nesting pairs in 1973, 40–45 in 1974 and 50 or more in 1975. The breeding stock of the lower Severn (Somerset and Gloucestershire) has remained small, the major expansion having occurred in the W Midlands, notably among the small reeded meres of Cheshire, Shropshire and W Staffordshire. Leicestershire is currently the most eastern county in which the Ruddy Duck breeds, since 1973, and Hertfordshire is the only one where it has nested but has as yet failed to colonise. In autumn the smaller breeding waters are deserted, and large flocks congregate on Belvide and Blithfield Reservoirs (Staffordshire) and on Blagdon and Chew Valley Reservoirs (Somerset). It is then possible to assess the total post-breeding population, which by the 1975/76 winter had reached 350 birds. This is one of the few British breeding species whose distributions are known to have changed markedly since *Atlas* fieldwork ended. In 1974, one pair nested successfully on Lough Neagh (Northern Ireland).

Though a recent addition to the British avifauna, the way in which the Ruddy Duck has established itself so quickly and so firmly indicates that it is here to stay.

The spread of Ruddy Ducks in Britain and Ireland

	First breeding	Breeding pairs 1975
Somerset	1960	5–6
Stafford	1961	10–15
Gloucester	1962	1
Shropshire	1965	15
Hertford	1965	—
Cheshire	1968	12–15
Worcester	1971	3–4
Leicester	1973	2–3
Warwick	1974	1–2
Northern Ireland	1974	?
Derby	1975	1
Montgomery	(summered 1974)	?
Hereford	(summered 1975)	?

Number of 10-km squares in which recorded:
20 (0·5%)
Possible breeding   6 (30%)
Probable breeding   4 (20%)
Confirmed breeding   10 (50%)

Reference
HUDSON, R. 1976. Ruddy Ducks in Britain. *Brit. Birds* 69: 132–143.

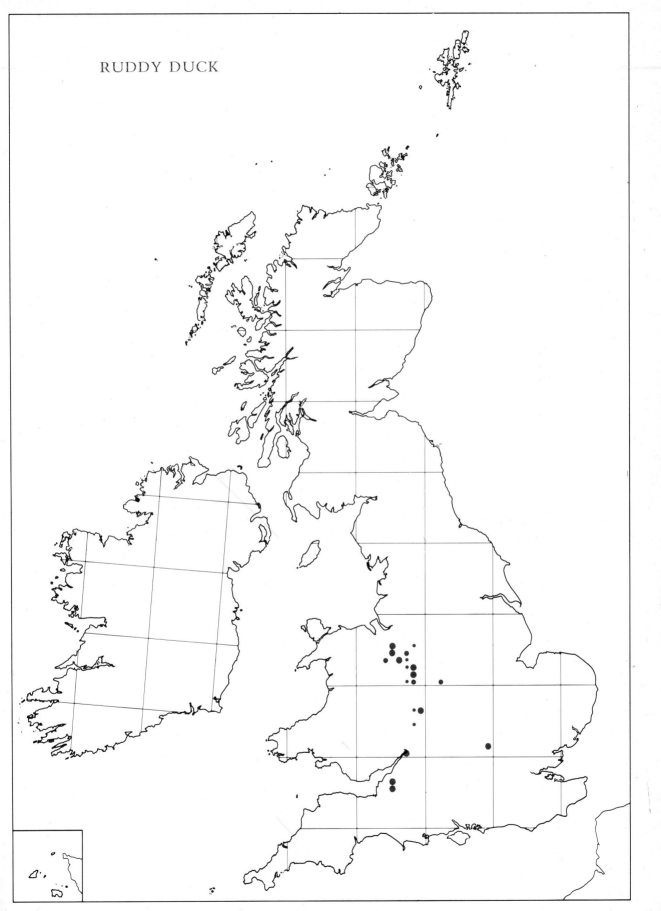

RUDDY DUCK

Red-breasted Merganser

Mergus serrator

HB.

Outside the breeding season the Red-breasted Merganser is usually to be found along coasts and in estuaries, whereas the related Goosander *M. merganser* occurs mainly on freshwater. These habitat differences are also noticeable to a considerable de-degree among nesting birds. Some Mergansers do nest far inland on the larger river systems, on lochs and in remote glens right up to the very sources of the burns, but this habitat is more typical of the Goosander, and breeding Mergansers are commonest in coastal districts, especially where there are sheltered sea lochs, inlets and firths studded with islets. In marine habitats in SW Scotland, this is often the most numerous breeding duck. Mergansers and Goosanders are subjected to considerable, though largely ineffective, persecution because of their predilection for young Salmon; but this human antagonism is less serious for the present species since much of the summer feeding takes place in tidal waters.

Whereas Goosanders nest typically in tree-holes, Mergansers nest on the ground amongst long grass, heather, gorse, brambles or other vegetation, often so dense that the approach to the site is effectively a tunnel. Pairs will also use Rabbit burrows, tree roots, boulders, or clumps of marram on sand-dunes. Nests are by no means easy to find, especially when on large islands, and the simplest way of proving breeding is to wait for the ducklings to appear. Broods may be taken considerable distances, however, so that the natal locality may be uncertain in some cases. It is by no means unusual for several broods to coalesce, and one female seen in the course of *Atlas* fieldwork was in charge of 51 unfledged young.

Unlike the Goosander, the present species has a long history of residence here. Ornithological exploration had shown by 1870 that it had a wide breeding range in the Scottish highlands and islands, south to Ayrshire and Wigtownshire in the west, Perthshire in the central Highlands, and the Dornoch Firth in the east. Nevertheless, a major phase of increase and expansion was apparent by the 1880s. Red-breasted Mergansers were breeding in Morayshire

and Banffshire by 1892, Aberdeenshire and Kincardineshire by 1913 and Dumfriesshire by 1928. The spread is continuing locally, but the species is still absent from most of SE Scotland, the southernmost breeding record on that side coming from Loch Leven (Kinross) in 1970. The *Atlas* map also shows how thinly distributed (indeed often absent) it is over large tracts of the central and eastern Highlands, but the important concentration in W Scotland is unmistakeable. Ireland too has long provided breeding haunts; a major increase since 1900 has extended the range to Antrim, Armagh, Cavan, Cork, Derry and Wexford, but the species is still absent from large areas of the south and east.

Breeding in England was first proved in 1950, with an advance across the Solway Firth to Ravenglass (Cumberland). During the next 10–15 years the Lake District was colonised, and since 1957 one to three pairs have bred annually in contiguous parts of NW Yorkshire. The *Atlas* map shows presence in the Peak District, and breeding was confirmed in 1973 when a pair and duckling were seen in the Goyt Valley (Derbyshire). This is the southern nesting limit in England at present, apart from an isolated instance in Lincolnshire in 1961. N Wales also was colonised in the 1950s, breeding having occurred in Anglesey since 1953, Merionethshire since 1957, and Caernarvonshire since 1958. By 1969 Red-breasted Mergansers were breeding in N Cardiganshire, and possibly also in Montgomeryshire, where a family was seen on the River Dyfi near Llanwrin in 1970. It remains to be seen whether they will spread into S Wales: in 1967 and 1970, juveniles hardly able to fly were found in late summer on the Glamorgan side of the Burry Inlet.

Little information is available on breeding densities. The respectable size of the British and Irish populations is indicated, however, by July–August flocks of 200–500 birds off Traeth Lafan (Caernarvonshire) and at various regular points around the Scottish and Irish coasts, while up to 1,500 have been seen at that season off Kintyre (Argyllshire). An estimate based on 3–5 pairs per 10-km square of confirmed or probable breeding would total about 2,000–3,000 pairs. This is consistent with the 1,000–2,000 pairs in Britain alone, estimated by Atkinson-Willes (1970).

Number of 10-km squares in which recorded:
  915 (24%)
Possible breeding   273 (30%)
Probable breeding   139 (15%)
Confirmed breeding   503 (55%)

References

ATKINSON-WILLES, G. L. 1970. Wildfowl situation in England, Scotland and Wales. *Proc. Int. Reg. Meet. Conserv. Wildfowl Res., Leningrad 1968*: 101–107.

MILLS, D. 1962. The Goosander and Red-breasted Merganser in Scotland. *Wildfowl Trust Ann. Rep.* 13: 79–92.

MILLS, D. H. 1962. The Goosander and Red-breasted Merganser as predators of Salmon in Scottish waters. *Freshwater and Salmon Fisheries Research* no. 29.

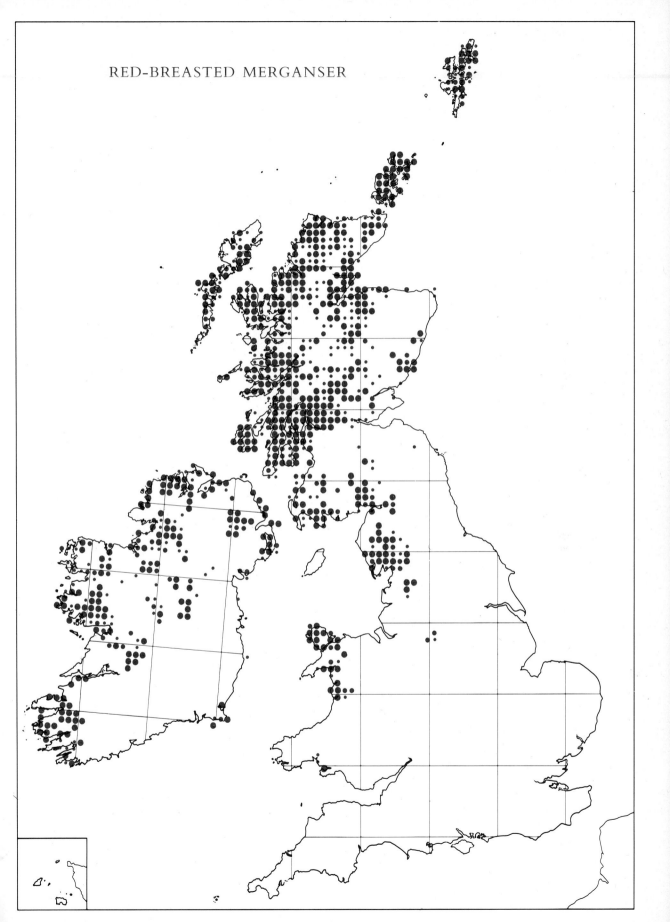

RED-BREASTED MERGANSER

Goosander

Mergus merganser

Goosanders are usually found on large clear rivers, lakes and lochs. They are much less marine than Red-breasted Mergansers *M. serrator*, but may occur on sea-lochs, especially at their heads or where rivers flow into them. The nest site is most commonly a hole in a tree, so rivers and lochs with wooded shores or islands are especially favoured. The nest may also be amongst boulders, in a hole in the ground, or in a cavity in a bank, so that treeless areas are sometimes frequented, though less often.

Where more than one pair is nesting, the males tend to form feeding flocks, which are very obvious on rivers and lochs. The incubating female can be followed back to the nest when it is in an open area, but on wooded rivers this is less easy. As with most other ducks, the easiest way of proving breeding is observation of the female with a brood of ducklings. These may have travelled a considerable distance from the actual nest site, however, and such records can usually be accepted as confirmed breeding only from places where adults have been seen earlier in the season. The numerous records of presence without confirmed breeding in the northern half of Scotland are thought to relate to potential breeding birds.

The first recorded nesting of Goosanders in these islands was in Perthshire in 1871. There was a very large influx in the winter of 1875/76, with firm colonisation following; and Berry (1939) noted that the establishment of the Scottish breeding population involved what '. . . appears to have been the nearest approach to mass emigration which a study of European Anatidae has revealed'. During the ensuing 60–70 years, breeding was confined to Highland counties; and then, as now, they avoided rugged sea-coasts and islands where the Red-breasted Merganser holds sway. Breeding Goosanders had spread to Loch Lomond by 1922, Dumfriesshire by 1936, and the Tweed area by 1930. Further spread across the border into England followed, with confirmation of breeding in Northumberland and the Lake District in 1941 and 1950 respectively, and subsequent rapid colonisation of both. Numbers there continue to increase, despite persecution on some rivers, and Goosanders began breeding in Co Durham in 1965, NW Yorkshire in 1970, and N Lancashire in 1973. The solid blocks of confirmed breeding in S Scotland and N England suggest that this region, though colonised for less than 40 years, is now the species' stronghold in Britain.

A high proportion of the food of Goosanders is provided by young Salmon. Though about a quarter of the diet also consists of various predators of Salmon, this species (like the Red-breasted Merganser) is regarded by water-bailiffs as vermin and is not afforded protection by the Protection of Birds Act, 1954–67. The large number of possible breeding records in the northern part of the range may partly reflect the results of efficient keepering by fishery interests, and this may also explain a decrease in the extreme north, especially Sutherland. Goosanders seem to be surviving this legal persecution, however, for there are signs of a continuing spread. The first ever Welsh and the single Irish breeding records occurred during 1968–72.

Counts of five Scottish rivers in Sutherland, Ross-shire and Aberdeenshire have shown a density of one or two pairs every 16 km, but higher densities have been reported elsewhere. Parslow rated the species as 'scarce', with 100–1,000 pairs. The upper limit is reached, however, by an average of only four pairs per 10-km square, which could be less than half the actual figure. One may surmise that the British population is about 1,000–2,000 pairs, and in excess of the 500–1,000 pairs estimated by Atkinson-Willes (1970).

Number of 10-km squares in which recorded:
412 (11%)

Possible breeding	152 (37%)
Probable breeding	56 (14%)
Confirmed breeding	204 (50%)

One dot has been moved by one 10-km square (the Rare Breeding Birds Panel's recommendation was accurate plotting), and the dot within the shaded square is conventionally placed centrally (as recommended by Major R. F. Ruttledge and D. Scott)

References

ATKINSON-WILLES, G. L. 1970. Wildfowl situation in England, Scotland and Wales. *Proc. Int. Reg. Meet. Conserv. Wildfowl Res., Leningrad 1968*: 101–107.

BERRY, J. 1939. The status and distribution of wild geese and wild duck in Scotland. *Internat. Wildfowl Inquiry*. Vol. 2. Cambridge.

MILLS, D. 1962. The Goosander and Red-breasted Merganser in Scotland. *Wildfowl Trust. Ann. Rep.* 13: 79–92.

MILLS, D. H. 1962. The Goosander and Red-breasted Merganser as predators of Salmon in Scottish waters. *Freshwater and Salmon Fisheries Research* no. 29.

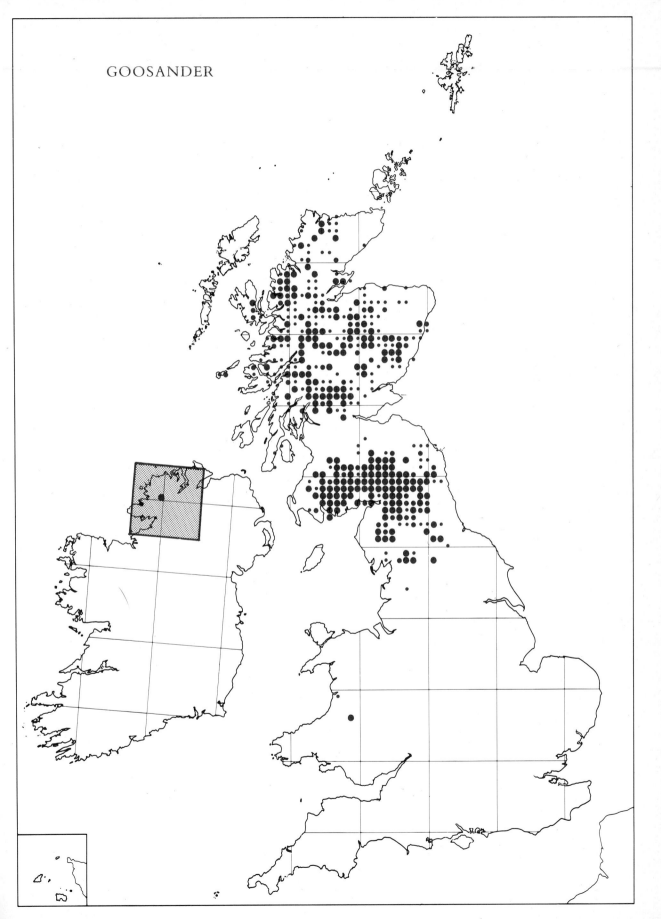

GOOSANDER

Shelduck

Tadorna tadorna

The Shelduck differs from all our other breeding ducks, except the Eider *Somateria mollissima*, in that the overwhelming majority nest in maritime counties and adjacent to tidal water. The preferred habitat is a sheltered estuary, where it nests on stabilised sand-dunes or adjacent grazing marshes; densities are low along coasts flanked by cliffs, though a few pairs breed around sea-lochs. To an increasing extent, Shelducks have been showing an inclination to breed inland on downs and commons, valley farmland, and in the neighbourhood of reservoirs, sugar beet factories or large sewage-farms, but even now very few nest more than 20 km from tidal water. Typically, the nest is a subterranean burrow such as that of the Rabbit, but the species can be catholic where a wide choice of sites is available. In a detailed study on the Isle of Sheppey (Kent), Hori (1964) found nests among stacks of hay and straw (25%), in Rabbit holes (25%), under miscellaneous objects and buildings (21%), in tree holes up to 5 m above ground (13.5%), among tree roots (12.5%), and in the open (3%).

Shelduck pairs sometimes nest in close proximity; in Kent, Hori (1969) found several instances of communal nesting (one 'dump' nest contained 32 eggs), and one shepherd's shed accommodated up to four pairs annually. Nevertheless, the species exhibits marked territorial behaviour, which appears to have the function of linking breeding density to food availability. Young (1970) found that Aberdeenshire territories are established in muddy intertidal areas where the marine mollusc *Hydrobia ulvae* (a staple food) is present; Jenkins *et al* (1975) discovered a similar state of affairs in the Firth of Forth, and concluded that the number of breeding pairs is determined by competition for feeding space in late winter, with successful birds obtaining territories over the best feeding areas and excluding non-breeders. In contrast, N Kent pairs establish their territories on freshwater grazing marshes, where much of their feeding takes place, although they continue to eat *Hydrobia* to some extent in the intertidal zone; and Hori thought that, in his study area, territory was more important for the maintenance of the pair bond. Territories are abandoned after hatching, and in July the well-known moult migration begins: ducklings are gathered into crèches in the care of a few adults, while most other full-grown birds move to the Heligoland Bight for the annual moult.

The Shelduck declined in many parts of Britain and Ireland during the 19th century, and subsequent widespread increases can be seen as a recovery under protection given both at home and in the Heligoland Bight. Such increases have been reported in almost every regional avifauna written in the last 30–40 years, and have been especially marked in S and E England, while the penetration into the southwest, as far as the Isles of Scilly, is a comparatively recent development. A feature of this increase has been the tendency to colonise inland places, especially noticeable in the Fens, where Shelducks now nest 30–32 km up the Rivers Nene and Ouse in the non-maritime counties of Cambridgeshire and Huntingdonshire. The most extreme case of inland nesting on the *Atlas* map comes from Warwickshire, where one or two pairs have bred annually in recent years, over 100 km from the coast.

Since Shelducks do not nest until two years old, each summer population includes a substantial proportion of non-breeders. In late winter and spring there are roughly 50,000 Shelducks in Britain and Ireland; from observations in Kent and Lancashire, Yarker and Atkinson-Willes (1971) assumed that it was normal for slightly under half of these to establish territories, implying a total of about 12,000 breeding pairs. The *Atlas* recorded confirmed or probable breeding in 864 squares, which, on the above estimate, would imply an average of 13–14 pairs per occupied square. This is not impossible, for the Birds of Estuaries Enquiry has revealed that in SE England densities of 20 pairs per 10-km square are by no means unusual on saltmarsh, and reach an average of 50 pairs per 10-km square in N Kent and the eastern side of the Wash, while even higher densities are recorded for Tentsmuir (Fife) and W Sussex.

Number of 10-km squares in which recorded: 1,023 (26%)
Possible breeding   159 (16%)
Probable breeding   120 (12%)
Confirmed breeding   744 (73%)

References
HORI, J. 1964. The breeding biology of the Shelduck *Tadorna tadorna*. *Ibis* 106:333–360.
HORI, J. 1969. Social and population studies in the Shelduck. *Wildfowl* 20: 5–22.
JENKINS, D., M. G. MURRAY and P. HALL. 1975. Structure and regulation of a Shelduck *Tadorna tadorna* population. *J. Anim. Ecol.* 44: 201–231.
YARKER, B. and G. L. ATKINSON-WILLES. 1971. The numerical distribution of some British breeding ducks. *Wildfowl* 22: 63–70.
YOUNG, C. M. 1970. Territoriality in the Common Shelduck *Tadorna tadorna*. *Ibis* 112: 330–335.

SHELDUCK

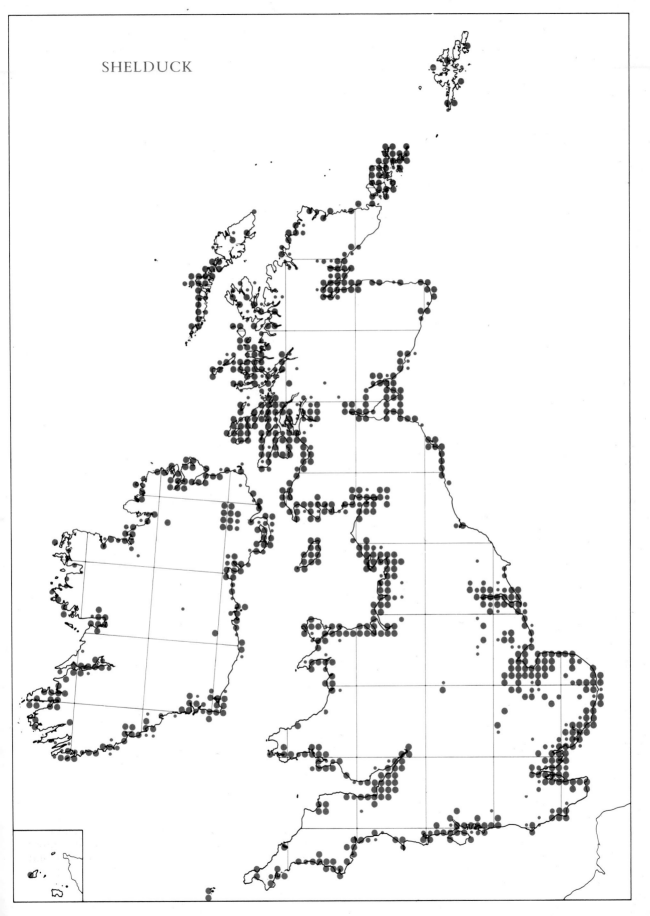

Egyptian Goose

Alopochen aegyptiaca

This is an introduced species, but is the least well documented of our aliens, and one which county bird reports hardly mentioned until 1971 when it gained admittance to the British and Irish list.

Egyptian Geese are related to the shelducks and are not true geese. They are native to Africa south of the Sahara and to Egypt, where they are now scarce. Importations into England began in the 18th (possibly 17th) century, so that by 1785 they had become familiar ornamental waterfowl on 'gentlemen's ponds'. In the 19th century there were full-winged, freely-breeding colonies on the lakes of private estates at Holkham, Gunton, Blickling and Kimberley (Norfolk), Bicton and Crediton (Devon), Woburn (Bedfordshire) and Gosford (East Lothian). Egyptian Geese from Bicton used to wander all over Devon and Dorset, while small flocks (presumably from Gosford) wintered regularly on the Northumberland coast, where local wildfowlers knew them as 'Spanish Geese' (Fitter 1959, Perry 1946).

Despite this proven ability to disperse over quite large areas, it is only in Norfolk that a feral population has become well established, and even there it is uncertain to what extent redistribution by man has been involved, though some natural dispersion has certainly occurred. The species' main feral centres in Norfolk are now around Holkham, where there is a notable concentration, and among the Brecks and Broads, where they are more scattered. Egyptian Geese were seen at Fritton Lake and Sotterley (NE Suffolk) in 1972, and a pair bred near Aldeburgh in the following year; a natural spread from Norfolk cannot be taken for granted because there are waterfowl collections in Suffolk. During 1968–72 they were reported from several other widely scattered localities, usually close to waterfowl collections, in the southern half of England; only one involved confirmed breeding, and none is believed to represent a viable feral population.

In their African home, Egyptian Geese frequent rivers, lakes and marshes, and use a bewildering variety of nest sites: on the ground (reedbeds, matted vegetation near water, small islands, mammal burrows, among boulders), on inland cliffs and ruined buildings, or in trees (sometimes a hole, or the old nest of another species) (Pitman 1965). They are thoroughly at home in trees, often perching there, and tree nests may be up to 25 m above ground. The Norfolk feral population lives on lakes in wooded parkland, broads, breckland meres, and some gravel pits—a similar habitat, in fact, to that of the local Canada Geese *Branta canadensis*, although trees are less important to the latter. It is not known whether these feral birds in Norfolk use the diversity of sites recorded in Africa: the only information available concerns two ground nests, of which one was on a dry hummock overlooking water, and the other on a small man-made island; in both instances the nest was in matted vegetation so thick that it provided a tunnel substitute (M. D. England *in litt*). In Norfolk the Egyptian Geese draw attention to themselves in spring through their noisy displays and savage territorial fighting, on water and ashore, but then virtually disappear until the time comes to escort their goslings to water.

There is no reliable estimate for the number of feral nesting pairs in Norfolk. When the breeding season is over, the geese tend to gather in flocks, especially for the moulting period and it is then that one can make some assessment of the population size. Atkinson-Willes (1963) estimated a total of 300–400 birds. In the 1973/74 winter there were reports of about 100 birds at Holkham and 140 at Beeston; doubtless there were smaller flocks elsewhere, and it seems certain that the population was then at least equal to Atkinson-Willes' figure. So little attention has been paid to this species, however, especially before 1968, that it is impossible to confirm an impression that there may have been a modest increase in recent years as a result of the series of mild winters.

Number of 10-km squares in which recorded: 18 (0.5%)
Possible breeding   4 (22%)
Probable breeding   3 (17%)
Confirmed breeding   11 (61%)

References

ATKINSON-WILLES, G. L. 1963. *Wildfowl in Great Britain*. Nature Conservancy Monograph 3. London.
FITTER, R. S. R. 1959. *The Ark in our Midst*. London.
PERRY, R. 1946. *A Naturalist on Lindisfarne*. London.
PITMAN, C. R. S. 1965. The nesting and some other habits of *Alopochen, Nettapus, Plectropterus* and *Sarkidiornis*. *Wildfowl Trust Ann. Rep.* 16: 115–121.

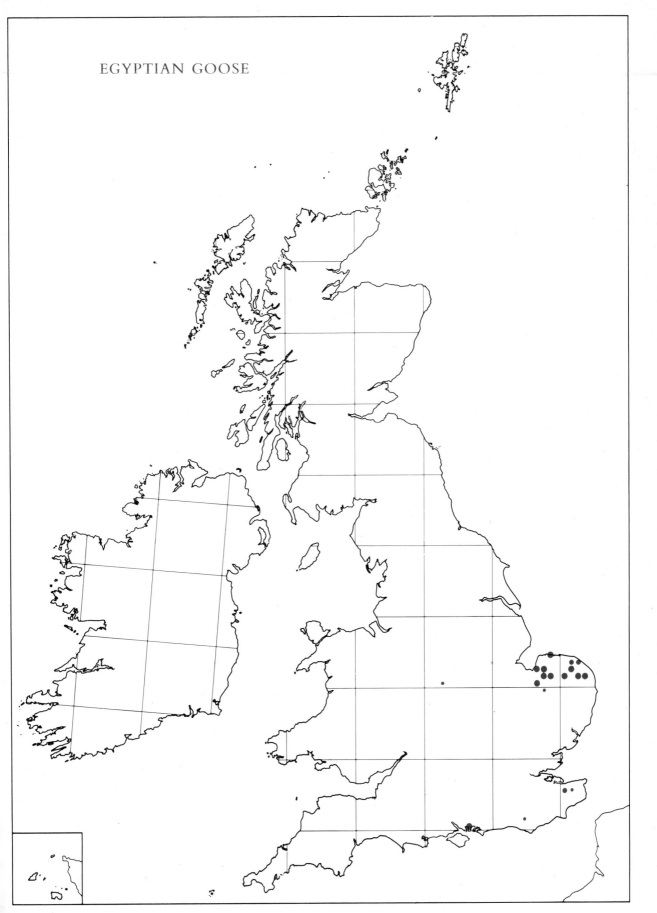

EGYPTIAN GOOSE

Greylag Goose

Anser anser

The Greylag is our only indigenous goose, and before the big drainage schemes of the early 19th century it nested as far south as the fens of Cambridgeshire and Lincolnshire. One suggested derivation of the name Greylag is the grey goose that lagged behind when other species returned north. By the early 20th century, man had restricted the breeding range to the remoter parts of the Scottish Highlands and western islands, but since the 1930s feral stocks have become established in many parts of Britain, and to a lesser extent in Ireland, so that the breeding range is now wider than at any time in recorded history.

The habitat in Scotland is hilly heather-moor and flow country with scattered lochs and, in the Outer Hebrides, lochs adjacent to moorland and machair (herb-rich grassland). Unlike other grey geese, this species will also breed on small coastal islands. Feral birds occupy a wide variety of freshwater sites, from upland lochs to lowland reservoirs, broads, flooded gravel pits and protected park lakes. The majority of nest sites are on islands, though some pairs breed in long vegetation around loch shores. In a detailed study of a feral population in SW Scotland, 476 nests were all adjacent to water and grassland; 415 were on wooded islands (unwooded islands being occupied by gulleries), 30 around the margins of lochs that lacked islets, 23 in vegetation along slow-flowing rivers, seven on moorland, and one in woodland (Young 1972a).

The wild population is now small, being confined to Wester Ross, Sutherland and Caithness (where stocks have been supplemented by releases of feral birds), and to the Outer Hebrides, where the headquarters is in the Loch Druidibeg NNR on South Uist. In about 1930, eggs and later young were brought from South Uist to an estate at Lochinch, near Stranraer (Wigtownshire); and in 1933, Greylags were also introduced to Monreith in the same county. This feral population has prospered: numerous lochs have been colonised naturally, and the birds have now spread over four contiguous counties (Wigtown, Ayr, Kirkcudbright and Dumfries) (Young

1972b). In 1961, it became necessary to halt the increase in the original Lochinch area, much pasture having been converted to arable, and, since that year, surplus eggs and young have been donated to WAGBI, which has used them to found colonies elsewhere in Britain. By 1970, WAGBI had released 938 hand-reared Greylags at 33 sites in 13 English and Welsh counties (Ellwood 1971).

Other sources have contributed, of course, and the substantial E Norfolk feral population stems largely from the descendants of two pricked geese brought from Scotland before the 1939–45 war, while a semi-feral colony at Castlecoole (Co Fermanagh) is believed to date from about 1700 (Fitter 1959). Full-winged Greylags are kept in a number of ornamental waterfowl collections and sometimes breed beyond the confines of the estates; thus the pairs which breed on Tring Reservoirs (Hertfordshire) are believed to be from Whipsnade Zoo, and to return there in winter. Such cases as these blur the distinction between feral and captive categories. A total of 39 released in Kent in 1973 were of the eastern, pink-billed *A. a rubrirostris*, imported from Belgium, where there is an expanding feral stock of this race.

Probably under 200 pairs of wild Greylags breed in Scotland. The majority are in the Outer Hebrides, where the species has increased under protection, despite some conflict with crofters due to the geese grazing on newly-sown grass in spring and on cereals in late summer and autumn. There are at least 70 pairs in the Loch Druidibeg NNR, and this may constitute half of the Hebridean population (Newton and Kerbes 1974). During 1968–72 there were about 60 pairs breeding in Caithness, a mixture of wild and feral birds. Feral groups are now widely scattered, though there are notable concentrations in Co Down, Kent, Norfolk, the Lake District and SW Scotland. The last group is the largest, and in July 1971 consisted of some 130 nesting pairs with 300 goslings, plus a further 600 failed breeders and non-breeders (Young 1972b). It seems likely that there are now about 700–800 breeding pairs in Britain and Ireland, of which at least 75% are derived from introduced stock.

Number of 10-km squares in which recorded:
 208 (5%)
Possible breeding   75 (36%)
Probable breeding   7 (3%)
Confirmed breeding   126 (61%)

References

ELLWOOD, J. 1971. Goose conservation. *WAGBI Rep. and Year Book* 1970–71: 59–60.

FITTER, R. S. R. 1959. *The Ark in our Midst.* London.

NEWTON, I. and R. H. KERBES. 1974. Breeding of Greylag Geese (*Anser anser*) on the Outer Hebrides, Scotland. *J. Anim. Ecol.* 43: 771–783.

YOUNG, J. G. 1972a. Breeding biology of feral Greylag Geese in south-west Scotland. *Wildfowl* 23: 83–87.

YOUNG, J. G. 1972b. Distribution, status and movements of feral Greylag Geese in southwest Scotland. *Scott. Birds* 7: 170–182.

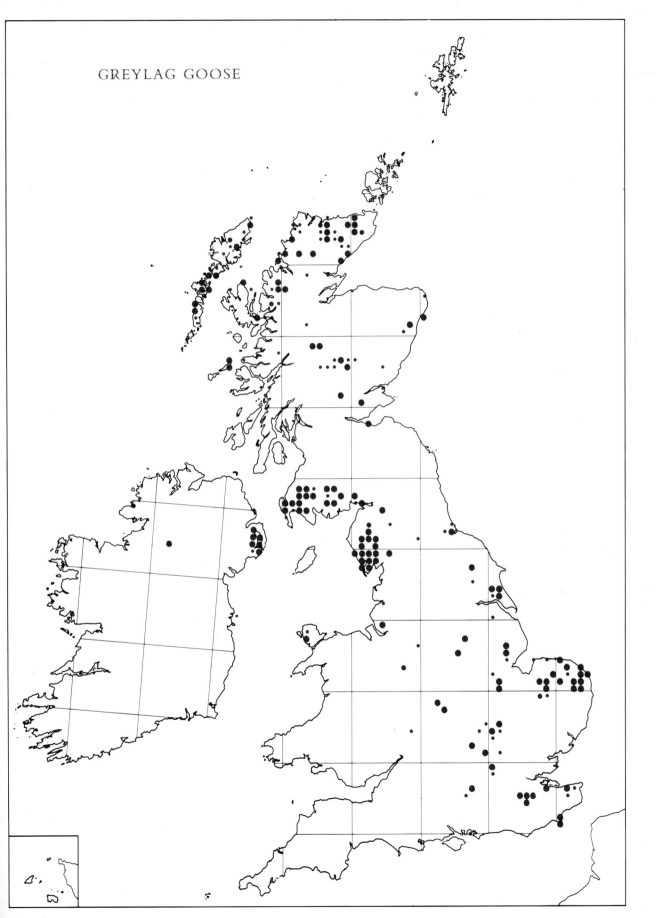

GREYLAG GOOSE

Canada Goose

Branta canadensis

The Canada Goose is a N American species which was brought to Britain as an ornamental bird to grace the parks and estates of wealthy landowners; it is known to have been in captivity in England during the reign of Charles II, and by 1785 was breeding freely. Few people bothered to write about it during the 18th and 19th centuries, so we have only an imperfect knowledge of the development towards feral status, though by the 1840s there were wandering flocks at large in England, and by the 1890s they were breeding ferally in scattered localities as far north as Westmorland (Fitter 1959).

As late as the 1940s, Canada Geese were predominantly birds of protected parks and large estates. Due partly to transportation by man in the last 30 years, however, there has been a more marked tendency to breed on reservoirs with natural margins, flooded gravel pits, rural meres, town lakes, marshes and slow-flowing rivers. The nest is generally close to water, most often on an island, and usually sheltered by rank vegetation or low scrub.

The first national Canada Goose census was organised by the BTO in July 1953 (Blurton Jones 1956) when there were 2,600–3,600 in Britain, including about 350 pairs and about 750 goslings. It was noticed that these were divisible into sub-populations, each based on a group of waters and more or less isolated from others. Feeding flocks foraged over restricted areas, and colonisation of new waters occurred only within the flock's foraging range. Canada Geese are long-lived, with few predators and a high potential breeding rate, so this sedentary behaviour acts as the main factor limiting population growth: high densities lead to maximum compression of territory sizes and restrict the number of pairs able to nest, resulting in a 'reservoir' of birds unable to breed for lack of space.

Since about 1950, however, a moult migration has gradually evolved among the non-breeders of the central Yorkshire sub-population, of which an increasing number (700 in 1974) spend the moulting period from June to August on Beauly Firth (Inverness-shire), 400–450 km to the north of their home range (Walker 1970). In the 1930s there had been 2,000 or more resident Canada Geese on private estates in Scotland, but these largely disappeared during the 1939–45 war, when winter feeding had to be discontinued, and by 1953 they had dwindled to some 150 birds, mainly in Dumfriesshire.

It was about the time of the 1953 BTO enquiry that farmers began to complain of damage by Canada Geese, which grazed on cereal crops and puddled the fields in wet weather. Various control methods were, and still are, tried, including egg destruction and mass winter shoots, but during the 1950s and early 1960s a favourite practice was to round up a proportion of a local flock during the summer moult, when the geese are flightless, and transport them elsewhere. Initially there was no problem in finding new sites, geese being welcomed by landowners with suitable lakes and by wildfowling clubs which hoped to establish flocks for sport. In the event, wildfowlers have been disappointed by Canada Geese, which do not present sporting shots, since they lack regular daily flighting patterns, often walking from the roosting water to the feeding field; when they fly, it is usually at tree-top height. Nevertheless, this large-scale redistribution in response to local overstocking led to the major increases which occurred during the next two decades. Depleted colonies soon built up again (erstwhile non-breeders now having room to establish territories of their own), new colonies grew at release points, and there was some settlement of intervening areas.

The Wildfowl Trust organised a Canada Goose survey during the years 1967–69, combining data from July counts at breeding waters (when the birds are less mobile but more scattered) with midwinter censuses of flocks (Ogilvie 1969). By this period, the total had trebled to 10,000–10,500 individuals: 700 in Wales, 100 in Scotland, 70 in Ireland, and over 9,000 in England. The sub-population structure was still evident, the largest groups being in N Norfolk (700–800), Derbyshire (900) and central Yorkshire (1,300). Norfolk is the only English county in which a big decline has been noticed: 1,700–2,000 had been present at Holkham in 1965. Merne (1970) has since revised the figures for Ireland: over 200 full-winged birds are based on waterfowl collections there, the more important flocks being in Co Cork, Co Down and Co Fermanagh; those at Strangford Lough (Down) are now truly feral.

Number of 10-km squares in which recorded:
687 (18%)
Possible breeding   143 (21%)
Probable breeding   38 (6%)
Confirmed breeding   506 (74%)

References
BLURTON JONES, N. G. 1956. Census of breeding Canada Geese 1953. *Bird Study* 3: 153–170.
FITTER, R. S. R. 1959. *The Ark in our Midst.* London.
MERNE, O. J. 1970. The status of the Canada Goose in Ireland. *Irish Bird Rep.* 17 (1969): 12–17.
OGILVIE, M. A. 1969. The status of the Canada Goose in Britain 1967–69. *Wildfowl* 20: 79–85.
WALKER, A. F. G. 1970. The moult migration of Yorkshire Canada Geese. *Wildfowl* 21: 99–104.

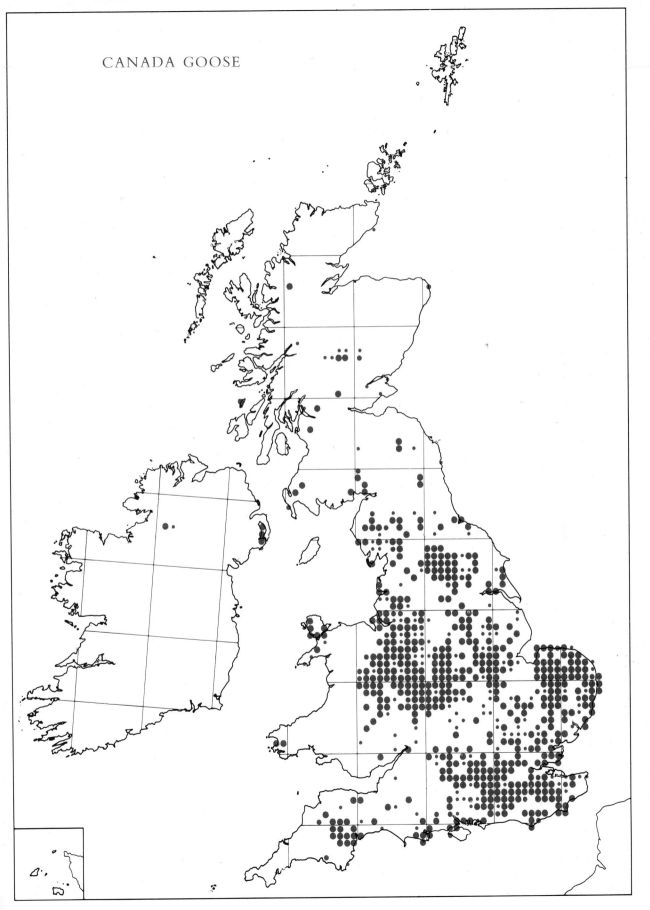

CANADA GOOSE

Mute Swan

Cygnus olor

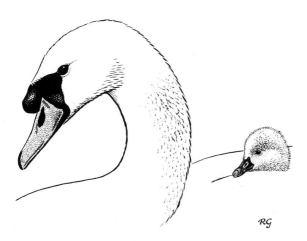

The Mute Swan, with its large size and strikingly white plumage, is one of the easiest species to census or survey. Historically, it is an indigenous bird which was brought into semi-domestication in mediaeval times, but, having long since lost its former culinary prestige, has been reverting to the wild state for two or three centuries. At present our Mute Swans run the whole gamut from tame urban birds to the shy breeders of Scottish and Irish islands. With the provisos that they do not normally breed higher than 300 m, and that waters must be large enough for their pattering take-off runs, these swans are to be found on almost any type of freshwater with subaqueous vegetation, ranging from pools and gravel pits to the largest lakes and reservoirs. They occur commonly on slow-flowing rivers, canals and low-lying marshes, while some breed even on sheltered tidal waters such as sea-lochs and the upper reaches of estuaries.

The nest must rank as one of the easiest to find, being a huge pile of dead and fresh plant material built close to the water. In open situations the incubating bird is often very obvious; nests on scrub-grown islets or within reed-beds may be missed on a cursory inspection, though the aggressive behaviour of the patrolling cob soon reveals the presence of a breeding pair.

Mute Swans breed over the whole of Britain and Ireland, apart from unsuitable upland areas and some off-lying islands such as the Shetland group, where introduction has always failed, and Lewis (Outer Hebrides). The broad limits of distribution have remained fairly constant since the 1939–45 war, though breeding occurred at three sites in 1969 in Banffshire, where there were few previous records.

In the spring of 1955 the BTO organised a census of Mute Swans in Britain (Campbell 1960, Rawcliffe 1958). The total population of England and Wales was about 14,300–15,300 birds, including 3,000–3,500 breeding pairs, and in Scotland there were 3,500–4,000 birds, including 463 known nesting pairs. Densities were highest in SE England and through the Thames Valley into the Midlands as far as Cheshire, and also in Norfolk and Somerset. A partial repeat census in 1956, coupled with a long series of figures available from the London area, indicated that a considerable increase was occurring, perhaps by as much as 16% per annum.

Shortly afterwards, farmers and fishermen began to complain of damage by swans. This initiated a further sample census in 1961 (Eltringham 1963); additionally, analyses have been made of the Wildfowl Trust's winter waterfowl count data over the 15 seasons 1954/55 to 1968/69 (Ogilvie 1967, 1972). From these sources it is clear that Mute Swans continued to increase until the 1959/60 winter, after which a rapid decline set in, and by the 1961/62 season they were back to the 1954 level. There was a further decrease of about 25% between 1961 and 1965, which has been attributed to the cold winters of 1961/62 and 1962/63. Since then, the population has been more or less stable. The evidence indicates that, throughout this period, the numbers of nesting pairs dropped by only a small percentage, the major decline having been amongst the flocks of non-breeders. Three causes for the decrease were suggested by Minton (1971): the cold winters of the early 1960s, increased casualties from hitting power lines (to which immatures are especially prone), and a lower production of young due to increased nest destruction by man.

The Irish population has been estimated at 5,000–6,000 birds (Ogilvie 1972), but no information is available on recent trends or the age structure of the flocks. The breeding population of Britain and Ireland may now total about 5,000–6,000 pairs.

Number of 10-km squares in which recorded: 2,258 (58%)
Possible breeding   206 (9%)
Probable breeding   75 (3%)
Confirmed breeding   1,977 (88%)

References
CAMPBELL, B. 1960. The Mute Swan census in England and Wales 1955–56. *Bird Study* 7: 208–223.
ELTRINGHAM, S. K. 1963. The British population of the Mute Swan. *Bird Study* 10: 10–28.
MINTON, C. D. T. 1971. Mute Swan flocks. *Wildfowl* 22: 71–88.
OGILVIE, M. A. 1967. Population changes and mortality of the Mute Swan in Britain. *Wildfowl Trust Ann. Rep.* 18: 64–73.
OGILVIE, M. A. 1972. Distribution, numbers and migration. pp 29–55 in SCOTT, P. and WILDFOWL TRUST, *The Swans*. London.
PERRINS, C. M. and C. M. REYNOLDS. 1967. A preliminary study of the Mute Swan *Cygnus olor*. *Wildfowl Trust Ann. Rep.* 18: 74–84.
RAWCLIFFE, C. P. 1958. The Scottish Mute Swan census 1955–56. *Bird Study* 5: 45–55.

Whooper Swan *Cygnus cygnus,* **see page 447**

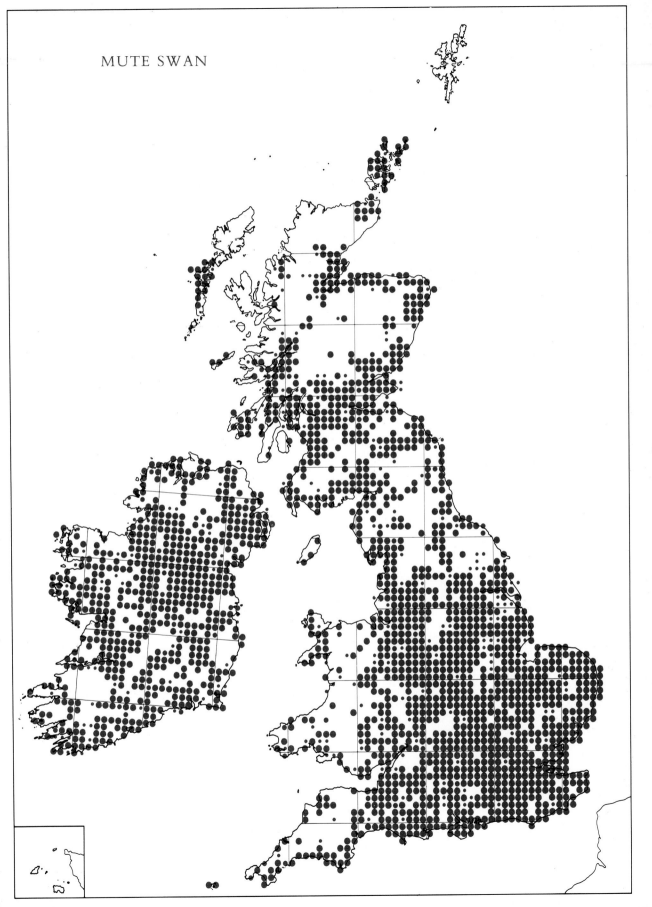

MUTE SWAN

Golden Eagle

Aquila chrysaetos

Golden Eagles formerly occupied the mountains of Ireland, Wales and England, though they were outnumbered by White-tailed Eagles *Haliaeetus albicilla* in Scotland and perhaps Ireland. Persecution in the 18th century, due to the spread of sheep farming, was aggravated by game preservation and the greed of collectors, so that Golden Eagles were exterminated in many former haunts, including all those in Wales and England, by the middle of the 19th century. A few pairs hung on in Ireland until the last in 1912. A recovery began in Scotland about the time of the 1914–18 war, probably because of a reduction in the activities of gamekeepers. The 1939–45 war provided another respite and, in the following years, there was recolonisation of former sites in the Hebrides and SW Scotland, while one pair nested in Co Antrim during 1953–60. Since 1969, a pair has nested in England for the first time for over 100 years, successfully rearing young each season during 1970–72.

Where they are numerous, Red Grouse *Lagopus lagopus* and Ptarmigan *L. mutus* form an important part of the diet, and it is claimed that the appearance of a Golden Eagle over a grouse moor can spoil a day's shoot. The presence of eagles is usually tolerated in deer forests, as they clear up the gralloch remaining after a successful stalk. They do occasionally kill young lambs, although such meat most frequently comes their way as carrion on overstocked sheepwalks. Here, as on heavily stocked grouse moors, they merely capitalise on the natural wastage which occurs in any animal population existing at a level beyond that which the environment can support. Thus, the antagonism of some gamekeepers and shepherds is largely unwarranted; and illegal killing, which continues on less enlightened estates, cannot be justified. It is unlikely that the density of Golden Eagles would increase significantly even if there were an immediate cessation of persecution; instead, there would probably be a welcome extension of range.

Chlorinated hydrocarbons, used in sheep dips, caused a serious decline in breeding success in the early 1960s. With this threat diminishing, the greatest problem now facing Golden Eagles, apart from illegal destruction, is disturbance by the increasing number of tourists.

Though it is not difficult for a knowledgeable searcher to find eyries, the cautious attitude of birdwatchers is demonstrated by the fact that a quarter of the confirmed breeding records shown on the map were originally submitted in confidence.

Although a few Golden Eagles prefer sea cliffs, most live in hill or mountain country, nesting on crags or in trees, usually with an extensive and uninterrupted view. The hunting area is sometimes vast, from 5,000 to 7,000 ha, though in some areas it may be as small as 2,000–2,500 ha, and in general the territories overlap (Newton 1972). A pair may have several eyries, and so may nest in more than one 10-km square over a series of years. Some squares held more than one pair, however, and, bearing these facts in mind, the 236 squares with confirmed breeding in 1968–72 may represent about that many pairs. Nicholson (1957) suggested a mid-1950s total of about 190 pairs, while Everett (1971) quoted C. E. Palmar's and Dr Adam Watson's later estimates of over 250 and nearly 300 pairs.

This species is afforded special protection in Great Britain under Schedule I of the Protection of Birds Act, 1954–67.

Number of 10-km squares in which recorded:
395 (10%)
Possible breeding   108 (27%)
Probable breeding   51 (13%)
Confirmed breeding   236 (60%)

Twenty dots have been moved by up to two 10-km squares and four dots (three of confirmed breeding and one of probable breeding) have been omitted (the recommendation of the Rare Breeding Birds Panel and M. J. Everett was that 17 dots should be moved by up to two 10-km squares)

References
BROWN, L. H. 1969. Status and breeding success of Golden Eagles in north-west Sutherland in 1967. *Brit. Birds* 62: 345–363.
BROWN, L. H. and A. WATSON. 1964. The Golden Eagle in relation to its food supply. *Ibis* 106: 78–100.
EVERETT, M. J. 1971. The Golden Eagle survey in Scotland in 1964–68. *Brit. Birds* 64: 49–56.
GORDON, S. 1955. *The Golden Eagle, King of Birds*. London.
LOCKIE, J. D. and D. A. RATCLIFFE. 1964. Insecticides and Scottish Golden Eagles. *Brit. Birds* 57: 89–102.
LOCKIE, J. D., D. A. RATCLIFFE and R. BALHARRY. 1969. Breeding success and organo-chlorine residues in Golden Eagles in west Scotland. *J. Appl. Ecol.* 6: 381–389.
NEWTON, I. 1972. Birds of prey in Scotland; some conservation problems. *Scott. Birds* 7: 5–23.
NICHOLSON, E. M. 1957. The rarer birds of prey. Their present status in the British Isles. Golden Eagle. *Brit. Birds* 50: 131–135.
WATSON, A. 1949. The Golden Eagle in the Highlands. *Bird Notes* 23: 262–264.

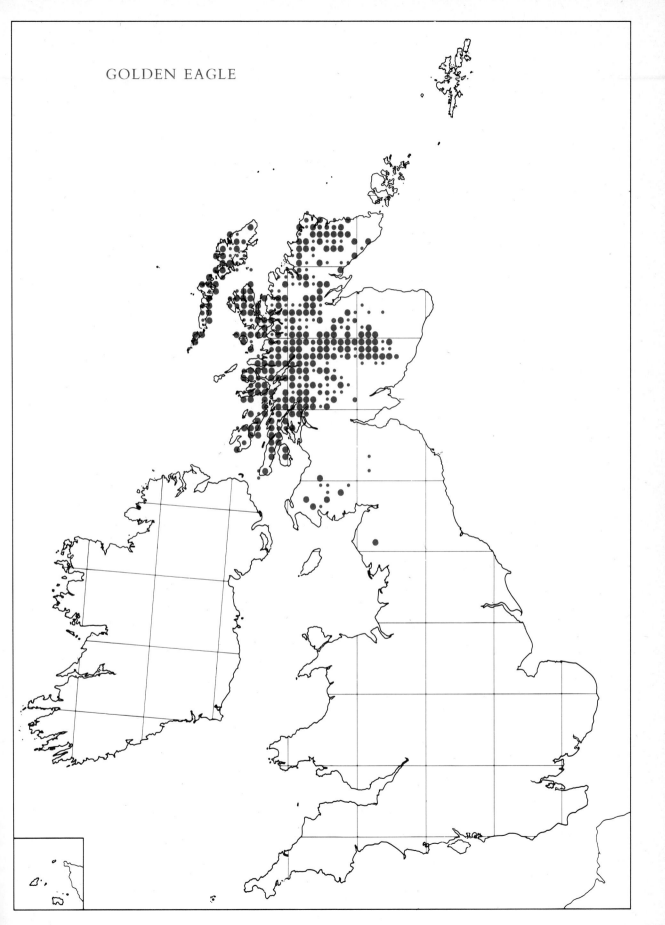

GOLDEN EAGLE

Buzzard

Buteo buteo

Although they need trees or crags as nesting sites, Buzzards are not at their commonest in forested or mountainous regions. The densest concentrations are where the habitat is diverse, as in the wooded farmland of SW England and the valleys of Wales, the Lake District and W Scotland. The bare mountains and moorlands of Sutherland and Caithness support only a few pairs.

Except where the population is very sparse, Buzzards are easy to locate as they soar effortlessly in spirals and mew loudly; nests are often not difficult to find and well-grown young may be noisy in and just out of the nest, making confirmation of breeding a relatively simple task.

In the early 19th century, Buzzards were common throughout most of mainland Britain and fairly general in Ireland. By the second half of that century there had been a substantial decline and contraction, attributed to persecution. Breeding in Ireland was restricted to N Ulster, and much of lowland England was devoid of Buzzards. The contraction continued until the start of the 1914–18 war and the position during the early part of this century represented the lowest ebb of the population in recorded times. The reduction in the number of gamekeepers during that war had an immediate effect and Buzzards returned to areas which they had not occupied for many years. A more enlightened attitude prevailed thereafter, and keepering never regained the level of the late 19th and early 20th centuries. Buzzards continued to regain ground and even spread (*eg* to the Outer Hebrides after 1930). By 1949–54 the numbers and range were larger than they had been for over 100 years, and Moore (1957) calculated that there were 20,000–30,000 birds (probably 12,000 breeding pairs). Keepering still has a limiting effect, however, with many potential colonists being killed when they disperse into vacant areas: a total of 223 Buzzards killed on just four estates in NE Scotland in 1968, for instance (Picozzi and Weir 1976).

Different phases in the contraction and subsequent growth of the population are shown in the maps on page 455.

Although Buzzards are catholic feeders, taking advantage of whatever prey is locally available, there is no doubt that the almost plague proportions of the Rabbit in some regions by the mid-1950s had boosted the population to an unnaturally high level. The decline in Rabbits during 1955–56, due to myxomatosis, affected the Buzzards strikingly, and in some areas the size of the breeding population, the number of eggs laid and the number of young reared all dropped by about half. In Lakeland, a later decline was noted, from the late 1950s, attributed to organochlorine poisoning, occasioned by the Buzzards turning their attention more to mutton carrion impregnated by dieldrin and aldrin used in sheep-dips. The use of these pesticides in sheep-dips was banned in 1966 and numbers and breeding success have shown recovery since.

N Ulster was recolonised in the early 1950s and numbers there now are higher than for 80–90 years. By the time of the *Atlas* survey, Buzzards were found in the breeding season in more than one-third of Britain and Ireland, and the 1970 population was estimated by Tubbs (1974) to be 8,000–10,000 pairs, corresponding to about seven to nine pairs per 10-km square in which breeding was probable or confirmed.

Number of 10-km squares in which recorded:
  1,451 (38%)
Possible breeding   318 (22%)
Probable breeding   192 (13%)
Confirmed breeding   941 (65%)

One dot has been moved by one 10-km square (the Rare Breeding Birds Panel's recommendation was accurate plotting)

References

ASH, J. S. 1960. Bird of prey numbers on a Hampshire game preserve during 1952–59. *Brit. Birds* 53: 285–300.

DARE, P. 1957. The post-myxomatosis diet of the Buzzard. *Devon Birds* 10: 2–6.

DAVIS, T. A. W. and D. R. SAUNDERS. 1965. Buzzards on Skomer Island, 1954–64. *Nature in Wales* 9: 116–124.

HOLDSWORTH, M. 1971. Breeding biology of Buzzards at Sedbergh during 1937–67. *Brit. Birds* 64: 412–420.

MOORE, N. W. 1957. The past and present status of the Buzzard in the British Isles. *Brit. Birds* 50: 173–197.

PICOZZI, N. and D. WEIR. 1976. Dispersal and causes of death in Buzzards. *Brit. Birds* 69: 193–201.

PRESTT, I. 1965. An enquiry into the recent breeding status of some of the smaller birds of prey and crows in Britain. *Bird Study* 12: 196–221.

TUBBS, C. R. 1972. Analysis of nest record cards for the Buzzard. *Bird Study* 19: 96–104.

TUBBS, C. R. 1974. *The Buzzard*. Newton Abbot.

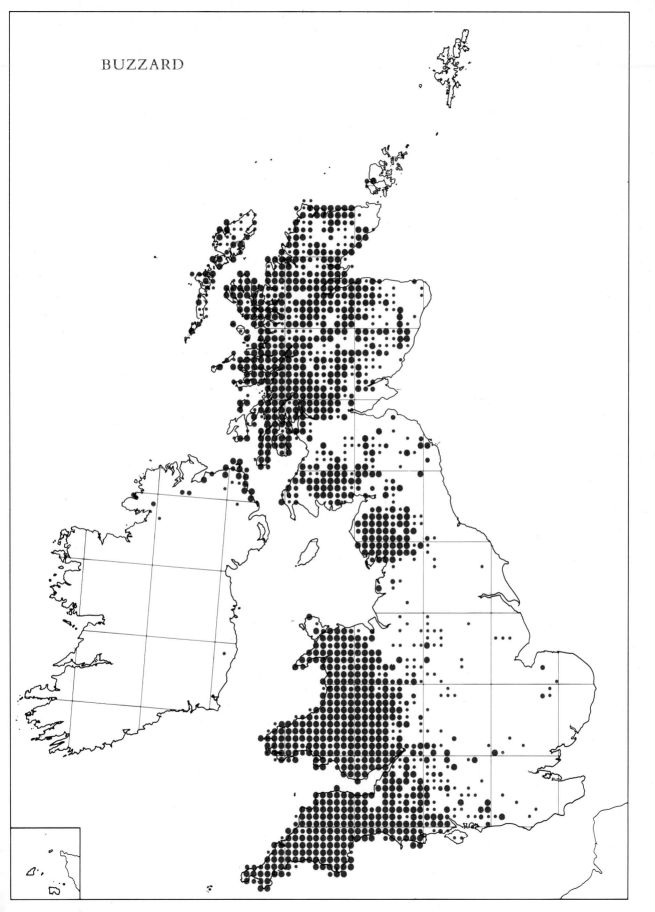

BUZZARD

Sparrowhawk

Accipiter nisus

Typically woodland birds, hunting by swift dashes through the trees, Sparrowhawks occur most commonly in coniferous or mixed woods, but may also be found wherever there is tree cover, even in shelter-belts on farmland and suburban gardens. Few places in Britain and Ireland are unsuitable for the species, and until the 1950s its status in almost the whole of these islands was frequently summarised as 'very common and widespread'.

Perhaps more than any other raptor, the Sparrowhawk has been persistently persecuted by game-keepers and farmers, females often being shot on the nest. Despite this, the species remained common, even in the heavily keepered areas of SE England and East Anglia, until a marked decline became evident in 1959–60. The species then disappeared from more than a dozen counties in E and S England, and there were less catastrophic decreases in SW and N England. Prestt (1965) summarised the effect of the change during 1953–63 by saying, 'There is now not a single county remaining in England where this species can be considered a common breeding bird.' He concluded that, since the species had weathered previous persecution by game preservation interests, the sudden dramatic collapse must have another cause. Toxic chemicals, particularly chlorinated hydrocarbons, were blamed, as the timing of their use coincided with that of the reported deaths, the reduced fertility and the general decline, which was greatest in the arable areas of E England (Cramp 1963, Ratcliffe 1970, Newton 1973).

The decline was so great that the Sparrowhawk, formerly the only raptor without it, was given legal protection in Britain in 1963. There are now restrictions on the use of chlorinated hydrocarbons, which can be taken in sublethal amounts by insectivorous and seed-eating birds, but then accumulated to a lethal level by predators higher up the food chain. Such action may have come just in time, for the 1968–72 distribution shows the beginning of re-colonisation in most of the eastern counties where the species was extinct in the early 1960s. The large number of small dots (presence in the breeding season

without further proof of breeding) also reveals the potential for a complete recovery if the Sparrowhawk is given a chance. There has already been a marked resurgence in Ireland, where this is probably now the commonest bird of prey.

A clue to the species' resilience comes from comparisons drawn by Newton (1974) between pairs nesting more than 20 km from arable farmland and those on or close to it. Nesting success had not decreased with the former group at any stage during the 'pesticides era'. Thus, since breeding adults do not range far for their food, and their prey species are themselves mostly sedentary, such pairs will continue to produce surplus young which can disperse and attempt to breed in areas depopulated by pesticides, or can colonise areas rendered free from pollution.

The chance of encountering a hunting Sparrowhawk during *Atlas* fieldwork was low in many areas, but searches for displaying birds soaring over suitable woods early on fine mornings in March or April sometimes pinpointed territories. Plucking posts near the nest were sometimes an aid to its location.

By 1972, the increase in the number of observations in areas from which Sparrowhawks had been absent for 10–15 years was gathering momentum, and recent searches have revealed concentrations of 15–20 nests in quite small areas, even in the English Home Counties. Many of the 10-km squares for which breeding was not proved may well have contained breeding pairs. Certainly, Parslow's category of 1,000–10,000 pairs, before the recovery had got under way—which implies an average of roughly five pairs per occupied 10-km square at most—is now too low. The breeding population may have reached 15,000–20,000 pairs by 1972.

This species is afforded special protection in Great Britain under Schedule 1 of the Protection of Birds Act, 1954–67.

Number of 10-km squares in which recorded:
2,626 (68%)
Possible breeding   732 (28%)
Probable breeding   438 (17%)
Confirmed breeding   1,456 (55%)

References
CRAMP, S. 1963. Toxic chemicals and birds of prey. *Brit. Birds* 56: 124–138.
NEWTON, I. 1973. Success of Sparrowhawks in an area of pesticide usage. *Bird Study* 20: 1–8.
NEWTON, I. 1974. Changes attributed to pesticides in the nesting success of the Sparrowhawk in Britain. *J. Appl. Ecol.* 11: 95–102.
PRESTT, I. 1965. An enquiry into the recent breeding status of some of the smaller birds of prey and crows in Britain. *Bird Study* 12: 196–221.
RATCLIFFE, D. A. 1970. Changes attributable to pesticides in egg breakage frequency and eggshell thickness in some British birds. *J. Appl. Ecol.* 7: 67–115.

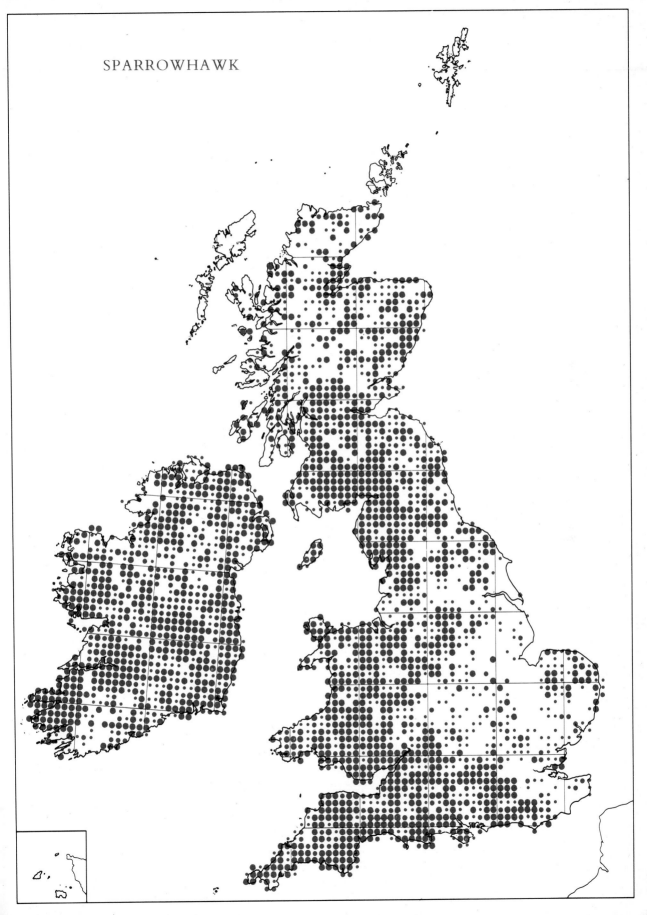

SPARROWHAWK

Goshawk

Accipiter gentilis

Goshawks frequent extensive woodland. Though this may be coniferous, mixed or broad-leaved, beech and pine are the most favoured. The nest is usually placed high up (often 12–20 m) in a fork, close to the main trunk, and may be very difficult or even impossible to see from below. The birds' flight is usually low, careering between the trees. For these reasons the presence of Goshawks is easily overlooked, the best chance of locating a pair being in March and April, when display flights high over the large territory may be seen.

The past history of Goshawks in Britain has been open to controversy, partly because the name 'Goose Hawk', applied locally to the Peregrine *Falco peregrinus*, was sometimes abbreviated to Goshawk: some old records, such as those of cliff-nesting birds in Orkney, clearly refer to Peregrines. Nesting certainly took place in the pine forests of the Scottish Highlands until about the 1880s, but ceased to be regular in England rather earlier. The decline to extermination preceded that of other raptors, so that the history of the species is neither well documented nor fully understood.

Falconry was a major national field-sport throughout mediaeval times, though it suffered a slow decline after the invention of firearms. As the Goshawk decreased gradually during this later period, the British stock was perhaps always largely dependent on falconers' birds to maintain its numbers. The species may also have become a threat to poultry and gamebirds, thereby suffering persecution both on smallholdings and the larger estates.

A tiny pocket of up to three pairs bred in Sussex from at least 1938 (possibly as early as 1921) until 1951. During much of this time, their existence was known only to falconers, demonstrating how easily this species can remain undetected by birdwatchers, even in a well-watched county. Up to 1967 there were a few other records of nesting at scattered localities, but it was only during 1968–72 that regular breeding in Britain was rediscovered. The map shows a healthier situation than there has been for at least 90 years.

Since the Goshawk is known to be decreasing on the Continent, natural recolonisation is unlikely.

Some breeding records are known to have resulted from falconers' birds which had escaped or had been deliberately released so that the young could be taken later from nests. A sample suggests that 50% of all Goshawks kept by members of the British Falconers' Club are lost or released; thus it seems likely that most if not all recent records originated in this way, though a small feral population now seems to have become established.

While there is plenty of suitable Goshawk habitat in Britain, re-establishment has certainly been aided by forestry enterprises, which provide the birds with areas where they enjoy protection and relative freedom from disturbance. The Goshawk feeds mostly on larger prey than is captured by its smaller relative, the Sparrowhawk *A. nisus*, particularly birds approximating in size to Moorhens *Gallinula chloropus* and Stock Doves *Columba oenas*. Although Pheasants *Phasianus colchicus* are sometimes taken, Goshawks also feed readily on Woodpigeons *Columba palumbus* and in consequence are likely to be tolerated or even actively encouraged by farmers.

The greatest risks to British Goshawks now come from falconers, egg-collectors and gamekeepers, though like Sparrowhawks they may have suffered as a result of absorbing toxic pesticides with their prey. Disturbance by birdwatchers may not in itself do much harm, but it can lead to discovery of a site by others with a less benevolent interest. The Goshawks' future may be helped by the fact that they often use alternative sites several kilometres apart in successive years. This, however, together with the large territory required, may have resulted in over-representation of their true distribution in any one year during 1968–72. There are probably fewer pairs than the 35 occupied 10-km squares of the map, even allowing for any which remain undiscovered, but the total certainly exceeds ten.

This species is afforded special protection in Great Britain under Schedule I of the Protection of Birds Act, 1954–67.

Number of 10-km squares in which recorded: 35 (0.9%)
Possible breeding   4 (11%)
Probable breeding   20 (57%)
Confirmed breeding   11 (31%)

Two dots (both confirmed breeding) have been omitted and 16 dots have been moved by up to two 10-km squares (the recommendation of the Rare Breeding Birds Panel and R. F. Porter was that eight dots should be moved by up to two 10-km squares)

References

HOLLOM, P. A. D. 1957. The rarer birds of prey. Their present status in the British Isles. Goshawk. *Brit. Birds* 50: 135–136.

KENWARD, R. E. 1974. Mortality and fate of trained birds of prey. *J. Wildl. Manage.* 38 (4): 751–756.

VAN BEUSEKOM, C. F. 1972. Ecological isolation with respect to food between Sparrowhawk and Goshawk. *Ardea* 60: 72–96.

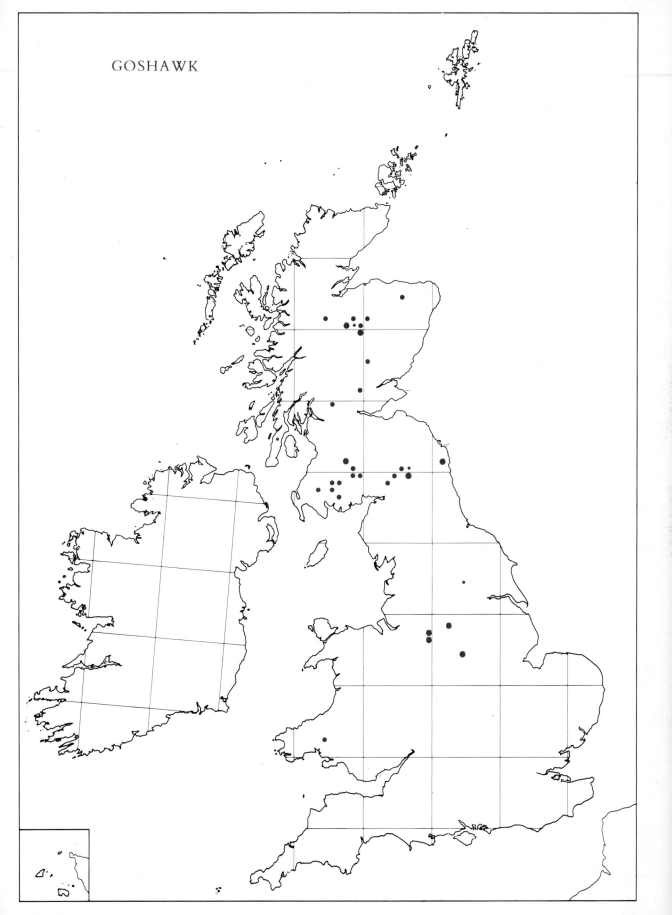

GOSHAWK

Red Kite

Milvus milvus

As a breeding bird, the Red Kite is confined largely to Europe. Man has been responsible for its marked reduction and even extermination in many parts, so that today it must be considered an endangered species. Due probably to this persecution, the patchy European range contracted during the 19th century. There followed a recovery during the first half of the present century in some areas, but this has been arrested or reversed in recent years (Glutz von Blotzheim *et al* 1971) and former breeding haunts in Norway, Denmark, Belgium and other parts of NW Europe have not been reoccupied.

The Red Kite was a familiar raptor throughout much of England, Scotland and Wales (though absent from Ireland) up to the end of the 18th century, scavenging in towns and cities. Persecution, largely in the cause of game-preservation, led to a rapid decline until the species was extinct as a breeding bird in England by the 1880s and in Scotland by 1890.

By the beginning of the 20th century there were apparently only a dozen birds left in Wales. Though recorded numbers varied from three to 12 pairs, there was little change until the early 1950s, despite the expenditure of much time and money on their protection. In 1954 at least 15 pairs were present, 12 of which reared a total of 15 young, and at the end of that season the total Welsh population was estimated to be 55 birds (Salmon 1970). There were setbacks in the following years, attributed to the reduction of Rabbits by myxomatosis as well as to human interference and, perhaps, the adverse effects of toxic chemicals. A welcome increase took place, however, so that 19–26 pairs nested annually during 1968–72, rearing an average of 16 young each year. By August 1972 the population stood at about 80 birds.

Mature oakwoods on steep valley slopes are the usual nesting habitat of the small relict Welsh population. These provide nesting and roosting sites and are therefore the focal point for the resident Red Kites throughout the year. Adjacent marginal hill land (*ffridd*) and, to a lesser extent, mountain sheep-walks provide the greater part of the food, both carrion and live. Although similar food supplies and habitats are available elsewhere in Britain, the breeding range in Wales has changed little in recent years, with in-filling rather than spread as a result of the increase in numbers.

The Welsh Red Kites are strongly prone to desert their nests at the slightest disturbance. It is, therefore, essential that, no matter how well intentioned, investigation of suspected pairs should be avoided. Almost all the Welsh data shown on the map were supplied by the Kite Committee, which co-ordinates the protection and study of this vulnerable stock. The activities of egg-collectors, the taking of young into captivity, and disturbance at the nest (all illegal activities, but still occurring) are strong threats to Red Kites; to these have been added the rapid transformation of their habitat, particularly afforestation of the upland sheep-walks where they feed, the growth of tourism in central Wales and strychnine poisoning from bait put out for Foxes.

The present level of breeding success is still lower than in the early 1950s, with the rate of hatching failure noticeably high, though the brood size of successful nests has tended to increase. The survival rate of immatures is low and recent ringing recoveries have confirmed a suspected southeasterly movement of juveniles, starting a few weeks after fledging. Such emigration may produce additional hazards. At present the number of survivors reaching breeding age only just exceeds adult deaths (Davies and Davis 1973). The recovery of a German-ringed immature in Radnorshire in July 1972 was the first proof of any contact between the Welsh and Continental stocks. At its present level of about 26 pairs, the Kite population is still at a vulnerable stage in its recovery and disturbance of nesting birds must be avoided.

This species is afforded special protection in Great Britain under Schedule I of the Protection of Birds Act, 1954–67.

Number of 10-km squares in which recorded:
  34 (0·9%)
Possible breeding   14 (41%)
Probable breeding   1 (3%)
Confirmed breeding   19 (56%)

The Welsh dots are conventionally placed centrally in a circle of radius 50-km and the other dots have been moved by up to two 10-km squares (as recommended by the Rare Breeding Birds Panel and the Kite Committee)

References
BIJLEVELD, M. 1974. *Birds of Prey in Europe*. London.
DAVIES, P. W. and P. E. DAVIS. 1973. The ecology and conservation of the Red Kite in Wales. *Brit. Birds* 66: 183–224, 241–270.
GLUTZ VON BLOTZHEIM, U., K. M. BAUER and E. BEZZEL. 1971. *Handbuch der Vögel Mitteleuropas*. Vol. 4. Frankfurt-am-Main.
SALMON, H. M. 1970. The Red Kites of Wales: the story of their preservation. pp 67–79 in LACEY, W. S. (ed), *Welsh Wildlife in Danger*. Bangor.

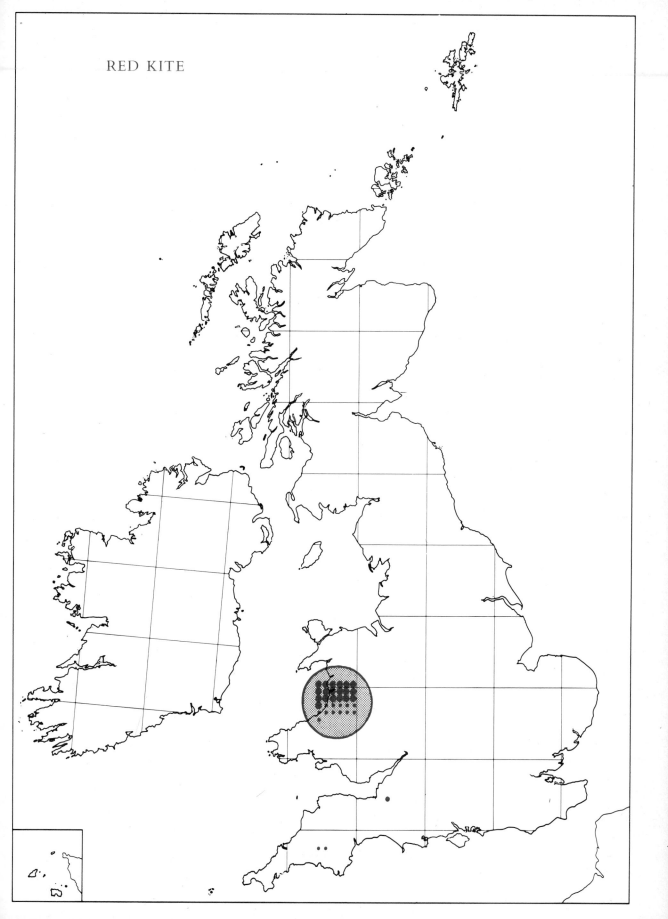

RED KITE

Honey Buzzard

Pernis apivorus

The favourite breeding habitat of the Honey Buzzard is a complex mosaic of mature woodland and open ground. Broad-leaved woodland appears to be preferred, especially beech, but sometimes mixed or even pure conifer stands are occupied. Typical situations include those where mature trees are well spaced, dissected by rides or glades and flanked by heath, or grouped into clumps and small woods on agricultural land.

Honey Buzzards feed chiefly on the ground at the nests of bees and wasps, also consuming other large insects, small mammals, birds, snakes, lizards and amphibians. They spend considerably less time in the air than many raptors and are easily overlooked by the casual observer; nevertheless, pairs are best located by the distinctive display flights or, later in the season, when young are on the wing. The arrival of Honey Buzzards in this country, and the timing of their breeding cycle, appear to be geared to the maximum production of bee and wasp larvae. Thus, they do not usually come until May, and young can be found in the nest from late June through to the middle of September (Campbell and Ferguson-Lees 1972).

Even when a pair has been located, discovery of the nest site and proof of breeding may be difficult, especially as disturbance must be avoided at all costs. The foraging area may be as much as 10 km² in extent. The nest is often not particularly large and usually well hidden among dense foliage at a height of 10–25 m in a tree. Adults are unobtrusive in the vicinity of the nest and it seems likely that some breeding pairs remain undetected each year.

Ever since Gilbert White wrote his account of the celebrated pair which nested 'upon a tall slender beech near the centre of Selborne Hanger in the summer of 1780', the temptation has been to assume that the Honey Buzzard was formerly well established as a British breeding bird. The past status is not precisely known, but it seems probable that this raptor was never numerous. It was perhaps rather more widespread than today, but still rare during the 19th century, when nesting was reported from S and E England north to Durham, Ross-shire and Aberdeenshire.

As recently as the mid-1950s, the Honey Buzzard was recorded as casual and very irregular (Hollom 1957), but it was then made known that a few pairs were established in one area. The situation up to 1967 was summarised by Parslow: 'For at least the last 30–40 years it has maintained a population of several pairs in the New Forest (Hampshire) and has sometimes bred elsewhere in southern England north to the Welsh border, as well as almost certainly Fife in 1949.' This statement would hold true for 1968–72.

The successful tenure of the small but vulnerable New Forest population is no doubt due to the existence of suitable nesting habitat and food supplies combined with sympathetic keepering, protection by conservationists and an absence of farm chemicals. There are no published details of breeding biology or population trends in Britain, but on the Continent the breeding density is highly variable and thought to be related to food supply (Munch 1955) and climatic conditions (Suter 1962), as a result of which the species is more numerous in dry than in wet years. Although the precise status of the species in Britain is not known, it is doubtful from *Atlas* records if the population exceeds a dozen pairs in any year.

This species is afforded special protection in Great Britain under Schedule I of the Protection of Birds Act, 1954–67.

Number of 10-km squares in which recorded:
12 (0.3%)
Possible breeding 4 (33%)
Probable breeding 1 (8%)
Confirmed breeding 7 (58%)

Within the shaded 100-km squares, dots are conventionally placed centrally; two other dots have been moved by up to two 10-km squares (the recommendation of the Rare Breeding Birds Panel, R. F. Porter and Dr D. A. Ratcliffe was that one dot should be moved by up to two 10-km squares and the others plotted accurately). This is the only species for which we know that records have been withheld from the *Atlas*, and this map is therefore incomplete to an unknown extent. Conventional plotting is used in deference to this attitude in some quarters, and we apologise to the observers who supplied records and requested accurate plotting

References

HOLLOM, P. A. D. 1957. The rarer birds of prey. Their present status in the British Isles. Honey Buzzard. *Brit. Birds* 50: 141–142.

MUNCH, H. 1955. *Der Wespenbussard*. Wittenberg-Lutherstadt.

SUTER, H. 1962. *Die Brutvögel der Schweiz*. Aarau.

WHITE, G. 1780. *The Natural History of Selborne* (Letter XLIII). London.

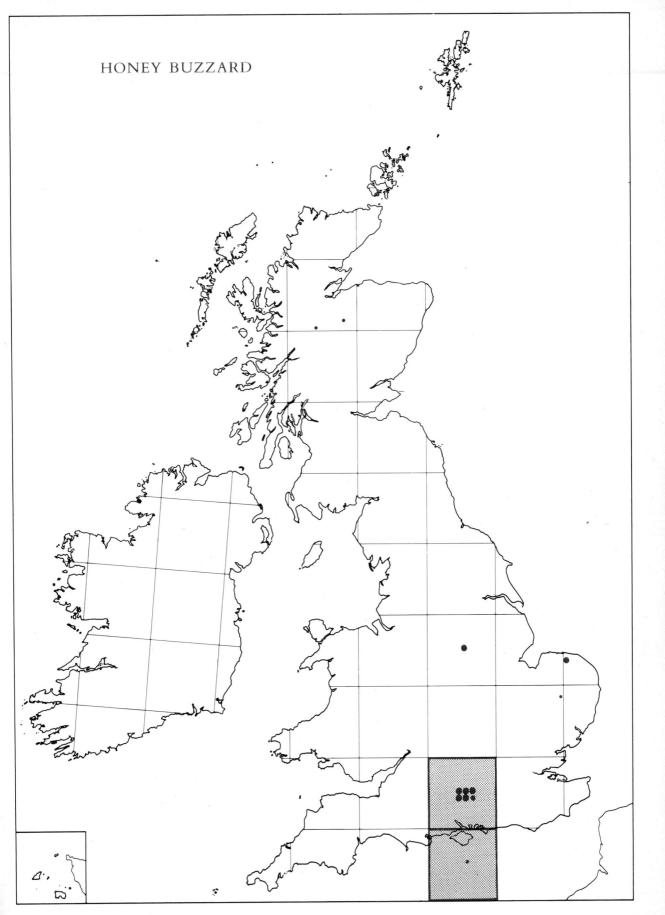

HONEY BUZZARD

Marsh Harrier

Circus aeruginosus

This spectacular raptor breeds almost exclusively in extensive *Phragmites* reed-beds; such terrain is well suited to its glide-and-pounce hunting technique, though it is by no means unusual for the Marsh Harrier to hunt for small birds and mammals over adjacent open country as well. The specialised habitat inevitably restricts both breeding distribution and numbers in these islands, while its sensitivity to disturbance is a further limiting factor.

The Marsh Harrier was widespread in Britain and Ireland 200–300 years ago, but the drainage of fens, and attendant destruction of the extensive reed-beds that the species needs, severely reduced its numbers in Britain. Spanish Marsh Harriers have taken to nesting in corn fields where their traditional wetlands have been reclaimed, but the British stock has shown no such flexibility. To this melancholy state of affairs was added direct persecution during the Victorian era by gamekeepers, trophy-hunters and egg-collectors. It is hardly surprising that the Marsh Harrier became temporarily extinct in England in the closing years of the 19th century. Extinction in Ireland followed by 1917, even though ideal habitat exists in the midlands to the present day. It may be that no natural factors were involved, the Marsh Harrier disappearing in the face of man's insatiable demand for more cultivable land, sport and cabinet specimens.

The growth of the conservation movement in the 1920s led to the protection of occasional pairs attempting re-establishment in Norfolk, and, thanks to the determined efforts of the owners of Hickling and Horsey Broads, the Marsh Harrier regained its place as a regular breeding bird in Britain. Up to four pairs bred annually in the Norfolk Broads from 1927 onwards, and during the late 1930s the species returned to the reedy meres of E Suffolk. By the 1950s there were up to 12 nests each year in East Anglia, as well as signs that the Marsh Harrier was beginning to spread to other areas. Nests were found in Anglesey in 1945, Kent in 1946, and on more than one occasion in Hampshire during the 1950s, while breeding took place in Poole Harbour (Dorset) in 1950 and subsequently, with five pairs there in 1954. Nicholson (1957) wrote optimistically, 'now appears to have a fair prospect of recovery under vigilant protection'.

Sadly the hoped-for revival was not to be. In Norfolk, the numbers slumped suddenly from a normal five nests in 1959 to one (which was unsuccessful) in 1960, and none in 1961; there have been only a few attempts in that county since, and 1961 was also the last year in which any bred in Dorset. Since then Marsh Harriers have bred regularly only in Suffolk, and it is fortunate that the principal locality, Minsmere, where they have nested since 1955, is an RSPB reserve. It is unlikely that there were more than half a dozen nests in Britain in any year during 1968–72, and the Marsh Harrier's status as a breeding bird is precarious. The only slight cause for optimism comes from the fact that an instance of the probable breeding of one pair in W Britain (not mapped here) was confirmed in 1973 and 1974.

Though disturbance of potential sites by holiday-makers, especially on the Norfolk Broads, may have been largely to blame for the modern decline, other factors may be influencing the birds. The early 1960s was a period when naturalists had particular cause to worry about the effects of pesticides on raptors. At the time of the Marsh Harrier's desertion of Norfolk, there were complaints that Coypus had seriously damaged reed and sedge beds, but Coypu numbers have been drastically reduced since the severe winter of 1962/63 and the harriers have not resettled, even though several non-breeders are seen each summer.

Though they are large raptors, Marsh Harriers can be remarkably inconspicuous as they glide low over reed-beds when hunting. It is possible that an undetected pair may occasionally nest away from the traditional East Anglian sites, like those found in Lincolnshire in 1962, Yorkshire in 1963, possibly Scotland in 1966, and Fenland in one year during the *Atlas* survey. Nevertheless, records of mere presence probably relate mainly, if not wholly, to migrants and summering immatures, though these have significance as prospecting individuals which might remain to breed in undisturbed areas if given a chance.

This species is afforded special protection in Great Britain under Schedule I of the Protection of Birds Act, 1954–67.

Number of 10-km squares in which recorded: 27 (0·6%)
Possible breeding   20 (74%)
Probable breeding   3 (11%)
Confirmed breeding   4 (15%)

Two dots have been moved by up to two 10-km squares and one dot (probable breeding) in W Britain has been omitted (as recommended by the Rare Breeding Birds Panel and R. F. Porter)

References

COLLING, A. W. and E. B. BROWN. 1946. The breeding of Marsh and Montagu's Harriers in North Wales in 1945. *Brit. Birds* 39: 233–243.

MACMILLAN, A. T. 1968. Possible nesting of Marsh Harriers in Scotland. *Scott. Birds* 5: 25–26.

NICHOLSON, E. M. 1957. The rarer birds of prey. Their present status in the British Isles. Marsh Harrier. *Brit. Birds* 50: 142–143.

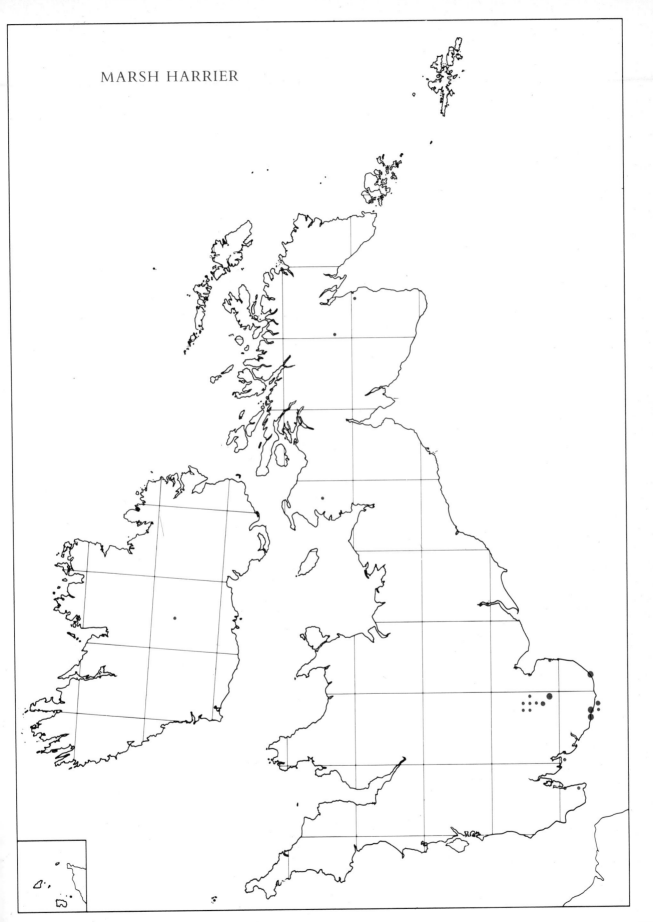

MARSH HARRIER

Hen Harrier

Circus cyaneus

In Britain, Hen Harriers are usually found on rolling moorland, particularly where this has patches of rushes and sedges. Bracken-covered hillsides and peat bogs are also frequented in a few places. Rank heather or a mixture of heather and rushes are favoured nest sites, but in recent decades they have nested increasingly in newly afforested areas, especially where a well-grown field layer offers shelter to such prey as small birds and mammals. In Ireland, dry heather near young conifer plantations, or, in the absence of heather, a strong growth of gorse, form the Hen Harrier's main habitats; most sites are at 200–250 m and there appears to be a preference for areas overlying Old Red Sandstone. Two hundred years ago, the Hen Harrier bred throughout Britain in such diverse habitats as the dry chalk downs of S England and the reeded fens and marshes of East Anglia.

The pale grey and white adult male is easy to see from a distance, as it floats casually, hunting low over the hill-sides. The courtship displays early in the nesting season, and later the aerial food-passes from male to female, help to indicate the location of the nest site. Most female and some male Hen Harriers are demonstrative towards human beings near the nest, particularly after the young have hatched. Nests on open moorland may then be found fairly easily.

Though formerly widespread, this and other ground nesting species were inevitably affected by the agricultural revolution with its associated land reclamation, while during the 19th century the Hen Harrier, together with most other raptors, suffered greatly from direct persecution. Latterly, the main threats came from gamekeepers on grouse moors, and the activities of egg-collectors. By the beginning of the 20th century, the Hen Harrier's range here was virtually confined to Orkney, the Outer Hebrides and Ireland. The survival of a viable population in Orkney may be attributed to the absence of large sporting estates, and particularly to its assiduous protection by the late George Arthur and the late Eddie Balfour, to whom ornithologists owe much. In the Outer Hebrides, gamekeepers were more concerned with wildfowl than Red Grouse *Lagopus lagopus*;

consequently, Hen Harriers were seldom destroyed.

The small number of gamekeepers remaining on the moors during the 1939–45 war, and the reduced number employed since then, resulted in less persecution of raptors. Decreased burning of heather also led to an increase in the amount of the tall, rank heather favoured for nesting. These two factors seem likely to have helped in the post-war recolonisation of the Scottish mainland by the Hen Harrier, although illegal persecution still continues on most grouse moors. The reafforestation of many moorlands since the war must also have speeded recolonisation, since Hen Harriers breed unmolested in these young plantations. It is an open question whether the recolonising birds were initially mainly from Orkney or, as suggested by Richmond (1959), from Norway.

The virtual absence of the Hen Harrier from much of central and NW Scotland probably reflects topography rather than persecution. Having established itself on the Scottish mainland during the 1950s, the Hen Harrier extended its range southwards in the 1960s and the years 1968–72 saw the first breeding records in this century for Co Durham, W Yorkshire, Lancashire, Cardiganshire and Norfolk, while in August 1974 a family party was seen on the N Staffordshire moors. In Ireland too they have been increasing apace since 1950; they were nesting in at least six counties by 1964 and in 13 counties by 1971. The 1964 estimate of 35 pairs (Ruttledge 1966) is considered to have been too low; there were probably about 75 pairs then, and about 200–300 pairs by the early 1970s (D. Scott *in litt*).

In 1974 there were 62 known nests in Orkney, averaging more than four for each occupied 10-km square. An average of two nests per 10-km square of proved or probable breeding during 1968–72 would lead to a guess of 500–600 nests per annum.

This species is afforded special protection in Great Britain under Schedule I of the Protection of Birds Act, 1954–67.

Number of 10-km squares in which recorded:
543 (14%)
Possible breeding 261 (48%)
Probable breeding 101 (19%)
Confirmed breeding 181 (33%)

Within the shaded 50-km squares, the dots are conventionally placed centrally; and nine other dots have been moved by up to two 10-km squares (the recommendation by the Rare Breeding Birds Panel, R. F. Porter, Major R. F. Ruttledge and D. Scott was accurate plotting)

References

BALFOUR, E. 1957. Observations on the breeding biology of the Hen Harrier in Orkney. *Bird Notes* 27: 177–183, 216–224.

BALFOUR, E. and M. A. MACDONALD. 1970. Food and feeding behaviour of the Hen Harrier in Orkney. *Scott. Birds* 6: 157–166.

CAMPBELL, J. W. 1957. The rarer birds of prey. Their present status in the British Isles. Hen Harrier. *Brit. Birds* 50: 143–146.

RICHMOND, W. K. 1959. *British Birds of Prey*. London.

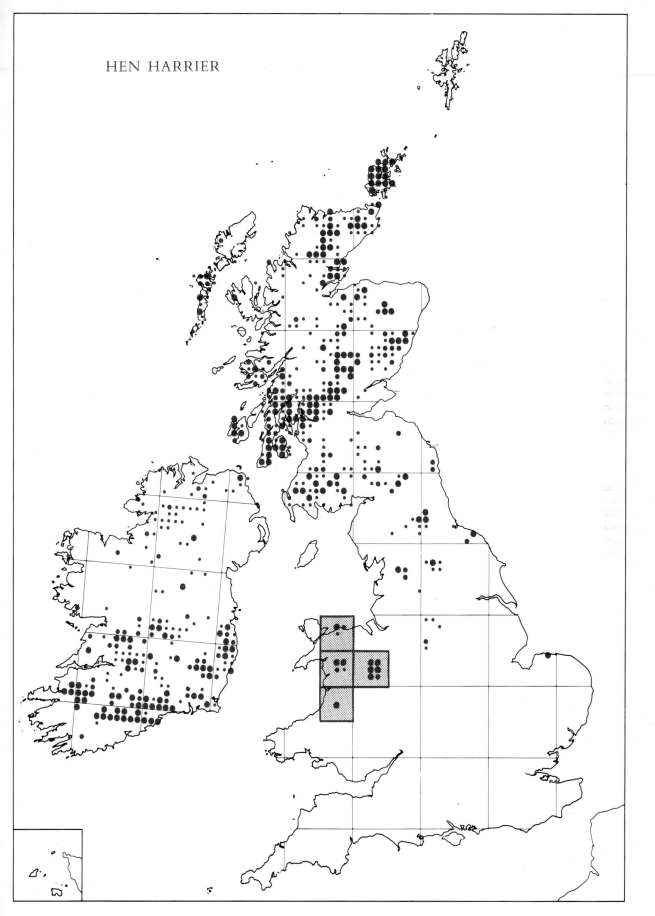

HEN HARRIER

Montagu's Harrier

Circus pygargus

This bird differs from the other two British breeding harriers in being exclusively a summer migrant, returning in April and departing in September–October. The breeding habitats are varied, overlapping with the Marsh Harrier *C. aeruginosus* in the reed-beds of fens and marshes, and with the Hen Harrier *C. cyaneus* on moorland. It is more usual for our Montagu's Harriers to nest in drier situations, however, and most are found in young forestry plantations and on gorse-covered heaths. British nests have also been found on dunes, rough pasture and arable land amidst growing crops. As with other harriers, it is by no means rare for non-breeding birds, probably mainly immatures, to summer in traditional nesting haunts.

This was the last of the British breeding harriers to be identified, for it was not until 1802 that Colonel George Montagu, working in Devon, finally cleared up the confusion that had existed between it and the Hen Harrier. Montagu's has probably always been the scarcest of the three British species. During the 19th century, it was persecuted by gamekeepers and egg-collectors and suffered from land reclamation, just as did all other large raptors. In the period from the 1890s until the 1914–18 war, breeding was regular only on the Norfolk Broads, where there were three or four nests each year. From this low ebb, numbers increased slowly in East Anglia and half a dozen other counties in S England and S Wales, until in the 1930s there were perhaps 15–25 pairs nesting annually; the species had perhaps never been very much commoner than this.

Whether the cause was climatic, respite from gamekeepers during the 1939–45 war, or the increase in afforestation, there was a sudden upsurge of numbers in the late 1940s and early 1950s. At this time, the centre of population shifted from East Anglia (the former Norfolk Broads stronghold was deserted in 1957) to SW England, from the New Forest westwards. Breeding also occurred then in a good many other counties (though irregularly in most) north to Anglesey in the west and Northumberland in the east, as well as in central and SW Scotland; and from

1955 onwards one or two pairs have nested sporadically in Ireland. By the mid-1950s there were estimated to be at least 40–50 (and perhaps 70–80) pairs breeding annually, with up to 20 of them in Devon and Cornwall (Nicholson 1957, Brown 1964).

Montagu's Harriers seem to have a mobile population which may be difficult to follow from year to year. Nevertheless, it is clear that a steady and continuing decline soon followed the mid-1950s' peak; by 1968 there were only nine pairs in the Devon-Cornwall stronghold. Most of the *Atlas* dots probably date from that year, after which the decline accelerated and Devon was deserted; thus, the map greatly exaggerates the current status of the Montagu's Harrier. Not unnaturally, ornithologists are somewhat secretive about this species, but published records for the most recent five-year period are as follows:

1970 5–8 pairs. Nests were found in Cornwall (2), Hampshire, Norfolk and E Yorkshire; while single pairs summered, without proof of breeding, in Wales and at additional sites in Cornwall and Hampshire.

1971 4–6 pairs. Single pairs bred in Ireland, Norfolk, Hampshire and Cornwall; and birds summered at two other Cornish sites.

1972 5–6 pairs. Four pairs bred in Cornwall and one in Norfolk; a pair summered in S Lincolnshire without evidence of nesting.

1973 2–3 pairs. Two nests (both unsuccessful and one female was unmated) were found in Norfolk; a pair seen in Cornwall was not known to have bred.

1974 No confirmed nesting records anywhere, though single pairs were seen in early summer in Cornwall and Suffolk.

From this melancholy picture, one can conclude that the Montagu's Harrier is now our rarest diurnal bird of prey, and that there is a very real danger of breeding ceasing here altogether.

This species is afforded special protection in Great Britain under Schedule I of the Protection of Birds Act 1954–67.

Number of 10-km squares in which recorded:
  51 (1%)
Possible breeding 20 (39%)
Probable breeding 18 (35%)
Confirmed breeding 13 (25%)

Three dots have been moved by one 10-km square (as recommended by the Rare Breeding Birds Panel and R. F. Porter); within the shaded 100-km square, the dot is conventionally placed centrally (as recommended by Major R. F. Ruttledge and D. Scott)

References

BIJLEVELD, M. 1974. *Birds of Prey in Europe*. London.

BROWN, P. 1964. *Birds of Prey*. London.

NICHOLSON, E. M. 1957. The rarer birds of prey. Their present status in the British Isles. Montagu's Harrier. *Brit. Birds* 50: 146–147.

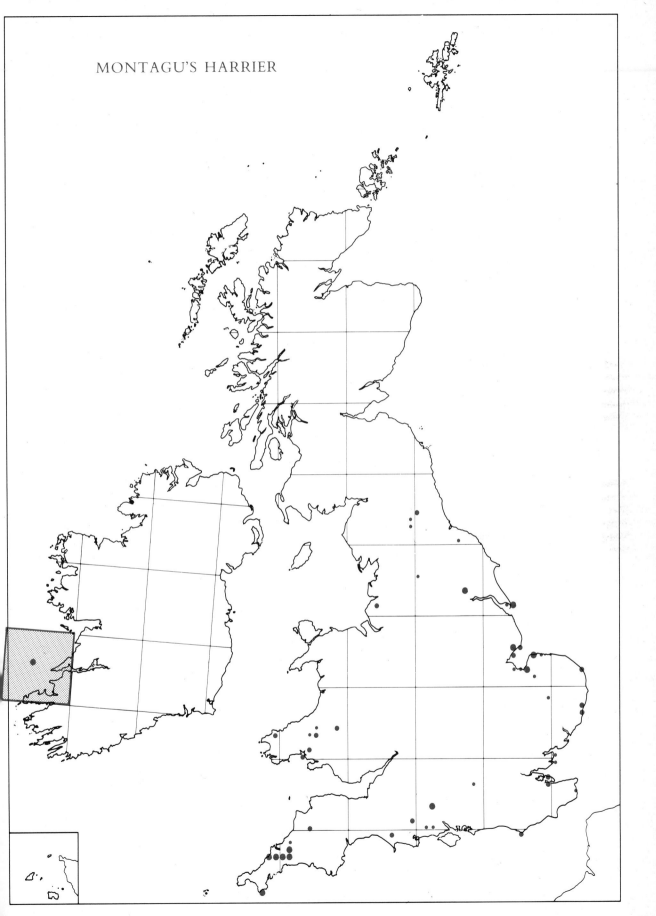

MONTAGU'S HARRIER

Osprey

Pandion haliaetus

Successful nesting by Ospreys depends upon the presence of open water that is suitably stocked with fish, and freedom from excessive human disturbance. Persecution is the chief factor responsible for the present irregular breeding distribution in Europe (Voous 1960). In Scandinavia, where the Osprey has managed to persist and even increase in the present century, new threats have arisen from toxic chemicals applied in agriculture and forestry, and mercurial compounds associated with the cellulose industry (Bijleveld 1974). The recent colonisation of Scotland, therefore, marks a bright spot in the general European scene.

Although Ospreys always nest in the general vicinity of water, the actual platform may be several kilometres away. Former Scottish sites included crags and ruins on islands or promontories in lochs, as well as trees, but all recent nests have been on the tops of conifers. Elsewhere in its wide range, the species nests in bushes, on telegraph poles and pylons, on specially provided cart-wheels affixed to stakes, and even on flat shingle and sand. The same eyrie may be used for many years, sticks being added annually until the platform reaches large proportions. Despite its considerable size, the nest can be remarkably inconspicuous, especially when a hillside or bog is clothed with a scatter of suitable trees. During the building and repairing phases, the adults may be seen carrying sticks to the nest. Similarly, throughout the incubation and first half of the fledging periods, when the male catches virtually all the fish and regularly hunts over the same stretch of water, he can be watched back to the nesting place. Great care must be taken, however, not to disturb this rare and sensitive raptor at the nest.

Ospreys bred commonly in Scotland well into the 19th century. Then, with the development of the gun and the increase in gamekeeping, they were widely persecuted as competitors for fish stocks, many estates placing a bounty on their heads. Nests were disturbed by egg- and skin-collectors, until the species was eliminated, the pair present and presumed to be nesting at Loch Loyne (Inverness-shire/Ross-shire) in 1916 probably being the last one.

In the 1950s there was an increase in the number of spring and summer records of Ospreys in Scotland, following an upsurge in the Scandinavian population in the previous decade. A pair probably raised two young at one site in 1954, but the record was not documented. Then, from 1955, the annual attempts of a pair to nest at Loch Garten (Inverness-shire) were thwarted by egg-collectors and disturbance by thoughtless birdwatchers, allowing Hooded Crows *Corvus corone cornix* to rob the nest. After four unsuccessful years, three young were raised in 1959, through a combination of the birds' persistence and the intensive wardening organised by the RSPB, who have continued to guard this site to the present day.

Recolonisation has continued steadily: at least seven pairs nested in 1971 and 1972 and birds were present at 16 or more sites in 1973, when ten pairs reared 21 young; and a similar number was recorded in 1974. The site at Loch Garten and, more recently, another at Loch of Lowes (Perthshire) are accessible to public viewing from hides. Over half a million people have taken advantage of these facilities and this has doubtless taken the pressure off other Osprey sites, thus encouraging the growth of the new Scottish population. Ringing recoveries show that a high proportion of Scottish-bred young fall victim to hunters when migrating south through Iberia and W Africa. The recolonisation has been linked by Williamson (1975) with a recent climatic change: the blocking anticyclone, which has been a feature of spring weather in NW Europe since the mid-1960s, displacing Scandinavian migrants to augment the Scottish stock; and he has shown a strong correlation between the rise in incidence of spring migrants since 1969–70 and the recent growth in the number of breeding pairs.

This species is afforded special protection in Great Britain under Schedule I of the Protection of Birds Act, 1954–67.

Number of 10-km squares in which recorded:
  24 (0.6%)

Possible breeding	13	(54%)
Probable breeding	4	(17%)
Confirmed breeding	7	(29%)

Within the shaded 100-km squares, the dots are conventionally placed centrally (except for NH91, the well known Loch Garten site) (as recommended by the Rare Breeding Birds Panel)

References

BIJLEVELD, M. 1974. *Birds of Prey in Europe*. London.

BROWN, P. and G. WATERSTON. 1962. *The Return of the Osprey*. London.

MEAD, C. J. 1973. Movements of British raptors. *Bird Study* 20: 259–286.

SANDEMAN, P. W. 1957. The rarer birds of prey. Their present status in the British Isles. Osprey. *Brit. Birds* 50: 147–149.

WATERSTON, G. 1966. *Ospreys in Speyside*. RSPB, Edinburgh.

WILLIAMSON, K. 1975. Birds and climatic change. *Bird Study* 22: 143–164.

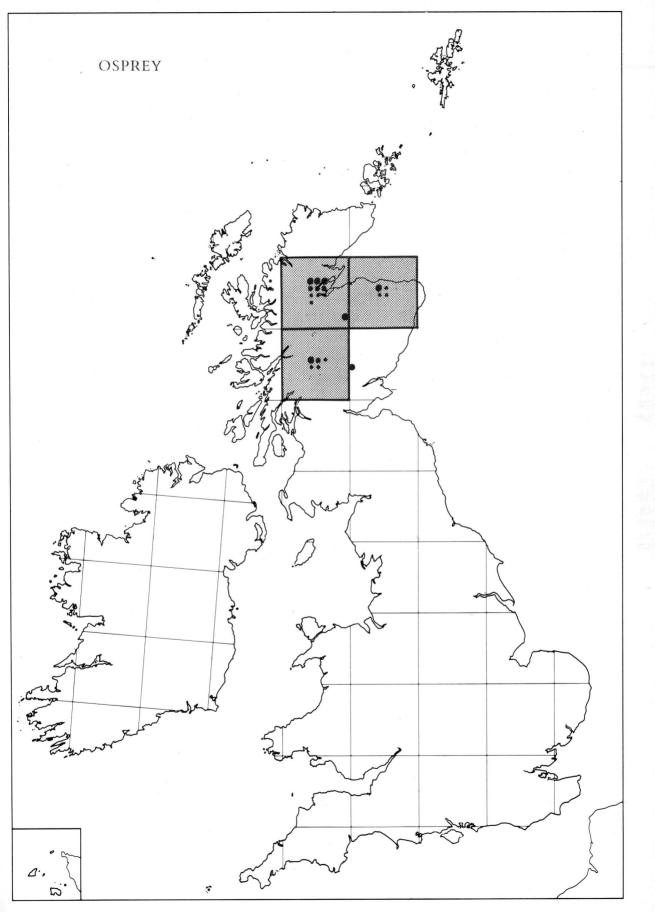

OSPREY

Hobby

Falco subbuteo

The Hobby, an attractive small falcon, is a trans-Saharan migrant which is present in its restricted breeding area for only five months of the year. A superb aerial performer, it is quite often seen during the summer in localities where none is known to nest, and it may be that such sightings involve roaming immatures summering in Britain but still too young to breed. Nevertheless, the *Atlas* map reveals quite a widespread breeding area, mainly in S England.

The Hobby has declined over Europe as a whole, but to a much lesser extent than the Peregrine *Falco peregrinus* and the Sparrowhawk *Accipiter nisus*. This difference may be attributed in part to the Hobby's diet, which is composed chiefly of large insects and small birds, particularly hirundines and Swifts *Apus apus*; it includes relatively few seed-eating birds, apart from Skylarks *Alauda arvensis* which are the staple food in some areas, so that there is a lower exposure to the toxic influences of chemicals.

Hobbies are found typically on the dry heaths and downlands of S England, where they require areas of open country for hunting, combined with isolated clumps, shelter-belts or tall trees in hedgerows for nest sites. Returning migrants often arrive late, usually not until May. Hobbies have a precise breeding season, most pairs laying in mid-June, hatching in mid-July, and fledging young in mid-August. Before laying, they engage in a varied pattern of aerobatic display flights, often incorporating food-passes, and this is a help in locating the nesting area. Later, the general position of the nest may be determined from the flight paths of the male carrying food, and the adults are usually very noisy with well-grown nestlings or newly fledged young.

The southern counties of Berkshire, Dorset, Hampshire, Surrey, Sussex and Wiltshire probably support more than three-quarters of the British population. Unoccupied nests of Carrion Crows *Corvus corone* in Scots pines provide a large proportion of the nesting sites. The open woods and heaths of the New Forest (Hampshire), which are free from the pressures of agrochemicals and gamekeeping, annually support

15–30 pairs. Elsewhere, Ministry of Defence training grounds on heaths and downs in Dorset, Wiltshire and Surrey, where public access is restricted, afford relatively unmolested haunts.

Outside the main breeding range, mixed farmland is the chief substitute habitat. Few pairs apparently nest north of a line from the Wash to the Severn, though in the past there has been sporadic breeding in Wales, N England, and once Scotland (Perthshire 1887). Location of farmland pairs is difficult, however, and it seems likely that some are overlooked, for suitable habitat is extensive and of a kind unlikely to attract ornithologists.

It is the Hobby's misfortune to have attractive eggs, prized by collectors. The species has been persistently robbed since the 19th century, despite recent legal protection. Females will often lay again if robbed early in the season, however, which could explain how the species has been able to withstand this constant persecution. Without it there might have been a welcome extension of range, for the Breckland of East Anglia is apparently ideal country, yet there has been only a handful of breeding records there in this century, and none during 1968–72. The scatter of records in Speyside (Inverness-shire) hints at the intriguing possibility of future colonisation there, perhaps analogous with that of the Osprey *Pandion haliaetus* and other boreal species, for Hobbies nest farther north in Sweden and Finland than those seen in Scotland.

At present, the trend appears to be towards a slight increase, with a westerly extension of range. The first records of breeding in Cornwall were five in the 1960s up to 1966 (and at least one more since 1970), and there has been an increase in Devon since 1968. Hobbies were known to be present at 51 sites in 15 counties in 1973, excluding Sussex and Hampshire, and in 1974 presence was reported at about 98 sites in 17 counties. By no means all of these involved confirmed breeding but, bearing in mind the difficulties of locating isolated pairs, the present population is probably close to, or may exceed, 100 pairs.

This species is afforded special protection in Great Britain under Schedule I of the Protection of Birds Act, 1954–67.

Number of 10-km squares in which recorded:
  261 (7%)
Possible breeding   123 (47%)
Probable breeding   43 (16%)
Confirmed breeding   95 (36%)

Three dots have been moved by up to two 10-km squares (as recommended by the Rare Breeding Birds Panel and R. F. Porter)

References
BIJLEVELD, M. 1974. *Birds of Prey in Europe.* London.
BROWN, P. E. 1957. The rarer birds of prey. Their present status in the British Isles. Hobby. *Brit. Birds* 50: 149.
BROWN, P. 1964. *Birds of Prey.* London.
SHARROCK, J. T. R. *et al.* 1975. Rare breeding birds in the United Kingdom in 1973 and 1974. *Brit. Birds* 68: 5–23, 489–506.

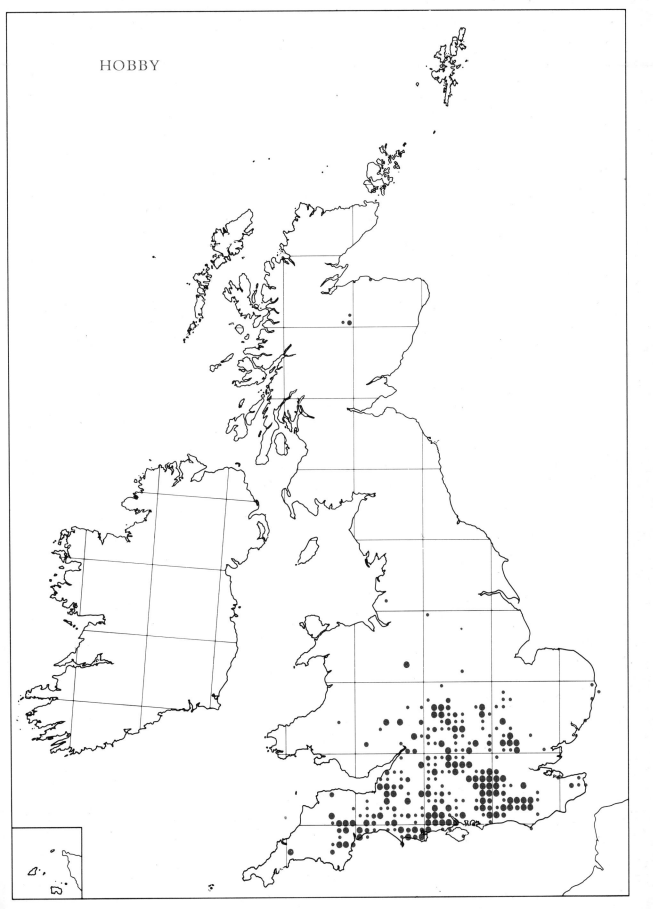

HOBBY

Peregrine

Falco peregrinus

Peregrines nest on inland crags and sea-cliffs, and occasionally on quarry faces. The adults are usually conspicuous and noisy around the nest site which, if used for several years, may have prominent green stains below it and thus be visible at considerable ranges. Cliff eyries are traditional and, in some cases, occupation can be traced back to mediaeval times; 41 out of 49 sites recorded in the 16th–19th centuries were still occupied in 1930–39.

In the Middle Ages, Peregrines were greatly prized for falconry and were protected by severe penalties. As sportsmen turned to guns, so persecution grew, but there is no evidence of a catastrophic decline such as affected some other raptors, perhaps because adult mortality in such a wide-ranging species was quickly made good by recruitment from areas where persecution was less intense. About 700 pairs bred in Britain and Ireland during 1930–39, and the total had probably been around this level since 1900.

Although the Peregrine has been recorded taking a wide range of bird prey, from Goldcrest *Regulus regulus* to Mallard *Anas platyrhynchos*, it feeds mostly on medium-sized birds, especially pigeons. The military use of the homing pigeon *Columba livia* during the 1939–45 war brought the Peregrine into conflict with the national interest in the United Kingdom. About 600 were shot and numerous eyasses and eggs destroyed. This action officially extended over the whole of the United Kingdom, but was most concentrated on the south coast of England.

In consequence, by 1944 the English population had been reduced to about 48% of its 1939–40 level, but it increased again to 65% by 1948–49 and 76% by 1955. The war-time decreases elsewhere had been less and had probably been made up by about 1955; indeed, in most parts of Scotland, the war years may even have been beneficial to Peregrines, giving them a respite from keepers' activities.

From about 1956, ornithologists detected a decline in breeding numbers. On the other hand, racing pigeon enthusiasts claimed that a growing Peregrine population was seriously affecting their sport. The Home Office asked the Nature Conservancy to institute an enquiry into its numbers, and this work was carried out by the BTO in 1961–62. The survey showed that the decline, first noticed in the south in about 1956, was real and had spread northwards. By 1961 there was only about 60%, and by 1962 only 50%, of the 1939 population left in Britain.

A characteristic pattern of failure, which included egg-breakage in the nest, infertile eggs and even inability to lay, often preceded disappearance or became habitual in such birds as remained. Further surveys in 1963–64 and 1965–66 suggested that the decline had been halted after a low ebb in 1963, with the level down to 44% of that in 1939, and only 16% of the pairs rearing young. A more comprehensive survey in 1971 revealed a slow recovery, the total then standing at 54% of the 1939 figure, with 25% rearing young. Sites which were regularly occupied in 1900–50, but where breeding was not confirmed in 1968–72, are mapped on page 456. The situation in Ireland paralleled that in N Britain, with about 70 pairs in the mid-1960s, compared with 190 in 1950, and 70% of known sites occupied in 1971.

Though at first there was heated controversy over the causes, it is now generally accepted that this dramatic decline was due primarily to the organochlorine pesticides accumulated by Peregrines from their prey. The current recovery probably results from partial bans on the use of some of these chemicals.

This species is afforded special protection in Great Britain under Schedule I of the Protection of Birds Act, 1954–67.

Number of 10-km squares in which recorded:
  634 (16%)
Possible breeding   202 (32%)
Probable breeding   104 (16%)
Confirmed breeding   328 (52%)

---

22 dots have been moved by one 10-km square; within the circle, dots are conventionally placed centrally (the recommendation of the Rare Breeding Birds Panel and Dr D. A. Ratcliffe was accurate plotting); in the Republic of Ireland, dots are conventionally placed within the shaded 100-km squares (as recommended by J. Temple Lang, Major R. F. Ruttledge and D. Scott)

References
FERGUSON-LEES, I. J. 1951. The Peregrine population of Britain. *Bird Notes* 24: 200–205, 309–314.
FERGUSON-LEES, I. J. 1957. The rarer birds of prey. Their present status in the British Isles. Peregrine. *Brit. Birds* 50: 149–155.
GILBERTSON, M. 1969. The distribution of the Peregrine Falcon in Northern Ireland. *Irish Nat. J.* 16: 131–133.
LANG, J. T. 1969. Peregrine survey—Republic of Ireland 1967–68. *Irish Bird Rep.* 16: 8–12.
RATCLIFFE, D. A. 1963. The status of the Peregrine in Great Britain. *Bird Study* 10: 56–90.
RATCLIFFE, D. A. 1965, 1967, 1972. The Peregrine situation in Great Britain. *Bird Study* 12: 66–82; 14: 238–246; 19: 117–156.

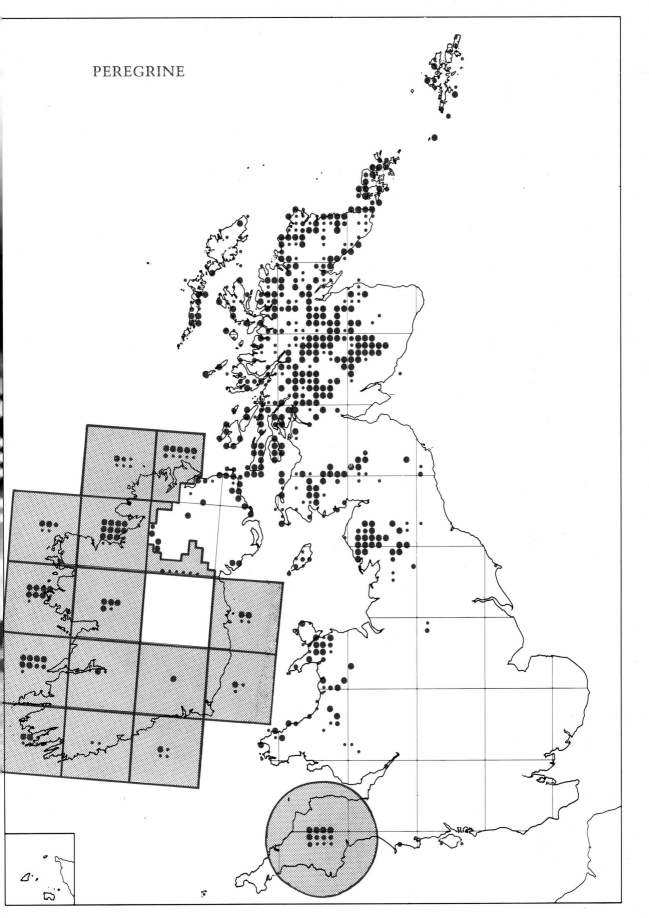

PEREGRINE

Merlin

Falco columbarius

Merlins are hunters of small birds on high moorland, fell country and extensive blanket-bog, though some nest locally in sand-dunes, on rough ground about sea-cliffs, and among trees along forest edges. The breeding distribution today reflects the preferred habitats, with no suitable tract of upland country entirely lacking the species. Thus, breeding was confirmed or suspected over much of Scotland (including most of the larger islands), N England south to the Peak District (Derbyshire/Staffordshire), Wales, Shropshire, and SW England (confirmed breeding only on Exmoor). The species is patchily but widely distributed in Ireland. The close proximity of new forestry plantations is attractive because the control of heather-burning leads to the deep growth favoured for nesting, while ploughing in preparation for planting concentrates the Meadow Pipits *Anthus pratensis* and other passerine birds which form its staple prey.

This tiny falcon is very elusive and the nest can be difficult to find, as is reflected by the high proportion of possible breeding records—nearly half of the total. The same section of moor or fell is often used year after year, though the actual nesting place may vary. Throughout the winter such high, open ground is practically birdless, and the Merlin usually moves to a lower altitude until an adequate abundance of prey is re-established in spring.

Once back on the breeding territory, the pair is relatively unobtrusive. Aerial displays are infrequent, but the male does make distinctive short flights between perches regularly uttering his characteristic high-pitched chatter. The birds hunt by means of low, dashing flights, grasping pipits, larks, chats and other small birds in mid-air. In the vicinity of the nest they may become unusually aggressive towards man, crows and other raptors. The nest is usually a scrape in a relatively bare patch among a moderate to thick cover of heather, less often bracken or grasses; it is characteristically, though not invariably, positioned on sloping ground or at the top of a hillock, where the incubating bird has a good view of the surrounding terrain. Old crows' nests in trees, in bushes and on platforms on low crags are sometimes occupied. Rock outcrops are often used as a look-out post by the off-duty bird.

Evidence bearing on the former status of the Merlin in Britain and Ireland is slender, but it was probably never very common. Despite feeding almost exclusively on small birds, the Merlin's affinity with grouse moors has inevitably meant persecution by gamekeepers, though perhaps to a lesser extent than other raptors. What little quantitative evidence exists is based largely on local opinion, but points to a slow and steady decline since about 1900, becoming most marked since about 1950, and affecting numbers throughout the range. This decline has been attributed mainly to a loss of satisfactory breeding areas (Prestt 1965). Afforestation of moorland and increasing disturbance by tourists and hill-walkers may be responsible for losses on moors in parts of Northumberland, Durham and Fife, the coastal dunes of S Wales, NW Devon, the mosses of S Lancashire and some places in Ireland. Merlins have been lost as breeding birds from many other apparently suitable areas, however, and other factors are clearly operating. The regular winter movement of Merlins to lowland areas, particularly coastal farmland, may be significant, since they feed largely by harrying the winter flocks of finches, buntings, pipits and larks, and are then exposed to the risk of accumulating toxic residues from such prey (Newton 1973).

Any estimate of the total number of breeding Merlins is not easy because of the high proportion of 'possible' records. Since the bird is easily overlooked, it may be permissible to allow an average of one breeding pair for every 10-km square in which a Merlin was seen in suitable breeding habitat during 1968–72, but even this would give a total of less than 850 pairs. Parslow suggested about 500 pairs. Probable or confirmed breeding was established in over 400 10-km squares, and some of these certainly held more than one pair, so the 1968–72 population may have been about 600–800 pairs.

This species is afforded special protection in Great Britain under Schedule I of the Protection of Birds Act, 1954–67.

Number of 10-km squares in which recorded:
  843 (22%)
Possible breeding   402 (48%)
Probable breeding   159 (19%)
Confirmed breeding   282 (33%)

Though some records were originally submitted in confidence, all dots are now shown accurately (as recommended by the Rare Breeding Birds Panel)

References
NEWTON, I. 1973. Egg breakage and breeding failure in British Merlins. *Bird Study* 20: 241–244.
PRESTT, I. 1965. An enquiry into the recent breeding status of some of the smaller birds of prey and crows in Britain. *Bird Study* 12: 196–221.

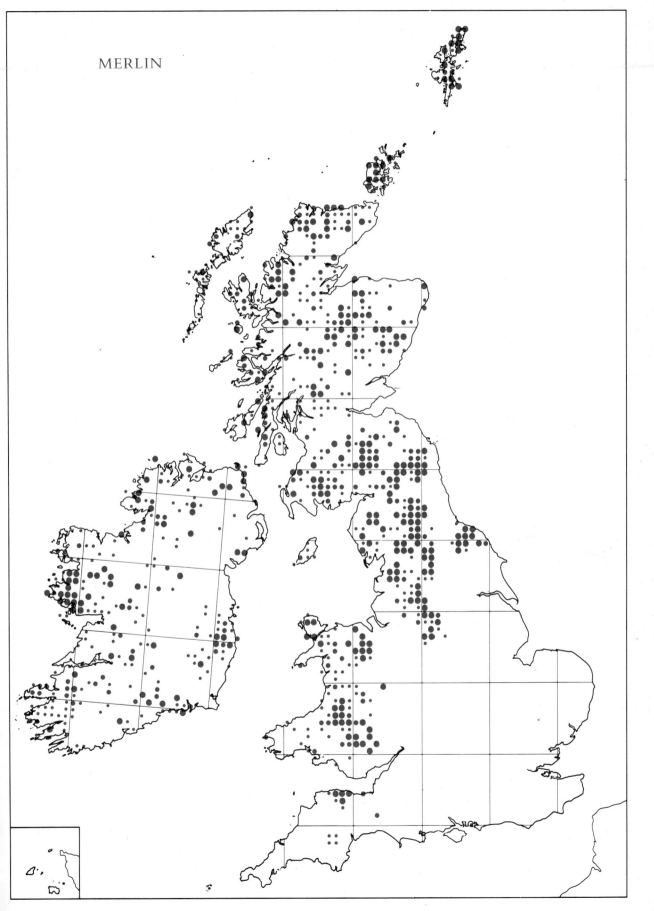

MERLIN

Kestrel

Falco tinnunculus

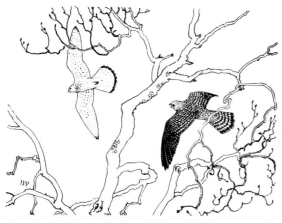

The Kestrel is the most widespread and numerous raptor in Britain, though locally it may be outnumbered by the Sparrowhawk *Accipiter nisus*, which is probably the commonest raptor in Ireland, or by the Buzzard *Buteo buteo*. Kestrels breed in such a wide variety of habitats—woods, moors, sea-cliffs, islands, farmland, parks and even the centres of cities —that there are few parts of Britain and Ireland where they do not occur. Kestrels were recorded in over 90% of the squares during 1968–72, the main areas of absence being Shetland (where they last nested in the late 19th or early 20th century) and much of the Outer Hebrides. Their choice of nest site is catholic, including holes in trees, ledges and holes of cliffs, quarries and even tall buildings, and disused nests of other birds (especially crows). In some places they also nest on the ground.

In certain areas the population fluctuates according to the numbers of Short-tailed Voles, their main prey in Britain, so that long-term trends are not easy to detect (see graph). In Ireland and the Isle of Man, where voles do not occur, the Wood Mouse is the staple diet. Urban Kestrels prey largely on small birds.

Decreases in the number of Kestrels were detected, mainly in the E English counties, from about 1956 onwards, an exception being pockets of mainly non-agricultural land within these areas—*eg* the Broads and Breckland in East Anglia (Cramp 1963, Prestt and Bell 1966). There was a coincident decline in parts of Ireland. Post-mortem tests confirmed certain per-sistent organochlorine pesticides as the cause of death and, as in the cases of the Sparrowhawk and the Peregrine *F. peregrinus*, the use of these pesticides was considered to be responsible for the decline. Other hazards are persecution by gamekeepers (though this is far less severe now than formerly) and the species' popularity with novice falconers who take some young birds for training, a practice which is both regrettable and illegal.

The lack of confirmed breeding records in much of the fen country of E England suggests that Kestrels are very scarce here: this may in part result from a continuing decrease due to certain agricultural pesticides, but it may also reflect a loss of habitat over a wide region of intensive arable farming. In such places, with large fields and few trees, the provision of nest-boxes on poles, as in the Netherlands and elsewhere on the Continent, would be advantageous to this wholly useful species. One recent change has been beneficial: Kestrels have taken to hunting over the broad, grassy verges of motorways.

The low density of dots in the W Highlands reflects the scarcity which is apparent even to the casual observer in this mountain and moorland region. This may be related to the high precipitation's adversely affecting both the Kestrel's hunting technique and the above-ground activity of its prey.

Taking all Common Birds Census areas, there was an average of 75 pairs of Kestrels per 10-km square in 1972. Even if the density over the whole of Britain and Ireland was about half of this figure, the total would be at or above the upper limit of Parslow's 10,000–100,000 pairs.

Number of 10-km squares in which recorded:
3,546 (92%)
Possible breeding   452 (13%)
Probable breeding   450 (13%)
Confirmed breeding   2,644 (75%)

References

CRAMP, S. 1963. Toxic chemicals and birds of prey. *Brit. Birds* 56: 124–139.

PRESTT, I. 1965. An enquiry into the recent breeding status of some of the smaller birds of prey and crows in Britain. *Bird Study* 12: 196–221.

PRESTT, I. and A. A. BELL. 1966. An objective method of recording breeding distribution of common birds of prey in Britain. *Bird Study* 13: 277–283.

SNOW, D. W. 1968. Movements and mortality of British Kestrels *Falco tinnunculus*. *Bird Study* 15: 65–83.

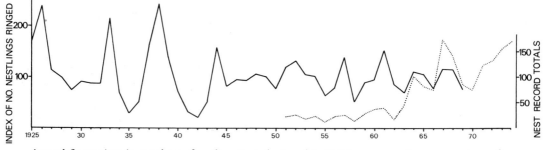

Annual fluctuations in numbers of nestling Kestrels ringed in Britain, expressed as a percentage of an 11-year sliding average (solid line), and numbers of nest record cards returned (broken line)

KESTREL

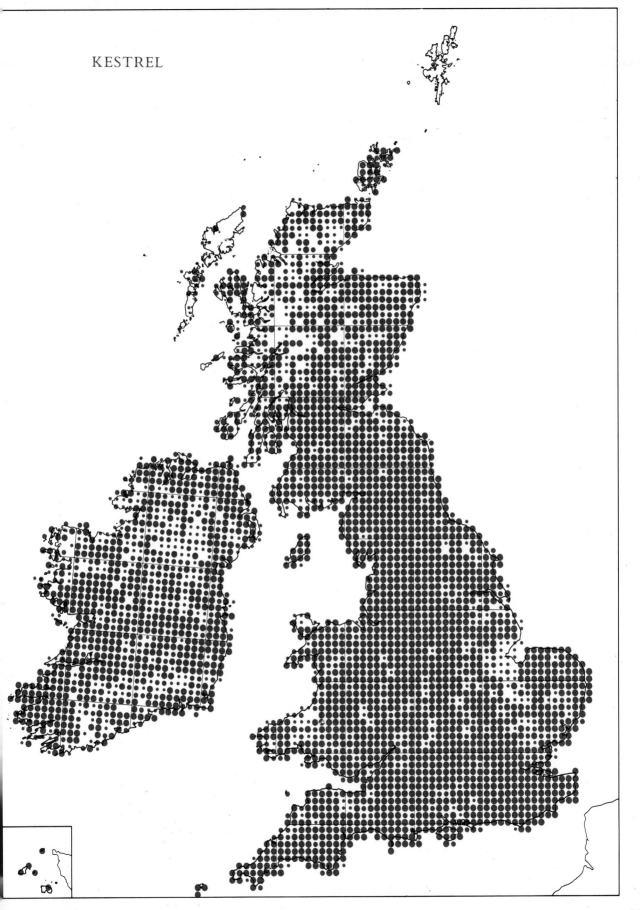

Red Grouse

Lagopus lagopus

The Red Grouse was once considered to be the only species entirely restricted to these islands. It is now, however, regarded merely as a distinct race, *L. l. scoticus*, of the Willow Grouse or Willow Ptarmigan, with a range extending across America and Eurasia.

The Red Grouse is characteristic of open, treeless moorland dominated by heather, but with crowberry and bilberry providing alternative foods. In the wetter climates of W Ireland and W Scotland (and locally in Wales) it occurs also on blanket-bog with sparse heather, or among patches of heather in otherwise grassy areas. There are hills in the Cairngorms where heather occurs up to 900 m in sheltered places, while arctic-alpine vegetation flourishes down to 600 m on exposed slopes; in such uplands Red Grouse may overlap altitudinally with Ptarmigan *L. mutus*, though their differing ecological requirements keep them separate (Watson 1966). The number on any particular moor is determined by the underlying substrate. Densities are highest over base-rich rocks (such as diorite and epidiorite) which influence soil fertility and consequently the nutrient quality of the heather; on such ground there may be up to 50–60 pairs per km², which is as high a figure as can be achieved on artificially managed moors (Jenkins and Watson 1967). Conversely, there are fewer grouse in natural circumstances on ground which overlies granite or thick peat; in Co Mayo there may be as few as one pair per 60 ha (Watson and O'Hare 1973). Grouse moors lie mostly between 300 and 600 m, but can range from sea-level to 800 m.

Attempts to introduce Red Grouse to Exmoor in the early 1820s were a failure, though further introductions there and on Dartmoor in 1915–16 were successful. Their presence in SW England probably represents the only major change in this century.

Numbers have decreased markedly in Ireland since about 1920, and in Britain since about 1940, following a very productive period between the two wars. Concern about this state of affairs led to the establishment of the Nature Conservancy Unit of Grouse and Moorland Ecology, which has been studying the species intensively since the late 1950s. Though landowners thought initially that disease and predation were responsible for the big drop in 'bags', it is now known that these factors affect only the non-breeding surplus remaining after the shooting season. The breeding population of a moor is determined by the number of cocks holding territories, and birds which fail to secure territories are driven into marginal areas where, progressively weakened and exposed to predators, such as Foxes and Golden Eagles *Aquila chrysaetos*, they soon die. Being non-dispersive birds (80–90% die within $1\frac{1}{2}$ km of where they were ringed), the surplus does not move to other moors, and has been eliminated by April. The average annual mortality is about 65%.

In some districts, increased grazing by sheep and cattle has had a deleterious effect on the habitat; but it has been shown conclusively that the major reason for decline is deterioration of heather quality, itself related to a reduction in the number of keepers employed on grouse moors. In order to hold a large number of grouse a moor must be carefully managed; this may involve the application of fertilisers, drainage where there is excessive water-logging, and above all rotational burning to ensure a continuous succession of young heather shoots. But the balance between burnt and unburnt ground is critical, since old, deep heather is needed for shelter and nesting.

Human disturbance, now increasing due to tourism, appears to have little adverse effect (Picozzi 1971); nor is there any evidence that climatic factors have depressed the food supply. There were suspicions that the decline of the Irish stock (formerly regarded as a separate race *L. l. hibernicus*) resulted from an inherent loss of vigour, despite frequent introductions of Scottish birds, but this has been disproved experimentally, according to Watson and O'Hare (1973). Although there are many large areas of Britain and some in Ireland where the needs of the Red Grouse have shaped the way man manages the land, there may now be fewer than half a million breeding pairs.

Number of 10-km squares in which recorded:
1,503 (39%)
Possible breeding   161 (11%)
Probable breeding   204 (14%)
Confirmed breeding   1,138 (76%)

References

JENKINS, D. and A. WATSON. 1967. Population control in Red Grouse and Rock Ptarmigan in Scotland. *Finn. Game Res.* 30: 121–141.

JENKINS, D., A. WATSON and G. R. MILLER. 1967. Population fluctuations in the Red Grouse *Lagopus lagopus scoticus*. *J. Anim. Ecol.* 36: 97–122.

PICOZZI, N. 1971. Breeding performance and shooting bags of Red Grouse in relation to public access in the Peak District National Park, England. *Biol. Conserv.* 3: 211–215.

WATSON, A. 1966. Hill birds of the Cairngorms. *Scott. Birds* 4: 179–203.

WATSON, A. and P. J. O'HARE. 1973. Experiments to increase Red Grouse stocks and improve the Irish bogland environment. *Biol. Conserv.* 5: 41–44.

YALDEN, D. W. 1972. The Red Grouse (*Lagopus lagopus scoticus*) in the Peak District. *Naturalist* 922: 89–102.

RED GROUSE

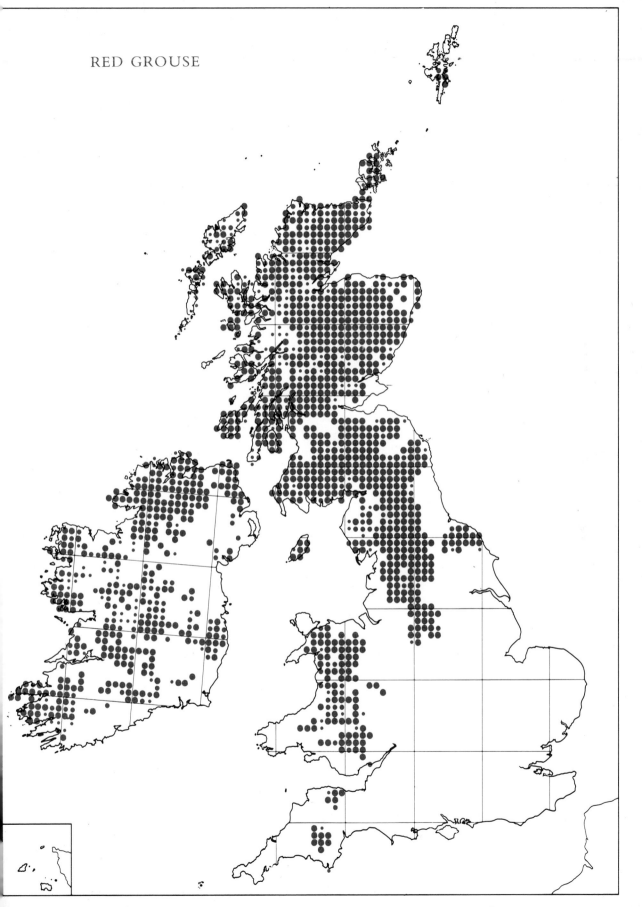

Ptarmigan

Lagopus mutus

The Ptarmigan is confined to the arctic-alpine heath in the Scottish Highlands, where abundant growth of bilberry and crowberry, often mixed with heather, provides the bulk of its food. The altitudinal zone varies considerably, since the arctic-alpine heath descends to lower levels in N and NW Scotland than in the Cairngorms and Grampians of the central Highlands. Ptarmigan may be found from 760 to 1,240 m in the Cairngorms, but as low as 180–300 m near Cape Wrath (Sutherland).

The problem in locating Ptarmigan is usually a matter of reaching their breeding grounds, rather than of finding them once there. While many *Atlas* fieldworkers made the necessary climbs, the data mapped also include observations supplied by gamekeepers and mountaineers. The map agrees so closely with the one published by Watson (1965) that it would be superfluous to reprint the latter.

The males occupy territories as soon as the ground is free of snow, defending them with threats, fighting and aerial chases, as well as by beating the bounds or, as Watson (1965) described it, 'walking parallel to their neighbours in prolonged disputes along the boundaries'. In display, they mount steeply upwards, and then descend, croaking, on rapidly beating wings. Breeding males secure large territories, while less vigorous individuals must make do with small ones and remain unmated. The females lay in early May in good years, but towards the end of the month in poor years; the species rarely calls and is reluctant to fly at this time. The males keep watch and lead away intruders; they usually desert when the family is a few days old, but may rejoin it before the young fledge. Breeding success is no better at low than at high densities, or in good than in bad summers despite the higher average clutch size then (7–8 eggs compared with 4–6 in poor years). Snowstorms and cold, wet June days cause high chick mortality. Broods break up between August and October and large winter flocks, sometimes over 100 strong, are formed.

Today, the most southerly outpost of the Ptarmigan is Ben Lomond (Stirlingshire); formerly, the species was more widespread, breeding on the hills of SW Scotland until 1830, and in the Isles of Arran and Rhum. It ceased to breed in the Outer Hebrides in 1938. There is no evidence of range contraction on the mainland, except in the very south. Numbers are known to fluctuate: the species was abundant in the years around 1923, 1934 and 1940, and Watson (1965) considered that the area of suitable habitat is so restricted in the far south and west that local extinctions are likely in years when the population is low. Watson (1972), however, has suggested that the early 19th century increase in sheep grazing may have had an important effect on the hills of SW Scotland, reducing the Ptarmigan's food plants below the level required to maintain a viable group. Reintroductions have been attempted, but have not been successful.

Within the main range, Scotland provides a favourable habitat. The evidence given by A. Watson shows that the density is much lower in the sub-arctic environment of Iceland, and lower still in arctic regions. An appendix to his 1965 paper gives a detailed distribution in Scotland, county by county. The densest recorded population is on the high ground of Aberdeenshire; but Sutherland, Ross-shire, Inverness-shire, Banffshire and Perthshire also have good numbers. He estimated that the spring breeding population in the Cairngorms massif may vary from 1,300 birds in a poor year to 5,000 in a good one, with about 15,000 in a peak autumn.

The high exposed road to Applecross (W Ross) crosses good Ptarmigan country, but probably much the easiest places to see the species nowadays are in the neighbourhood of ski-lifts at Cairngorm and Cairnwell. The rapid growth of tourism in Scotland has already brought skiers, climbers and hill-walkers into the Ptarmigan's haunts, but the birds on the high tops are confiding and there is no evidence that human pressures have had an adverse effect. Eventually, excessive trampling in the vicinity of the ski-lifts may damage the vegetation irreparably, but there will still be vast areas over which the Ptarmigan and its main predators, the Fox and Golden Eagle *Aquila chrysaetos*, can live their lives undisturbed.

Parslow placed the Ptarmigan in his category 10,000–100,000 pairs. Even the lower limit of this range would necessitate an average of over 50 pairs per 10-km square, and this, in view of the limited area of suitable ground in many squares, seems likely to overestimate the situation in poor years.

Number of 10-km squares in which recorded:
195 (5%)
Possible breeding   33 (17%)
Probable breeding   24 (12%)
Confirmed breeding   138 (71%)

References

WATSON, A. 1965. Research on Scottish Ptarmigan. *Scott. Birds* 3: 331–349.

WATSON, A. 1966. Hill birds of the Cairngorms. *Scott. Birds* 4: 179–203.

WATSON, D. 1972. *Birds of Moorland and Mountain*. Edinburgh and London.

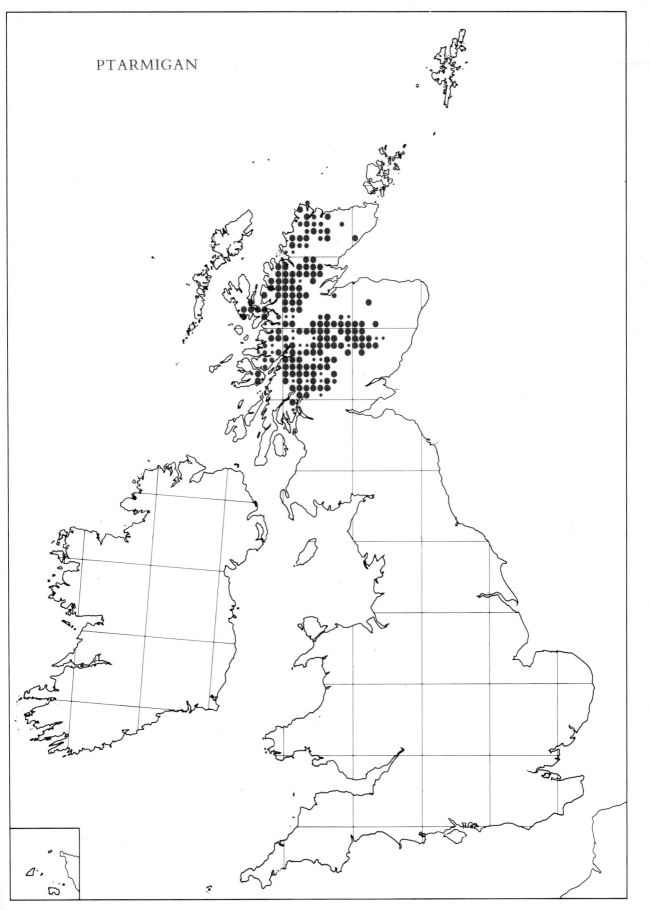

PTARMIGAN

Black Grouse

Lyrurus tetrix

The habitats of the Black Grouse include moorland dominated by heather but with some trees or scrub, bogs with rushes, conifer plantations up to 20 years old, mature open pine forest with heavy undergrowth, and open birch woodland. Optimum habitat appears to be a mosaic of these different types, and densities are highest in the interface between forest and moorland. Black Grouse often feed on adjoining marginal agricultural land. Rather few nest above 400 m, though the upper limit is about 600 m.

Early morning communal displays at leks announce the presence of Black Grouse; though the bubbling or crooning song of the cocks is soft, the combined sound carries a long way—400 m or more on a still day. Nevertheless, the species can be very retiring when at low density. As would be expected, most of the *Atlas* records of mere presence or probable breeding are from fringe areas where numbers are small; note, for instance, the low proportion (28%) of squares with confirmed breeding in Wales.

Black Grouse were formerly much more widespread, occurring east to Lincolnshire and Norfolk and south to Cornwall, Dorset and Hampshire; but they disappeared from many English counties in the late 19th and early 20th centuries (Gladstone 1924). There was a simultaneous decline in Scotland following a period of increase and abundance in the late 1880s and early 1890s (Rintoul and Baxter 1927). The reasons for this decline and range contraction, which are not well documented, are not understood; habitat changes due to man have been suggested, but probably this is not the whole story. Disappearances were hastened on the one hand by shooting, and masked on the other by attempted reintroductions. In Hampshire, to take just one example, the indigenous stock probably died out in 1909, but some are said to have been seen in 1918–19 and again in 1954, with a reputedly unsuccessful release in the 1930s.

The tide appears to have turned, however, increases having been noticed since the late 1940s in Wales and the 1950s in Scotland. Black Grouse are now present in many areas from which they were believed to be absent 30 years ago. The most widely held view is that this results from the greatly increased area of young afforestation since 1945; but Johnstone (1967) thought that the correlation might be more apparent than real, more Black Grouse being seen since foresters began to visit such areas regularly.

Deliberate restocking of some formerly occupied areas may have been a contributory factor. Indeed, it may be that the widespread distribution in the 19th century was partly an artifact resulting from local introductions and the planting of hawthorns to provide winter food. It is noteworthy that repeated introductions (or perhaps reintroductions) into Ireland in the 18th and 19th centuries always failed (Barrett-Hamilton 1899).

The small, isolated population on Exmoor (Somerset/Devon) may no longer be viable without periodic reinforcements by hand-reared birds, such as were made in 1969 and 1971. The species is thought to have become extinct on Dartmoor in the 1950s, but a nest was found in 1968; it is possible, however, that Exmoor birds wander to Dartmoor and breed there occasionally.

The Black Grouse, like the Capercaillie *Tetrao urogallus*, has a bad reputation among foresters because of the damage sometimes inflicted on growing trees by eating the buds and young shoots. Johnstone (1967) showed that heather was the most important item, especially in winter. Conifer buds and shoots comprised only a small part of the diet, and only locally did the damage reach a level where economic loss might result. Such depredations arose mainly when hard weather with heavy snowfalls cut short the natural supply and forced the grouse into plantations for food and shelter.

Parslow placed the Black Grouse in his category of 10,000–100,000 pairs. This would imply broad limits of 17–85 pairs per occupied 10-km square; and there can be little doubt that the real figures lie well within the lower halves of these ranges.

Number of 10-km squares in which recorded:
603 (16%)
Possible breeding   140 (23%)
Probable breeding   177 (29%)
Confirmed breeding   286 (47%)

References

BARRETT-HAMILTON, G. E. H. 1899. The introduction of the Black Grouse and of some other birds into Ireland. *Irish Nat.* 1899: 37–43.

GLADSTONE, H. S. 1924. The distribution of Black Grouse in Great Britain. *Brit. Birds* 18: 66–68.

JOHNSTONE, G. W. 1967. Blackgame and Capercaillie in relation to forestry in Britain. *Forestry Suppl.* 1967: 68–77.

RINTOUL, L. J. and E. V. BAXTER. 1927. On the decreases of Blackgame in Scotland. *Scott. Nat.* 1927: 5–13, 45–52, 69–75.

SITTERS, H. P. 1974. *Atlas of Breeding Birds in Devon.* Plymouth.

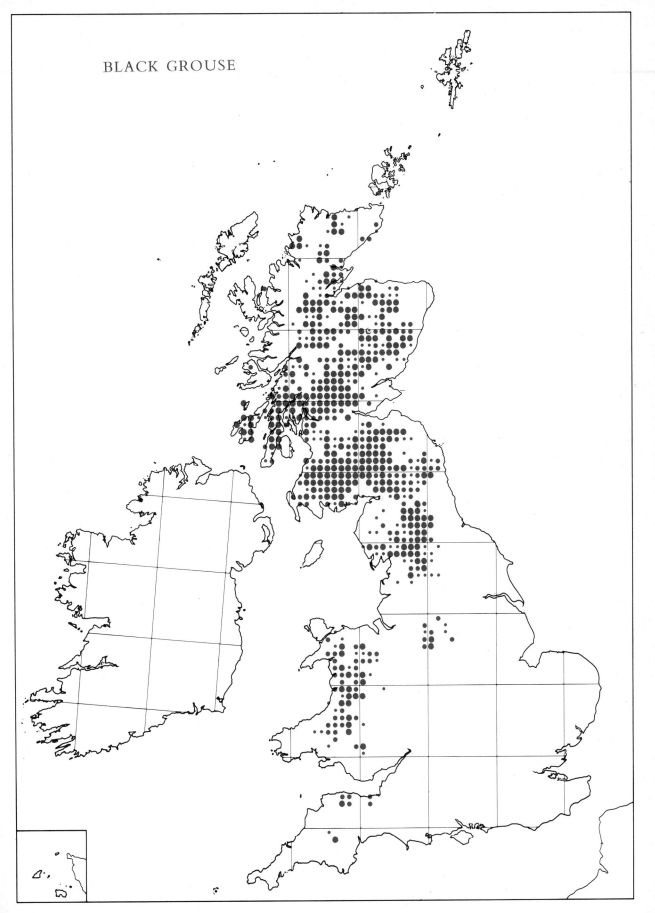

BLACK GROUSE

Capercaillie

Tetrao urogallus

The map shows that Capercaillies are confined almost entirely to E central Scotland, where they are the descendants of introduced stock. While their natural habitat is old woods of Scots pine, with a good undergrowth of heather and bilberry, interspersed with open glades, they now also frequent plantations of larch and spruce 20–30 years old, especially where there is some mixture with Scots pine.

The species was widespread and common in Scotland and Ireland (though absent from England) at the close of the 17th century, but the large-scale felling of natural pine forest had brought it to the verge of extinction in both countries by 1760. A few lingered until at least 1771 in the Abernethy and Glenmoriston forests (Inverness-shire), and the last known indigenous Scottish Capercaillies were shot on Deeside (Aberdeenshire) in 1785. It was at about this time (perhaps as late as 1790) that the Irish population became extinct. The largest reintroduction, of Swedish stock, was made by Lord Breadalbane at Taymouth Castle, Aberfeldy (Perthshire) in 1837–38, and since then the Capercaillie has recolonised much of its former ground, assisted by further successful reintroductions in Angus (1862–65), Kincardineshire (1870), Morayshire (1883) and Inverness-shire (1895), as well as other supplementary releases.

Today, the Capercaillie is present throughout the E Highlands from the Moray Firth to the upper reaches of the Forth, being particularly abundant in the valleys of the Spey, Don, Dee and Tay. There are outlying groups in suitable woods elsewhere, from near sea level in the Culbin Forest to altitudes of 450–460 m, but the species seems unable to establish permanent breeding haunts in the maritime climate zone of the W Highlands (Palmar 1965). Efforts at introduction in England and reintroduction in Ireland have always failed, but an attempt is currently being made in Grizedale Forest (N Lancashire), where 35 were released in 1971 and nesting was reported to have taken place in 1973 (Grant and Cubby 1973).

The history of the Scottish population was well documented by Harvie-Brown (1879) and Pennie (1950–51), and the 1879 and 1949 distribution maps are shown on page 456. The spread which followed reintroduction reached its maximum extent about 1914, but was then halted by the felling of timber on many private estates, particularly during the 1914–18 and 1939–45 wars. During the spread, females often preceded males into new areas, where they paired with male Black Grouse *Lyrurus tetrix*.

The cock Capercaillie's song is a curious mixture of brittle notes, cork-popping sounds and gobbling noises, delivered with distended throat-feathers, drooping wings and widely fanned tail. Several males may display together at a lek, visited by croaking females. The nest is usually between the exposed roots of a tree, but sometimes away from trees in heather, bilberry or juniper.

The establishment of the Forestry Commission in 1919 was a potential boon to this and other forest species, and in recent years the maturation of the early plantations, together with the growth of the forestry industry in general, have encouraged the Capercaillie's spread. Since most of its winter food comprises shoots, needles, seeds and young cones of Scots pine, larch and Douglas fir, its presence in commercial stands is a mixed blessing; happily, however, it is tolerated by the Forestry Commission and most private owners. Damage is most frequent in spring when the bursting buds and new shoots are eaten. Recovery from such attacks depends much on the vigour of the trees; in an actively growing stand there may be little trace of the depredations after five or six years, whereas thin, struggling plantations may suffer serious check (Palmar 1965).

These huge birds are sometimes caught unawares, but they are usually shy in the breeding season and can be surprisingly elusive when at a low density. Their presence is always known to foresters, gamekeepers and landowners, however, and much of the success of the *Atlas* survey, with nearly two-thirds of the records relating to proved breeding, is due to them.

March counts in 1965–66 in the Black Wood of Rannoch (Perthshire), one of the finest remnants of the old Caledonian forest, gave density figures approximating to 17–20 birds per km^2 (Johnstone and Zwickel 1966). Parslow put the species in the range 1,000–10,000 pairs.

Number of 10-km squares in which recorded:
182 (5%)
Possible breeding   48 (26%)
Probable breeding   18 (10%)
Confirmed breeding   116 (64%)

References

GRANT, W. and J. CUBBY. 1973. The Capercaillie reintroduction experiment at Grizedale. *WAGBI Rep. and Year Book* 1972–73: 96–99.

HARVIE-BROWN, J. A. 1879. *The Capercaillie in Scotland*. Edinburgh.

JOHNSTONE, G. W. and F. C. ZWICKEL. 1966. Numbers of Capercaillie in the Black Wood of Rannoch. *Brit. Birds* 59: 498–499.

PALMAR, C. E. 1965. *The Capercaillie*. Forestry Commission Leaflet no. 37.

PENNIE, I. D. 1950–51. The history and distribution of the Capercaillie in Scotland. *Scott. Nat.* 62: 65–87, 157–178; 63: 4–17, 135.

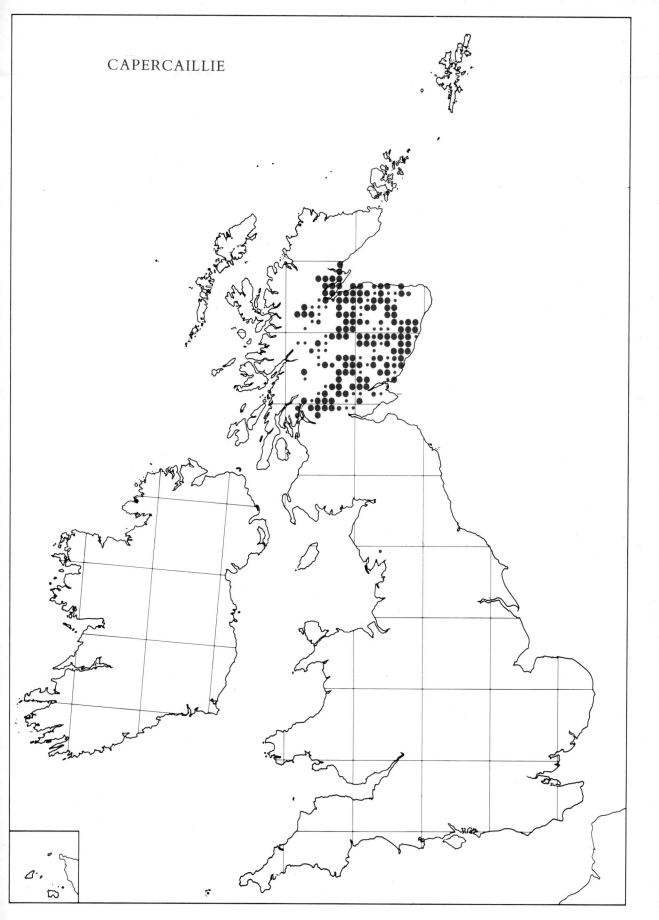

CAPERCAILLIE

Red-legged Partridge

Alectoris rufa

Red-legged Partridges are commonest on agricultural land, but they also occur on sandy heaths, chalk downland, coastal shingle and dunes, and occasionally in woods with large glades or wide rides. On the whole they prefer drier situations than Grey Partridges *Perdix perdix*: their ranges overlap to a large extent in England, but the aversion of Red-legs to areas of high rainfall is shown by their inability to become established in most parts of the north and west, despite various attempts to introduce them there.

This is not a native species, its British population being derived entirely from liberated stock and their progeny. The first recorded attempt at introduction was in 1673 and there were several others in Essex, Surrey and Sussex (possibly elsewhere) before the first real success in Suffolk in 1790. This was achieved with several thousand eggs imported from France for local hatching and rearing. Although subsequent colonisation stems from this source, over 60 further introductions between 1830 and 1958 are on record, mostly in England, but including Wales, Scotland, and at least once in Ireland (Galway). Such liberations still continue, with birds from commercial game-farms used to augment stocks. A series of releases in Scotland since 1972 has involved localities as far north as Caithness, and some have been turned down recently in the Isle of Man. In the final *Atlas* year (1972) it became known that game-farm stocks included the closely related Chukar *A. chukar* (*Brit. Birds* 65: 404–405). These, and *chukar* × *rufa* hybrids, have been released on some occasions, and have bred successfully in the wild, though they produce far fewer young than do pure Red-legged Partridges (G. R. Potts *in litt*). Such hybrids will usually not have been distinguished by *Atlas* fieldworkers.

There has been some antagonism from conservative sporting elements who hold that the Red-legged Partridge affords poor sport compared with the native Grey Partridge, and attempts have been made to eliminate it in a few areas. Numbers reached a maximum in about 1930, followed by a decline and slight contraction of range. This trend has reversed since about 1959, with some marked increases, especially in NW Norfolk. The distribution by 1972 was probably as widespread as it had ever been, and the Common Birds Census has shown that in recent years, within the main part of its range, this has been a more successful species than the Grey Partridge (see graph on page 142).

The 1968–72 map could be regarded as presenting the species' adopted range in England, since small-scale introductions outside the main part have always eventually failed. The proportion of confirmed breeding records is greatest from Lincolnshire south to London, thence eastwards through East Anglia, suggesting that this is the region where the bird is most numerous. There is confirmation in the returns made to the National Game Census, with average county bags of over 7.5 birds per km² only in that region, the highest total in 1961–62 being 36 birds per km² in Hertfordshire, though falling steeply to two or fewer per km² in the S England counties west of London.

East Anglia probably provides the optimum conditions of intensive agriculture in a continental type of climate. The soils are often sandy or calcareous and dry, and the rainfall is the lowest in Britain. The wetter, heavier soils of the Weald are shunned. Howells (1963) concluded that the distribution of Red-legged Partridges coincided with an annual rainfall of less than 35 inches (89 cm), and that a lower precipitation in the breeding season was favourable to chick survival.

Though remaining in cover rather more than Grey Partridges, Red-legs are easy to see when the crops are short in early spring, especially since they are noisy at that season. Clutches are often laid in two nests, so that male and female each raise a brood. Nests at the bottoms of hedges or in nettlebeds are not always easy to find, and proof of successful breeding comes most readily from seeing broods; in the event, proof was obtained for no less than 75% of occupied 10-km squares. From a count of these, the National Game Census figures and the average CBC figure in 1972 of 1.2 pairs per km², one may surmise a total population of between 100,000 and 200,000 pairs.

Number of 10-km squares in which recorded:
  919 (24%)
Possible breeding   124 (13%)
Probable breeding   109 (12%)
Confirmed breeding   686 (75%)

References

ANON. 1971. National Game Census. *Game Conserv. Ann. Rev.* 1970: 19–22.

BLANK, T. H. and R. P. BRAY. 1970. The National Game Census. *Game Conserv. Ann. Rev.* 1969/70: 30–37.

HOWELLS, G. 1963. The status of the Red-legged Partridge in Britain. *Game Res. Assoc. Ann. Rep.* 2: 46–51.

POTTS, G. R. 1970. Recent changes in the farmland fauna with special reference to the decline of the Grey Partridge. *Bird Study* 17: 145–166.

POTTS, G. R. 1972. Factors governing the chick survival rate of the Grey Partridge (*Perdix perdix*). *Actes Congr. Int. Biol. Gibier Xe, Paris May 1971*: 85–96.

POTTS, G. R. 1973. Pesticides and the fertility of the Grey Partridge, *Perdix perdix. Reprod. Fert.*, suppl. 19: 391–402.

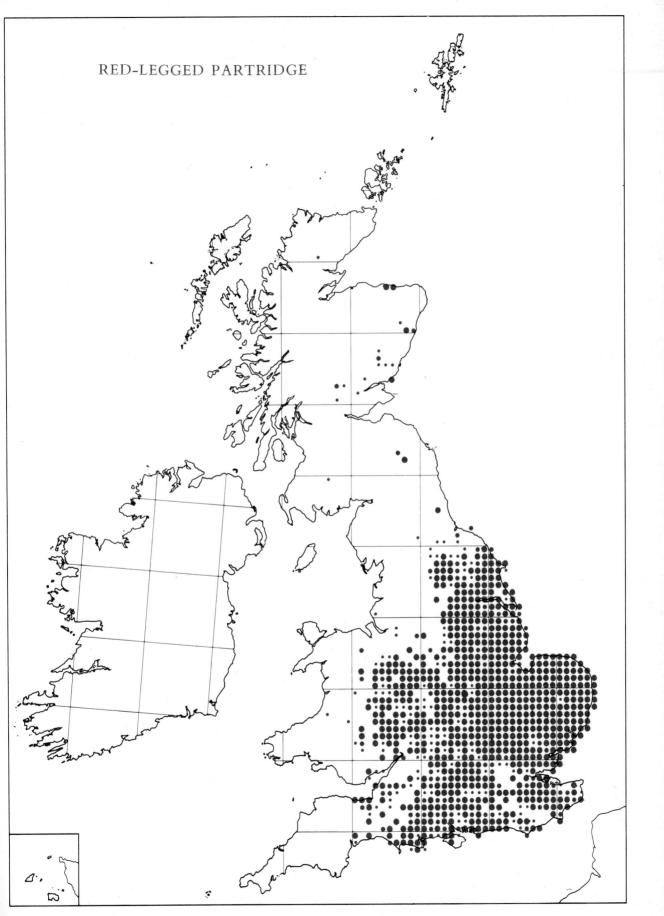

RED-LEGGED PARTRIDGE

Partridge

Perdix perdix

Although found principally in areas of mixed cultivation where hedgerows and some marginal cover remain, the native Partridge (now usually referred to as the Grey Partridge) breeds regularly on moorland up to an altitude of 500 m. It also occurs in rough pasture and on heaths, commons, sand-dunes and brecks, and even on allotments and other open land in the suburban zone.

The map shows that the Grey Partridge still has a widespread and almost continuous distribution in England, despite having been on the decline for a long period. It is rare or absent over large areas only in W Scotland and parts of Wales, and in Ireland where the decline started in the 19th century. By the 1920s the Irish decline was so serious that protective legislation prohibiting or restricting shooting of Grey Partridges was introduced in 1930; without this, and also restocking, the species would probably have become extinct there. Even now, it is very sparsely distributed and scarcer than the map suggests, with only a few pairs in many of the occupied squares in the west and west midlands of Ireland. The decrease in England became particularly evident during the 1960s and has been measured by spring counts carried out by the Game Research Association and the Common Birds Census (see graph). The causes of this continuing fall in numbers are complex. Changes in agricultural practice, such as stubble-burning and autumn ploughing, and the greater application of insecticides and herbicides, are partly to blame; but the recent run of cold, late springs has also been detrimental to the survival of young. Potts (1970) has shown that the Grey Partridge's nesting is not adjusted to late springs, so that in most recent years there has been a shortage of food, particularly arthropods, for the newly hatched young. The situation has been aggravated because tenthredinid sawfly larvae, one of the staple foods at this season, are much scarcer than formerly as a result of soil disturbance by autumn ploughing.

As well as short-term variables such as chick survival and shooting pressure, land use and altitude are important factors affecting numbers of Grey Partridges. High densities occur on land providing plenty of cover in early spring, but lower ones where there are large areas under plough and on upland farms. The type of field boundary is also critical, with the greatest number of nests where there are low incomplete hedges (Southwood and Cross 1969). The highest densities and best nesting success are on farms comprising a mosaic of small fields; the modern practices of removing hedges and grassy tracks and sowing large areas of spring corn are, thus, detrimental to Grey Partridges.

Presence in March is a good indication that a territory has been established; the nest site is selected by the female in April and the eggs usually laid late in that month. At this time, nests can be found by looking for tracks through the vegetation or watching the female in the early morning, as she moves directly to the nest when she has finished feeding.

The Common Birds Census shows densities varying from 1.6 pairs per km² on a Dorset dairy farm to 7.2 pairs per km² on Suffolk arable; in 1972 the average density for farmland plots was 2.76 pairs per km². This species is likely to be underestimated, however, because observers usually may not wander at will into crop fields. Densities of 40 pairs per km² have been reported from managed estates in Hampshire and East Anglia (Blank and Ash 1962). Basing an estimate on these counts, the total British and Irish population could reach or even exceed 500,000 pairs.

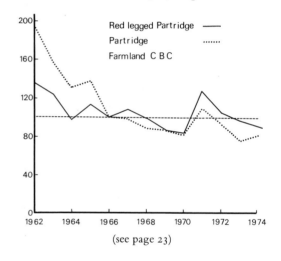

(see page 23)

Number of 10-km squares in which recorded:
2,261 (59%)
Possible breeding   168 (7%)
Probable breeding   156 (7%)
Confirmed breeding   1,937 (86%)

References

BLANK, T. H. and J. S. ASH. 1962. Fluctuations in a Partridge population. pp 118–130 in LECREN, E. D. and M. W. HOLDGATE (eds), *The Exploitation of Natural Animal Populations*. Oxford.

POTTS, G. R. 1970. Recent changes in the farmland fauna with special reference to the decline of the Grey Partridge. *Bird Study* 17: 145–166.

SOUTHWOOD, T. R. E. and D. J. CROSS. 1969. The ecology of the Partridge. III. Breeding success. *J. Anim. Ecol.* 38: 497–509.

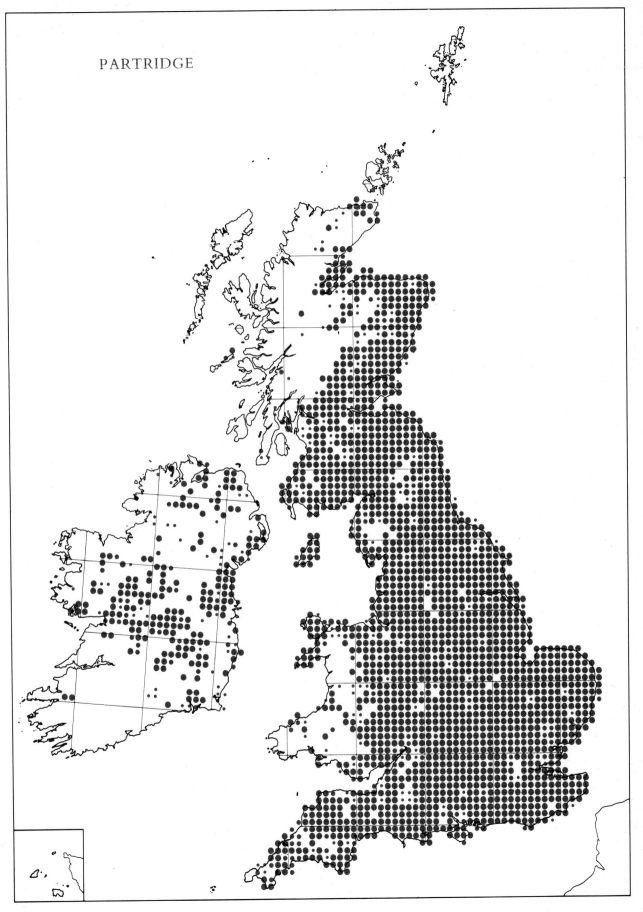

PARTRIDGE

Quail

Coturnix coturnix

The Quail is found in all kinds of herbaceous vegetation in open country, from rough tussocky grassland to hay fields and cereal crops, but in Britain and Ireland the most frequented habitats are corn and hay fields. A comparison of the Quail map with that of the distribution of calcareous soils (see overlay) shows clearly, for S England at least, the known preference of the species for rolling chalk downland. The large open fields on the chalk may present warmer and drier conditions than those in the surrounding lowland. There is a strong tendency for Quails to concentrate in small areas, late males presumably being attracted by the calling of earlier arrivals.

Quails were probably common in Britain and Ireland until the end of the 18th century. A decline in Britain in the first half of the 19th century contrasted strangely with a progressive increase in Ireland at that time, until they were said to be ten times commoner there than in England. Overwintering in Ireland was so frequent that the species was regarded as a resident. A reversal, the cause of which is unknown, started in about 1865, and in this century Quails have actually been rarer in Ireland than Britain. Agricultural changes may have had a deleterious effect, but earlier grass cutting, which is certainly detrimental to successful nesting, should have been counterbalanced by an increased acreage of corn. Quails have always been prized for food, and perhaps the increasing use of firearms against migrants passing through the poorer countries of S Europe has contributed to the decline.

Though there were some years of abundance (*eg* 1870 and 1893), the Quail was at a very low level in both Britain and Ireland between the 1860s and about 1942, since when there has been an upward trend. About twice as many were recorded in 1947 as in any previous year in this century; 1953 saw an even greater number, at least double that of 1947, while another invasion in 1964 produced about twice as many records as in 1953, with well over 600 individuals heard calling. In the *Atlas* period, 1970 was another good year, probably equalling 1964. These occasional invasions are not fully understood, but appear to be associated with warm, dry springs and SE winds.

Most records in Britain and Ireland refer to males calling at dusk or dawn. This is by no means an indication of breeding, however, since unmated males may move considerable distances (40 km or more) and it seems that calling ceases once pairing has taken place. Such records, treated here as probable breeding, made up 60% of those obtained during 1968–72. Proved breeding came almost entirely from a few sightings of broods or nests cut out during farming activities, and made up only 15%.

The *Atlas* map, including as it does one of the best years for the Quail this century (1970), and also combining the records from the four other years, exaggerates the normal distribution. A comparison of the main map with the inset map of the records in 1968–69 and 1971–72 shows the areas from which the species is absent in normal years.

This species is afforded special protection in Great Britain under Schedule I of the Protection of Birds Act, 1954–67.

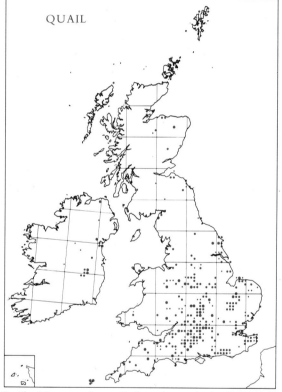

Quail *Atlas* records, excluding those obtained in 1970, which was a 'Quail year'

Number of 10-km squares in which recorded:
  438 (11%)
Possible breeding   110 (25%)
Probable breeding   262 (60%)
Confirmed breeding   66 (15%)

References
MOREAU, R. E. 1951. The British status of the Quail and some problems of its biology. *Brit. Birds* 44: 257–276.
MOREAU, R. E. 1956. Quail in the British Isles, 1950–53. *Brit. Birds* 49: 161–166.

Bob-white Quail *Colinus virginianus*, **see page 451**

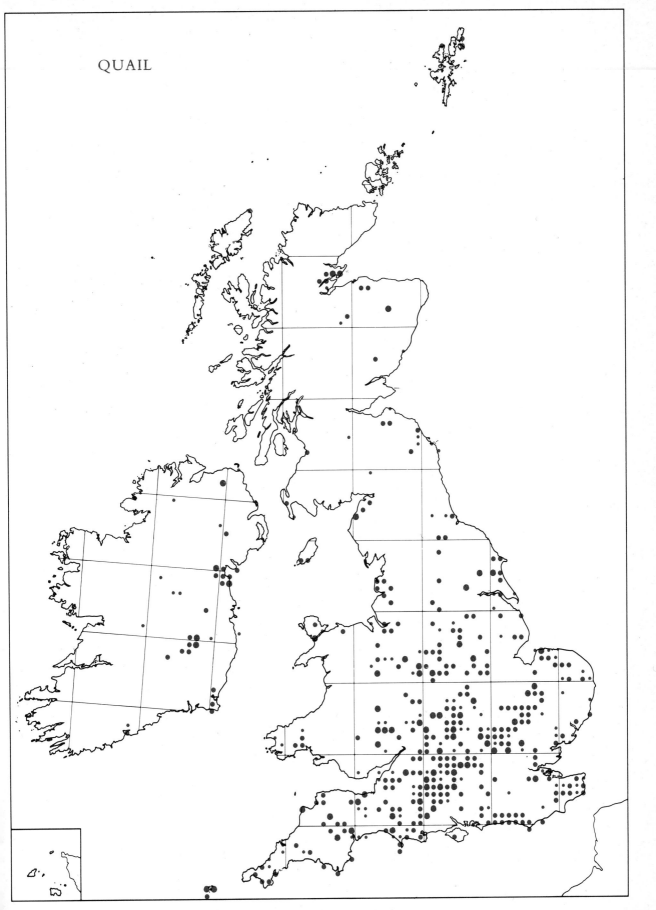

QUAIL

Pheasant

Phasianus colchicus

In Britain and Ireland, Pheasants are now mainly birds of wooded agricultural land, and the parkland and policies of large estates and demesnes. Reed-beds along rivers (an original habitat in Asia) are not much frequented except in the fens of E England. Similarly, though some wild populations in the natural range occupy largely treeless areas, these are mostly shunned here, though a few Pheasants do occur on open blanket-bog and moorland.

Pheasants were probably first introduced to Britain by the Normans in the late 11th century and seem to have been fairly well established over much of England by the late 16th century, when they were taken to Scotland, Wales and Ireland. They did not become common in much of Wales, however, until the second half of the 19th century. The early introductions were of *P.c. colchicus* from the Caucasus, but since the late 18th century most of those acclimatised have been *P.c. torquatus* from China. Several other races have been introduced and all interbreed freely, but the white neck ring of *torquatus* is now a feature of most of the feral males of Britain and Ireland.

The management of Pheasants is carried out on such an extensive scale that ornithologists tend to dismiss them as an entirely unnatural part of our avifauna. Though the density of the population is much lower away from areas of game preservation, the birds can sometimes survive well. For example, about 30 pairs live on Brownsea Island (Hampshire) after 30–40 years with no management whatsoever (Lachlan 1970). In areas where Pheasants are reared, the usual practice is to catch adults in the late winter and early spring so that they can breed in the safety of predator-proof enclosures. Nowadays, the eggs from these pairs are normally collected and hatched artificially in incubators.

The economics of game preservation are harsh. Even with modern aids, which enable a single game-keeper to rear and release as many as 2,000 a year, each young Pheasant let out of the release pen probably costs £5 or £6 and, even in the best-managed shoot, rather less than half the released birds actually fall to the guns. It is little wonder that shooting on a large scale remains a luxury sport. The pressures on the gamekeeper to ensure that plenty of Pheasants are available used to result in the destruction of large numbers of innocent birds and mammals which were thought to hazard stocks of game. In recent years several species, regarded by the older gamekeepers as their sworn enemies, have received legal protection; and, more important, the attitude of some game-keepers is changing. Research on the impact of the Sparrowhawk *Accipiter nisus*, considered to be the worst avian predator of live Pheasants, has shown that sensible management can keep losses to a minimum. At a Sparrowhawk's nest in Dumfriesshire, only 50 m from a release pen, no Pheasants were brought to the young; but, after they had fledged, the juveniles took 12 of the 350 Pheasants released (Young 1972).

Game preservation is often blamed for the destruction of raptors which the birdwatcher would like to see, but this is only one side of the coin. The countryside as a whole benefited greatly (and still does in many areas) from the activities of the gamekeeper. Populations of many species derive profit from the small areas of cover retained for gamebirds to breed and roost in, and from areas planted with roots, sunflowers and other crops to provide food for Pheasants.

The National Game Census has shown that bags vary annually from about 200 to 400 Pheasants per 400 ha. The bulk of this variation is due to fluctuations in the wild population, which makes up about 65%–75% of the national bag, and about one-third of the bag even in areas where rearing and release are carried out on a large scale. It is clear that there is now a thoroughly naturalised, self-supporting, feral population, though clearly at a higher level than if all rearing and release were to be discontinued. Decreases were noted in the 1914–18 and 1939–45 war years, due to a reduction in Pheasant rearing.

Except where they are very scarce, Pheasants are conspicuous birds, the males strutting in open fields and crowing noisily, and the females with broods affording easy proof of breeding. Landowners and gamekeepers often supplied data to *Atlas* field-workers, so that the map is probably virtually complete. Parslow described the species as 'numerous', indicating over 100,000 pairs in Britain and Ireland, and there may be as many as 500,000.

Number of 10-km squares in which recorded:
  3,105 (80%)
Possible breeding   175 (6%)
Probable breeding   212 (7%)
Confirmed breeding   2,718 (88%)

References
FITTER, R. S. R. 1959. *The Ark in our Midst*. London.
LACHLAN, C. 1970. Wild Pheasants on Brownsea Island. *Game Res. Ass. Ann. Rev.* 1969/70: 59–67.
MATHESON, C. 1963. The Pheasant in Wales. *Brit. Birds* 56: 452–456.
MIDDLETON, A. D. 1963. National Game Census. *Game Res. Ass. Ann. Rep.* 3: 48–57.
YOUNG, J. G. 1972. The Pheasant and the Sparrowhawk. *Birds* 4: 94–99.

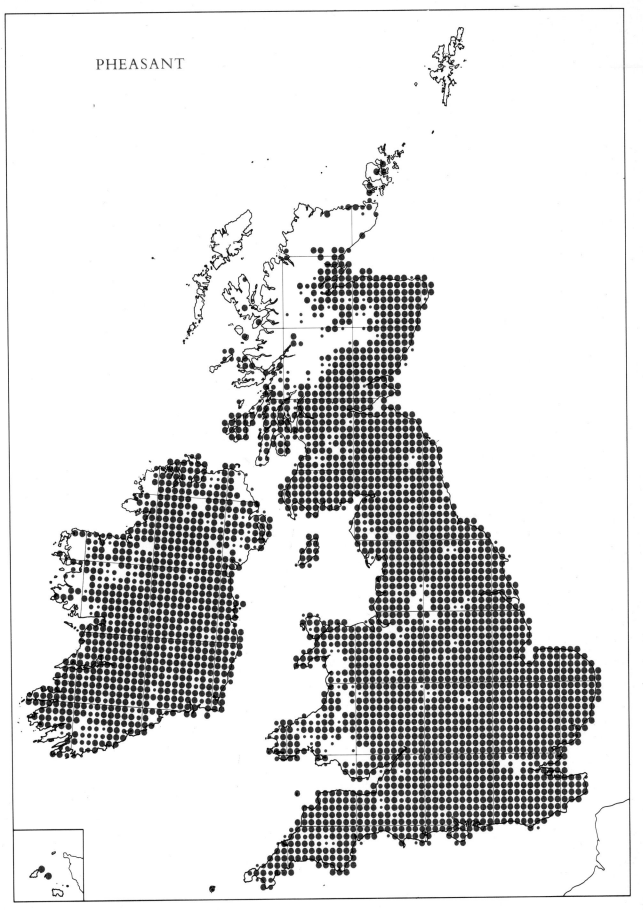

PHEASANT

Golden Pheasant

Chrysolophus pictus

The Golden Pheasant is native to the uplands of central China. There its natural habitat is bushes, bamboo thickets, and similar low but dense scrub on rocky slopes and in valleys. It is not a forest species. British feral birds, on the other hand, are found in coniferous woods, especially forestry plantations, and to a lesser extent in mixed deciduous/coniferous woods. The Asian range overlaps that of Lady Amherst's Pheasant *C. amherstiae*, which is the scarcer of the two; their habitats appear to be similar, but it is said that they do not normally occur on the same mountain. The two interbreed freely both in captivity and under feral conditions, and it is unfortunate that in Britain few populations of either are isolated from the other. One hopes that any future liberations of the Golden Pheasant will be made in areas well away from those where Lady Amherst's Pheasant is established, and *vice versa*.

Golden Pheasants were first imported in the 18th century, but there do not appear to have been any attempts at naturalising the species until the 1880s, when birds were introduced to several estates in the W Highlands, including the island of Gigha (Harvie-Brown and Buckley 1892). Nothing more is recorded about these attempts, so presumably they soon failed. About 1895 some Golden × Lady Amherst's hybrids were released near Newton Stewart (Galloway); these established themselves and eventually reverted to the pure Golden Pheasant type (Maxwell 1905). It is believed that this is the origin of the thriving feral population which now lives in the Kirroughtree Forest/Penninghame/Creetown triangle (Wigtownshire/Kirkcudbrightshire). These have increased and spread in recent years due to extensive afforestation, but are most numerous in 15–30 years-old stands of Scots pine and larch.

Probably the most successful feral stock is that in the Brecklands of Norfolk and Suffolk. Birds were turned down in the late 1890s, and other releases followed during the heyday of the big sporting estates; these thrived despite little positive protection, and by 1950 Golden Pheasants were common and increasing as new pine woods were planted on the heathy Brecks (Edlin 1952). This expansion continues alongside further afforestation, and up to 60 birds have been seen together. The presence of a few pairs in the Sandringham/Wolferton area, at least since 1967, is believed to be due to a separate introduction.

Other pre-1940 attempts to naturalise Golden Pheasants in Gloucestershire, Bute and Kent appear to have lasted only for a limited time. This also applies to the New Forest, where Edlin (1952) reported a 'colony' at Hinton Admiral, arising from birds which left a nearby estate when its pine woods were damaged by fire; but these had disappeared before *Atlas* fieldwork began. The Galloway and Breckland populations are probably the only viable ones at present, other mapped sites representing recent liberations (which may or may not succeed) or escapes. This is now the commonest ornamental pheasant in captivity, being kept in garden aviaries as well as in large collections.

Though Golden Pheasants were turned down partly for sport, they are primarily ornamental. They are long-legged and agile, slipping easily through thickets and tangled undergrowth, preferring when alarmed to run rather than fly, and for this reason they provide poor shooting. Though less shy and skulking than Lady Amherst's Pheasants, one can surmise that a certain degree of secretiveness is necessary for the survival of the gaudy males, which would make conspicuous targets in the open. It may well be that predation, not least by man, is a contributory factor to the tendency for small introductions to fail in unprotected environments. Cock Golden Pheasants can be very aggressive (to people as well as to other pheasants), and wandering birds are disliked by gamekeepers for this reason, though they are sometimes tolerated because of their attractive appearance. The nest of this species is hard to find, a difficulty exacerbated by the apparent habit of females of sitting continuously throughout incubation, without taking food or water (Goodwin 1948).

The total British and Irish population may number between 500 and 1,000 pairs, but these skulking birds are difficult to assess quantitatively. This species has so far received little attention, for it was not admitted to the British and Irish list until 1971.

Number of 10-km squares in which recorded:
29 (0.8%)
Possible breeding   9 (31%)
Probable breeding   5 (17%)
Confirmed breeding   15 (52%)

References

EDLIN, H. L. 1952. *The Changing Wild Life of Britain*. London.

FITTER, R. S. R. 1959. *The Ark in our Midst*. London.

GOODWIN, D. 1948. Incubation habits of the Golden Pheasant. *Ibis* 90: 280–284.

HARVIE-BROWN, J. A. and T. E. BUCKLEY. 1892. *A Vertebrate Fauna of Argyll and the Inner Hebrides*. Edinburgh.

MAXWELL, H. 1905. Naturalization of the Golden Pheasant. *Ann. Scott. Nat. Hist.* 1905: 53–54.

WAYRE, P. 1969. *A Guide to the Pheasants of the World*. London.

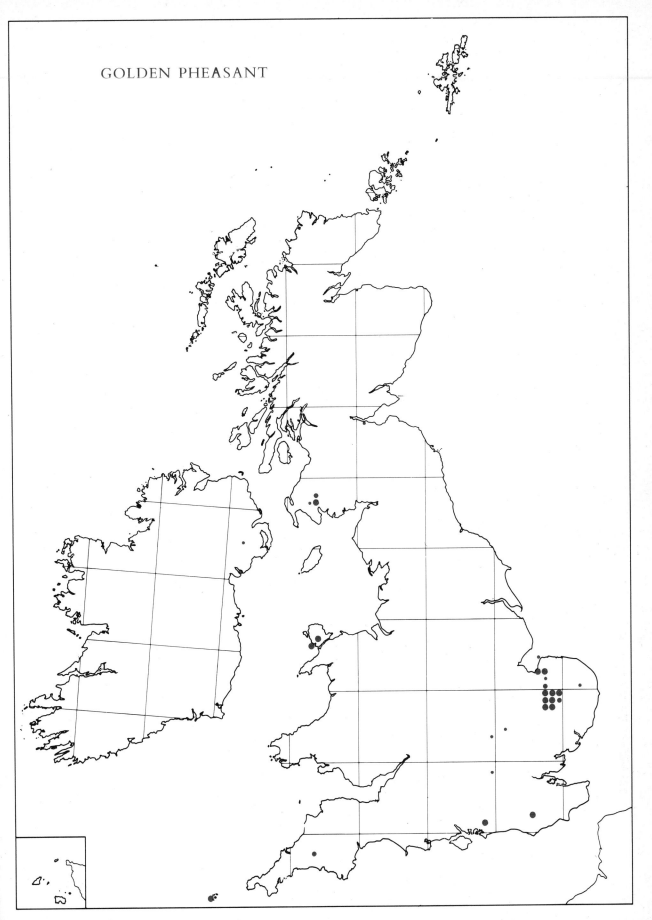

GOLDEN PHEASANT

149

Lady Amherst's Pheasant

Chrysolophus amherstiae

This species is native to SW China (Szechwan, Yunnan and W Kweichow) and adjacent parts of Tibet and upper Burma. It inhabits rocky mountain slopes between 2,000 m and 4,000 m and occurs at higher altitudes than the Golden Pheasant *C. pictus* where their ranges overlap. In England the introduced feral population inhabits deciduous, young coniferous or mixed woodland with dense undergrowth, particularly brambles and rhododendrons.

Lady Amherst's Pheasants were first brought to England in 1828, but they were a considerable rarity for a long time, and were first bred successfully in captivity as late as 1871. Thereafter a captive stock was amassed, but an initial shortage of females led to some early crossing with Golden Pheasants and, as a consequence, pure *C. amherstiae* unfortunately became somewhat rare. The two species interbreed freely where they occur together, so that feral populations cannot co-exist in the pure state.

The first known attempts to liberate Lady Amherst's Pheasants were made around the turn of the century at Mount Stuart (Bute) and Woburn (Bedfordshire). The former failed due to interbreeding with Golden Pheasants, but the Woburn stock endured and eventually spread beyond the confines of the estate (Fitter 1959). More were released in Whipsnade Park (Bedfordshire) in the 1930s. These Woburn and Whipsnade birds formed the basis of the present healthy feral population now living in Bedfordshire (where they extend north to Maulden Woods and Old Warden near Biggleswade), adjacent parts of Buckinghamshire (Brickhill Woods and Mentmore Estate), and Hertfordshire (Ashridge Estate). Recent increases in these places are perhaps due partly to the mild winters of the last decade. Extensive Forestry Commission and private plantations provide plenty of suitable habitat.

In 1971 there were some Lady Amherst's Pheasants hybridising with Golden Pheasants in Galloway; it is not recorded whether there had been a recent release of the former, or whether this was a reminder that the original Galloway stock was of *C. pictus* × *amherstiae* hybrids (see under Golden Pheasant). Some Lady Amherst's Pheasants were liberated at Elveden in the Suffolk Brecks in 1950; these seem to have disappeared within a few years, which was only to be expected since Golden Pheasants were already well established there. The Lady Amherst's Pheasants registered by the *Atlas* in NW Norfolk presumably stemmed from a later release; it seems probable that this species was turned down in more than one Norfolk locality about this period, for in 1973 successful breeding was reported farther east, at Guist (near Fakenham) and Quidenham (near East Harling), which are 40 km apart. Unfortunately, none of these is properly isolated from Norfolk's feral Golden Pheasants. Another release in the New Forest may fare better in the absence of Golden Pheasants, though numbers are still small; during the 1950s some Lady Amherst's Pheasants spread beyond their home estate at Exbury, occurring within a 12–15 km radius, and a flock of 11 (including three males) was seen there in January 1973.

The male Lady Amherst's Pheasant is perhaps the most beautiful of all British breeding birds, and the species was introduced for ornamental rather than sporting purposes. It is, indeed, disliked by many gamekeepers because it competes for winter food with the Pheasant *Phasianus colchicus*, and provides very poor sport since it runs and skulks rather than flies when disturbed. Attempts to exterminate it have been made in at least one area, but have failed because of these very habits. In other instances, however, pairs which have spread into new areas have been welcomed because of their attractiveness and novelty.

As previously indicated, the main risk to the species comes from hybridising with the Golden Pheasant. The British population of Lady Amherst's Pheasant (which is probably in the region of 100–200 pairs) is not completely pure even now, and misguided introductions of Golden Pheasants which have taken place in Bedfordshire on several occasions since 1949 could lead to further degeneration of the stock.

This introduced species was admitted to the British and Irish list as recently as 1971, and no studies have yet been made of its habits and breeding biology.

Number of 10-km squares in which recorded:
13 (0.3%)
Possible breeding   4 (31%)
Probable breeding   3 (23%)
Confirmed breeding   6 (46%)

References
CHENG TSO-HSIN. 1963. *China's Economic Fauna: Birds*. English translation 1964. Washington.
DELACOUR, J. 1951. *The Pheasants of the World*. London.
FITTER, R. S. R. 1959. *The Ark in our Midst*. London.
SMYTHIES, B. E. 1953. *The Birds of Burma*. Edinburgh and London.

Reeves's Pheasant *Syrmaticus reevesi*, **see page 451**

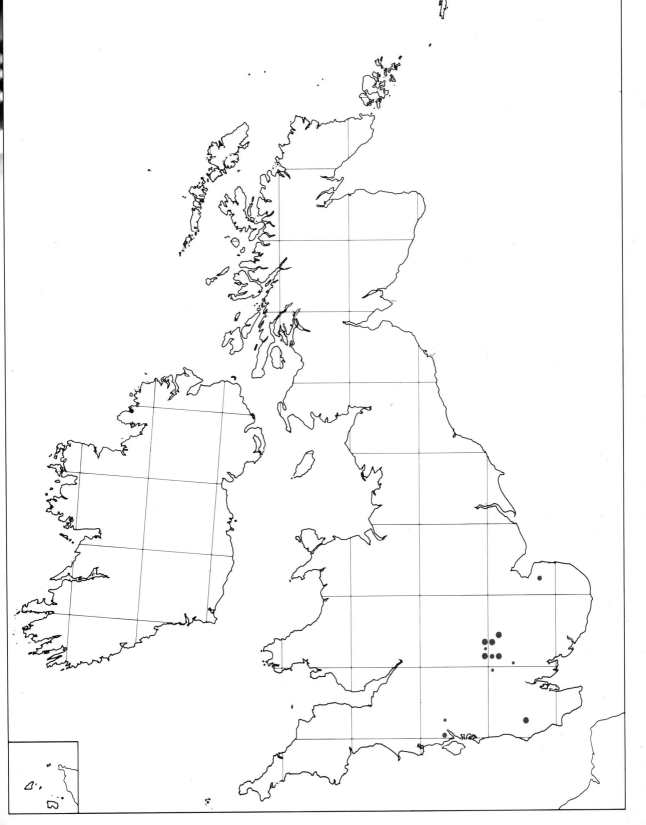

LADY AMHERST'S PHEASANT

Water Rail

Rallus aquaticus

Water Rails are found among dense aquatic vegetation, such as reed-beds of *Phragmites* and *Typha* on the margins of lakes, rivers and overgrown canals, and in carrs, osier beds, ballast pits, swamps, fens and acid bogs with cotton-grass, bog myrtle, *Sphagnum* mosses and sallows. Their long-toed feet allow them to cross soft mud or, when they occasionally come into the open, to walk over floating vegetation without sinking. Their slender bodies, strangely flattened in the vertical plane, are well adapted to rapid, furtive movement between the reed stems, and their white-striped flanks and habit of 'freezing' when disturbed camouflage them well.

Apart from bleak, mountainous country, such as the Pennines, Border hills and Scottish Highlands, and the high ground in N Wales, most parts of Britain contain potential Water Rail haunts, though the scarcity of the species in Devon is surprising, for there is much apparently suitable ground. The extensive drainage in the 18th and, especially, 19th centuries, not just of reed-bed areas but also of swampy fields, must have caused a reduction in numbers. The flooded gravel pits of S England and the Midlands are compensating for this loss, however, as more and more of them become overgrown. The distribution of dots often follows the natural flow of river systems, and the occasional remarkably straight lines, several squares in extent, usually represent the orderly nature of canal systems in the lowlands. Many of these canals are now disused and, in their overgrown state, represent a further valuable addition of suitable habitat. The British distribution may be as extensive now as at any time in this century, although apparently suitable sites often remain unoccupied. In Ireland, there is far more Water Rail habitat than in Britain: many 10-km squares there were surveyed in only a few hours and this elusive species must often have been missed.

Severe winters undoubtedly reduce Water Rail numbers temporarily, although many of the individuals which die may be overwintering migrants from the Continent. Such high mortality is difficult to understand, as Water Rails lead rather sheltered lives and show a dietary catholicism embracing much plant and animal matter and extending to predation on other birds, especially at times of stress.

In Sussex, the county total was estimated as not more than 50 pairs in 1938 and 15–25 pairs in 1962–66. There are few data from elsewhere, but Water Rails are elusive and status changes may go undetected because of the difficulty of locating them. This is probably most easily accomplished at dusk or at night when sharming (squealing, grunting and screaming noises) reveals their presence. Proof of breeding, however, involves a good deal of luck and patience, since the nest is one of the most difficult to find even if the haunt can be entered—and reed-beds ought not to be trampled.

The nest, though smaller, recalls that of the Moorhen *Gallinula chloropus*, being built of dead reeds and sedges and lined with smaller fragments; it is usually well hidden among tussocks of reeds, sedges or grasses, with the surrounding vegetation drawn over it. So slim is the Water Rail that well-marked paths are not formed, and the incubating bird may return and enter from any direction. It has been suggested that this species may be one where several cock's nests are made and only one occupied, but this will not have influenced the map in any way, as proof of breeding by finding the nest was so unusual. Most of the confirmed records came from views of adults with young on the margins of marshes at dusk.

Atlas data confirm that Water Rails are commoner in Ireland than in Britain. They were found in 27% of Irish squares compared with 22% of British ones and, although confirmed breeding records made up 23% of the total in both countries, a further 54% of the Irish records referred to probable breeding, compared with only 33% in Britain. David Scott (*in litt*) considers that there are 'undoubtedly more than 1,000 pairs breeding in Ireland' and that the species is much more widespread there than the map suggests. With Water Rails discovered in over 900 squares (and probable or confirmed breeding in over 500), it seems likely that this easily overlooked species numbers at least 2,000 pairs in Britain and Ireland; the upper limit is guesswork, but a personal view is that it is unlikely to exceed 4,000 pairs.

Number of 10-km squares in which recorded:
911 (24%)
Possible breeding   346 (38%)
Probable breeding   356 (39%)
Confirmed breeding   209 (23%)

References

ANON. 1967. A summary of the breeding survey of Water Rails, 1962–66. *Sussex Bird Rep.* 19: 53–54.

FLEGG, J. J. M. and D. E. GLUE. 1973. A Water Rail study. *Bird Study* 20: 69–79.

PERCY, LORD WILLIAM. 1951. *Three Studies in Bird Character*. London.

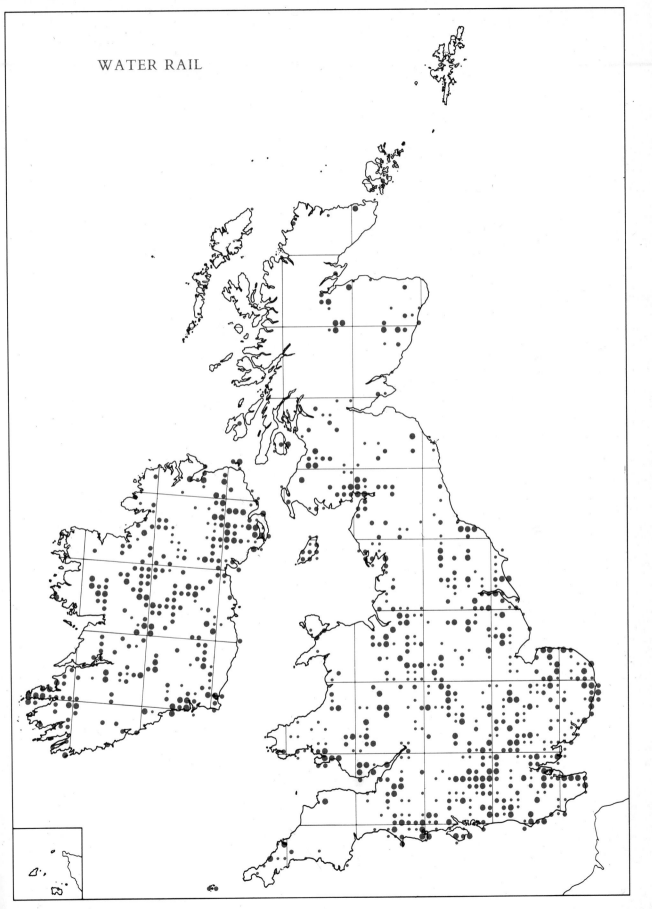

WATER RAIL

Spotted Crake

Porzana porzana

Spotted Crakes always breed in wet sites with a dense tangled cover of sedges and other plants, but apparently rather infrequently in reed-beds. The presence of trees and bushes does not discourage them and willow carr is just as likely to be frequented as marshes, fens, quaking bogs or the swampy margins of rivers or lakes. This is one of the most difficult species to see and its status here is not well understood.

Almost the only way to discover breeding Spotted Crakes is to listen for their characteristic 'whiplash' call, often made at night. Holmes (1949) noted that an apparently unmated male spent the whole of a mid-June night uttering this 'h'wit, h'wit' call, sometimes in excess of once per second. Despite many hours of observation he obtained only one fleeting glimpse of the bird, and the chances of seeing one in the course of *Atlas* fieldwork must have been slight. Proof of breeding by finding the nest is almost impossible; even the most skilled oologists were seldom successful, and a deliberate search would cause a level of disturbance which is totally unacceptable nowadays. Of the two proved breeding records, that in Northamptonshire was purely fortuitous, when two *Atlas* workers had the exceptional good fortune to see an adult and a juvenile in a maze of small ditches and drains on damp waste ground in late July 1970. The map must inevitably under-record such an extraordinarily elusive species, but, as will be seen later, it does indicate that a change in distribution may have occurred relatively recently.

Spotted Crakes probably bred locally but fairly commonly in many parts of England and Wales, Scotland (especially Kirkcudbrightshire and Dumfriesshire) and Ireland (Co Roscommon and perhaps Leix, Louth and Fermanagh) up to the middle of the 19th century. The drainage of most of their former haunts during the 18th and 19th centuries was probably the main reason for their reduction to the state of a rare and possibly not annual breeder here, although fluctuations in the limits of the breeding range on the Continent may indicate a more widespread cause. A brief resurgence came during 1926–37, with breeding in at least ten counties of England and Wales, including four or five pairs in Somerset in 1930 (Palmer and Ballance 1968). It is generally accepted that numbers again declined, but Buxton (1948), writing about the Horsey area of the Norfolk Broads, thought that it was quite untrue to say that the Spotted Crake was a rare bird there; it was simply that 'they are impossible little brutes to see'.

Within the last 10–15 years, there may have been another slight resurgence in the number summering, although the increasing army of birdwatchers and the greater interest shown in breeding season studies are doubtless contributory factors. It is notable that several of the regions where Spotted Crakes were reported in the past have few, if any, occupied 10-km squares: there is, for instance, not a single record in East Anglia, where there still appear to be many suitable sites.

The small cluster of dots in SW Scotland shows a traditional area with a history going back for many years. Though those in the Northern and Western Isles may have related mainly to migrants, just over half of the 1968–72 records were in Scotland, at a time when few were recorded at English or Welsh haunts; none was recorded in summer in Ireland, though there were single August records in 1968 and 1969. This northern bias has been correlated with a recent expansion of the species in Sweden (Sharrock *et al* 1975). One Sutherland site held Spotted Crakes each summer during 1966–70, but such regular occupation is the exception rather than the rule and there is probably now no place in Britain where these birds are recorded annually in summer. It is an exceptionally difficult species to locate, however, and probably commoner than is suggested by a mere two confirmed breeding records in five years.

This species is afforded special protection in Great Britain under Schedule I of the Protection of Birds Act, 1954–67.

Number of 10-km squares in which recorded:
39 (1%)

Possible breeding   12 (31%)
Probable breeding   25 (64%)
Confirmed breeding   2 (5%)

Though some records were originally submitted in confidence, all dots are now shown accurately (as recommended by the Rare Breeding Birds Panel)

References

BUXTON, A. 1948. *Travelling Naturalist*. London.

HOLMES, P. F. 1949. Voice of Spotted Crake. *Brit. Birds* 42: 364–365.

HUTSON, A. M. and J. GOODERS. 1970. Possible breeding of Spotted Crake in the London area. *London Bird Rep.* 34: 86–88.

PALMER, E. M. and D. K. BALLANCE. 1968. *The Birds of Somerset*. London.

SHARROCK, J. T. R. *et al.* 1975. Rare breeding birds in the United Kingdom in 1973 and 1974. *Brit. Birds* 68: 5–23, 489–506.

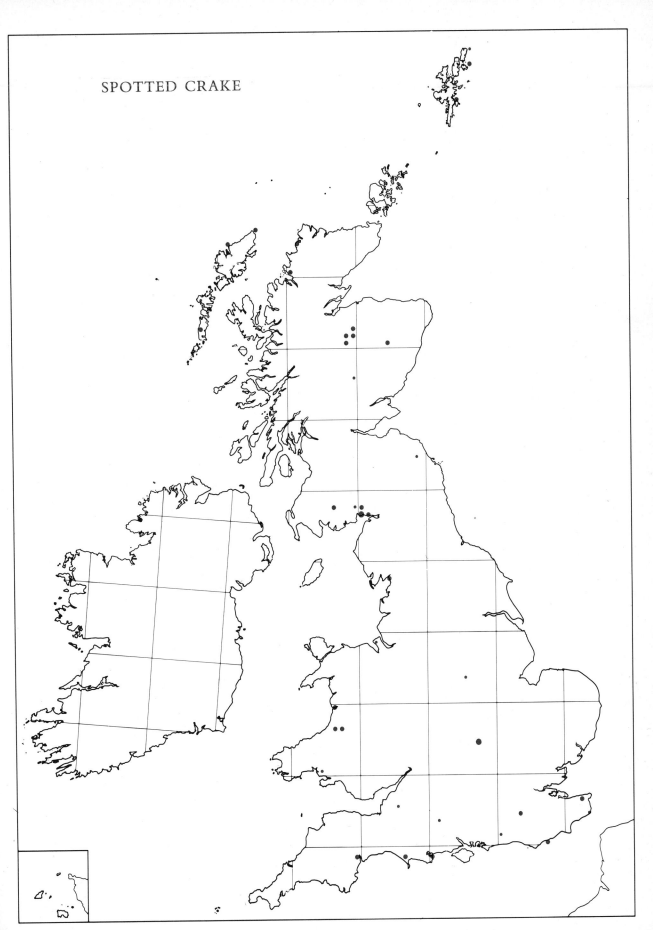

SPOTTED CRAKE

Corncrake

Crex crex

The vernacular name is something of a misnomer. While Corncrakes breed in various sorts of tall vegetation from sedgy meadows to beds of nettles, by far the commonest habitat in Britain and Ireland is fields of grass grown for hay or seed, and only rarely corn. Wet, marshy fields, occupied in parts of the Continent, are seldom used here, except in the Outer Hebrides.

As with the Quail *Coturnix coturnix*, the male's song (a harsh, repeated 'crek crek'), usually heard from dusk to dawn, but also during the day, is the best method of locating the birds, and proof of breeding comes mainly from information given by farmworkers who see the nests or broods during haycutting. The preference for hay may have been the cause of the species' downfall. A decline was first noticed in the second half of the 19th century in the areas of greatest cultivation, in SE England, and the species' range has contracted westwards until it is now common only in parts of Ireland and the Scottish islands (*cf* map on page 456). A similar decline has occurred in a number of N European countries, beginning later, in the first few decades of this century. In every case it has been attributed largely to the mechanisation of farm operations. This not only destroys adults, nests and small young (whereas hand-scything allowed the handler to spare nests and gave adults and young time to escape), but has allowed mowing to take place progressively earlier in the year, at a more vulnerable period in the breeding season, mostly in June rather than mid-July. The increasing production of silage, for which the grass is cut even earlier (and repeatedly) is blamed in some areas. This has probably had more effect in reduction of suitable habitat than in destruction of nests, however, for Corncrakes occur less often in the lush meadows of grass destined for silage than in grass for hay or seed; and the repeated cutting may remove nesting cover at a critical time in the breeding season.

Corncrakes (and indeed all rails) seem particularly liable to be killed by hitting overhead cables. The network of such wires which has developed in Europe with the widespread use of electricity may well have contributed to the decrease. Whatever the causes, the decline continues. The conspicuous gap in inland Co Cork is of recent origin, *Atlas* fieldworkers in 1969–70 often being informed by local inhabitants that Corncrakes had been present until 1966–67. Even on Cape Clear Island in the west of that county, where 'crekking' had been heard in all but one of the hay fields in 1967 (a total of at least 20 males), only two were heard in 1973, though the same number of suitable hay fields remained. During that period there was a reduction in Corncrakes on Rhum (Inverness-shire) and Inishbofin (Galway), and dramatic declines even between 1969 and 1972 in parts of mainland Ireland.

In view of the decrease and withdrawal to the west and north, there were a surprising number of records during 1968–72 in central and S England. Though many of these related only to crekking, the existence of cases of confirmed breeding shows that not all (perhaps not most) were due to migrants. In Devon, for instance, the breeding records were the first since 1938. Nevertheless, without a change in habitat preference, which might occur through selection against birds using hay fields, the species' future here seems bleak. It is interesting, therefore, that in some Irish cities (*eg* Dublin) Corncrakes have taken to breeding on waste ground around factories and are commonly heard in some suburban areas.

Some 10-km squares, particularly in such areas as Northern Ireland where Corncrakes are still common (though scarcer than formerly), held 20 or 30 crekking males during the *Atlas* period. It seems unlikely, however, that the average was more than five in squares with probable or confirmed breeding. On this basis, the number in 1968–72 was probably about, or just above, the mid-point in Parslow's category of 1,000–10,000 pairs.

This species is afforded special protection in Great Britain under Schedule I of the Protection of Birds Act, 1954–67.

Number of 10-km squares in which recorded:
  1,489 (39%)
Possible breeding   170 (11%)
Probable breeding   909 (61%)
Confirmed breeding   410 (28%)

References

BRAAKSMA, S. 1962. Voorkomen en levensgewoonten van de Kwartelkoning (*Crex crex* L.). *Limosa* 35: 230–259.

NORRIS, C. A. 1945. Summary of a report on the distribution and status of the Corncrake (*Crex crex*). *Brit. Birds* 38: 142–148, 162–168.

NORRIS, C. A. 1947. Report on the distribution and status of the Corn Crake. *Brit. Birds* 40: 226–244.

SHARROCK, J. T. R., H. M. DOBINSON and M. P. TAYLOR. 1968. Corncrakes on Cape Clear Island, 1967. *Cape Clear Bird Obs. Rep.* 9: 48–49.

VON HAARTMAN, L. 1958. The decrease of the Corncrake (*Crex crex*). *Soc. Scien. Fennica Comment. Biol.* 18(2): 1–29.

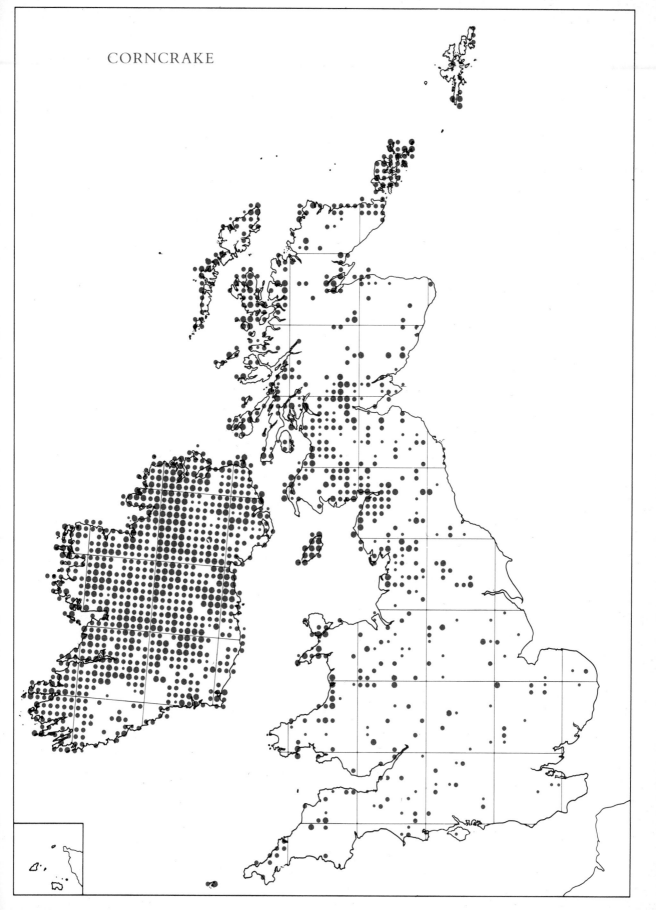

CORNCRAKE

Moorhen

Gallinula chloropus

Moorhens inhabit almost any piece of freshwater from large lakes to tiny farmyard ponds, large rivers to muddy ditches, and extensive reed-beds to small damp areas in grassy fields. Man-made waters, such as overgrown ballast pits and canals, attract large numbers and this is much the commonest riparian species in lowland Britain. The Waterways Bird Survey in 1975 gave figures ranging from 206 territories per 100 km of river and stream in the E Midlands to 296 territories per 100 km in S England, the species being less frequent in the north and west.

In some parts of their range Moorhens are shy, skulking birds, seldom seen; they become accustomed to man if not persecuted, however, and in Britain and Ireland are usually conspicuous, often feeding in open fields and along roadside verges, even inhabiting lakes in the centres of cities. They may nest at pools up to 600 m above sea-level, but usually avoid fast-flowing streams and rivers, so that the main areas lacking Moorhens are the Scottish Highlands, the mountains of central Wales, the higher parts of Dartmoor and Exmoor, and Mayo, Galway and the highlands of Kerry in the extreme west of Ireland.

The breeding season is long, egg-laying starting in middle or late March and continuing until early August, with a peak in Britain in the last week of April and the first three weeks of May. There is a high rate of egg predation, especially early in the season, which produces a large number of repeat layings; although some pairs rear two broods, and exceptionally three, the proportion doing so is probably small. 'Dump-nesting' (*ie* more than one female laying in a single nest) is not uncommon and, although the normal clutch size averages seven, there are many records of 13–20 eggs in individual nests (Huxley and Wood 1976).

The ease with which nests may be found varies as the breeding season progresses. Many early ones are very conspicuous until emergent vegetation provides them with concealment. Moorhens make display platforms and brood nests as well as the actual nest for eggs. Display platforms may be built from late February onwards and consist mainly of dead twigs,

sedges and reeds; they are used for sexual display and coition, and as many as five may be present within a territory. The egg nest is a platform of dead or green water plants, lined with finer leaves or grasses, formed into a shallow depression. If the water level rises during incubation, the nest may be built up to avoid flooding. It is often placed among the vegetation fringing lakes, rivers and canals, or may be supported by a fallen branch or hanging bramble. On marshes and bogs, and in wet corners in fields, the nest may be placed in a tussock; in town parks it is often on a small island. Nests are occasionally found up to 8 m above the ground in dense bushes, sometimes in old nests of Magpie *Pica pica* or Woodpigeon *Columba palumbus*. Nests floating in deep water may have a ramp· so that the parents can enter without damaging the sides. The brood nests, of which there may be several depending upon the number of young, are similar to egg nests, though some have ramps, and are built shortly after the chicks hatch.

In Britain and Ireland, Moorhens are largely sedentary and may defend a territory throughout the year, the winter ones being much smaller than the breeding territories. Wood (1974) found this for some pairs in his study area, though others defended territories from March until only October or November, feeding during the winter in neutral areas.

Except where isolated pairs exist outside the main range, Moorhens are very common in Britain and Ireland, and it is not surprising that 94% of the *Atlas* records refer to confirmed breeding. Though the species suffers setbacks in severe winters, recovery is rapid and there is very little evidence of any marked long-term change in status. Breeding was first recorded in Shetland in 1890 and, over the whole of Scotland, a marked increase occurred during 1900–40, though there may have been a slight decline since.

Farmland Common Birds Census areas showed an average density of 3.8 pairs per km^2 in 1972. Even one-quarter of this level would give a total British and Irish population of about 300,000 pairs, which may be compared with Parslow's range of 100,000–1,000,000 pairs.

Number of 10-km squares in which recorded:
3,149 (82%)
Possible breeding   117 (4%)
Probable breeding   68 (2%)
Confirmed breeding   2,964 (94%)

References
ANDERSON, A. 1963. Moorhens at Newburgh. *Scott. Birds* 3: 230–233.
HOWARD, E. 1940. *A Waterhen's Worlds*. Cambridge.
HUXLEY, C. R. and N. A. WOOD. 1976. Aspects of the breeding of the Moorhen in Britain. *Bird Study* 23: 1–10.
RELTON, J. 1972. Breeding biology of Moorhens on Huntingdonshire farm ponds. *Brit. Birds* 65: 248–256.
WOOD, N. A. 1974. The breeding behaviour and biology of the Moorhen. *Brit. Birds* 67: 104–115, 137–158.

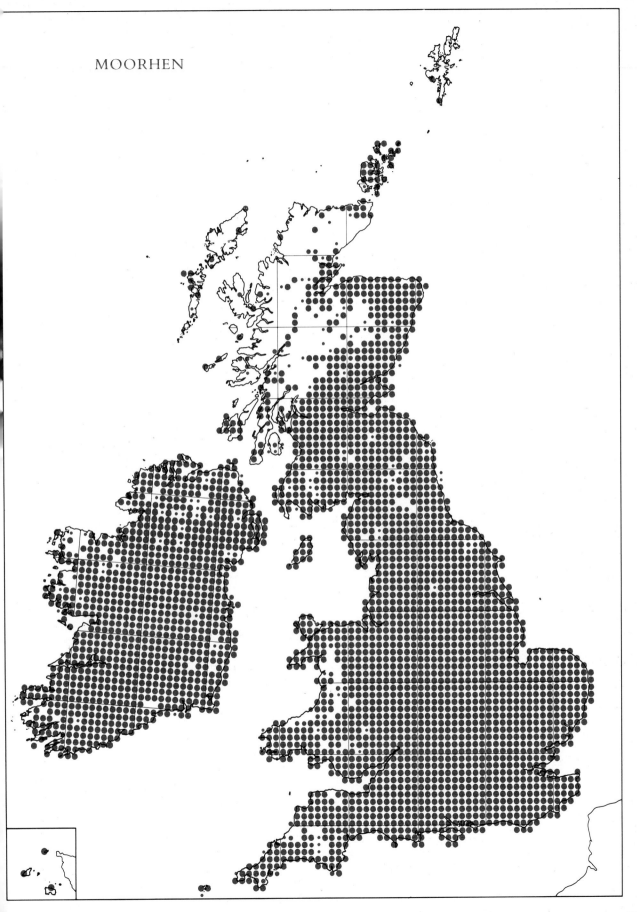

MOORHEN

Coot

Fulica atra

Over much of Britain and Ireland the Coot is one of our most familiar freshwater birds. Its somewhat narrow choice of habitat, its size and often conspicuous behaviour together encourage the belief that the map offers a reliable picture of its distribution.

Although it breeds in all mainland counties, in Scotland it is very scarce to the north and west of the Great Glen, and absent from many of the islands in the Hebrides and Shetland. The white areas on the map faithfully reflect the land above about 230 m, such as the Pennines and the Wicklow and Mourne Mountains. There is no reason to suppose that altitude, as such, is a bar to the Coot, for it is common on Malham Tarn (W Yorkshire) at 380 m and Baxter and Rintoul (1953) recorded nesting above 500 m in Scotland. The explanation is more likely to be ecological, most highland waters being deep and lacking both submerged and emergent vegetation.

Largely vegetarian in diet, the Coot is a bottom feeder, or more correctly a bottom harvester, for it surfaces before eating. There can be no doubt that it finds feeding most easy in relatively shallow, eutrophic waters; Dewar (1924), who made a special study of its diving behaviour, believed that it rarely penetrated much deeper than about 2 m, though other observers have recorded depths of over 7 m. It will also graze on grassland in winter.

Apart from its feeding requirements, this species is dependent on vegetation for security when breeding. Moorhens *Gallinula chloropus* often seem to thrive with little more than a wet ditch. Coots, on the other hand, although occasionally found breeding on streams less than 1 m wide, usually require a water area of not less than 0.5 ha. Apart from lakes and large ponds, they have sometimes nested on land-locked arms of the sea, and also breed on reed-fringed drainage dykes of coastal marshland. They are not averse to running water, provided the current is slow, and occur on the quieter stretches of rivers and navigation canals.

The nests are frequently in sites similar to those of the Great Crested Grebe *Podiceps cristatus*, but then usually built up from the bottom rather than floating.

Often, too, collapsed reeds, fallen branches and the like support them clear of the water and offer concealment. Many are conspicuous, however, and it is obvious that the essential requirement is a water barrier to hamper terrestrial predators. The usually 4–8 elongated oval eggs are stone-coloured with blackish-brown speckles which are generally smaller, more uniform in size, and more numerous than on those of the Moorhen.

Although large winter flocks form on reservoirs, these mostly lack suitable breeding sites due to their concrete embankments, so the summer population is small. In town park lakes, too, Coots occur first as winter visitors and then the abundance of artificial food often leads them to attempt nesting in atypical sites, including grassy banks and even flower-beds. Such behaviour is to be noted in St James's Park, London, yet the first settlement there was not natural, pinioned Coots being introduced and eggs from Richmond Park placed under Moorhens.

The vast growth in the civil engineering and building industries during the last 40 years has created an almost insatiable demand for sand and ballast, and the flooded workings have become a characteristic feature of the landscape near many large urban areas, especially in SE England. Often with islands, and swiftly colonised by annual and then perennial vegetation, these ballast pits have provided an ideal new habitat for the Coot. Since the occupation of such pits does not lead to evacuation of adjacent waters, it is evident that locally there must have been big increases in the population. Viewing the national situation, however, Parslow concluded that there was little indication of marked change. There is evidence that in the earlier years of the century the Coot was firmly established in Shetland, even though in small numbers; and, if Voous (1960) is correct in thinking that temperature controls the northern limit, which approximates to the 16°C July isotherm, the retreat from the northwest may well be correlated with a decline in mean summer temperatures beginning in the 1940s. Elsewhere in Europe, the species is said to have been spreading northwards in this century, but there is little to indicate whether or not this is a continuing trend.

Parslow estimated the population at 10,000–100,000 breeding pairs. In the absence of population density figures, one may subjectively conclude that the Coot's status is currently nearer the upper than the lower figure.

Number of 10-km squares in which recorded:
2,256 (58%)
Possible breeding   149 (7%)
Probable breeding   84 (4%)
Confirmed breeding   2,023 (90%)

References

BROWN, R. G. B. 1955. The migration of the Coot in relation to Britain. *Bird Study* 2: 135–142.
DEWAR, J. M. 1924. *The Bird as a Diver*. London.
SAGE, B. L. 1969. Breeding biology of the Coot. *Brit. Birds* 62: 134–143.

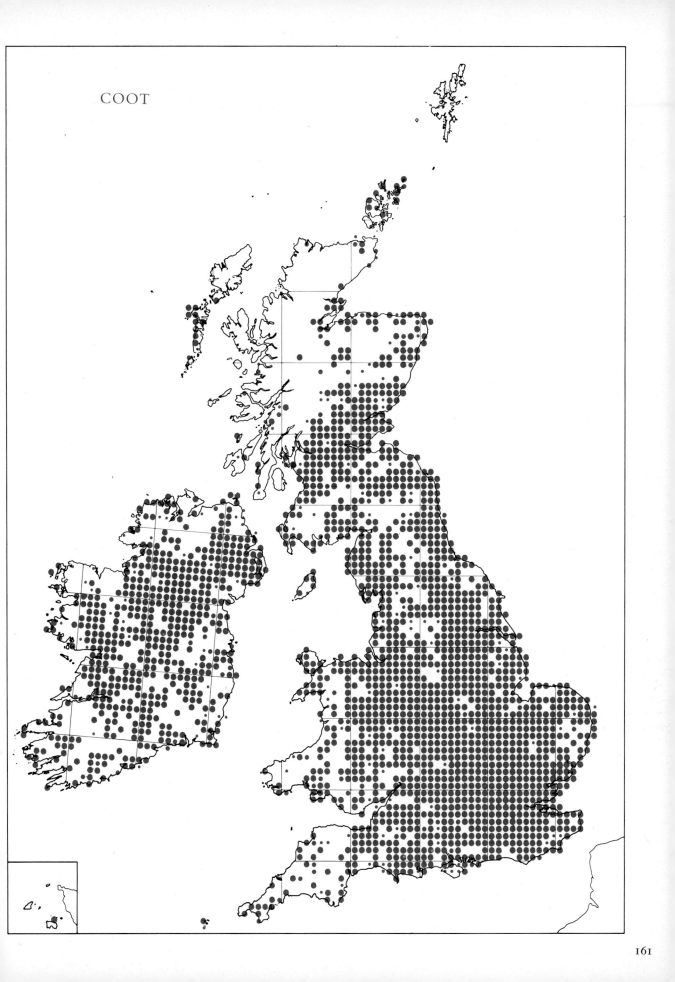

COOT

RAR

Oystercatcher

Haematopus ostralegus

Oystercatchers are basically coastal birds, nesting on rocky, pebbly or sandy shores, salt-marshes and the well-vegetated tops of small islands. Where inland nesting occurs—widely in N England and Scotland—sites include lake shores, gravel pits, shingle banks in the lower reaches of river valleys, and adjacent pasture and arable fields or moorland. Nests have even been found on sloping cliffs, in open woods away from water, and atypically on stumps and in the hollowed top of a post, on stone walls on St Kilda and on roof-tops in Aberdeen.

It is likely that few breeding areas were overlooked during 1968–72 and that the map is virtually complete, because Oystercatchers are large, conspicuous and noisy birds, enjoying spectacular communal piping displays on their breeding grounds. Though the nest is not always easy to find, it is less difficult than for most waders. When the young have left it, the adults mob intruders noisily, or indulge in false-brooding and other distraction behaviour. Later, the flying young are themselves conspicuous. Breeding is therefore easy to prove, as shown by the high proportion (78%) of confirmed records.

On the coast, Oystercatchers are vulnerable to disturbance and in many parts of S Britain decreases in breeding strength have been attributed to growing pressures from holiday-makers and development. In some places nesting is now almost confined to nature reserves or offshore islets. The absence from long stretches of coastline in E and S England may be explained largely by disturbance or a lack of suitable feeding habitats. In Ireland, nesting is less prevalent on the mainland coast than on islands, but the gap on the south coast between Cape Clear Island and extreme E Waterford is difficult to explain, for Oystercatchers were absent from that area before recent increases in human holiday pressure.

In most of Britain there has been a marked increase and spread since 1900, and particularly since 1940, due in part to relaxed predation by man. Inland breeding has been widespread in the eastern parts of N Scotland since the 18th century (probably earlier), but such colonisation elsewhere has progressed only since late in the 19th century, beginning with the rivers flowing into the Solway (Buxton 1962). The scattered *Atlas* records inland south of a line from the Dee to the Humber refer mostly to new sites colonised during 1968–72, mainly gravel pits. In other southern areas, such as East Anglia, coastal fields are now used for nesting, whereas formerly breeding

was confined strictly to the shore. A similar move to inland areas has taken place in NW Europe—*eg* the Netherlands, S Sweden and NW Germany (Voous 1960)—and it has been suggested that a behavioural change has occurred within the species, enabling Oystercatchers to exploit habitats that were not previously tolerated (Heppleston 1972); but it is difficult to know to what extent such movements are a direct response to human disturbance in the preferred coastal habitat. In Ireland there were only four cases of inland breeding before 1953, so there may be signs of the same trend in that country too.

Dare (1966) estimated that at least 19,000 (and possibly 30,000–40,000) pairs of Oystercatchers bred in Britain and Ireland in the period 1960–65, about 70% of them in Scotland. An average as low as 20 pairs per 10-km square with confirmed or probable breeding would give a current total exceeding 30,000 pairs.

Number of 10-km squares in which recorded:
    1,802 (47%)
Possible breeding   219 (12%)
Probable breeding   174 (10%)
Confirmed breeding   1,409 (78%)

References

BUXTON, E. J. M. 1962. The inland breeding of the Oystercatcher in Great Britain, 1958–59. *Bird Study* 8: 194–209.

DARE, P. J. 1966. The breeding and wintering populations of the Oystercatcher (*Haematopus ostralegus* Linnaeus) in the British Isles. *Fishery Invest. London*, Ser. II, 25 (5): 1–69.

HARRIS, M. P. 1967. The biology of Oystercatchers *Haematopus ostralegus* on Skokholm Island, S Wales. *Ibis* 109: 180–193.

HEPPLESTON, P. B. 1972. The comparative breeding ecology of Oystercatchers (*Haematopus ostralegus* L.) in inland and coastal habitats. *J. Anim. Ecol.* 41: 23–51.

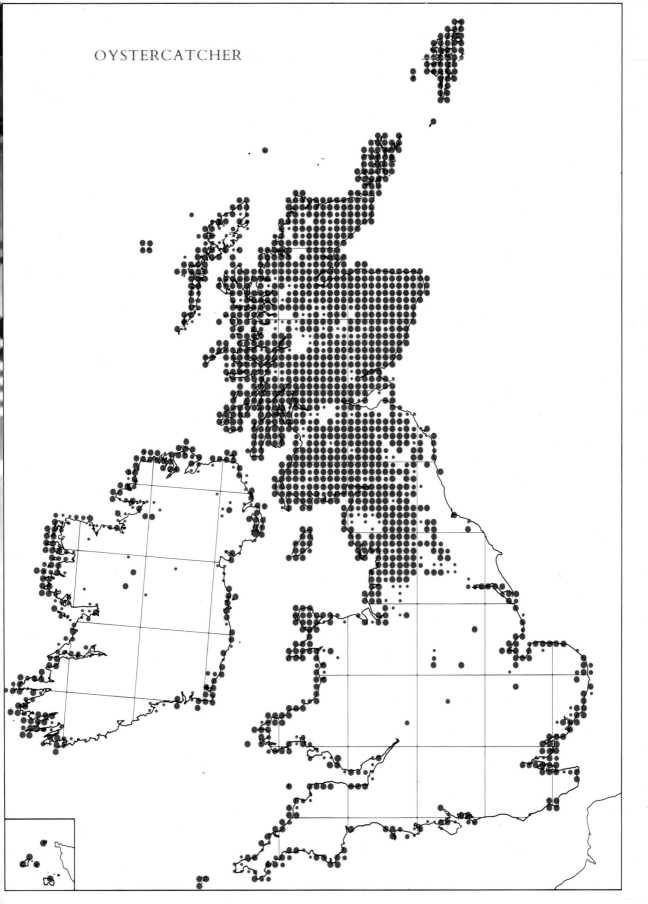

OYSTERCATCHER

Lapwing

Vanellus vanellus

Though Lapwings breed in a great variety of habitats, these all have in common relatively short vegetation (or patches of bare ground) for feeding. Over much of lowland Britain, they were once typical birds of farmland—permanent pasture, ploughed land and, during March and April when the first eggs are laid, young corn. They are still present in these habitats, but often in scattered small groups, leaving large and apparently suitable expanses without any. In some parts of the country, most nesting pairs are found on waste areas, such as those associated with gravel pits, sewage farms and refuse tips, or on the margins of large bodies of water. In upland Britain, Lapwings may be found in all but the most exposed areas and are often concentrated along valley bottoms where the mosaic of arable and pasture provides ideal conditions for both feeding and nesting. In Ireland, they are especially found on poor, wet ground with short vegetation, at the margins of lakes or on waste ground at the edges of moors, often in association with Redshanks *Tringa totanus*.

There should be no problem in recording such a conspicuous inhabitant of open ground: its pied plumage, aerial displays and habit of mobbing intruders with loud 'peewit' cries force attention, so that the map clearly reflects its true distribution, showing absence from only 15% of the 10-km squares in Britain and Ireland. The nest and newly hatched young are also relatively easy to find; hence the high proportion (86%) of confirmed breeding.

Apart from setbacks due to severe winters such as that of 1962/63, the general trends seem to be a gradual decrease in southern areas and an increase in the north. The latter may be the result of climatic amelioration, as has been claimed for the Fenno-Scandian population (Kalela 1949), but the decrease in the south has been attributed largely to changes in land-use and farming practice: the replacement of permanent pasture by arable, the drainage of damp meadows and reclamation of waste ground, and the repeated use of machinery for cultivation early in the season when Lapwings are nesting.

The scarcity of breeding Lapwings in western areas, such as Cornwall and Pembrokeshire, is difficult to explain. Decreases have been noted over the past 20–30 years, and particularly since the early 1960s, when the severe winters of 1961/62 and 1962/63 reduced numbers drastically. Recovery has been slow (see graph). The SW Ireland gap sets a particular problem, agricultural changes having been less there than anywhere else in Britain and Ireland. The absence from parts of NW Scotland probably reflects the unsuitability of habitats compared with NE Scotland. Parslow noted the Lapwing's almost complete disappearance from a wide area of SW Suffolk and central Essex even before the 1961/62 winter, but there are only two 10-km squares where the species was absent there during 1968–72, although a lower proportion of the records are of proved breeding than in the rest of E England. The lack of penetration into the environs of London is marked.

Parslow placed Lapwing breeding numbers in the category 100,000 to one million pairs, and Fisher, quoted in Spencer (1953), estimated 175,000 pairs in the 1930s. On farmland Common Birds Census areas in 1972, there was an average density of 3.4 pairs per km^2. Even one-fifth of this, over all the occupied 10-km squares, would give a total British and Irish breeding population of over 200,000 pairs.

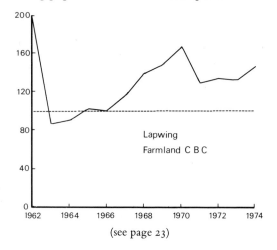

(see page 23)

Number of 10-km squares in which recorded:
3,264 (85%)
Possible breeding   171 (5%)
Probable breeding   279 (9%)
Confirmed breeding   2,814 (86%)

References
ENNION, E. A. R. 1946. *The Lapwing*. London.
KALELA, O. 1949. Changes in geographic ranges in the avifauna of northern and central Europe in relation to recent changes in climate. *Bird Banding* 20: 77–103.
LISTER, M. D. 1964. The Lapwing Habitat Enquiry 1960–61. *Bird Study* 11: 128–147.
NICHOLSON, E. M. 1938. Report on the Lapwing Habitat Enquiry, 1937. *Brit. Birds* 32: 170–191, 207–229, 255–259.
SPENCER, K. G. 1953. *The Lapwing in Britain*. Hull.

LAPWING

Ringed Plover

Charadrius hiaticula

The Ringed Plover breeds in the N temperate, subarctic and arctic regions from extreme NE Baffin Island in Canada eastwards across the Palearctic to the Bering Sea. Apart from a few pairs which nest in Brittany, Britain and Ireland are at the extreme southwestern edge of the species' range. This probably accounts for its scarcity in Pembrokeshire, Devon and Cornwall, and perhaps Cork, though there is less suitable habitat there, and coverage may have been less complete.

In Britain, the Ringed Plover breeds primarily on the coast, although during the last 20 years there has been an increasing tendency to nest inland, particularly in N England and Scotland. In England and Wales, over 90% are coastal, of which 70% are found on sandy, shingle or shell beaches. Since the pressures on this habitat have become considerable, many Ringed Plovers, particularly in S England, have taken to nesting within power-station and oil-refinery compounds, and on farmland adjacent to sea-walls. Inland, a wide variety of sites is chosen: in Scotland and N England many breed on the shingle banks of rivers and natural lakes, but in England more are found on reservoirs, gravel pits and other places modified by man's activities—the same habitats as are occupied by Little Ringed Plovers *C. dubius*. An inland population on the Brecks, which numbered some 400 pairs in the early part of this century, has greatly declined, however, due to farming and forestry, and now numbers only a handful of pairs.

Ringed Plovers return to their territories from late February or early March, although inland breeders may not do so until late April or even May. The male makes several scrapes within the territory and egg-laying reaches a peak during late April. Late breeders can still be found with chicks in early September. In most years, second broods are raised in much of England, although inland breeders usually have only a single brood. The high incidence of repeat clutches, however, complicates this picture (Prater 1974). Ringed Plovers are highly territorial during the early part of the breeding season, but often less so after late June. The relative ease with which nests and young can be found, and the striking broken-wing distraction display, resulted in a large proportion of proven breeding records during the *Atlas* fieldwork. Many nests are lost, about 60% due to predation by gulls, crows, Foxes, Brown Rats and other mammals, about 17% washed away by spring tides and the remainder destroyed, deliberately and accidentally, by man.

Alexander and Lack (1944) thought that the population had remained unchanged during the hundred years to 1940, but a reduction in that period has since been documented in SW England (Penhallurick 1969). Parslow noted that a decrease had occurred in many areas during the latter part of it and especially during the subsequent 30 years. Trends are difficult to assess because numbers fluctuate considerably from year to year and the pattern varies between adjacent populations. The only widespread synchronous change occurred in 1963, after the severe winter of 1962/63, when breeding numbers in much of England were reduced by up to a third, although over the country as a whole there was apparently only a small decrease. The increase in inland nesting, and the association with industrial complexes and farmland on the coast, indicate that the species has developed a flexibility which may enable some range expansion to be achieved.

Parslow put the population in the range 1,000–10,000. In a census in 1973–74, Prater (1976) found 1,878 pairs in England, 186 pairs in Wales, 75 in the Isle of Man and 93 in N Ireland, and estimated 3,565 pairs in Scotland, giving a total for the UK of about 5,800 pairs. The Republic of Ireland holds an unknown number, but it is unlikely that the combined figure exceeds 8,000 pairs. Numerically the Outer Hebrides is the most important area, with high densities on the machair of the Uists. Norfolk, Orkney and Shetland also have large numbers.

Number of 10-km squares in which recorded:
  1,229 (32%)
Possible breeding   161 (13%)
Probable breeding   152 (12%)
Confirmed breeding   916 (75%)

References

ALEXANDER, W. B. and D. LACK. 1944. Changes in status among British breeding birds. *Brit. Birds* 38: 62–69.

PENHALLURICK, R. D. 1969. *Birds of the Cornish Coast.* Truro.

PRATER, A. J. 1974. Breeding biology of the Ringed Plover *Charadrius hiaticula. Proc. I.W.R.B. Wader Symp. Warsaw 1973*: 15–22.

PRATER, A. J. 1976. The breeding population of Ringed Plovers in Britain. *Bird Study* 23 (in press).

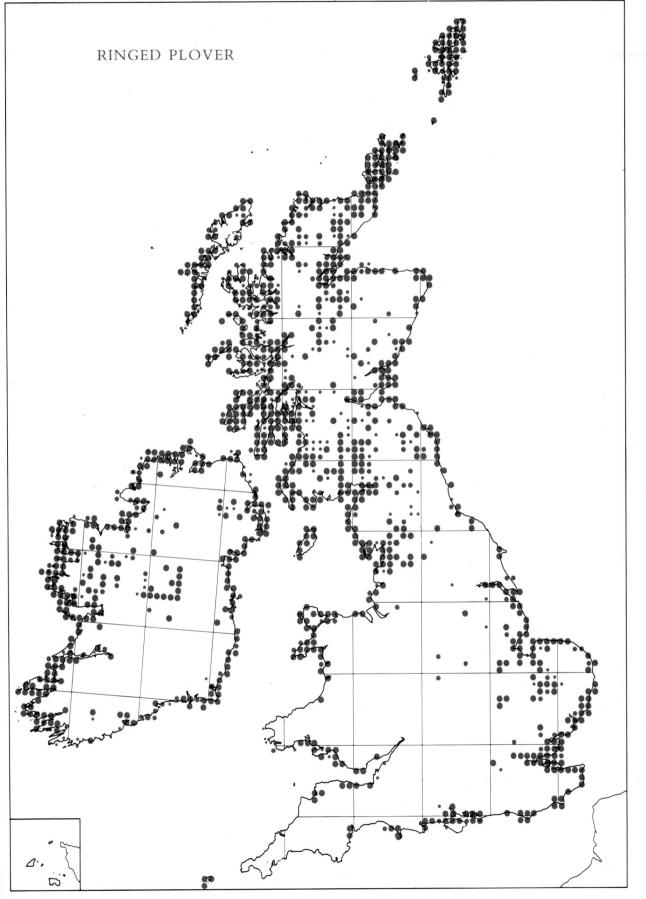

RINGED PLOVER

Little Ringed Plover

Charadrius dubius

Little Ringed Plovers were unknown as breeding birds in Britain before 1938 and, indeed, were extreme rarities even as migrants, as they still are in Ireland. In 1938 a pair nested at a reservoir at Tring (Hertfordshire) and in 1944 two pairs bred at Tring and another in Middlesex. Since then, as shown by the graph (right) and maps (page 457), colonisation has continued apace until by 1972 over 400 pairs summered in Britain.

On the Continent, Little Ringed Plovers traditionally nest on shingle beds in rivers, some on or close to the coast. Though such haunts have occasionally been used in Britain, the vast majority of breeding records have been at gravel pits and, to a lesser extent, at other man-made sites such as industrial tips and waste ground, sewage farms and reservoirs. Similar sites have been utilised increasingly on the Continent over the last 30 years. Such places are usually prone to a good deal of disturbance and the Little Ringed Plover's toleration of this in England, and its readiness to lay repeat clutches when first nests are destroyed, have doubtless been factors in the species' success story. In W Germany, however, Holzinger (1975) found that, if disturbance was severe during the incubation of the first clutch, many birds vacated their territories and bred elsewhere. The spread here has coincided with a period of growth in the building industry, with its requirement for increased supplies of gravel and the consequent rapid rise in the number of suitable pit margins for nesting.

Though not now the rarity that it once was, the Little Ringed Plover is still much sought after by birdwatchers, and has the advantage of breeding in a distinctive habitat which also attracts migrant waders. The spread, therefore, has been well documented (Parrinder 1964, Parrinder and Parrinder 1969, 1975) and the *Atlas* map gives what is probably a nearly complete picture of the 1968–72 distribution, with presence in 7% of the 10-km squares. The rate of increase during 1948–62 was about 15% per annum with, as would be expected, the greatest increase in the newly settled northern areas in the later years.

Location is easy because of the restricted habitat; the birds are noisy and conspicuous when displaying,

and again when they have young, though they are very quiet in the period between. Nevertheless, they are seldom present at a gravel pit without the workmen being aware of their existence. In the open habitat, adults can be watched back to the nest and, even if this cannot be found, they indicate its presence by anxiety calls and distraction displays. It is not surprising, therefore, that breeding was confirmed in over 80% of the squares in which the species was found.

This species is afforded special protection in Great Britain under Schedule I of the Protection of Birds Act, 1954–67.

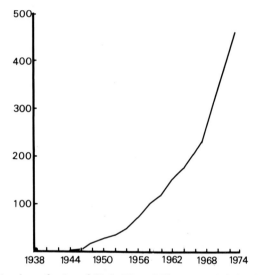

Number of pairs of Little Ringed Plovers in Britain since the first breeding in 1938

Number of 10-km squares in which recorded:
  288 (7%)
Possible breeding   28 (10%)
Probable breeding   23 (8%)
Confirmed breeding   237 (82%)

Though some records were originally submitted in confidence, all dots are now shown accurately (as recommended by the Rare Breeding Birds Panel)

References

HÖLZINGER, J. 1975. Investigations on the behaviour of Little Ringed Plover *Charadrius dubius* during disturbed and undisturbed incubation. *Anz. Orn. Ges. Bayern* 14: 166–173.

PARRINDER, E. R. 1964. Little Ringed Plovers in Britain during 1960–62. *Brit. Birds* 57: 191–198.

PARRINDER, E. R. and E. D. PARRINDER. 1969. Little Ringed Plovers in Britain in 1963–67. *Brit. Birds* 62: 219–223.

PARRINDER, E. R. and E. D. PARRINDER. 1975. Little Ringed Plovers in Britain in 1968–73. *Brit. Birds* 68: 359–368.

STALKER, D. 1969. Little Ringed Plovers breeding in Clyde. *Scott. Birds* 5: 282–283.

Kentish Plover *Charadrius alexandrinus*, **see page 448**

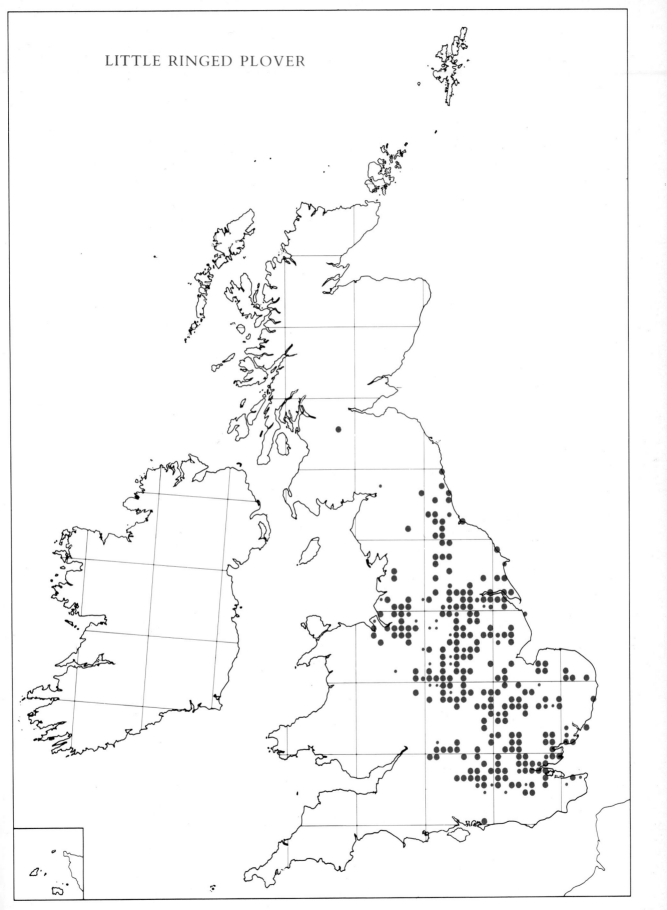

LITTLE RINGED PLOVER

Golden Plover

Pluvialis apricaria

Golden Plovers are typical of the flat or gently sloping moorland of N and W Britain and Ireland; in the south of their range they generally keep to the highest land (up to 1,300 m), but in N Scotland and W Ireland, as in subarctic regions, they may breed almost at sea level.

The beautiful aerial display is the best guide to the territory: with deliberate, spasmodic wing beats the bird drifts slowly on the wind, or maintains a nearly stationary position, whistling 'pee-per-yur' at regular short intervals. This may be followed by a silent flight on faster-beating wings. At other times the call, always with a melodious flute-like quality, becomes a trilling, repetitive 'pee-yur-ee-oo'. Every territory has a prominent, moss-topped look-out hummock on which the alert off-duty bird stands guard.

Although Campbell and Ferguson-Lees (1972) noted that this is probably the hardest of the commoner wader nests to find, nearly two-thirds of *Atlas* records referred to confirmed breeding. This was largely through observations of the charming downy young or of the adults' anxious distraction behaviour, which includes injury-feigning patterns of at least three distinct types (Williamson 1948). The three or four eggs hatch more nearly simultaneously than those of other waders, and the parents divide the brood between them. The breeding grounds are vacated soon after the young fledge in mid-July, although in years when severe weather occurs in June, causing a high mortality among the downy chicks, the moors may be deserted several weeks earlier.

Throughout their breeding range in central and S Europe, Golden Plovers have become less widespread and their numbers have diminished during this century. This decline is probably a relatively recent phenomenon and may be due in part to the climatic amelioration and in part to the large-scale planting of conifers in many upland areas, such as the high country on either side of the England/Scotland border. Suitable parts of Exmoor (Somerset) and SW Ireland (Cork, Kerry and Tipperary) have been evacuated for 30–60 years, and contraction of range has also occurred in Wales. The only notable gain has been on Dartmoor (Devon), where a small group seems now to be established, breeding having been first confirmed in 1950. There appears to have been a general decline in N Scotland, though the species is still much commoner there than elsewhere. In the 1930s, a few pairs nested on forest bog in the Spey Valley, but deserted in the following decade. Density is now greater on the E Grampian moors and E Sutherland/Caithness flows than in the NW Highlands, where the species is often sparsely and patchily distributed. In the past, observers have spoken of 'a Golden Plover on every tussock' which, while clearly an overstatement, could not apply anywhere today.

The only quantitative survey in England relates to the Peak District National Park (mainly Derbyshire), where in 1970–73 some 380–400 pairs were estimated within the park's 1,400 km² (Yalden 1974). This is a density of 0.28 pairs per km², though not all of this area could be regarded as suitable ground. Ratcliffe (1976) has estimated densities ranging from as high as five to seven pairs per km² on the Pennines, southern uplands of Scotland and E Highlands, down to less than one in N and W Scotland. The highest density he found was 16 pairs per km² in a limestone region of the Pennines (W Yorkshire).

Dr D. A. Ratcliffe (*in litt*) and A. J. Prater have estimated the following approximate totals of pairs:

SW England		10
Wales		600
N England		7,500
S Scottish uplands		3,800
Scottish Highlands	S of Great Glen	8,700
	N of Great Glen	6,800
Hebrides, Orkney and Shetland		2,000
Ireland		600
		30,010

The total of about 30,000 pairs is well above Parslow's range of 1,000–10,000.

Number of 10-km squares in which recorded:
915 (24%)
Possible breeding   110 (12%)
Probable breeding   209 (23%)
Confirmed breeding   596 (65%)

References

NETHERSOLE-THOMPSON, D. 1961. pp 206–214 in BANNERMAN, D. A. *The Birds of the British Isles*, vol. 10. Edinburgh and London.

NETHERSOLE-THOMPSON, D. and A. WATSON. 1974. *The Cairngorms.* London.

RATCLIFFE, D. A. 1976. Observations on the breeding of the Golden Plover in Great Britain. *Bird Study* 23: 63–116.

WILLIAMSON, K. 1948. Field-notes on the nidification and distraction display in the Golden Plover. *Ibis.* 90: 90–98.

YALDEN, D. W. 1974. The status of Golden Plover (*Pluvialis apricaria*) and Dunlin (*Calidris alpina*) in the Peak District. *Naturalist* no. 930: 81–91.

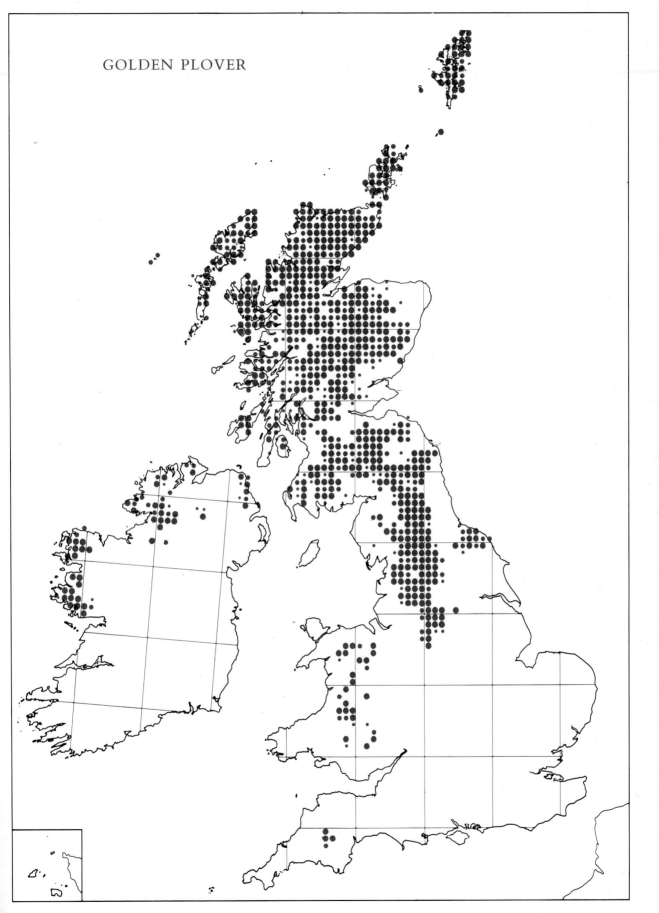

GOLDEN PLOVER

Dotterel

Eudromias morinellus

Dotterels inhabit some of the wildest and most desolate places in Britain. In Scotland they are birds of the round-topped mountain massifs—especially 'whale-backed' plateaux—largely above 850–900 m in the central Highlands and a little lower elsewhere; they occupy the montane zone of short grassland, moss and lichen heath, and occasionally dwarf shrub heather. These are the places where snow lasts longest in late spring and summer, so the Dotterels tend to nest away from gullies and hollows where drifts occur, preferring the drier, wind-swept tops.

Dotterels were formerly more common and widespread in Britain than now, trips of up to 200 being regularly seen (and shot) on migration in N England and S Scotland in the 19th century, though even then the species seems likely to have been only a sparse nester in N England. Continued shooting once the birds had been reduced to rarity level, as a table delicacy and especially for feathers for fishing, together with the activities of egg-collectors and trophy hunters, were probably the major reasons for its decline and contraction to the relatively small areas in the Highlands which afford optimum conditions.

The main haunts are increasingly being invaded by holiday-makers as tourism spreads in the Highlands, access roads and ski-lifts bringing the nesting grounds within easier reach, and this development must be closely watched. Nevertheless, these tame and confiding plovers sometimes nest close to well-trodden paths without apparent detriment, though nowadays such nests have been harried by crows attracted to the vicinity by hikers' scraps.

It may be that the ameliorating climate during the first half of this century played a part in the range-contraction of the Dotterel for, coincident with the recent cooling conditions in spring and early summer, resumption of breeding has taken place in N England and the first proof of nesting has been obtained in Sutherland (1967), Kirkcudbrightshire (1967), Wales (1969), and Selkirk/Peebles (1970).

There are no published records of breeding in Ireland, but, if the current trend continues, suitable mountains there may reward the diligent searcher, for the distribution in Britain is probably more extensive now than at any time in this century.

Though mountain-top birds in Britain, Dotterels breed down to sea-level on the arctic tundra of Scandinavia and the USSR and even below sea-level on the polders of the Netherlands since 1961, in areas where trips had previously occurred on passage.

Similar regular migration haunts in East Anglia have been closely watched, especially during *Atlas* field-work, but no comparable colonisation has yet been recorded.

The main problem in locating Dotterels in their remote and desolate mountain-top habitat, subject to severe weather even in midsummer, is its inaccessibility. Dotterels usually arrive on the fells during the first two weeks of May, just as the first snow-free ground is appearing above the 900 m contour.

Soon after laying the eggs, the females leave almost all duties to the males and, banding together, move considerable distances; so the presence of several females may not always provide an accurate reflection of breeding distribution. Proof of breeding is relatively easy to obtain only when the male is accompanying chicks and his beautiful injury-feigning distraction display is seen. The male alone usually incubates the eggs (although the female may help in about 6% of cases) and his very tameness may constitute a difficulty, for so well camouflaged is he and so tightly does he sit that one can walk past him time after time.

In the light of these problems, the *Atlas* picture is a very satisfactory one. Though undoubtedly incomplete, the pattern is evident, with records in fewer than 50 10-km squares. Nethersole-Thompson assessed the regular breeding pairs in each area as: Ross-shire 6–8, Inverness north of the Great Glen 3–4, Monadliath 6, E Cairngorms 5–7, W Cairngorms 7–8, E Grampians 10–15, Central Grampians 10–15, W Grampians 8–10 and England 1. The total population is probably between 60 and 80 pairs, although in exceptional years up to 100 pairs may breed.

This species is afforded special protection in Great Britain under Schedule I of the Protection of Birds Act, 1954–67.

Number of 10-km squares in which recorded:
46 (1%)
Possible breeding   14 (30%)
Probable breeding   6 (13%)
Confirmed breeding   26 (57%)

Within the shaded 100-km squares, the dots are conventionally placed centrally; and six other dots have been moved by one 10-km square (as recommended by the Rare Breeding Birds Panel and Dr D. A. Ratcliffe)

References
NETHERSOLE-THOMPSON, D. 1973. *The Dotterel*. London.
SOLLIE, J. F. 1961. Twee broedgevallen van de Morinelplevier (*Charadrius morinellus*) in de Noordoostpolder. *Limosa* 34: 274–276.

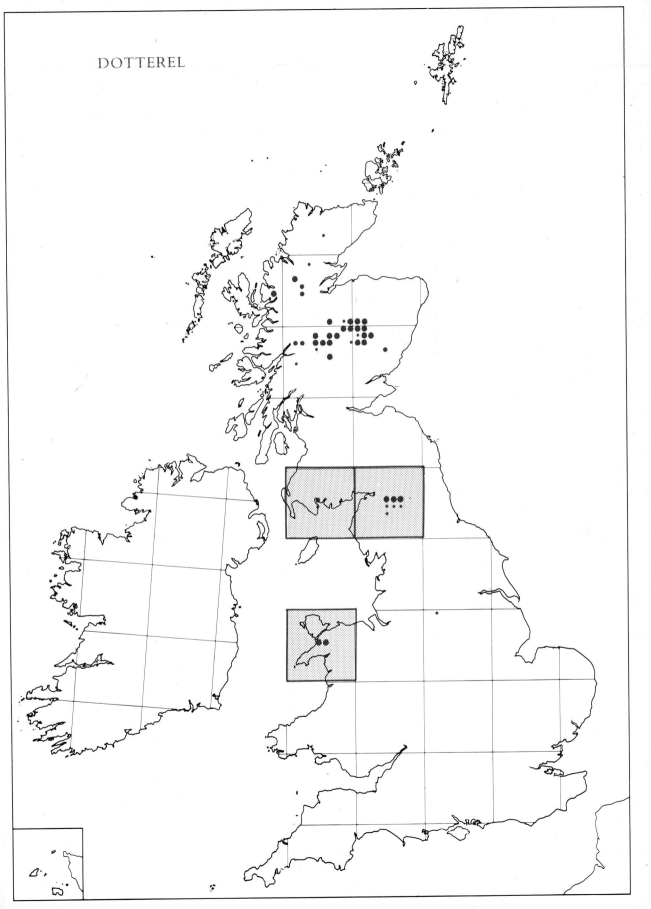

DOTTEREL

Snipe

Gallinago gallinago

RAR

Although sometimes breeding in dry meadows or on dry and occasionally stony moorland, the Snipe is typically a bird of wet ground such as rushy fields, water-meadows, washes, blanket-bogs, salt-marshes, and the marshy edges of rivers and lakes.

There was a decrease in the early 19th century, presumably associated with extensive drainage, but at the turn of the century an increase and spread reversed the trend, with colonisation of a number of inland counties in S England. This spread seems to have ceased in the 1930s or 1940s, and there has been a marked decline in some areas since—*eg* Sussex (Shrubb 1968)—possibly due to more drainage of rough, wet fields on lowland farms since the 1939–45 war. Parslow (1967) mentioned that nesting might no longer be annual in Bedfordshire, but happily this is not the case. Since 1967, breeding has occurred on the Isle of Wight, where the only previous instance was in 1919. The Snipe is still found in the breeding season in four-fifths of the 10-km squares in Britain and Ireland. In Wales, N Britain and Ireland, where the species has always been more numerous, there is no evidence of any marked change.

On St Kilda, and perhaps also in Shetland, breeding adults have plumage characteristics of the Faeroese race *C. g. faroeensis*. There, and elsewhere in the north and west, adults flushed from eggs or chicks are highly prone to a beautiful distraction display in which the bird moves in a crouched posture with its wings spread and the colourful tail-feathers expanded in a broad fan; often it emits a curious, low, guttural call during the performance. Like some other moorland waders, the parents divide the brood between them soon after the hatch, and go their separate ways, the two halves of the family feeding and roosting up to 100 m or more apart, thus reducing the risk of total loss of the brood to ground predators. Roosting in a 'form' hollowed out of long grass or other vegetation seems to be general, and an adult Snipe will lie up in this manner during the daytime.

Breeding Snipe are easy to locate by the drumming noise, produced by the vibrating outer tail-feathers, which accompanies the advertisement-flight, and the loud 'chip-per, chip-per' call uttered from the ground, a post or wall, or even in flight. These noises may be heard at any time of the day or night, but are particularly evident at dawn, or just after nightfall and in damp, drizzling conditions. Nearly one-third of the *Atlas* records related to probable breeding, and most of these were drumming birds.

The nest is often hard to find, for although some birds flush readily, going off silently with a halting, 'impeded' flight, others sit very tightly. The fact that most of the confirmed breeding records referred to nests may indicate just how common the Snipe is in some areas, especially on the damp moors of N Scotland and in Ireland; and it may also reflect the long breeding season, with hatching almost continuous from May through to mid-August. The discovery of downy, silver-spangled, russet chicks, perhaps the most attractive of all young waders, provided the second commonest method of confirmation. The young first fly when about three weeks old, though seven weeks pass before they attain a weight and wing-length comparable with the adults.

Parslow placed the Snipe in the category 10,000–100,000 pairs. They are certainly at the upper end of this range, for an average of 30–40 breeding pairs in the squares in which breeding probably or certainly took place in 1968–72 gives a very rough estimate of 80,000–110,000 pairs.

Number of 10-km squares in which recorded:
  3,130 (81%)
Possible breeding   360 (12%)
Probable breeding   1,010 (32%)
Confirmed breeding   1,760 (56%)

References

CARR-LEWTY, R. A. 1943. The aero-dynamics of the drumming of the Common Snipe. *Brit. Birds* 36: 230–234.

MASON, C. F. and S. M. MACDONALD. 1976. Aspects of the breeding biology of the Snipe. *Bird Study* 23: 33–38.

SHRUBB, M. 1968. The status and distribution of Snipe, Redshank and Yellow Wagtail as breeding birds in Sussex. *Sussex Bird Rep.* 20: 53–60.

TUCK, L. M. 1972. *The Snipes.* Canadian Wildlife Service Monograph Ser. no. 5. Ottawa.

WILLIAMSON, K. 1950. The distraction behaviour of the Faeroe Snipe. *Ibis* 92: 66–94.

WILLIAMSON, K. 1960. The development of young Snipe studied by mist-netting. *Bird Study* 7: 63–76.

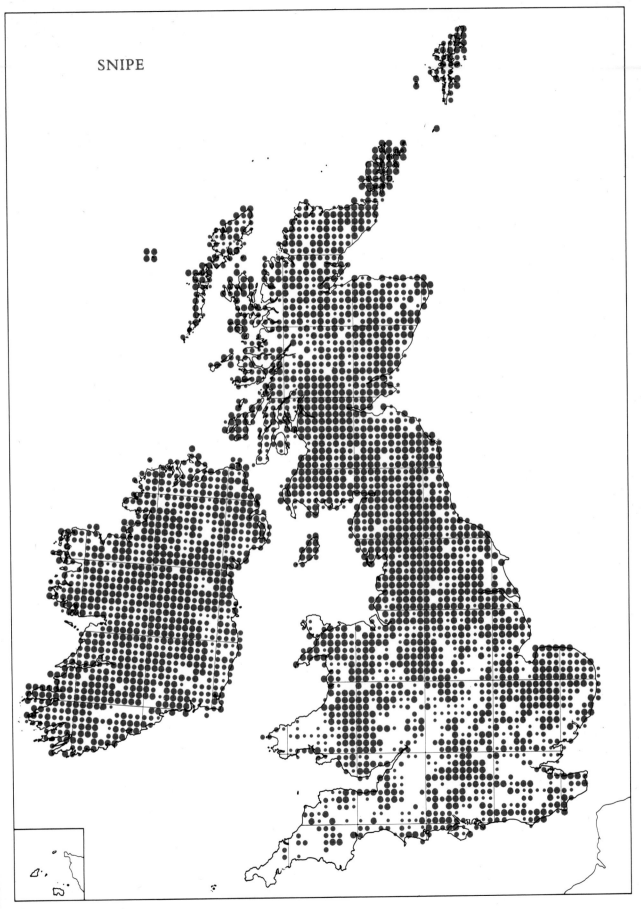

SNIPE

Woodcock

Scolopax rusticola

R.A.R

Its crepuscular habits and strange, roding advertisement flight, with slow, owl-like wing action and accompanying squeak-and-croak call, give this forest wader a special fascination.

Deciduous woodland, with a combination of dry ground for nesting, wet areas for feeding, wide rides or other open spaces, and an open canopy, provides the typical habitat, which therefore ranges from large broad-leaved woods in S England to thin birch woods and scrub in N Scotland. Mixed deciduous and coniferous stands and young forestry plantations are commonly frequented, as occasionally are bracken-covered hillsides, moorland, and even open fields.

Until the late 1820s, Woodcocks had been noted breeding here regularly only in England. Though it is difficult to know how thoroughly Wales, Scotland and Ireland had been searched previously, there was a marked increase and spread during the remainder of the 19th century, so that by the mid-1930s breeding had occurred in every mainland county of Britain and Ireland. The cause of the spread is not known, but it may have been helped by the cessation of shooting in the breeding season and by the management of estates for Pheasants *Phasianus colchicus*. Little change in distribution or numbers has been recorded in the past 30 years. Though the felling of old woodlands has produced local decreases, the spread of young conifer plantations has probably more than compensated for this, and Woodcocks must now occur in many places where there was little or no suitable habitat a few decades ago.

The distribution maps for 1940 (see page 458) and 1968–72 (opposite) are similar, though there is a suggestion of infilling and expansion from the established centres. Woodcocks were present in the breeding season in nearly 60% of the 10-km squares in Britain and Ireland during 1968–72. There was still a gap, however, in what appears to be eminently suitable country in S Suffolk and N Essex. Absence from the fens of E England is a feature shared by many species, and may be due not only to the general paucity of woods, but perhaps also to the fact that existing ones are too damp. Past data for Ireland are too scanty to allow comment on the Cork/Kerry gap.

Breeding has never become established in Cornwall, and Devon records are very few; the gap in SW England, therefore, probably represents an uncolonised area rather than a contraction of range.

Woodcocks are well camouflaged and the nest is seldom found except by chance. Breeding was nevertheless confirmed for half of the squares in which the species was recorded during *Atlas* fieldwork, due in most cases to downy young being seen. The roding flights, mainly at dusk and dawn, provide the best way of locating the species in the breeding season and, although these were not considered a certain indication of nesting, such observations added a further 35% of squares in the probable breeding category. Since suitable woodland usually has to be visited at dusk to see roding Woodcocks and thereby prove their presence, this species is probably underrecorded in those areas covered by roving expeditions; this applies especially to much of Ireland.

Incubating Woodcocks sit tight, rising silently when approached too closely. The nest is a mere hollow lined with dead leaves, most often among dead bracken or a light covering of brambles. The breeding season is extensive and eggs may be found from early March to mid-July, the peak being between mid-March and mid-April (Morgan and Shorten 1974). The young are led from the nest after hatching and it has now been firmly established that adults will sometimes carry their small young in flight away from danger.

Most British and Irish Woodcocks are believed to be sedentary. Of those that do migrate from N England and Scotland, two-thirds are thought to go to Ireland, half the remainder to S England and the rest to France, Spain and Portugal. In the autumn, large numbers come into Britain from Scandinavia, Russia and Germany, many going to W Britain and Ireland, and it is in Ireland that the greatest numbers are shot.

Estimation of the numbers of breeding pairs of such a secretive and crepuscular species can be attempted only tentatively. Parslow placed it in the range 10,000–100,000 pairs; guessing at an average of 10–25 pairs in each 10-km square in which breeding probably occurred, one may surmise that the British and Irish population lies in the lower half of his range.

Number of 10-km squares in which recorded:
2,190 (57%)
Possible breeding   323 (15%)
Probable breeding   769 (35%)
Confirmed breeding   1,098 (50%)

References

ALEXANDER, W. B. 1945–47. The Woodcock in the British Isles. *Ibis* 87: 512–550; 88: 1–24, 159–179, 271–286, 427–444; 89: 1–28.

MORGAN, R. and M. SHORTEN. 1974. Breeding of the Woodcock in Britain. *Bird Study* 21: 193–199.

SHORTEN, M. 1974. The European Woodcock (*Scolopax rusticola* L.); a search of the literature since 1940. *Game Conservancy Rep.* no. 21: 1–93.

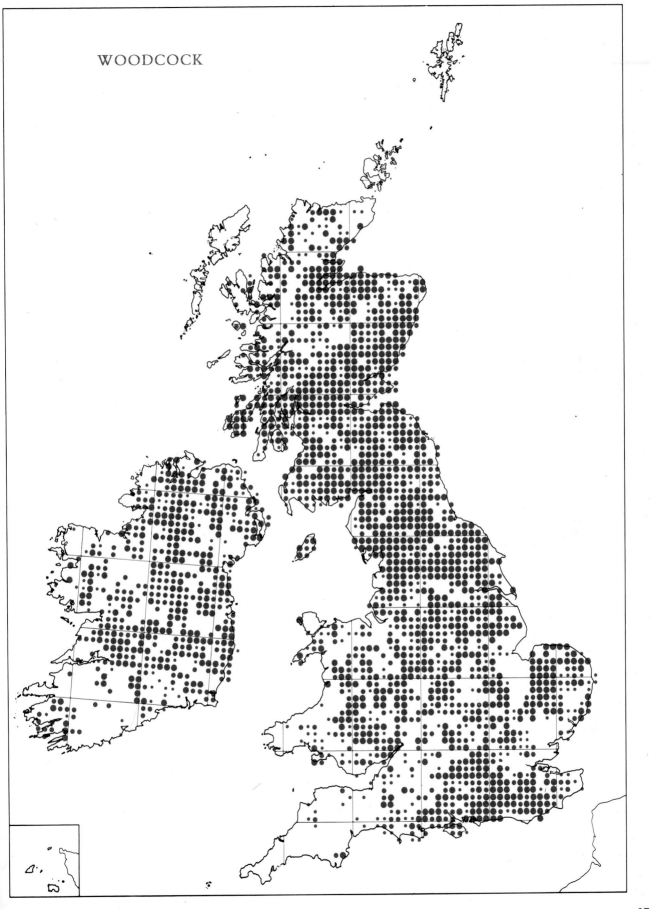

WOODCOCK

Curlew

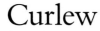

Numenius arquata

At one time Curlews were restricted mainly to damp upland moors, but they are now also found in many lowland regions, inhabiting rough, damp pastures, mosses, bogs, heaths and, in some areas, fields of arable crops down to sea level. The population in the lowlands may now even outnumber that on upland moors, where the density is generally lower. The species breeds in good numbers up to 550 m, with a few as high as 760 m.

Most of our breeding Curlews return to the nesting grounds early in the year, many by early February in lowland areas, although some upland sites are not occupied until early April. At this time the wonderful bubbling song, as the bird rises steeply on trembling wings, hangs suspended, then planes slowly earthwards over the breeding territory, draws attention from a considerable distance. During incubation, however, the Curlew is often fairly secretive. The sitting bird slips off the nest long before an intruder is near, so that it is usually difficult to locate the actual spot, although the presence of quiet and watchful birds indicates that a nest is near. Towards the end of incubation and when young are present, usually from the end of May through June (and even as late as July), the parents are much more conspicuous as they utter loud, barking cries of warning. By late July, most of the breeding grounds have been vacated, the adults and young having moved first down to the lowland fields, and then to the coasts and estuaries for the winter.

There has been a dramatic increase and spread in this century—particularly into the lowlands—but opinions differ whether the upland population has declined during this period. Inland breeding started in Wiltshire in about 1916 and Curlews settled the heaths of Sussex and Hampshire in the 1930s and the Breckland of Norfolk and Suffolk in the late 1940s. In S Scotland, this species has become noticeably commoner on bracken-clad slopes and rushy hollows of the foothills. The extensive peat moorland of the Outer Hebrides is currently being colonised. The expansion has slowed down recently, perhaps since the 1950s; this may be due mainly to the rapid decline of areas of potential colonisation because of drainage and urbanisation. Recent decreases in parts of SW England and the W Midlands are probably attributable to these causes. The Curlew is also fairly susceptible to severe weather. After the severe winter of 1962/63 large decreases were noted in Devon

(Sitters 1974), Herefordshire, Wiltshire, Scotland and Ireland (Dobinson and Richards 1964).

In adjacent Continental countries, the Curlew has also had a chequered history. In the Netherlands, Braaksma (1960) noted a big reduction during the present century, due mainly to habitat loss, to a level of 2,500–3,000 pairs. In Denmark, on the other hand, an opposite trend has been observed: breeding was not proved until 1925—approximately the time of the start of our birds' movement into the lowlands—and afterwards numbers increased steadily to 25 pairs in 1940, 50 in 1950 and 95 in 1960, but with little growth since (Pedersen 1966).

Curlews are nowhere commoner than in the undulating drumlin areas of the north of Ireland, where the rough grass fields have dry nesting sites and damp feeding areas in close proximity. The calcareous mires and limestone lings in the W Yorkshire Pennines have a density of 14–18 pairs per km² (Williamson 1968); yet traditional Curlew country of upland moors in the Scottish Highlands and Ireland will sometimes reveal only one or two pairs in a whole day's hill-walking. This is particularly noticeable in W Sutherland and Ross-shire, where the sparse population is reflected on the map by scattered blank squares and records of probable breeding, a feature shared with other species (*eg* Black-headed Gull *Larus ridibundus* and Redshank *Tringa totanus*). Watson (1954) found 113 pairs in 259 km² on the borders of Banffshire and Aberdeenshire, an average of 0.44 pairs per km². Densities may range from one pair per 10-km square in many areas of S England and NW Scotland, to 40–50 pairs in good breeding country in E Scotland and up to 1,000 pairs in the few most suitable areas. An average of 15–25 pairs per 10-km square would give a total of about 40,000–70,000 pairs in Britain and Ireland.

Number of 10-km squares in which recorded: 2,784 (72%)
Possible breeding   372 (13%)
Probable breeding   542 (19%)
Confirmed breeding   1,870 (67%)

References

BRAAKSMA, S. 1960. De verspreiding van de Wulp (*Numenius arquata* L.) als broedvogel. *Ardea* 48: 65–90.

PEDERSEN, E. T. 1966. Stor Regenspove (*Numenius arquata* L.) som ynglefugl i Danmark. *Dansk Orn. Foren. Tidsskr.* 59: 235–258.

SITTERS, H. 1974. *Atlas of Breeding Birds in Devon.* Plymouth.

STANFORD, J. K. 1955. The Common Curlew as a Wiltshire breeding bird. *Wilts. Arch. Nat. Hist. Mag.* 56: 30–34.

WATSON, A. 1954. Curlew nesting in cornfields. *Scott. Nat.* 66: 125.

WATSON, D. 1972. *Birds of Moor and Mountain.* Edinburgh.

WILLIAMSON, K. 1968. Bird communities in the Malham Tarn region of the Pennines. *Field Studies* 2: 651–668.

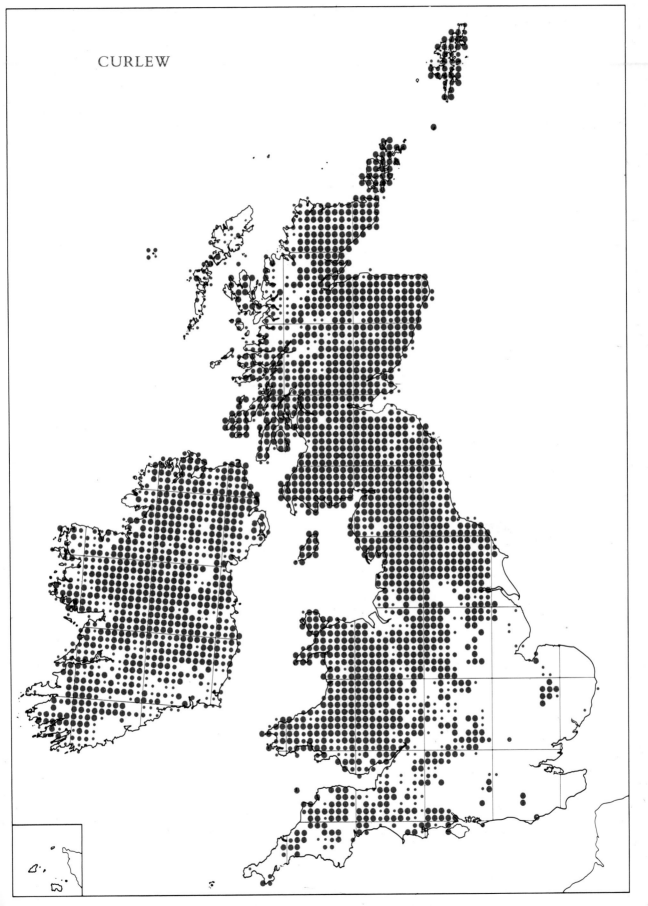

CURLEW

Whimbrel

Numenius phaeopus

RAR.

The Whimbrel is generally regarded as the ecological replacement of the larger Curlew *N. arquata*, living farther north and at higher altitudes; although this is true of the European tundra zone beyond about 65°N, and of the Norwegian fells, there is a very considerable region of overlap of the two species in the northern half of the Curlew's distribution (see maps in Voous 1960). Some of this overlap may be recent, for the Curlew is known to have spread northwards in Fenno-Scandia during the climatic amelioration of this century.

In Britain, the Whimbrel nests on moorland, frequently in dry grass and heather, but sometimes among old peat-haggings and on boggy ground broken up by peaty channels. Such habitat exists in much of N Scotland but, being a boreal species, it hardly penetrates Scotland beyond the northern and western isles, and is common only in parts of Shetland. On Unst, where both species are found, the Whimbrel nests at a higher level on the hillsides, the Curlew occupying the damp, rush-grown fields and heaths of the valley bottoms (Williamson 1951). Whimbrel families descend to the valleys after breeding, and birds have been discovered nesting near sea level in NE Scotland, as they do commonly in Iceland where the Curlew is absent.

Nesting pairs are not difficult to locate after their arrival from Africa in late April and early May. In the beautiful song-flight, the male often describes the same circular course time after time. The flight is a steady climb on quickly beating wings, followed by a fast declining glide; it may be silent, but is more often punctuated by a mournful 'koo', the intervals becoming shorter and the recital more impassioned as the climactic bubbling trill is reached. Nesting takes place from mid-May in virtually all parts of the European range, and unfledged young may still be found in mid-August. The nest is often in long grass close to, or immediately beside, a small pool or flooded peat-cutting. The incubation period is 27–28 days. The parents may divide a brood of three or four chicks and go their different ways, as do Curlews, the family reuniting when the young are fledged, having sometimes travelled a distance of 2 km or so (Williamson 1946). Adults are very demonstrative, even aggressive, when the nest or young are threatened, flying close to the observer and using the whinnying

call, or a shrill, barking cry if very excited. Fledging takes between five and six weeks. The species' conspicuousness is reflected in the low proportion of probable breeding records, most being of confirmed breeding or possible breeding, the last perhaps referring chiefly to late migrants.

There was a marked decline late in the 19th century. Small numbers then bred in Orkney, but had ceased to do so by the 1880s. There was a decrease in Shetland between 1889 and 1930, with a withdrawal from Yell, Hascosay, Noss and perhaps other islands (Venables and Venables 1955). The close correspondence of dates suggests that the climatic amelioration may have adversely affected this boreal species; and indeed the trend has now reversed, coincident with the recent cooler springs and early summers. The Shetland population has probably trebled since the early 1950s, when the Venables noted that there were 50–55 pairs in four localities. While the population may well be responding to climatic or other natural events, the protection provided by law, and the sympathetic attitude of Shetlanders to wildlife, must be contributory factors.

Outside Shetland, where there were about 150 pairs in 1970, and the Isle of Lewis (Outer Hebrides), where a few pairs have nested since 1957, breeding is sporadic. The Orkney, St Kilda and Scottish mainland records refer to fewer than half a dozen pairs. Successful breeding took place on Fair Isle in 1973 and 1974. The present population is certainly under 200 pairs (30% of this total being on Unst), even if some birds eluded discovery during 1968–72.

This species is afforded special protection in Great Britain under Schedule 1 of the Protection of Birds Act, 1954–67.

Number of 10-km squares in which recorded:
59 (2%)

Possible breeding	28 (47%)
Probable breeding	9 (15%)
Confirmed breeding	22 (37%)

One dot has been moved by up to two 10-km squares (as recommended by the Rare Breeding Birds Panel)

References

GUDMUNDSSON, F. 1957. Icelandic birds. XV. The Whimbrel (*Numenius phaeopus*). *Náttúrufraeðingurinn* 27: 113–125.

HEADLAM, C. G. 1971. Whimbrels breeding at sea-level in northern Highlands. *Scott. Birds* 6: 279–280.

VENABLES, L. S. V. and U. M. VENABLES. 1955. *Birds and Mammals of Shetland*. Edinburgh.

WILLIAMSON, K. 1946. Field-notes on the breeding biology of the Whimbrel *Numenius phaeopus* (Linnaeus). *North-West Nat.* 21: 167–184.

WILLIAMSON, K. 1951. The moorland birds of Unst, Shetland. *Scott. Nat.* 63: 37–44.

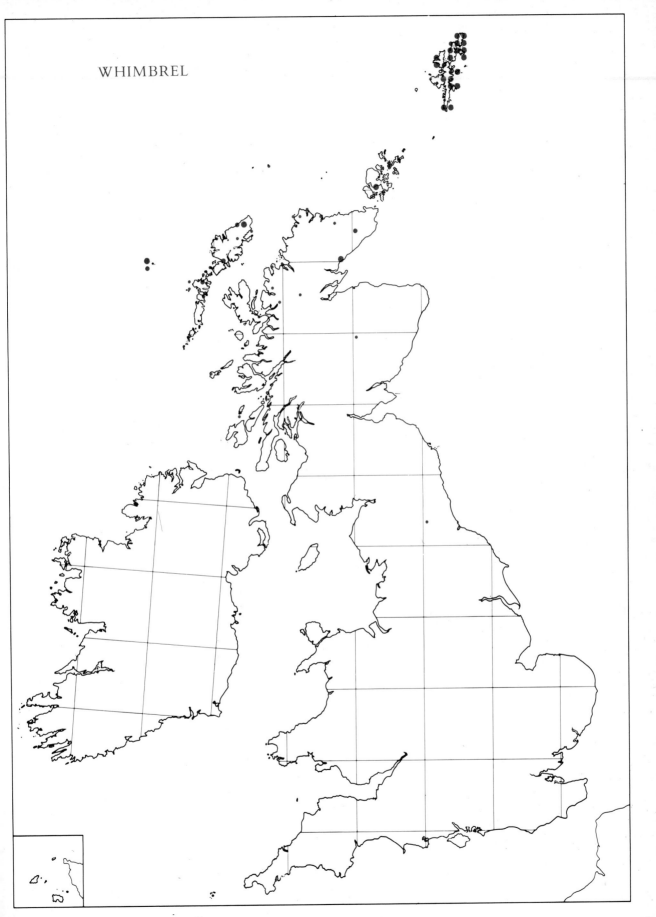

WHIMBREL

Black-tailed Godwit

Limosa limosa

In England, Black-tailed Godwits breed in damp, undulating meadows, the nest being placed on a hummock or dyke-bank if the terrain is too wet. Fields which are grazed in spring, cut for hay late in the summer and flooded throughout the winter produce the tussocky structure favoured by this species. In N Scotland, on the other hand, the habitat is usually damp moorland and blanket-bog.

Suitable habitat is so restricted in England, and the birds are so vocal and conspicuous in display, that the map probably gives a full picture of the 1968–72 distribution. Breeding was formerly far more widespread, and until the early 19th century took place commonly over much of East Anglia as well as in parts of Yorkshire. Drainage, egg-collecting and shooting have been blamed for the extinction of the species as a regular breeder in England by the late 1820s or 1830s. There were only half a dozen scattered records in the next century, but then, from about 1940, the numbers seen on passage and in winter increased enormously (Prater 1975) and isolated breeding became more frequent.

A pair nested unsuccessfully in the Ouse Washes (Cambridge/Norfolk) in 1952, but four pairs bred in the following year and increasing numbers annually since then. The birds and the site have been carefully protected since 1953; indeed, it was not until 1958 that the fact of breeding was announced, and another 11 years before the actual locality was disclosed in 1969. By that time, the ground was safely in the ownership of three conservation organisations—the RSPB, the Wildfowl Trust, and the Cambridge and Isle of Ely Naturalists' Trust. This is still the major locality, holding about 85% of the British breeding birds (see graph). Nesting by a few pairs occurs regularly now at a few other sites, and irregularly at several more (eight or nine during 1968–72).

Increasing numbers of Black-tailed Godwits have wintered here since the 1940s, mainly at the harbours of the English Channel coast and in S Ireland (see graph), and there is a large spring and autumn passage. It has been shown that the wintering birds belong to the Icelandic race *L. l. islandica* (William-

son and Ruttledge 1957, Vernon 1963), and that the pattern reflects the remarkable recent expansion of this population due to the climatic amelioration (Prater 1975). Judging by their richer and more contrasting breeding dress, those which breed on moorland in Caithness, Orkney and Shetland are also derived from Icelandic stock. It has been suggested that this may also be true of the colonists of East Anglia, despite the similarity in habitat preference to their neighbours of the typical race in the Netherlands (Harrison and Harrison 1965).

This species is afforded special protection in Great Britain under Schedule I of the Protection of Birds Act, 1954–67.

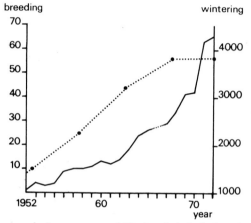

Increases during 1952–72 of Black-tailed Godwits wintering in Britain and Ireland (Icelandic race *L. l. islandica*: dotted) and pairs breeding on the Ouse Washes (solid)

Number of 10-km squares in which recorded:
    47 (1%)
Possible breeding   21 (45%)
Probable breeding   12 (26%)
Confirmed breeding   14 (30%)

Thirty-four dots have been moved by one 10-km square (as recommended by the Rare Breeding Birds Panel) and four dots in Ireland (all of possible breeding) have been omitted (as recommended by Major R. F. Ruttledge and D. Scott)

References

CONDER, P. 1962. The return of the Black-tailed Godwit. In BROWN, P. and G. WATERSTON, *The Return of the Osprey*. London.

COTTIER, E. J. and D. LEA. 1969. Black-tailed Godwits, Ruffs and Black Terns breeding on the Ouse Washes. *Brit. Birds* 62: 259–270.

HARRISON, J. M. and J. G. HARRISON. 1965. The juvenile plumage of the Icelandic Black-tailed Godwit and further occurrences of this race in England. *Brit. Birds* 58: 10–14.

PRATER, A. J. 1975. The wintering population of the Black-tailed Godwit. *Bird Study* 22: 169–176.

VERNON, J. D. R. 1963. Icelandic Black-tailed Godwits in the British Isles. *Brit. Birds* 56: 233–237.

WILLIAMSON, K. and R. F. RUTTLEDGE. 1957. Icelandic Black-tailed Godwits wintering in Ireland. *Brit. Birds* 50: 524–526.

Green Sandpiper *Tringa ochropus*, **see page 448**

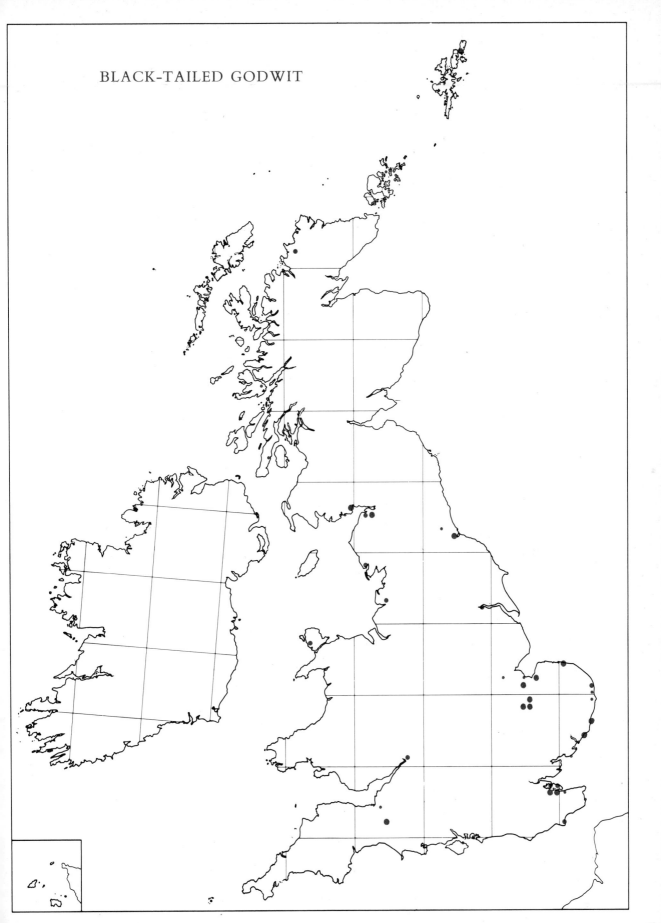

BLACK-TAILED GODWIT

Wood Sandpiper

Tringa glareola

The breeding habitat ranges from relatively open, boggy moorland to small, wet clearings in conifer and birch woods. The majority of Wood Sandpipers nest on the ground in wet situations, and these are where they have been found in Britain, but a small proportion use old tree nests of other species, especially Fieldfares *Turdus pilaris* (Ferguson-Lees 1971). British sites are usually close to eutrophic lochans with marshy areas of reeds and sedges providing suitable places for feeding.

Wood Sandpipers are often fairly easy to locate up to mid-June, when the conspicuous song flight is distinctive, with frequently repeated, mellow, double notes uttered during a gliding descent on down-curved wings. During the incubation period, however, they are much less vocal, and therefore relatively inconspicuous. After the eggs hatch, the adults sometimes become extremely noisy in defence of their broods, mobbing intruders with a harsh and rapid 'chip chip' call, though other pairs may remain silent and unobtrusive. Passage birds may occur, and even sing and display, in suitable breeding areas at any time from late April, but then move on. Some of the possible and probable records during 1968–72 are likely to have referred to such migrants.

A pair of Wood Sandpipers bred in Northumberland in 1853, and possibly at the same site in 1857. It was not until 1959, however, that another pair was proved to breed, when two young were seen in a marshy area in Sutherland. A pair bred at this same locality in each of the three following years, and birds were present there and breeding was proved in other years into the early 1970s. A nest was found in W Inverness in 1960, in the following year a second pair in Sutherland successfully reared two young and, later, breeding probably occurred in Perthshire.

During 1968–72, the maxima in any one season were five occupied sites, 16 or more birds present and five pairs proved to breed, but there were wide fluctuations from year to year, 1969 being particularly poor and 1972 particularly good (see table). By 1972, 13 years had elapsed since the first confirmed instance of nesting this century and, though breeding has probably occurred annually in recent years, colonisation cannot yet be regarded as firmly established.

Although Wood Sandpipers may have been missed at remote sites during *Atlas* fieldwork, the map combining five years' records probably exaggerates the picture in any one year.

This species is afforded special protection in Great Britain under Schedule I of the Protection of Birds Act, 1954–67.

Number of 10-km squares in which recorded:
  18 (0.5%)
Possible breeding   4 (22%)
Probable breeding   9 (50%)
Confirmed breeding   5 (28%)

All dots have been moved by one 10-km square (as recommended by the Rare Breeding Birds Panel)

References

DOWNHILL, I. R. and G. HALLAS. 1959. Wood Sandpiper breeding in Sutherland. *Scott. Birds* 1: 150–151.

DOWNHILL, I. R. and I. D. PENNIE. 1963. Wood Sandpipers breeding in Sutherland. *Scott. Birds* 2: 309.

FERGUSON-LEES, I. J. 1971. Studies of less familiar birds. 164. Wood Sandpiper. *Brit. Birds* 64: 114–117.

THOM, V. M. 1966. Probable breeding of Wood Sandpipers in Perthshire. *Scott. Birds* 4: 228.

Wood Sandpipers in suitable breeding areas in Scotland 1968–74

Numbers refer to occupied sites, birds (in brackets) and pairs proved breeding. P = present: probably only one or two birds

This table has been compiled from 'Scottish Bird Reports' and *Atlas* data, but may be incomplete

	1968	1969	1970	1971	1972	1973	1974
Aberdeenshire	—	—	—	—	—	1 (1) 0	—
N Argyllshire	1 (3) 0	—	—	—	—	—	—
Caithness	—	—	—	—	2 (4) 1	1 (1) 0	2 (2) 0
E Inverness-shire	1 (8–12) 2	2 (2) 0	—	1 (1) 0	1 (3) 1	1 (1) 0	1 (3) 1
Outer Hebrides	—	1 (P) 0	—	—	—	—	—
Perthshire	1 (1) 0	—	1 (5) 0	1 (P) 0	—	—	—
Ross-shire	—	—	—	1 (P) 0	1 (6) 3	—	—
Sutherland	2 (4) 1	—	1 (2) 0	1 (2) 1	1 (2) 0	—	—
Minimum totals	5 (16) 3	3 (3) 0	2 (7) 0	4 (5) 1	5 (15) 5	3 (3) 0	3 (5) 1

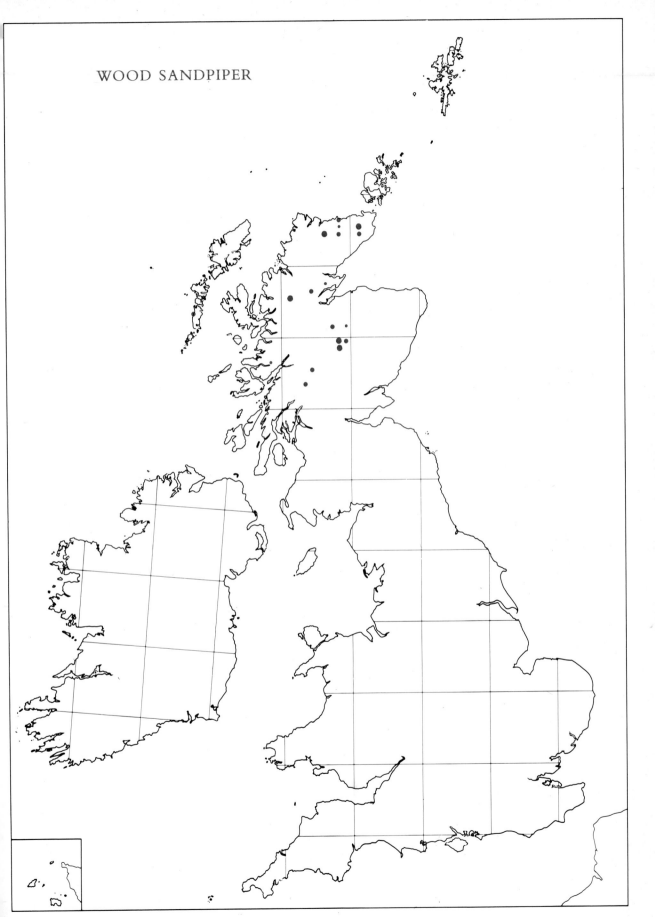

WOOD SANDPIPER

Common Sandpiper

Tringa hypoleucos

The Common Sandpiper is typical of upland streams, rivers and clear lakes, with exposed alluvial deposits and stony rather than muddy or marshy shores. It is often the only breeding bird on the bare margins of upland lochs. It also frequents the shores of Scottish sea lochs and, particularly in SW Ireland, coastal shingle bars. In Ireland, lowland rivers and streams and, above all, the lowland lakes of Connacht, the Shannon, Co Clare and the midlands have a far higher density than upland streams and rivers. In lowland Britain, river banks and, occasionally, flooded gravel pits may be just suitable.

In the Pennines, Cuthbertson *et al* (1952) found that only about a quarter of the river systems supported Common Sandpipers. The unsuitable areas were generally narrow becks, rivers with a fall of over 40 m per km, streams with heavily vegetated or steep-sided rocky banks, and those above 540 m, though in Scotland the species penetrates to 650 m.

Presence is not difficult to detect, as the adults bob conspicuously at the water's edge or on partly submerged stones, showing their white under tail-coverts, and frequently utter their high-pitched 'willy-wicket' song. Breeding is usually also easy to deduce from the adults' agitated behaviour when they have young, although it may be difficult to locate the chicks themselves, since they are adept at diving into cover. The scattered records of possible and probable breeding in the lowlands presumably refer mainly to passage birds. Yet this is not always so, for two pairs summered in Surrey in 1969: song and display were noted, and in one case distraction display confirmed breeding. There have been similar instances elsewhere, the most recent in Norfolk in 1962 and 1963.

The earliest returning birds are difficult to separate from the small wintering population that has built up here during the last few decades. In England and Ireland the main arrival is in mid-April, but in Scotland about a fortnight later.

The distribution is not known to have changed markedly in this century in Britain, though breeding on Dartmoor has not been recorded since 1962, before the severe winter of 1962/63. Where changes in status have been noted, however, these refer to decreases, which have occurred over the whole range from Orkney, E Scotland and the Lake District to S Wales and SW England. Most losses appear to have taken place during the period between the 1930s and 1950s. In Ireland, there seems to have been a contraction in range since the 1950s: the area of scarcity during about 1900–60, encompassing Carlow, Kilkenny, Waterford and Wexford, appears now to have extended to include Kildare, Louth, Meath and even E Cork.

The BTO Waterways Survey in 1974 showed an average of 0.83 pairs per km of river and stream in N England and N Wales, compared with only 0.1 pairs per km in the Midland counties. Sedbergh School surveys in the W Yorkshire Pennines during 1939–51 revealed an average density of 0.21 pairs per km on 480 km of rivers and becks, but the species was found along only 96 km of the total length, giving an average of 1.05 pairs per km; the greatest densities were found in the lower river valleys where, over a 12 km stretch of the River Lune, there were 3.32 pairs per km. Along 400 km of the River Esk (Midlothian), only 90 km were colonised, by a total of 50 pairs, giving an average of 0.2 pairs per km, or 0.55 pairs per km of occupied banks. A general figure is probably about 0.2–0.4 pairs per km of river bank or, considering only the suitable areas, about 0.5–1.0 pairs per km.

It is very difficult to estimate the size of the present British and Irish population. The Esk area covered approximately four 10-km squares, and the Lune two squares: this would give averages of 13 pairs and 50 pairs per 10-km square respectively. Although this is a minute sample from which to extrapolate, it is likely that the average lies between 10 and 30 pairs per 10-km square. This gives an upper limit to the British and Irish breeding population of 50,000 pairs, which is thus in the lower half of Parslow's category of 10,000–100,000 pairs.

Number of 10-km squares in which recorded:
 1,858 (48%)
Possible breeding   277 (15%)
Probable breeding   319 (17%)
Confirmed breeding   1,262 (68%)

References

COWPER, C. N. L. 1973. Breeding distribution of Grey Wagtails, Dippers and Common Sandpipers on the Midlothian Esk. *Scott. Birds* 7: 302–306.

CUTHBERTSON, E. I., G. T. FOGGITT and M. A. BALL. 1952. A census of Common Sandpipers in the Sedbergh area, 1951. *Brit. Birds* 45: 171–175.

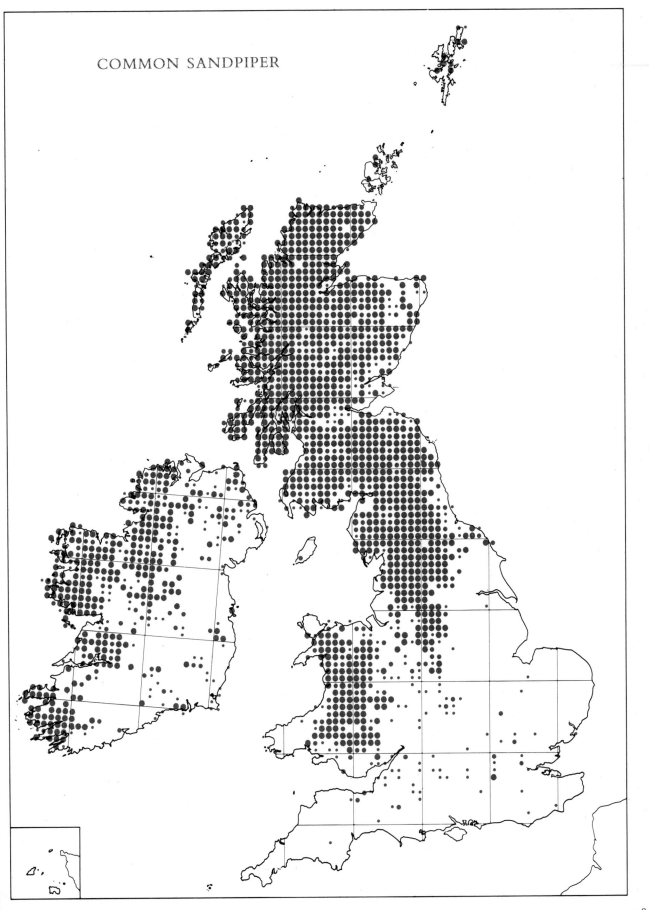

COMMON SANDPIPER

Redshank

Tringa totanus

The old evocative names of 'watchdog of the marshes' and 'yelper' conjure up an accurate picture of the Redshank noisily proclaiming the invasion of its nesting ground by an intruder. Though some single pairs on isolated patches of marshy ground may have evaded the *Atlas* fieldworkers, the extreme conspicuousness of this species whenever its breeding areas are approached is likely to have resulted in an accurate picture of its 1968–72 distribution.

The usual habitat is damp (but not wet) marshland and grassy fields, generally without lush vegetation. This may vary from a small patch of winter flooding in an otherwise dry field to water-meadows, estuarine marshes and saltings, but rushy fields and wet pastures together make up the commonest habitat, where the nest is frequently placed in a prominent tussock of sedge or grass. In S England, recently flooded gravel pits often provide ideal conditions for a few years.

The Redshank is one of the earliest waders to return to its nesting grounds: it may even be displaying before January is out in some parts of S England, though the end of February in the lowlands, and March in the hills, are the more usual times for settling down. Eggs are customarily laid in late April or May, so that chicks are about from mid-May onwards in lowland fields and during June in moorland regions. Pairs nesting on tidal saltmarshes have a variable breeding success, those at the lowest levels being usually flooded out by the highest of the late May and June spring tides; many birds, however, are able to lay again and complete the breeding cycle by mid-July. Most breeding sites are deserted by that time, though it is difficult to be sure of this in coastal saltmarshes owing to the presence of non-breeders and post-breeding gatherings.

The species has had a somewhat chequered history in Britain. There was a huge decrease at the beginning of the 19th century, presumably linked with extensive drainage. From then until about 1842, the distribution seems to have been confined to counties bordering the North Sea, from Orkney south to Kent. From about 1865, there was a gradual spread to the west and southwest, continuing until about 1940. There has probably been little general change since then (though some new counties have been colonised), decreases from habitat alterations mostly being matched by in-

creases elsewhere. In S England, however, inland breeding has certainly become scarcer, and Redshanks now have a markedly coastal distribution, while numbers have dropped since the last stages of the expansion of the 1930s (*eg* Shrubb 1968).

This is now a markedly commoner bird in the north than in the south, as reflected in the density of dots in N England and Scotland. By comparison, Redshanks are scarce in Ireland, with remarkably little coastal breeding and the main inland sites centred on the Connacht lakes and Lough Neagh; the western limit of breeding was documented by Ruttledge (1961). During 1968–72, Redshanks were located in the breeding season in half of the squares in Britain and Ireland. They may be badly affected by severe winters: in Devon, where small numbers had bred since the beginning of the century, there were no indications of nesting after the severe winter of 1962/63, until a pair held territory again in 1973. Parslow suggested a connection between the mild winters of the period of expansion and the harder winters which occurred after 1940, at which time expansion ceased and the distribution became more coastal in the south. Even so, Redshanks are now more numerous than they were at the end of the 19th century and the decline (if any) has been less marked than in some countries on the Continent.

Greenhalgh (1971) found that on the Ribble Estuary (Lancashire) densities were nearly twice as great on the natural saltings as on the wet, reclaimed marsh: 22.5 pairs per km^2 and 12.2 pairs per km^2 respectively. Extensive areas of saltmarsh support large numbers of breeding Redshanks: 1,500 pairs on the Wash, for instance. Some estimated averages per 10-km square are: the Wash 160 pairs, NW England 150 pairs, and Essex 55 pairs. Many inland haunts in the south have low numbers, which reduces the average, perhaps to 20–25 pairs per 10-km square. Extrapolation from these figures suggests a total British and Irish population of about 38,000–48,000 pairs, in the lower part of the range 10,000–100,000 pairs given by Parslow and reasonably consistent with winter counts on estuaries and similar haunts.

Number of 10-km squares in which recorded:
1,925 (50%)
Possible breeding   327 (17%)
Probable breeding   333 (17%)
Confirmed breeding   1,265 (66%)

References

GREENHALGH, M. E. 1971. The breeding bird communities of Lancashire saltmarshes. *Bird Study* 18: 199–212.

HALE, W. G. 1956. The lack of territory in the Redshank, *Tringa totanus*. *Ibis* 98: 398–400.

RUTTLEDGE, R. F. 1961. The breeding range and status of the Redshank in western Ireland. *Bird Study* 8: 2–5.

SHRUBB, M. 1968. The status and distribution of Snipe, Redshank and Yellow Wagtail as breeding birds in Sussex. *Sussex Bird Rep.* 20: 53–60.

THOMAS, J. F. 1942. Report on the Redshank Inquiry, 1939–40. *Brit. Birds* 36: 5–14, 22–34.

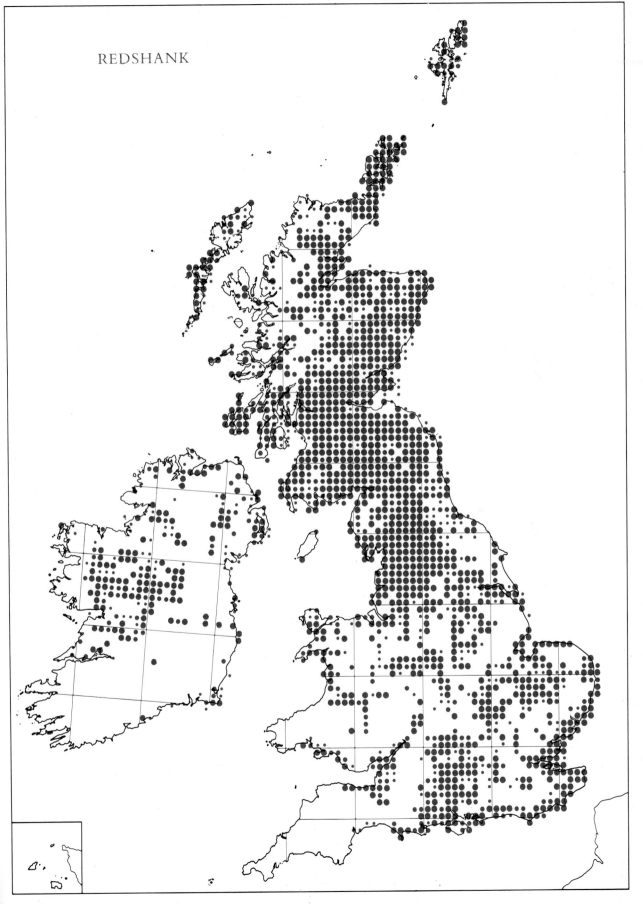

REDSHANK

Greenshank

Tringa nebularia

Greenshanks are birds of wild country. The habitat varies from rough, boggy, moorland slopes, with rocky ridges and occasional clumps of trees, to flat and unbroken flows. Some in the Spey Valley nest in forest bogs, as in N Europe, and they are found occasionally well inside open canopy pine woods; in Deeside, a few pairs occur in forest meadows. In the Spey Valley, with its abundance of fallen timber, the Greenshanks usually place their nests against dead wood, and favourite nesting sites in Sutherland and Perthshire are close to old snow-fencing alongside railways, or adjacent to stones on open heather moors. In all cases, the mottled, grey-brown plumage of the sitting birds forms a superb camouflage against lichen-covered timber or rocks. They dislike nesting in rank heather and, if it grows too tall, even traditional ground may be abandoned. Moorland burning can have a beneficial effect, increasing the number of pairs until such time as the new growth becomes too long (Nethersole-Thompson and Nethersole-Thompson 1943). They nest from a few metres above sea level in the NW Highlands regularly to a height of 480 m, and up to 630 m in the Cairngorms.

It is easy to find Greenshanks on their breeding grounds. They call noisily if flushed while feeding and have a wonderful, switchback song flight which attracts attention. The nest is one of the most difficult to find of all in Britain and Ireland, and indeed this species is the nest searcher's blue riband bird. Few *Atlas* records refer to nests; fortunately, adults become noisily agitated when small young are approached, so that the discovery of a nest is not essential to prove breeding. Distraction and aggressive behaviour provided much of the evidence for confirmed breeding. It has to be remembered, however, that Greenshank families, like those of many other waders, may move several kilometres from the home area, deserting the relatively dry, open moor to concentrate on loch shores or along burns.

Although the bulk of the population winters south of the Sahara, Greenshanks return to their breeding grounds remarkably early: the first are often back in late March, and almost all are on their territories by mid-April. This has led to speculation that the birds which winter in Britain, and especially in Ireland, may belong to the Scottish breeding population, for the main passage of Greenshanks on the Continent takes place during late April and early May. The chicks hatch, and adults are very noisy, over about a month from late May: during studies spanning 16 years, Nethersole-Thompson (1951) noted that the first young hatched in the period 22nd–31st May. Late clutches may result in chicks still being present at the end of July; by then many pairs will have left the breeding grounds, although some juveniles remain throughout August.

Though their eggs were much sought by oologists in the 19th and early 20th centuries, the limited evidence suggests that the Greenshank's numbers increased and its range expanded during that period. There have been local decreases in the south of the range in Inverness-shire, but no marked change in the main part north of the Great Glen, and probably an increase in the Outer Hebrides where breeding may not have been regular during the 1940s (see map on page 458). Greenshanks were proved to breed in 15 10-km squares in Lewis, Harris and N and S Uist during 1968–72, but they remained absent from Orkney and Shetland. No confirmed records came from S Aberdeenshire, or the Lammermuir Hills (E Lothian/Berwickshire) where breeding was recorded in the 1920s. There has been a notable range extension into Ireland, however, where a single pair has now nested annually for several years at one locality.

Nethersole-Thompson (1951) found that Greenshanks usually hold large territories, and that there may be only one pair in 1,500–3,500 ha. In typical habitats, however, a pair occupies 100 to 300 ha, and the highest recorded density was four pairs in 160 ha. In many cases, feeding birds could be found 3 or 4 km from the nest site. He estimated that there were probably about 300–500 pairs nesting in Scotland. Numbers now may be slightly higher than this in good years, and a guess at two to four pairs per 10-km square in which probable or confirmed breeding was recorded in 1968–72 would give a total of about 400–750 pairs.

This species is afforded special protection in Great Britain under Schedule I of the Protection of Birds Act, 1954–67.

Number of 10-km squares in which recorded:
254 (7%)
Possible breeding   66 (26%)
Probable breeding   53 (21%)
Confirmed breeding   135 (53%)

Within the shaded 100-km square, the dot is conventionally placed centrally (as recommended by Major R. F. Ruttledge and D. Scott); all other dots are shown accurately (as recommended by the Rare Breeding Birds Panel)

References
NETHERSOLE-THOMPSON, D. 1951. *The Greenshank*. London.
NETHERSOLE-THOMPSON, C. and D. NETHERSOLE-THOMPSON. 1943. Nest-site selection by birds. *Brit. Birds* 37: 70–76, 88–94, 108–113.

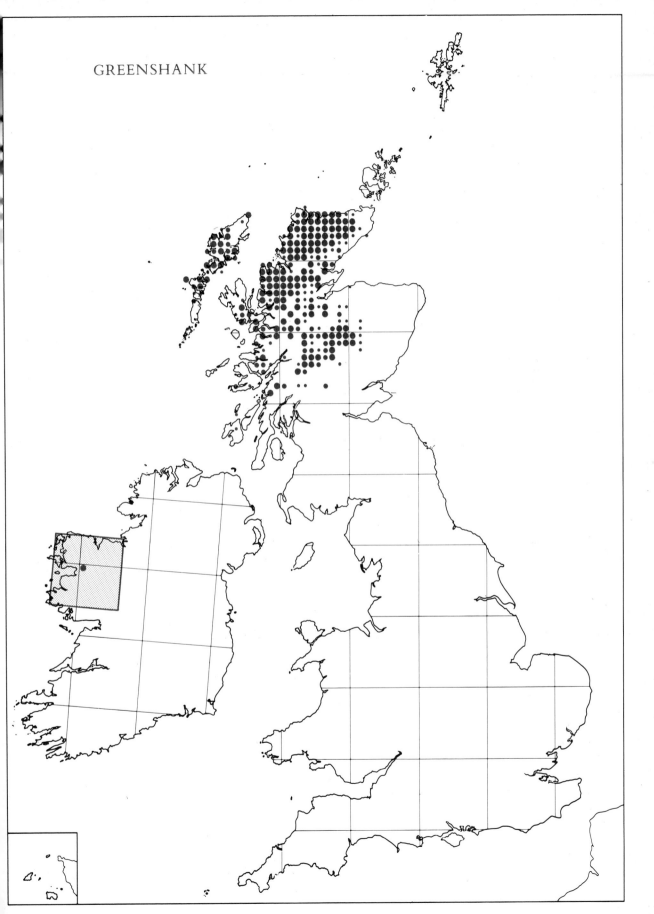

GREENSHANK

Temminck's Stint

Calidris temminckii

R.A.R.

Temminck's Stints are mainly tundra breeders, nesting from Norway eastwards to NE Siberia. They are scarce and very locally distributed in S Scandinavia, so that the few British ones are at the extreme west of the range and at least 5° of latitude farther south. They breed in a wide variety of situations, ranging from coastal plains in Finland to 1,000 m above sea level in N Scandinavia. The habitat is usually rather limited, however, being principally the mossy bogs and wet grassland with willow scrub which are associated with river valleys.

The trilling song and moth-like aerial display are distinctive and, if the nest is in open terrain, the species' tameness makes it quite easy to find by watching back. Males may also trill from vantage points on the ground (Southern and Lewis 1938). Initial location, however, depends almost entirely on chance where the population is thinly dispersed. Temminck's Stints are among the latest birds to nest, reaching their breeding grounds in late May or early June. The eggs are usually laid during the second half of June. Like some populations of Sanderlings *C. alba*, Temminck's Stints lay two clutches of eggs, within a two-week period (Hildén 1965). Hildén's subsequent studies (1975) have shown a most remarkable breeding strategy, well described in his summary as a double-clutch system associated with successive bigamy: 'Every female pairs in rapid succession with two males on different territories and lays one clutch on each. Every male also pairs successively on the same territory with two females and fertilizes one clutch of each. The first clutch is incubated by the male, the second by the female, and both take sole responsibility for their brood. Exceptions to the normal schedule occur fairly often, chiefly due to the polygynous tendency in males. They court every female that enters their territory, so two females occasionally lay their first clutches on the same territory.' Chicks are usually found from mid-July to early August.

The only recorded instances of nesting in Britain before 1968 were in Inverness-shire in 1934, 1936 and 1956 (with presence, but no nest found, in 1935 and 1947) and in Yorkshire in 1951. In all proven breeding records the eggs were found, but in none were they successfully hatched: two clutches were collected after they were presumed to have been deserted, one failed due to a predator, and the sitting bird was killed on the fourth. During the six years 1969–74, however, one or two pairs were present annually at one site in Scotland. Disturbance was kept to a minimum to give the birds an opportunity to establish themselves, and successful breeding was confirmed once, two downy chicks being seen on 16th July 1971 and ringed six days later. The description of this case in Easter Ross (Headlam 1972) makes interesting reading in light of the research into the phenomenon of a double clutch in this species in Finland. At no time were two adults seen together during the two weeks that careful observations were made, although two were watched 200 m apart. It seems likely that there was one pair with a double clutch.

Other sightings of Temminck's Stints in suitable breeding habitat during 1968–72 may have referred merely to passage birds, but there can be little doubt that the species has bred undetected on many more occasions than the few which have been discovered and reported by ornithologists.

Temminck's Stints have a relatively long life expectancy. Hildén (1972) found that most adults live to be five to eight years of age. This is surprising in view of their potentially high productivity, but it does indicate that pairs may have a good chance of establishing a regular breeding population if they are allowed to nest undisturbed.

This species is afforded special protection in Great Britain under Schedule I of the Protection of Birds Act, 1954–67.

Number of 10-km squares in which recorded:
    4 (0.1%)
Possible breeding   2 (50%)
Probable breeding   1 (25%)
Confirmed breeding   1 (25%)

One dot has been moved by up to two 10-km squares (as recommended by the Rare Breeding Birds Panel)

References

BANNERMAN, D. A. 1961. *The Birds of the British Isles.* Vol. 9. Edinburgh and London.

HEADLAM, C. G. 1972. Temminck's Stints breeding in Scotland. *Scott. Birds* 7: 94.

HILDÉN, O. 1965. Zur Brutbiologie des Temminckstrandläufers, *Calidris temminckii* (Leisl.). *Orn. Fenn.* 42: 1–5.

HILDÉN, O. 1972. Mortality and average life expectancy of Temminck's Stint (*Calidris temminckii*). *Proc. Int. Orn. Congr.* 15, abstracts: 650.

HILDÉN, O. 1975. Breeding system of Temminck's Stint *Calidris temminckii*. *Orn. Fenn.* 52: 117–146.

SHARROCK, J. T. R. 1974. *Scarce Migrant Birds in Britain and Ireland.* Berkhamsted.

SOUTHERN, H. N. and W. A. S. LEWIS. 1938. The breeding behaviour of Temminck's Stint. *Brit. Birds* 31: 314–321.

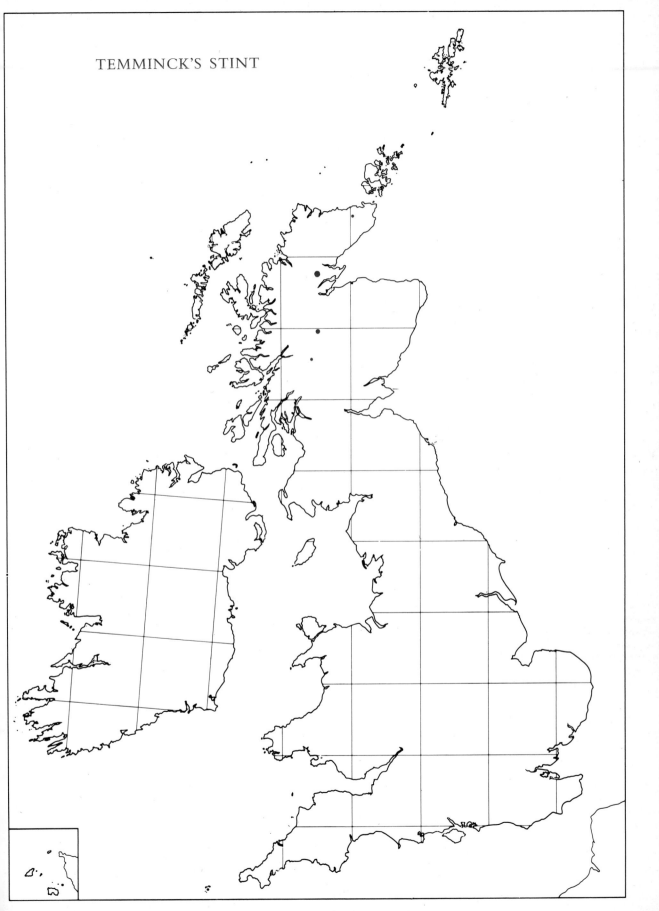

TEMMINCK'S STINT

Dunlin

Calidris alpina

The typical habitat of the Dunlin in Britain is poorly drained upland moors, with scattered small pools, particularly good examples being the Pennine mosses of N England and the flow country of N Scotland. In contrast, Dunlins are rarely moorland birds in Ireland, where the habitat is usually callow land—lowland rough grass near lakes and turloughs or marshes. They breed round the grassy edges of some Scottish lochs, as they do at the loughs of Connacht and Ulster, and are to be found in good numbers near sea level on the machair of the Outer Hebrides, also in lesser strength on the extensive saltmarshes from the Solway Firth south to the Ribble Estuary (Lancashire). As they are often semi-colonial, a small patch of suitable ground may hold several pairs.

It is remarkably easy to overlook breeding sites unless the Dunlin's trilling song is heard, for the adults often stand silently some way from the nest. Sometimes a useful clue can be obtained by listening to the local Skylarks *Alauda arvensis*, which, when Dunlins are nesting nearby, frequently include an excellent imitation of the trill in their songs. Similarly, Golden Plovers *Pluvialis apricaria* can be of practical help to the Dunlin-seeker, for the smaller birds follow the plovers when they circle an intruder into their territory: in some places the Dunlin is known as the 'plover's page'. Since Dunlins sing and display while still on passage, a score of trilling birds may be recorded in May in a locality which later holds but one or two breeding pairs, or even none at all; this is especially liable to occur in coastal areas or beside inland lakes. The nest is not easy to find and the tiny young are well camouflaged, but anxious adults often come very close to an observer.

After wintering in S Europe and N Africa, the return to lowland breeding grounds is in late April, with most back by early May; those which nest at high altitudes—up to 1,000 m in the Cairngorms—arrive a week or two later. Egg-laying begins shortly after they have settled in mid-May, so that hatching takes place mainly during the first half of June. Even at this early period, failed breeders may be leaving the breeding grounds; Dunlins suffer a fairly high failure rate since many nests are made in wet, grassy areas which become flooded during heavy rain. At the end of June some females leave their broods, and by the end of July virtually all have gone.

The scattered records and low proportion of proved breeding reflect both the difficulty in locating the dispersed pockets of birds and their relative scarcity. The map suggests that Dunlins are now more common on the Pennines and in extreme NE Scotland (Shetland, Orkney and Caithness) than elsewhere. The British and Irish breeding populations are at the extreme southwestern edge of the species' range in the Palearctic, and indeed the Dartmoor birds form the most southerly group in the world. Our Dunlins belong to the southern race *C. a. schinzii*, which ranges north to Iceland in the west and S Finland in the east. Throughout this range, numbers have fluctuated markedly in recent times. There has been a decline in Denmark, due primarily to drainage of nesting areas (Dybbro and Jørgensen 1971). In S Finland, on the other hand, Soikkeli (1964) traced a growth from the first breeding in the 1940s to a total of more than 200 pairs, and he considered this expansion to be due to the milder spring and summer weather, combined with loss of habitat farther south and west in Europe.

While breeding was not proved on Dartmoor until 1956, it has probably occurred there at least since 1937, judging by the agitated behaviour of the birds encountered by some observers (Moore 1969). It seems likely that Dunlin numbers have decreased in many parts of their British and Irish range in this century, although Yalden (1974) considered that those in the Peak District had remained fairly stable, or had even increased slightly, since 1900. Reafforestation of moorland may have had some effect in certain areas of Britain, but the lack of precise information makes assessment of changes extremely difficult. Though 100 or more pairs may be present in some 10-km squares, the average is probably only about 10–20 and the total population of Britain and Ireland is probably some 4,000–8,000 pairs.

Number of 10-km squares in which recorded:
537 (14%)
Possible breeding   137 (26%)
Probable breeding   155 (29%)
Confirmed breeding   245 (46%)

References

DYBBRO, T. and O. H. JØRGENSEN. 1971. The distribution of Black-tailed Godwit, Dunlin, Ruff and Avocet in Denmark 1970. *Dansk Orn. Foren. Tidsskr.* 65: 116–128.

GREENHALGH, M. E. 1969. The populations of Redshank and Dunlin on saltmarshes in northwest England. *Bird Study* 16: 63–64.

MOORE, R. 1969. *The Birds of Devon.* Newton Abbot.

SOIKKELI, M. 1964. The distribution of the Southern Dunlin (*Calidris alpina schinzii*) in Finland. *Ornis Fenn.* 41: 13–21.

YALDEN, D. W. 1974. The status of Golden Plover (*Pluvialis apricaria*) and Dunlin (*Calidris alpina*) in the Peak District. *Naturalist* no. 930: 81–91.

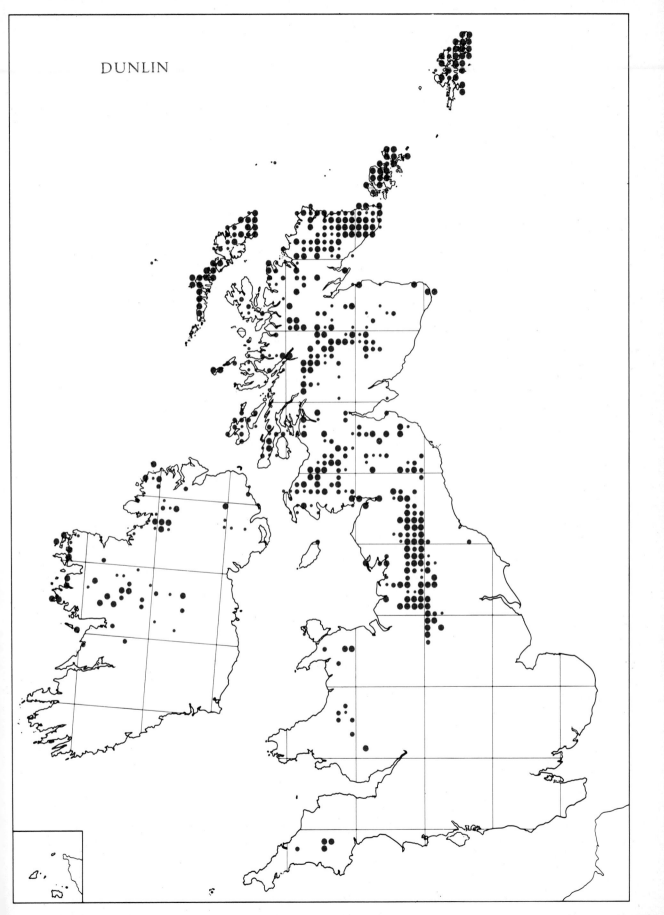

DUNLIN

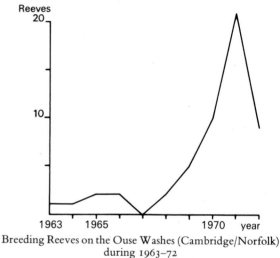

Ruff

Philomachus pugnax

The main breeding habitat in Britain and adjacent Continental countries is low-lying, wet, grassy meadows, which were once fenland and marshes, but are now usually grazed in summer and flooded in winter.

Ruffs formerly bred in many places in Britain from Northumberland to SW England, but declined through the 18th and 19th centuries, largely due to the drainage of suitable nesting areas. The final stages of extinction were probably hastened by the activities of collectors. The species bred regularly in Norfolk up to 1871, continued spasmodically until 1890, and nested again in 1907 and 1922. Outside Norfolk, the only breeding records after the 1860s were in Durham in 1902 (possibly 1901 and 1903) and probably in Suffolk in 1898 and Lancashire in 1910. Attempts at reintroduction, using imported eggs, in Norfolk in 1939 and 1957 were unsuccessful.

Then began the present period of recolonisation. The number wintering in Britain had been increasing since the 1950s (Prater 1973). After several years in which breeding was suspected, this was proved on the Ouse Washes (Cambridge/Norfolk) in 1963, the first time for 41 years.

The Ruffs first appear at their leks as soon as they come back from African wintering grounds in late March. Within two weeks virtually all the males have arrived, but the females (Reeves) rarely appear before the second week of April. The peak activity at leks is from mid-April to the end of May, but in some cases occupation continues until mid-June. Lek sites can be recognised by having many patches of almost bare earth about 30 cm in diameter and 1–1.5 m apart. Each male occupies its own patch or 'residence' and stays on it for the duration of the lek display, which is most vigorous just after sunrise. Ruffs in optimal summer dress are very much more successful in enticing females; and this usually means that one-year old birds with their smaller ruffs and head tufts are less successful than adults. After copulation the Reeves fly into the surrounding fields where they make their nests and incubate in almost complete isolation from the males. They are very inconspicuous, usually sitting tight or slipping unnoticed from their nests before an intruder is near. Once the young have hatched, however, the Reeve is much more obtrusive and flies around the intruder uttering low calls (Andersen 1951).

It is possible that occasional instances of breeding

were overlooked between 1922 and 1963, and that the 1968–72 map is incomplete. Breeding at the Ouse Washes has continued, with up to 103 males at the leks (1969) and up to 21 breeding Reeves (1971) (see graph). The main sites are now under the management and protection of conservation bodies.

Elsewhere, breeding is not regular and involves only a few Reeves, but points to the possibility of future range expansion. It is noteworthy that there has never been any suspicion of nesting in Scotland, even though the bulk of the world's population breeds on marshy tundra in N Europe and Asia. The British stock is most likely an offshoot from colonies in the Netherlands and Denmark.

This species is afforded special protection in Great Britain under Schedule I of the Protection of Birds Act, 1954–67.

Breeding Reeves on the Ouse Washes (Cambridge/Norfolk) during 1963–72

Number of 10-km squares in which recorded:
  14 (0.4%)
Possible breeding   6 (43%)
Probable breeding   2 (14%)
Confirmed breeding   6 (43%)

Four dots have been moved by up to two 10-km squares (as recommended by the Rare Breeding Birds Panel)

References

ANDERSEN, F. S. 1951. Contributions to the biology of the Ruff (*Philomachus pugnax*). *Dansk Orn. Foren. Tidsskr.* 45: 145–173.

COTTIER, E. J. and D. LEA. 1969. Black-tailed Godwits, Ruffs and Black Terns breeding on the Ouse Washes. *Brit. Birds* 62: 259–270.

HOGAN-WARBURG, A. J. 1966. Social behavior of the Ruff *Philomachus pugnax* (L.). *Ardea* 54: 109–229.

PRATER, A. J. 1973. The wintering population of Ruffs in Britain and Ireland. *Bird Study* 21: 245–250.

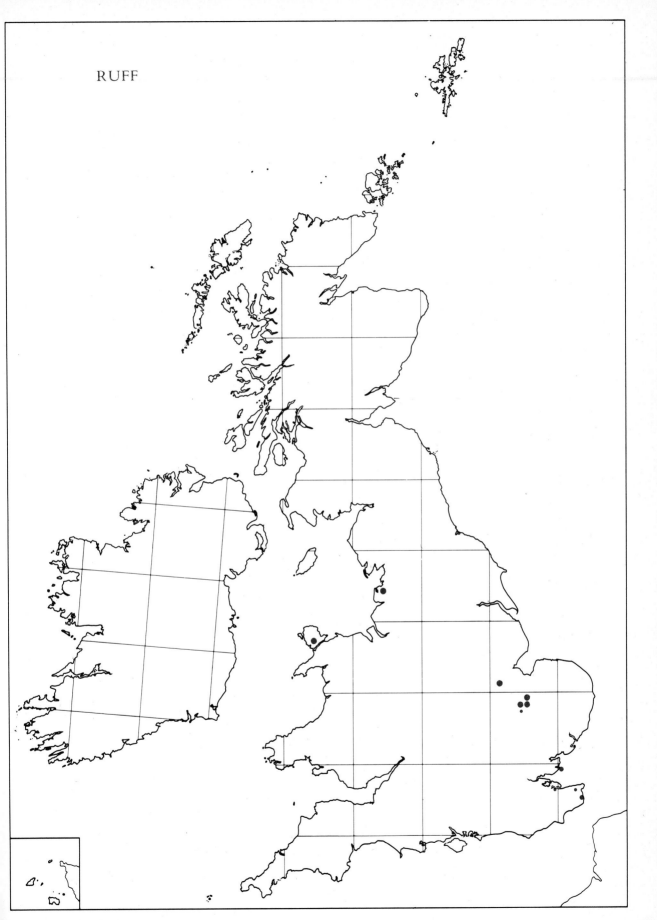

RUFF

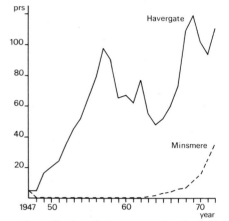

Avocet

Recurvirostra avosetta

In England, the highly specialised breeding habitat is shallow, brackish lagoons with low, muddy islands and gently sloping, sparsely vegetated banks, close to the coast. There are now few suitable sites in Britain and Ireland, even within nature reserves, where these birds are safe against reclamation, drainage and other disturbance.

Avocets formerly bred regularly, but perhaps never commonly on the coast of E England from the River Humber south to Sussex. A decline came in the late 18th and early 19th centuries, and the last instances of nesting in that period were in Norfolk about 1824, at the mouth of the River Trent about 1837, and in Kent in 1842. The reasons for this disappearance are not fully understood, since the period of extensive drainage and the heyday of oology both came later. It is known, however, that both Avocets and their eggs were harvested for food, and this may have contributed towards the extinction of colonies.

It was nearly 100 years before Avocets bred again, when two pairs nested, somewhat unexpectedly, in Co Wexford in 1938. Recolonisation of the English east coast began in the early 1940s, when most of this area was closed to the public during the war period. Not all records may be known, therefore, but breeding was confirmed during 1941–46 in both Essex and Norfolk. In 1947, four pairs nested at Minsmere, and four or five pairs on Havergate Island, both in Suffolk. Breeding has since been annual at Havergate and, from 1963, at Minsmere, building up to over 100 pairs at the former and 35 pairs at the latter by 1972 (see graph). Spasmodic nesting has occurred elsewhere in East Anglia and in Essex and Kent since the 1950s, but the only regular sites remain those which were colonised in 1947.

The recolonisation of England can be attributed to the increase of Avocets in the Netherlands, Denmark and adjacent countries. A rise in Denmark from 750 pairs in 1920 to 2,300 in 1970 was probably aided by the protection afforded by war-time access restrictions (Dybbro and Jørgensen 1971); in the Dutch strongholds, numbers increased fourfold between the 1920s and 1969 (Tjallingii 1970); and Avocets colonised Estonia, where they are still increasing, in 1962 (Kallas 1974). In England, the credit for their firm establishment as regular breeders must go to the RSPB who have afforded the birds encouragement at the two major sites, by protection and the maintenance of suitable breeding conditions. The two records of summering pairs in 1968–72 suggest the possibility of future range expansion, but because they are so conspicuous these attractive birds will have to be safeguarded from disturbance and egg-collectors wherever they attempt to nest.

This species is afforded special protection in Great Britain under Schedule I of the Protection of Birds Act, 1954–67.

The number of pairs of Avocets nesting in Suffolk since breeding first occurred in 1947

Number of 10-km squares in which recorded:
8 (0.2%)
Possible breeding   1 (13%)
Probable breeding   2 (25%)
Confirmed breeding   5 (63%)

References

BROWN, P. E. and E. LYNN-ALLEN. 1948. The breeding of Avocets in England in 1947. *Brit. Birds* 41: 14–17.

BROWN, P. E. 1949. The breeding of Avocets in England, 1948. *Brit. Birds* 42: 2–12.

BROWN, P. E. 1950. *Avocets in England*. RSPB, London.

DAVIES, G. 1962. The return of the Avocet. In BROWN, P. E. and G. WATERSTON, *The Return of the Osprey*. London and Glasgow.

DYBBRO, T. and O. H. JØRGENSEN. 1971. The distribution of Black-tailed Godwit, Dunlin, Ruff and Avocet in Denmark 1970. *Dansk Orn. Foren. Tidsskr.* 65: 116–128.

KALLAS, J. 1974. Nesting ecology of the Avocet in Käina Bay. *Estonian Wetlands and their Life*: 119–138. Tallinn.

TJALLINGII, S. T. 1970. Inventarisatie van de in 1969 in Nederland broedende Kluten. *De Levende Natuur* 73: 222–229, 251–255.

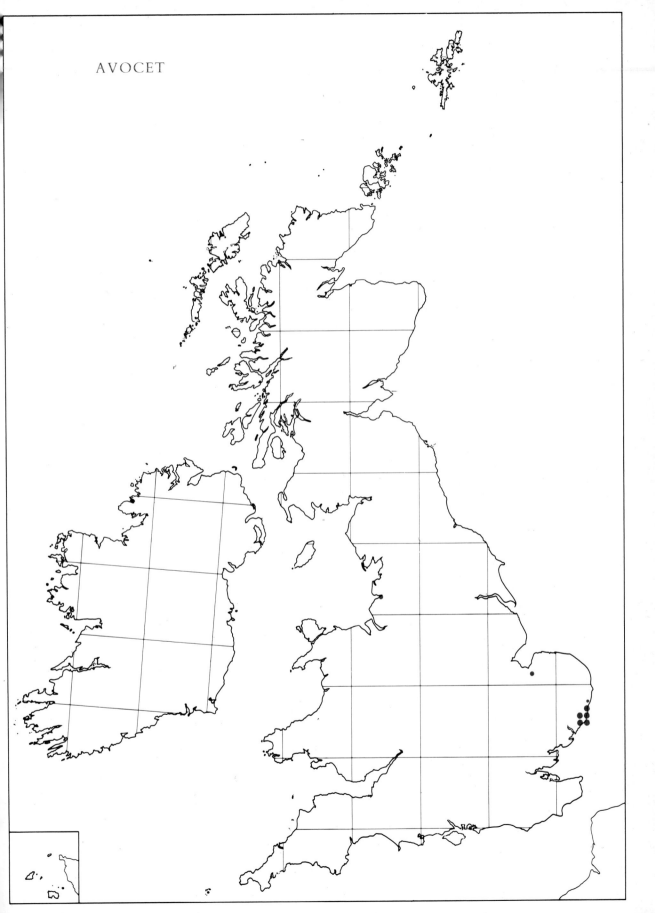

AVOCET

Red-necked Phalarope

Phalaropus lobatus

Breeding is usually associated with shallow pools created by peat cutting, small lochans and shallow bays of larger lochs. Emergent vegetation is normally present, although breeding birds will sometimes feed on lochs where there is little or none, and they may even do so on the sea. The nest may be in the surrounding marshland or in rough damp grazing pasture, often at some distance from open water.

The Red-necked Phalarope is one of the latest species to arrive in spring and, although some females, following their reversed sexual role, may defend territory during mid-May, most do not appear until the end of the month along with the males. Late birds may not be seen before mid-June, but nest building and egg laying start soon after their appearance on the breeding grounds, probably much of the courtship having taken place previously.

Although usually very tame, this charming, tiny wader can be easily overlooked as it swims among water plants, feeds along the edge of a pool, or walks on seaweed close to the tide's edge. The male incubates and can be watched back to the nest; with young, he becomes very agitated when approached, flying around and calling noisily. Initial location of pairs and confirmation of breeding once the young have hatched is usually fairly easy, but observation during incubation can be more difficult. There is also the complication of occasional migrants on passage to and from northern breeding grounds.

Since breeding sites may be associated with tiny pools—perhaps only 15 m across—some pairs may have been overlooked during 1968–72. There is considerable loyalty to traditional sites, however, and the map probably shows the situation in any typical year in the period, although numbers vary annually. Everett (1971) calculated that the total British and Irish population was 54–65 pairs in 1968, 28–41 pairs in 1969 and about 45 pairs in 1970.

Though precise figures are not available, there was a major decline in numbers during the first part of the 19th century (Saxby 1874, Buckley and Harvie-Brown 1891). This decline may have been due mainly to collecting, and a partial recovery in the early part of the 20th century seems likely to have resulted from protection. A large colony was discovered in Co Mayo in 1900, but numbers declined from about 50 pairs in 1905 and 40 in 1929 to only one to three pairs by 1966. There was then a short-lived revival during 1967–71, with up to 25–30 adults (1970) and

three to five pairs nesting; but the last year of the *Atlas* period saw none breeding there for the first time since their discovery, and only one bird appeared briefly in 1973.

The Red-necked Phalarope is a common breeding bird of the Holarctic region with the bulk of the population between 60°N and 70°N. In a few places, however, it extends south to 52°N and 54°N. Thus those in Ireland are at the extreme southern edge of the range. On the other hand, most of Shetland lies north of 60°N and within the main breeding zone. In Ireland and Scotland, climatic factors must play an important part in this species' fluctuations and the present cooling trend may prove advantageous. One other possible reason for the decrease and lack of recruitment into our Red-necked Phalarope breeding population from the north may be the migration routes used. The Fenno-Scandian population migrates southeast away from Britain: there are many ringing recoveries of Norwegian and Finnish phalaropes in the valley of the Dnepr, which flows into the Black Sea. Similarly, most Icelandic birds may take an oceanic route or combine with those from Greenland and migrate south off the east coast of N America. The presence of suitable habitat and freedom from disturbance are vital if the species is to maintain its present slender foothold in Britain and Ireland.

This species is afforded special protection in Great Britain under Schedule I of the Protection of Birds Act, 1954–67.

Number of 10-km squares in which recorded:
  22 (0·5%)
Possible breeding   2 (9%)
Probable breeding   3 (14%)
Confirmed breeding   17 (77%)

Five dots (all of confirmed breeding) have been omitted (as recommended by the Rare Breeding Birds Panel, M. J. Everett, Major R. F. Ruttledge and D. Scott)

References

BUCKLEY, T. E. and J. A. HARVIE-BROWN. 1891. *A Vertebrate Fauna of the Orkney Islands*. Edinburgh.

EVERETT, M. J. 1971. Breeding status of Red-necked Phalarope in Britain and Ireland. *Brit. Birds* 64: 293–302.

HILDÉN, O. and S. VUOLANTO. 1972. Breeding biology of the Red-necked Phalarope *Phalaropus lobatus* in Finland. *Orn. Fenn.* 49: 57–85.

SAXBY, H. L. and S. H. SAXBY 1874. *The Birds of Shetland*. Edinburgh.

WATSON, D. 1972. *Birds of Moor and Mountain*. Edinburgh.

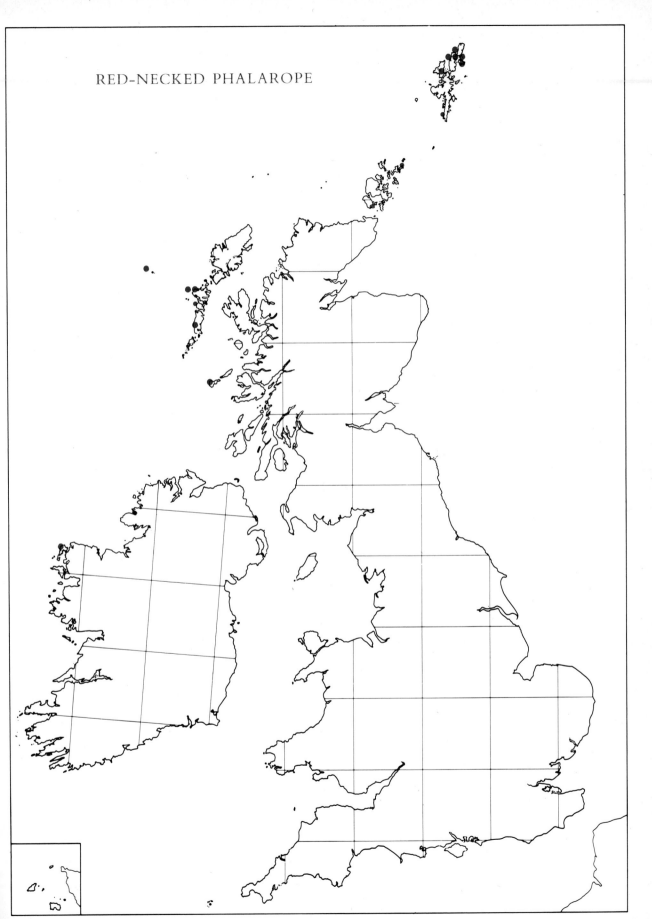

RED-NECKED PHALAROPE

Stone Curlew

Burhinus oedicnemus

Stone Curlews are birds of dry, stony, open ground, and in England there is a clear association with calcareous soils, mainly chalk downland, sandy heaths and shingle. The period between the wars, when marginal land was no longer cultivated, saw an increase. The reduction in Rabbit numbers from myxomatosis in the mid-1950s, allowing scrub to develop and engulf some downland sites, affected the species adversely. With increased cultivation and afforestation of marginal land, Stone Curlews have decreased further. Nowadays, many occupy cultivated fields and, to a lesser extent, the wide fire-breaks in forestry plantations. Despite these developments, the total distribution has changed relatively little since Yorkshire lost its small breeding population in 1938 (see maps on page 458).

In Britain, the Stone Curlew is at the northwestern edge of its range, which extends south and east to N Africa, Arabia and India. Although a few may overwinter in some years in S England, the species is basically a migrant, the majority arriving in March or early April. Stone Curlews are crepuscular and nocturnal in their habits and can be very difficult to see during the day, when they often lie up in the concealment of short cover. Their presence may be established during nocturnal visits to potential breeding areas because of their loud, eerie and penetrating calls. Their pale brown plumage provides excellent camouflage, and those with eggs or small chicks may run long distances before flying while the observer is still far off. Patient watching back from a concealed position can confirm breeding and two-thirds of the records reached this category.

In the typical open terrain of down or heathland, Stone Curlews usually make their nest scrapes on a small patch of bare earth just below the top of a ridge. In such a position the sitting bird's head may be visible from one side, but from the other the whole body will merge with the background. Most now breed on cultivated land and the nest may be hidden by the growing crop before the chicks hatch in the second half of May. This species still suffers at the hands of egg-collectors and, in some areas, early clutches may also be destroyed by rolling; repeat nests, as well as some genuine second broods, extend the breeding season into late August. When the chicks have hatched, they may be walked some way from the nest by their parents and proof of breeding can again be obtained by watching from a distance.

It is difficult to assess the number of Stone Curlews breeding in any area. There is every likelihood that non-breeders call and hold territories, and that the breeding birds may vary their calling, both quantitatively and in character, at different stages during their nesting cycle. Furthermore, in some areas there may be quite large gatherings of fledged young (and possibly also non-breeders) at a time when other pairs are still incubating fresh clutches or caring for small young. Some recent all-night expeditions have shown that peak vocal activity may be as late as 03.00 hours; thus, listening only during the evening and earlier part of the night may result in serious underestimates of the numbers present. Observers who have tried all-night vigils feel that Parslow's figure of 200–400 pairs in the late 1960s is too low.

Detailed studies in several areas have indicated that breeding densities of one pair per 100–200 ha may be attained regularly. On this basis, the population in Britain during the late 1930s may have been between 1,000 and 2,000 pairs. Since then, newly planted forests have effectively banished the species from some large tracts of traditional habitat (particularly in the Brecklands of East Anglia) and gradual declines have been reported from Dorset, Sussex and Berkshire. Even so, the present breeding population is probably not less than 300 pairs, and may exceed 500.

This species is afforded special protection in Great Britain under Schedule I of the Protection of Birds Act, 1954–67.

Number of 10-km squares in which recorded:
94 (2%)
Possible breeding 12 (13%)
Probable breeding 19 (20%)
Confirmed breeding 63 (67%)

Though some records were originally submitted in confidence, all dots are now shown accurately (as recommended by the Rare Breeding Birds Panel and R. F. Porter)

References
GLUE, D. E. and R. A. MORGAN. 1974. Breeding statistics and movements of the Stone Curlew. *Bird Study* 21: 21–28.
MORGAN, R. A. 1975. Breeding bird communities on chalk downland in Wiltshire. *Bird Study* 22: 71–83.
SCOTT, R. E. 1965. Some observations on the Stone Curlew at Dungeness. *Bird Notes* 31: 261–265.

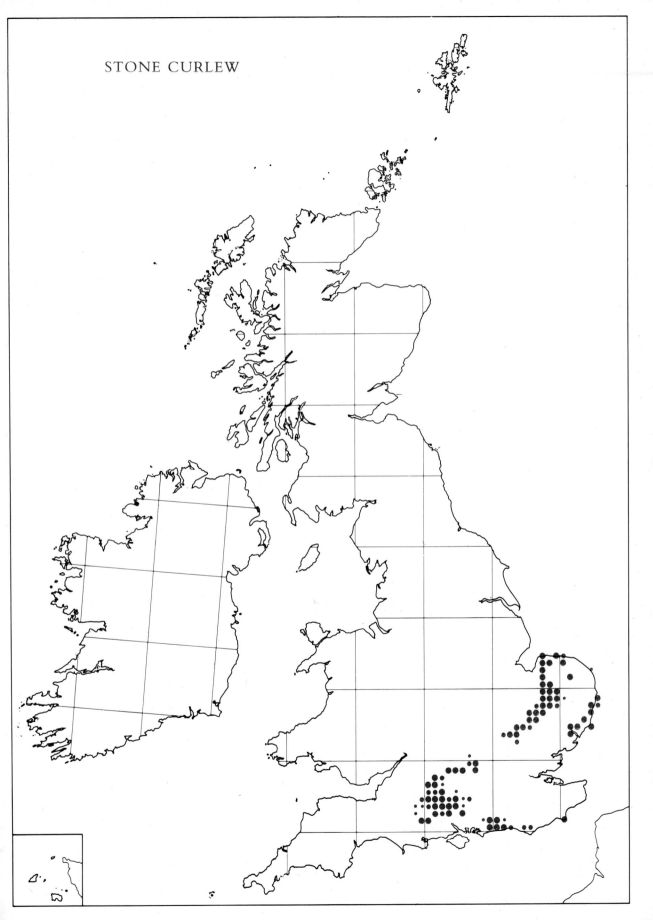

STONE CURLEW

Great Skua

Stercorarius skua

The Great Skua has its closest relatives in the southern hemisphere, the form inhabiting Tristan da Cunha and Gough Island being so similar in structure and plumage as to suggest that the species' arrival in the north (though it certainly took place before the Viking era) must be a recent event in evolutionary terms. Its distribution is restricted to S Iceland, Faeroe, Shetland and Orkney, with peripheral footholds elsewhere in N and W Scotland, SE Greenland, and Bear Island. Against this distribution, the more euphonious name 'Bonxie', a relic of the Norse language and still in common use in Shetland, is often preferred.

Early in the 19th century, Bonxies appear to have been fairly common in Shetland, where crofters regarded them with favour because they drove the dreaded White-tailed Eagles *Haliaeetus albicilla* from the lambing grounds (Stenhouse 1926). After the demise of the eagle, however, man's hand turned against them: the eggs were increasingly sought, first by hungry crofters and later by oologists, and in some places the young were tethered beside the crofts to be fattened on household scraps for the table. By 1850, only two small groups remained, on Foula and at Hermaness on Unst. About 1890, the Edmonstons of Buness, who owned Hermaness, employed a watcher to protect the remaining birds, a responsibility later taken over by the RSPB and pursued vigorously to the present day. This colony then numbered nine pairs, and the one on Foula less than 100 pairs. From these small nuclei, a period of spread began, with birds settling Fetlar, Yell, Hascosay, Noss, and Ronas Hill on Mainland (where a colony had existed formerly). The species occupied Hoy (Orkney) in 1914 and Fair Isle in 1921, and first bred on the Scottish mainland in Caithness in 1949. Within recent years a few pairs have spread to Lewis and St Kilda (Outer Hebrides) and sites in W Sutherland. Meanwhile, the colony on Foula grew to an estimated 2,500 pairs by 1973. A parallel decline and increase took place in the Faeroe Islands, especially at its classical site, Skuvoy. Only four pairs remained there in 1897, but with protection the species has recovered and there were about 530 pairs in 1961.

The Bonxie is a pirate in the same sense as the Arctic Skua *S. parasiticus*, but it is also a predator, killing birds as big as Kittiwakes *Rissa tridactyla* and Oystercatchers *Haematopus ostralegus*, taking the young of Arctic Skuas and moorland waders, and raiding Kittiwake colonies for the eggs. Its large size ($1\frac{1}{2}$–2 kg), mottled brown plumage (varying from ochraceous to russet shades) and broad, rounded wings give it a silhouette recalling that of a Buzzard *Buteo buteo*. Its flight is powerful, enabling it to harry the larger gulls, as well as Kittiwakes and terns, in attempts to deprive them of food.

The Bonxies return to their moors early in April. The chief display—used as a territorial advertisement, as an agonistic display against other skuas, large birds and even passing aircraft, and as a greeting ceremony between mates—is a posture in which the head is bowed and the wings uplifted in a V to show the white bases of the primary feathers. The figure is accompanied by a tuneless, repeated 'ek, ek, ek', during which the head is raised. The territory is large, even where many pairs are nesting together, and nearly always embraces a mound which the off-duty bird uses as a look-out point. This becomes the focus of repeated, low, menacing, aggressive flights against intruders and, although most Bonxies veer off at the last moment, painful blows are sometimes delivered. All colonies have a fair proportion of non-breeders, since Bonxies do not nest until they are 4–6 years old (Williamson 1965).

The colonies in Scotland were assessed at 3,170 pairs by Operation Seafarer in 1969–70, but are now probably closer to 3,800 pairs, two-thirds of the total being on Foula. It is not certain that the recent rapid increase in Britain represents a real growth in the world population, five-eighths of which formerly nested in S Iceland, since Dickens (1964) has pointed out that the colonies there have decreased greatly since about 1930, and particularly during 1954–63. Furness (1974) considered that there was no need to hypothesise a population shift from Iceland to Shetland, believing that the increase and spread in the south of the range is independent of the Icelandic stock and due entirely to protection.

Number of 10-km squares in which recorded:
    85 (2%)
Possible breeding   15 (18%)
Probable breeding   10 (12%)
Confirmed breeding   60 (71%)

References

BAYES, J. C., M. J. DAWSON, A. H. JOENSEN and G. R. POTTS. 1964. The distribution and numbers of the Great Skua (*Stercorarius s. skua* Brünn.) breeding in the Faeroes in 1961. *Dansk. Orn. Foren. Tidsskr.* 58: 36–41.

DICKENS, R. F. 1964. The North Atlantic population of the Great Skua. *Brit. Birds* 57: 209–210.

FURNESS, R. W. 1974. The ecology of the Great Skua on Foula. *Field Studies Rep.* no. 25. Brathay Trust, Ambleside.

STENHOUSE, J. H. 1926. The Great Skua in Shetland. *Scott. Nat.* (1926): 169–173.

VENABLES, L. S. V. and U. M. VENABLES. 1955. *Birds and Mammals of Shetland.* Edinburgh.

WILLIAMSON, K. 1965. *Fair Isle and its Birds.* Edinburgh.

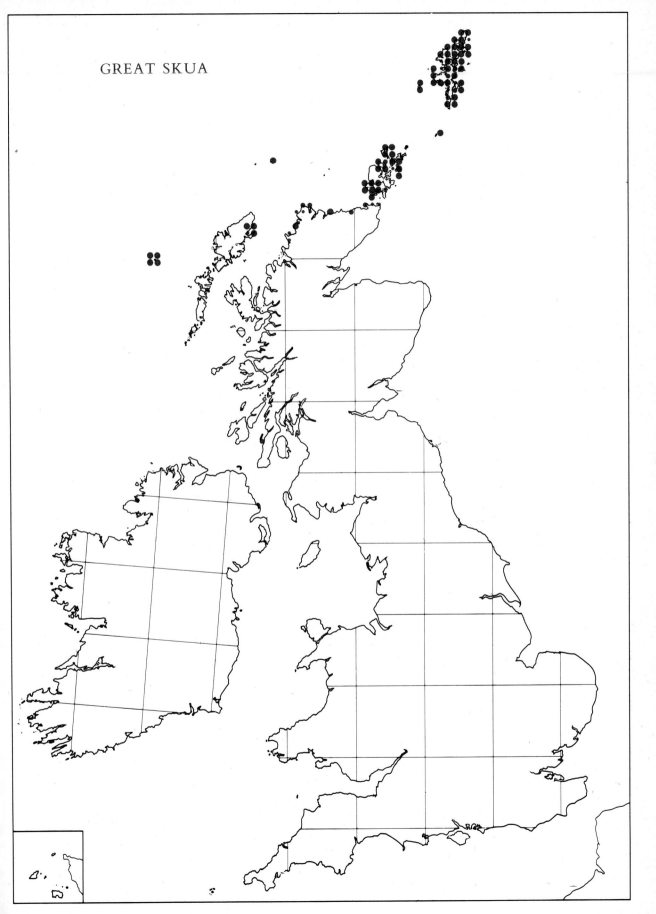

GREAT SKUA

Arctic Skua

Stercorarius parasiticus

The nesting habitat of the Arctic Skua is moorland, varying from blanket-bog to drier heather moor and cliff-top brows. Where the terrain is flat and uniform, the nest is often located close to a small prominence— a mossy tussock or hillock used as a look-out—and it may also be near a small pool. The Arctic Skuas of the northern tundra mainly prey on small mammals (especially Norwegian Lemmings), but British birds, even at inland colonies, apparently feed mainly at sea by forcing terns, Puffins *Fratercula arctica* and Kittiwakes *Rissa tridactyla* to disgorge captured fish. Small song birds, such as Wheatears *Oenanthe oenanthe*, are occasionally hunted down, and crowberries and other moorland fruits are eaten in late summer. Several colonies in Caithness are well inland, the farthest 30 km from the sea.

These large and elegant birds are polymorphic, the pale phase having a creamy face and nape contrasting with a dark brown cap and white underparts, often with a buff or pale brown breast band, while the dark-phase birds are a uniform dark brown. The majority are intermediate, with the belly paler and more buffish-brown than the crown, mantle and wings, and with some lightening of colour on the cheeks and nape. The dark morphs and intermediates, which predominate in Britain, are more difficult to locate against the old heather and peaty soil of the nesting grounds than are the pale morphs, which become commoner towards the north and east of the Eurasian range.

Arctic Skuas customarily breed in loose colonies, within which each pair defends a territory. They are extremely demonstrative when the nest or young are approached, dive-bombing sheep, dogs and even human intruders. This aggressive flight often culminates in physical attack. Against man, they will also react with violent and realistic injury-feigning; this, together with their propensity for attacking Hooded Crows *Corvus corone cornix* (and indeed any large bird which flies over the nesting ground) with loud staccato cries, renders the colonies easy to locate. Moreover, the yodelling song given when off-duty birds and non-breeders visit territories of established pairs, can be heard at a considerable distance. The map, therefore, probably provides an accurate picture of the 1968–72 distribution.

It is thought that numbers were formerly larger in the Outer Hebrides and on the Scottish mainland, but there has been an increase in Orkney (especially at the main colony on Hoy) and in Shetland, despite the expansion of the Great Skua *S. skua*. The best documented increases are in Orkney, from 80 pairs in 1941 to about 190 in 1961, 230 in 1969–70 and 622 in 1974; and on Fair Isle, from 15 pairs in 1949 to 106 pairs in 1973. While persecution may have caused a decline in the 19th century (and, even now, some gamekeepers and shepherds do not look on the species with favour), this attractive bird seems to be currently holding its own and seems to be increasing. The possibility of new colonies forming outside the present range should be borne in mind. Though there were no relevant Irish records during 1968–72, one or two birds summered (but probably did not breed) at one Irish locality every year during 1960–67, and the records of possible breeding at several sites in Sutherland, on Rannoch Moor and on the coast of N Argyll may be indications of a future spread.

Although in general the Arctic Skua has a preference for heather moor, and the Great Skua for grass moor (often on somewhat wetter ground), there is considerable overlap, especially on islands where the population of the latter is expanding. The length of the vegetation, providing cover for the growing chicks, appears to be the most important criterion, the Great Skua requiring 10 cm or more of growth, whereas the Arctic can do with less (Furness 1974). Earlier arrival, in late March and April, gives the larger species a distinct advantage, since its territories are already well established when the Arctic Skuas return in May. Interspecific competition thus results in the displacement of Arctic Skuas, and those nesting close to Great Skua colonies are also subject to predation of their chicks. Nevertheless, there is no real evidence of any fall in numbers as a consequence of this competition.

The Operation Seafarer census in 1969–70 registered a British population of 1,090 pairs, mostly in Shetland and Orkney, which makes this our rarest seabird.

Number of 10-km squares in which recorded:
139 (4%)
Possible breeding   40 (29%)
Probable breeding   13 (9%)
Confirmed breeding   86 (62%)

References
FURNESS, R. W. 1974. The ecology of the Great Skua on Foula. *Field Studies Rep.* no. 25. Brathay Trust, Ambleside.
SOUTHERN, H. N. 1943. The two phases of *Stercorarius parasiticus* (Linnaeus). *Ibis* 85: 443–485.
WILLIAMSON, K. 1949. The distraction behaviour of the Arctic Skua. *Ibis* 91: 307–313.
WILLIAMSON, K. 1965. *Fair Isle and its Birds*. Edinburgh.

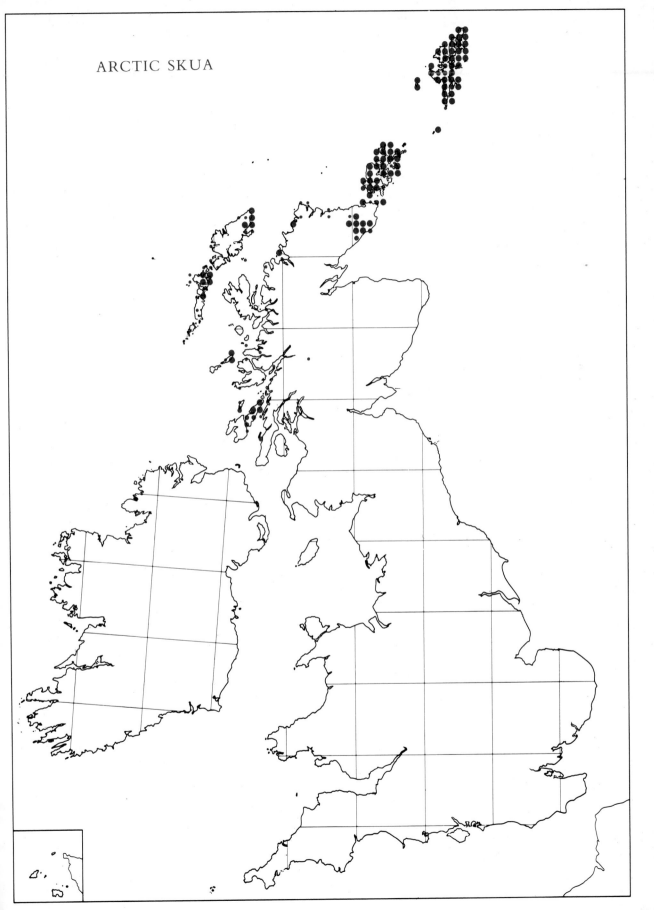

ARCTIC SKUA

Great Black-backed Gull

Larus marinus

Despite a marked and widespread increase since 1880, the Great Black-backed Gull remains the scarcest of our long established breeding gulls. Special enquiries were held into its status in England and Wales in 1930 and 1956, between which years there was a threefold increase, mainly among island breeding groups. Unfortunately, no comprehensive survey of Scotland was carried out until Operation Seafarer in 1969–70, so it is not possible to quantify the increase there. Seafarer produced an estimate of 22,000 pairs, of which about 16,000 were in Scotland, with the largest concentrations in the Outer Hebrides, Orkney, W Sutherland, Pembrokeshire and the Isles of Scilly. The biggest colony is of 2,000 pairs on North Rona (Outer Hebrides). There has been a noticeable spread to the eastern side of Scotland since 1960, but the population is still very small south of the Moray Firth. In Ireland, five new counties were colonised between 1900 and 1951.

The increase in Britain and Ireland during this century is considered to be part of a general expansion over most of the species' range, which is confined mainly to coasts on both sides of the N Atlantic between latitudes 40°N and 76°N, and longitudes 80°W and 40°E. The global range is thus much more restricted than those of our other breeding gulls. It is also much more maritime, the Great Black-backed rarely nesting inland, except in Sweden, Iceland, Ireland and at Lake Huron in Ontario (Canada).

The northern spread, exemplified by an increase in Iceland and the Faeroe Islands, and the colonisation of Bear Island and Spitsbergen since 1930, is thought to be related to the gradual amelioration of the N Atlantic climate. During 1921–42, the southern limit of the American breeding range also moved from Nova Scotia to Long Island, a distance of 720 km; this is thought to have been due to successful exploitation of the abundance of edible refuse and sewage outfalls in the vicinity of coastal towns (Gross 1955). Another factor in the general spread may have been the relaxation of the persecution sustained in the 19th century. Over a long time scale the present increase may be a return to a former status.

The most remarkable feature of the distribution in Britain and Ireland is the Great Black-backed Gull's almost complete absence from the south and east coasts of England between the Isle of Wight and Berwickshire. This is probably due to the dearth of rocky coasts which supply good nesting sites, such as the tops of stacks and small islands. Individuals do spend the summer, however, at such seabird stations as the Farne Islands (Northumberland). In Ireland, a few pairs nest on islands in freshwater lakes especially in Co Donegal, Co Fermanagh, Co Galway, Co Mayo and on Lough Neagh. According to Davis (1958), all the traditional inland breeding localities in England have been deserted in the present century, particularly since the late 1930s, although colonisation occurred in 1949 at Tarnbrook Fell (Lancashire) over 16 km from the nearest tidal water and already the site of a colony of Lesser Black-backed Gulls *L. fuscus*. The *Atlas* survey showed that this colony still held 35 pairs in 1972. Occasional breeding attempts are made in the east, as at Minsmere and Havergate (Suffolk) and near Blakeney (Norfolk), but the birds have not succeeded in establishing themselves. One pair nested on a temporary island in Chew Valley Reservoir (Somerset) in 1956.

In some areas, Great Black-backed Gulls breed socially in either homogeneous or mixed colonies, but in others single pairs are common or even usual. Finding nests is not too difficult; if a pair is seen on an island or headland, it is best to check the highest point, as this is the most likely site.

The food is varied and includes fish, other birds' eggs and young, and marine invertebrates, such as crabs, mussels, limpets and annelids. Carrion (often dead sheep and lambs) is also taken. There is little doubt that Manx Shearwaters *Puffinus puffinus*, Puffins *Fratercula arctica* and Rabbits, when plentiful, provide much of the food of the Great Black-backed Gulls which nest among them; but, although they may create disturbance, it is not likely that these most predatory gulls are an important factor in the current decline of some large Puffin colonies (Evans 1975). Nevertheless, Davis (1958) estimated that in the mid-1950s at least 4,000 shearwaters and up to 1,000 Puffins were killed annually by the 220–250 pairs of Great Black-backed Gulls on Skomer (Pembrokeshire).

Number of 10-km squares in which recorded:
  870 (23%)
Possible breeding   167 (19%)
Probable breeding   43 (5%)
Confirmed breeding   660 (76%)

References

DAVIS, T. A. W. 1958. The breeding distribution of the Great Black-backed Gull in England and Wales in 1956. *Bird Study* 5: 191–215.

EVANS, P. G. H. 1975. Gulls and Puffins on North Rona. *Bird Study* 22: 239–247.

GREENHALGH, M. E. 1974. The Pennine gullery. *Bird Study* 21: 146–148.

GROSS, A. D. 1955. Changes of certain seabird populations along the New England coast of North America. *Proc. Int. Orn. Congr.* 11: 446–449.

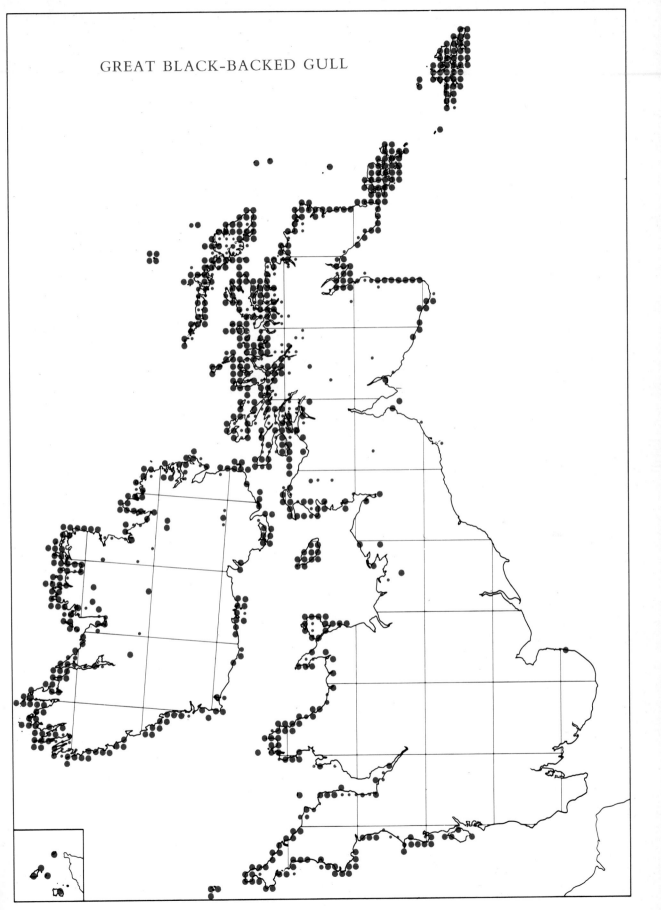

GREAT BLACK-BACKED GULL

Lesser Black-backed Gull

Larus fuscus

Typically, coastal colonies of Lesser Black-backed Gulls are on the flatter parts of sand-dune systems or the relatively flat and unbroken grassy slopes of undisturbed coasts or offshore islands. The Herring Gull *L. argentatus*, whilst almost always also present, is far more likely to be found on the cliffs themselves or on rocky bluffs intruding into the summit grassland. Nests in Lesser Black-backed Gull colonies are usually more closely packed than are those of the Herring Gull, and the grass-lined scrapes are often superbly situated, with the handsome slate-grey and white gull sitting against a colourful backdrop of thrift, bluebells, and red and white campions.

The absence of Lesser Black-backs from some coastal areas (particularly in the more populous areas of S and W England and Wales), where the Herring Gull can flourish by nesting on the cliffs, is clearly seen if the maps for the two species are compared. Operation Seafarer in 1969–70 counted 47,000 pairs of coastal-nesting Lesser Black-backs, 15% of the Herring Gull total.

It is also clear from a comparison of the two maps that Lesser Black-backed Gulls occur in a greater number of inland squares than do Herring Gulls, particularly relative to the total of squares occupied. Inland breeding, especially in the north and west of Britain, is confined largely to high moorland and a few lakes: these colonies, like the coastal ones, are compact and some are large, reaching several thousands of pairs. The inland colonies in Ireland are much smaller and are mostly on lowland lakes. The greater proportion of the breeding population is confined to relatively few areas: the Isles of Scilly, S Wales and the Bristol Channel islands, the islands of the Clyde and the Forth estuaries, and above all Walney Island (Lancashire), which holds about one-third of the British and Irish total. On buildings, this is a less widespread breeding species than the Herring Gull and is normally found in rather small groups.

The Lesser Black-backed Gull is a migrant and, although there is increasing evidence that more may be overwintering in Britain and Ireland, and that the range of migratory dispersal may be diminishing,

they still return to the colonies two or three weeks later than Herring Gulls. It could be argued that, in the numerous mixed colonies of the two species, the sedentary Herring Gull should derive territorial advantage from this, and thus be more successful, especially as it does not risk the hazards of migration or of being shot in its wintering area. Whether or not this is the case, there is ample evidence that the present rate of increase of the Herring Gull is paralleled by that of the Lesser Black-back, as some colonies have doubled in size in only six or seven years. This general picture of increase contrasts with the situation in Orkney and Shetland, where marked decreases, perhaps associated with changes in the fishing industry (or, alternatively, with the increase of the Great Skua *Stercorarius skua* and Great Black-backed Gull *L. marinus*), occurred earlier this century and have left the population more or less stable at a low level.

Equally interesting in this context are the feeding habits of the Lesser Black-back, compared with those of the Herring Gull whose increase in numbers is often attributed to man's wasteful habits (Brown 1967, Harris 1965). In winter and summer, Lesser Black-backed Gulls tend to feed much less by scavenging than do Herring or Great Black-backed Gulls. They plunge-dive for fish, or feed on terrestrial or shore invertebrates collected from rough grassland or the beach, even though on many occasions the easier pickings of fish offal or refuse tips are close at hand.

Since both species are often present in the same colony, mixed pairings might be expected. Such pairs, however, are very rare: in part, the later return of the Lesser Black-back acts as an isolating mechanism, while Harris (1970) has shown that the colour of mantle and wings at a distance, and of eye-ring and mandible at close quarters, are important recognition features. Experiments with cross-fostered eggs of both species on Skokholm (Pembrokeshire) during 1962–66 produced some 900 young gulls. Their winter movements were more closely akin to those of the foster-parents than to the movements of their own species, and (as might be expected) they readily formed mixed pairs in later years when they returned to breed.

Number of 10-km squares in which recorded:
867 (22%)
Possible breeding 313 (36%)
Probable breeding 68 (8%)
Confirmed breeding 486 (56%)

References

BROWN, R. G. B. 1967. Species isolation between the Herring Gull *Larus argentatus* and the Lesser Black-backed Gull *L. fuscus*. *Ibis* 109: 310–317.

CRAMP, S. 1971. Gulls nesting on buildings in Britain and Ireland. *Brit. Birds* 64: 476–487.

HARRIS, M. P. 1965. The food of some *Larus* gulls. *Ibis* 107: 43–53.

HARRIS, M. P. 1970. Abnormal migration and hybridization of *Larus argentatus* and *L. fuscus* after interspecies fostering experiments. *Ibis* 112: 488–498.

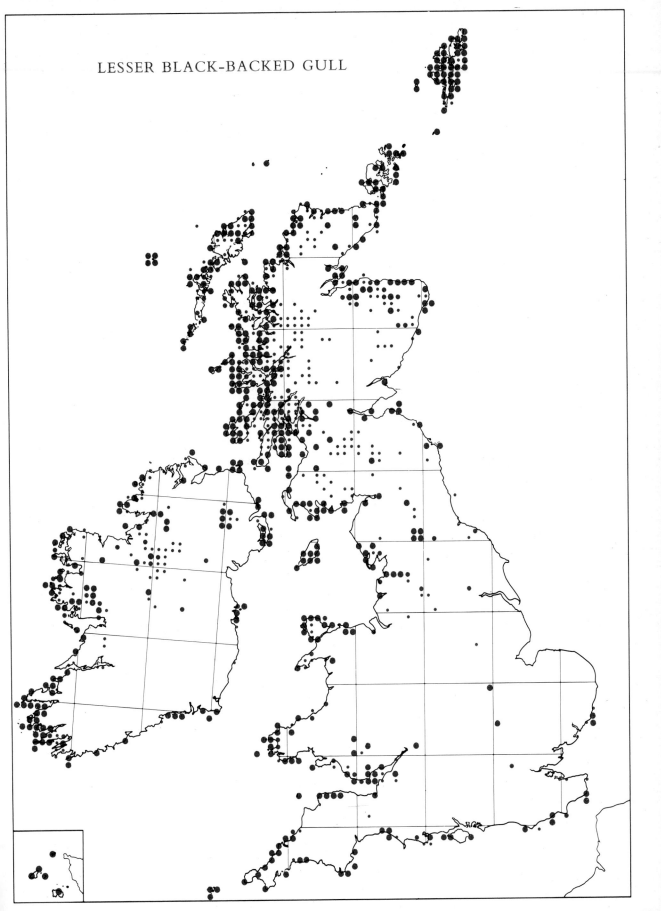

LESSER BLACK-BACKED GULL

Herring Gull

Larus argentatus

Our breeding Herring Gulls are largely concentrated on rocky coasts where there are substantial cliffs, but to the north and west they also frequent low, rocky islets, coastal dunes and shingle beaches. Breeding pairs are often widely scattered over suitably broken terrain provided it is undisturbed by man—hence the wide belt of the northwest coastal distribution. Elsewhere, some huge and dense congregations occur, and there are major colonies many thousands of pairs strong in the Irish Sea basin, the Bristol Channel and NE Scotland. Operation Seafarer found the Herring Gull to be the second most numerous gull, with over 300,000 pairs estimated for the coastal regions in 1969–70.

Saltmarsh colonies are infrequent, which helps to explain the largely blank area in E England from S Yorkshire to the Thames estuary. The relatively recent colonies at Orfordness (Suffolk) and on the shingle at Dungeness (Kent) may, however, indicate that in time, if the species continues to increase at its present rate, even this area may be occupied.

Of more recent origin are Herring Gull colonies inland and on buildings. Only 33 squares contain truly inland records of confirmed breeding, mostly in the central Irish wetlands, and only one colony, on the Pennine moors, is at all substantial in size. The habit of nesting on buildings was recorded first in the 1920s, principally at south coast seaside resorts. Although colonies were originally quite small, the largest (at Dover, Kent) numbered about 225 pairs by 1968–70 and the average for 55 colonies on buildings in 1969–70 was 22 pairs (Cramp 1971). The unpleasant combination of noise (which starts in the small hours of summer mornings) and excrement has naturally led to a sharp fall from favour for this once popular bird.

Such versatility in breeding has been accompanied by changes in winter distribution and feeding. No winter town refuse tip is likely to be without feeding Herring Gulls, and the proximity of suitable reservoirs for roosting has given rise to concern for public health. Recent estimates of major colonies show continuing growth of 13–15% per annum (see graph) and this is paralleled by increases in wintering birds. These increases are only partly correlated in time with the greater availability of fish offal and domestic refuse, but it may be that the present highly adaptable scavenging behaviour took several years to

develop and spread through the population (Harris 1970).

Herring Gulls are relatively sedentary in Britain and Ireland, and return early (sometimes in February) to their breeding grounds. This early establishment of territory, coupled with rapidly increasing numbers (which Parslow thought may well have doubled in the last 20 years), has given rise to considerable concern. In some places, the grassland in which Puffins *Fratercula arctica*, Manx Shearwaters *Puffinus puffinus* and Storm Petrels *Hydrobates pelagicus* burrow is eroded following tussock-pulling by displaying gulls, and in many others the sheer weight of numbers of gulls is considered to have excluded late-arriving, less robust seabirds such as terns, as on the Isle of May in the Firth of Forth. Control measures, including culls of breeding birds, are being undertaken in several areas to reduce hazards to human health and the risk of bird/aircraft collisions; and also to protect sensitive species such as terns and auks from displacement, predation and kleptoparasitism.

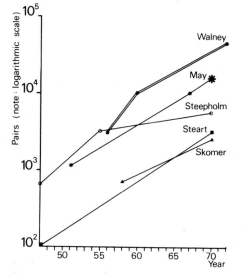

Rates of increase of some Herring Gull colonies since 1947. Note that the Walney Island colony also contains Lesser Black-backed Gulls

Number of 10-km squares in which recorded: 1,152 (30%)

Possible breeding	183 (16%)
Probable breeding	35 (3%)
Confirmed breeding	934 (81%)

References

CRAMP, S. 1971. Gulls nesting on buildings in Britain and Ireland. *Brit. Birds* 64: 476–487.

HARRIS, M. P. 1970. Rates and causes of increase of some British gull populations. *Bird Study* 17: 325–335.

PHILLIPS, N. R. 1968. After the *Torrey Canyon. Ann. Rep. Cornwall Bird-watch. Pres. Soc.* 37 (1967): 90–129.

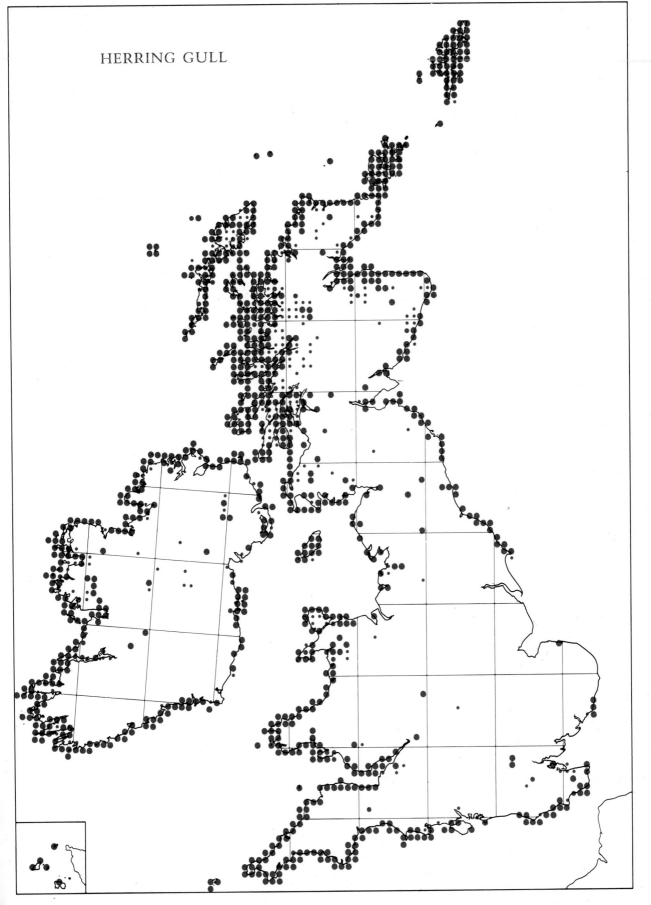

HERRING GULL

Common Gull

Larus canus

The Common Gull breeds on both inland hills and coasts. In many parts of Scotland and NW Ireland, it breeds commonly along the shore or on small in-shore islands, in the same situations as many Herring Gulls *L. argentatus*. Indeed, mixed colonies often occur. The Common Gull is much less marine in character, however, and the coastal colonies are seldom large. Over much of the hill country of Scotland, small groups or even single pairs may be found breeding on moorland, sometimes at a small pool or lochan but often on open ground and particularly on shingle bars or small islets in streams or rivers. The largest concentrations in Ireland are on the large lakes of Connacht. Unlike those of the other small inland-breeding gull, the Black-headed *L. ridibundus*, however, Common Gull colonies are seldom dense and are usually relatively small.

Despite the name, Common Gulls are certainly not the commonest of our gulls, but the map shows that they are the most widely distributed north of the Scottish lowlands.

The return of the adults to their nesting sites starts in February or early March, but is not complete until April, with egg-laying towards the end of that month or in early May. At the highest inland sites, over 900 m in Scotland, first eggs may not be laid until June. The nest is usually on the ground and may be on sand or shingle, amongst rocks, tide-wrack or flood debris, or in almost any sort of low vegetation; nesting in stunted willow bushes on islands is not infrequent in Ireland. Some are simple scrapes, but most pairs use weeds and grasses and may form substantial structures. Exceptionally, nesting in trees has been recorded: old nests of Rooks *Corvus frugilegus* were occupied at an Irish site, and there have been several Scottish records of Common Gull nests up to 10 m above ground on the flat branches of pines. Man-made structures such as dam-walls, piers and jetties may be used on occasion; but there are few British records of roof-nesting, though this is common in Scandinavia.

Since incubating birds are very conspicuous, especially on open moorland, confirmation of breeding is readily obtained once a colony has been located. In most areas at least some of the breeding groups are associated with shingle bars or rocky islands along watercourses, and these were often the easiest sites for *Atlas* workers to find. Many more Common Gulls winter in Britain and Ireland than breed here; mass return movements to the Continent during the first half of April are observed on radar screens, though often the birds are flying too high to be seen by bird-watchers (Bourne and Patterson 1962). It is quite common for summering birds to remain behind in areas where none breeds (Vernon 1969).

The Common Gull has long been a component of our northern avifauna, but the species has increased and spread beyond its traditional strongholds in Scotland and Ireland during the last 100 years or so. In Scotland, expansion has been greatest in the southwest, but its continuance is suggested by the first breeding records on Fair Isle in 1966 and 1973–74, and the first for over 110 years on St Kilda in 1963. In SW Ireland, seven 10-km squares were occupied during 1968–72 in an area where only one colony was known 20 years earlier and only three in 1955. The colonies along the Ulster coast were first occupied in 1934 and have gradually increased and expanded.

In England, the best established breeding site, on shingle at Dungeness (Kent), was founded in 1919. The colonising birds almost certainly came from extensive Continental breeding stations in similar habitat; for example, Fisher and Lockley (1954) quoted an estimate of 500,000 pairs in Denmark, and several hundred pairs breed on the Dutch coastal dunes. Sporadic nesting in several parts of N England during the last 50 years, and particularly the last 15 (Dobbs *et al* 1968), has presumably been due to temporary settlements by Scottish stock; but similar instances in East Anglia and Nottinghamshire probably stemmed from Continental winter visitors that remained behind to breed.

There are few data relating to numbers breeding in these islands. Cramp *et al* (1974) gave the coastal total as 12,400 pairs; but most Common Gulls nest inland. An astonishing assembly was discovered inland in Aberdeenshire in 1972, involving 3,000–4,000 pairs nesting over a wide area of grouse moor (Swann 1974). In most parts of Scotland, each occupied 10-km square will hold several small colonies; and an average of 50 pairs per square would imply a total British and Irish population of 50,000 pairs. Thus, Parslow's upper limit of 10,000 pairs was clearly much too low.

Number of 10-km squares in which recorded:
1,054 (27%)
Possible breeding   249 (24%)
Probable breeding   59 (6%)
Confirmed breeding   746 (71%)

References

BOURNE, W. R. P. and I. J. PATTERSON. 1962. The spring departure of the Common Gull from Scotland. *Scott. Birds* 2: 1–15.

DOBBS, A., J. T. RADFORD and P. WOODCOCK. 1968. Common Gulls breeding in Nottinghamshire. *Brit. Birds* 61: 83–84, 267.

FISHER, J. and R. M. LOCKLEY. 1954. *Sea-Birds.* London.

SWANN, R. L. 1974. Gulls breeding inland in Aberdeenshire. *Scott. Birds* 8: 75–76, 281.

VERNON, J. D. R. 1969. Spring migration of the Common Gull in Britain and Ireland. *Bird Study* 16: 101–107.

Mediterranean Gull *Larus melanocephalus* **and Little Gull** *Larus minutus,* **see page 448**

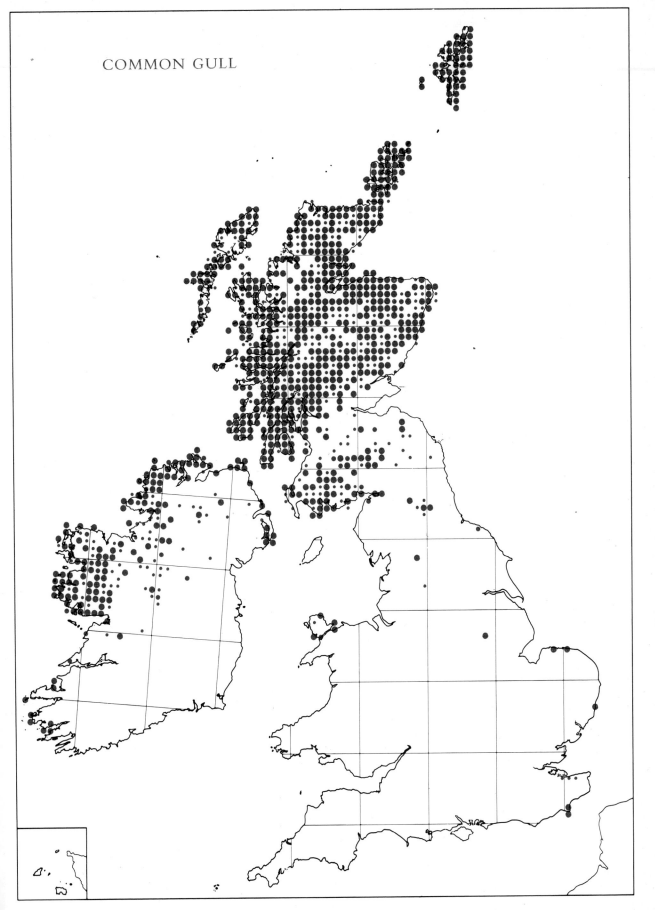

COMMON GULL

Black-headed Gull

Larus ridibundus

Although not our most numerous gull, the Black-headed has the widest inland breeding distribution. It is absent from the rocky coasts and inshore islands of N and W Britain, the characteristic nesting places of other gulls, but there are some small colonies in such locations in Ireland and it is versatile in its choice of breeding grounds. Over much of the north and west, Black-headed Gulls breed in colonies in reeds and sedges surrounding tarns, or in boggy lakes and marshes, at up to 700 m. In S and E England, although increasing, inland breeding is less common and the majority of colonies are coastal. These are usually on saltmarshes or amongst sand-dunes and some contain many thousands of pairs. In the south, inland colonies tend to centre on gravel and clay diggings or sewage farms. In all cases, colonies are both conspicuous and noisy, and even those high in the hills are easily pin-pointed by following the flight-lines of birds returning to eggs or young.

Colony size ranges from less than a dozen to over 20,000 pairs. Gribble (1976) showed that 23% contained less than ten pairs, 44% less than 100, 26% between 100 and 1,000 pairs, and only 7% in excess of 1,000 pairs. Although the percentage distribution has not changed much since 1938, the number of colonies containing 1,000–10,000 pairs has doubled in recent years.

In most situations, the nests are vulnerable to changes in water level, be it spring tides in an estuary or heavy rain flooding a highland pool, and consequently they tend to be substantial mounds of dead vegetation, sometimes over 30 cm high. Although loss of eggs and young is often considerable, Black-headed Gulls are relatively long-lived and sufficiently productive for the numbers to be increasing rapidly.

It is astonishing today to realise that a steady population decline during the 19th century brought the Black-headed Gull close to extinction here. The 20th century has seen a remarkable reversal of fortunes. Recent censuses in England and Wales have produced the following totals of pairs:

1938	35,000–40,000	(Hollom 1940, Marchant 1952)
1958	46,000–51,000	(Gribble 1962)
1973	100,000–110,000	(Gribble 1976)

It may be suggested that the favourable forces of conservation, a marked reduction in shooting and harvesting of eggs, and the creation of much new habitat have caused this increase, but at Needs Oar Point (Hampshire), the largest colony, licensed egg-harvesting still takes place, and the colony has continued to expand rapidly (see graph for increases at this and other sites). There has been a parallel expansion in numbers and range elsewhere in Europe, often in areas remote from man's influence. One-hundred fold increases have been documented this century in Finland and Sweden. In Iceland, where the species first bred in 1911, this is now the commonest gull, and with the recent expansion of the polar easterlies it has become the commonest Palearctic vagrant in eastern N America.

No reliable figures exist for inland colonies, but about 74,500 coastal pairs were counted by Operation Seafarer during 1969–70. The total in Britain and Ireland is probably between 150,000 and 300,000 pairs.

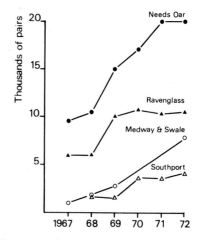

Rates of increase of some Black-headed Gull colonies since 1967

Number of 10-km squares in which recorded:
1,736 (45%)
Possible breeding 628 (36%)
Probable breeding 95 (5%)
Confirmed breeding 1,013 (58%)

References

FLEGG, J. J. and C. J. COX. 1975. Mortality in the Black-headed Gull. *Brit. Birds* 68: 437–449.

GRIBBLE, F. C. 1962. Census of Black-headed Gull colonies in England and Wales, 1958. *Bird Study* 9: 56–71.

GRIBBLE, F. C. 1976. Census of Black-headed Gull colonies in England and Wales in 1973. *Bird Study* 23: 139–149.

GURNEY, R. 1919. Breeding stations of the Black-headed Gull in the British Isles. *Trans. Norfolk and Norwich Nat. Soc.* 10: 416–447.

HOLLOM, P. A. D. 1940. Report on the 1938 survey of Black-headed Gull colonies. *Brit. Birds* 33: 202–221, 230–244.

MARCHANT, S. 1952. The status of the Black-headed Gull colony at Ravenglass. *Brit. Birds* 45: 22–27.

BLACK-HEADED GULL

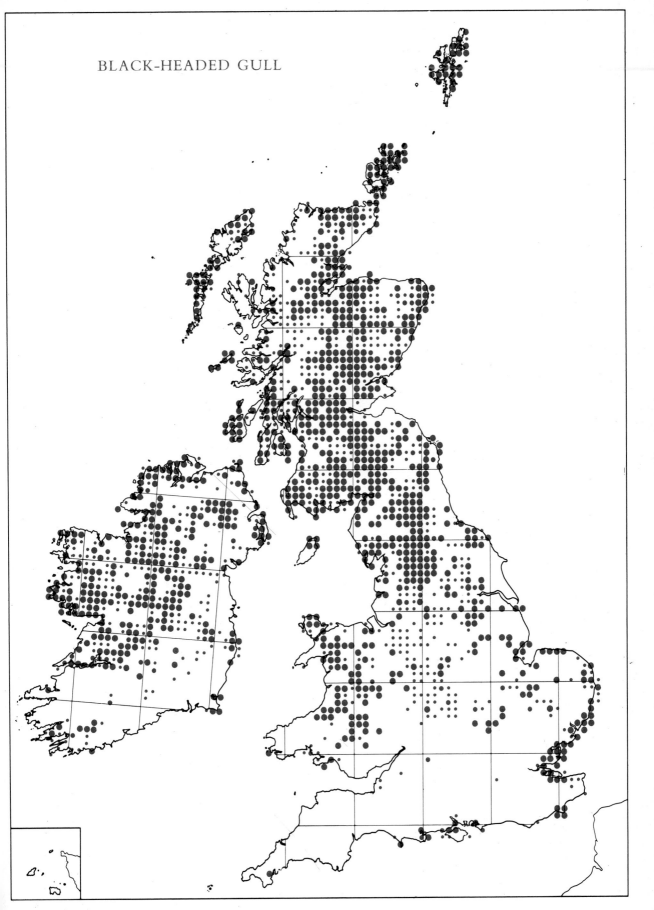

Kittiwake

Rissa tridactyla

The Kittiwake is the most maritime of our gulls, nesting almost exclusively on coasts, feeding offshore, performing transoceanic flights, and seldom venturing inland at any season. It breeds typically on precipitous seacliffs, the nests being placed on ledges and projections; in such situations it is possible that Kittiwakes sometimes have to compete for nest sites with other seabirds, especially Guillemots *Uria aalge*, although characteristically they prefer much fractured faces offering minimal nest-holds, which other seabirds would find impossible to use.

Before Kittiwakes began their present phase of expansion, their breeding stations were mainly on cliffs over 60 m high, but colonists of new areas have often had to accept cliffs of lesser proportions. This has resulted in many breeding stations being nearer to human habitations, and during the last 40 years Kittiwakes have nested regularly on warehouses and similar buildings where vertical walls and window-sills act as cliff and ledge substitutes. Along the tidal River Tyne, Kittiwakes now nest on warehouse frontages as far upstream as Newcastle and Gateshead, 17 km from the river mouth. They have also begun nesting on even lower structures, such as harbour walls (Caithness), a pier pavilion (Suffolk), and intermittently on sand or shingle (Norfolk).

There have been two modern surveys of the breeding distribution and numbers, a BTO enquiry in 1959 (Coulson 1963) and Operation Seafarer in 1969–70 (Coulson 1974): both revealed a continuing major increase in the range and total numbers. There can be no doubt that this population growth began as a recovery from the effects of the enormous human predation of the last century. As early as 1802, Kittiwakes and other seabirds were being shot for sport, and the industrial revolution provided better public transport and more lethal weapons with which to reach and attack the colonies. The position was exacerbated by the growth of the millinery trade, which demanded huge quantities of Kittiwakes' wings, particularly those of juveniles. Plumage preparation became a cottage industry at Clovelly (Devon), whose source of birds—up to 700 a day—was Lundy. The large colonies at Flamborough Head (Yorkshire) and Ailsa Craig (Ayrshire) were drastically reduced, and elsewhere stretches of former breeding cliffs were deserted.

A slow recovery began about 1900, with the gradual easing of shooting pressure following a series of bird protection acts. Initially, the Kittiwake colonies increased in size, and only after 1920 were new ones founded; but it was not until the 1959 enquiry that ornithologists realised the magnitude of the increase that was taking place. With almost complete protection from man and few natural predators (except for Bonxies *Stercorarius skua*), higher adult survival and breeding success rates have enabled Kittiwakes to achieve this increase.

The 1959 enquiry produced an estimate of 170,000–180,000 breeding pairs in Britain and Ireland, though it was suspected at the time, and is now known, that the Scottish population was underestimated. The most reliable figures were for England and Wales, a total of 37,000 breeding pairs, of which just over half were on Flamborough Head. From the known histories of the main colonies, it was calculated that Kittiwakes were increasing by at least 3% per annum in numbers of both colonies and pairs.

A decade later, Operation Seafarer produced a revised estimate of 470,000 pairs: Scotland about 370,000, England and Wales about 57,000, Ireland about 43,000, and the Channel Islands 12. Three-quarters are on North Sea coasts from Shetland southwards. Thus, there were about 62,000 pairs between Yorkshire and Berwickshire, 63,000 between Kincardineshire and Banffshire, 52,000 in Caithness, 42,000 in Shetland, and the impressive total of about 128,000 pairs in Orkney. In contrast, small colonies are characteristic of W Scotland, the Hebrides, and Ireland.

Comparing data from colonies covered by both enquiries, it is clear that the numbers of nesting Kittiwakes increased by 49% over the 10-year period, an average now of over 4% per annum. As remarked by Coulson (1974), it is a sobering thought that Kittiwakes had been increasing at a rate of nearly 50% per decade for half a century before ornithologists became aware of it.

Number of 10-km squares in which recorded:
   383 (10%)
Possible breeding   67 (17%)
Probable breeding   12 (3%)
Confirmed breeding   304 (79%)

References
COULSON, J. C. 1963. The status of the Kittiwake in the British Isles. *Bird Study* 10: 147–179.
COULSON, J. C. 1974. Kittiwake *Rissa tridactyla*. pp 134–141 in CRAMP, S., W. R. P. BOURNE and D. R. SAUNDERS, *The Seabirds of Britain and Ireland*. London.

Black Tern *Chlidonias niger*, **see page 449**

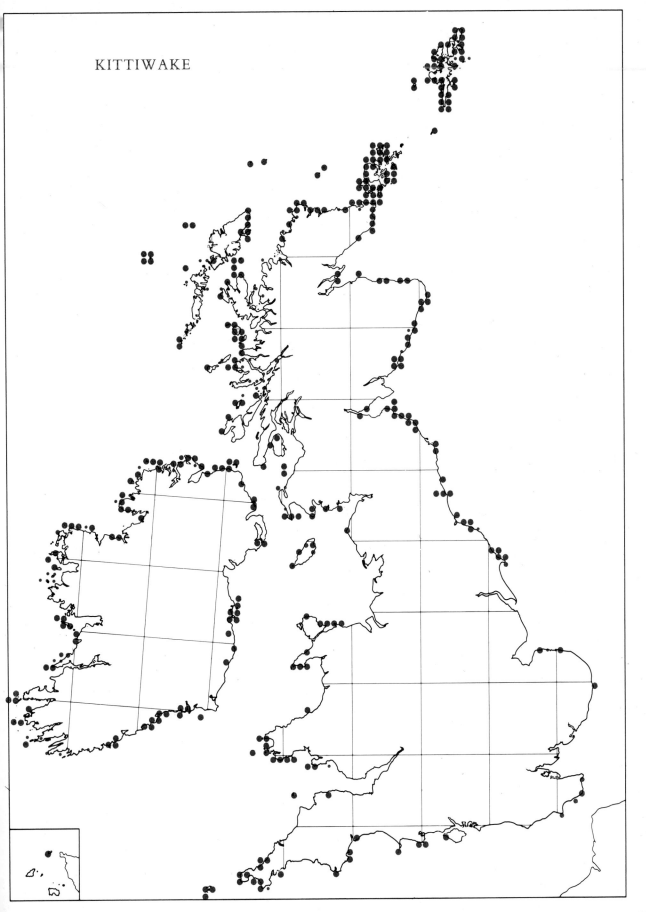

KITTIWAKE

Common Tern

Sterna hirundo

PJG

Common Terns are the most widely distributed of our breeding terns. Most are on the coast, but inland nesting is frequent in some areas. The species breeds over most of Europe, Asia and N America between 30° and 65°N, with some farther south in the Caribbean, N Atlantic and Africa. Over much of this range, colonies are often far from the sea and sometimes at a great height, up to 4,500 m (Voous 1960); but most of those inland in Britain and Ireland are below 300 m.

The species is replaced by the Arctic Tern *S. paradisaea* at higher latitudes, and Britain and Ireland lie within the zone of overlap. Common Terns outnumber Arctic at most colonies, except in N and W Scotland and on Coquet Island and the Farnes (Northumberland). Outside Scotland, there are only 16 10-km squares with Arctic but no Common Terns, and almost 300 with Common but no Arctic. There is evidence that the proportion of Common Terns in S Britain and Ireland has increased during the last hundred years. Arctic Terns, for example, are now absent from the Isles of Scilly where they previously formed the majority.

There are considerable problems in identifying the two species, although separation of the adults during the breeding season is easier than of autumn birds on passage, and their distinctive calls are helpful. The adults are quite conspicuous and breeding sites are reasonably predictable, so that few will have been missed. Some colonies are large, and the Common Tern mixes with other species on coastal islands, sand or shingle banks, sand-dunes and saltmarshes. Few inland colonies contain other species and most are rather small, on islands in lakes or on shingle banks in rivers. Careful observation from a distance is the best way to establish the specific identity of the birds, since recognition of eggs or chicks is difficult.

Inland breeding has decreased in recent years in Ireland, but has become more frequent in Scotland and England. The inland nesting in E England is mostly on islands in sand, clay or gravel pits. In some instances, these islands have been provided for the terns; in at least one place, specially built rafts have been colonised (Eades 1972).

During the 19th century, like many other seabirds, Common Terns undoubtedly decreased. Egg-gathering for food and shooting for sport, as well as the Victorian millinery trade, were the probable causes (Fisher and Lockley 1954). All species were protected by the Sea Birds Protection Bill of 1869, the first English legislation to deal with wild birds as anything other than game, and this probably marked the turning point in their fortunes. The population of Common Terns may have reached a peak in the 1930s and then declined; but assessment is difficult since, like other terns, the species may fluctuate widely at some colonies from year to year and few were counted systematically. In the last few decades, the Common Tern has seldom nested in Wales (apart from Anglesey) or in SW England (apart from the Isles of Scilly), and its absence from apparently suitable sites in this region is notable (*cf* Little Tern *S. albifrons*).

Within the last 50 years, some colonies have built up, but, possibly at their expense, others have declined. A notable casualty was the Isle of May (Firth of Forth) which held 5,000–6,000 pairs in the late 1940s, less than 30 years after recolonisation, and which was deserted in 1956 through competition for nest sites with the Herring Gulls *Larus argentatus* that increased greatly in the 1940s. At sites where Herring Gulls may have affected the tern populations, recent practice has been to cull the gulls and, in some cases, terns have returned. On the Isle of May, large-scale culls of Herring Gulls have been carried out, but it is too early yet to say whether the terns will be able to nest again; a pair of Common Terns did lay eggs on the island in June 1973 (Eggeling 1974), but the fate of the nest was not known. An encouraging feature of modern conservation has been the success of artificially prepared areas in attracting breeding terns, the scrape at Minsmere (Suffolk) being a notable example (Axell 1973).

The coastal breeding population of Britain and Ireland was estimated to be 14,700 pairs in 1969–70 during Operation Seafarer. Recent data on colonies which provided over half this total have shown annual fluctuations of up to 15% (Lloyd *et al* 1975). Since about 150 inland 10-km squares were found to contain breeding Common Terns, it is probable that the total breeding population in Britain and Ireland currently fluctuates between 15,000 and 20,000 pairs.

Number of 10-km squares in which recorded:
893 (23%)

Possible breeding   256 (29%)
Probable breeding   81 (9%)
Confirmed breeding   556 (62%)

One dot has been moved by one 10-km square (as recommended by the Rare Breeding Birds Panel)

References

AXELL, H. E. 1973. In *Manual of Wetland Management*. IWRB, Slimbridge.

EADES, R. 1972. An artificial raft as a nesting site for terns on the Dee. *Seabird Group Rep.* 2: 45.

EGGELING, W. J. 1974. The birds of the Isle of May—a revised assessment of status. *Scott. Birds* 8: 93–148.

LLOYD, C. S., C. J. BIBBY and M. J. EVERETT. 1975. Breeding terns in Britain and Ireland in 1969–74. *Brit. Birds* 68: 221–237.

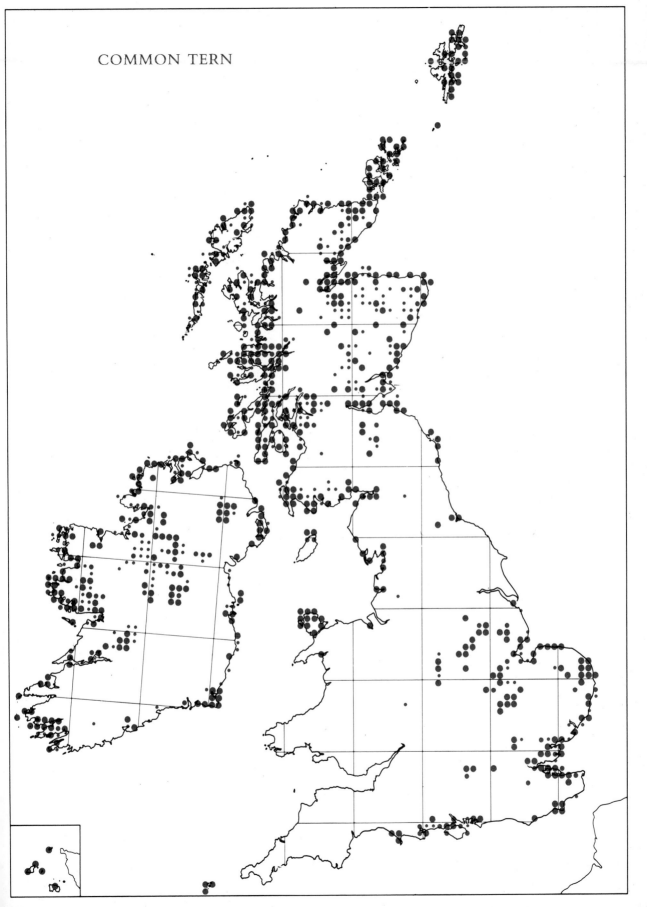

COMMON TERN

Arctic Tern

Sterna paradisaea

PJG

The Arctic is the most numerous tern in Britain and Ireland. Nearly all the colonies are on or close to the coast, apart from a few inland in Ireland and, to a lesser extent, Scotland. Elsewhere, the species has a circumpolar distribution, and often breeds well inland, particularly in Siberia and N America. The northernmost colonies, in Greenland, are within 700 km of the North Pole. Britain and Ireland are on the southern edge of its range and it is only in Scotland that it is more numerous than the Common Tern *S. hirundo*, its close relative and temperate zone counterpart.

Away from N and W Scotland, most of the breeding records are from mixed colonies where the Common Tern predominates. Notable exceptions are in Anglesey and on the Farne Islands (Northumberland). There are only 16 10-km squares outside Scotland with confirmed breeding records for Arctic Terns but not Common. The breeding sites are like those of other terns but, since so many nest in N Scotland, small turf-covered or rocky islands, or moorland areas on larger islands, are used more often.

The birds return in May and many have eggs by the end of that month. The young fledge from July onwards and leave the country, with their parents, rather earlier than the other terns. They are phenomenal migrants and some of even the most northerly breeding populations winter off the antarctic pack ice.

Arctic and Common Terns are so similar that identification is always a problem, even though easier during the breeding season than at other times. Outside Scotland, Common Terns are generally much the more numerous, but the presence of even a few Arctics within a mixed colony can often be realised first through hearing the adults' distinctive screaming 'kee-arr' calls among the more grating cries of the Common Terns. Then, by patient observation from outside the colony, confirmation of identification on physical characters and proof of breeding are often possible. Searching within the colony is not helpful since the eggs and young of the two species are much alike, and, in any case, prolonged disturbance can cause predation by gulls and desertion. Nesting grounds are often revealed by following the flight-lines of adults, which are quite easily observed when fishing. Clearly, however, single pairs or even small numbers of Arctic Terns nesting in large colonies of Common Terns are likely to have been missed sometimes and so the distribution map probably lacks a few dots outside the main area.

There is some evidence that Arctic Terns have retreated from areas in S Britain and Ireland where they nested in the 19th century. They are not now present on the Isles of Scilly, where they used to outnumber Common Terns, and Ruttledge (1966) recorded the desertion at that time of many inland sites in Ireland. It seems possible that this species was affected by the same factors that caused the general decline in tern numbers in the 19th century and then, during the climatic amelioration, found itself at a disadvantage in relation to the more southerly Common Tern, when the numbers of the other tern species began to recover.

Since the Arctic Tern's stronghold is in N and W Scotland, however, detailed historical information for the major part of the population is lacking. In SE Scotland, colonies were probably at their highest level during 1930–50 and have subsequently declined; for example, none has nested on the Isle of May since 1957. At the same time, the situation in Ireland has deteriorated both on the coast and inland. All these areas combined will not, however, have held a population approaching that recently found breeding in Orkney, and so the general trends up to 1969 cannot even be guessed. In Orkney, the vast colonies on the Westray group of islands were believed to contain almost 28,000 pairs in 1969, though estimation of numbers was so difficult that a much lower figure was given in the results of Operation Seafarer. A recent reassessment, however, following further counts in Orkney during 1974, suggests that the 1969 figure may even have been an underestimate and a revised total of over 50,000 pairs for Britain and Ireland in 1969 has now been given (Lloyd *et al* 1975). This may have fallen to about 40,000 by 1974, for the largest Orkney colony has suffered considerable disturbance by cattle, people and Arctic Skuas *Stercorarius parasiticus*.

Number of 10-km squares in which recorded:
536 (14%)
Possible breeding 89 (17%)
Probable breeding 34 (6%)
Confirmed breeding 413 (77%)

Though some records were originally submitted in confidence, all dots are now shown accurately (as recommended by the Rare Breeding Birds Panel)

References
LLOYD, C.S., C. J. BIBBY and M. J. EVERETT. 1975. Breeding terns in Britain and Ireland in 1969–74. *Brit. Birds* 68: 221–237.
MEAD, C. 1974. *Bird Ringing*. BTO Guide no. 16, Tring.
PENHALLURICK, R. D. 1969. *Birds of the Cornish Coast*. Truro.

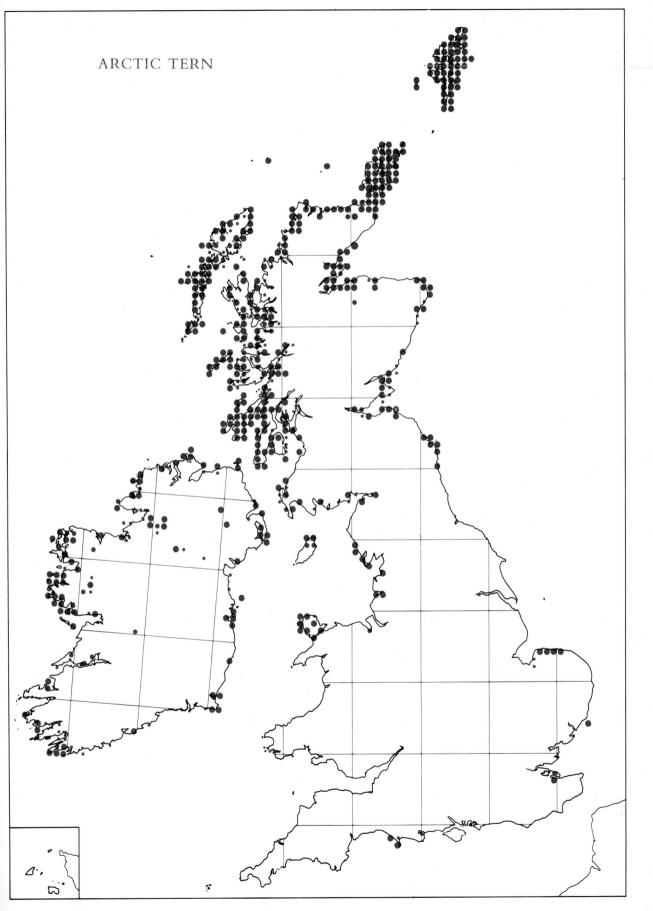

ARCTIC TERN

Roseate Tern

Sterna dougallii

The Roseate Tern is one of the rarest breeding sea-birds in Britain and Ireland. Only about a dozen colonies are used regularly by more than a handful of birds. All these are situated on islands, but a few pairs nest sporadically (or at least attend during the breeding season) at coastal colonies of other terns. Britain and Ireland are the stronghold of the European population, the only other area of regular breeding being in Brittany.

The islands with the main colonies are rocky or sandy, either offshore or in sea lochs or harbours. Almost always they hold other species of terns and sometimes Black-headed Gulls *Larus ridibundus* as well, with the Roseates often forming a tight group within the mixed colony (Williamson *et al* 1943). The inaccessibility of present colonies is an indication of the vulnerability of this species to disturbance on the breeding grounds. A majority of the main sites are managed as reserves, but wardening at small islands is not easy, and the birds remain at risk to casual visits by yachtsmen and fishermen. They are also exposed to flooding by storms or high tides, particularly on low, sandy islands.

Roseate Terns are seldom observed on migration, possibly because their numbers are swamped by the similar and much more numerous Common and Arctic Terns *S. hirundo* and *S. paradisaea*. They arrive much later than the other species, and eggs are generally not laid until the end of May or early June. These are more pointed than those of the other terns, and the nestlings with their hairy down (like young Sandwich Terns *S. sandvicensis*) are easily distinguished. Proof of breeding at the main colonies is thus simply achieved, but isolated pairs, nesting within colonies of the other species could easily be missed.

As if the hazards to this rare species through interference and inclement weather when nesting were not enough, ringing has shown very real threats to its continued existence in Europe through trapping activities in W Africa (Mead 1971). Youths, particularly in Ghana, catch terns for food and, whilst this affects other species as well, the Roseates seem to be particularly at risk. In some years, more than 2.5% of all the young ringed in Britain and Ireland have been killed during their first few months of life by trappers in W Africa. It is, of course, impossible to assess how many more have been trapped and not reported.

The rarity of the Roseate Tern and its vulnerability to disturbance have been appreciated for many years,

and the suppression of the exact location of some of the main colonies has created difficulties in following the species' history. It is clear that it declined during the 19th century but rallied during the first part of the 20th. A peak may have been reached in the early 1960s, when as many as 3,500 pairs may have bred. As with other species of terns (particularly Sandwich), however, apparently quixotic shifts of colonies from place to place cast some doubt on assessments of the total population made from data gathered over a period of several years. The results of Operation Seafarer in 1969–70 gave 2,367 pairs, but a recent revision (Lloyd *et al* 1975) put the 1969 population at about 2,500 pairs. Whichever figure is taken, this probably represents a substantial real decrease since the early 1960s. Subsequent counts showed that this decline continued and only about 50% of the 1969 population bred in 1972. There was then evidence of a slight recovery in 1973–74 (see table).

This species is afforded special protection in Great Britain under Schedule I of the Protection of Birds Act, 1954–67.

National totals of breeding pairs of Roseate Terns at the twelve main colonies in Britain and Ireland 1969–74

Data from Lloyd *et al* 1975. Each ★ represents a colony not counted in that year

	1969	1970	1971	1972	1973	1974
Scotland	111	129	88	75	52★	91
England	335	204	112	114	110	81
Wales	202	256	206	156	165	251
Ireland	1,828	1,816★	1,380★	808★★	914★	991
Totals	2,476	2,405★	1,786★	1,153★★	1,241★★	1,414

Number of 10-km squares in which recorded:
62 (2%)
Possible breeding   16 (26%)
Probable breeding   5 (8%)
Confirmed breeding   41 (66%)

One dot (confirmed breeding) has been omitted (as recommended by the Rare Breeding Birds Panel, Major R. F. Ruttledge and D. Scott)

References

LLOYD, C. S., C. J. BIBBY and M. J. EVERETT. 1975. Breeding terns in Britain and Ireland in 1969–74. *Brit. Birds* 68: 221–237.

MEAD, C. J. 1971. Seabird mortality as seen through ringing. *Ibis* 113: 418.

WILLIAMSON, K., M. N. and D. H. RANKIN. 1943. Field-notes on the breeding ground of the Roseate Tern (*Sterna dougalli* Mont.). *North-West. Nat.* 18: 29–32.

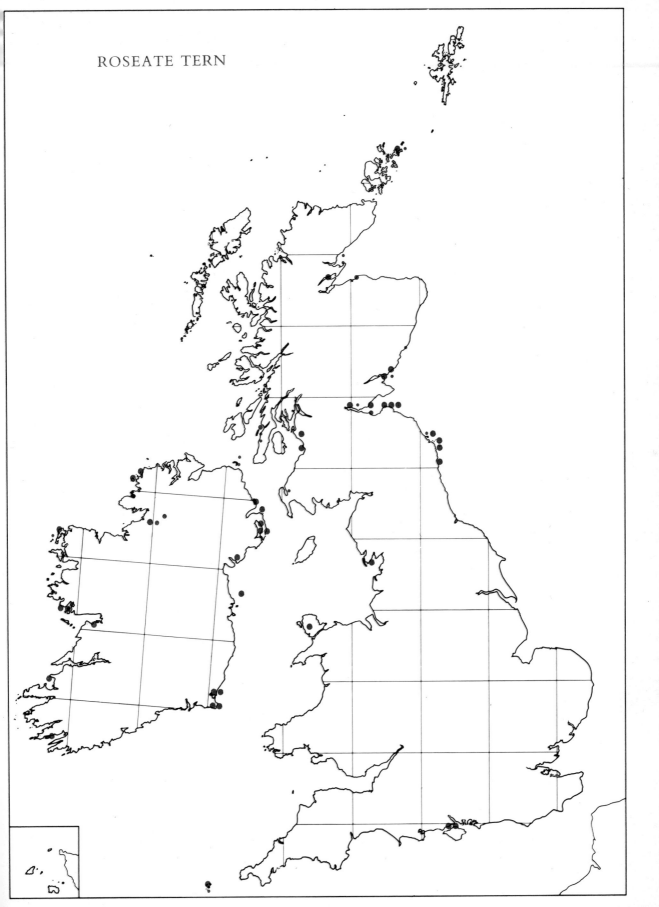

ROSEATE TERN

Little Tern

Sterna albifrons

PJG

The Little Tern is almost exclusively a coastal breeding species in Britain and Ireland, although in other parts of the world, and even as close as France, many are found beside lakes and rivers far from the sea.

Little Tern colonies are not as dense and compact as those of our other terns. The scrapes are invariably on sand or shingle almost completely clear of vegetation and many are within a few metres of the high tide mark. Thus, they are vulnerable to being buried in sand when there are strong winds, and to high tides and storms. At a few sites the nests may be some hundreds of metres from the shore, either on extensive shingle areas, as at Dungeness (Kent), or on similar substrates associated with river systems or gravel extraction. At two Scottish sites, the crumbling bases of war-time hangers on disused airfields are used, and nests have recently been found in growing corn in the Outer Hebrides. The farthest inland breeding recorded in Britain has been at freshwater sites in East Anglia, 7 km and 10 km from the sea.

The absence of Little Terns from SW Britain and SW Ireland may be due to exposure to Atlantic swells on rather steeply shelving shores; the lack of records in the Bristol Channel and NE Ireland is more puzzling, but may also be caused by conditions offshore.

Colonies are generally rather small and, of 149 counted during the 1967 survey, only ten (6.7%) held more than 25 pairs, while 64 (43.0%) held five or fewer (Norman and Saunders 1969). Little Terns usually fish close inshore, or in coastal creeks and lagoons or other shallow water. They are conspicuous and noisy at the colony and thus easy to find, and breeding may readily be proved from a distance. Searching for nests can be hazardous to the birds since both the eggs and young are well camouflaged and the searcher can easily crush them.

Unfortunately, protection under the law falls far short of the help this species needs. Disturbance by holiday-makers has driven it from many beaches where it used to breed, and egg-collecting is a continuing threat: more than 50 nests were robbed in Essex in 1974 (R. M. Blindell, in Lloyd *et al* 1975); such disturbance was cited as a threat to 53 (35%) of the colonies visited during the 1971 survey. Many colonies are now protected by simple fences and notices explaining to the public the damage their presence might unwittingly cause, and several are wardened. Such protection has often been successful in increasing both breeding success and the numbers nesting.

The total breeding in Britain and Ireland undoubtedly decreased during the 19th century, but began to recover before it ended. The peak population during the present century was probably reached in the late 1920s or early 1930s. The species then declined to about 1,600 pairs in 1967 (Norman and Saunders 1969), but improved to just over 1,800 by Operation Seafarer in 1969–70. At that time it was our second rarest regular breeding seabird, after the Arctic Skua *Stercorarius parasiticus*. This level, of about 1,800 pairs, seems to have been maintained during the early 1970s (Lloyd *et al* 1975) and the Roseate Tern *S. dougallii*, which has declined further since Operation Seafarer, is now scarcer in Britain and Ireland.

This species is afforded special protection in Great Britain under Schedule I of the Protection of Birds Act, 1954–67.

Pairs of Little Terns in Britain and Ireland 1969–71

Data from Lloyd *et al* 1975. ★ Incomplete counts

	1967	1969–70	1971
Outer Hebrides	25★	66	30★
N/NE Scotland	20	43	40
SW Scotland	51★	69	59★
E/SE Scotland	76	73	106
NE England	20	21	22
Lincolnshire to Kent	651	731	746★
Sussex to Dorset	366	365	311
Lake District	59	105	163
Isle of Man	14	20	—
Wales	35	25	29
E/S Ireland	53	165	153
W/N Ireland	57	131	26★
Totals	1,427★	1,814	1,685★

Number of 10-km squares in which recorded: 232 (6%)
Possible breeding   45 (19%)
Probable breeding   24 (10%)
Confirmed breeding   163 (70%)

Ten dots have been moved by one 10-km square (the recommendation of the Rare Breeding Birds Panel, Major R. F. Ruttledge and D. Scott was accurate plotting)

References

LLOYD, C. S., C. J. BIBBY and M. J. EVERETT. 1975. Breeding terns in Britain and Ireland in 1969–74. *Brit. Birds* 68: 221–237.
NORMAN, R. K. and D. R. SAUNDERS. 1969. Status of Little Terns in Great Britain and Ireland in 1967. *Brit. Birds* 62: 4–13.

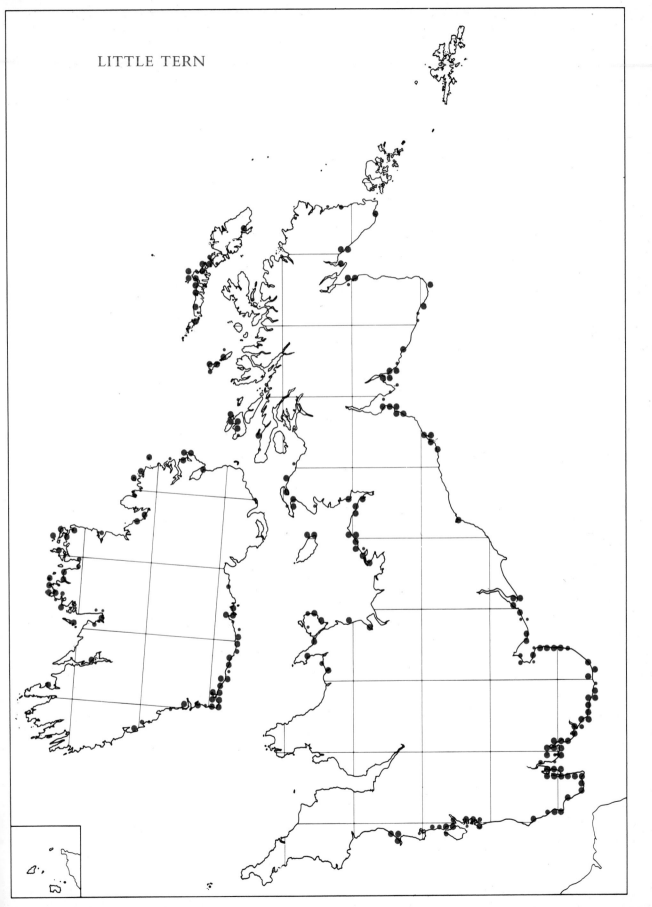

LITTLE TERN

Sandwich Tern

Sterna sandvicensis

The Sandwich Tern almost always breeds in coastal colonies in Britain and Ireland. Most of these are on sand or shingle bars, but off rocky shores some are on turf-covered islands. At many sites the species associates with other terns and there is some evidence that it seeks the proximity of colonies of Black-headed Gulls *Larus ridibundus*. The terns benefit from the aggression shown by the somewhat larger gulls in protecting nests, but they also suffer food piracy (Smith 1975). There are several records of colonies of Sandwich Terns moving with Black-headed Gulls when the latter shifted their breeding places.

Most colonies are in traditional areas, although the actual location of the nests may vary from year to year as erosion or accretion alters the physical characteristics of the shore. Many have a long history of occupation, but the species is notoriously fickle and what seems to be slight disturbance can cause complete desertion, sometimes when the eggs have already been laid. Colour-ringing has shown that the displaced terns may eventually breed at quite distant colonies, over 100 km away (Lloyd *et al* 1975).

Sandwich Terns dive into the sea to catch small fish, particularly sand-eels and sprats (Pearson 1968). Even at inland nesting sites on freshwater loughs in Ireland, the adults fish at sea and commute up to 20 km to the colony (Cramp *et al* 1974). They are thus highly mobile, and the presence of non-breeders in summer, far from active colonies, can mislead the ornithologist who attempts to survey numbers and distribution. Nevertheless, searching traditional sites and colonies of other terns or Black-headed Gulls, and watching for the regular movement of adults feeding young, have probably ensured complete coverage. Proof of breeding, once the colony has been reached, is easy since the Sandwich Tern's egg is much bigger than those of the other species, while the chicks have a characteristic hairy appearance shared only with the much less common Roseate *S. dougallii*. Access to a colony is sometimes difficult and disturbance must always be kept to a minimum.

Breeding Sandwich Terns return from their wintering area off W Africa during early April and many colonies are occupied by the end of that month or the beginning of May. Sometimes, mass occupation is quickly followed by egg-laying. Breeding is highly synchronised within dense groups of nests and it is at this stage that disturbance, whether by man or ground predators such as Foxes, can be particularly harmful. The terns often nest in rather inaccessible situations, however, and fortunately many colonies are protected in reserves. The nestlings may gather into large crèches, which seems likely to be a defence against predators. After the juveniles have fledged, they are still accompanied by their parents and start their autumn migration in August or September (Langham 1971).

Operation Seafarer produced a total of 11,860 pairs in 1969–70. It was considered that the population then was higher than at any previous time during this century, and the history of well-documented colonies showed a continuing increase from the early 1920s. The most recent survey (Lloyd *et al* 1975) covered the years 1969–74 at colonies which contained over 90% of the total found by Seafarer. Their results showed a peak population in 1971–72, about 20% higher (see table), but decreases in 1973–74 brought the totals to within 10% of the Seafarer figures.

Total numbers of Sandwich Terns breeding at the main sites in each country during 1972

Data from Lloyd *et al* 1975. * None of the small colonies in W Ireland was counted

Country	Total pairs	Occupied colonies
Scotland	1,855	6+
England	10,367	11
Wales	201	1
Ireland*	1,774+	3+
Totals	14,197+	21+

Number of 10-km squares in which recorded:
181 (5%)
Possible breeding   89 (49%)
Probable breeding   18 (10%)
Confirmed breeding   74 (41%)

Though some records were originally submitted in confidence, all dots are now shown accurately (as recommended by the Rare Breeding Birds Panel)

References

LANGHAM, N. P. E. 1971. Seasonal movements of British terns in the Atlantic Ocean. *Bird Study* 18: 155–175.

LLOYD, C. S., C. J. BIBBY and M. J. EVERETT. 1975. Breeding terns in Britain and Ireland in 1969–74. *Brit. Birds* 68: 221–237.

PEARSON, T. H. 1968. The feeding biology of sea-bird species breeding on the Farne Islands, Northumberland. *J. Anim. Ecol.* 37: 521–552.

SMITH, A. J. M. 1975. Studies of breeding Sandwich Terns. *Brit. Birds* 68: 142–156.

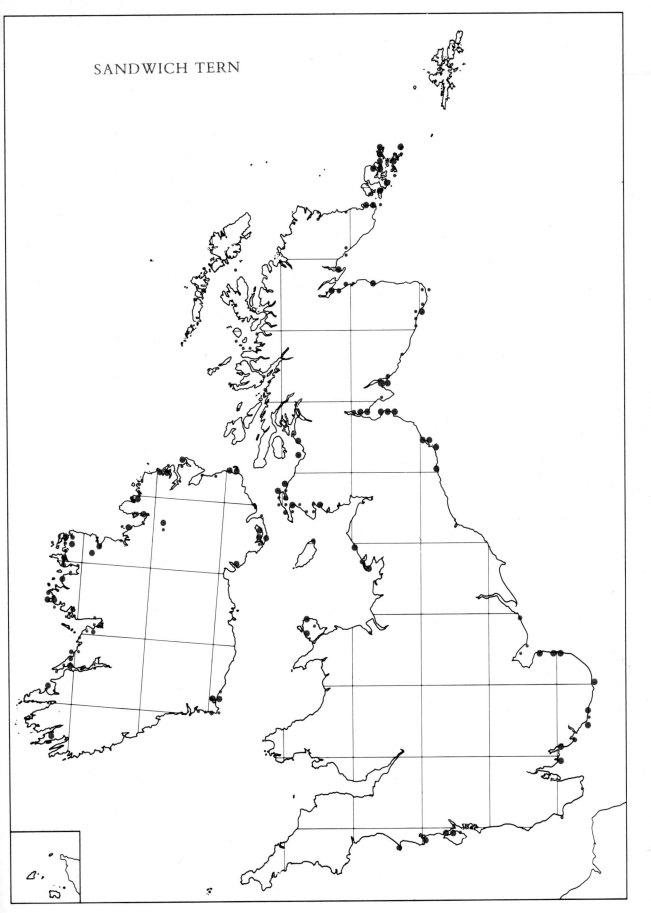

SANDWICH TERN

Razorbill

Alca torda

As a breeding bird, the Razorbill is confined to the N Atlantic coasts and islands, and it seems certain that the colonies in Britain and Ireland hold a very material proportion of the world population, perhaps about 70%, with 12% in Norway and 9% in North America (Lloyd 1976).

Razorbills breed on offshore rocky islets and stacks, and on cliffs in areas remote from man, particularly where the faces have cavities and where sheer drops are broken by rock chutes or scree, or capped with boulder tumbles. Such habitat preferences are less restrictive than those of the Guillemot *Uria aalge*, and result in the slightly more widespread distribution of the Razorbill, although its total numbers may be only about one quarter of those of the Guillemot.

Although isolated pairs may nest in the darker and more recessed parts of the open ledges favoured by Guillemots, most seem to prefer a rock roof over their heads, serving as protection against predation from gulls and skuas on the sitting bird or the unattended egg or chick; the single large egg lacks the anti-roll design subtleties of the Guillemot's. Concealment, and the tendency to nest singly or in small dispersed colonies, make Razorbills relatively difficult auks to survey and almost impossible subjects when it comes to assessing population size. In the south, pairs nesting on the cliff face can be clearly distinguished amongst the chocolate-coloured Guillemots *Uria aalge albionis*, but in the north *U. a. aalge* is almost as black-backed as the Razorbill.

The absence of Razorbills from E England, and from much of the south coast, reflects the lack of suitable cliffs, the record of probable breeding on the E Kent chalk cliffs being an exception. The historical record of Razorbill numbers and distribution is poor, but the finding of quantities of bones in Romano-British middens close to coastal settlements (*eg* in the Isles of Scilly) indicates that numbers may once have been much higher in the south. These archaeological finds are an early indication of the human exploitation of Razorbills for food. This certainly continued into the 19th century in the remoter parts of Scotland,

where seabirds formed an important item of diet on some of the small inhabited islands. During the middle of the 19th century this and other seabirds were menaced by the increasing human population and its mobility. There are, for instance, many examples of seabirds at colonies being used as targets for shooting practice, and trains were even hired to transport people to such sporting events. In addition, local people often took the eggs and sold them either for food or as souvenirs.

It was at this time that the colonies on the chalk cliffs of Sussex declined and were finally extinguished. Since the 1940s, there have been decreases all along the south coast, perhaps associated with increased human pressures, perhaps with levels of oil or other pollutants in the English Channel, or perhaps with more subtle changes in food availability (Lockley *et al* 1949). Recent censuses, starting with Operation Seafarer in 1969–70 and continuing to the present at several sample colonies, show that elsewhere in Britain and Ireland there is little evidence of population change.

Operation Seafarer established that most colonies were small, well under 10,000 pairs; only Horn Head (Donegal) was larger than this, with an estimated 45,000 pairs. Acknowledging the difficulties in counting this species, it was estimated that the 1969–70 population totalled approximately 144,000 pairs.

Like Guillemots, Razorbills make irregular visits to their colonies long before most species are contemplating breeding, and mild days in January and February may see many back on the rocks around the nesting cavities. The eggs are normally laid in April or early May, and the chicks hatch from early June. The chicks descend to the sea when half-grown at three to four weeks old—a journey undertaken after dark to avoid the predatory attentions of Great Black-backed Gulls *Larus marinus*. The range of the chick and its attendant parents at sea is unknown, so sight records of adults with unfledged young cannot necessarily be relied on as an indication of breeding nearby.

Number of 10-km squares in which recorded:
  384 (10%)
Possible breeding   57 (15%)
Probable breeding   15 (4%)
Confirmed breeding   312 (81%)

References
LLOYD, C. S. 1974. Movement and survival of British Razorbills. *Bird Study* 21: 102–116.
LLOYD, C. S. 1976. An estimate of the world breeding population of the Razorbill. *Brit. Birds* 69: 298–304.
LOCKLEY, R. M., G. C. S. INGRAM and H. M. SALMON. 1949. *The Birds of Pembrokeshire*. Haverfordwest.
MEAD, C. J. 1974. The results of ringing auks in Britain and Ireland. *Bird Study* 21: 45–86.

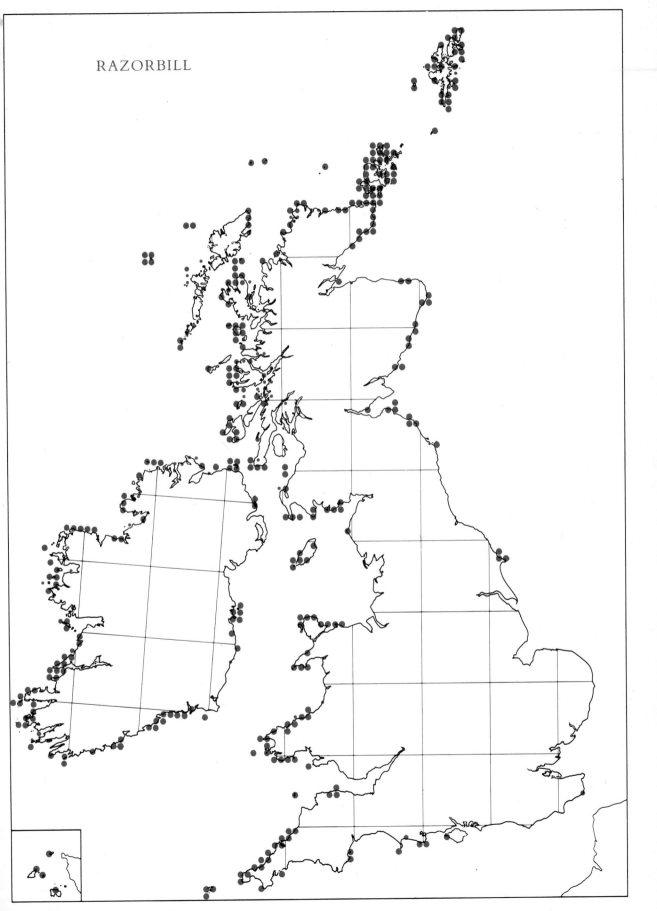

RAZORBILL

Guillemot

Uria aalge

The Guillemot is one of our most spectacular and most strikingly adapted seabirds. Two geographical races breed in Britain and Ireland, the southern brown-backed *U. a. albionis* extending southwards from S Scotland and the northern black-backed *U. a. aalge* through the rest of Scotland. Ireland, Wales and England together have only a fifth of our total Guillemot population, but this forms a substantial part of the southern race, which has a restricted distribution elsewhere (Cramp *et al* 1974). The bridled variant, with a prominent white eye-ring and curved line running backwards almost to the nape, constitutes less than 1% of breeding birds in S England, but increases with latitude to about 26% in Shetland, 34% in the Faeroe Islands, and 50%–70% in Iceland (Southern and Reeve 1941). The proportions may vary with climatic fluctuations, since Southern (1962) showed that the lines joining areas with similar proportions of bridled birds slope steeply from southwest to northeast and appear to follow surface water isotherms.

Guillemots breed colonially on ledges of vertical or near-vertical cliffs on the rocky parts of the British and Irish coasts, and on offshore islands and stacks; they may even lay in most years on Rockall, 300 km west of St Kilda, though it is improbable that eggs or young ever survive on this stormswept stack. The single, colourful egg is markedly pear-shaped, so that when knocked it revolves like a top in a tight circle centred on the small end, rather than rolling off the ledge into the sea. When the adults are facing the cliff, their chocolate-brown or black backs provide fair camouflage, but normally many birds have the white underside facing out to sea, and their upright stance when incubating or brooding makes them look, from a distance, like rows of milk-bottles on doorsteps. In small colonies, the number of non-breeding birds present, and the apparently low breeding success of the others, may make the location of an egg or chick to prove breeding quite difficult. This is not usually a problem in larger colonies.

On sea stacks, the flat summit (as well as the ledges) may be covered in a dense carpet of birds standing shoulder to shoulder. Guillemot colonies are not only crowded (and smelly late in the season) but also noisy, as these are the most vociferous of the Atlantic auks, filling day and night with a mixture of moos, raucous trumpetings, and growlings.

The type of rock, and the way it weathers and becomes fragmented at fault or intrusion lines, can be of major importance. For example, Skokholm (Pembrokeshire) is formed of steeply inclined strata of Old Red Sandstone, which fragments to give knife-edges pointing skyward and quite unsuitable for nesting Guillemots, save for a single tiny colony of about 100 pairs. Skomer, only 3 km distant, is granite with much more regular, near-horizontal fault lines, giving many flat ledges and allowing the establishment of flourishing colonies amounting to about 4,000 pairs.

Operation Seafarer revealed the Guillemot as the most numerous of our seabirds, with an estimated total in Britain and Ireland of 577,000 pairs in 1969–70. Roughly 80% are in Scotland, including 25% in Orkney, where the biggest colonies are on Westray (70,000 pairs) and Marwick Head (25,000 pairs). These and other large northeastern colonies would be extremely vulnerable to any accidents during the extraction of North Sea oil. Earlier hazards were also due to man, the notoriously high levels of egg-collecting and shooting for sport on Bempton Cliffs (Yorkshire) are an odious example from Victorian times. More common throughout the N Atlantic has been the regular harvesting of eggs (and sometimes adults) for food by remote island communities, apparently carried out for centuries with no signs of ill effect.

Southern colonies in Britain and Ireland seem to have decreased markedly during the last century, but these form a relatively small proportion of the population as a whole. Elsewhere, at the present time, there are heartening signs of stability, or even of an increase despite occasional pollution calamities (see map 28 in Cramp *et al* 1974).

Number of 10-km squares in which recorded:
382 (10%)
Possible breeding 80 (21%)
Probable breeding 13 (3%)
Confirmed breeding 289 (76%)

References
BIRKHEAD, T. R. 1974. Movements and mortality rates of British Guillemots. *Bird Study* 21: 241–254.
FISHER, J. 1956. *Rockall*. London.
KAY, G. T. 1947. The young Guillemot's flight to the sea. *Brit. Birds* 40: 156–157.
MEAD, C. J. 1974. The results of ringing auks in Britain and Ireland. *Bird Study* 21: 45–86.
SOUTHERN, H. N. 1962. Survey of bridled Guillemots, 1959–60. *Proc. Zool. Soc. Lond.* 138: 455–472.
SOUTHERN, H. N. and E. C. R. REEVE. 1941. Quantitative studies in the geographical variation of birds—the Common Guillemot (*Uria aalge* Pont.). *Proc. Zool. Soc. Lond.* (A) 111: 255–276.
TUCK, L. M. 1960. *The Murres*. Ottawa.

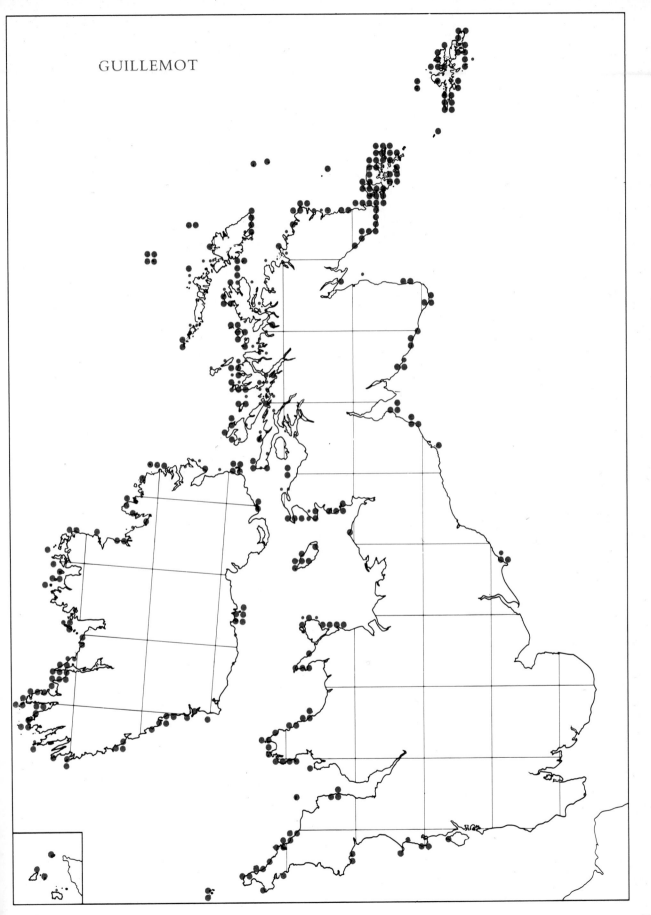

GUILLEMOT

Black Guillemot

Cepphus grylle

The handsome Black Guillemot has a circumpolar distribution extending southwards in seas with a surface temperature of 0°C–15°C in August. Interestingly, its range here—and indeed in the whole of the NE Atlantic—is almost contained within that region of former Viking influence which has left us, in various forms derived from the Old Norse, the name Tystie which is still in general use in Norway, Iceland, the Faeroes, Shetland and the Hebrides.

In Britain and Ireland, at the southern limit of its range, the Tystie has a much more restricted distribution than the other auks. It is completely absent as a proven breeding species on the east coast south of Banffshire, but on the west side nests as far south as the Isle of Man and Anglesey. It occurs almost all round the Irish coast, and birds have been observed in suitable habitat at St David's Head (Pembrokeshire).

The Tystie is a bird of rocky and boulder-strewn coasts, particularly where there are sea lochs and harbours with water shallow enough to provide plenty of fish, such as Butterfish, which form its staple diet, particularly when feeding young. Nest sites are typically in holes and crevices, often in caves or blow-holes, or under boulders on storm-beaches or fallen slabs at the foot of block-screes. Holes in harbour walls have been adopted at Port Patrick (Wigtownshire) and Bangor (Down) and in a wooden pier at Greenore (Louth). Ruined buildings 100 m from the cliff have been used on North Rona (Outer Hebrides). Other unusual sites have included a Shetland inter-island ferry boat, old cannons, drainage holes in the stone retaining wall of a railway embankment and old Rabbit burrows (Campbell and Ferguson-Lees 1972). The species has nested in piles of driftwood in Iceland, and will take to artificial sites made of stones.

Before nesting, Tysties gather on the sea near the cliffs and communal displays are frequent. Often, these take the form of complex water dances in which several pairs participate in processional swimming and underwater chases with the white wing patches and bright red legs prominently displayed (Armstrong 1940, Williamson 1965). The nest is often inaccessible, but the strong smell of guano—arising from the latrine adjacent to the nest—usually gives its position away. Later in the season, breeding may be proved by watching the parents flying with fish to the hidden young. Two eggs are usually laid on the bare rock, or sometimes on broken shells or jetsam which have been thrown into the cavity by the waves. Nests on storm-beaches and at the foot of talus slopes are subject to heavy losses when spring tides and stormy weather coincide.

In a study of the Black Guillemots of Kent Island in the Bay of Fundy (Canada) the average incubation period, which starts after the laying of the second egg, was 29 days, both adults sharing (Winn 1950). The fledging period is usually 34–36 days, the young remaining in the nest until they are able to fend for themselves. The breeding haunts are vacated from late July onwards, but the birds do not move far; winter occurrences as far south as the Thames Estuary and English Channel are few, and even the arctic Tysties move no farther south than the edge of the pack ice.

Operation Seafarer was the first census of this species so it is not possible to comment, other than briefly, on population trends. There is evidence of a decline in some areas: for example, the Tystie disappeared as a breeder from parts of SE Scotland in the last century, and nesting has not been recorded in Yorkshire since 1938. Decreases have also been noted in Ross-shire and the northern parts of W Inverness-shire, but there have been increases farther south in that county, and in the Firth of Clyde. For a time Wales lacked breeding Tysties, but some recent colonisation has occurred. Because of its habit of breeding in small groups and scattered pairs, the species is more subject to temporary fluctuations, and even disappearance from some areas, than are the other auks, which usually nest in much larger colonies. During Operation Seafarer in 1969–70, a total of 8,340 pairs was counted, including a large colony of as many as 340 pairs on Auskerry (Orkney).

Number of 10-km squares in which recorded:
540 (14%)
Possible breeding   119 (22%)
Probable breeding   70 (13%)
Confirmed breeding   351 (65%)

References

ARMSTRONG, E. A. 1940. *Birds of the Grey Wind.* London.

SALOMONSEN, F. 1944. The Atlantic Alcidae. *Göteborgs Kungl. Vet. Vitt. Samh. Handl.* 6 (3): 1–138.

SLATER, P. J. B. and E. P. SLATER. 1972. Behaviour of the Tystie during feeding of the young. *Bird Study* 19: 105–113.

WILLIAMSON, K. 1965. *Fair Isle and its Birds.* Edinburgh.

WINN, H. E. 1950. The Black Guillemots of Kent Island, Bay of Fundy. *Auk* 67: 477–485.

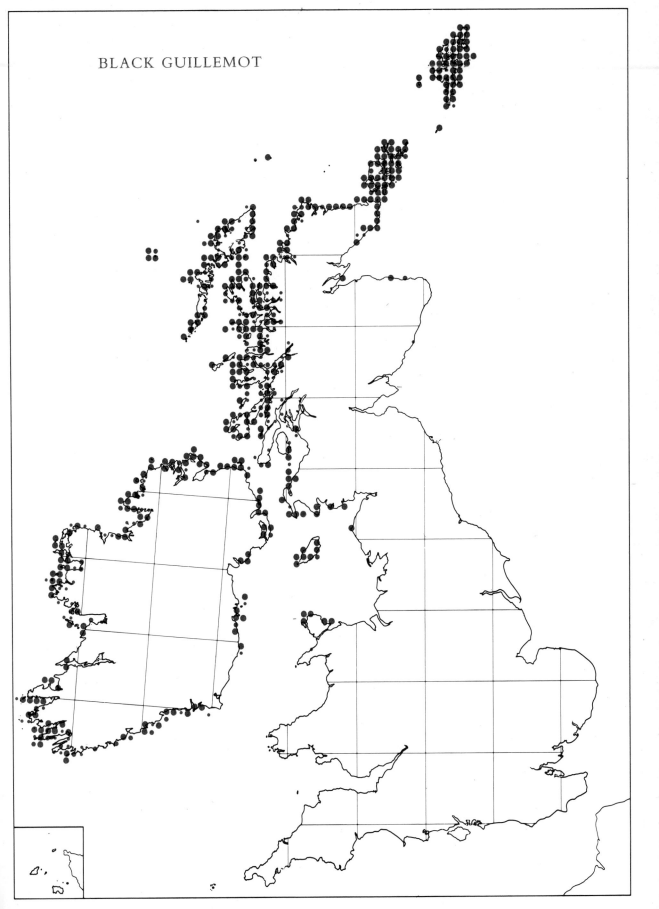

BLACK GUILLEMOT

Puffin

Fratercula arctica

Despite its ability to arouse enthusiasm and fascination in the birdwatcher, thus making it one of our most popular birds, the handsome and charming Puffin is most difficult to study in any detail. Its comings and goings about the colony are notoriously fickle, and it nests in a burrow or cavity usually rather longer than a human arm and too deep and dark to permit eggs or young to be seen. Fortunately, most colonies are reasonably large and, once the chicks have hatched (usually during June), some adults can be seen visiting their burrows with sand-eels or similar small fish held crosswise in their beaks. This suffices to confirm breeding.

Comparison of the Puffin map with those for the Guillemot *Uria aalge* and the Razorbill *Alca torda* shows that, while the basic west-coast pattern is retained (with an increasing density of occupied squares towards the north), the total number of squares with positive records is considerably reduced. Almost one-third of the confirmed breeding records refer to offshore islands rather than to mainland 10-km squares in both Britain and Ireland.

Most colonies are in remote, often near-inaccessible places, perhaps because the Puffin is more sensitive to human disturbance than are the other auks. It may be all the more subject to disturbance because of its preference for grassy slopes, many of which are capable of supporting sheep throughout the summer. In that case, however, it is difficult to understand the stability of colonies on remote islands, well-stocked with sheep, during the 18th and 19th centuries—particularly those such as St Kilda, where the birds filled a vital role in human economy, being harvested for food and feathers. Furthermore, by virtue of its habitat, the species is more vulnerable to predation, especially by Great Black-backed Gulls *Larus marinus*, though the extent to which this may affect the total size or success of a colony is unresolved (Evans 1975).

Although a few Puffins nest in holes in cliff-faces, and sizeable colonies occur in screes and boulder-tumbles at the head and foot of the cliffs, Puffins are primarily burrowers in grassland. They may excavate these burrows themselves, or may commandeer from Rabbits or Manx Shearwaters *Puffinus puffinus*. The slopes are usually covered in thrift, sea-campion, other maritime plants and even bluebells, flourishing on guano deposits and forming an attractive backdrop for the social gatherings and communal fly-pasts that are so much a part of the Puffin's life. Where, however, massive reductions in the population have taken place, the ground quickly becomes overgrown with sorrel (Flegg 1972).

As with the other auks, colony declines have long been reported in S Britain—perhaps due to pollution, perhaps to disturbance and, in the case of the Puffin (but not the cliff nesters), due to the introduction of Brown Rats (*eg* Lundy, Calf of Man). An unusual additional cause has been suggested for Grassholm (Pembrokeshire), now famed for its Gannets *Sula bassana*, but once equally well known for its Puffins (Drane 1894). Here, over-intensive burrowing by the birds may have made the soil too friable, allowing desiccation and subsequent wind and rain erosion of the soil mantle, and leaving the bedrock exposed (Lockley 1957).

More seriously, surveys have shown evidence of sharp decreases during the last decade in several colonies in the north and west—areas long considered to be the stronghold of Puffins in Britain and Ireland. In some cases, these declines have approached calamitous levels, even on remote island colony complexes such as St Kilda and the Shiants. Declines have also been reported from the Atlantic shores of the USA, Canada and Newfoundland. In many cases, the causes are obscure. There is historical evidence, however, of sudden population collapses, so let us hope that recovery will ultimately follow the recent declines.

The number of Puffins visible at a colony can fluctuate markedly even in a single day, and rarely bears much relation to the actual breeding strength. Schofield (1975) has suggested that adult activity is greatest at the time when the season's young are ready to leave their burrows and make for the sea, a hazardous journey which must be performed by night. Estimations of population are, therefore, difficult. Operation Seafarer conservatively put the 1969–70 figure at just under 500,000 pairs—a grand total less than several of the individual colony totals estimated by Fisher and Lockley (1954).

Number of 10-km squares in which recorded:
248 (6%)
Possible breeding   31 (13%)
Probable breeding   13 (5%)
Confirmed breeding   204 (82%)

References

BROOKE, M. DE L. 1972. The Puffin population of the Shiant Islands. *Bird Study* 19: 1–6.

DRANE, R. 1894. Natural history notes from Grassholm. *Trans. Cardiff Nat. Soc.* 26: 1–13.

EVANS, P. G. H. 1975. Gulls and Puffins on North Rona. *Bird Study* 22: 239–247.

FISHER, J. and R. M. LOCKLEY. 1954. *Sea-Birds*. London.

FLEGG, J. J. M. 1972. The Puffin on St Kilda, 1969–71. *Bird Study* 19: 7–17.

LOCKLEY, R. M. 1957. Grassholm: some facts and a legend. *Nature in Wales* 3: 382–388.

SCHOFIELD, P. 1975. Puffins on St Kilda in 1972. *Bird Study* 22: 233–237.

PUFFIN

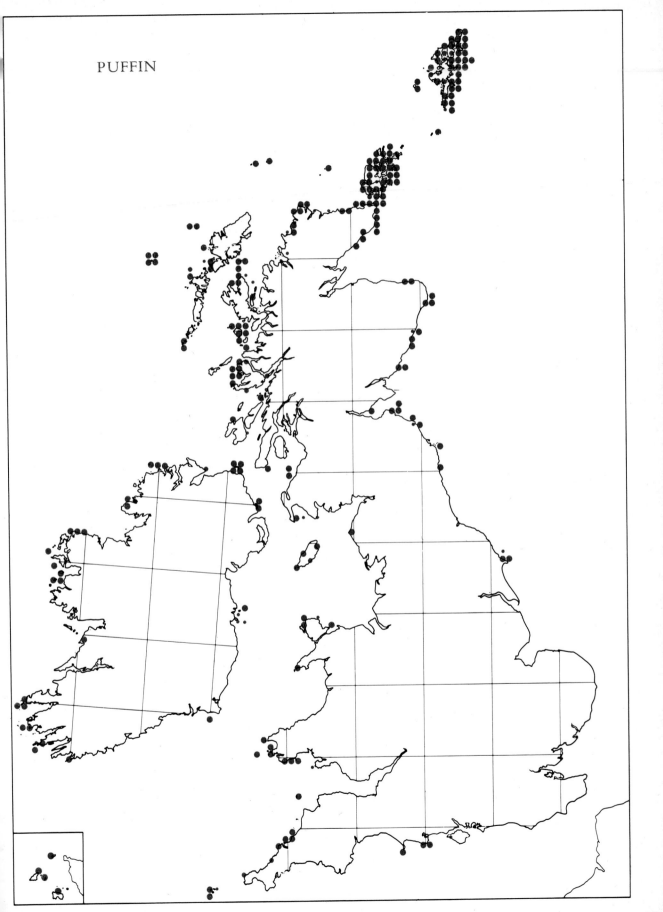

Stock Dove

Columba oenas

Although the Stock Dove was originally a bird of open or savanna woodland, its most frequent habitats in Britain are now parkland and farmland with old trees. The species is adaptable in its nest-site selection, and old nests or dreys, and holes in cliffs, quarries and old buildings are all used, as well as the normal holes in trees; some nest on the ground under bushes and in burrows. In Ireland, the majority nest in holes in buildings, and old castles are especially favoured.

Stock Doves have expanded their range very markedly since the early 19th century, when they were confined to S and E England. The spread really got under way in the second half of the 19th century and has been attributed to the increase in arable farming at that time. Reduction of competition with Feral Pigeons *C. livia*, previously widespread in rural areas, may also have been an important factor. N and SW England were colonised in the 1870s, and the first known cases of nesting in Scotland and Ireland were about 1866 and 1877 respectively. This expansion continued, though at a reduced rate, until about the 1930s in Britain and the 1950s in Ireland, though local decreases sometimes took place against the general trend. From about 1957 to at least 1960 there was a sudden general decline, especially marked in much of E England, with near extinction in some areas such as Essex. The species disappeared completely from the central London parks, where it had increased and spread since 1950. Stock Doves farther west in Britain were apparently unaffected. This collapse has been attributed to the use of pesticides, particularly organochlorine seed dressings. The Common Birds Census index of annual population changes shows a steady recovery from 1964, numbers on the census plots increasing by a factor of four by 1974 (see graph). The *Atlas* map indicates that the distribution is about as extensive as it was before the crash in the mid-1950s. The numerical level has, however, not necessarily recovered in all areas.

The colonisation of Scotland took place from the south and round the coasts, thence inland up the glens, with a separate centre around the Moray Firth. Irish colonisation started in the north (Down and Louth in 1877, Antrim in 1889, Armagh in 1890) and east (Wicklow in 1890, Carlow in 1894), and continued westwards until W Kerry and W and N Mayo were reached in the 1950s. The distribution map, therefore, reflects the present stage of an expansion which, although interrupted, has lasted over 100 years and may well continue. The strange gap covering much of Leitrim and Cavan, and parts of the adjoining counties, is a quirk for which there is no apparent explanation. Though hills and bogs abound, other parts of this area seem very suitable and there is no barrier to colonisation from the east.

Stock Doves are scarcer than Woodpigeons *C. palumbus* everywhere in Britain and Ireland, but their far-carrying song and display flights make location just as easy. Where scarce, however, the nest is often not easy to find, and records of mere presence are likely to be indications of unconfirmed breeding rather than of non-breeding birds. Taking all Common Bird Census areas, there was an average of just over one pair per km[2] in 1972. If the average density over the whole of the Stock Dove's British and Irish range was only half of this, the total would be just above the upper limit of Parslow's assessment of 10,000–100,000 pairs, made in 1967 when numbers were much lower.

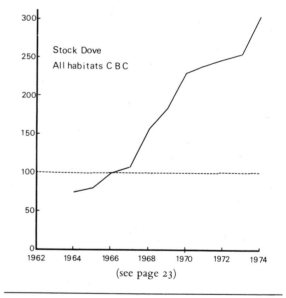

Stock Dove
All habitats C B C

(see page 23)

Number of 10-km squares in which recorded:
2,503 (65%)
Possible breeding 364 (15%)
Probable breeding 399 (16%)
Confirmed breeding 1,740 (70%)

References
CAMPBELL, B. 1951. A colony of Stock Doves. *Bird Notes* 24: 169–176.
MURTON, R. K. 1966. Natural selection and the breeding seasons of the Stock Dove and Wood Pigeon. *Bird Study* 13: 311–327.

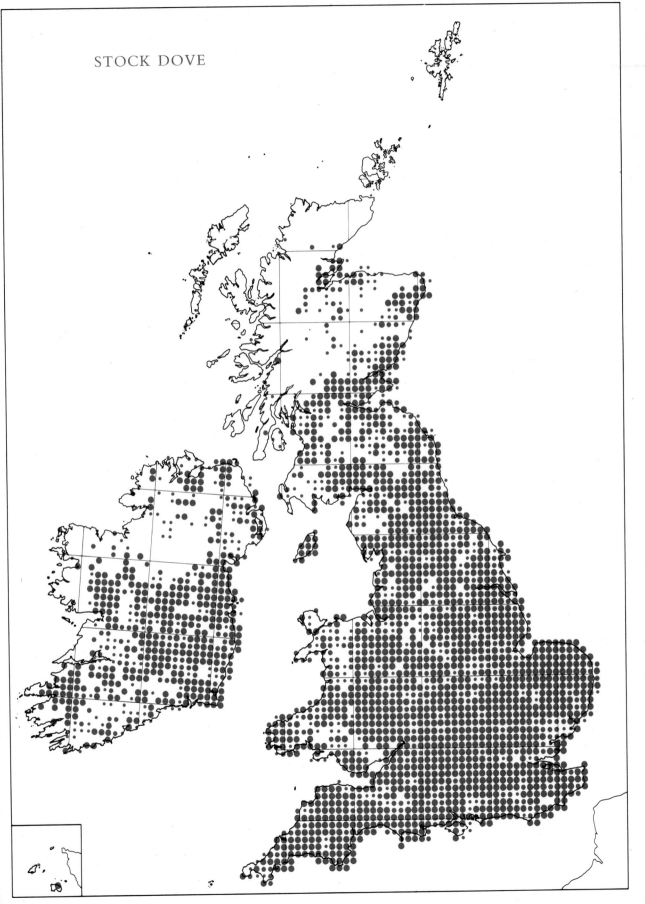

STOCK DOVE

Rock Dove and Feral Pigeon

Columba livia

Rock Doves and Feral Pigeons are elements of a single species, and they are treated together here. Ornithologists have for many years shown a considerable interest in the Rock Dove, but the Feral Pigeon has been largely ignored in British and Irish distributional literature. Yet, as discussed by Murton and Westwood (1966), there is now some difficulty in defining just what constitutes a wild Rock Dove population. Until the agricultural revolution which accompanied the Napoleonic Wars, semi-domesticated dovecote pigeons were an important part of rural economies, the birds being free to find their own food in the fields. From the earliest times, there must have been contact between dovecote birds and wild Rock Doves, leading to interbreeding and assimilation. In the present century, many lost racing pigeons have attached themselves to Rock Dove and Feral Pigeon colonies. All of this must have influenced the genetic composition of wild populations, even in remote parts of the highlands and islands.

Among Feral Pigeons, the commonest plumage types are the 'blue' (which resembles the wild Rock Dove apart from the thicker bill and enlarged cere common to all domestic and semi-domestic strains) and the 'blue chequer' (in which the wing coverts are spotted with black). Especially in urban areas, there are also individuals showing pronounced melanism, varying degrees of albinism, and even erythrism.

Feral colonists on the coastal cliffs of England, Wales, Isle of Man and S Scotland have the feeding and nesting habits of their Rock Dove predecessors, and clearly are now their ecological substitutes.

Hewson (1967) attempted to define the status of the Rock Dove in Scotland. Recognising that proportions of birds with wild-type characters decrease from north to south, he adopted the expedient of including as Rock Doves those colonies in which 80% or more of the birds had the wild-type plumage (two black wing-bars, unspotted wing coverts, and white lower back and underwing). On this criterion, Rock Doves now occur northwards from Bute and Argyll in the west and from Sutherland in the east, as well as on all crofted northern and western islands. It is clear that

the Rock Dove genotype has survived best in areas where dovecotes were always scarce, and where arable land is restricted to narrow and comparatively treeless coastal strips, so that competition for food with other pigeons is minimal.

In Ireland, too, Rock Doves are essentially birds of coastal cliffs and marine islands, and are said to be more numerous in the north and west than in the south and east. Feral Pigeons are fairly widespread, however, especially in the eastern half; and even in remote districts Rock Doves have interbred with feral birds, so that the influence of domestic strains is widely apparent (Ruttledge 1966). According to *Atlas* contributors, there is likely to be less contact between Rock Doves and Feral Pigeons in the south and west, from Co Waterford round to Co Donegal.

The habitat of true Rock Doves is coastal cliffs, where they nest colonially on ledges or crevices in sea caves or, occasionally, sheltered cliff ledges or among boulders. Rural colonies of Feral Pigeons, which more often than not behave as perfectly wild birds, utilise similar nest sites in cliff situations, while inland colonies occupy old or ruined buildings. Urban populations almost invariably nest on ledges and crannies in buildings, which thus provide a cave substitute. This species is particularly notable for its extended breeding season. Egg-laying can occur throughout the year, each pair producing five clutches on average; only about 25% of pairs in rural colonies engage in winter breeding, though more do so in urban areas. Melanic morphs are more likely to be continuous breeders than those with wild-type plumage, which helps to explain the dominance of melanics in town populations (Murton and Clarke 1968).

There are no sample counts on which to base an estimate, but some urban 10-km squares may hold thousands of birds and the total breeding population of Britain and Ireland could exceed 100,000 pairs.

Number of 10-km squares in which recorded: 1,904 (49%)
Possible breeding   415 (22%)
Probable breeding   196 (10%)
Confirmed breeding   1,293 (68%)

The dotted line on the map shows very approximately the limits of wild Rock Doves, confined mostly to the north and west coasts

References

GOODWIN, D. 1952. The colour-varieties of Feral Pigeons. *London Bird Rep.* 16 (1951): 35–36.

GOODWIN, D. 1954. Notes on Feral Pigeons. *Avic. Mag.* 60: 190–213.

HEWSON, R. 1967. The Rock Dove in Scotland in 1965. *Scott. Birds* 4: 359–371.

MURTON, R. K. and S. P. CLARKE. 1968. Breeding biology of Rock Doves. *Brit. Birds* 61: 429–448.

MURTON, R. K. and N. J. WESTWOOD. 1966. The foods of the Rock Dove and Feral Pigeon. *Bird Study* 13: 130–146.

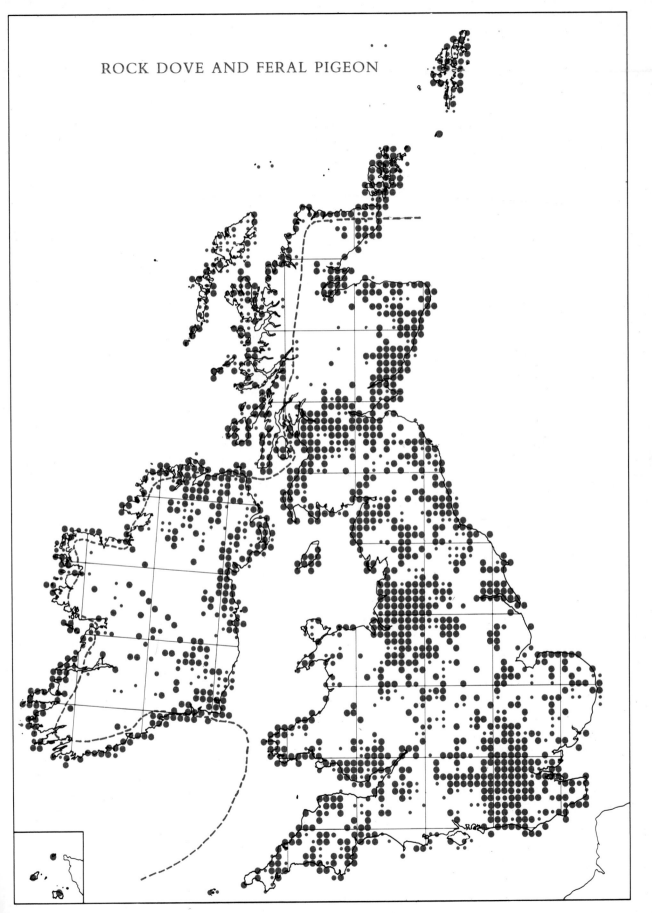

ROCK DOVE AND FERAL PIGEON

Woodpigeon

Columba palumbus

The Woodpigeon was originally a bird of the deciduous forest, but is now typically a farmland species where it is, undoubtedly, the worst avian pest in Britain and Ireland. In areas where extensive woods remain, a few Woodpigeons may spend much of their lives within them, but the majority now use trees mainly for roosting and nesting. All save the remotest areas of cultivated land are within their reach. If woods are lacking, they will readily nest in spinneys, hedges, isolated trees, tall heather or, if all else fails, on the ground. Within cities, they usually nest in trees or shrubs in gardens, but will use trees along busy streets or ledges on buildings.

The very wide distribution of Woodpigeons and their abundance are of quite recent origin. Murton (1965) has pointed out that they began to be mentioned as pests of crops some 200 years ago. By the middle of the 19th century, when the practice of growing turnips for use as winter fodder and of undersowing corn with clover was normal, the Woodpigeon steadily increased and consolidated its breeding range. By the turn of the century, it was nesting in the Outer Hebrides, Sutherland and Orkney and, although its spread across Ireland had been slower, it was already present in parts of the extreme west. Within the last 20 years, it has spread even farther north in Britain, with breeding proved before, but not during, 1968–72 in Shetland (and subsequently in the Faeroe Islands), and to the south and west in Ireland, with Cape Clear Island colonised in 1963. The colonisation of urban areas began about 150 years ago in many parts of Europe, and within the last century uncharacteristically tame birds have joined the long-established Feral Pigeons *C. livia* breeding in such cities as London.

Undoubtedly, new supplies of food were crucial in permitting this tremendous range-expansion and staggering increase in numbers. The original woodland populations relied upon natural foods during the winter, and such items as acorns and beech-mast might be available in large quantities in some years, but would fail almost completely in others. Obviously, the stand-by foods of ivy berries, weed seeds and leaves would not support a large population and any tendency to increase was quickly checked. The pre-existing adaptation which allowed Woodpigeons to feed on green-stuffs found naturally in woodland glades meant, however, that new agricultural crops such as turnips, kale, other brassicas and clover, which stand green through the winter, could be exploited. This allowed a greater percentage of the autumn population to survive through the winter, and was of crucial importance. The benefits of agriculture do not stop there, for cereal crops, ripening in July and August, are available as spilt grain on the stubbles for several weeks, providing an excellent food supply for late breeders.

It is hardly surprising that the Woodpigeon has increased to pest status and is estimated to cause well over £1 million damage each year. Control techniques have included the poking out of occupied nests, large-scale co-ordinated winter shoots, and the use of stupefying baits. The first method is expensive and would need to be practised over wide areas to be effective. The second, as Murton (1966) has shown, usually takes place in the autumn and early winter and removes individuals which would, in any case, die during the period of food-shortage in February and March. The use of stupefying baits is still in an experimental stage.

Proof of breeding for the *Atlas* was easily obtained, at any time of the year, by finding the characteristic and conspicuous nests in almost any kind of cover. In some conifer plantations surrounded by farmland, dozens of nests may be present in a very small area. Where Woodpigeons are scarce, their nests may be difficult to find, however, and most of the possible breeding records in the Highlands probably refer to single pairs whose nesting site in a remote oak or birch wood was not discovered. On farmland, the breeding season is at its peak from July to September, but in towns, where the birds feed mainly on bread, it is much earlier (Cramp 1972).

Woodpigeons are neither the most widespread nor the commonest species of bird in Britain and Ireland. Murton (1966) estimated that the British population was 5,000,000 birds in July and had doubled by the end of September. This suggests an average of 1,000 pairs per occupied 10-km square. Although the species is not normally counted during Common Birds Census work, since the majority breeds much later than most other birds, several estimates of densities in excess of 50 pairs per km² have been made. These figures, from arable areas in lowland England, would more than compensate for the 10-km squares with sparse populations in other habitats. It seems likely that the total British and Irish breeding population is about 3,000,000 to 5,000,000 pairs.

Number of 10-km squares in which recorded:
3,536 (92%)
Possible breeding   107 (3%)
Probable breeding   104 (3%)
Confirmed breeding   3,325 (94%)

References
CRAMP, S. 1972. The breeding of urban Woodpigeons. *Ibis* 114: 163–171.
MURTON, R. K. 1965. *The Woodpigeon*. London.

WOODPIGEON

Turtle Dove

Streptopelia turtur

Turtle Doves require open areas for feeding on the ground and shrubs or trees for nesting. Their main food plant is fumitory, which is found on light, dry and disturbed soils. Thus, they are associated with agriculture, and find typical arable farmland ideal.

Alone among European doves and pigeons, the Turtle Dove is a summer migrant, wintering mainly in Africa and returning to breed in late April or early May. The characteristic purring song is reminiscent of high summer, and makes initial location easy. First clutches are laid in May (Murton 1968) and new nests may be found through to the end of August; most pairs raise two broods and some three. The nest is an insubstantial twig platform often in a hedgerow shrub such as hawthorn or elder. Most are below 3 m, although a few may be as high as 6 m and there is one record for 12 m; except where breeding density is low, nest-finding probably provides the easiest means of confirming breeding. Overshooting migrants often linger well outside the normal range during the summer, and rather few of the *Atlas* records of possible breeding plotted in such areas will have referred to nesting pairs.

During the 19th century, the Turtle Dove increased and spread as new methods of arable cultivation developed through the country. The breeding distribution may have been static during the first four decades of the present century, but, in the last 30 years or so, there have been further slight expansions. The first breeding records for Scotland, all in the southeast, were from Berwickshire in 1946, Roxburghshire in 1951 and East Lothian in 1958; and the *Atlas* map indicates that these areas may continue to have a scattering of nesting pairs. In Ireland, however, where there were old nesting records from Cos Kerry and Down, and small concentrations existed for a few years from 1939 and again during 1955–57 in Co Dublin, breeding was confirmed in only four 10-km squares during 1968–72. This seems surprising because migrants are commonly seen in spring on the S and E coasts and many stay throughout June.

In England and Wales, there have been some slight fluctuations on the periphery of the Turtle Dove's range. The map perhaps indicates a slight increase in Wales, following a decline there during the 1950s and early 1960s. The blank area around London shows that the species cannot live in areas which have become completely built-up. Also, being essentially a lowland bird, it is unable to inhabit uplands such as the Pennines, which accounts for the wedge separating the populations breeding in S Lancashire and Yorkshire.

The dependence on the seeds of the fumitory, which are available for most of the period that the Turtle Dove is present in Britain, is not complete; but Murton *et al* (1964) found them to account for 30–50% of its diet. The map of this plant's distribution over much of England and Wales (Perring and Walters 1962) coincides quite well with the bird's presence. Many other food items are, however, consumed. Norris (1960) also suggested a relationship with summer temperatures (19°C July isotherm) and precipitation (below 102 cm of rain annually) which can be seen on the overlays.

The Common Birds Census index for the Turtle Dove has shown a steady increase from 1962 to the present, and the *Atlas* period was a time of good population levels. Densities on individual sites may exceed 30 pairs per km², but in 1972 the farmland and woodland averages were 1.4 and 2.2 pairs per km². Unlike its relative the Collared Dove *S. decaocto*, which forms dense concentrations in limited areas, the Turtle Dove is distributed continuously over suitable farmland and woodland, with probably well over 500 pairs in favourable 10-km squares. Even taking into account its greater scarcity towards the periphery of its range, an estimate of 100 pairs per occupied 10-km square may be conservative, which suggests that there are over 125,000 pairs in Britain, above Parslow's range of 10,000–100,000.

Number of 10-km squares in which recorded:
1,287 (33%)
Possible breeding   158 (12%)
Probable breeding   254 (20%)
Confirmed breeding   875 (68%)

References
MURTON, R. K. 1968. Breeding, migration and survival of Turtle Doves. *Brit. Birds* 61: 193–212.
MURTON, R. K., N. J. WESTWOOD and A. J. ISAACSON. 1964. The feeding habits of the Woodpigeon *Columba palumbus*, Stock Dove *C. oenas* and Turtle Dove *Streptopelia turtur*. *Ibis* 106: 174–188.
NORRIS, C. A. 1960. The breeding distribution of thirty bird species in 1952. *Bird Study* 7: 129–184.
PERRING, F. H. and S. M. WALTERS. 1962. *Atlas of the British Flora*. London and Edinburgh.

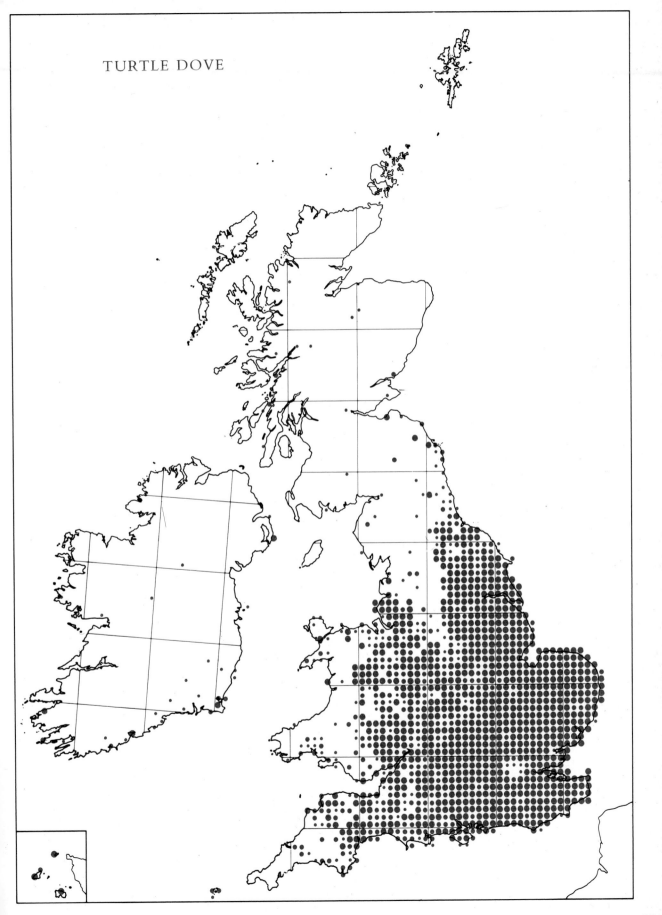

TURTLE DOVE

Collared Dove

Streptopelia decaocto

Collared Doves are closely associated with human habitations, especially where grain is readily available through processing (mills, maltings), spillage (as in docks), or use as livestock feed (farms, garden hen-runs, and rearing pens for Pheasants *Phasianus colchicus*). These doves are now a familiar sight and sound in suburbia and villages, though scarcer or even absent as breeding birds from city centres and open countryside (but the presence of farm buildings can lead to concentrations even in bare and exposed places). In many areas their appetite for grain and their monotonous cooing have resulted in their being regarded as pests, and treated accordingly.

Yet it was in 1955, only 13 years before *Atlas* fieldwork started, that the first Collared Doves nested in Britain. The colonisation of Britain and Ireland has been one of the most dramatic events witnessed by present-day ornithologists, but is just one stage in an even more dramatic range-extension northwestwards across Europe. Until about 1930, when explosive expansion began, these doves were restricted in Europe to Turkey and parts of the Balkans (Albania, Bulgaria and Yugoslavia). They reached Hungary in 1932, Czechoslovakia in 1936, Austria in 1938, Germany in 1943, the Netherlands in 1947, Denmark in 1948, Sweden and Switzerland in 1949, France in 1950, and Belgium and Norway in 1952—thus spreading over 1,600 km in less than 20 years. Early in the 1970s the species even bred in the Faeroe Islands and Iceland. The European spread and the colonisation of Britain and Ireland have been well-documented by Fisher (1953), Stresemann and Nowak (1958) and Hudson (1965, 1972); the settlement here is illustrated by the series of maps on page 459.

When Collared Doves reached these islands, they found an ecological niche not filled by any other bird and, in the absence of competition, proceeded to demonstrate the potential for geometric population increase that is presumed to be inherent in all species.

During their first decade here, they increased and spread at the incredible rate of 100% per annum. Of course, it was inevitable that this rate of increase would slow down as optimum habitat became fully exploited, and by 1970 the species was expanding at under 50% (possibly only 25%) per annum. Town suburbs and villages were colonised first, especially those in low-lying areas of coastal counties. Collared Doves are particularly fond of parks and large gardens where ornamental evergreen trees (such as cypresses and pines) provide sheltered nesting and roosting sites.

Though the period of explosive expansion is over, Collared Dove numbers are still increasing. Nowadays, this is most apparent through in-filling in rural areas; the Common Birds Census recorded a five-fold increase on farmland during 1969–73. The *Atlas* distribution map still shows concentration in the coastal belt and avoidance of upland areas, which were even more evident in the incomplete map for 1968–70 (see Hudson 1972). It is particularly striking that this recent colonist now has a much more extensive British and Irish distribution than that of the Turtle Dove *S. turtur*.

Collared Doves are easy to locate because of their persistent cooing and the males' repeated alighting call. While nests in deciduous trees may be easy to see, those in evergreens are more difficult; recently fledged juveniles are readily seen, however, and, at the height of the breeding season, successive broods may follow so closely that the female may be attending fledged young in off-duty spells from incubating the next clutch. It is such prolific breeding which helped to provide the surplus of birds required for dynamic expansion.

At the present time, numbers are not easy to determine. Hudson thought that there were about 3,000 pairs (19,000 birds in autumn) in 1964, and 15,000–25,000 pairs in 1970. By 1972 there may well have been up to 30,000–40,000 pairs; this would imply an average of around 25–30 pairs per 10-km square with probable or confirmed breeding, which may not be excessive and is certainly exceeded in many coastal counties.

Number of 10-km squares in which recorded: 2,653 (69%)
Possible breeding   420 (16%)
Probable breeding   506 (19%)
Confirmed breeding   1,727 (65%)

References
FISHER, J. 1953. The Collared Turtle Dove in Europe. *Brit. Birds* 46: 153–181.
HUDSON, R. 1965. The spread of the Collared Dove in Britain and Ireland. *Brit. Birds* 58: 105–139.
HUDSON, R. 1972. Collared Doves in Britain and Ireland during 1965–70. *Brit. Birds* 65: 139–155.
STRESEMANN, E. and E. NOWAK. 1958. Die Ausbreitung der Türkentaube in Asien und Europa. *J. Orn.* 99: 243–296.

Ring-necked Parakeet *Psittacula krameri* **and Budgerigar** *Melopsittacus undulatus*, **see page 452**

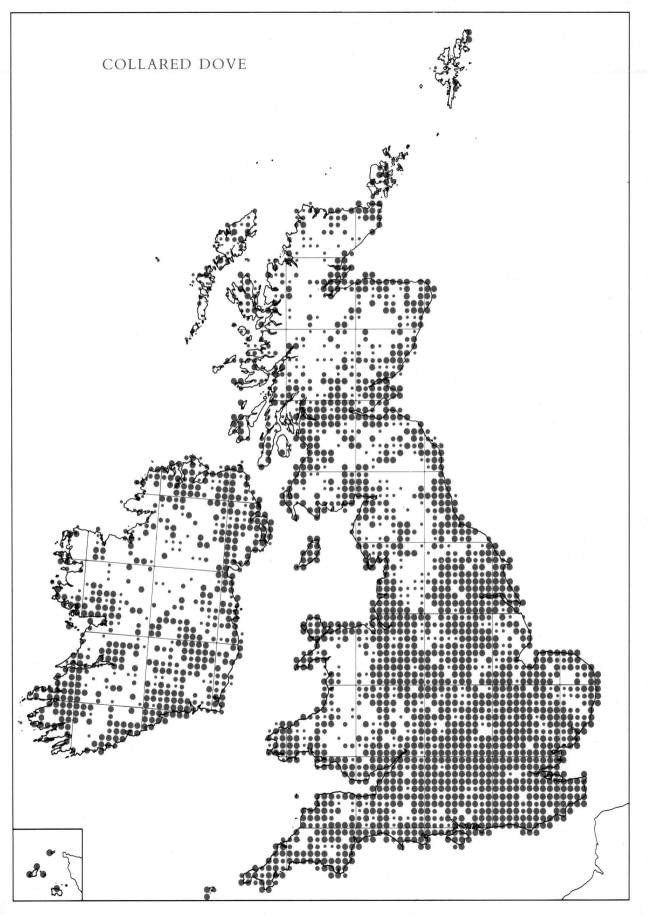

COLLARED DOVE

Cuckoo

Cuculus canorus

Apart from city centres, there is virtually no habitat in Britain and Ireland where Cuckoos do not occur. While the familiar song is far-carrying, making it easy to establish presence and probable breeding, confirmation is much more difficult unless the loud food-begging calls of the young are heard. These facts are reflected in the map, with presence in over 90% of the squares, but breeding proved in less than half.

Cuckoos winter in Africa and arrive over here during April. The female returns to the same area in consecutive years and concentrates on a particular host species, normally the one which was her own foster parent. From a vantage point she watches for birds in the process of building. When a nest is ready, she first removes one of the host's eggs and, still holding this in her bill, lays her own in its place, often all the time being mobbed by the host birds. Chance (1922) recorded that a single Cuckoo was able to lay 25 eggs in a season when nests of the hosts had been deliberately robbed to provide a continuous supply at a suitable stage. In normal circumstances, however, many fewer than this are laid in a season, though Wyllie (1975) recorded a minimum of 12 produced by one female; he also noted nestling predation, which would force the hosts to re-nest.

The extensive list of hosts ranges in size from Blackbird *Turdus merula* to Wren *Troglodytes troglodytes*. Some unusual species include Red-backed Shrike *Lanius collurio*, Hawfinch *Coccothraustes coccothraustes* and Ring Ouzel *Turdus torquatus*. Small insectivorous species are usually selected and those Cuckoo eggs laid in seed-eating finches' nests are not normally successful even if they hatch. Certain species will not be duped by the Cuckoo, and Chance listed Spotted Flycatcher *Muscicapa striata* and Blackcap *Sylvia atricapilla* among those regularly rejecting its egg.

The commonest hosts, with 2.2–3.1% of their nests parasitised in Britain, are Dunnocks *Prunella modularis*, Meadow Pipits *Anthus pratensis* and Reed Warblers *Acrocephalus scirpaceus*; Meadow Pipits are by far the commonest hosts in Ireland. Apart from these and the closely related Rock and Tree Pipits *Anthus spinoletta* and *A. trivialis*, and the rare Marsh Warbler *Acrocephalus palustris*, all other species have less than 1% of their nests parasitised (Glue and Morgan 1972). The Meadow Pipit is the most frequent dupe in coastal areas and on lowland heath and moorland, while the Dunnock is the commonest in woodland, around habitations and on farmland. Robins *Erithacus rubecula* and Pied Wagtails *Motacilla alba* are not infrequent fosterers in woods and inhabited areas respectively. In British freshwater habitats, the most frequent host is the Reed Warbler, but some Cuckoos select the Sedge Warbler *A. schoenobaenus* instead.

In Britain the Dunnock may have become a regular victim only relatively recently, which could explain why the eggs of Dunnock-Cuckoos are so unlike those of their hosts. That the Cuckoo is capable of laying a blue egg like the Dunnock's is shown by the fact that on the Continent it will do so in nests of the Redstart *Phoenicurus phoenicurus*. Before the clearing of the primaeval forest, the Robin was perhaps of greater importance, as it is today in deciduous areas in most of Europe.

A widespread decrease has been reported since about 1953 (perhaps earlier in SW England) and this has affected E England especially. A decrease has been noted in Ireland during this century, but breeding in Shetland has become more frequent since about 1947. The Common Birds Census revealed little change during 1968–72. With records in over 3,500 10-km squares, Parslow's inclusion of the Cuckoo in the range of 1,000–10,000 breeding pairs must be a gross underestimate, since even a modest 5–10 pairs per 10-km square would give a total of 17,500–35,000 pairs in Britain and Ireland.

Number of 10-km squares in which recorded: 3,532 (91%)
Possible breeding   174 (5%)
Probable breeding   1,746 (49%)
Confirmed breeding   1,612 (46%)

References
BAKER, E. C. S. 1942. *Cuckoo Problems*. London.
CHANCE, E. P. 1922. *The Cuckoo's Secret*. London.
CHANCE, E. P. 1940. *The Truth about the Cuckoo*. London.
GLUE, D. and R. MORGAN. 1972. Cuckoo hosts in British habitats. *Bird Study* 19: 187–192.
HARRISON, C. J. O. 1968. Egg mimicry in British Cuckoos. *Bird Study* 15: 22–28.
LACK, D. 1963. Cuckoo hosts in England. *Bird Study* 10: 185–202.
WYLLIE, I. 1975. Study of Cuckoos and Reed Warblers. *Brit. Birds* 68: 369–378.

CUCKOO

Barn Owl

Tyto alba

Barn Owls are found in a wide variety of chiefly agricultural habitats, particularly where areas of rough waste ground and suitable nesting places occur. The nest may be in an artificial site, such as an old barn, derelict building, ruin, or haystack, or in a natural one, such as a hollow tree or a cavity in a cliff face. Though nests in old trees are common (39% of 282 sites on nest record cards), these are usually isolated rather than in dense woodland. Competition with the larger Tawny Owl *Strix aluco*, which will kill Barn Owls, whether for food or as competitors (Mikkola 1976), is thus largely avoided. The occupation of nest boxes by both species has become commoner in recent years.

Breeding Barn Owls can be located by watching at dusk for adults hunting or carrying food, by searching for the characteristic black, shiny pellets at daytime roosts, or by listening for the territorial shrieks of adults and the snoring voices of young in the nest. Despite these clues, pairs may be easily overlooked. The records from *Atlas* fieldworkers were augmented by reports received as a result of appeals on radio, and in various farming and country journals. Most of the replies came from Britain and it should be borne in mind that the Irish picture was not significantly added to in this way. The apparent concentration in Co Kerry is probably largely explained by the local *Atlas* organiser having many contacts in the farming community there. An enquiry relating to 1953–63 (Prestt 1965) indicated that Barn Owls were commonest in SW England, S Wales, S Yorkshire, NW England and S Scotland. The proportion of confirmed breeding records in the *Atlas* shows a similar distribution.

Those nesting in Ross-shire (and also SE Sutherland immediately before the *Atlas* period) probably represent the most northerly breeding Barn Owls in the world. Numbers and range may be limited by the effects of severe winters—not surprising since this is a mainly tropical species—and in this connection it is noticeable that the proportion of proved breeding records is greater in the milder maritime zone of SW Scotland than in the colder SE Scotland. The relative lack of suitable breeding sites, plus winter severity at high altitudes, results in avoidance of parts of the Pennines and the mountains of Wales and Scotland. This owl's degree of abundance in various parts of England and Wales in 1932 (see page 460), based on analysis of returns from 4,000 observers, shows similarities with the distribution indicated by the *Atlas* map.

Though now generally appreciated as a beneficial species, with a diet consisting mostly of Short-tailed Voles, Common Shrews and Wood Mice in Britain, and Wood Mice and Brown Rats in Ireland and the Isle of Man (Glue 1974), Barn Owls were formerly much persecuted, along with all other predators. Even today, the recoveries of ringed individuals show that these protected birds are still shot and trapped, while many more succumb on our roads and railways (Glue 1971).

Short-term fluctuations caused by hard winters or by variations in the density of small rodents tend to mask long-term trends, but there seems no doubt that the Barn Owl has continued to decline in most parts of both Britain and Ireland during this century. Decreases have been attributed largely to loss of habitat, human disturbance, severe winters and, in E England during the late 1950s and early 1960s, toxic chemicals. In Prestt's (1965) enquiry, the Barn Owl came second only to the Sparrowhawk *Accipiter nisus* in the high proportion of returns (76%) reporting a decrease during 1953–63, and this was additional to the long-term decline which was worrying ornithologists even in the 1930s.

Blaker (1934) attempted to estimate the Barn Owl population of England and Wales and arrived at a figure of 12,000 pairs. Parslow commented that some sample areas showed a decline to considerably under half the number found in 1932, and placed the species in the range 1,000–10,000 pairs. At a conservative two to four pairs per occupied 10-km square, the current total would be about 4,500–9,000 pairs.

This species is afforded special protection in Great Britain under Schedule I of the Protection of Birds Act, 1954–67.

Number of 10-km squares in which recorded: 2,279 (59%)
Possible breeding   480 (21%)
Probable breeding   419 (18%)
Confirmed breeding   1,380 (61%)

References
BLAKER, G. B. 1934. *The Barn Owl in England and Wales*. RSPB, London.
GLUE, D. E. 1971. Ringing recovery circumstances of some small birds of prey. *Bird Study* 18: 137–146.
GLUE, D. E. 1974. Food of the Barn Owl in Britain and Ireland. *Bird Study* 21: 200–210.
MIKKOLA, H. 1976. Owls killing and killed by other owls and raptors in Europe. *Brit. Birds* 69: 144–154.
PRESTT, I. 1965. An enquiry into the recent breeding status of some smaller birds of prey and crows in Britain. *Bird Study* 12: 196–221.
PRESTT, I. and A. A. BELL. 1966. An objective method of recording breeding distribution of common birds of prey in Britain. *Bird Study* 13: 277–283.

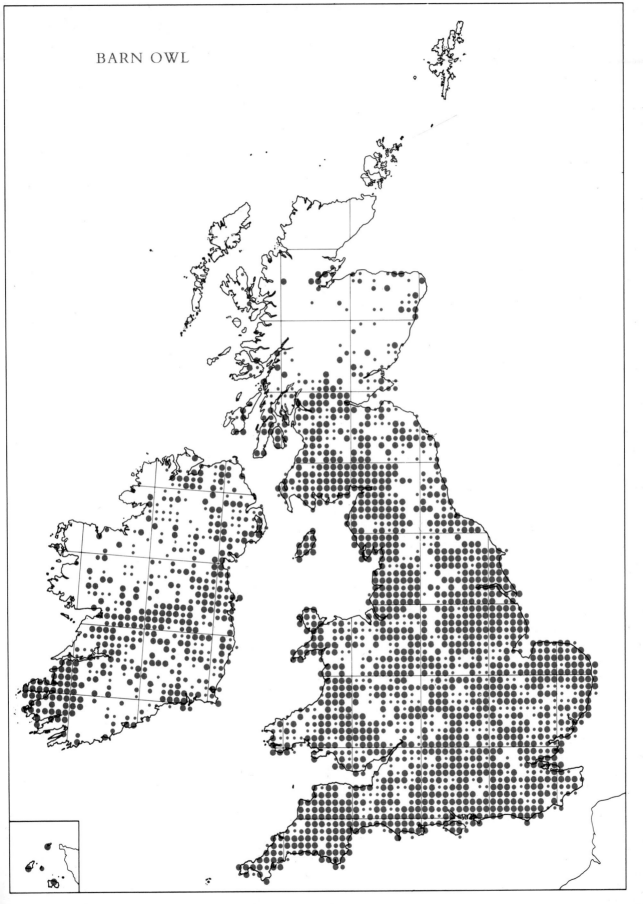

BARN OWL

Snowy Owl

Nyctea scandiaca

The Snowy Owl nests chiefly in the tundra zone where its food consists principally of lemmings. In the subarctic, Snowy Owls occasionally breed where alternative mammalian prey such as hares, Rabbits, mice and voles are plentiful; they will even do so where rodents are scarce, as in central Iceland. The numbers attempting to nest and the sizes of the broods reared vary annually with the fluctuating abundance of the prey: in poor lemming years, few of these owls breed and, instead, they wander widely in search of food.

Throughout the last century, the Snowy Owl was an irregular visitor to Britain and Ireland. Witherby *et al* (1938–41) described it as an 'almost regular winter visitor to Shetlands and frequent Orkneys and Hebrides, often on mainland of Scotland and in Ireland', but over 20 years later Hollom (1962) noted it as 'rare and irregular even in the north of Scotland'. Its decreasing incidence during this century was no doubt due to the 'warming up' of the Arctic between about 1900 and 1940. In Ireland, for example, there were 50 records before 1950, but only one in the following 15 years. Then, after a series of winter invasions in Scandinavia during 1960–63 (Nagell and Frycklund 1965), Snowy Owls appeared for several summers on various of the Scottish islands and were also increasingly reported from other countries including Estonia, Finland, Germany and the Netherlands. Finally, a nest was found on the Shetland island of Fetlar in June 1967, the first confirmed evidence of breeding here.

The typical tundra or Scandinavian high fell habitat commonly occupied by the Snowy Owl is paralleled on Fetlar by bare moorland of rough grass and heather with rocky outcrops and boulder-strewn slopes 150 m above sea level. Nests on Fetlar have been bare scrapes in patches of short grass, usually close to exposed slabs of rock. In 1967, seven eggs were laid. The female incubated with a commanding view of the surrounding terrain, and the male sat sentinel nearby, except during the short periods when he was hunting. That year, five young reached the free-flying stage and, though this output

has never been repeated, 16 young were raised during the following eight years, apparently by the same pair of owls (Tulloch 1975). Bigamy is not uncommon in Snowy Owls and, since 1973, a second female (believed to be from an earlier brood) has laid eggs close to the first territory, but these have invariably failed to hatch. In 1976, no male was present and there was no attempt at nesting.

The Snowy Owl events on Fetlar provide one of the conservation success stories of our time and, without the help provided by the RSPB, it is likely that history would have recorded no more than an instance of 'attempted breeding'. The island is small, some 8 km by 6.4 km, and the nest site is on open ground grazed by ponies and sheep and traversed by local crofters and birdwatchers. Shortly after the nest was discovered in 1967, a hide was positioned and a round-the-clock watch maintained to eliminate the inevitable disturbance that such a rare and attractive bird would unwittingly bring upon itself.

Even after the young have left the nest, accidents may happen. Young Snowy Owls on Fetlar have on two occasions received medical attention after becoming entangled with barbed wire, and the adult male was also once restored to health after having damaged a wing. The future of the Snowy Owl in Scotland may well depend on the fortunes of those young so far raised. In recent years, summering individuals have appeared elsewhere in Shetland, including Fair Isle, as well as in the central and NE Highlands and the Hebrides.

This species is afforded special protection in Great Britain under Schedule I of the Protection of Birds Act, 1954–67.

Number of 10-km squares in which recorded:
5 (0.1%)
Possible breeding   4 (80%)
Probable breeding   0
Confirmed breeding   1 (20%)

Three dots have been moved by up to two 10-km squares (as recommended by the Rare Breeding Birds Panel)

References

HOLLOM, P. A. D. 1962. *The Popular Handbook of British Birds*. London.

NAGELL, B. and I. FRYCKLUND. 1965. Invasionen av Fjälluggla (*Nyctea scandiaca*) i södra Skandinavien vintrarna 1960–63. *Vår Fågelvä*. 24: 26–55.

SHARROCK, J. T. R. and E. M. SHARROCK. 1976. *Rare Birds in Britain and Ireland*. Berkhamsted.

TULLOCH, R. J. 1968. Snowy Owls breeding in Shetland in 1967. *Brit. Birds* 61: 119–132.

TULLOCH, R. J. 1975. Fetlar's Snowies. *Birds* 5: 24–27.

WATSON, A. 1957. The behaviour, breeding and food-ecology of the Snowy Owl *Nyctea scandiaca*. *Ibis* 99: 419–462.

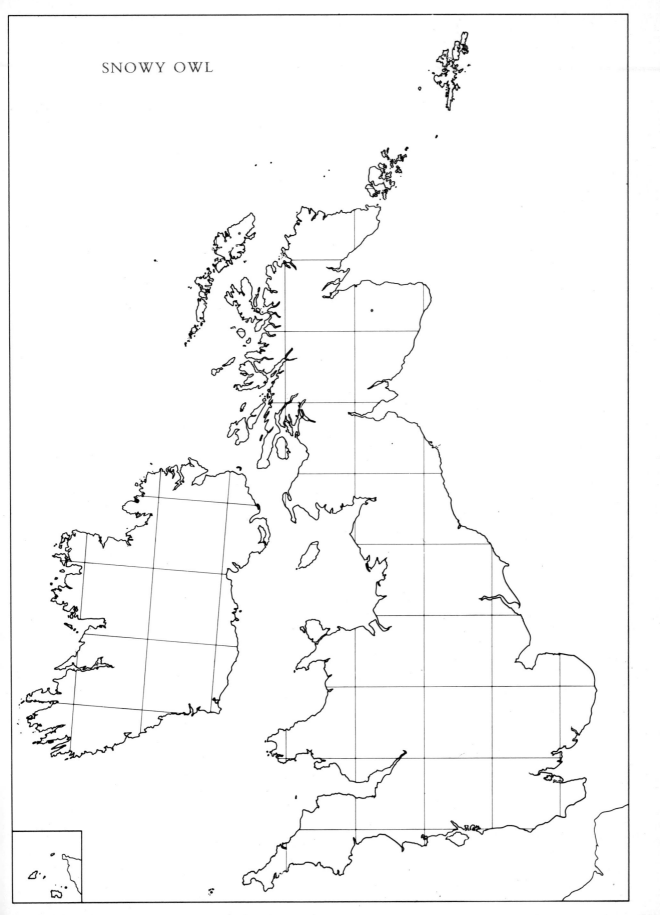

SNOWY OWL

Little Owl

Athene noctua

In Britain, Little Owls are characteristic of agricultural countryside well endowed with hedgerow trees and farm buildings. Old orchards and parkland are other favourite haunts, but these owls also frequent industrial waste ground, sand dunes, moorland edges, old quarries, sea-cliffs and inshore islands. They occur in relatively bare country, especially in such regions as Cornwall and the Lleyn Peninsula (Caernarvonshire), and yet sometimes penetrate to the centres of our towns and cities. The nest is most often in a hole in a tree, pollarded willows being favoured in some areas. Less often it is in an old building, a stone wall or a rock cleft, while hay and corn stacks and even Rabbit burrows are sometimes used.

Though found throughout the Continent north to Denmark, Little Owls are not indigenous to Britain. Charles Waterton released five in Walton Park (Yorkshire) in 1842, but the experiment failed. Forty were set free in Kent by E. B. Meade-Waldo during 1874–80, with some success, and others abortively in Norfolk and Sussex in the 1870s. Extensive introduction of Dutch Little Owls by Lord Lilford near Oundle (Northamptonshire) during 1888–90 resulted in a spread of breeding to Rutland by 1891 and Bedfordshire by 1892. Further introductions took place in Yorkshire, Hampshire and Hertfordshire in the 1890s, but by the end of the century regular breeding was established only in Kent, Bedfordshire, Northamptonshire and Rutland. Subsequently, the spread was explosive and, partly aided by further releases in Essex, Hampshire, Sussex, Yorkshire and probably other counties, the range extended westwards to the River Severn and northwards to the River Trent by 1910. A decade later, Little Owls were present in every county south of the River Humber excepting parts of Wales and the SW Peninsula, which, however, had been colonised by 1930. The rate of spread then slowed, and the northwards expansion to the Scottish border counties occupied the following two decades. (See map on page 460.) Even in the early 1970s, confirmed Scottish breeding records were sparse and only as far north as Midlothian, though a single dead juvenile was reported from Perthshire.

While the range was still expanding northwards in the 1940s, decreases were noted in some southern and western counties; these may have resulted from the cold winters at this period, since numbers were especially low after the hard weather of 1946/47, as indeed they were following the severe winter of 1962/63. Marked sudden decreases also occurred, especially in SE England, in the decade 1956–65, and these may have had an origin in pesticide contamination of prey. Signs of a slight recovery have been noted in some areas, but in S England at least the subjective impression remains that Little Owls are considerably scarcer now than in the 1950s, when they were a not uncommon sight on the tops of fences, walls and telegraph poles in broad daylight.

Little Owls will take prey up to the size of a half-grown Rabbit, and small birds and mammals are an important part of their diet. They also feed on earthworms, slugs, snails, beetles and other invertebrates, as shown by a special enquiry into their feeding habits organised by the BTO (Hibbert-Ware 1937–38). Some years ago, a pair of Little Owls resident on Skokholm (Pembrokeshire) fed almost entirely on Storm Petrels *Hydrobates pelagicus*, while at Dungeness (Kent) others have been found preying on Common Terns *Sterna hirundo*.

The habit of perching prominently, often near the nest, makes location easier in daytime than it is for other owls and, once the approximate site is known, it is not difficult to find nests which are in tree-holes. Nests in buildings, quarries and walls are more difficult to find and this may partly explain the lower proportion of confirmed breeding records in Cornwall and mid-west Wales, though it is also likely that Little Owls are scarcer there than in the main range.

The species is quite common in the fens of E England, partly a reflection of its frequent use of pollarded willows as nest sites, and partly perhaps a result of the scarcity of the Tawny Owl *Strix aluco* in this open habitat. Elsewhere, there may well be interspecific competition for nest sites and food, and the Little Owl is a not infrequent prey of the Tawny (Mikkola 1976).

Parslow included the Little Owl in the range 1,000–10,000 pairs. It seems certain that the total is near the upper figure and could even exceed it, since a conservative 5–10 pairs per occupied 10-km square suggests a population of about 7,000–14,000 pairs.

Number of 10-km squares in which recorded: 1,381 (36%)
Possible breeding   202 (15%)
Probable breeding   239 (17%)
Confirmed breeding   940 (68%)

References
FITTER, R. S. R. 1959. *The Ark in our Midst.* London.
HIBBERT-WARE, A. 1937–38. Report of the Little Owl food inquiry, 1936–37. *Brit. Birds* 31: 162–187, 205–229, 249–264.
MIKKOLA, H. 1976. Owls killing and killed by other owls and raptors in Europe. *Brit. Birds* 69: 144–154.
WITHERBY, H. F. and N. F. TICEHURST. 1908. The spread of the Little Owl from the chief centres of its introduction. *Brit. Birds* 1: 335–342.

LITTLE OWL

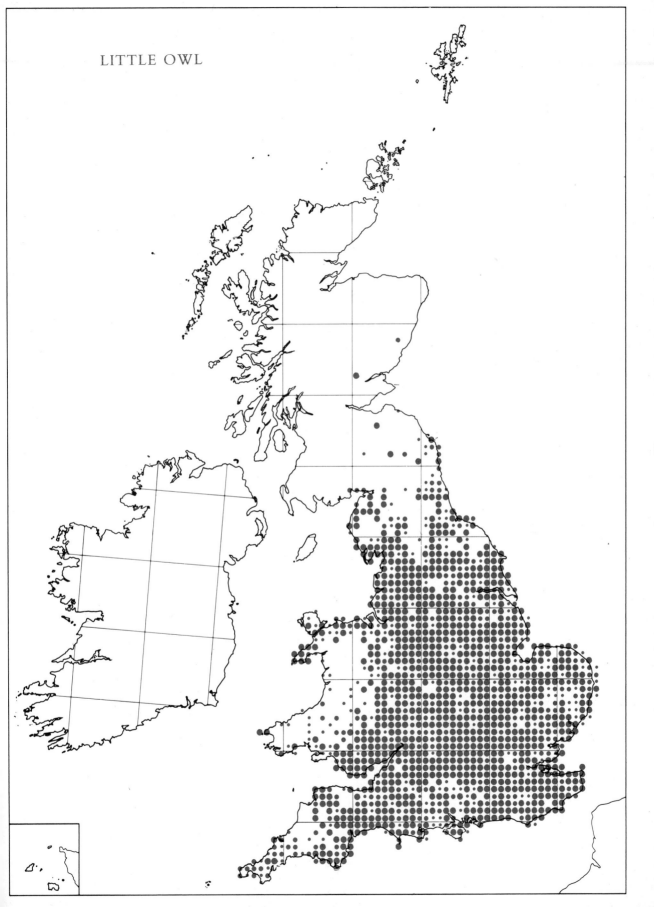

Tawny Owl

Strix aluco

Most Tawny Owls inhabit deciduous or mixed woodland, though they may be not uncommon in mature coniferous plantations. They are also found in tree-dotted farmland and in parks, large gardens and churchyards, frequently in built-up areas. Exceptionally, isolated pairs may nest in open country, breeding in old buildings or holes in quarries or cliffs. The nest is most often in a hole, frequently opening upwards (chimneys are occasionally used), but Tawny Owls sometimes take over large, disused nests of other species, particularly those of Carrion or Hooded Crows *Corvus corone*, Magpies *Pica pica*, Sparrowhawks *Accipiter nisus* and Buzzards *Buteo buteo*, in that order of frequency. In the absence of old timber, Tawny Owls will resort to nesting on the ground, sometimes in the entrance to a Rabbit burrow, among bracken or heather, or in the shelter of old tree roots.

The diet varies according to the prey available. In woodland it is composed very largely of small mammals, particularly Wood Mice and Bank Voles, together with a few small birds; but in some urban situations House Sparrows *Passer domesticus* and Brown Rats are the usual prey. Invertebrate foods, particularly earthworms, form a greater part of the diet than that of the other native owls.

The Tawny Owl is a highly territorial and sedentary species, single-brooded, but failing to breed during years of food shortage. More than three-quarters of the *Atlas* records referred to confirmed breeding, a much higher proportion than for the other owls. The nocturnal hooting and 'kewick' calls make location of the breeding territory easy. This species is consistently the first of the six British breeding owls to lay, with a mean first egg date of 25th March (from nest record card data). Incubation spans four weeks, both parents feed the owlets for four to five weeks before they fledge and for up to a further 13 weeks (Southern *et al* 1954, Glue 1973). Fledged owlets are very noisy from mid-May to early August.

This species was much persecuted in the 19th century, and unfortunately this has not entirely ceased.

Ringed birds are regularly found shot and even more die on roads and railways. A general increase in numbers took place in many areas during 1900–30 (up to about 1950 in some places), perhaps aided by the climatic amelioration of the first part of this century, when the species also extended its northern limit in Europe. In recent years, however, numbers and distribution have remained more or less stable, apart from some strictly local changes. Surveys in 1963 (Prestt 1965) and 1964 (Prestt and Bell 1966) showed that Tawny Owls were considered to be common everywhere within the British range except in the N Midlands (including Lincolnshire) and SE England (including London), with presence in more than 60% of surveyed 10-km squares everywhere except in NE England (100-km square NZ) and the E Midlands (squares TF and TL).

The Tawny Owl's sparse distribution in the fens of E England may reflect the shortage of suitable nesting sites and the virtual absence of mature woodland. There is a similar situation in the Highlands and N Scotland, though in Sutherland and Caithness it is very common where there are birch woods in the glens. The Tawny Owl has never been recorded in Ireland, where its niche is filled by the Long-eared Owl *Asio otus*, and only once (1961) in the Isle of Man. An attempt to introduce the species to Ireland (near Belfast in 1900) failed, not surprisingly since four of the nine released are *known* to have been shot. Even on the Isle of Wight, where two or three occur in most years, breeding has not yet been proved.

Parslow placed the Tawny Owl in the range 10,000–100,000 pairs and, as Tawny Owls outnumbered Little Owls *Athene noctua* by two to one in Common Birds Census areas (farmland and woodland combined) in 1971–72, it would be surprising if the species were not in the upper half of this range.

Number of 10-km squares in which recorded:
2,305 (60%)
Possible breeding   163 (7%)
Probable breeding   349 (15%)
Confirmed breeding   1,793 (78%)

References

GLUE, D. E. 1971. Ringing recovery circumstances of some small birds of prey. *Bird Study* 18: 137–146.
GLUE, D. E. 1973. Seasonal mortality in four small birds of prey. *Ornis Scand.* 4: 97–102.
HARRISON, C. J. O. 1960. The food of some urban Tawny Owls. *Bird Study* 7: 236–240.
PRESTT, I. 1965. An enquiry into the recent breeding status of some of the smaller birds of prey and crows in Britain. *Bird Study* 12: 196–221.
PRESTT, I. and A. A. BELL. 1966. An objective method of recording breeding distribution of common birds of prey in Britain. *Bird Study* 13: 277–283.
SOUTHERN, H. N. 1954. Tawny Owls and their prey. *Ibis* 96: 384–410.
SOUTHERN, H. N., R. VAUGHAN and R. C. MUIR. 1954. The behaviour of young Tawny Owls after fledging. *Bird Study* 1: 101–110.

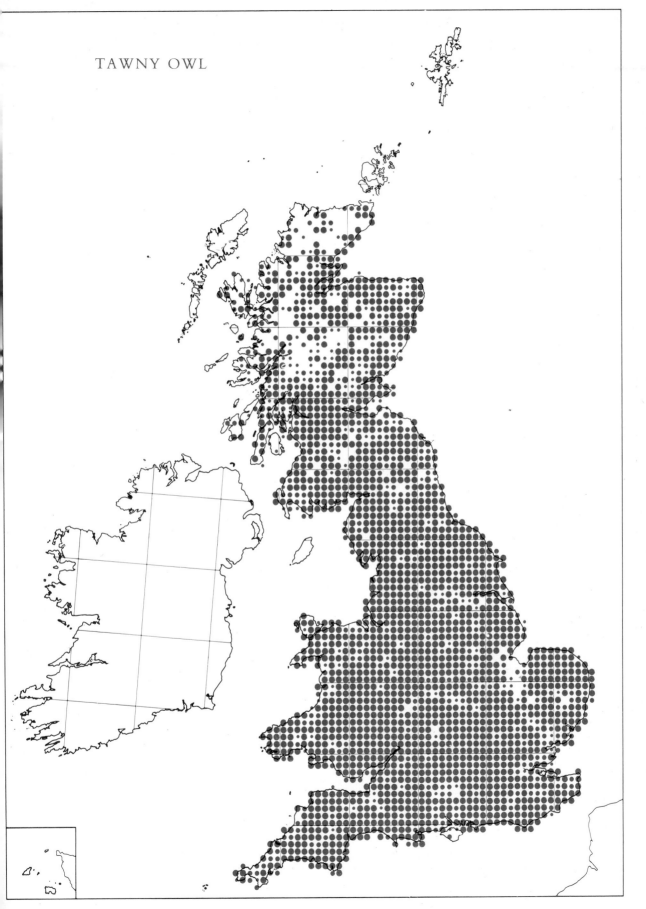

TAWNY OWL

Long-eared Owl

Asio otus

In Britain today, Long-eared Owls are found in coniferous woods and commercial plantations, but they are possibly more numerous in small, isolated groups of trees, such as farm shelter-belts and clumps on hill grazing land and moorland. That this apparent preference has been enforced by competition with the larger Tawny Owl *Strix aluco*, which is predominantly the owl of broad-leaved situations, seems highly likely, for in Ireland and the Isle of Man, which are without Tawny Owls, the Long-eared is widely distributed throughout all kinds of arboreal habitats. It may be that the Long-eared Owl can make do with smaller woods, and has the advantage when old timber with potential Tawny Owl nest-holes is scarce or absent. The place-name 'Hoo Wood', thought to be a reference to the nocturnal hooting of Long-eared Owls, occurs commonly in parts of S England where the species is now scarce, and may reflect the situation in former times before the expansion of the Tawny Owl's range. Nevertheless, the Long-eared occasionally inhabits a mainly deciduous environment, and pairs have been found in open farmland, among low bushes on sand-dunes and marshes, and in hawthorn and elder scrub. Ivy-covered trees are especially favoured for roosting.

The old nests of other birds are taken for breeding, and nest record cards show that use is most often made of those of Carrion or Hooded Crows *Corvus corone*, Magpies *Pica pica*, Woodpigeons *Columba palumbus* and Sparrowhawks *Accipiter nisus*. The incubating female often sits very closely, the male roosting against the trunk of a nearby tree; since neither is easily flushed, the nest may be difficult to find. This is the most nocturnal of all our owls and day-time foraging is rarely observed. Territories can be located quite early in the year by listening at night for the distinctive, triple hoot, and also between May and July for the hunger-note of the young, which sounds like an unoiled gate. Systematic rapping of tree-trunks in a suitable wood will sometimes displace roosting birds (Campbell and Ferguson-Lees 1972). Due to the difficulty of locating scattered pairs,

the map undoubtedly gives an incomplete picture of the species' true distribution, which could probably be revealed only by a special survey.

Though Long-eared Owls are certainly more widespread than the *Atlas* data suggest, they are equally clearly rather scarce birds, especially in central and SW England, Wales and, surprisingly, W Scotland. Even in the eastern halves of England and Scotland the breeding distribution is extremely irregular, with the exception of concentrations in areas such as the Weald of Kent, the Norfolk/Suffolk Breckland, N and S Humber, coastal Aberdeenshire, the Moray Firth and the Lancashire mosslands and N Solway shore in the west. This patchy distribution is the result of a substantial decline since about 1900, coinciding with the timing of the Tawny Owl's increase. In S England and Wales this had become most noticeable by about 1930, and in N England by the 1950s, but the losses affected virtually all counties. In sharp contrast, there is no evidence of a general reduction of breeding numbers in Ireland, where the Long-eared Owl occurs widely with apparent concentrations in Ulster and the southwest. It is the commoner of the two breeding owls of Ireland, and was found there in about three-quarters of the number of squares in which Barn Owls *Tyto alba* (easier to find and reported by farmers and others) were located, compared with about one-third of such squares in Britain. Recent local increases in Ireland have been attributed to additional habitat provided by maturing forestry plantations; similar forestry development in parts of Britain must also have been beneficial.

The marked difference in the fortunes of the Long-eared Owl in Britain as opposed to Ireland argues strongly in favour of the success of the Tawny Owl in interspecific competition. The former is killed by the latter on occasions, and in Europe Mikkola (1976) has noted that the Long-eared occurs much more often than any other owl as a victim of larger owls and birds of prey.

With *Atlas* records in over 900 10-km squares, it seems reasonable to suggest that the British and Irish population of this elusive owl is over 3,000 pairs, but most unlikely to exceed 10,000 pairs.

Number of 10-km squares in which recorded:
942 (24%)
Possible breeding   270 (29%)
Probable breeding   175 (19%)
Confirmed breeding   497 (53%)

Though some records were originally submitted in confidence, all dots are now shown accurately (as recommended by the Rare Breeding Birds Panel)

References

GLUE, D. E. and G. J. HAMMOND. 1974. Feeding ecology of the Long-eared Owl in Britain and Ireland. *Brit. Birds* 67: 361–369.

MIKKOLA, H. 1976. Owls killing and killed by other owls and raptors in Europe. *Brit. Birds* 69: 144–154.

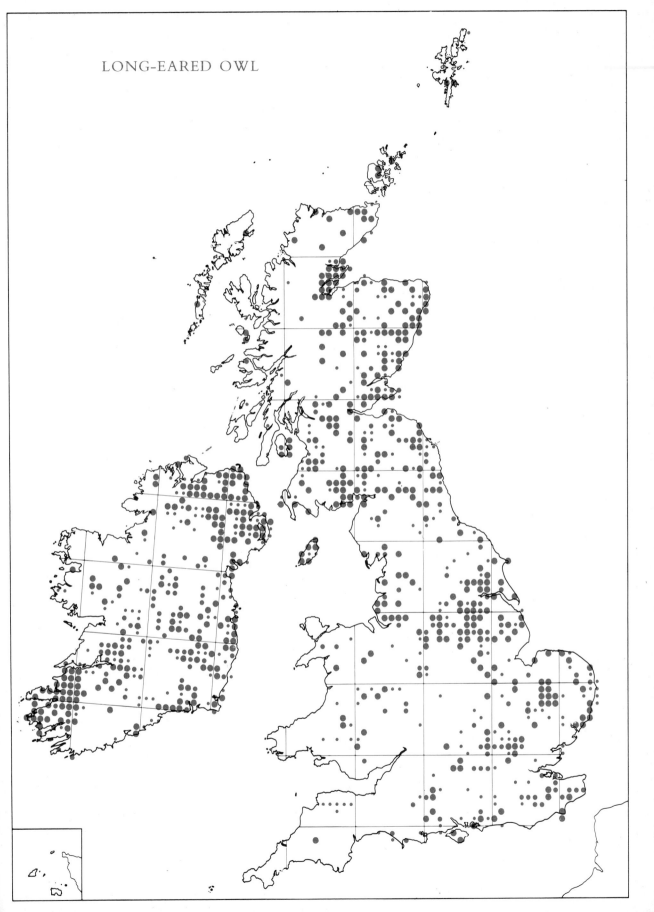

LONG-EARED OWL

259

Short-eared Owl

Asio flammeus

The basic requirements for successful nesting by the Short-eared Owl appear to be substantial tracts of open country remote from excessive human disturbance where there is also a good food supply of rodents. Consequently, they inhabit relatively inaccessible habitats in Britain, such as moorland, heaths, newly afforested hillsides, large areas of rough grazing land, marshes, bogs, sand-dunes and islands. Proof of breeding is not easy to secure. Territorial birds quarter the ground rather like harriers during the breeding season, from March to early August. Although primarily crepuscular in habit, they can also be seen hunting during daylight hours, but isolated pairs are easily overlooked. The nest is usually a mere scrape amongst ground vegetation, but is sometimes a substantial platform; it is not easy to find as most incubating females sit very tight. The immediate area of the site is best found by watching very carefully for the male as he carries food to the nest. When they have young, both adults will rise to mob intruders noisily, and many nests are found in this way by forestry workers, gamekeepers and fell walkers.

In Britain, the diet of breeding and wintering birds consists mainly of Short-tailed Voles, with Common Shrews usually of secondary importance. The number of breeding owls may increase dramatically, especially in northern areas, when there is a vole plague (Adair 1892, Goddard 1935, Lockie 1955). Such conditions existed in the Eskdalemuir area of Dumfriesshire during 1969–70 (Picozzi and Hewson 1970) and it seems likely that this temporary peak contributed towards the high proportion of confirmed breeding records in SW Scotland shown here. In the Orkney archipelago, the Orkney Vole serves instead as the main prey; while on the Isle of Man, on Scottish isles which lack Short-tailed Voles, and also in the arable areas of East Anglia, the principal food is the Brown Rat (Glue 1970, 1972).

The absence of voles in Ireland must be an important reason for the lack of regular breeding there by Short-eared Owls. The only instances of nesting were in 1923 (Co Mayo, unsuccessful) and 1959 (Co Galway), in which year individuals were seen on single days in summer in Cos Antrim, Donegal and Wicklow. Others were reported in summer in the 1960s. There was sporadic nesting in Shetland in the 19th century, but there has been no breeding record since.

Coastal nesting in E England is of fairly recent origin. Regular breeding in N Norfolk and also on the Brecks dates from the 1930s; the Kent, Essex and Suffolk coasts were colonised in the 1940s and 1950s, and the Wash region of Norfolk and Lincolnshire in the 1960s. Elsewhere, changes are less easy to detect, because of the periodic fluctuations brought about by variations in vole numbers. The general trend, however, has been towards an increase, and there can be no doubt that this is due mainly to the larger areas of young forestry plantations now available. In their early stages, these provide perfect Short-eared Owl habitat: since grazing animals are excluded, the grass grows long and encourages a rapid propagation of the moorland vole population. Like the Hen Harriers *Circus cyaneus* which have also taken to these young plantations, the owls have found a haven from persecution. Short-eared Owls are probably more firmly established now than at any time for at least 100 years.

Parslow placed this owl in the range 1,000–10,000 pairs. With presence in about 800 10-km squares in 1968–72, but probable or confirmed breeding in less than 550 (a proportion of which are probably not occupied annually), it is likely that in poor vole years the British population is near to the lower limit of about 1,000 pairs.

Number of 10-km squares in which recorded:
  802 (21%)
Possible breeding   260 (32%)
Probable breeding   173 (22%)
Confirmed breeding   369 (46%)

Though some records were originally submitted in confidence, all dots are now shown accurately (as recommended by the Rare Breeding Birds Panel)

References

ADAIR, P. 1892. The Short-eared Owl (*Asio accipitrinus* Pallas) and the Kestrel (*Falco tinnunculus* Linnaeus) in the vole plague districts. *Ann. Scott. Nat. Hist.* 1892: 219–231.

GLUE, D. E. 1970. Prey taken by Short-eared Owls at British breeding sites and winter quarters. *Bird Study* 17: 39–42.

GLUE, D. E. 1972. Bird prey taken by British owls. *Bird Study* 19: 91–95.

GODDARD, T. R. 1935. A census of Short-eared Owl (*Asio f. flammeus*) at Newcastle, Roxburghshire, 1934. *J. Anim. Ecol.* 4: 113–118, 289–290.

LOCKIE, J. D. 1955. The breeding habits of Short-eared Owls after a vole plague. *Bird Study* 2: 53–69.

PICOZZI, N. and R. HEWSON. 1970. Kestrels, Short-eared Owls and Field Voles in Eskdalemuir in 1970. *Scott. Birds* 6: 185–190.

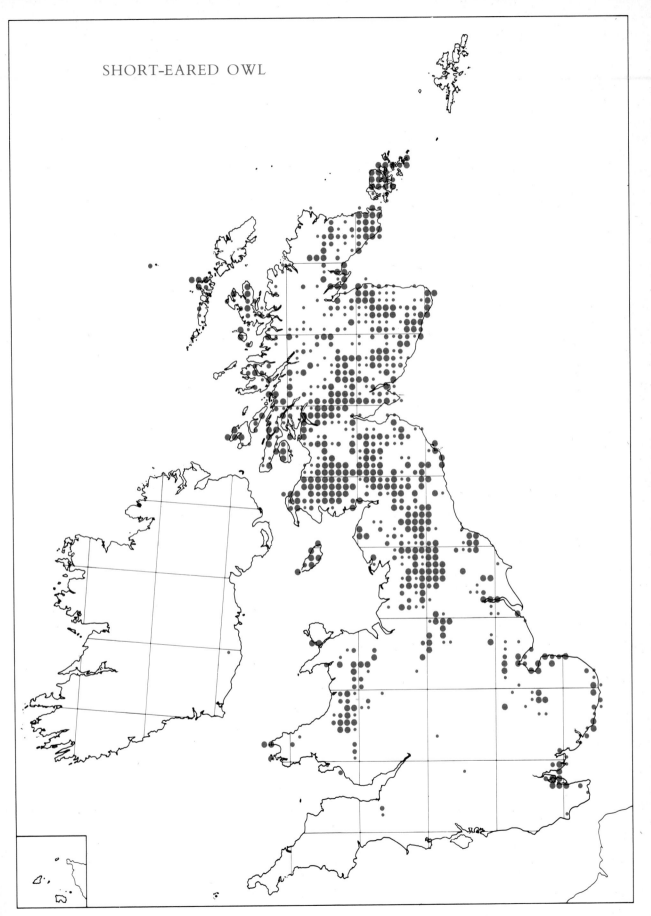

SHORT-EARED OWL

Nightjar

Caprimulgus europaeus

The Nightjar is typically a bird of dry, sandy heaths with scattered trees, and comparison of the *Atlas* map with the overlay of lowland heath shows a good correlation within Britain. A wide variety of other habitats may be occupied, however, including open woodland (occasionally even dense coppice), commons, sand-dunes, shingle, industrial tips and chalk downland. In the west of Britain and in Ireland, moorland, including wet blanket-bog, may be the most frequented habitat, even when what might be regarded as typical areas are available nearby. Perhaps the most favoured sites nowadays are recently felled woods, and forestry plantations in their early stages.

Nightjars are crepuscular and nocturnal, and night expeditions are usually required to locate them. Their churring song, which can be heard from their arrival in mid-May until early August, is far-carrying (up to two km on a calm night), so that visits to suitable locations can often quickly establish presence. Adults and young are well camouflaged and incubating birds sit tight, flushing only when approached to within about 2 m, so that actual proof of breeding is not easy to obtain, as witness the fact that only 31% of *Atlas* registrations fell into this category. For these reasons, most of the probable breeding records, and perhaps many of the possible ones, are likely to refer to nesting birds.

Compared with numbers at the end of the 19th century, when this was considered to be a common bird, there has been a widespread drastic decline. This began in some areas before the 1914–18 war, became general by about 1930 and has been very pronounced since 1950. Norris (1960) showed that in 1952 the species was represented by probably over ten pairs (certainly over five pairs) in only 20 out of 99 50-km squares surveyed, seven of them south of a line from the Thames to the Severn. In a 1957–58 survey (see map on page 460), 30 counties reported a decrease in the previous decade, these being mostly in Scotland, N and E England, and N and SW Wales; only 23 counties reported no change, mainly in S and SW England, the West Midlands, central

Wales and Ireland; and only in Herefordshire had there been a possible increase. Over most of Britain and Ireland, Nightjars are now uncommon birds: in Essex, for example, they dropped from 18–20 pairs in 1952 to not more than three 20 years later.

While the 1968–72 map confirms this general picture, there seems to have been a further decrease in the eastern Highlands of Scotland and in W Ireland (E Galway and Mayo), which were two of the 20 areas of higher density in Norris's survey. This species was almost certainly under-recorded in Ireland in 1968–72, however, due to rather fewer night expeditions being made there than in Britain. The Nightjar is now very scarce in Scotland, where the majority are to be found in Galloway, Ayrshire, Bute and S Argyllshire, all areas recolonised since 1957–58.

We still do not know the ultimate factors responsible for this long-term decline, which has been shared by certain other insectivorous summer migrants, notably Wryneck *Jynx torquilla* and Red-backed Shrike *Lanius collurio*. The felling of woods, increased building on heaths and commons, and disturbance by trippers at weekends and during holidays may have contributed; but while other commonland and moorland species, such as Hen Harrier *Circus cyaneus* and Short-eared Owl *Asio flammeus*, have actually increased with afforestation, the expansion of this habitat has done no more for the Nightjar than help it to maintain numbers locally. Nor is there any obvious correlation with climatic change, which might influence the level of insect food, for Nightjars, like Red-backed Shrikes, were declining during the warmer period of climatic amelioration which was so marked up to the 1939–45 war. Pesticides may have been a contributory factor in the 1950s and 1960s, but these cannot have done more than exacerbate a situation which already existed.

A thorough census of Nightjars is urgently needed to establish the present situation, which subjective impressions suggest is worse than the 1968–72 map indicates. The population is certainly within the category of 1,000–10,000 pairs given by Parslow and, on the basis of 5–10 pairs per occupied 10-km square, may lie between about 3,000 and 6,000 pairs, though even this could be too optimistic a figure now.

Number of 10-km squares in which recorded:
  656 (17%)
Possible breeding   135 (21%)
Probable breeding   317 (48%)
Confirmed breeding   204 (31%)

References

LACK, D. 1930. Some diurnal observations on the Nightjar. *London Nat.* 1929: 47–55.
NORRIS, C. A. 1960. The breeding distribution of thirty bird species in 1952. *Bird Study* 7: 129–184.
STAFFORD, J. 1962. Nightjar Enquiry, 1957–58. *Bird Study* 9: 104–115.

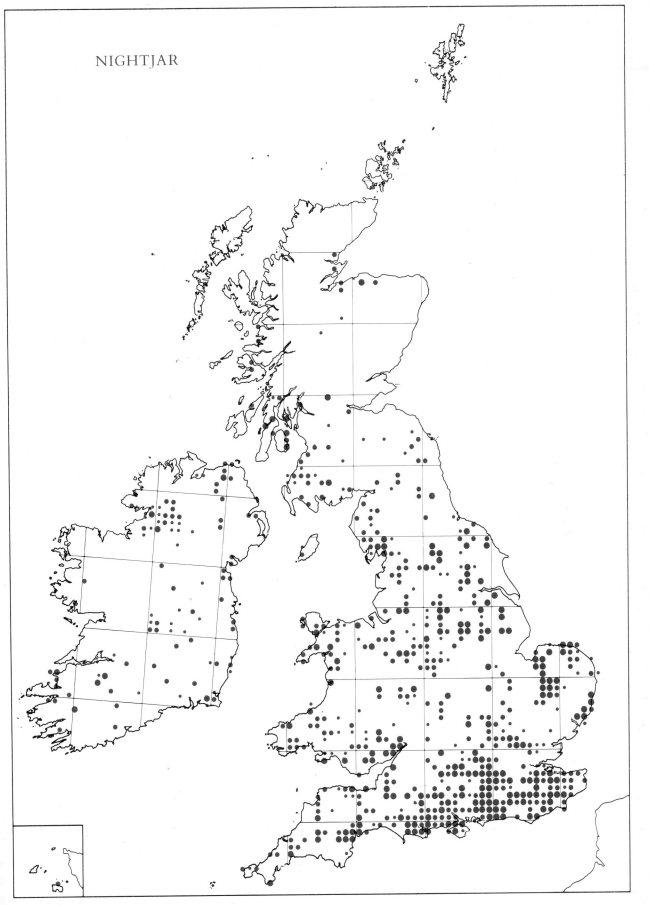

NIGHTJAR

Swift

Apus apus

Screaming parties of Swifts are such a familiar feature of cities, towns and villages alike that they tend to be taken for granted. With the nest site usually under the eaves or in some similar, small crack in an old building, areas of long-established human occupation are much more suitable than new housing estates and tower blocks. In some areas, there are small colonies in crevices in sea-cliffs, and occasionally in inland cliffs and quarries, but these are very much in the minority. Hole-nesting in trees is common in some regions of the Continent—indeed, nesting in man-made sites is almost unknown in parts of eastern Europe—but no such case was recorded in Britain or Ireland during 1968–72.

Locating breeding Swifts is easy, because of their noisy chases. Since the *Atlas* instructions stated that 'Adult(s) entering or leaving nest-site in circumstances indicating occupied nest' should be taken as confirmation of breeding, nest examination was not essential, and proof was easy to obtain even though Swifts are with us for only about 16 weeks of the year. They have a low annual mortality rate (probably about 15%) and may not breed for their first two or three summers, so that the traditional colonies tend to be stable and new sites are only gradually occupied. Such first- and second-year Swifts pioneering new sites may occasionally have been recorded as breeding, since they are very noisy and persistent during the seasons before they first lay eggs. The records of mere presence are mostly in areas where nesting in natural sites or isolated buildings is possible, but often rather unlikely.

Swifts are highly mobile, and, apart from coming to the nest, never willingly alight. They are aerial feeders and observations from aircraft and by radar have shown that they regularly reach heights of over 1,000 m (Eastwood 1967). Radar has also plotted their course as they drift inland on the rising air of sea-breeze fronts, feeding on insects carried up to the inversion level (Simpson 1967); or ascend on fine evenings from the towns where they breed, to spend the night drifting on the wing. Cold, wet and windy conditions during the summer create great difficulty for the adults, but the nestlings can survive such lean spells with little food intake for several days. Lack (1956) showed that the period between hatching and flying might be as short as 35 days during a good summer or as long as 56 days if the weather was bad. During adverse spells, large concentrations of feeding Swifts may congregate at favoured feeding areas, usually bodies of water such as reservoirs.

Apart from impressions of an increase and westwards spread in Ireland since 1932, there is little evidence of any long-term change in the Swift's numbers or distribution. During the last 15 years or so, however, the demolition of old houses and other buildings and their replacement by modern shops, flats and offices, even in rural towns and villages, has severely reduced the number of breeding sites available. A few modern buildings incorporate unintentional nest sites in ventilation louvres, but most are totally unsuitable. In Amsterdam, when the pantiles used for roofing many of the older buildings had to be replaced by modern materials, the same problem was solved by an ordinance making re-roofing illegal unless access for Swifts was retained. In England, they will take to nest-boxes readily and these are sometimes included by the architect. One modern factor favourable to the Swift is the increasingly tight control on atmospheric pollution, which has undoubtedly allowed the species to build up its numbers in colonies closer to the centres of such large conurbations as London. Indeed, since Swifts feed at higher altitudes than House Martins *Delichon urbica*, where smoke pollution decreases rapidly, they are often able to penetrate urban areas, and many Victorian and Edwardian terrace properties hold good colonies.

Actual census results are sparse. The problems associated with prospecting non-breeders have already been mentioned, but multiple nests reached by a single hole are another. A survey of at least 85% of the suitable areas in Sussex during 1968–70 revealed a total of about 4,000 Swifts performing low, screaming flights during the first half of June. Allowing for non-breeders and then extrapolating this density to the other 10-km squares where breeding was proved, this gives a British and Irish breeding population of about 100,000 pairs. Although some fringe areas may be more sparsely occupied than Sussex, density will be higher in many urban complexes, so this seems a reasonably conservative assessment.

Number of 10-km squares in which recorded:
3,073 (80%)
Possible breeding   440 (14%)
Probable breeding   181 (6%)
Confirmed breeding   2,452 (80%)

References
EASTWOOD, E. 1967. *Radar Ornithology*. London.
GOODERS, J. 1968. The Swift in Central London. *London Bird Rep.* 32: 93–98.
HUGHES, S. W. M. 1971. Surveying a breeding population of Swifts. *Sussex Bird Rep.* 23: 61–69.
LACK, D. 1956. *Swifts in a Tower*. London.
PERRINS, C. M. 1971. Age of first breeding and adult survival rates in the Swift. *Bird Study* 18: 61–70.
SIMPSON, J. E. 1967. Swifts in sea-breeze fronts. *Brit. Birds* 60: 225–239.

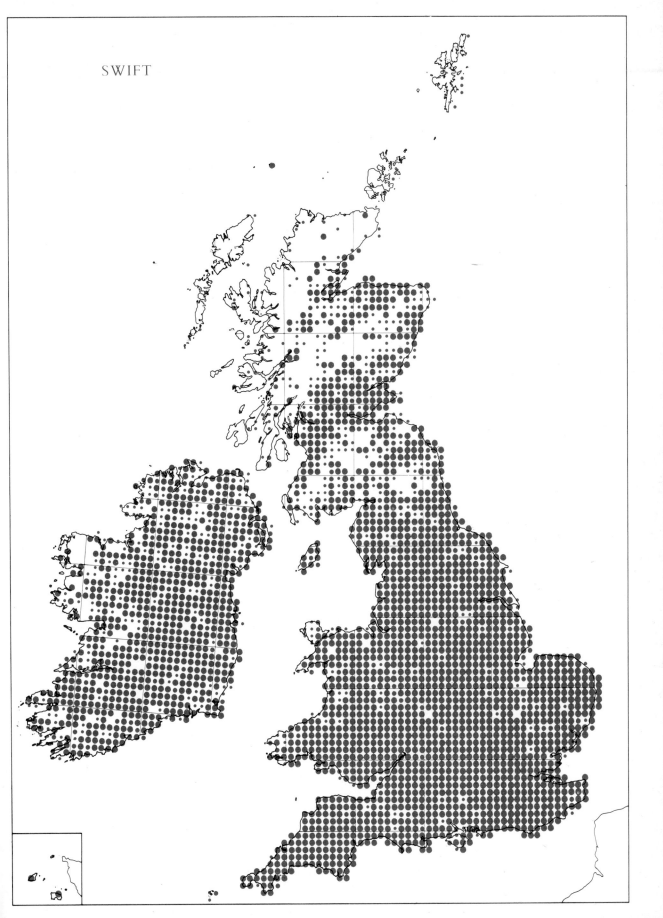

SWIFT

Kingfisher

Alcedo atthis

Kingfishers are found only in the vicinity of water, usually slow-flowing rivers, canals, lakes, ponds and flooded gravel-pits, but also sometimes on fast-flowing streams in the more mountainous regions of Wales, Scotland and Ireland. After a wet spring, they may nest alongside ditches which dry up later in the summer to leave nothing more than the occasional puddle. Provided that an alternative feeding area is available nearby, broods can be reared successfully in such situations. The nest is usually in an exposed bank bordering water, but occasionally may be 250 m or more away; sometimes this involves the adults in flying through woodland between the feeding and nesting sites.

Though the high-pitched flight call is very distinctive and the nest-hole (often with the dark slime of droppings and disgorged fish offal running from it) can be easy to find, an observer briefly visiting an area is quite likely to overlook the species. This may partly explain the apparent sparseness in Ireland (presence in 50% of squares), where much of the fieldwork was carried out by roaming observers, compared with England and Wales (71%) where most cover was achieved by people in their local squares.

The species is severely affected by hard winters: in 1962/63, for example, there were reports of heavy losses and even total extermination in some regions. Recovery may be fairly rapid, however, as shown for the River Thames after 1939/40 (Venables and Wykes 1943) and 1962/63 (Meadows 1972). This is due to a high reproductive potential: during a season extending from March to mid-September, two and sometimes three broods are raised and an average of 1.5 young per pair survive to breed. Also, although two-thirds of the ringing recoveries refer to distances of less than 9 km, a proportion of the population is more mobile, especially in the autumn, and movements of up to 250 km have been recorded, enabling recolonisation of depleted areas (Morgan and Glue in prep.).

Hard winters and river pollution have been taken to explain a marked decrease in Scotland since about 1947, followed by a recent recovery. The isolated breeding in Easter Ross was the most northerly ever recorded in Britain and related to a pair whose nest was washed out by a flood after the clutch had hatched in 1970. The Irish population is not subject to dramatic fluctuations (Ruttledge 1968), since winters there are less severe than in Britain and coastal feeding places remain unfrozen even when inland waters are iced over.

River pollution has resulted in some local decreases, and the complete absence of records from the block of ten 10-km squares in the region of Bradford and Leeds, where Kingfishers have not returned since the 1962/63 winter, suggests that water pollution may have had a serious effect there. Tiny streams in suburbia and even the centres of towns may be occupied in some areas, however, and human activities have provided new habitats, such as gravel pits and reservoirs.

Numbers are almost certainly in the upper half of Parslow's range 1,000–10,000 pairs, since an average of three to five pairs per occupied 10-km square would give a total of 5,000–9,000 pairs in Britain and Ireland.

This species is afforded special protection in Great Britain under Schedule I of the Protection of Birds Act, 1954–67.

Number of 10-km squares in which recorded:
1,819 (47%)
Possible breeding   418 (23%)
Probable breeding   325 (18%)
Confirmed breeding   1,076 (59%)

References

EASTMAN, R. 1969. *The Kingfisher*. London.

MEADOWS, B. S. 1972. The recovery of the Kingfisher in London after the 1962/63 hard winter. *London Bird Rep.* 36: 60–65.

MORGAN, R. A. and D. E. GLUE. In prep. Breeding, mortality and movement of Kingfishers. *Bird Study*.

RUTTLEDGE, R. F. 1968. The Kingfisher population. *Irish Bird Rep.* 15: 11–14.

VENABLES, L. S. V. and U. M. WYKES. 1943. An index to the Thames Kingfisher recovery. *Brit. Birds* 36: 153–155.

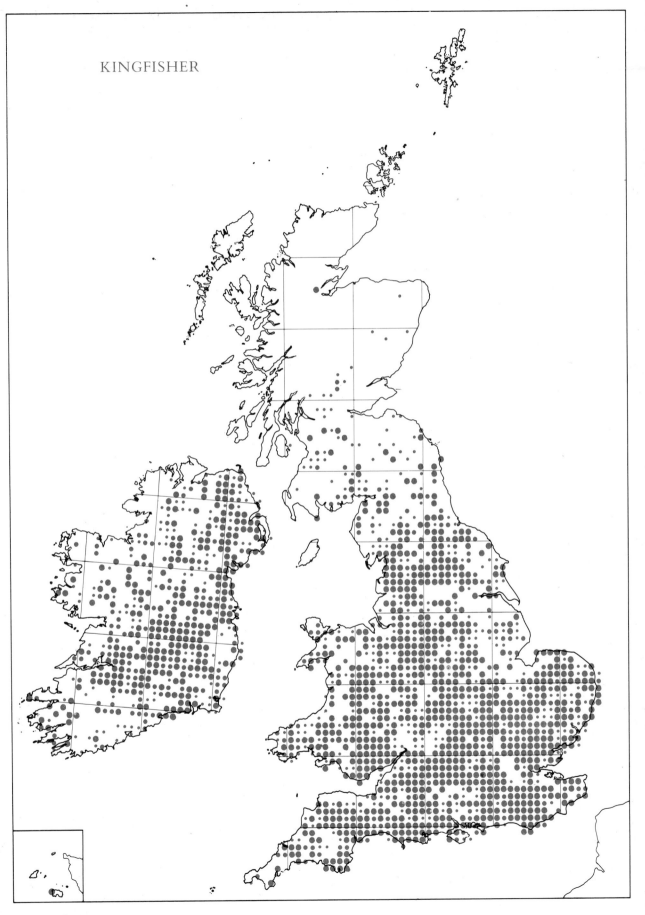

KINGFISHER

Hoopoe

Upupa epops

To those for whom the name Hoopoe evokes a picture of olive trees on a sun-baked Mediterranean hillside, the small number of records during 1968–72 will occasion no surprise. Perhaps the surprise is that the Hoopoe should breed with us at all, for in these islands it is at the extreme northwest of its range, limited no doubt by the paucity of its favourite prey, grasshoppers, crickets and small lizards.

Clegg (1942), analysing over 1,100 records in Britain and Ireland, found that 88% were reported from the counties south of a line from the Wash to N Wales, and that 68% of these southern records occurred from March to May. The pattern during 1958–67 is mapped (right). It thus seems likely that the Hoopoe arrives in Britain and Ireland as an over-shooting migrant and that occasionally, in warm, dry springs, it is tempted to stay and breed.

Hoopoes nest in all sorts of open, wooded country, but in Britain they tend to favour large gardens, parkland with scattered trees, and sites such as pollarded willows alongside water-courses. The nest itself is built in a hole, often in an old and partly rotten tree, or in a wall, building, thatch or similar site. The song is a deep, resonant 'hoo-hoo-hoo', exceedingly far-carrying and highly distinctive. Hoopoes have the habit of feeding conspicuously in the open on lawns and pathways, so that they are likely to be spotted even by people who usually take little notice of birds, while their exotic appearance makes it probable that observations will be reported. Both parents feed the young, and this period is the best in which to locate the nest and prove breeding, as the adults are extremely secretive earlier in the cycle (though the male feeds the incubating female on the nest, and watching back can be successful at this stage). It is unlikely that there were more than a handful of overlooked cases of breeding during 1968–72, and the instances of possible breeding seem more probably to have referred to migrants.

Considering that, on average, about 100 Hoopoes are recorded each spring in Britain and Ireland, only a very small proportion ever stay to nest. Fewer than 30 cases of proved breeding are known for the last 140 years, an average of two per decade. There was an unusual number during the two decades at the turn of the century, with at least eight in the 12 years 1895–1906, and another small upsurge in the 1950s, with four breeding records. Past instances were usually in S English counties, mostly Hampshire and Sussex. Breeding has never been proved in Ireland and has only once been suspected (1934). The two confirmed breeding dots mapped here refer to nesting at the same Cornish site in 1968 and 1969 (where nesting also occurred in 1962), and in Sussex in 1971.

This species is afforded special protection in Great Britain under Schedule I of the Protection of Birds Act, 1954–67.

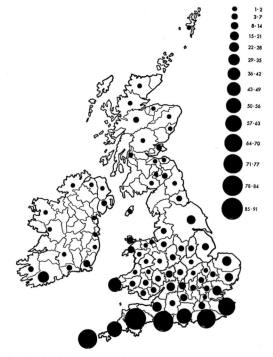

Distribution by counties of March–June records of Hoopoes during 1958–67 (from Sharrock 1974)

Number of 10-km squares in which recorded:
4 (0.1%)
Possible breeding 2 (50%)
Probable breeding 0
Confirmed breeding 2 (50%)

All dots have been moved by one 10-km square (as recommended by the Rare Breeding Birds Panel)

References
GLEGG, W. E. 1942. A comparative consideration of the status of the Hoopoe (*Upupa epops epops* Linn.) in Great Britain and Ireland over a period of a hundred years (1839–1938), with a review of breeding records. *Ibis* 84: 390–434.
SHARROCK, J. T. R. 1974. *Scarce Migrant Birds in Britain and Ireland*. Berkhamsted.

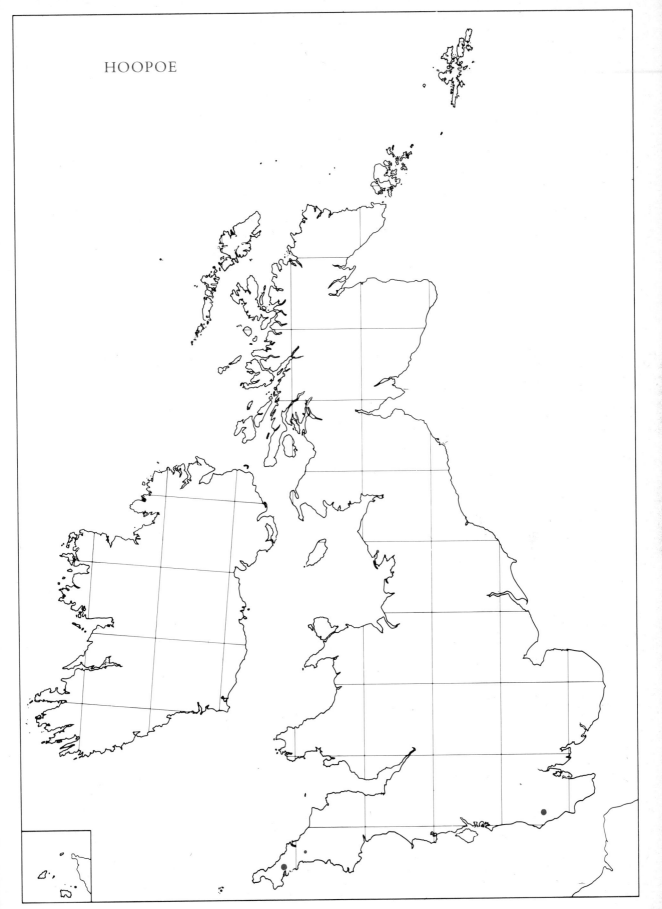

HOOPOE

Green Woodpecker

Picus viridis

The Green Woodpecker is the largest of the woodpeckers nesting in Britain and, like the others, it does not breed in Ireland. Although sometimes found in deciduous woods, this species is more typical of wooded areas with open ground. Parkland, and farmland with plenty of mature trees in the hedgerows, are ideal. Dry heath is also favoured, provided mature trees are available for nesting. These habitats are preferred since this species feeds much more on the ground, especially on ants, than do the other woodpeckers.

The Green Woodpecker is very noisy and its 'yaffle', a loud, laughing cry, is one of the most familiar sounds of the countryside. This only indicates its presence, however, and proof of breeding may be much harder to obtain. Drumming is so rare that it is seldom an extra aid to location of the nest. The hole itself is often difficult to find since it may be high up in a tree. Proof of breeding is readily obtained only during the short time when the young are calling in the nest, or when they are still being fed, out of the nest, by their parents.

Nevertheless, two-thirds of the *Atlas* records related to confirmed breeding. The highest concentration of these was to the south and west of a line from the River Dee to the Wash, especially in S Wales and south of the Severn and Thames valleys, suggesting that this is where Green Woodpeckers are commonest. This accords with the findings of Norris (1960). The species' absence from much of the fen country of E England probably reflects a lack of suitable habitat.

There have been large-scale changes in distribution in N England over the last 150 years, but the species has only recently spread to Scotland. In the early part of the 19th century, it bred in S Northumberland and E Cumberland, but neither farther north nor in other parts of the Lake District. Later, it became rare in Northumberland and remained so until about 1925, but then began to expand northwards. About 1945, the pace increased and Lakeland was colonised. The species then spread south into Lancashire, and north

into Scotland, first breeding in Selkirkshire in 1951. It is now well-established on the margins of the oakwoods beside Loch Lomond (Stirlingshire) and by 1973 was breeding in Kinross, Angus and Aberdeen/Kincardine: there had also been a recovery from a temporary lapse in the Lothians and increased settlement of N Perthshire. The *Atlas* map clearly demonstrates the probable routes of this remarkable range expansion—into SW Scotland from Cumberland and into the central lowlands and E Scotland from Northumberland. The species advanced over 200 km in 20 years (see map on page 460).

The sparseness in coastal Lancashire and much of NE England and the Midlands dates mainly from the severe winter of 1962/63. The reasons for the population's lack of recovery after that are not at all clear, but may be associated with the fortunes of the ants on which the species feeds. It is possible that the increase and spread in Scotland is associated with new coniferous afforestation encouraging the wood ant.

The Green Woodpecker bred for the first time on the Isle of Wight in 1910, and in about 1945 was reported to be spreading westwards in SW England. Two factors which may have caused a serious check, however, were the decline in sheep husbandry and the reduction of Rabbits through myxomatosis. Both these mammals produce a closely grazed turf which, because of its higher exposure to the sun, supports far bigger and more varied ant populations than long-grass swards.

The Common Birds Census results from woodland confirm that, by 1966, the species had still not completely recovered its numbers from the reverse imposed by the two cold winters of three and four years earlier. Over the next two years, the population increased by about 50% and then remained at about the same level up to 1974. Since Green Woodpeckers have large territories, the individual CBC results do not give an accurate indication of the breeding densities met with in Britain. In suitable areas, such as the New Forest (Hampshire), several birds can be heard calling at once during the breeding season. It seems likely that at least ten pairs and possibly as many as 20 may, on average, breed in each occupied 10-km square. On this assumption, there would be about 15,000–30,000 pairs; Parslow's estimate of 1,000–10,000 pairs must surely be too low.

Number of 10-km squares in which recorded:
  1,623 (42%)
Possible breeding 219 (13%)
Probable breeding 332 (20%)
Confirmed breeding 1,072 (66%)

References

BLEZARD, E. 1951. Status of Green Woodpecker in northern England: Lakeland. *Brit. Birds* 44: 26.
NORRIS, C. A. 1960. The breeding distribution of thirty bird species in 1952. *Bird Study* 7: 129–184.
TEMPERLEY, G. W. 1951. Status of Green Woodpecker in northern England: Northumberland and Durham. *Brit. Birds* 44: 24–26.

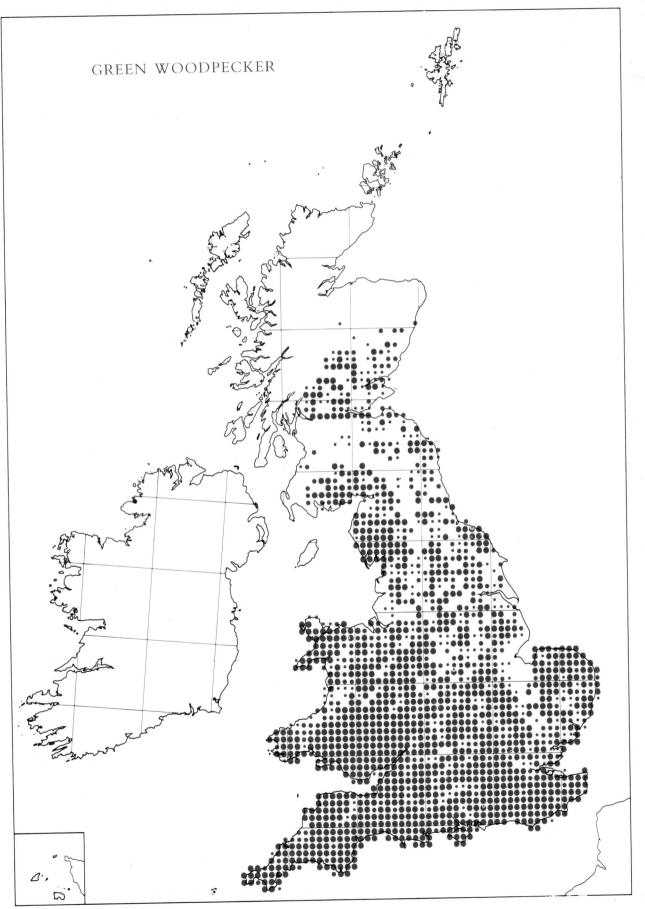

GREEN WOODPECKER

Great Spotted Woodpecker

Dendrocopos major

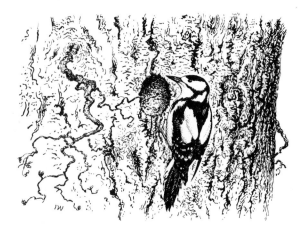

More strictly a woodland species than the Green Woodpecker *Picus viridis*, the Great Spotted is found in both deciduous and coniferous areas. Since the 1950s, it has become commoner in suburban parks and gardens near town centres, but still usually shuns small, isolated clumps and hedgerow trees on farmland during the breeding season.

The drumming and loud distinctive 'tchick' call make location relatively easy, even where there is only an occasional pair in extensive woodland. The young are very noisy in the nest when well-grown, and the adults are easy to follow as they carry food; nest location is therefore not difficult, and this is reflected in the map. Old nesting holes often house other species: Starlings *Sturnus vulgaris* are the most frequent, but tits and, in certain areas, Tree Sparrows *Passer montanus* and Pied Flycatchers *Ficedula hypoleuca* also use them. It was important during the *Atlas* survey to avoid recording holes made before 1968 as proof of breeding in 1968–72.

Like the other woodpeckers, there have never been any breeding records from the Isle of Man or Ireland. The Irish *Atlas* record relates to an unmated male which partly excavated a hole. Migrants may occur almost anywhere, especially in years of autumn invasions by the northern race *D. m. major*. Such irruptions are sometimes on a big scale, as in 1949 and 1962. The scarcity or absence of breeding birds in the Fens of E England and in some coastal and highland areas of Scotland mostly reflects the shortage of suitable habitat.

Early Scottish writers mentioned the species as breeding in the remnant woods as far north as Sutherland during the 17th and 18th centuries. In the first part of the 19th, it was still present from Fife in the south to Ross-shire in the north, but it may have disappeared from Scotland by 1860, apart from a few pairs which are said to have survived in the remoter parts of Moray. By the early 19th century, the Great Spotted Woodpecker had apparently disappeared from much of England north of Cheshire and Yorkshire. Extensive coppicing and tree-felling, competition with the increasing numbers of Starlings for newly excavated nest-holes, and predation by Red Squirrels were all blamed for the decline. In the 1870s a few breeding pairs were discovered in the old woods of the Spey Valley, and in 1887 nesting was re-established in Berwickshire, after recolonisation of the N English counties. By 1900, Great Spotted Woodpeckers had arrived at the Forth and were spreading west; 30 years later, they had reached Argyllshire and spread through Inverness-shire to Sutherland. The climatic amelioration from 1890 to the middle of the 20th century coincided with this northward spread to the limit of suitable breeding areas and, clearly, the extensive reafforestation of much of Scotland will provide good habitat as the trees mature. An increase has been noted since the 1920s in most counties of S Britain and this is probably continuing. The first breeding on the Isle of Wight was in 1926.

Norris (1960) showed that the Great Spotted Woodpecker was generally scarcer than the Green Woodpecker in 1952, but the Common Birds Census figures for 1968–72 suggest approximately equal numbers in woodland (ratio of 1 to 1.1). A personal impression, based on fieldwork in many parts of Britain, is that the Great Spotted has now become the commoner. The CBC annual index remained steady during 1965–72, but then increased by about 40%, this level being maintained in 1974. The jump may have been caused by the epidemic of Dutch elm disease making available a greater supply of larval and adult invertebrates in the dead and dying elms. Parslow placed the Great Spotted in a higher category, 10,000–100,000, than the Green and an average of 15–20 pairs per occupied 10-km square would give a total population of between 30,000 and 40,000 pairs.

Number of 10-km squares in which recorded:
2,053 (53%)
Possible breeding 274 (13%)
Probable breeding 278 (14%)
Confirmed breeding 1,501 (73%)

References

HARVIE-BROWN, J. A. 1880. On the decrease in Scotland of the Greater Spotted Woodpecker. *Zoologist* (3) 4: 85–89.

HARVIE-BROWN, J. A. 1892. The Great Spotted Woodpecker (*Picus major* L.) in Scotland. *Ann. Scott. Nat. Hist.* 1892: 4–17.

HARVIE-BROWN, J. A. 1908. The Great Spotted Woodpecker's resuscitation in Scotland since 1841 or 1851. *Ann. Scott. Nat. Hist.* 1908: 210–216.

NORRIS, C. A. 1960. The breeding distribution of thirty bird species in 1952. *Bird Study* 7: 129–184.

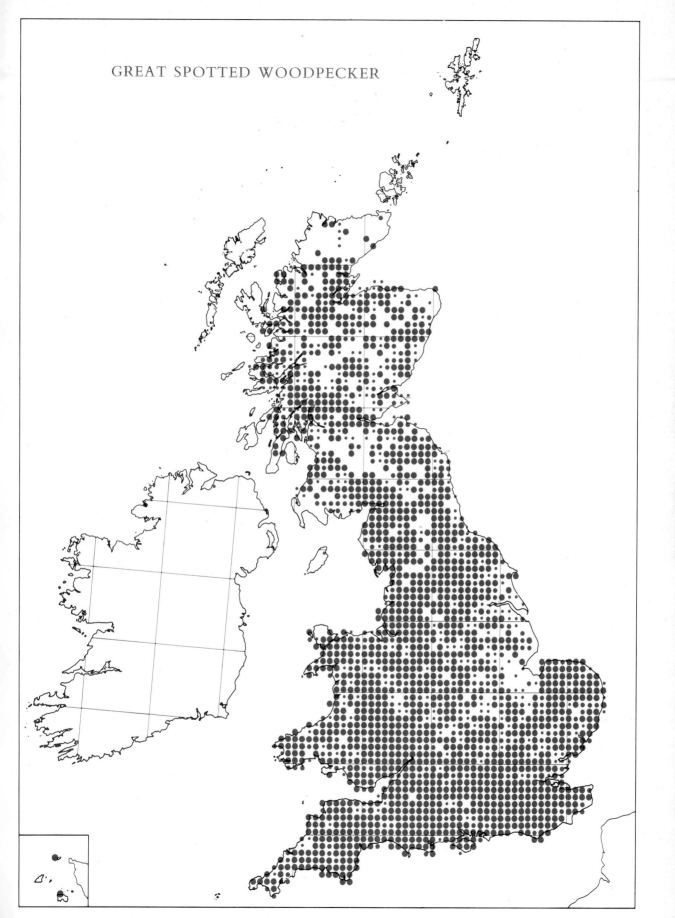

GREAT SPOTTED WOODPECKER

Lesser Spotted Woodpecker

Dendrocopos minor

Woodland occupied by Lesser Spotted Woodpeckers is often similar to that holding Great Spotted *D. major* and the two species commonly occur together, distinctions in food, feeding habits and choice of nest site apparently preventing conflict. Lesser Spotted Woodpeckers are also typical of parkland and old orchards, and in some areas they particularly favour mature alders, even where these merely form a straggling line along a stream.

Drumming, high up and often on a relatively slender, dead branch, is quieter than that of the Great Spotted, but higher pitched and sounds rather more brittle; the 'pee-pee-pee' call is not unlike that of a Wryneck *Jynx torquilla*, but weaker and less resonant. The sparrow-sized Lesser Spotted is rather retiring and, where numbers are low or pairs are widely separated, periods of drumming or calling may be very restricted, sometimes to just a few days in early spring. Its shyness is also demonstrated by the frequency with which individuals have been caught in mist-nets in areas where their presence had not been previously suspected. Except in orchards, the nest hole is often very much higher (up to 25 m) than those of the other two British woodpeckers (1–15 m). This makes it considerably more difficult to find, even when the birds have been located, and the best technique is careful observation and listening in drumming or calling areas during the period of excavation. Fortunately, although the nest is often high, it is quite commonly in the underside of a branch (rather than in the main trunk), so that the entrance is visible. Even though accurate measurement of hole-diameter is rarely possible, careful estimates will allow identification, as the Lesser Spotted's is normally less than 4 cm across, compared with the 5.5–6.5 cm of the Great Spotted and Green Woodpeckers. The male has a wonderful floating display flight, which makes him look like a miniature Hoopoe *Upupa epops*, but it is seldom observed.

There is little doubt that Lesser Spotted Wood-peckers were under-recorded during *Atlas* fieldwork, due to the difficulty of locating them and proving breeding. The proportion of confirmed breeding is low compared with the other two woodpeckers, but they are mainly sedentary, so that a high proportion of the records of possible and probable breeding are likely to have related to nesting birds.

The range and numbers are not known to have changed markedly since ornithological recording began, although the Lesser Spotted Woodpecker was described as being 'tolerably common' in almost all English woodlands towards the end of the 19th century and Batten (1972) showed that this was the dominant woodpecker in his London study area between 1850 and 1900. There have been local fluctuations, sometimes on quite a large scale: for example, the decreases due to loss of old parkland and orchards, such as the grubbing up in Hereford-shire and Somerset of over-mature cider-apple orchards planted during the Napoleonic wars. Recently there have been increases, perhaps due to Dutch elm disease: a virulent form, killing infected trees in a matter of weeks, appeared in localities in SE and SW England in 1969, spreading across much of lowland England during the years of the *Atlas* fieldwork. In one seriously affected 52 ha wood of oak and elm in SE England, where there were one to three pairs in the decade up to 1968, the breeding strength had risen to perhaps 15 pairs by 1970 (Flegg and Bennett (1974). The woodpeckers have probably benefited in such cases from the abundant supply of invertebrate food.

The Scottish records (presence only) follow the first observations in that country in autumn/winter 1966/67, September 1968 (two) and January 1970 (three). These are so far north of the largely sedentary English population as to give rise to speculation that they may be from Scandinavia rather than England (*cf* Wryneck *Jynx torquilla*).

Even within the area of range overlap with the other two species, this is probably the rarest of Britain's woodpeckers, though its unobtrusive nature exaggerates this impression. It is clearly commonest in the region immediately to the south and west of London, where breeding was confirmed in a large block of contiguous 10-km squares. Allowing for the probability of under-recording, the average number of pairs per occupied 10-km square is probably in the range of five to ten, which would suggest a total British population of 5,000–10,000 pairs.

Number of 10-km squares in which recorded:
 889 (23%)
Possible breeding   247 (28%)
Probable breeding   214 (24%)
Confirmed breeding   428 (48%)

References

BATTEN, L. A. 1972. Breeding bird species diversity in relation to increasing urbanisation. *Bird Study* 19: 157–166.

FLEGG, J. J. M. and T. J. BENNETT. 1974. The birds of oak woodlands, pp 324–340 in MORRIS, M. G. and F. H. PERRING (eds), *The British Oak*. Faringdon.

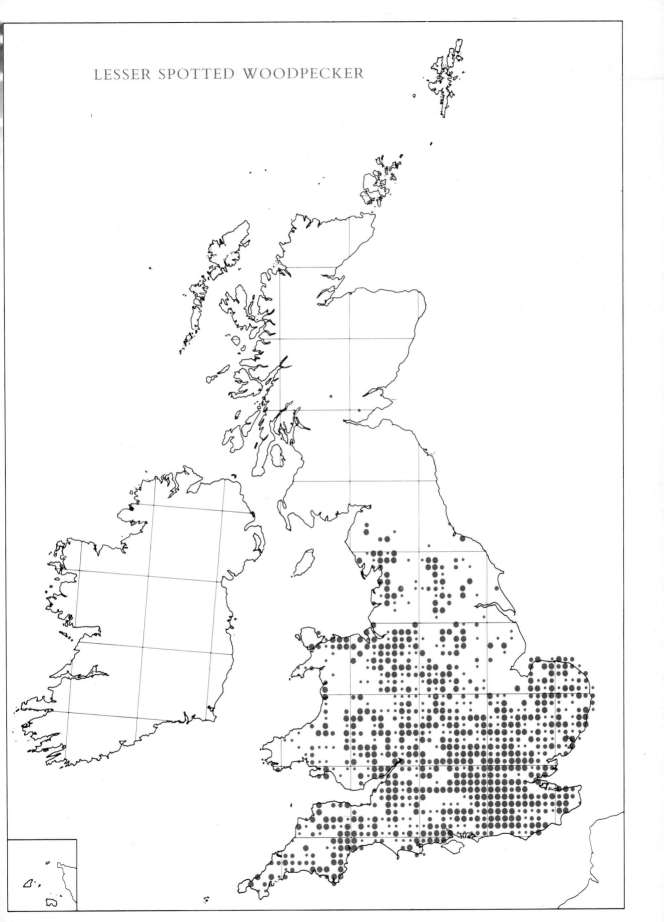

LESSER SPOTTED WOODPECKER

Wryneck

Jynx torquilla

Though breeding in woodland is not unknown, the usual habitats of the Wryneck in S England are large gardens, old orchards and parkland. Nesting has also been noted on commons, heaths and marginal land where there is a mixture of scrub and open ground. These areas have in common the presence of trees with suitable holes for nesting, and relatively short grass, where the major food, various species of ants and their larvae, is to be found. In N Scotland, open woodland of pine and birch provides these requirements.

When they first arrive, in early April, Wrynecks may be easy to locate because of the loud, ringing 'quee-quee-quee' song of both sexes—rather like the voice of a distant falcon. This ceases as soon as the clutch is complete and, unless pairs are stimulated by the proximity of others, they may remain quiet for much of the spring. The apparent disappearance of pairs located early in the season is thus an encouraging rather than disappointing sign, but it limits the period during which discovery can be made. When not vocal, the birds are difficult to find because of their cryptic colouration and retiring nature.

Wrynecks were once common in central and SE England and breeding occurred north to the Lake District and Co Durham, and west to Devon; of all the counties in England and Wales, only Cornwall and Northumberland lack a breeding record. Since about 1830, numbers have declined and the range has gradually contracted southwards, as documented in detail by Monk (1963) and Peal (1968), and shown in the maps on page 461. Recently this has been very rapid, numbers falling from 150–400 pairs in England in 1954–58 (only 100–200 in the last of those years) to not more than 40–80 pairs in 1966, and none reported in 1974. Thus, the prophecy by Monk (1955), that, if the rate of decline continued, there might be none left in 25 years, seems to have come true six years earlier than he predicted. The *Atlas* map, by combining sporadic records for the five-year period 1968–72, greatly exaggerates the true picture for any one year. It may well display the Wryneck's last days as an English breeding bird.

But the picture is not entirely black. Since the early 1950s there have been occasional reports of singing birds inland in Scotland, and in 1969 three out of five territorial pairs bred successfully in Inverness-shire (Burton *et al* 1970), while others were heard in song elsewhere in that and subsequent seasons. Attempted breeding (in a nest-box) occurred in E Ross-shire in 1974 and six other singing males were heard in that county, Inverness-shire and Perthshire. There can be little doubt that this continuing influx is due to Scandinavian migrants. Strangely, the future of the Wryneck in Britain may now depend upon the successful colonisation of Scotland, where it never nested even when it bred commonly throughout England 150 years ago.

The reasons put forward for the collapse in the southern population have included pesticides, destruction of habitat, competition with other species for nest sites, climatic change, a reduction in food supply, mortality on passage or in winter quarters, and increased predation. Several can be discounted, however. Pesticides were not in general use until the decline was well under way, though they have been used against ants for many years and England (1971) thought they had had an important impact. Though many old orchards have gone, there is still plenty of suitable habitat, and there has been no widespread increase in the numbers of predators. Wrynecks are aggressive and quite well able to oust Starlings *Sturnus vulgaris* and tits from nest-holes (although young Wrynecks have been killed by tits building a nest on top of them). The decline has lasted some 140 years and has encompassed most of W Europe, but is still something of a mystery. The major factor may be the tendency towards a more maritime climate, with a preponderance of cool, cloudy summers, denying the ants' nests the warm sunshine required for the development of eggs and larvae.

This species is afforded special protection in Great Britain under Schedule I of the Protection of Birds Act, 1954–67.

Number of 10-km squares in which recorded:
48 (1%)
Possible breeding   22 (46%)
Probable breeding   12 (25%)
Confirmed breeding   14 (29%)

Though some records were originally submitted in confidence, all dots are now shown accurately (as recommended by the Rare Breeding Birds Panel)

References

BURTON, H., T. LLOYD-EVANS and D. N. WEIR. 1970. Wrynecks breeding in Scotland. *Scott. Birds* 6: 154–156.

ENGLAND, M. D. 1971. Wryneck in focus. *World of Birds* 1: 3–6.

MONK, J. F. 1955. Wryneck survey. *Bird Study* 2: 87–89.

MONK, J. F. 1963. The past and present status of the Wryneck in the British Isles. *Bird Study* 10: 112–132.

PEAL, R. E. F. 1968. The distribution of the Wryneck in the British Isles, 1964–66. *Bird Study* 15: 111–126.

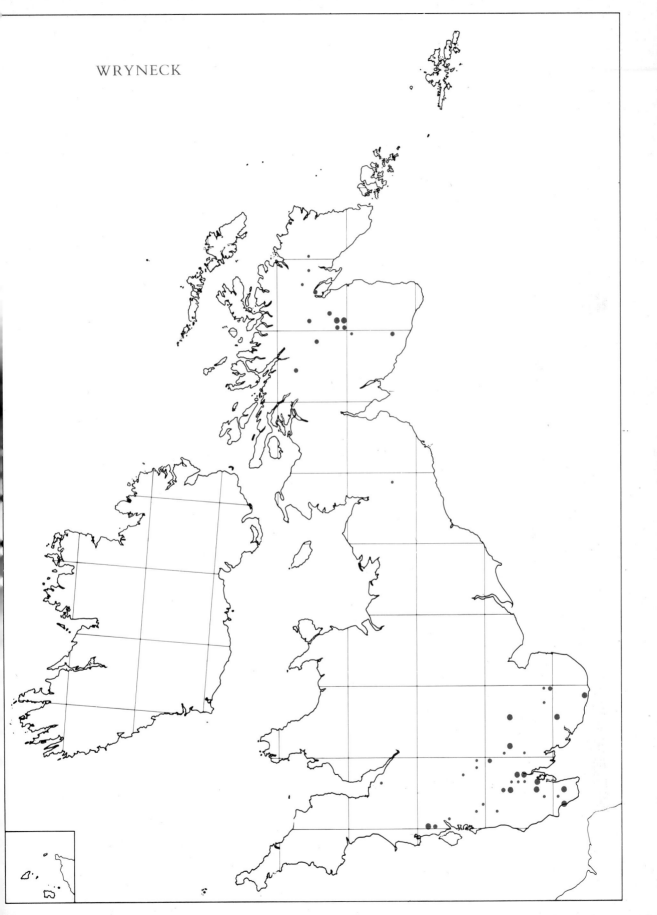

WRYNECK

Woodlark

Lullula arborea

Woodlarks breed usually in dry sites on sand, gravel or chalk where a combination of short grass for feeding, longer grass for nesting, and suitable song-posts are available. These last may consist of scattered trees or bushes, or even fence-posts on heathland. Most pairs probably now nest on heaths, commons or downland with scattered trees, and in areas of recently felled woodland. In Wales and Sussex, some pairs formerly bred in areas with much wet and boggy land, although the actual nest sites were on raised, dry outcrops. Woodlarks usually nest in places where the terrain is broken or sloping.

The distinctive song is a rich, flowing series of notes uttered from a song-post, in flight or even from the ground. Displaying birds are sometimes quite easy to locate early in the season, but, while song from some pairs may be almost continuous, others may remain silent for long spells. They are easy to miss and most surveys of the species have recorded that nesting areas are occupied sporadically from year to year (*eg* Sitters 1975). This could be due to territories shifting, and Harrison and Forster (1959), reporting a five years' occupation of a Surrey territory, considered that its continual use was due to its suitability rather than the persistence of a single pair. First clutches are laid in early April and sometimes three broods are reared. Watching for the adults taking food to the young is probably the only sensible way to prove breeding, since this is one of the more difficult passerine nests to find. It is likely, however, that most records of possible or probable breeding refer to nesting pairs, rather than to transient birds.

Woodlarks have shown very marked fluctuations, as documented by Parslow. During the first part of the 19th century, they were said to breed in most counties of England and Wales, and sparsely in Ireland. By the middle of that century, breeding had ceased in NW England and Ireland; and, apart from Wexford about 1905 and Cork in 1954, it has not since been proved in either region. An increase began in the 1920s and, despite heavy mortality in years with severe winters, this seems to have reached a peak in the early 1950s (see maps on page 462). There were breeding records from Yorkshire (1945–

58) and Lincolnshire (1946–59), but a withdrawal then set in and numbers decreased even in southern counties. The two successive cold winters of 1961/62 and 1962/63 seem to have accelerated this decline. The London area held 45 pairs in 1950, but probably fewer than nine in 1961, and none in 1964. The peak population in Sussex was 50–100 pairs in the 1940s, declining to 20 pairs by 1962 and only four in 1964; special efforts were made to look for the species during 1967–69, but probably not more than ten pairs were present.

Although severe winters are clearly implicated in the short-term fluctuations, the increase during the period 1939–50, which included the notoriously cold winters of the 1940s, suggest that winter severity may not be the only cause of long-term change. Yeatman (1971) noted that Woodlarks had declined recently over most of the northern part of their European range—Germany, Switzerland, Belgium, the Netherlands and N France. Loss of habitat to agriculture and afforestation may have had an adverse effect, and the low numbers of Rabbits following myxomatosis may have resulted in less of the close-cropped ground favoured by the species. Long-term climatic factors may well be implicated, however, as in the declines of Wryneck *Jynx torquilla* and Red-backed Shrike *Lanius collurio*; and cooler and possibly wetter weather in spring and summer may underlie the contraction in range.

Census work in recent years in S England (Sitters 1975, Hughes 1970) suggests that the density during the *Atlas* period was about one to 2.5 pairs per 10-km square. Sites occupied in one year were often vacant the next, so the map may exaggerate the picture in any single year, though this was doubtless partly offset by squares in which the species was entirely missed. Only about 100 occupied territories were known in 1965, but it seems likely that the population during 1968–72 was probably between 200 and 450 pairs.

This species is afforded special protection in Great Britain under Schedule I of the Protection of Birds Act, 1954–67.

Number of 10-km squares in which recorded:
  188 (5%)
Possible breeding   32 (17%)
Probable breeding   94 (50%)
Confirmed breeding   62 (33%)

Though some records were originally submitted in confidence, all dots are now shown accurately (as recommended by the Rare Breeding Birds Panel and R. F. Porter)

References
HARRISON, C. J. O. and J. FORSTER. 1959. Woodlark territories. *Bird Study* 6: 60–68.
HUGHES, S. W. M. 1970. The decline of the Woodlark as a Sussex breeding species. *Sussex Bird Rep.* 22: 65–68.
SITTERS, H. P. 1975. Results of the 1974 Devon breeding status survey. *Devon Birds* 28: 35–43.
YEATMAN, L. J. 1971. *Histoire des Oiseaux d'Europe*. Paris.

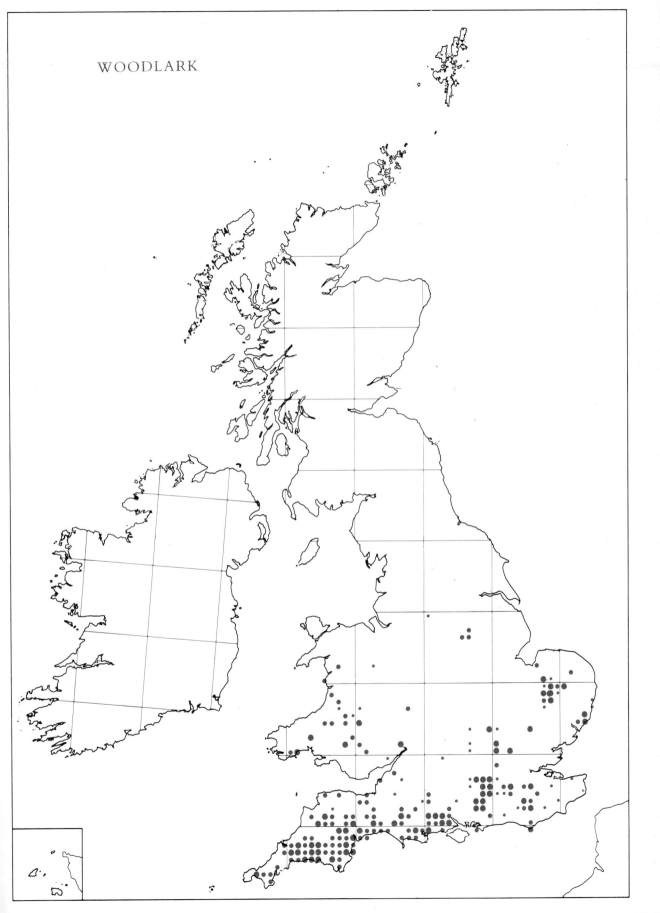

WOODLARK

Skylark

Alauda arvensis

Skylarks are well adapted to nesting in open country since the familiar song is habitually given in flight and they do not require song-posts. This does not mean that they are restricted to large tracts of featureless ground without trees, bushes, hedges or fences. They readily nest on farmland with hedgerows, where they prefer the bigger fields; they are numerous on chalk downland, even if there is a thin scatter of scrub; they are at home on salt-marsh and in sand-dunes and inhabit coastal and inland heaths; they also nest in the developing scrub surrounding ballast pits, on upland pasture and moorland, and up to the arctic-alpine level in the Cairngorms at 1,000 m or more. Indeed, the *Atlas* has shown that this is the most widely distributed bird in Britain and Ireland, having been recorded in more 10-km squares than any other species. The essential need is to have areas of short vegetation to feed in, and undisturbed pasture and grass-leys are preferred to newly cultivated fields (Robson and Williamson 1972).

There are few species so easily found and recorded, at least to the level of probable breeding. The song is audible over a wide area, and the song period extends into the late summer. Where Skylarks are particularly common, the explosion of sound, as dozens begin to sing at dawn, drowns the voices of other species. In areas where they nest sparsely, however, proof of breeding may be time-consuming to obtain, and this has resulted in a lack of confirmed breeding records for parts of Ireland and upland Britain and a few suburban areas. The probable records must surely relate to breeding birds, however.

Skylarks may have declined in Ireland during the early 1960s, and the use of certain pesticides has been blamed for a concurrent decline on the Continent. In Britain, the pattern of distribution has hardly altered over the years, but Nethersole-Thompson and Watson (1974) thought that breeding on some of the higher land in Scotland may have started only in the 1940s. Locally, Skylarks have been affected by agricultural changes and the current move towards larger fields may actually be in their favour. Recent trends towards more frequent ploughing and

the raising of cereal and root crops may have led to changes in habitat preference in certain areas.

At first sight this may seem an unlikely bird to be dubbed an agricultural pest, but the Skylark has become just that to some specialist farmers. From time to time, during the last 50 years or so, there have been reports of grazing Skylarks damaging seedlings of arable crop plants such as lettuces and peas; but recent reports from areas where sugar-beet is the main crop are more serious. Formerly, beet seeds were sown continuously in drills, and the young plants thinned out at a later stage (after the period of vulnerability to bird damage) to leave the more healthy ones. Since the early 1970s, however, a more usual procedure in mechanised farming has been the precision drilling of single seeds in pelleted form, properly spaced out; with fewer sugar beet seedlings available for grazing, bird damage inevitably affects plants which should provide the grower with his crop, reducing the yield in patches over a very wide area which may total some thousands of hectares annually (Dunning 1974).

The Common Birds Census index for farmland Skylarks was at its lowest in 1963 (about 64% of the maximum in 1968). This was probably the effect of the cold winters of 1961/62 and 1962/63, although the then widespread use of persistent pesticides may have contributed. Otherwise, this index has fluctuated rather little, with only a 14% difference between maximum and minimum values during 1965–74. The CBC and other studies have provided much information on breeding densities in Britain. Farmland areas in 1972 averaged 18.4 pairs per km², but Hardman (1974) recorded almost 90 and Robson and Williamson (1972) almost 50 pairs per km² on their plots in Warwickshire and Westmorland respectively. In other habitats, densities of about 75 pairs per km² have been found on areas as varied as coastal dunes, salt-marsh and chalk downland. Skylarks may be rather sparsely distributed over impoverished upland areas, however, where densities are often only a tenth or less of lowland figures. Over the whole of Britain and Ireland, the average number of Skylarks in each occupied 10-km square is probably between 500 and 1,000 pairs. Thus the total population probably lies between 2,000,000 and 4,000,000 pairs.

Number of 10-km squares in which recorded:
3,775 (98%)
Possible breeding   35 (1%)
Probable breeding   481 (13%)
Confirmed breeding   3,259 (86%)

References

DELIUS, J. D. 1965. A population study of Skylarks *Alauda arvensis*. *Ibis* 107: 466–492.
DUNNING, R. A. 1974. Bird damage to sugar beet. *Ann. Appl. Biol.* 76: 325–335.
HARDMAN, J. A. 1974. Biology of the Skylark. *Ann. Appl. Biol.* 76: 337–341.
ROBSON, R. W. and K. WILLIAMSON. 1972. The breeding birds of a Westmorland farm. *Bird Study* 19: 202–214.

Shore Lark *Eremophila alpestris*, **see page 449**

SKYLARK

Swallow

Hirundo rustica

Swallows are among the most familiar of our summer visitors. Their arrival, starting in force early in April, heralds the spring; this, together with their association with man's buildings for breeding, gives them a very special place in public affection.

Apart from the centres of towns, the most exposed mountains and remote islands, the Swallow may be found nesting almost everywhere in Britain and Ireland where there are barns and outhouses. Natural sites are now very rare in Britain, though there have been a few records of nests affixed to trees, on sea-cliffs, and in caves in mountainous districts. Elsewhere in its range, where buildings are not available, it often uses natural sites and may even breed on the sides of large nests built by raptors (Dementiev and Gladkov 1954). Before man began to clear the forests and build huts and houses, very few can have bred in Britain and Ireland, unless tree-nests were common. Certainly the association with man-made structures is very old and there are a number of references to it in Roman and Greek literature.

The nest is usually inside a building of some description. Farmsteads, particularly those holding stock, are the most frequented sites, but porches, garages, sheds and even occupied bedrooms may be used. In many districts, the beams under road and railway bridges across rivers and streams are favoured, as by the House Martin *Delichon urbica*, and in low coastal regions of Britain the provision of pill-boxes, for defence against invasion during the 1939–45 war, enabled Swallows to breed in areas where none could have done so previously.

The nest is made of pellets of mud mixed with saliva and fibrous material to bind it together; it is strongly built and often survives from year to year. The lining consists of fine hairs and feathers. Nests with eggs and young may be found from early May to mid-September (Boyd 1936) and two broods are usual, successful pairs commonly rearing three. The nesting season may be 15–20 days later in N Scotland than in S England (Adams 1957).

Ringing of British birds and recoveries in Britain and Ireland of Swallows marked in winter indicate a recent shift, in all likelihood induced by a climatic change, in the main wintering quarters in S Africa; most recoveries were formerly from the Transvaal, but since 1962 SW Cape Province has also come into the picture.

A detailed ringing study (Boyd 1936) has shown that adults will return to the same farm (even to the same nest) in subsequent years, but that young birds disperse more widely. Swallows feed almost exclusively on the wing, often associating with cattle and horses, whose movements disturb insects from the grass. In cold, windy weather, especially early in the season, they often congregate over water where flying insects are more abundant.

The map shows that Swallows, though found almost everywhere in England, Wales and Ireland, are absent from some parts of Scotland. Many of the inland areas are too high and exposed, and nests at over 500 m are rare in Britain. It is likely that rather more Swallows are present in N Scotland than was the case in the 19th century, and nesting is now regular on Orkney, where it used to be sporadic. There were gaps in the distribution along the western seaboard of Ireland 50 years ago, but breeding is now regular there.

The Swallows' return is so eagerly awaited that local declines, often due to the expansion of urban areas or changes in agricultural practice, have frequently led to reports of widespread decreases. There is, however, little evidence of any long-term change in the last 50 years. The Common Birds Census index declined sharply after 1968, which was a peak year, and in 1974 dropped to two-thirds of the 1973 level. Census data on 11 extensive areas in 1935, totalling more than 20,000 ha, gave densities of up to 10.8 pairs per km², with an average of about 2.0 (Boyd 1936). CBC data on farmland in 1972 showed a mean density of 2.6 pairs per km². These figures imply a total population of over 500,000 pairs, but probably less than one million—the upper limit of Parslow's range.

Number of 10-km squares in which recorded:
3,592 (93%)
Possible breeding   91 (3%)
Probable breeding   45 (1%)
Confirmed breeding   3,456 (96%)

References
ADAMS, L. E. G. 1957. Nest records of the Swallow. *Bird Study* 4: 28–33.
BOYD, A. W. 1936. Report on the Swallow Enquiry. *Brit. Birds* 30: 98–116.
DEMENTIEV, G. P. and N. A. GLADKOV (eds). 1954. *Birds of the Soviet Union*. Vol. 6. Moscow. (Translation, Jerusalem 1968.)
MEAD, C. J. 1970. The winter quarters of British Swallows. *Bird Study* 17: 229–240.

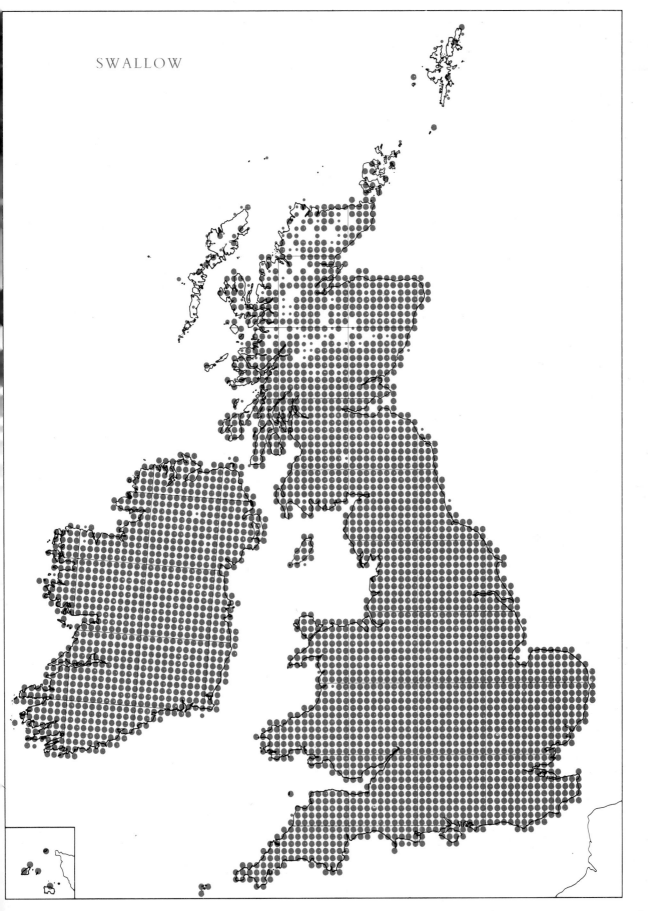

SWALLOW

House Martin

Delichon urbica

The House Martin is a widespread and common species occurring across the Palearctic region. Although it breeds north of the Arctic Circle in Scandinavia, only very small numbers occur in N and NW Scotland, and it is infrequent in Orkney, Shetland and the Outer Hebrides.

The House Martin has a close association with man, the great majority of its nests being built under the eaves of houses, but there are still a number of colonies to be found on inland and sea-coast cliffs, which are presumably the natural habitats. These were used more widely earlier in this century, when there were records from virtually all counties with sea-cliffs in Britain north to the Great Glen, and in several places in Ireland, the Isle of Man and the Channel Islands.

House Martins return to their colonies soon after the main influx in mid-April or early May. Prospecting for new sites and repairing old nests may take several weeks, and in S Britain the first clutches are laid in late May or early June, the mean date being 29th May. The young hatch two weeks later and fledge after a further 30 days, generally about mid-July. The majority of pairs (87%) have second clutches, although 9% move to a different area, and these are started only a week after the first broods leave the nest. With such a long incubation and fledging period, second broods are rarely on the wing before mid-September, and some as late as mid-October (Bryant 1975). As the nests are almost invariably in the open and adult activity nearby is unceasing, proof of breeding is easy to obtain.

In a detailed study in E Lancashire, Bouldin (1959) found that nests faced all compass directions to an almost equal extent. Colony size varies from a single nest up to 500 or more, but large colonies are very scarce. In Bouldin's survey there were 380 colonies (61%) involving fewer than four nests, and only eight with more than 30 nests, the most being 65. Colonies are generally smallest in urban areas and increase in size through suburban areas of major towns to reach their largest in rural districts and small villages. Most of the large colonies are associated with farmyards or bridges over rivers. Bouldin also found that there were considerable fluctuations in the numbers breeding in each colony in successive years, 30%

decreasing and a similar percentage increasing, while about 20% were deserted. The total population of his study area of 1,370 km² remained stable, however, showing a maximal variation of 10% between years.

Very few studies have revealed any long-term changes in the population level, despite the general observation that several large colonies have decreased markedly; but there has been an increase in Inner London. Cramp (1950) noted that none was breeding there, nor had done so since 1889, London's House Martins being found in just ten 1-km squares in the suburbs. By 1965, a small colony had started in the northern part of Inner London, and others were breeding in a further 38 1-km squares of the metropolis. Since then, a steady spread and growth in numbers has been noted. The martins' distribution was inversely correlated with atmospheric pollution, most colonies being located in smokeless zones, so that the spread appears to be related to the implementing of the Clean Air Act (1956) and the consequent increase of aerial plankton.

There are, unfortunately, no recent estimates of the density of House Martins in sample areas, most of the information relating to the mid-1960s. Bouldin gave an average figure of 2.21 nests per km², although if bleak moorland was excluded the density was 3.34. Boyd (1935) recorded an average of 2.72 per km² from a number of rural areas, while London averaged 0.31 (Cramp and Gooders 1967). Numbers probably reach their highest in mixed farmland in the lowlands, for which the only pointer to density is provided by Alexander (1933) for a part of Oxfordshire where there was an average of 5.23 nests per km². In view of the low density in many upland districts it seems likely that the general figure may lie between 100 and 200 pairs per 10-km square, corresponding to a total for Britain and Ireland in the region of 300,000–600,000 pairs.

Number of 10-km squares in which recorded:
3,325 (86%)
Possible breeding   151 (5%)
Probable breeding   40 (1%)
Confirmed breeding   3,134 (94%)

References

ALEXANDER, W. B. 1933. A census of House Martins: are their numbers decreasing? *J. Min. Agric.* 40: 8–12.

BOULDIN, L. E. 1959. Survey of House Martin colonies in east Lancashire. *Brit. Birds* 52: 141–149.

BOULDIN, L. E. 1968. The population of the House Martin *Delichon urbica* in east Lancashire. *Bird Study* 15: 135–146.

BOYD, A. W. 1935. Report on the Swallow Enquiry, 1934. *Brit. Birds* 29: 3–21.

BRYANT, D. M. 1975. Breeding biology of House Martins *Delichon urbica* in relation to aerial insect abundance. *Ibis* 117: 180–216.

CRAMP, S. 1950. The census of Swifts, Swallows and House Martins 1949. *London Bird Rep.* 14: 49–57.

CRAMP, S. and J. GOODERS. 1967. The return of the House Martin. *London Bird Rep.* 31: 93–98.

JOURDAIN, F. C. R. and H. F. WITHERBY. 1939. Cliff-breeding in the House Martin. *Brit. Birds* 33: 16–24.

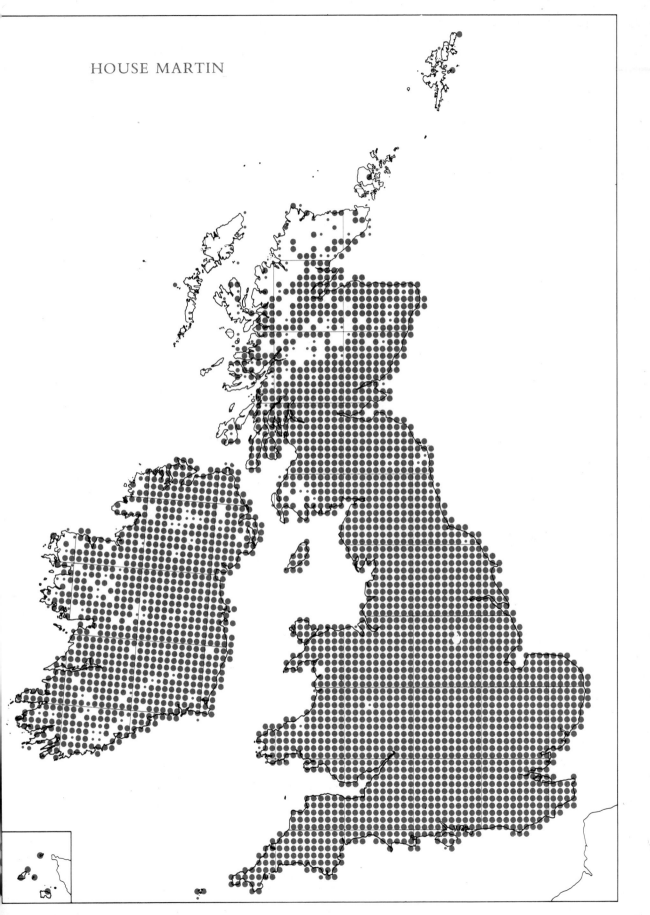

HOUSE MARTIN

Sand Martin

Riparia riparia

Sand Martins nest in burrows which they excavate in vertical banks. They are colonial, ten to 50 pairs usually nesting together, although single pairs have been known to breed successfully and, when the population is at a high level, some colonies may contain several hundred birds. The need for a suitable sand-face for burrowing restricts the breeding range, and the species is absent from large areas in S and E England where chalk and limestone formations predominate. Sandy sea-cliffs are often used. Colonies above 400 m are infrequent, and there are few breeding records from the more distant Scottish islands.

Colonies exploiting natural sand-banks along rivers and streams are rare in S England, but are frequent in wilder areas of the north and west, where a higher rainfall leads to spate conditions so that erosion of alluvial deposits creates fresh, clear, vertical faces for the nests. The Sand Martin must often be an opportunist nester, since many banks, whether natural or man-made, change drastically from year to year and the location of the colony must move as old sites deteriorate and new ones are exposed.

In S England, man-made sites far outnumber natural ones. Throughout the country, sand and gravel pits, quarried for construction work or industrial purposes, are readily colonised, the regular removal of material ensuring fresh vertical cliffs for burrowing. Nest losses due to quarrying are generally avoided, since the workmen are usually very interested in the welfare of 'their birds'. Sand Martins exploit many other man-made situations where vertical banks have been exposed, such as railway and road cuttings, drainage excavations, silage pits and even the foundation trenches dug during building work. Sites of this kind may be colonised almost overnight, another reflection of the opportunist breeding habits of the species. The presence of workmen and heavy, noisy machinery close to the burrows does not deter the birds from breeding. Colonies in heaps of sawdust are quite common at sawmills, and piles of quarry-dust at a stone-crushing plant have been used. Drainage pipes set in stone-embanked rivers and other retaining walls are used in several places and these form some of the most permanent colonies of the species. The soil structure of the overburden at clay and chalk pits is seldom suitable, but occasionally groups are found in such situations. Where sand is obtained by dredging in water-logged pits, and no banks are available, Sand Martins commonly burrow in the heaps of washed sand, while in parts of Ireland the faces of peat-cuttings and the stacks of drying peat blocks enable Sand Martins to breed in bare bogland.

Sand Martins are aerial feeders and can often be seen hawking over water. Their breeding sites are not necessarily associated with water, but most of the suitable alluvial deposits are in river valleys. The nesting place may be several kilometres from the feeding area, but the birds can be followed readily and so breeding is easy to prove. Once the colony is found, other species associated with the Sand Martins may also be discovered. Mead and Pepler (1975) listed the species they found breeding in Sand Martin burrows, Starling *Sturnus vulgaris* and Tree Sparrow *Passer montanus* being the most frequent.

Sand Martins are among the earliest spring migrants, starting to reoccupy their colonies in early April in S England, but up to a month later in N Scotland. Breeding is well-synchronised within each colony and the first juveniles have fledged by the end of May. Two or three broods are raised by each successful pair. The young from the first brood wander extensively from late June onwards, calling at other colonies and founding the night-time roosts, usually in reed-beds, which are such a feature of the species' autumn migration.

Although it is easy to count the burrows at a colony, this does not necessarily give a good indication of the number of breeding pairs, and very detailed study is needed for a proper census. The species declined considerably between the 1968 and 1969 breeding seasons, at the time of the population crash of the Whitethroat *Sylvia communis*. Winstanley, Spencer and Williamson (1974) have correlated that with the drought in the Sahel region, and ringing recoveries have shown that this is where British Sand Martins go in the winter. Before the crash, there was probably an average of well over 100 pairs in each 10-km square in which breeding was proved, and the breeding population of Britain and Ireland may have approached 1,000,000 pairs. Currently, it must be at a much lower level, possibly only 250,000 pairs, with breeding sites and feeding areas available for exploitation in the event of a recovery.

Number of 10-km squares in which recorded:
2,889 (75%)
Possible breeding   392 (14%)
Probable breeding   83 (3%)
Confirmed breeding   2,414 (84%)

References

MEAD, C. J. and G. R. M. PEPLER. 1975. Birds and other animals at Sand Martin colonies. *Brit. Birds* 68: 89–99.

WINSTANLEY, D., R. SPENCER and K. WILLIAMSON. 1974. Where have all the Whitethroats gone? *Bird Study* 21: 1–14.

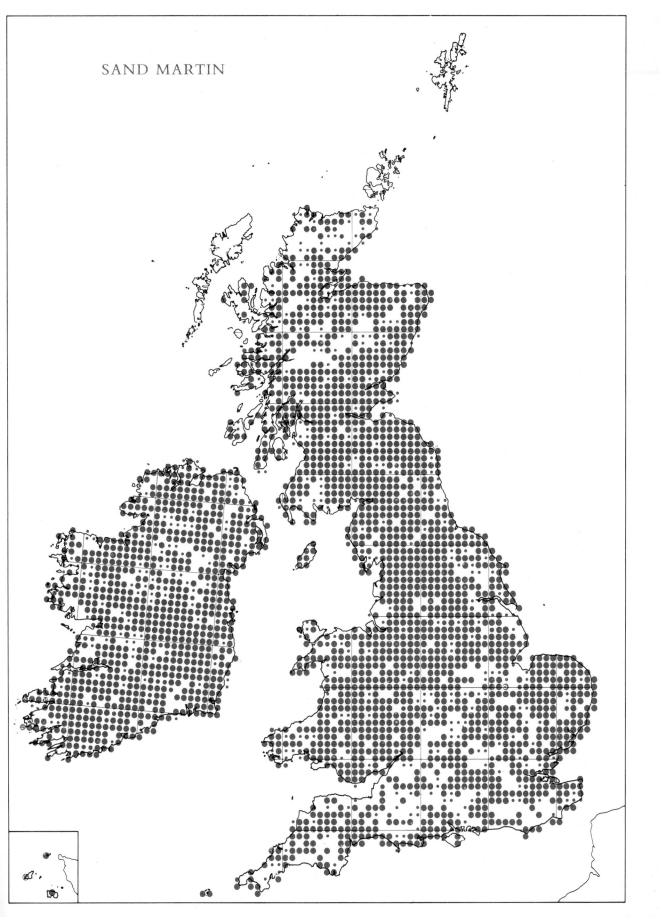

SAND MARTIN

Golden Oriole

Oriolus oriolus

The usual habitat of breeding Golden Orioles is mature woodland, varying from oak forest to dense, damp alder carr, but usually deciduous or mixed and much less often coniferous in type. Where the bird is common on the Continent, small clumps of trees, especially if close to water, may be occupied, but this is not usually the case in Britain, though large, well-timbered gardens and wooded parks have provided sites.

The fluted song is a loud, far-carrying and highly distinctive 'weela-weeo'. Although the brightly-coloured yellow and black male might be thought to be conspicuous, both sexes are remarkably well-camouflaged in the leaf canopy, and the voice is heard much more often than the birds are seen. The undulating flight and habit of sweeping upwards into the heart of a tree make confusion possible with the Green Woodpecker *Picus viridis*. For these reasons, breeding is easily overlooked and singing birds may well have been dismissed as spring migrants. Even when breeding is suspected, it is not easy to prove: of 15 possible cases during the 19 years 1949–67, breeding was proved in only four.

The Golden Oriole has increased in numbers in Denmark, and since 1944 has nested in S Sweden. It appears to be one of the species which have profited from the rise in mean spring temperatures in NW Europe since the 1930s. Like Hoopoes *Upupa epops*, migrants in spring show a tendency to overshoot to Britain and Ireland in anticyclonic weather, mainly to the south coast and East Anglia (see map). During the decade 1958–67, a total of 257 was reported in Britain and Ireland, an average of 26 per year; though the numbers reaching us are smaller than in the case of the Hoopoe, a higher proportion stays to breed. The majority came between mid-April and mid-July, and indeed 62% fell within the four weeks —critical for potential breeding records—from 7th May to 3rd June. In early spring the chief concentration is in the southwest, but towards the end there is a more uniform scatter with, if anything, an east coast bias (Sharrock 1974).

Golden Orioles may have been regular breeding birds in Kent in the middle and late 19th century, though in very small numbers, and one or two breeding records were claimed in about ten other counties, mainly in East Anglia and the E Midlands, but including Devon and the Isle of Wight, during 1840–90. There were then fewer until a steady increase occurred in the 1950s and 1960s. Those discovered during 1968–72 probably represented a larger number than in any other five-year period for at least 100 years. Though the majority were isolated instances, those in East Anglia involved a colonisation which probably began about 1967 and is still proceeding, with several singing males present and breeding proved annually in recent years. The first ever Scottish record of proved breeding was in Fifeshire in 1974, after singing had been heard at the same site in 1973.

This species is afforded special protection in Great Britain under Schedule I of the Protection of Birds Act, 1954–67.

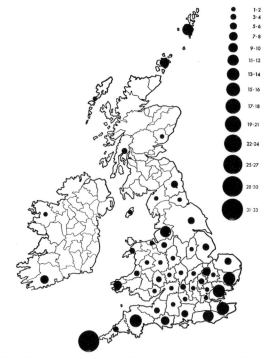

Distribution by counties of March–July records of Golden Orioles during 1958–67 (from Sharrock 1974)

Number of 10-km squares in which recorded:
10 (0.3%)
Possible breeding   4 (40%)
Probable breeding   1 (10%)
Confirmed breeding   5 (50%)

Three dots have been moved by up to two 10-km squares (as recommended by the Rare Breeding Birds Panel)

Reference
SHARROCK, J. T. R. 1974. *Scarce Migrant Birds in Britain and Ireland*. Berkhamsted.

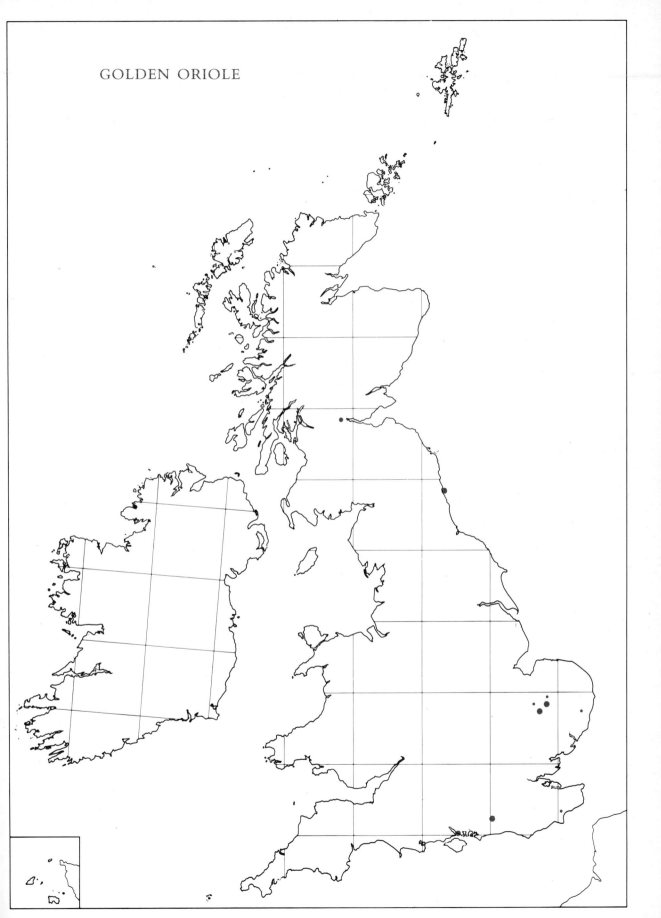

GOLDEN ORIOLE

Raven

Corvus corax

Before the early 19th century the Raven was widespread here, but, owing to years of persecution by man, its range has contracted. By the beginning of this century it was virtually restricted to the more remote coastal and upland districts in the west and north, and it is still most commonly known as a denizen of rocky crags, open moorland and steep sea-cliffs. In mountainous districts, large cliffs of 30 m or more with a wide outlook are normally chosen. Disused quarries with suitable ledges are also used. The bulky nest of sticks and heather stems mixed with earth and lined with moss, grass and wool, is normally situated on a ledge, often beneath an overhang. In an extensive study of upland Ravens, Ratcliffe (1962) found that the most favoured altitude is 380–450 m and that nests above 600 m are uncommon, probably due to the severe climate at this level when the Ravens are nesting. Eggs are sometimes laid as early as February, although Holyoak (1967) gave the mean first-egg date as the first week of March for Ireland, Wales and S England, and slightly later in the north.

Nesting in trees, which must have been a widespread habit when Ravens occupied much of lowland Britain, seems to occur mainly when cliff sites are lacking or subject to disturbance. In upland areas a stunted rowan or birch may be used, and a Cardiganshire nest was at only 3 m, in an elder bush growing in the garden of a derelict farmstead. A survey of Co Wicklow and part of Co Dublin showed that, of 45 nests, 22 were on inland cliffs, 14 in trees and the others in quarries, on sea-cliffs and on ruined buildings. In many parts of Ireland, ruined towers and castles are frequently used; the species is probably under-recorded there, since most fieldworkers initially expected to find Ravens at cliff sites, and not in trees or on buildings.

In upland districts, Ravens are most numerous where sheep carrion is fairly plentiful, especially in the form of placentae at lambing time. They occur at a reasonable density on grouse moors, if not persecuted by gamekeepers, but only in low numbers in the remote deer forest country of Scotland. Here, they may be in competition for nest sites and for food with the Golden Eagles *Aquila chrysaetos*, which are dominant. They often breed side by side with Peregrines *Falco peregrinus*, which will use old Ravens' nests. A feature of many territories is that four or five different nest sites may be used over a period of years. The amount of movement between different sites varies greatly: the same nest was occupied for nine consecutive years at one place in N Wales, while another pair was known to have used two sites alternately during eight successive years (Allin 1968).

The recent history of Raven populations in Britain shows a slow recovery since 1914 in the areas adjoining the main upland refuges—SW England, the Welsh borders and S Scotland. The recovery in Ireland seems to have been more rapid than in Britain. These recolonisations of lost ground have resulted in a return to tree-nesting, which represents a population overflow from areas where rock-nesting Ravens were at or near saturation (Ratcliffe 1962). E Britain has not followed this trend and in upland areas, such as the Yorkshire Pennines, there are still many deserted crags; Ratcliffe attributed this to the intensity of game-preservation, especially on grouse moors.

D. Nethersole-Thompson (in Ratcliffe 1962) noted the highest known breeding density of 15 pairs in a 27 km section of coast in Devon and Cornwall. A census of breeding Ravens in the Isle of Man revealed 33 occupied eyries, a density of 0.55 pairs per km^2, or 2.4 per 10-km square (Cowin 1941), while the Wicklow/Dublin study showed about 1.5 pairs per 10-km square. The average area of 139 territories studied in inland areas of England, Scotland and Wales by Ratcliffe (1962) was 20 km^2. On the basis of these surveys, an average of three pairs per 10-km square seems reasonable, and leads to an estimate for the total British and Irish population of about 5,000 pairs.

Number of 10-km squares in which recorded:
  1,697 (44%)
Possible breeding   346 (20%)
Probable breeding   202 (12%)
Confirmed breeding   1,149 (68%)

Though some records were originally submitted in confidence, all dots are now shown accurately (as recommended by the Rare Breeding Birds Panel)

References

ALLIN, E. K. 1968. Breeding notes on Ravens in north Wales. *Brit. Birds* 61: 541–545.

COWIN, W. S. 1941. A census of breeding Ravens. *Yn Shirragh ny Ree* no. 1: 3–6.

HOLYOAK, D. T. 1967. Breeding biology of the Corvidae. *Bird Study* 14: 153–168.

HOLYOAK, D. T. and D. A. RATCLIFFE. 1968. The distribution of the Raven in Britain and Ireland. *Bird Study* 15: 191–197.

HUME, R. A. 1975. Successful breeding of Ravens on city building. *Brit. Birds* 68: 515–516.

NOONAN, G. C. 1971. The decline and recovery of the Raven in Dublin and Wicklow. *Dublin and N Wicklow Bird Rep.* 2 (1970): 16–21.

RATCLIFFE, D. A. 1962. Breeding density in the Peregrine *Falco peregrinus* and Raven *Corvus corax*. *Ibis* 104: 13–39.

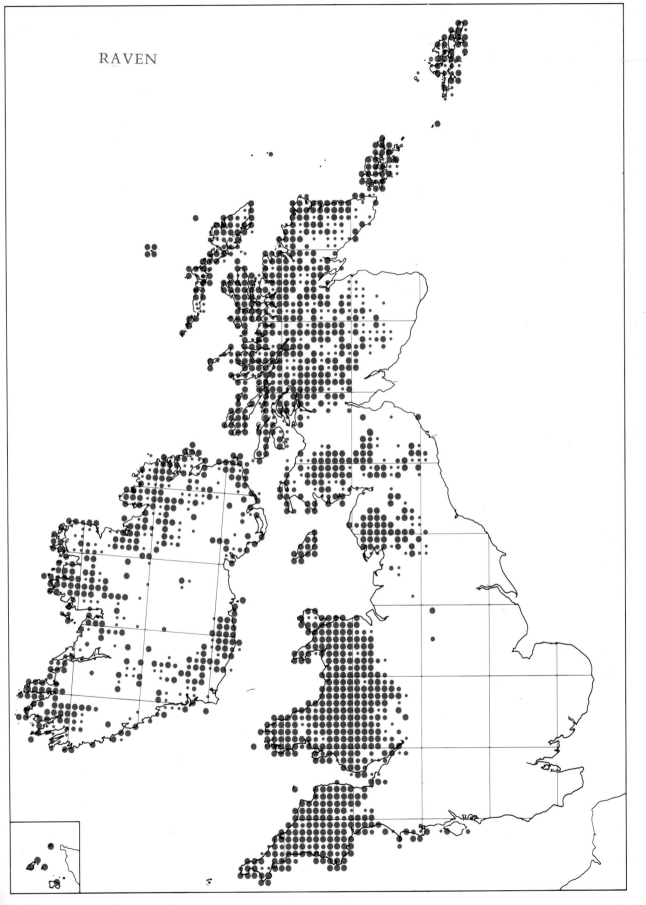

RAVEN

Carrion/
Hooded Crow

Corvus corone

The two forms of the European Crow, the all-black Carrion Crow *C. c. corone* and the grey-and-black Hooded Crow *C. c. cornix*, are easily distinguished by their obvious plumage differences. They are regarded as belonging to a single species, because they freely interbreed where they meet, producing fertile offspring.

The Carrion Crow inhabits W Europe, while the Hooded Crow lives in E and N Europe and most of the Mediterranean region. The two subspecies come into contact along a narrow corridor starting in E Ireland, embracing the Isle of Man, extending through Scotland, Denmark, central Germany and Austria, and following the southern slopes of the Alps to the Mediterranean near Genoa (Italy). Every combination of the parental characters (plus apparently typical Carrion and Hooded Crows) is found in the narrow zone of hybridisation.

The two forms are thought to have evolved during the last ice age, when the European Crow separated into isolated populations in the ice-free Iberian and Balkan Peninsulas. These populations were apart long enough to develop distinctive plumage differences, but not separate vocal and behavioural characters. Given time, further differences might have arisen, but when the ice eventually retreated, and the two populations expanded to meet in central Europe, they had not evolved biological incompatability and so successful interbreeding took place. Farther east, near the Yenesei River in central USSR, the all-black Carrion Crow is encountered once again, forming a second hybrid zone which extends for over 3,000 km (Voous 1960). The Hooded thus holds a central position, flanked on both east and west by the Carrion Crow.

The width of the zone of contact seems never to exceed 75–100 km and in some parts is probably even narrower. Mayr (1942) wrote: 'Even assuming that adult birds nest year after year in the same tree, and that the young settle down no farther than 500 m from the place of birth . . . the hybrid zone should now cover the whole width of Europe.' That it does not do so implies a reduced viability of the hybrids, as suggested by Meise (1928).

The hybrid zone is not stable and was pushed northwards in Europe during the climatic amelioration of the first half of this century. Between 1928 and 1974, its axis in Scotland shifted northwestwards. Meise gave the position of the axis in 1928, and a modern comparison can be made with the maps from the *Atlas* data and from Cook (1975): see page 294. At Dornoch (Sutherland), the proportion of the Carrion type in the population rose from 15% in 1955/56 to 35% in 1964 and 50% by 1974.

Although climatic factors have had an important influence, habitat preferences and altitude exert considerable modifying effects. Four lines of evidence indicate that the distribution of the two subspecies in Scotland is affected by altitude. First, the greatest displacement of the hybrid zone towards the northwest has been over low ground under 300 m in the east and southeast, where arable farming has intensified since the amelioration began; towards the predominantly high ground of Galloway in the southwest the zone has remained relatively fixed since 1928. Secondly, the corridor is much broader in the northeast, where there is a gradual transition from low to high ground, than in the southwest, where the transition is more abrupt. Thirdly, small populations of hybrids persist in certain upland areas to the south of the present axis, as on the Ochil and Pentland Hills; these could be relict populations, left behind by the northwards shift of the hybrid zone. Finally, the Isle of Arran, which lies at the southwest extremity of Scotland, shows a tendency for the Carrion Crow to decrease in frequency with increasing altitude and for the Hooded to predominate on the high ground (Cook 1975). In the Alps, there is a reversal of habitat preferences compared with the Scottish position, a narrow corridor separating the Hooded in the plains and the Carrion at higher levels (Mayr 1942).

It will be interesting to see what happens in this dynamic situation in the next few years, particularly as there is some evidence that the British and Irish climate has moved towards a cooler phase since the 1940s. There has been little change in the incidence of Carrion Crows in the Isle of Man during the last 50 years, and only a relatively minor infiltration of Ireland, the latter coinciding with a notable increase and spread of the Hooded Crow in the northwest.

Taking the two subspecies together, this is the most widespread member of the crow family in Britain and Ireland; indeed, it is the second most widespread bird of all, surpassed only by the Skylark *Alauda arvensis*. It does not show the local distribution in NW Scotland and the Scottish islands exhibited by both the Jackdaw *C. monedula* and the Rook *C. frugilegus*. Crows breed in all types of open country—agricultural, moorland, heathland and coastal—as well as in open rather than closed woodland and even in tree-lined avenues, parks and the squares of city centres.

The nest is usually placed high in the fork of a tall tree, although on rocky coasts and in treeless country cliff-ledges, small bushes, deep heather, buildings and even electricity pylons are used. Unlike the Rook and the Jackdaw, the Crow is a solitary nester, but the

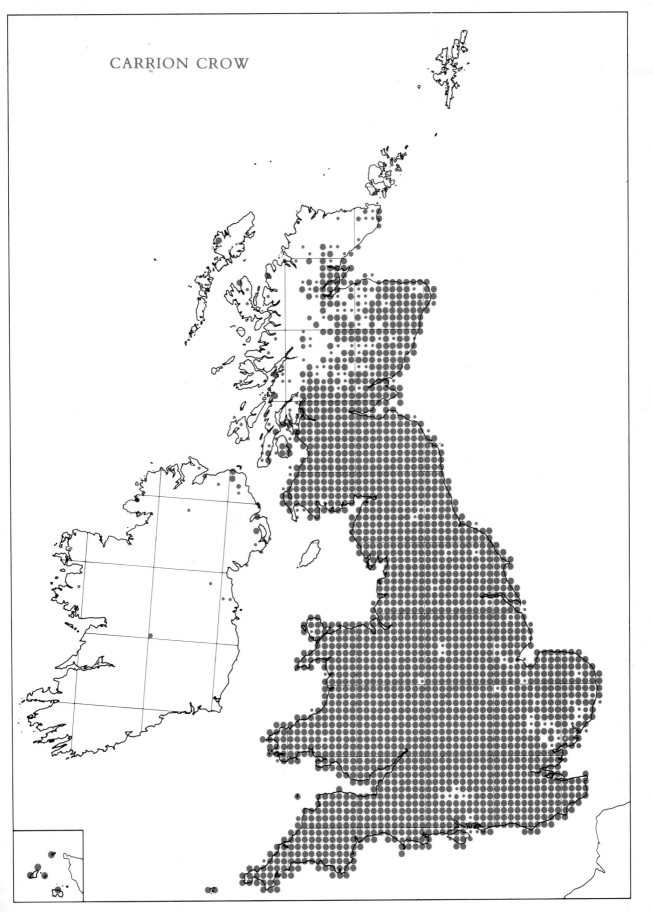

CARRION CROW

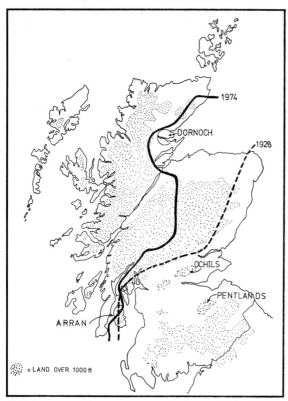

Shift in centre of Carrion × Hooded Crow hybrid zone,
1928–74 (from Cook 1975)

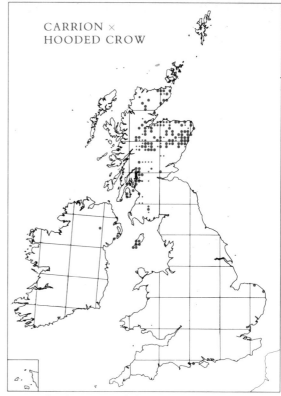

CARRION ×
HOODED CROW

Carrion × Hooded Crow, 1968–72

large nests of sticks, earth and moss, lined with wool
and hair, are easily found and most records refer to
proved breeding.

Crows are often responsible for considerable
predation on birds' eggs and young, and for this
reason they are regarded as enemies by the gamekeeper. In upland areas they feed alongside Ravens *C.
corax* on sheep carrion, and are unpopular with many
farmers because of reputed attacks on ewes and lambs.
It is thought that most of these attacks are caused by
non-breeding birds which are often attracted by the
feed put out for the sheep. Murton (1971) put the loss
of lambs to be well under 0.5% of those at risk.

Until this century, Crows were severely hampered
by persecution, but a decline in game-preservation,
especially during the 1914–18 and 1939–45 wars,
allowed them to increase. They have adapted very
well to the modern farm environment, and have become established in many town parks. A BTO
national survey showed an increase in most areas of
Britain between 1953 and 1963; except East Anglia,
where game-preservation was intensive (Prestt 1965).

The mean densities from Common Birds Census
plots in 1972 were 3.2 and 4.7 pairs per km^2 in farmland and woodland respectively. The species' adapt-
ability to a wide variety of habitats, and its high
densities in some coastal areas, probably result in an
average of 250 or more pairs per occupied 10-km
square and so about one million pairs in Britain and
Ireland, which is at the top of Parslow's range of
100,000–1,000,000. Of these, rather more than half
may be Carrion Crows. The figures below show
(a) all records combined, (b) Carrion Crows,
(c) Hooded Crows and (d) Carrion × Hooded
hybrids/mixed pairs.

Number of 10-km squares in which recorded:	(a)	(b)	(c)	(d)
	3,767	2,310	1,665	162
	(98%)	(60%)	(43%)	(4%)
Possible breeding	181	149	153	37
	(5%)	(6%)	(9%)	(23%)
Probable breeding	118	57	81	21
	(3%)	(2%)	(5%)	(13%)
Confirmed breeding	3,468	2,104	1,431	104
	(92%)	(91%)	(86%)	(64%)

References

COOK, A. 1975. Changes in the Carrion/Hooded
  Crow hybrid zone and the possible importance of
  climate. *Bird Study* 22: 165–168.
HOLYOAK, D. T. 1968. A comparative study of the food
  of some British Corvidae. *Bird Study* 15: 147–153.
LOCKIE, J. D. 1955. The breeding and feeding of Jack-
  daws and Rooks with notes on Carrion Crows and
  other Corvidae. *Ibis* 97: 341–369.
MACDONALD, D. 1965. Increase of Carrion Crow in
  south east Sutherland. *Scott. Birds* 3: 366.
MAYR, E. 1942. *Systematics and the Origin of Species.*
  New York.
MEISE, W. 1928. Die Verbreitung der Aaskrähe
  (Formenkreis *Corvus corone* L.). *J. Orn.* 76: 1–203.
MURTON, R. K. 1971. *Man and Birds.* London.
PRESTT, I. 1965. An enquiry into the recent breeding
  status of some of the smaller birds of prey and
  crows in Britain. *Bird Study* 12: 196–221.

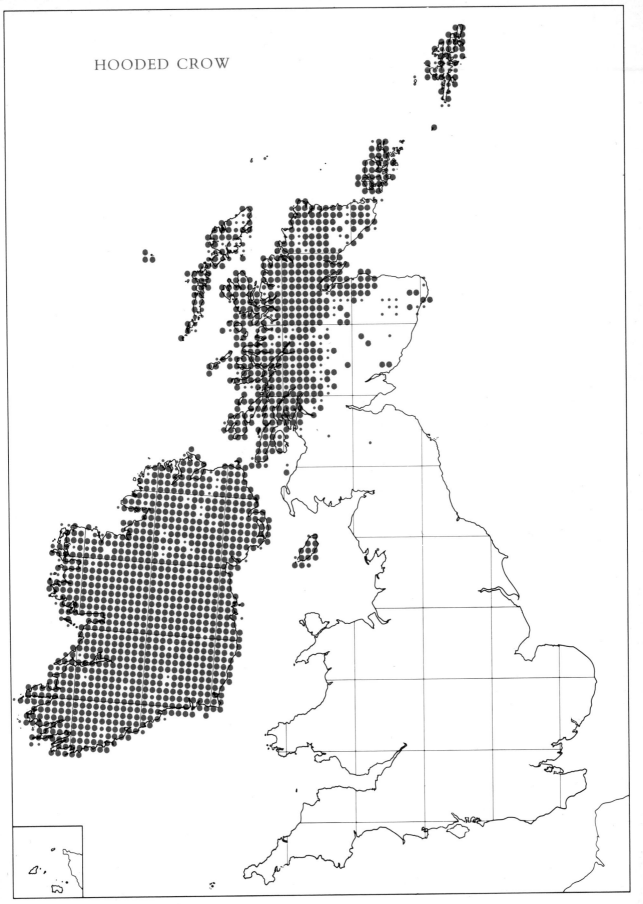

HOODED CROW

Rook

Corvus frugilegus

The noisy, highly gregarious Rook is widespread in all types of tree-clad agricultural country, but less so in areas of moorland, heath and marshes; heavily wooded countryside is generally avoided. The species is found in association with the smaller human settlements and even the outer suburbs of large towns.

Rooks are most commonly found nesting in dense colonies. This habit, together with the propensity for early nesting, before the appearance of leaves on the trees, means that there is no difficulty in proving breeding. Though the species occasionally nests singly, colonies may contain many hundreds of pairs, the largest in Britain being at Hatton Castle (Aberdeenshire), where 6,985 nests were counted in 1945 and 6,697 in 1957. Rookeries are more numerous but smaller in Ireland than in Britain, and few contain over 50 pairs (*cf* Grey Heron *Ardea cinerea*, page 54); the trend in Britain seems to be towards this situation. Although various trees are utilised, elms are a favourite, and it remains to be seen what the effect will be of the destruction wrought by Dutch elm disease.

The economic status of this species has been in dispute since James I of Scotland introduced an Act for its destruction in 1424 and at one time villagers set nets to trap the birds coming down to the corn. Nowadays, most persecution is by means of the gun, but the shooting of young at the rookeries is pointless, since a high proportion dies anyway during the first two months after fledging; the early removal of some of the young birds merely increases the remainder's chances of survival. At certain times Rooks can be injurious to agriculture, but this is usually on a small and local scale. On balance, the species is beneficial.

The Rook is scarce in the uplands of central Wales, the Scottish border, SW Scotland and particularly the northwest mainland and islands of Scotland. In both the Outer Hebrides (colonised 1895) and Shetland (colonised 1952), breeding is confined to single localities. Generally speaking, the Scottish population has seen a long-term increase and expansion of range, attributed to climatic amelioration and improvements in agriculture.

It was during the 1939–45 war that the first national investigation into the status of the Rook was carried out by the BTO. The results indicated a total population in Britain of just under 3,000,000 birds (Fisher 1948). A comparison of the figures from this wartime census with those obtained in the 1930s showed an increase of about 20%. The Rook population continued to increase, according to further censuses in Essex, Hertfordshire, and Nottinghamshire. Dobbs (1964) suggested that the growth in Nottinghamshire up to 1958 may have been associated with increased tillage improving supplies of earthworms, and that a decrease after 1962 was due to the extensive use of organochlorine seed-dressings. Local decreases were also recorded from SW Lancashire, Derbyshire and parts of Cheshire, where Henderson (1968) attributed the fall to a loss of farmland to town and industrial developments. In Hertfordshire, the number of nests increased by 84% between 1945 and 1960–61, but there was then a 32% decline by 1971, with a trend towards smaller colonies.

The reasons for these fluctuations remain obscure. Food is the most likely factor, but during 1945–61 (when Rooks increased) the acreage of cereals and grassland decreased, while during the next decade (a period when Rooks declined) the reverse occurred. Modern agricultural practices, such as stubble burning, probably result in less grain being available. In view of widespread reports of decline over the last 20 years, a national census was made in the United Kingdom in 1975. Preliminary analysis indicated minima of 236,769 occupied nests reported in W England and Wales (95% coverage), 250,000 nests in Scotland (98% coverage) and 55,022 nests in Northern Ireland (49% coverage). The data for E England are not yet available, but it seems likely that the total British and Irish population is about $1\frac{1}{2}$ million pairs.

Number of 10-km squares in which recorded:
  3,178 (82%)
Possible breeding   152 (5%)
Probable breeding   11 (0.3%)
Confirmed breeding   3,015 (95%)

References

DOBBS, A. 1964. Rook numbers in Nottinghamshire over 35 years. *Brit. Birds* 57: 360–364.
FISHER, J. 1948. Rook Investigation. *Agriculture* 55: 20–23.
HENDERSON, M. 1968. The Rook population of a part of west Cheshire 1944–68. *Bird Study* 15: 206–208.
HOLYOAK, D. T. 1972. Food of the Rook in Britain. *Bird Study* 19: 59–68.
MUNRO, J. H. B. 1971. Scottish winter Rook roost survey—southern Scotland. *Scott. Birds* 6: 438–443.
NICHOLSON, E. M. and B. D. NICHOLSON. 1930. The rookeries of the Oxford district. *J. Ecol.* 18: 51–66.
SAGE, B. L. 1972. The decline of the Rook population of Hertfordshire. *Trans. Herts. Nat. Hist. Soc.* 27: 1–17.
WATSON, A. 1967. The Hatton Castle rookery and roost in Aberdeenshire. *Bird Study* 14: 116–119.

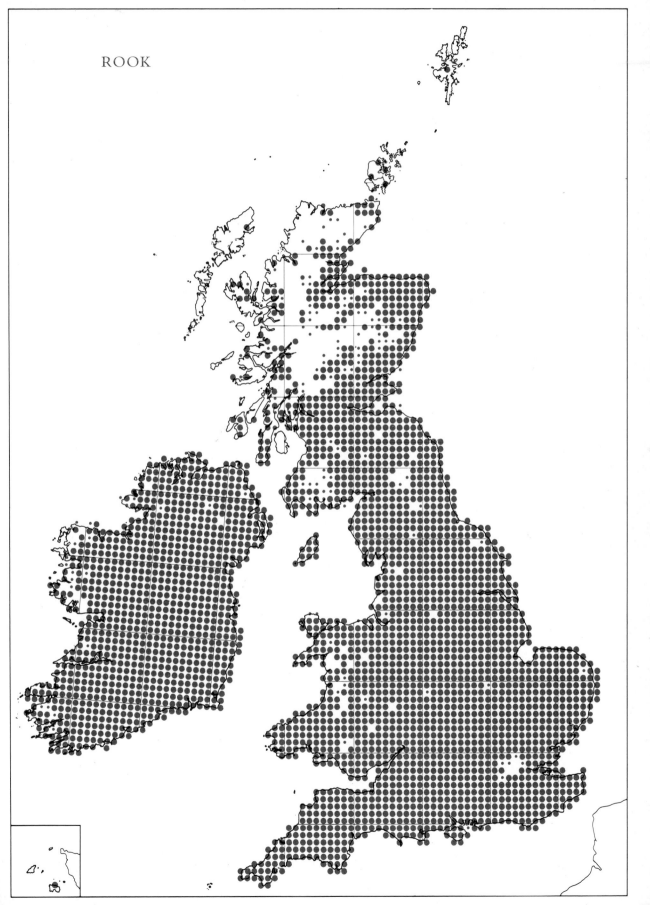

ROOK

Jackdaw

Corvus monedula

Its small size, pale eye, ash-grey nape and distinctive call at once distinguish the Jackdaw from other crows, with which it often associates. Both it and the Rook *C. frugilegus* are typical of the steppe fauna of central Europe and Russia, and it is likely that they originally spread here from those regions. Even in recent times, Voous (1960) found that the range had expanded generally in Europe and, in particular, had extended northwards in Fenno-Scandia, probably as a result of increased cultivation in forested regions and possibly aided by climatic amelioration.

Jackdaws breed in a variety of habitats, including woods, parkland, hedgerow trees, sea cliffs, inland crags, quarries and town centres, but in mountainous country on the Continent they do not usually nest above the tree line, being replaced there by the Chough *Pyrrhocorax pyrrhocorax* and the Alpine Chough *P. graculus*. Like Rooks, they are gregarious at all seasons and breed colonially, several and sometimes many pairs occupying the same or neighbouring trees, or single cliff or quarry faces.

Before breeding, they are often to be seen sitting near the entrances to prospective nests. These are usually in cavities or crevices, though more open structures are occasionally built in ivy or among dense conifer branches, and the same sites are used year after year. Ruined buildings, churches, castles and even the chimneys of occupied houses, which may become completely blocked by the accumulation of material, hold many colonies, but holes in trees are much favoured in woods and farmland areas, while Rabbit burrows are frequently adopted on cliff brows. Large cavities are filled with numerous twigs until a firm platform is constructed, but small ones may be lined with little more than wool and hair.

Lockie (1955) found that about half the feeding time throughout the year was spent on grassland, often in association with Rooks. Unlike the latter, however, Jackdaws are mainly surface feeders, taking mostly larvae of moths, butterflies and flies, as well as spiders. In May, some feed on defoliating caterpillars; subsequently, they eat the pupae in the oak and elm canopy. Because of the later abundance of its main foods, the Jackdaw's breeding season is considerably delayed by comparison with the Rook's, and most eggs are not laid before the second half of April.

The breeding range covers all counties of Britain and Ireland, but is as local as that of the Rook in NW Scotland, the Hebrides, Orkney and Shetland. Nevertheless, an increase and range extension have taken place in Scotland during this century. The first breeding in Shetland was in 1943 and, although none was proved during 1968–72, three pairs nested there in 1973. The six pairs which colonised Eigg (Inner Hebrides) in 1933 had risen to 100 by 1966 (Evans and Flower 1967). In Wales, Saunders (1962) recorded that the population on Skomer (Pembrokeshire) grew from 20 pairs in 1946 to 200–250 in 1961. Numbers have also increased in Ireland this century and this species is now strikingly commoner there than in many equivalent habitats in Britain.

The Common Birds Census registered a decline on farmland during 1968–70, but a recovery since (see graph). In 1972, the mean density on farmland was 1.6 pairs per km². With thriving populations in most other habitats, this order of density may well apply on average to all occupied 10-km squares, suggesting a total British and Irish population of about 500,000 pairs, near the middle of Parslow's range of 100,000–1,000,000 pairs.

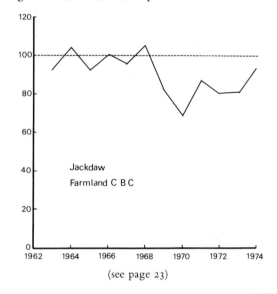

Jackdaw
Farmland C B C

(see page 23)

Number of 10-km squares in which recorded:
3,387 (88%)

Possible breeding	114	(3%)
Probable breeding	54	(2%)
Confirmed breeding	3,219	(95%)

References

EVANS, P. R. and W. U. FLOWER. 1967. The birds of the Small Isles. *Scott. Birds* 4: 404–445.

LOCKIE, J. D. 1955. The breeding and feeding of Jackdaws and Rooks with notes on Carrion Crows and other Corvidae. *Ibis* 97: 341–369.

SAUNDERS, D. R. 1963. Skomer bird report for 1962. *Nature in Wales* 8: 99–104.

JACKDAW

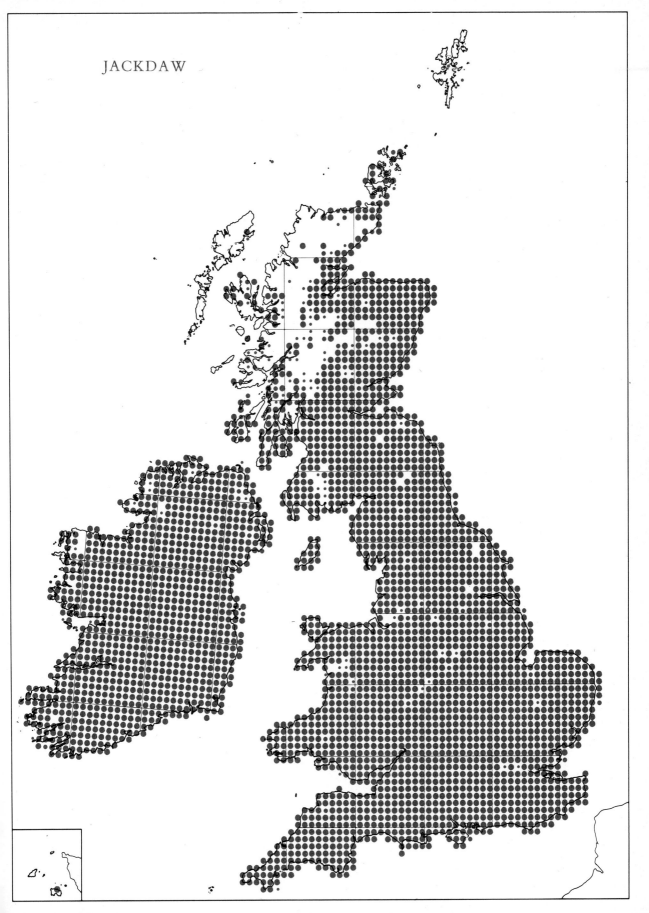

Magpie

Pica pica

The boldly pied plumage, long and wedge-shaped tail and harsh chattering combine to make the Magpie one of the most conspicuous members of our avifauna. Even when concealed by trees or bushes, Magpies often betray their presence by raucous cries, while pairs or family parties feeding in the open and on the ground are easily seen. All types of habitat within range of tree or bush cover are occupied, but there is probably a preference for poorly-managed farmland, particularly grassland with thick hedges and some trees, thickets, the outskirts of woods and, to a lesser extent, comparatively open country. The penetration of town parks and gardens, even city centres, and the exploitation of many coastal scrub habitats, where nests have been found on sea-cliffs, are features of this century.

Most Magpie nests are built in tall, isolated trees, thickets and hedges of thorn or single thorn bushes; conifers are often used, but in woods nests are usually confined to the periphery. Both birds can easily be watched back to the nest when building, which may begin as early as February; the nest may remain virtually complete but empty for up to two months before the eggs are laid (Campbell and Ferguson-Lees 1972). It is a sizeable construction of sticks, strongly lined with mud and a layer of grass roots; there is often a dome of twigs, usually thorny. Both parents chatter during nest-building and the male is vocal during the incubation period; this behaviour, together with the fact that most nests are bulky structures, relying on difficulty of access rather than concealment for protection, explains the high proportion of confirmed breeding records.

The current breeding distribution has been determined to a large extent by various of man's activities. During the Victorian era, Magpies were trapped and shot widely, mainly because of their feeding habits. While the diet is composed primarily of various invertebrates, chiefly insects, plus some small mammals, carrion, cereals, fruits and berries (Holyoak 1968), young birds and eggs are eaten during the breeding season, a fact which led to the elimination of the species from many game-rearing areas. Marked decreases were noted in certain parts of England and throughout the bird's range in Scotland during the 19th century. Like those of others of the crow family, numbers were at a low ebb in Britain (though not in Ireland) at the start of this century. The first signs of substantial increase were recorded during and after the 1914–18 war. These were attributed to lapses in keepering, and also probably an Act of 1911 which prohibited the use of poisoned bait (Parslow 1967). Magpies remained scarce in parts of E and S England until the 1930s, when, especially following the 1939–45 war, they increased rapidly in both range and numbers. The 1940s saw a general expansion into more open countryside and suburban areas, a process that has continued to the present day.

The Magpie has shown itself to be a very adaptable species in modern conditions, scavenging for food on the outskirts of towns and cities, and occupying the parks, allotments or larger gardens of cities such as Aberdeen, Dublin, Glasgow, London, Manchester and Sheffield. It is now a stealthy but regular visitor to many bird-tables in suburbia, and its opportunist nature is amply illustrated by recent cases in Manchester of egg-cartons delivered to doorsteps being opened and the contents consumed.

The history of the Magpie in Ireland is also one of successful expansion following persecution. The bird was first recorded in Co Wexford about 1676, but, three centuries later, it now breeds in every county, reaching even certain of the less remote islands and penetrating several large towns and cities. In Scotland, the species breeds rather locally on the mainland, but is absent from the islands. Again, its stronghold in many parts is the built-up area, where it is safe from the activities of game-preservers.

In England and Wales, the Magpie currently breeds in every county, but there is still evidence of the noticeable decline reported in some parts of E England, particularly East Anglia, since the late 1950s. The decreases appear to have affected rural rather than suburban areas and the most widely held reasons are the grubbing up of hedgerows and the increased use of pesticides (Prestt 1965). Even today, however, the Magpie is regularly shot in rural areas and is often the commonest victim at the gamekeeper's gibbet.

Common Birds Census data show mean densities of 2.3 pairs per km[2] on farmland and 2.8 in woodland in 1972. Even if the average is as low as 100 pairs per occupied 10-km square, the total British and Irish population is probably in excess of 250,000 pairs, well above the range 10,000–100,000 suggested by Parslow.

Number of 10-km squares in which recorded:
  2,899 (75%)
Possible breeding   160 (6%)
Probable breeding   97 (3%)
Confirmed breeding   2,642 (91%)

References

HOLYOAK, D. 1968. A comparative study of the food of some British Corvidae. *Bird Study* 15: 147–153.
PRESTT, I. 1965. An enquiry into the recent breeding status of some smaller birds of prey and crows in Britain. *Bird Study* 12: 196–221.

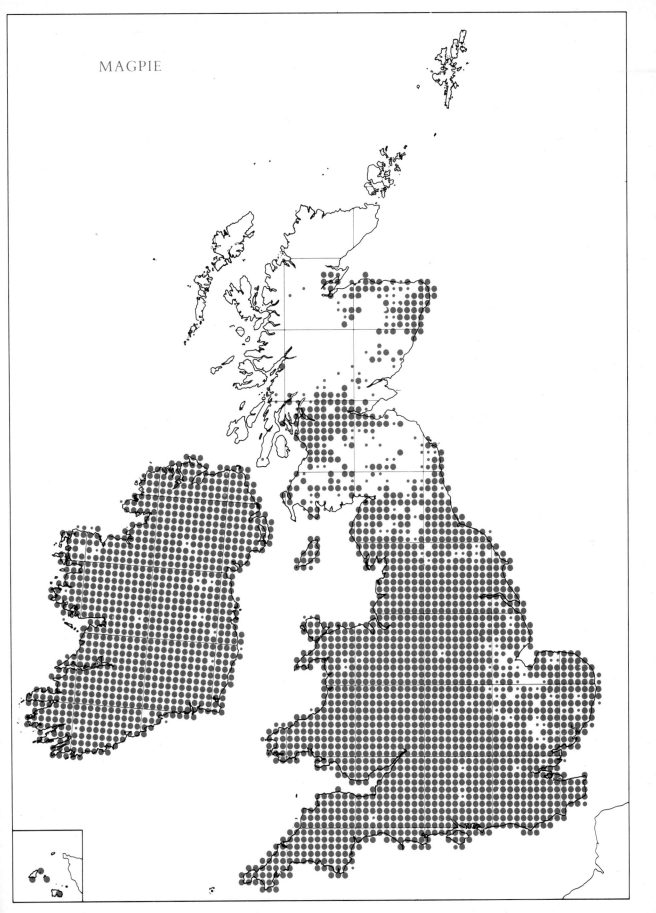

MAGPIE

Jay

Garrulus glandarius

The Jay is a restless, wary and difficult bird to observe when settled, and is usually first seen flying away uttering its harsh calls. This is the most arboreal member of the crow family; whilst perhaps characteristic of oak woods (which it helps to propagate by burying acorns as a winter food), it occurs in beech, chestnut and other woods, often favouring coppice-with-standards, and will nest in Scots pine and spruce plantations, suburban parks, and occasionally along farm hedgerows. Coniferous woodland is frequented as often as deciduous in Ireland and, as in Britain, afforestation benefits this species.

Evidence of breeding is often not easy to obtain. During the summer months the Jay is rarely found far from trees and its nest is the most difficult to find of all the crows, owing to the bird's secretive behaviour and liking for thick cover. Jays may be watched building, but most nests are found by methodical 'cold searching' in woods where they have been seen or heard (Campbell and Ferguson-Lees 1972). Incubating Jays sit very tightly and fly off only when the tree is climbed. Family groups of newly-fledged young offer the easiest proof of breeding.

Fieldwork for the *Atlas* has shown that the Jay is now both more common and more widespread than it was in the 19th century, when a marked general decrease was noted, probably due to persecution by landowners and gamekeepers, and for the taxidermy trade. Excluding local and temporary fluctuations, the evidence points towards a steady and widespread increase since 1914, with the suggestion that this may have accelerated since the 1940s.

Food, cover and persecution are key factors influencing the distribution. The Jay feeds extensively on large insects, such as caterpillars and beetles living in trees and bushes; also various fruits and seeds, including acorns, beech and hazel nuts, pine seeds and some grain (Owen 1956, Holyoak 1968). It is, however, the inclusion of garden soft fruits and the eggs and young of game-birds and song-birds in the diet that is the main cause of local destruction of the Jay by man.

Today, Jays are absent as breeding birds from very few areas of England and Wales. Upland sites in the N Pennines, lowland strips of the east coast, and the fens of E England are examples; all are areas where a lack of woodland (particularly the oak and its fruit, the acorn—an important winter food) may be a limiting factor. Most suburban areas have been colonised. Since first breeding in central London in 1930, Jays have steadily increased in numbers and now nest in most of the Royal Parks and in several other open spaces (Homes *et al* 1964). The trend towards a spread into orchards, shrubberies and large gardens, where Jays now sometimes come to bird-tables, is indicative of an adaptable species benefiting from a greater tolerance by man.

In Scotland, the Jay is strangely absent from several of the southern counties, but it has spread in recent decades, particularly in certain of the new coniferous forests. It now breeds as far north as N Argyll, central Perthshire and the Kincardine/Aberdeenshire border, having penetrated certain of the valleys in the Highlands, though not yet reaching the Grampians or farther north. The habitat requirements and general ecology of this distinct Scottish population merit further study, especially as there is some indication from the greyer mantle plumage of a closer affinity with the typical race of Scandinavia than with the English *G. g. rufitergum*.

Irish Jays belong to the race *G. g. hibernicus* which is somewhat darker than *G. g. rufitergum*. In Ireland, there has been a marked general expansion, especially since 1936, which has included the recolonisation of five counties in Ulster (Deane 1954) and the gradual occupation of new ground in the west. Today, the Jay is widely distributed in Ireland except in parts of the north and west, though it appears to be scarcer than in Britain.

The sedentary nature of the Jay probably explains its absence from the Isle of Man and the Scottish islands. Outside the breeding season, however, wandering pairs and small flocks can be seen in some years in the late summer and autumn (presumably times of food shortage) in regions where the species does not normally breed. With growing afforestation and reduced persecution, further increases in the range should occur. The average breeding density in Common Birds Census woodland plots in 1972 was 5.1 pairs per km². Since about 10% of Britain and Ireland is wooded, 50 pairs per occupied 10-km square may be a reasonable estimate. Thus, a total population of about 100,000 pairs is indicated, at the upper limit of Parslow's range of 10,000–100,000.

Number of 10-km squares in which recorded: 2,142 (55%)
Possible breeding 293 (14%)
Probable breeding 312 (15%)
Confirmed breeding 1,537 (72%)

References

DEANE, C. D. 1954. Handbook of the birds of Northern Ireland. *Belfast Mus. and Art Gallery Bull.* 1 (6): 119–194.

HOLYOAK, D. 1968. A comparative study of the food of some British Corvidae. *Bird Study* 15: 147–153.

HOMES, R. C. et al. 1964. *The Birds of the London Area since 1900.* London.

OWEN, D. F. 1956. The food of nestling Jays and Magpies. *Bird Study* 3: 257–265.

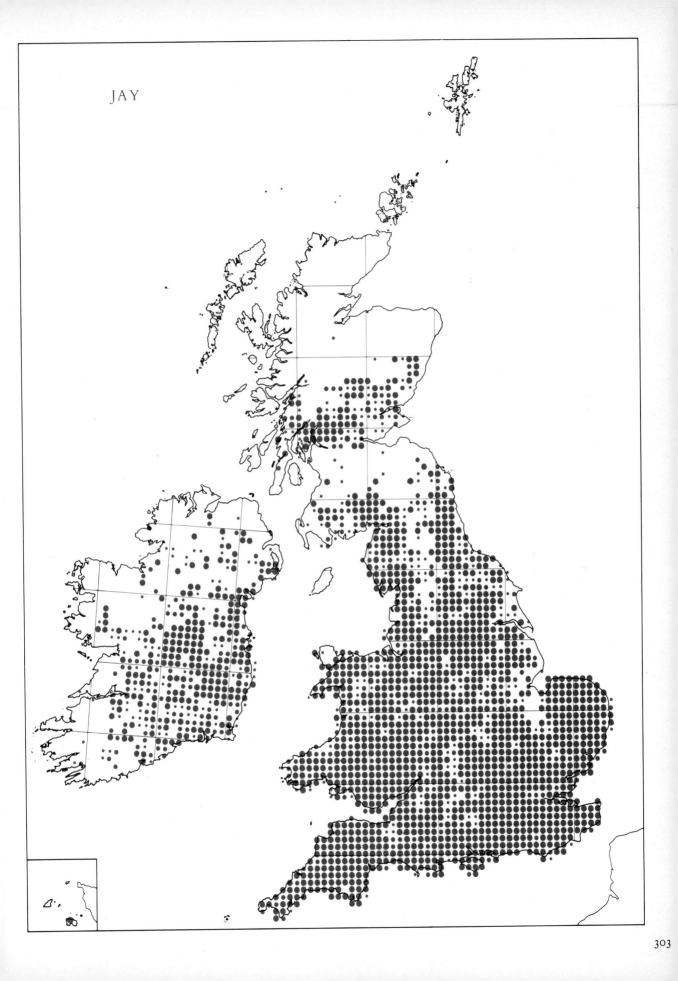

JAY

Chough

Pyrrhocorax pyrrhocorax

The Chough, a crow of great character and charm, is an integral part of the rugged coastal scenery of the maritime west, but is now lamentably restricted to Ireland, Wales, the Isle of Man and SW Scotland. The name, which must be onomatopaeic, should of course be 'chow', not 'chuff' as we now pronounce it; the common call-note is a clipped, high-pitched 'kwee-ow', and a harsher, truncated 'kar, kar' is used in alarm.

Although characteristically found in Britain and Ireland on sea-cliffs, nesting on ledges in caves or in cavities and crevices at greater heights, many Choughs inhabit inland sites, especially in Wales where one pair has been recorded 65 km from the sea. Inland nests are usually in quarry faces and old mine-workings, occasionally well below ground level in open shafts. Traditional sites on the Calf of Man and Cape Clear Island are in disused lighthouses, while derelict cottages are often occupied.

The hub of the social life of the Chough is the summer flock; as the members gather food, they stay close together in pairs, which at intervals rise, call and fly directly to the cliffs. Not all are breeders, since the flock has a proportion, perhaps at least 30% (Rolfe 1966), of non-breeders which, although they mate and prospect a site, do not nest until three years old (Holyoak 1972). Observation of the flock is the best way of pinpointing individual nest sites, though once located the actual crevice or cavern is likely to prove inaccessible.

The Chough's decline has been discussed in superficial terms, since there is a lack of factual data, by Ryves (1948), Rolfe (1966) and others. A popular belief that the species has had the worst of competition with the thrustful Jackdaw *Corvus monedula* does not stand up to examination, for their food requirements and nest-site preferences do not clash. There is certainly a coincidence, however, between the Chough's decline and the long run of cold winters during the 19th century; and the severe winter of 1962/63 saw a marked diminution in SW Scotland, from which the species has not recovered.

In the breeding season, Choughs rely on ants and their larvae, the down-curved bill and feeding method being well adapted to exploring ant galleries in close-cropped turf. It follows that this species does best in places where there is continual sheep grazing or nibbling by Rabbits, and it will be interesting to see if the recent introduction of Manx *loghtan* sheep to the Calf of Man improves the habitat for it. Holyoak (1972) thought that availability of food might be a limiting factor in spacing out the pairs: densities are certainly greater at the cliffs and on offshore islands than among the Welsh hills, where they nest at 250–380 m above sea level.

The range was formerly much wider than now, extending to the east coasts of Scotland (where there were also many inland sites) and Yorkshire, and the cliffs of Sussex, the Isle of Wight, Dorset and Devon. Some bred in N Devon until 1910, on Skye and Mull (Inner Hebrides) into the 1920s, and in Cornwall till 1952. In Ireland, some contraction has occurred, the species withdrawing from Cos Dublin, Londonderry, Wexford and Wicklow; but this country remains the heart of its range in these islands, with more than three times the number to be found in Britain, and Choughs are more than holding their own in the west and south.

A census in 1963 suggested a total breeding population of 700–800 pairs, with perhaps 400 non-breeders, distributed as follows: Ireland 567–682; Wales 98 (42 in Caernarvonshire and 33–36 in Pembrokeshire); Isle of Man 20; and S Argyllshire 11 (Cabot 1965, Rolfe 1966).

This species is afforded special protection in Great Britain under Schedule I of the Protection of Birds Act, 1954–67.

Number of 10-km squares in which recorded:
244 (6%)
Possible breeding 38 (16%)
Probable breeding 25 (10%)
Confirmed breeding 181 (74%)

Four dots have been moved by up to two 10-km squares (the Rare Breeding Birds Panel's recommendation was that three dots should be moved by up to two 10-km squares)

References
CABOT, D. 1965. The status and distribution of the Chough *Pyrrhocorax pyrrhocorax* in Ireland. *Irish Nat. J.* 15: 95–100.
COWDY, S. 1973. Ants as a major food source of the Chough. *Bird Study* 20: 117–120.
HOLYOAK, D. 1972. Behaviour and ecology of the Chough and the Alpine Chough. *Bird Study* 19: 215–227.
RALFE, P. G. 1905, 1924. *The Birds of the Isle of Man* and *Supplement*. Edinburgh.
ROLFE, R. 1966. The status of the Chough in the British Isles. *Bird Study* 13: 221–236.
RYVES, B. H. 1948. *Bird Life in Cornwall*. London.
WILLIAMSON, K. 1959. Observations on the Chough. *Peregrine* 3: 8–14.

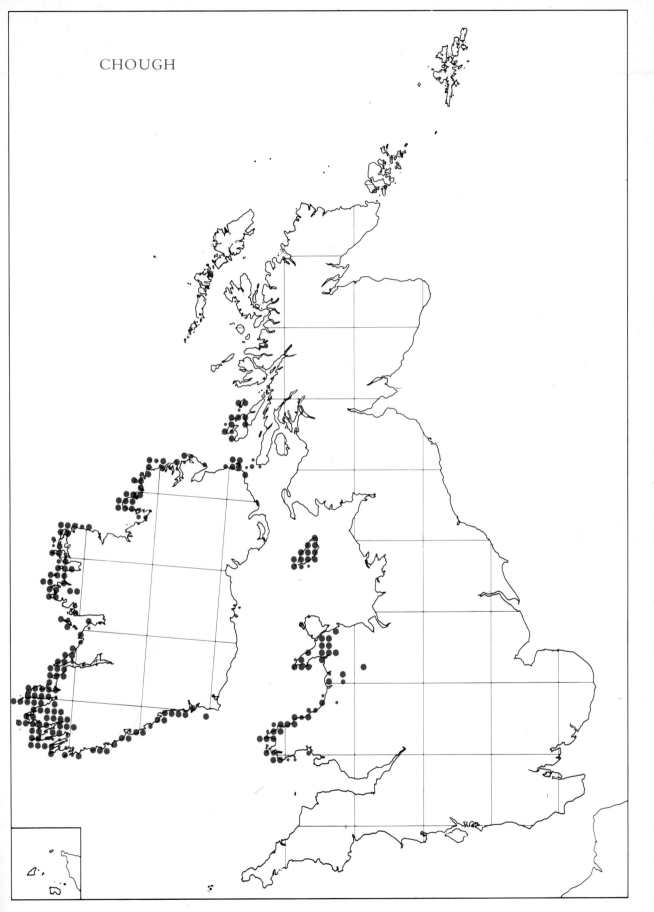

CHOUGH

Great Tit

Parus major

The Great Tit is found breeding in Britain and Ireland in almost any area with deciduous trees, whether woodland or parkland, and it also often occurs in coniferous woods. Snow (1954) pointed out that its large size (for a tit) and its habit of often taking food on the ground make it rather finch-like and better able than the other tits to adapt to habitats outside woods. It is commonly found in scrub and along hedgerows on farmland, and also in gardens and parks in towns and cities. At the eastern extremity of its extensive Eurasian range, it is abundant in coniferous forests.

A handsome and familiar bird, with a loud, far-carrying call and bell-like song, it is an easy species to find and identify. By early April, when *Atlas* workers were recommended to start their surveys, male Great Tits would have been singing for more than two months, and most pairs would have set up territories and chosen nesting holes.

The map shows an extensive range with gaps in some Highland squares. Few Great Tits seem to nest above 500 m and there can be little suitable habitat at this height. There have never been breeding records from the Northern Isles, and the Outer Hebrides have only recently been colonised (woodland at Stornoway). Breeding in the Inner Hebrides has been recorded for many years, but increased planting of trees may have extended the range. In the far north of mainland Scotland, Great Tits have extended their breeding distribution markedly in the last 50 years (Pennie 1962) This extension, paralleled in Norway, may have been helped by afforestation, but is probably also correlated with milder winter weather. In Ireland there are rather few Great Tits in the far west, where a number of 10-km squares contain little cover. It is from here, and the mainland of Scotland, that the excess of 10-km squares occupied by Blue Tits *P. caeruleus* and not by Great Tits derives. As in the case of the Blue Tit, breeding in the Isles of Scilly is recent, dating from the 1920s.

Although Continental Great Tits are regularly migratory, our birds are normally resident. In some years, numbers may build up and trigger an eruption, as occurred in 1957 (Cramp, Pettet and Sharrock 1960), but this did not happen here during 1968–

72. The Common Birds Census indices show the same trends as for Blue Tits, with the woodland population remaining quite stable and the farmland population increasing. By 1971, the farmland index had reached a level double that of 1962 (see graph).

The densities recorded on individual plots were almost always lower than for Blue Tits. A Sussex yew wood, however, and oaks in Wester Ross, actually held more Great Tits than Blue Tits: this is unusual in Britain, but is regular on the Continent, especially in beech woods. Woodland densities often exceed 50 pairs per km², but seldom reach 100. Farmland densities are sometimes very low but may, in favourable circumstances, be up to 20 pairs per km². In 1972, woodland plots averaged 27.7 and farmland plots 8.5 per km². These are respectively 65% and 58% of the mean densities for the Blue Tit. Since Great Tits are also well distributed in suburban areas, an average population of more than 1,000 pairs per occupied 10-km square seems to be a reasonable estimate, even allowing for some peripheral squares with small areas of potential breeding habitat. Thus, the British and Irish population is likely to be over 3,000,000 breeding pairs.

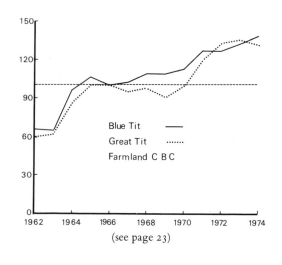

(see page 23)

Number of 10-km squares in which recorded:
  3,365 (87%)
Possible breeding   75 (2%)
Probable breeding   127 (4%)
Confirmed breeding   3,163 (94%)

References

BARNES, J. A. G. 1975. *The Titmice of the British Isles.* Newton Abbot.

CRAMP, S., A. PETTET and J. T. R. SHARROCK. 1960. The irruption of tits in autumn 1957. *Brit. Birds* 53: 49–77, 99–117, 176–192.

LACK, D. 1966. *Population Studies of Birds.* Oxford.

PENNIE, I. D. 1962. A century of bird-watching in Sutherland. *Scott. Birds* 2: 167–192.

ROYAMA, T. 1966. A re-interpretation of courtship feeding. *Bird Study* 13: 116–129.

SNOW, D. W. 1954. The habitats of Eurasian tits (*Parus* spp.). *Ibis* 96: 565–585.

GREAT TIT

Blue Tit

Parus caeruleus

In Britain and Ireland, the Blue Tit may be found almost anywhere provided that some trees, or at least large bushes, are present. Whilst it may be out-numbered by the Great Tit *P. major* in a few decidu-ous woods (as it is more generally on the Continent), and by the Coal Tit *P. ater* in coniferous woods, in-cluding yew, it is our most widely distributed and most numerous tit. Snow (1954) has shown that its deep and stubby beak is adapted for feeding in broad-leaved trees, and it is at a disadvantage com-pared with the Coal Tit, and locally the Crested Tit *P. cristatus*, when feeding in the narrow-leaved coni-fers. Mature stands of oak and beech, containing old trees with holes for breeding, may be the preferred habitat, but the Blue Tit has adapted well to coppice and coppice-with-standards woods. Lines of trees along roads, water-courses and hedgerows, clumps in parkland and on farms, as well as orchards and gardens are all attractive haunts to this versatile bird.

Both parents feed the young and their repeated visits make proof of breeding a very simple matter. For a few weeks after fledging, the family parties stay together, or join with others from the immediate vicinity. The 114 10-km squares where the species was seen but not proved to nest mostly have little suitable habitat; nevertheless, many may contain a few isolated breeding pairs.

Ever since ornithological recording started, the Blue Tit has been very widely distributed in Britain and Ireland. Commercial planting of trees, even if they are mostly of conifers, has enabled it to spread into some upland regions which were formerly with-out woods, and afforestation has probably been responsible for a recent increase in Sutherland and Caithness. Numbers have certainly built up in the Isle of Man as the planted woodlands have matured. There are no breeding records from Orkney or Shetland, although Blue Tits are now firmly estab-lished in the most extensive wood in the Outer Hebrides, around Stornoway Castle. Breeding began in the Isles of Scilly in the late 1940s.

The numbers of all species of tits may fluctuate

quite widely from year to year and, when populations are high in the autumn, eruptions may occur. The last time this happened was in 1957, huge numbers of Blue and Great Tits, with a few of other species, arriving from the Continent during the autumn. Several hundred Blue Tits passed through some coastal localities in a single day. Earlier in the autumn, native bred birds were unusually common, and some of these were caught up in the subsequent move-ments. There was a return to the Continent in the following spring. These movements, and associated paper-tearing and milk-bottle opening activities, were documented by Cramp *et al* (1960). Other eruptive movements have occurred on the Continent since, but none has involved our birds.

The Common Birds Census index shows that, while woodland populations have remained stable since 1964, those on farmland have been increasing gradually since 1962 and doubled that year's level by 1973 (see graph on page 306). The *Atlas* years span the latter part of this increase and spread into open habitats. The numbers breeding in a particular wood are limited by the availability of suitable holes, and the provision of nest-boxes, particularly in suburban gardens and commercial forests, can increase the breeding population considerably.

Densities vary greatly on CBC areas, as would be expected in a species which has such a catholic choice of habitat. Coniferous woods may have only ten pairs per km^2, but in deciduous woods with plenty of breeding holes there may be more than 100 pairs per km^2. Blue Tits are present in almost all farmland plots, with densities ranging from 2.6 to 34.7 pairs per km^2 (Westmorland and Suffolk respectively). Average figures in 1972 were 14.6 in farmland and 42.7 pairs per km^2 in woodland. Maximum numbers may be reached in suburban woodland and parkland. Densities in deciduous woods in Ireland are also very high, and it seems likely that an average of 2,000 breeding pairs per occupied 10-km square is a reason-able estimate, even allowing for a much sparser population in many occupied 10-km squares in moorland and upland areas. Thus, the British and Irish population is likely to be in excess of 5,000,000 pairs.

Number of 10-km squares in which recorded:
  3,473 (90%)
Possible breeding   60 (2%)
Probable breeding   54 (2%)
Confirmed breeding   3,359 (97%)

References
BARNES, J. A. G. 1975. *The Titmice of the British Isles.* Newton Abbot.
CRAMP, S., A. PETTET and J. T. R. SHARROCK. 1960. The irruption of tits in autumn 1957. *Brit. Birds* 53: 49–77, 99–117, 176–192.
LACK, D. 1968. *Ecological Adaptations for Breeding in Birds.* London.
SNOW, D. W. 1954. The habitats of Eurasian tits (*Parus* spp.). *Ibis* 96: 565–585.

BLUE TIT

Coal Tit

Parus ater

More than any of the other common tits, Coal Tits are associated with conifers. Beak length and depth, like those of the more locally distributed Crested Tit *P. cristatus*, are clearly adapted for finding food amongst bunches of needles (Snow 1964). Thus, Coal Tits are found both in semi-natural Scots pine forest and in more recent commercial forestry plantations, as well as where pines, firs, larches, yews, cypresses and various exotic conifers have been introduced to ornament gardens and parks. Only a few such trees are needed, and churchyards and vicarage gardens can provide oases of habitat suitable for this species and the Goldcrest *Regulus regulus*. This affinity is by no means absolute, however, and Coal Tits may be found in exclusively deciduous woodland. Indeed, in the sessile oakwoods of W Britain and Ireland, and the birch woods of N Scotland, it may be the most numerous tit, occasionally outnumbering the Blue Tit *P. caeruleus* and Great Tit *P. major* combined (Yapp 1962). These regions mostly lack both Marsh *P. palustris* and Willow Tits *P. montanus*, and it may be that competition with these two species helps to concentrate the Coal Tits in coniferous woodland over much of England and Wales.

The Coal Tit's loud, piping 'seetoo seetoo' song may be heard at long range, making location easy. Most Coal Tits lay their clutches rather earlier than either Blue or Great Tits. They will readily take to nest-boxes erected on trees, but many natural nests are in holes in the ground, among the roots of trees and coppice stools, and in crevices in dry-stone walls. Nest sites are generally lower than those of other tits.

The distribution in Britain and Ireland has probably not changed much for many years, except as a result of increased afforestation. Even as early as 1844, some Scottish naturalists were commenting on a growth in numbers as the result of 'the increasing age of the plantations and the immense quantity of wood which has lately been planted'. The Coal Tit is more widespread in upland areas than the other common tits and can be found nesting at higher altitudes, up to 600 m. Breeding was not proved in the Outer Hebrides during 1968–72, although the species nested at Stornoway Castle in 1966. Similarly, it nests only sporadically on Rhum in the Inner Hebrides. In the Channel Islands, breeding has occurred only on Jersey and Guernsey; and in the Isles of Scilly not at all. The rather thin distribution in parts of England, particularly in the Fenlands, Wales and NW Mayo, reflects shortage of suitable habitat.

During the five *Atlas* years, the Common Birds Census index increased from double to treble the 1964 level by 1972 (see graph). The Goldcrest, found in the same habitat and also benefiting from the run of mild winters, shows a similar CBC graph (see page 384). Both populations are currently so high that the levels preceding the two severe winters at the beginning of the 1960s have probably been surpassed two or three times over.

Woodland CBC plots hold up to 100 pairs per km² in favoured areas. The average in all woodland CBC plots (mostly in lowland Britain) was 12.5 pairs per km² in 1972. Even though there were many squares where *Atlas* fieldworkers had difficulty finding even a single pair, the high densities in coniferous woodland everywhere, and mixed or deciduous woodland in some areas, probably lead to an average of about 350 pairs per 10-km square. This would give a total in Britain and Ireland of about 1,000,000 pairs.

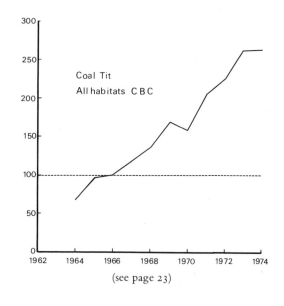

(see page 23)

Number of 10-km squares in which recorded:
3,250 (84%)
Possible breeding   172 (5%)
Probable breeding   231 (7%)
Confirmed breeding   2,847 (88%)

References

DEADMAN, A. J. 1973. The Coal Tit. *Forestry Commission Forest Record*, 85. HMSO.

SNOW, D. W. 1954. The habitats of Eurasian tits (*Parus* spp.). *Ibis* 96: 565–585.

YAPP, W. B. 1962. *Birds and Woods*. Oxford.

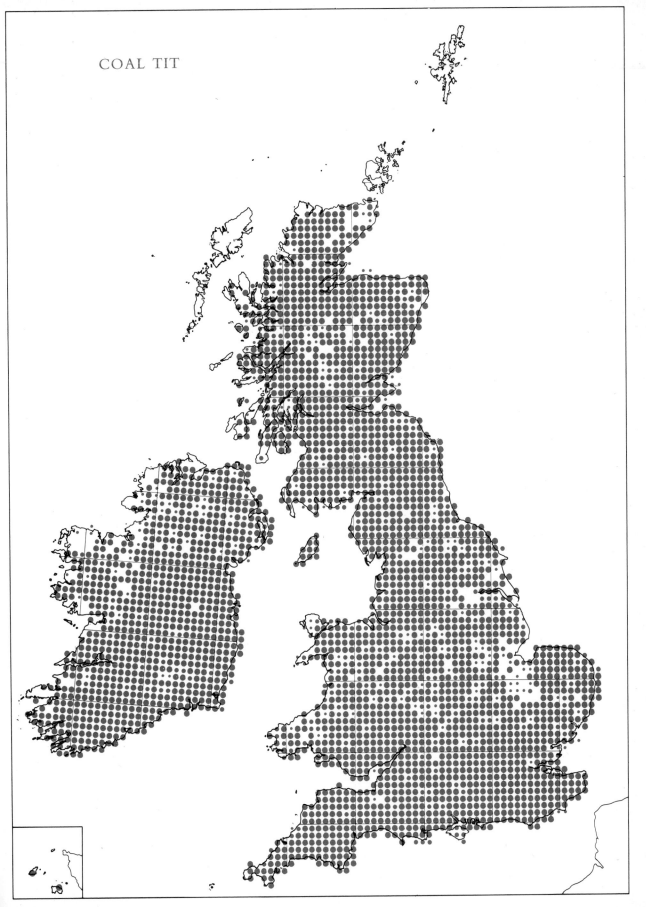

COAL TIT

Crested Tit

Parus cristatus

The Crested Tit is the rarest and most restricted in range and breeding habitat of the British tits. It is surprising that a species which breeds over most of Europe, ranging from S Spain through France to the middle of Scandinavia, should be completely absent from England and Wales, especially as apparently suitable habitat exists. Since it is the best adapted British tit for life in conifers (Snow 1954), recent commercial plantations of pines should provide areas where it would have an advantage over other species. There are so few records of vagrants in S Britain, and the species is so sedentary, however, that natural colonisation from the Continent is unlikely.

Its typical Scottish haunts are the open Scots pine forests, with dead and decaying wood available for nest sites, and rank heather, bilberry and juniper to provide winter shelter. New plantations, where the trees grow close together and ground cover is poor, are not occupied by the Crested Tit until they are about 20 years old. In such plantations, management demands removal of the rotten wood with the result that nest sites are at a premium and nest-boxes are needed.

When seen well, these are unmistakable little birds. The usual calls are rather similar to those of other tits and are not particularly distinctive, but Crested Tits do have a very characteristic, stuttering trill. Since they are sedentary, records of presence without actual confirmation of nesting are likely to refer to small pockets of breeding birds. The map is probably complete except that a few isolated pairs, away from the traditional haunts, may have been overlooked.

The paired adults select the nest site together but, in most cases, it is the female who excavates the hole. Of the other British tits, only the Willow Tit *Parus montanus* regularly excavates its own nest. At this stage, location can be easy since the sound of the female at work may carry 50 m. Of 324 nests recorded by Nethersole-Thompson, more than 90% were in pines (most often in stumps), and most of the rest were in the stumps of other trees or in fence-posts; a very few were in existing holes, and one was in the old drey of a Red Squirrel; most nests were less than 3 m up (but some reached 14 m) and two were in the ground under the roots of trees (Nethersole-Thompson and Watson 1974).

Since Crested Tits remain in the breeding area throughout the year, winter food supply may be a crucial factor. There are many cases of their coming to deer carcases and skins to take fat, and they often feed at bird-tables.

When there were large tracts of the ancient Caledonian pine forest in Scotland, the Crested Tit was probably more widely distributed. Destruction of this great forest from the Middle Ages through to the end of the 19th century gradually restricted the range. At one time it was thought to be confined to a 50 km length of the Spey Valley, though, even early in this century, there were some records from the Moray Firth and Easter Ross. Small populations may have survived away from the Spey and *Atlas* fieldworkers were apparently the first to prove breeding in NW Inverness-shire (the western cluster of four dots): this may represent either a relict population in an isolated remnant of the old forest cover or recolonisation via new linking plantations of exotic conifers. There is some evidence of a gradual spread and recovery in numbers within the last ten years.

D. Nethersole-Thompson, in Darling and Boyd (1969), recorded densities of about three pairs per 100 ha in traditional pine forest in good years. The numbers are reduced considerably by mortality during severe winters, but recover quickly. In 1964, he estimated that 300–400 pairs may have bred in Scotland. Since then, some extra groups have been discovered and nest-boxes have been used in some extensive, well-grown plantations. With presence discovered in nearly 50 10-km squares during 1968–72, one may hazard a guess at an average of at least 20 pairs per occupied 10-km square, and a total approaching or even exceeding 1,000 pairs.

This species is afforded special protection in Great Britain under Schedule I of the Protection of Birds Act, 1954–67.

Number of 10-km squares in which recorded:
46 (1%)
Possible breeding   14 (30%)
Probable breeding   5 (11%)
Confirmed breeding   27 (59%)

Though some records were originally submitted in confidence, all dots are now shown accurately (as recommended by the Rare Breeding Birds Panel)

References

CAMPBELL, B. 1958. *The Crested Tit*. Forestry Commission Leaflet, no. 41. London.

DARLING, F. F. and J. M. BOYD. 1969. *The Highlands and Islands*. London.

HAFTORN, S. 1954. Contribution to the food biology of tits especially about storing of surplus food. Part 1, the Crested Tit. *Norske Vid. Selsk. Skr.* 1953 (4): 1–123.

NETHERSOLE-THOMPSON, D. and A. WATSON. 1974. *The Cairngorms*. London.

SNOW, D. W. 1954. The habitats of Eurasian tits (*Parus* spp.). *Ibis* 96: 565–585.

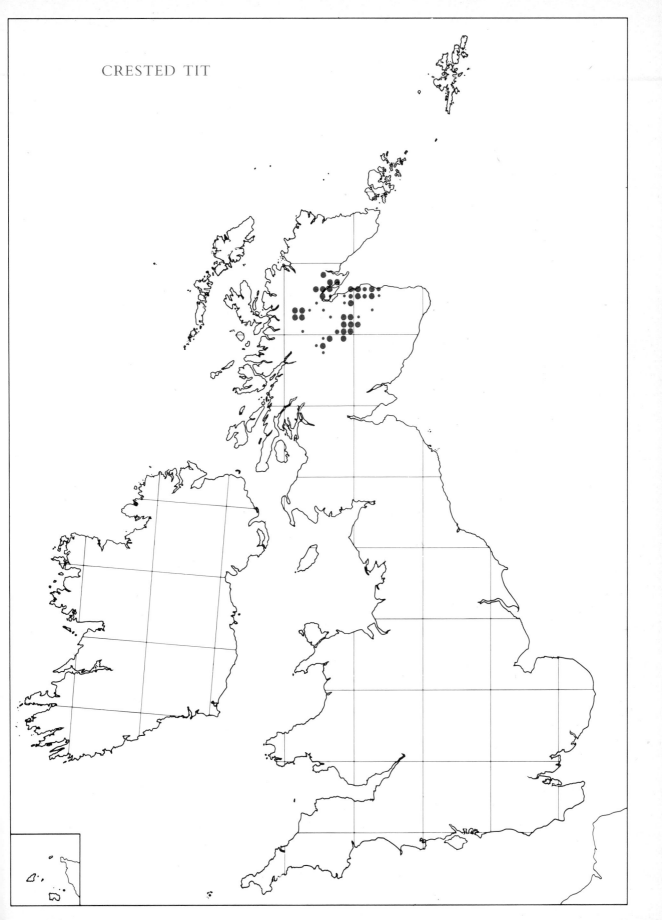

CRESTED TIT

Marsh Tit

Parus palustris

Marsh Tits are more strictly rural than the three commonest tits and do not usually breed in towns, although they wander to gardens at times. The vernacular name is something of a misnomer, for they are not marshland birds, and the usual habitat is deciduous woodland, especially alder, ash, birch and oak. They also occur in a variety of other habitats, though the presence of trees appears to be essential.

During the autumn and winter months, Marsh Tits join with other tits in flocks. Pairs tend to remain together within the flock, and pairing of new couples takes place in February and March, when territory owners can be heard loudly calling their diagnostic 'pitchou' notes. They are early songsters and the main song period extends until mid-May. Hole prospecting reaches a peak during March, with birds exploring likely clumps of alders and other suitable trees. Although Marsh Tits do not usually excavate their own nests as do Willow Tits *P. montanus*, they often chip pieces of wood away from the entrance. Many holes are visited at this time, but by the end of March the pair has usually made a selection, and much time is spent in the vicinity of the chosen site.

The holes vary in height from below ground level to over 10 m, but just over half of nest record cards refer to nests at under 1 m. All types of natural holes are used, including cavities under tree roots and in cliffs, while artificial sites may include dry-stone walls, nest-boxes and hollow metal posts. Competition for sites is often severe and, although Marsh Tits can hold their own against Blue Tits *P. caeruleus*, they give way to the larger Great Tits *P. major* and Nuthatches *Sitta europaea*. Territory-holding Marsh Tits are extremely aggressive towards neighbouring pairs and much calling and even fighting take place, especially early in the year. Non-territorial individuals are not challenged in the same way, and this floating population seems quickly to provide a new mate if one of a pair should die.

The size of territory in a small population studied in an Oxfordshire oak wood varied from as little as 0.5 ha to 6.5 ha, with a mean of 2.5 ha (Southern and Morley 1950). Most eggs are laid between early April and May, with over 60% of clutches started in the second fortnight of April in S England and Wales. The young fledge in early June and family parties are very noisy. Fledglings away from adults are difficult to separate from young Willow Tits, however, and a few such sightings which could not be assigned to either species are omitted from the maps. These sibling species present one of the most difficult identification problems facing *Atlas* fieldworkers, and this is discussed in detail under Willow Tit (see page 316).

There have been very few recorded changes in numbers or distribution in Britain. The second Scottish record, in 1945, related to breeding in Berwickshire, but this penetration across the border may have been previously overlooked. The absence of the Marsh Tit from large areas of Cumberland and Lancashire contrasts with the presence of the Willow Tit, but both are largely absent from the Fens of E England. There are no reliable records of either species in Ireland, though Marsh Tits are said to have been seen in four Irish counties in the 19th century and there was an unsuccessful attempt at introduction in Co Tipperary before 1953.

Parslow classed the Marsh Tit as 'fairly numerous', with 10,000–100,000 pairs. The British population is certainly in the upper half of this range, or above it, since even a conservative 50–100 pairs per 10-km square would give 70,000–140,000 pairs.

Number of 10-km squares in which recorded:
   1,366 (35%)
Possible breeding   162 (12%)
Probable breeding   180 (13%)
Confirmed breeding   1,024 (75%)

References

MORLEY, A. 1949. Observations on courtship feeding and coition of the Marsh Tit. *Brit. Birds* 42: 233–239.

MORLEY, A. 1950. The formation and persistence of pairs in the Marsh Tit. *Brit. Birds* 43: 387–393.

MORLEY, A. 1953. Field observations on the biology of the Marsh Tit. *Brit. Birds* 46: 231–238, 273–287, 332–346.

SOUTHERN, H. M. and A. MORLEY. 1950. Marsh Tit territories over six years. *Brit. Birds* 43: 33–47.

MARSH TIT

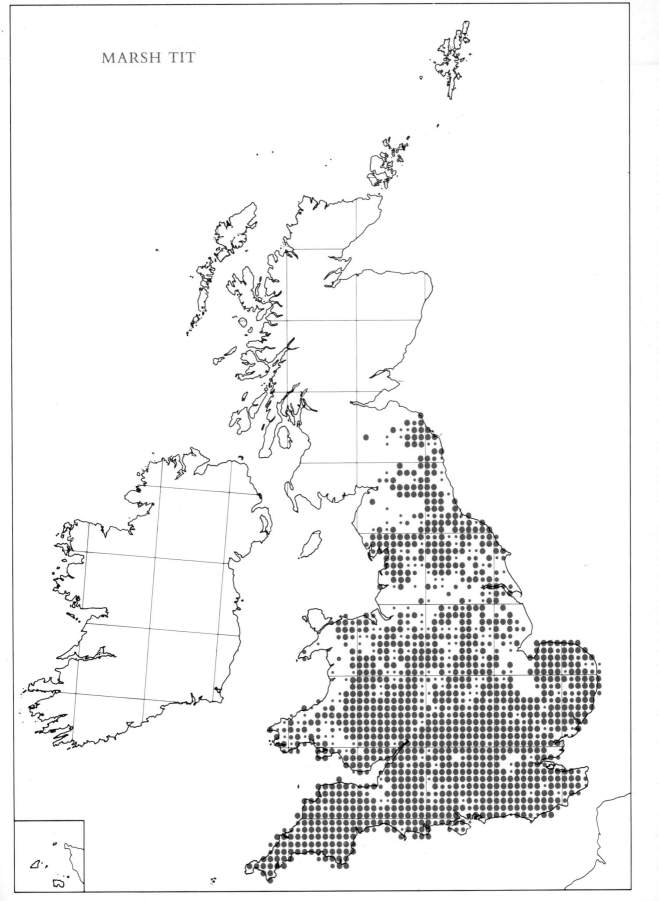

Willow Tit

Parus montanus

Willow Tits are widely distributed across Europe and Asia, but there has never been a record in Ireland. In N Europe they inhabit the dark, damp Norway spruce and birch forests, and also wooded mountain slopes up to 2,000 m in the Alps. In lowland regions, damp mixed woods of alder and birch, and willow thickets, are favoured by this species, which often breeds alongside the very similar Marsh Tit *P. palustris*. Of the two, the Willow Tit may have a greater affinity for waterside habitats, and it is frequently found at overgrown, flooded gravel pits. These are usually along river valleys, where the proximity of suitably decrepit trees may be the prime factor: unlike the Marsh Tit, the Willow regularly excavates its nest hole and so soft, rotten stumps, trunks or branches are needed, though gate-posts and fence-posts are sometimes used.

The most common nesting trees reported for Willow Tits are birch, willow, elder and alder. Many trial borings may be made in March and April until a suitably soft section is found. Like woodpeckers, they usually leave a pile of chippings below the nest hole, which draws attention to the site. Damp woods are especially likely to provide rotten timber, but drier types of deciduous woodland are also occupied. The Common Birds Census data suggest that Marsh Tits outnumber Willow Tits by about four to one in broad-leaved woods, but on farmland with hedgerows and copses the ratio is only 1.3 to one.

Willow Tits are rather less noisy and demonstrative than other tits, though their curious, distinctive buzzing calls may allow detection even when they are not seen. Separation of briefly seen, silent birds from Marsh Tits is often impossible; even in the hand identification rests on a combination of features, and Perrins (1964) said he knew of 'no single character that is absolutely diagnostic in the separation of these two species'. Even more recently, Campbell and Ferguson-Lees (1972) stated of the Willow Tit 'detailed distribution not yet worked out owing to confusion with Marsh Tit'.

The problem was recognised before the *Atlas* work began, so provisional maps were published at an early date (Sharrock 1970), and it was pointed out that the boundaries between their respective distributions looked suspiciously like an artefact, since they followed those of the counties in some parts of the country. This early warning probably helped to ensure a more critical examination of Marsh and Willow Tits in the last three seasons. The maps given here are the most accurate and reliable available, but it must be admitted that errors due to incorrect field identification probably have not been completely eliminated.

Marsh or Willow Tits occur in 55% of the squares in Britain and Ireland, 86% of these being in England and Wales. Both species occur in 64%, Marsh Tit alone in 23% and Willow Tit alone in 13%. There is thus a great deal of overlap in distribution, as there is in habitat. The history of both species is difficult to unravel because the Willow Tit was not separated from the Marsh Tit in Britain until 1900, and there has been much confusion between the two. One incontrovertible change, however, is the virtual disappearance of Willow Tits from the Scottish Highlands since about 1950, the decrease being first noted about 1918.

Within Britain, the annual ringing totals up to 1960 always included at least three times as many Marsh as Willow Tits (the average ratio was seven to one), but since 1965 the reverse has been the case, Willow Tits always outnumbering Marsh. It is impossible to be sure whether this reflects improving observer ability, changing trapping methods, a decline in Marsh Tits, a dramatic increase in Willow Tits, or some combination of these.

While appreciating that the identification problem makes assessment of the numbers of Willow Tits even more liable to error than those of most other species, one can attempt some deductions. Though rarer in woods, Willow Tits are usually commoner than Marsh Tits on farms; though scarcer over much of the shared range, they have been shown to be markedly commoner than Marsh in some well-worked areas (*eg* counties just to the north of London). An average of about 40–80 pairs per 10-km square, slightly lower than for Marsh Tits, would indicate a British population of about 50,000–100,000 pairs (compared with 70,000–140,000 pairs of Marsh Tits). Parslow rated both species as 'fairly numerous', implying 10,000–100,000 pairs.

Number of 10-km squares in which recorded:
  1,218 (32%)
Possible breeding   170 (14%)
Probable breeding   212 (17%)
Confirmed breeding   836 (69%)

References

PERRINS, C. M. 1964. Identification of Marsh and Willow Tits. *Ringers' Bull.* 2, no. 6: 10–11.

SHARROCK, J. T. R. 1970. Atlas—preliminary species maps. *BTO News* 40: 2–4.

WITHERBY, H. F. and E. M. NICHOLSON. 1937. On the distribution and status of the British Willow Tit. *Brit. Birds* 30: 358–364.

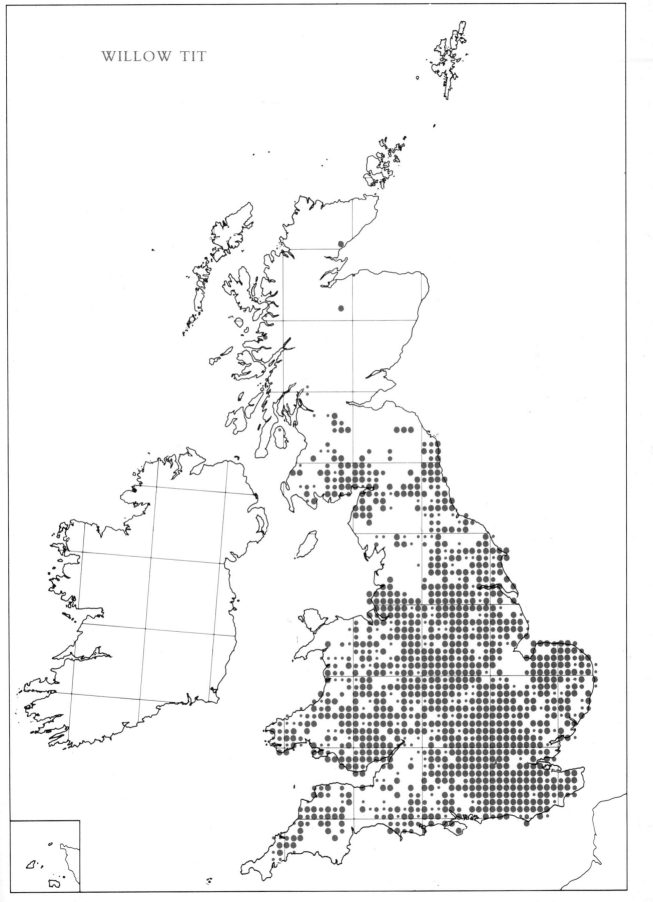

WILLOW TIT

Long-tailed Tit

Aegithalos caudatus

Long-tailed Tits may be present in any type of woodland, but are more typical of dense hedgerows, scrub or open canopy. Good numbers are found in such areas as overgrown gravel pits with plenty of thorn bushes, chalk scrub, and heath with scattered trees. Although its habits are superficially like those of the *Parus* tits and, indeed, they are often found together in mixed flocks, the Long-tailed Tit is only distantly related to them, being different in several aspects of structure and behaviour. For example, all *Parus* breed in holes, but the nest of this species is a marvellous ball constructed of moss, cobwebs, hair and lichens and lined with hundreds of feathers.

Nest-building may start early in March, and often takes three weeks or more. Most sites are in thorny bushes or shrubs, but some are in the forks of birches and other trees at heights of up to 20 m. Nests last well, so that proof of breeding can be obtained by looking for them when the leaves have fallen. Early nests are easily found before the vegetation comes into leaf and, not surprisingly, are often lost to predators. Evidence of successful breeding is provided by the parties of fledged young and adults.

Large clutches are laid and ten, 11 or even 12 eggs are frequently recorded. Nest losses seem to be heavy, however, and it may be that only about a third of the breeding pairs manage to raise young each year. Long-tailed Tits are almost always found in parties, which keep in touch with each other by characteristic, high-pitched, whistling and low, chattering calls. Quite commonly, several adults attend an active nest and it has been suggested that the high rate of nest predation has led to such co-operative breeding (Lack and Lack 1958). Recent studies of this phenomenon, which is apparently rare among temperate zone birds but much commoner among tropical species, interpret it as a strategem evolved to maximise nesting efficiency (Fry 1972). Detailed investigations of behaviour during the breeding season showed that breeding parties of Long-tailed Tits defend a territory, just as a normal pair of another species would do (Gaston 1973).

Such a tiny insectivorous resident species as the

Long-tailed Tit is naturally at risk during severe winters and up to 80% of the British population has often been wiped out by hard weather. The 1961/62 and 1962/63 winters had such an effect, but the Common Birds Census index had reached quite a high level when *Atlas* fieldwork started, and increased by 12% for farmland and 31% for woodland during the five years of the survey. The map thus shows the distribution at a time of high population. There is little evidence, however, that the general pattern has changed in recent years, apart from climate-induced fluctuations, although the breeding in W Sutherland and Caithness may be new. The gaps relate mostly to city centres or fenland and upland areas where suitable breeding habitat does not exist. The species has not, of course, been able to colonise the exposed treeless areas of the Scottish islands or the west coasts of Scotland and Ireland.

Published densities from CBC work range from two or three to 30 families per km^2 in wooded areas, and up to five families per km^2 on farms; the average for farmland in 1972, however, was only about one family per km^2. The total of almost 3,000 occupied 10-km squares might indicate a large population, but fieldwork in N Britain and Ireland, where the distribution is rather patchy, has suggested that some squares there may hold only 5–10 breeding pairs. On the other hand, many squares in lowland England and Wales, with extensive scrub and open woodland, contain several hundred breeding pairs. An average of 50 over the whole of Britain and Ireland would give a total population of roughly 150,000 families. This is considerably more than Parslow's range of 10,000–100,000, but that was based on 1966, only three years after the 1962/63 winter, and his assessment was almost certainly correct at that time.

Number of 10-km squares in which recorded:
2,916 (76%)
Possible breeding   194 (7%)
Probable breeding   123 (4%)
Confirmed breeding   2,599 (89%)

References

FRY, C. H. 1972. The social organisation of the bee-eaters (Meropidae) and co-operative breeding in hot-climate birds. *Ibis* 114: 1–14.

GASTON, A. J. 1973. The ecology and behaviour of the Long-tailed Tit. *Ibis* 115: 330–351.

LACK, D. and E. LACK. 1958. The nesting of the Long-tailed Tit. *Bird Study* 5: 1–19.

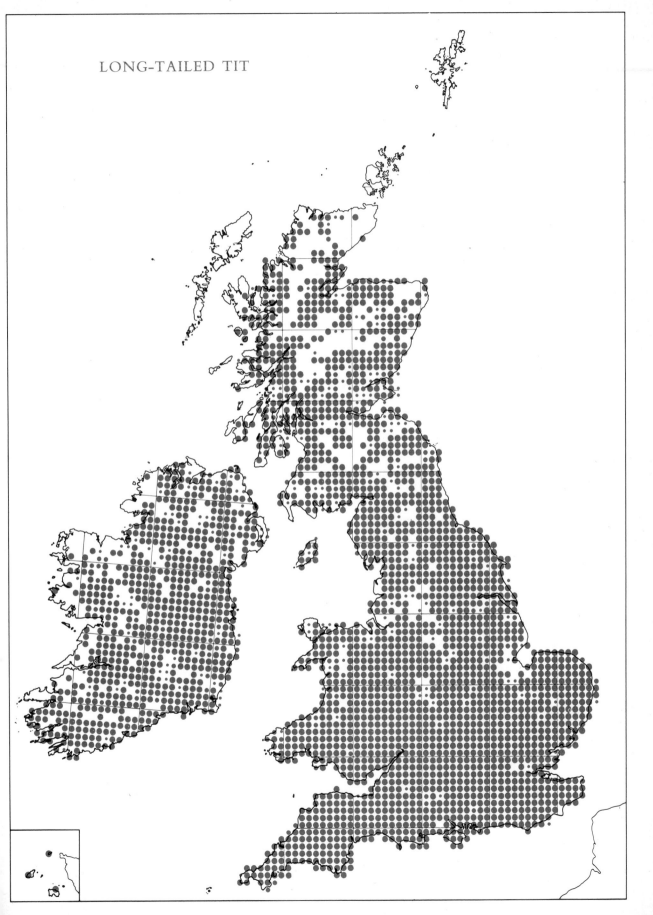

LONG-TAILED TIT

Nuthatch

Sitta europaea

Nuthatches occur most often in mature deciduous or mixed woodland, especially where there is beech, oak and sweet chestnut. Open parkland and hedgerows with scattered mature trees and even large gardens may also prove attractive. Even within the main range, however, many apparently suitable sites do not support Nuthatches: they have a patchy distribution belied by the solid cover of large dots indicating that breeding has been proved within the relatively large 10-km square unit.

The ringing calls and song in early spring make the displaying pairs easy to locate, but they become rather more silent in April and for the rest of the breeding season. The nest hole is chosen towards the end of March. It is usually in a tree, most often at a height of 3–10 m, and has an entrance rather wider than is necessary for the passage of the birds. Holes in buildings, walls or even straw stacks may also be used. Whatever the situation, mud is plastered either within the entrance, to reduce it to about 3 cm diameter, or in the nest-hole. Those which take over nest-boxes will often use mud to cement the roof on to the box, or the box to the tree. Astonishing quantities may be brought to the nest and then plastered with rapid prodding actions of the bill. Some nests in ricks had up to 4 kg of mud reinforcing their flimsy entrances (Walpole-Bond 1938).

Unlike other tree-climbing birds, the Nuthatch has a soft tail which is not used for support; the species may climb up or down trees, head first, searching for food on the bark. Larger, hard foods such as chestnuts, beech mast and hazel nuts are inserted into crevices in bark or masonry and are hammered with the bill to open them. The characteristic hammering may be heard at a long range but, unfortunately for *Atlas* workers, this behaviour is not normally associated with the breeding season. Nuthatches seem to be very sedentary, however, so the possible and probable records from 24% of the 10-km squares almost certainly refer to breeding birds.

Nuthatches apparently disappeared from the northern parts of their range in England during the 19th century, when they also left the parks of Inner London, possibly as a result of increasing atmospheric pollution (Homes *et al* 1964). Since about 1940 the species has extended north in N Wales, Cheshire and Lancashire, as well as into Durham and Northumberland from the outlying Yorkshire population, which may also have led to recent records in the Lake District (*cf* map on page 463). The gap through industrial Yorkshire (*cf* Kingfisher *Alcedo atthis*, page 266) may be due to atmospheric pollution reducing the food supply, though Great Spotted Woodpeckers *Dendrocopos major* are present in the area, so some suitable habitat with available food presumably exists there. The gaps in Lincolnshire and the Fenland of E England reflect the scarcity of woodland in those areas. Although Nuthatches have been recorded on the Isle of Wight, there has not yet been proof of breeding.

Since they are such attractive birds, there have been several attempts to introduce them to Scotland and Ireland. None has apparently been successful and the only records from Ireland followed these releases, over 60 years ago. The central Scottish *Atlas* records were unexpected and, whilst they may be the result of unrecorded introductions, it is possible that the birds were natural colonists. They might have come from the expanding population in N England, but could perhaps be immigrants from S Scandinavia, like the newly-discovered Scottish Wrynecks *Jynx torquilla*. Siberian Nuthatches are subject to eruptive movements westwards (Voous 1960) and the same may be true of Scandinavian ones. Baxter and Rintoul (1953) listed a few records of migrants and others seen during the winter, although only one instance where breeding started, in Wigtownshire in 1927.

There is rather little information on the density which breeding Nuthatches may reach. Where sites are freely available among mature deciduous trees, occupied nests may be close together. Many apparently suitable areas have no breeding Nuthatches, however, and the woodland Common Birds Census areas (including those without any) averaged only 3.1 pairs per km^2 in 1972. On this basis, with woodland accounting for about 10% of land, there may perhaps be an average of about 20 per occupied 10-km square, and the British population may number 20,000 or more pairs, rather higher than Parslow's range of 1,000–10,000.

Number of 10-km squares in which recorded:
1,175 (30%)
Possible breeding 114 (10%)
Probable breeding 167 (14%)
Confirmed breeding 894 (76%)

References

HOMES, R. C. *et al.* 1964. *The Birds of the London Area since 1900*. London.

WALPOLE-BOND, J. 1938. *A History of Sussex Birds*. London.

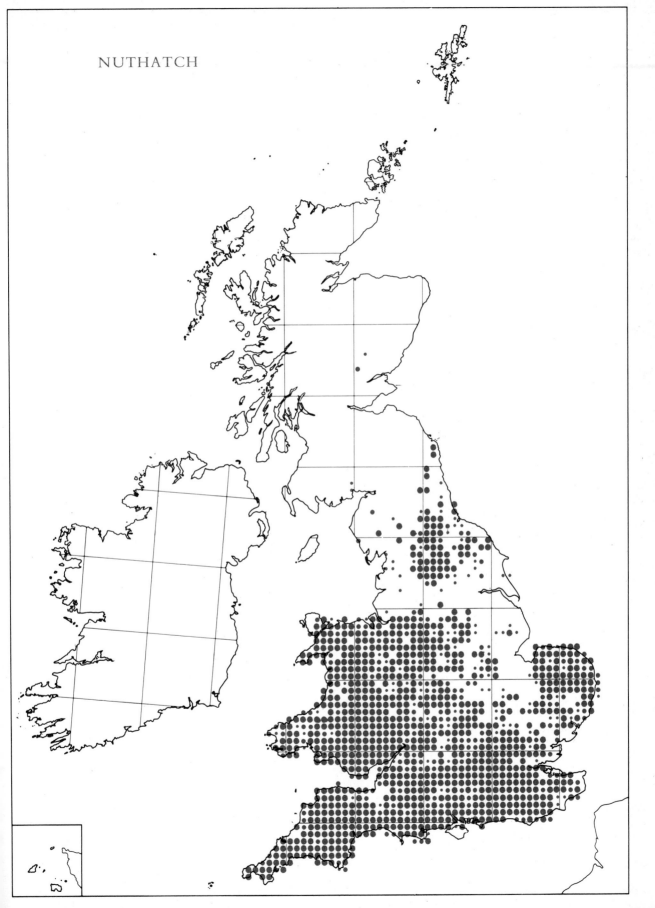

NUTHATCH

Treecreeper

Certhia familiaris

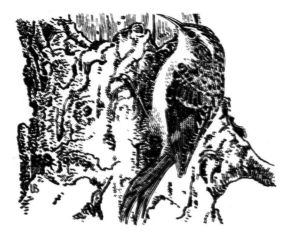

On the Continent, this species is usually found in upland coniferous forest and is replaced in lowland deciduous habitats by its sibling, the Short-toed Treecreeper *C. brachydactyla*. Presumably, after the last glaciation, the conifer-loving Treecreeper colonised Britain and Ireland in the train of the rapid northward expansion of Scots pine, but the land-bridge to the Continent was severed before the appearance of the Short-toed Treecreeper, moving more slowly in association with its favoured broad-leaved timber. When, with milder climate, deciduous forest appeared on this side of the English Channel, the Treecreeper took over the normal habitat of its sibling as well as its own.

Thus, in Britain and Ireland the Treecreeper has become typical of deciduous or mixed woodland, extending into almost any area where there are mature trees, including farmland, parks and large gardens. Treecreepers are also found in coniferous woods, but as these are usually managed, with commercial felling taking place before the trees are mature, nest sites are considerably fewer and the species' density is lower than in deciduous woods.

Treecreepers are most vocal and, therefore, most easily located early in the year from February to early April. The song and calls are high-pitched and distinctive, but tend to be overlooked by many observers. The nest, most often placed behind a flap of bark or in a slit in a tree, but also behind ivy, as well as in artificial sites, is usually very well concealed, though a few twigs may project and reveal its location. Old trees with loose bark in the midst of a wood of younger trees will often provide sites, and up to seven nests with eggs were found in a day of normal *Atlas* fieldwork by looking in such places. Nevertheless, the best period to attempt confirmation of breeding is when there are large young in the nest and the adults are carrying food, or just after the young have fledged, when they form noisy family parties. An incautious approach, however, may cause them to 'freeze' against the tree-boles or in a head-up position on a branch, like tiny Bitterns *Botaurus stellaris*.

Treecreepers are susceptible to hard winters, but, apart from the fluctuations these produce (see graph), there are few indications of changes in numbers or distribution, though Stornoway (Outer Hebrides) was colonised in 1962. The *Atlas* data suggest that Treecreepers are relatively scarcer in Ireland than in Britain; not only were they found in a lower proportion of 10-km squares (70% compared with 81%), but there was also a lower proportion of confirmed breeding records (66% compared with 82%). Apart from absence from the most mountainous and barest moorland areas of the Scottish Highlands, the main area of scarcity (rather than absence) is clearly in the Fens of E England, a feature of the distribution of several other woodland birds.

Treecreepers are common, though often overlooked, in most of lowland Britain and even in the sparse birch woods of the extreme north of Scotland. In the Channel Islands the species is replaced by the Short-toed Treecreeper (see page 450). Even allowing for a greater rarity in Irish squares, an average of 50–100 pairs per 10-km is likely, and a total British and Irish population of about 150,000–300,000 pairs in 1968–72 can be estimated, higher than the range 10,000–100,000 pairs given by Parslow.

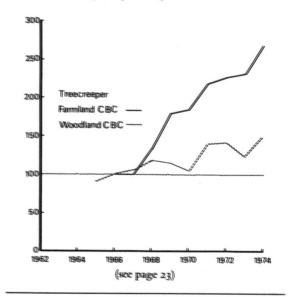

(see page 23)

Number of 10-km squares in which recorded: 3,002 (78%)
Possible breeding   293 (10%)
Probable breeding   348 (12%)
Confirmed breeding   2,361 (79%)

References

FLEGG, J. J. M. 1973. A study of Treecreepers. *Bird Study* 21: 287–302.

MEAD, C. J. 1975. Variation in some characters of three Palaearctic *Certhia* species. *Bull. Brit. Orn. Cl.* 95: 30–39.

MEAD, C. J. and D. I. M. WALLACE. 1976. Identification of European treecreepers. *Brit. Birds* 69: 117–131.

THIELCKE, G. 1972. Waldbaumläufer ((*Certhia familiaris*) ahmen artfremdes Signal nach und reagieren darauf. *J. Orn.* 113: 287–296.

Short-toed Treecreeper *Certhia brachydactyla*, **see page 450**

TREECREEPER

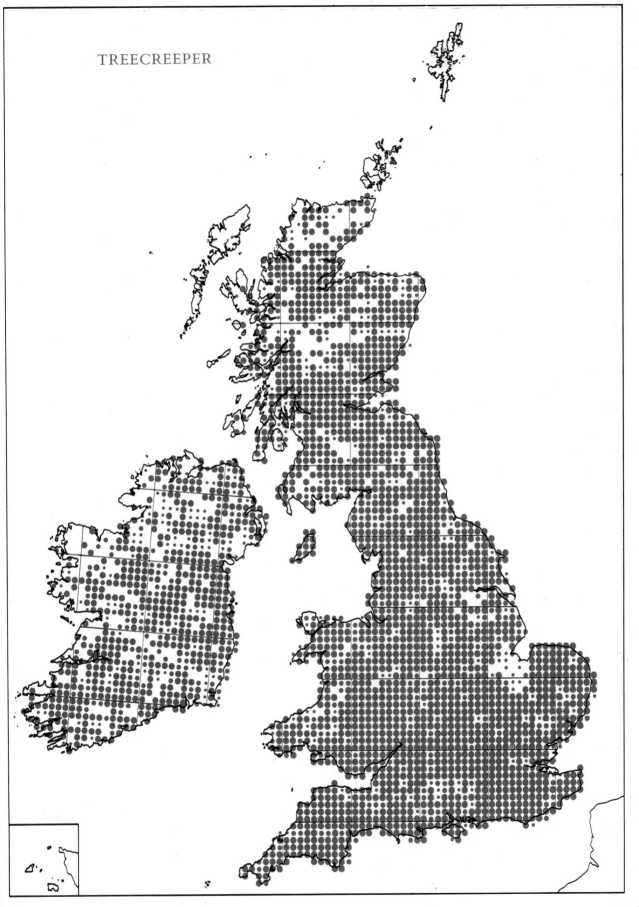

Wren

Troglodytes troglodytes

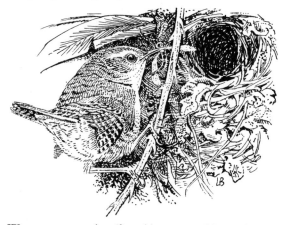

Wrens are severely affected by very cold weather (see Common Birds Census graph), but there had been unusually mild winters in the five years leading up to and also during the *Atlas* period. The resulting map shows the Wren to be the third most widespread species in Britain and Ireland, exceeded only by the Skylark *Alauda arvensis* and the Carrion/Hooded Crow *Corvus corone*.

The Wren is one of our most adaptable species. It may be found in almost every habitat from the seashore to boulder-fields high on the mountains. Only the very centres of cities and the most uniform open habitats with low vegetation are avoided. Even on bare moorland, however, the banks of small burns may provide enough of a break in the uniform cover for an occasional pair. In lowland Britain, woodland, no matter how small an area, is the preferred habitat, together with waterside vegetation. During recovery from the severe winter of 1962/63, garden and orchard sites proved rather less attractive, and field hedgerows were the last habitat to be occupied as the overspill increased (Williamson 1969).

Although mainland Wrens are quite mobile (Hawthorn and Mead 1975), the breeding groups on some Scottish islands have been isolated long enough to have become distinct geographical races. It is likely that the changes in size, song, plumage and habits have arisen in the last 6,000–7,000 years, since Wrens can hardly have reached these islands before trees and shrubs spread to them in about 5000 BC.

The loud, vehement song makes location of this species very easy where it is common, but there were more than 100 10-km squares, many in coastal or mountainous areas, where no Wren was recorded during 1968–72. The location of one or two of these tiny birds in such vast areas would be very difficult, and there must be a suspicion that sometimes they were overlooked. The breeding season starts with a first clutch in April and lasts into late June or early July, two broods being normal. Since the males build several 'cock's nests', building activity and unlined nests were not regarded as proof of breeding. The easiest confirmation comes from watching adults carrying food to young, or removing faecal sacs, or

by hearing the noisy, recently fledged broods, whose calls bear a resemblance to those of Treecreepers *Certhia familiaris*.

The extent to which Wrens may suffer through hard weather may be gauged by the CBC index. Between 1964, following two severe winters, and 1974, the index revealed a ten-fold increase (see graph) unmatched by any other common species. Apart from these periodic short-term fluctuations, there are no range or numerical changes on record. Perhaps the most immediately obvious blank on the map is Tiree, where the first recorded breeding was in 1952 (Boyd 1958), though none was found during 1968–72.

The Wren is perhaps the commonest nesting bird throughout Britain and Ireland today. Density figures are available for a very wide range of habitats. Scrub and woodland may have from 13 pairs per km^2 (deciduous woodland) to over 100 pairs per km^2. The average CBC densities in 1972 were 22.5 pairs per km^2 on farmland and 61.4 in woodland. There could well be an average of 3,000 pairs per 10-km square, and this suggests a current British and Irish population of about 10,000,000 pairs. This figure would drop dramatically after a severe winter.

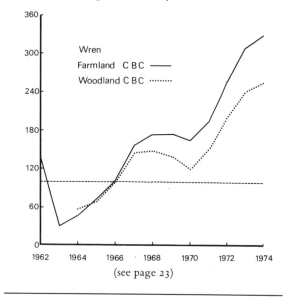

(see page 23)

Number of 10-km squares in which recorded: 3,755 (97%)
Possible breeding   32 (1%)
Probable breeding   145 (4%)
Confirmed breeding   3,578 (95%)

References
ARMSTRONG, E. A. 1955. *The Wren*. London.
BOYD, J. M. 1958. The birds of Tiree and Coll. *Brit. Birds* 51: 41–56, 103–118.
HAWTHORN, I. and C. J. MEAD. 1975. Wren movements and survival. *Brit. Birds* 68: 349–358.
WILLIAMSON, K. 1958. Population and breeding environment of the St Kilda and Fair Isle Wrens. *Brit. Birds* 51: 369–393.
WILLIAMSON, K. 1969. Habitat preferences of the Wren on English farmland. *Bird Study* 16: 53–59.

WREN

Dipper

Cinclus cinclus

Dippers are found mainly in the uplands, frequenting rocky or gravelly, fast-flowing streams and rivers of mountainous and hilly regions. The British and Irish distribution reflects this, there being good correspondence with the presence of land over 305 m (1,000 feet) (*cf* overlay). Some occur on lowland streams, however, especially where there are weirs or other fast-flowing stretches of water, but usually only if such places are contiguous with more typical habitat. Where hills come down to the sea, Dippers may even occasionally nest near sea-level and feed on the shore.

Bobbing on rocks in the centre of a river, or flashing upstream, Dippers are fairly easy to locate on suitable waters. They sing and hold territory during the winter (Hewson 1967), and pair and display together from January onwards. Nest-building may take place during February or March, and in mild years many pairs have complete clutches by the end of March. Two, sometimes three, broods are reared, and active nests or dependent young were easily found during *Atlas* fieldwork; adults carrying faecal sacs were also a common source of confirmed breeding records.

The nest is a characteristic ball of moss and grass, lined with leaves, resembling that of a large Wren *Troglodytes troglodytes*. Some are marvellously well-concealed under the roots of trees or within hanging vegetation beside the stream, but many are built in rock cracks and crevices, frequently beside or behind waterfalls, so that the parents have to fly through a curtain of falling water. Such natural sites are in the minority in many areas, with most built on ledges or in crevices in man-made structures, particularly under bridges or culverts, or in walls and weirs. Unless destroyed by floods, nests in sheltered positions may last for months, even years, and so proof of breeding may be sought even in the winter.

Except in fringe lowland areas, there have been few documented changes in distribution in Britain and Ireland. Although there were some instances of breeding earlier in this century in the Isle of Man and Orkney, regular nesting in both had ceased by 1950; the *Atlas* record of probable breeding in Orkney indicates an attempt to recolonise. In the Midlands and south-central England, there were a few nesting records earlier in this century, and the map shows a slight recent extension of range there. In Ireland, the Dipper is present in some lowland regions where the milder climate may enable it to survive the winters when equivalent habitat in Britain has become frozen over. Since it stays in its breeding area during the winter, this species can be severely affected by freezing conditions, although there are many records of its being able to feed under ice, provided some points of entry remain open. Dippers nest regularly at altitudes up to 600 m in parts of Scotland. It is possible that the mobility of the Grey Wagtail *Motacilla cinerea* provides the key to that species' better success in exploiting lowland waters, for in the uplands the two birds' requirements are very similar. River pollution has caused local extinctions in a few places, but most of the Dipper's upland streams and rivers remain unspoiled.

This bird's fascinating underwater feeding habits and its territorial behaviour during both summer and winter in a restricted habitat make it an ideal species for special study, and it has captured the imagination of several ornithologists. Shooter (1970) found in Derbyshire that the length of river occupied by each pair depended on the extent of shallows available for feeding, and averaged about 1.5 km of river. The BTO Waterways Survey produced a mean of about 35 territories per 100 km of river/stream in England, but 129 in more favoured parts of N Wales. Robson (1956) estimated that the density in N Westmorland was about 15 pairs per 10-km square. Other surveys indicate that this might be a reasonable estimate to take for the whole of Britain and Ireland, and it leads to a figure of about 30,000 pairs. Parslow's (1967) range of 1,000–10,000 pairs seems very pessimistic, even for the time, quite soon after the two cold winters, when he proposed it.

Number of 10-km squares in which recorded: 2,051 (53%)
Possible breeding   201 (10%)
Probable breeding   199 (10%)
Confirmed breeding   1,651 (80%)

References

COWPER, C. N. L. 1973. Breeding distribution of Grey Wagtails, Dippers and Common Sandpipers on the Midlothian Esk. *Scott. Birds* 7: 302–306.

HEWSON, R. 1967. Territory, behaviour and breeding of the Dipper in Banffshire. *Brit. Birds* 60: 244–252.

NETHERSOLE-THOMPSON, D. and A. WATSON. 1974. *The Cairngorms*. London.

ROBSON, R. W. 1956. The breeding of the Dipper in north Westmorland. *Bird Study* 3: 170–180.

SHOOTER, P. 1970. The Dipper population of Derbyshire, 1958–68. *Brit. Birds* 63: 158–163.

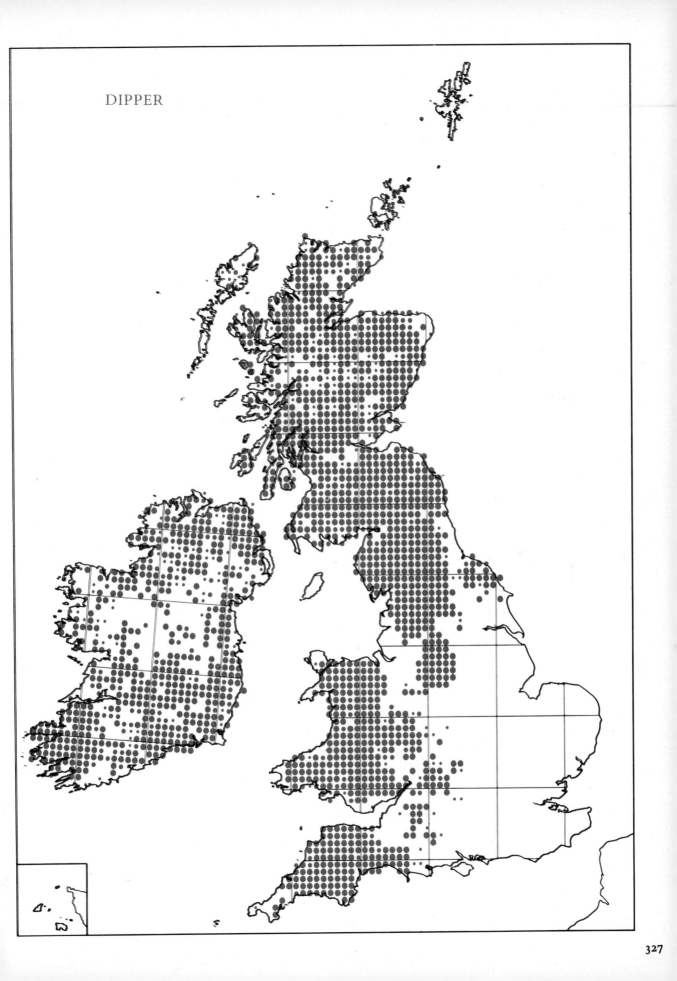

DIPPER

Bearded Tit

Panurus biarmicus

Bearded Tits (or Bearded Reedlings, as they are also known) are confined to reed-beds, usually extensive ones with *Phragmites* predominating. Their distinctive shape and twanging call, together with the restricted breeding habitat, make it unlikely that they were overlooked during the *Atlas* survey.

Early in the 19th century, this species could be found in suitable habitat over much of E England from Lincolnshire south through the coastal counties to Kent, thence west to Hampshire, as well as at inland sites in East Anglia and along the River Thames into Berkshire. The destruction of reed-beds by drainage and reclamation schemes, however, coupled with persecution of the species by collectors for both eggs and skins and by trappers for sale as cage-birds, led to a contraction of range and a decline in numbers. By the end of the last century, the Norfolk Broads were the stronghold, with only a few pairs remaining in Suffolk, Essex and a few south coast sites.

Bearded Tits are sometimes seriously affected by hard winters. Those of 1916/17, 1939/40 and 1946/47, for example, were particularly disastrous, while others which were as cold, or even colder, have had relatively little influence on numbers. Thus, after 1962/63, the worst winter of the century, the British population fell by little more than a half whereas it had been nearly extinguished by the less severe one of 1946/47. The determining factor is the amount of snow. Frosts alone, no matter how severe, rarely prevent the Bearded Tits from finding their staple winter diet of *Phragmites* seeds. Heavy snowfalls, or thick layers of glazed ice, on the other hand, cover the reed litter and shut off the food supply.

During this century, the winter of 1946/47 was undoubtedly the most damaging. The British population was reduced to a very few pairs in Suffolk, while only a single male was seen in Norfolk. The Dutch population fared almost as badly and the whole W European stock may have fallen to no more than 100 pairs. Recovery in England may have been assisted by birds from the Continent, for the numbers increased well until the North Sea floods of 1953

inundated and laid waste many breeding areas. Another quick recovery followed, and 185 pairs were estimated to be breeding in East Anglia by 1959. Following a productive nesting season, the fine, anticyclonic autumn of that year saw the start of the eruptive behaviour which has been a prelude to dispersal in most subsequent autumns. Small breeding groups became established elsewhere, and the expansion has continued, though checked for three or four years by the winter of 1962/63. In the Netherlands at this time, the vast tracts of suitable reed-beds produced by land reclamation in the IJsselmeer were estimated to hold 20,000 Bearded Tits during the autumn, and ringing began to show evidence of movements between there and England (Mead and Pearson 1974).

Whether the dramatic recovery from the ill-effects of the 1946/47 cold winter was due to the injection of new blood from central Europe, where the birds might be better adapted to cope with cold winters (Spitzer 1972), or to 'catastrophic selection' within the remnant population of East Anglia (Richards 1975), may never be known. It is certain, however, that this is now a dynamic species, having founded new colonies in Britain, settled in Denmark, and established a firm foothold in Sweden during the recent run of mild winters (Olsson 1975). Not only should the large traditional reed-beds, several of which are now nature reserves, keep their regular breeding stocks, but new sites are likely to be occupied if the present climatic regime in W Europe continues. It is likely that the breeding population of England was about 400 pairs in 1972.

This species is afforded special protection in Great Britain under Schedule I of the Protection of Birds Act, 1954–67.

Number of 10-km squares in which recorded:
  45 (1%)
Possible breeding   6 (13%)
Probable breeding   4 (9%)
Confirmed breeding   35 (78%)

Though some records were originally submitted in confidence, all dots are now shown accurately (as recommended by the Rare Breeding Birds Panel)

References

AXELL, H. E. 1966. Eruptions of Bearded Tits during 1959–65. *Brit. Birds* 59: 513–543.

MEAD, C. J. and D. J. PEARSON. 1974. Bearded Reedling populations in England and Holland. *Bird Study* 21: 211–214.

OLSSON, V. 1975. Bearded Reedling populations in Scandinavia. *Bird Study* 22: 116–118.

O'SULLIVAN, J. 1976. Bearded Tits in Britain 1966–74. *Brit. Birds* in press.

PEARSON, D. J. 1975. Moult and its relation to eruptive activity in the Bearded Reedling. *Bird Study* 22: 205–227.

RICHARDS, A. J. 1975. Bearded Reedling populations in England and Holland. *Bird Study* 22: 118.

SPITZER, G. 1972. Jahreszeitliche Aspekte der Biologie der Bartmeise (*Panurus biarmicus*). *J. Orn.* 113: 241–275.

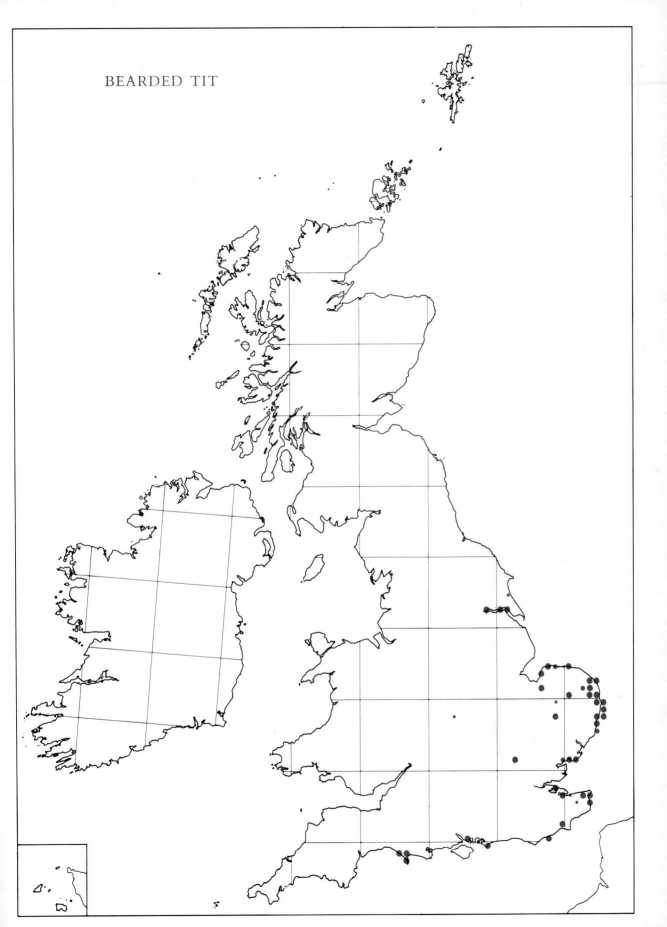

BEARDED TIT

Mistle Thrush

Turdus viscivorus

Mistle Thrushes are birds of woodland edge or open country with scattered trees and bushes. As such, they have adapted readily to farmland with its mosaic of open fields and hedgerows with trees. They thrive in the larger suburban parks and gardens, and are often to be seen feeding on lawns and playing fields in and near towns. In moorland regions and on islands, where trees are absent, they may nest in walls or among rocks and sometimes even on the ground.

The loud, rather repetitive, fluted song carries a long way, and is uttered from late December onwards from a high vantage point in a tree. The defiant notes, often heard in the teeth of a winter gale, have given the species the local name of 'storm-cock'. The breeding season begins early, eggs being laid at the end of February or in early March during warm springs; Snow (1969) showed that even in N Britain the first clutches are normally started before the end of March.

Two, sometimes three, broods are reared by each pair, and nesting activity persists until the end of June. The adults are often noisy at the nest, but the spotted juveniles, attended by their parents, perhaps afford the easiest confirmation of breeding. Early nests seem to be more successful than later ones, and Snow (1969) has suggested that this advantage arises in two ways: first, early nesting birds are likely to be the older, more experienced pairs; and, secondly, since so few other species are then nesting, predators will not be actively hunting for eggs and young.

The map shows a wide distribution in Britain and Ireland, a situation which would have astonished 18th century ornithologists, for this species was then apparently largely restricted to S England and Wales, being very scarce or absent in N England and Scotland. The first record of a Mistle Thrush in Ireland was not until 1800; breeding was proved a few years afterwards in Down and in 1807 in Louth.

It has been suggested that the past distribution, which was much like that of the mistletoe today, was imposed on the bird by its partiality to that plant. Despite its vernacular name, however, a survey of the fruit-eating habits of British thrushes (Hartley 1954) revealed no records of mistletoe being eaten by this species in Britain, and Hardy (1969) pointed out that there was every reason to suppose that the name came from its habit of feeding on the red berries of another species of mistletoe, which is a common parasite of olives in the Mediterranean countries. Mistle Thrushes probably prefer yew and holly berries where they are available, rather than the haws taken by Blackbirds *T. merula* and wintering Fieldfares *T. pilaris* and Redwings *T. iliacus*.

The increase and spread in the first half of the 18th century was staggering. Within about 40 years of first nesting in Ireland, all counties there had been colonised; in the same period, the Mistle Thrush also became a familiar bird in S Scotland and a few were recorded breeding farther north. The population growth continued steadily in both countries, so that by the 1950s the species was breeding in all mainland counties, though sparsely in the far north, and on many of the islands of the Inner Hebrides. The single record for the Outer Hebrides in the *Atlas* period is from the woodlands of Stornoway Castle, where sporadic nesting has been recorded for almost 70 years; there have been some Orkney breeding records in the past, but none during 1968–72.

The reasons behind this range extension are obscure, although as early as 1834 Sir William Jardine noted the species' frequency in Dumfriesshire as a 'consequence of the increased extent of plantations'. This can hardly be the only reason, however, since over much of Europe the Mistle Thrush has changed in recent times from being a shy bird of the mountains to one well able to live in close proximity to man. It is badly hit by severe weather, yet flourished despite the fact that the last century (with the exception of the 1850s) was notorious for hard winters. The Common Birds Census index in 1963, after the extreme winter of 1962/63, was less than a quarter of the 1962 level, which was not regained until 1968.

Mistle Thrush territories are generally large, and there are few CBC areas with densities of more than ten pairs per km². In 1972, the farmland average was 1.9 and the woodland 4.9 pairs. There are, however, some heathlands, as in the New Forest (Hampshire), where this species is more common than the Song Thrush *T. philomelos* and some moorland areas where it outnumbers both the Song Thrush and the Blackbird combined. Allowing an average of 100–200 pairs per occupied 10-km square, the total population may be about 300,000–600,000 breeding pairs, around the middle of the 100,000–1,000,000 pairs given as a range by Parslow.

Number of 10-km squares in which recorded:
3,395 (88%)
Possible breeding   93 (3%)
Probable breeding   104 (3%)
Confirmed breeding   3,198 (94%)

References

HARDY, E. 1969. Mistle Thrushes and mistletoe berries. *Bird Study* 16: 191–192.

HARTLEY, P. H. T. 1954. Wild fruits in the diet of British thrushes. *Brit. Birds* 47: 97–107.

SNOW, D. W. 1969. Some vital statistics of British Mistle Thrushes. *Bird Study* 16: 34–44.

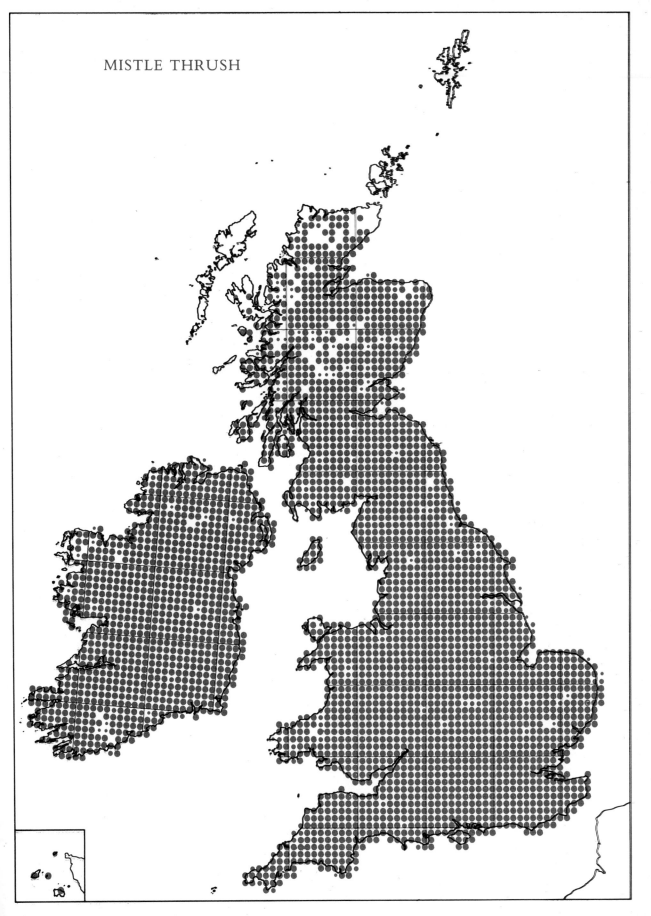

MISTLE THRUSH

Fieldfare

Turdus pilaris

In Scandinavia, breeding Fieldfares are to be found in habitats so diverse and far apart as the city parks and gardens of Stockholm and the willow/birch scrub of the low alpine zone above the tree limit in Lapland. Between these extremes, they also nest in birch, alder and mixed woods of valleys and hillsides, and in lowland farming country. In Britain, also, this species has already nested in a fairly wide range of habitats: scrub in moorland valleys, wooded hill slopes, farmland, forestry plantations and woodland edges. Scottish nests have been recorded on the ground (in grass tussocks and heather on the banks of a ditch or stream) and up to 8 m above the ground in elder, oak, sycamore and conifers. Like those of the Redwing *T. iliacus*, nest sites are often close to water.

The Fieldfare's nest is not unlike that of the Blackbird *T. merula*, reinforced with a layer of mud below the grass lining. The five or six eggs are usually similar in coloration to a Blackbird's. Incubation and fledging periods total about one month and there is sometimes a second brood in July. Like Mistle Thrushes *T. viscivorus*, adult Fieldfares can be very aggressive to other birds, and also to human intruders, in the vicinity of the nest and when they have newly fledged young.

Though bold and noisy on the nesting grounds, Fieldfares have an undistinguished song. The species is often a colonial nester on the Continent (especially in birch scrub or woods), which makes location easy, but isolated pairs in Britain are less easy to find. In late spring, paired birds appear to wander, showing interest in a place for a few days and then disappearing, so that definite territories are by no means easy to pinpoint. The scattered nature of the records suggests that there may well have been pairs, prospecting or settled, which were overlooked. Nevertheless, the *Atlas* map, being a composite of five years' records, inevitably exaggerates the picture for any one season.

The first known breeding in Britain was in 1967, a year in which Fieldfares were observed unusually late in spring: a nest, from which three young fledged, was found in Orkney in June and there is a distinct possibility that breeding also occurred in Co Durham, where a pair and three juveniles were seen in mid-July. Subsequently, breeding became annual in Shetland, with two or three pairs present in 1968, 1969 and 1970. Until the final *Atlas* year there had been only one confirmed nest on the Scottish mainland (E Inverness-shire in 1970), but in 1972 pairs were located in Banffshire, Aberdeenshire, N Kincardineshire and Perthshire. Details of some English breeding records remain confidential, but the southernmost were in Derbyshire in 1969 and 1970 (and probably again in 1974); in 1974, certainly one and probably two pairs nested in Staffordshire. By this last year, although no more than half a dozen pairs had been found breeding in any one season, the records were becoming more widely dispersed in Scotland and the N and S Pennines.

For over 100 years the Fieldfare has been slowly extending its breeding range westwards in Europe south of the Baltic. Formerly occurring from the USSR through Poland into E Germany, it spread into W Germany during the second half of the last century and continues to expand there. Switzerland was reached in 1923 and the French Jura in 1953, and there have been nesting records in the Netherlands. Fieldfares began breeding in Denmark in 1965 and colonisation has proceeded rapidly (Skov 1970); and in 1967, the year the species first nested in Orkney, they were also discovered in Belgium (Arnhem 1967). The 1968–72 distribution of British breeding records (all north of 53°N) points, however, to a link with Scandinavian rather than central European stock.

This species is afforded special protection in Great Britain under Schedule I of the Protection of Birds Act, 1954–67.

Number of 10-km squares in which recorded: 35 (0.9%)
Possible breeding   17 (49%)
Probable breeding   3 (9%)
Confirmed breeding   15 (43%)

Two dots have been moved by one 10-km square (as recommended by the Rare Breeding Birds Panel)

References

ARNHEM, R. 1967. Première découverte en Belgique d'une colonie de Grives Litornes (*Turdus pilaris*). *Aves* 4: 117–122.

BALFOUR, E. 1968. Fieldfares breeding in Orkney. *Scott. Birds* 5: 31–32.

PICOZZI, N. 1973. Fieldfares breeding on the Scottish mainland, 1972–1973. *Scott. Birds* 7: 406–408.

SKOV, H. 1970. Antallet af ynglende Sjaggere (*Turdus pilaris*) i Thy fordoblet. *Dansk Orn. Foren. Tidsskr.* 64: 271–272.

WEIR, D. N. 1970. Fieldfares breeding in East Inverness-shire. *Scott. Birds* 6: 212–213.

WILLIAMSON, K. 1975. Birds and climatic change. *Bird Study* 22: 143–164.

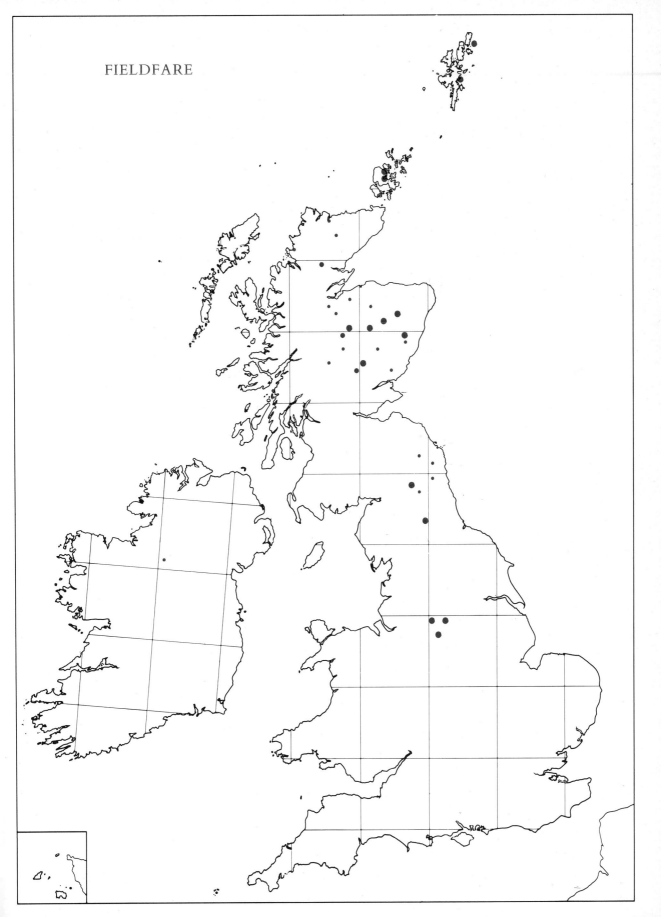

FIELDFARE

Song Thrush

Turdus philomelos

In Britain and Ireland, Song Thrushes breed in almost any habitat with trees or bushes. Woodland edges, farms, hedgerows and bushy commons are especially favoured, and suburban gardens and parks in city centres may hold good numbers. Bare moorland and mountain are almost the only unoccupied habitats on the mainland, but, provided that there is some heather or similar cover, even remote islands often have breeding pairs.

Robert Browning's 'That's the wise thrush; he sings each song twice over . . .' is so familiar that the repetitious phrases of the Song Thrush are known and correctly identified even by non–ornithologists. The majority of nests are built within 2 m of the ground, and the smooth mud lining and spotted, blue eggs are as diagnostic as the song. The conspicuous behaviour of the adults when feeding young, and their tendency to gather food on short grassland, makes confirmation of breeding straightforward, and it is likely that most of the gaps in the map represent genuine absence.

The *Atlas* maps of the Song Thrush and Blackbird *T. merula* are similar; note, however, the absence of Song Thrushes in Shetland, where up to two dozen pairs bred during this century until the severe winter of 1946/47, and their presence in some of the far northwest mainland 10-km squares, which still lack Blackbirds. There the Song Thrushes are mainly inhabitants of the sparse hillside birch woods; the spread of Blackbirds to such areas is relatively recent. Ginn (1969) and Parslow (1973) showed that, at about the time of the 1939–45 war, annual totals of ringed nestlings, which had been higher for the Song Thrush, changed to a 3:2 majority for the Blackbird. Song Thrush numbers appear to be far more seriously affected by cold winters, and there were three severe ones during 1939–48 which may have influenced this situation. In Ireland, however, they are markedly less common than Blackbirds and are apparently still declining in numbers, even though harsh winters are almost unknown there. The Common Birds Census, relating mainly to lowland Britain, showed that

Song Thrush numbers declined to 59% of their former level as a result of the 1962/63 severe winter. At such times of prolonged bad weather, enforced movements are made to the south and west (Spencer 1964). The population recovered, however, to reach a consistently high level during 1968–72 compared with the earlier part of the decade (see graph).

On individual CBC plots, farmland breeding densities of 5–20 pairs per km² are regularly reported, and the 1972 average was 13.5. In woodland plots, the highest densities may reach 120 pairs per km², but the 1972 average was 27.1. In suburban habitats in the London area, densities similar to or exceeding those in woodland have been found (Batten 1972). It thus seems likely that a mean figure of 1,000 pairs per occupied 10-km square should be allowed when estimating the British and Irish population. This gives a total of about 3,500,000 pairs, but the 1963 figure, following two harsh winters, may have barely exceeded 1,000,000 pairs.

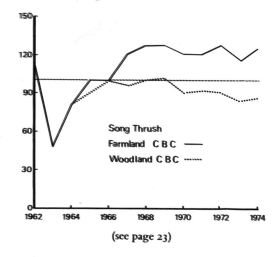

Song Thrush
Farmland C B C ——
Woodland C B C ------

(see page 23)

Number of 10-km squares in which recorded:
3,659 (95%)
Possible breeding   35 (1%)
Probable breeding   66 (2%)
Confirmed breeding   3,558 (97%)

References
BATTEN, L. A. 1972. The past and present bird life of the Brent Reservoir and its vicinity. *London Nat.* 50: 8–62.
GINN, H. B. 1969. The use of annual ringing and nest record card totals as indicators of bird population levels. *Bird Study* 16: 210–248.
HARTLEY, P. H. T. 1954. Wild fruits in the diet of British thrushes. *Brit. Birds* 47: 97–107.
MYRES, M. T. 1955. The breeding of Blackbird, Song Thrush and Mistle Thrush in Great Britain. Part 1. Breeding seasons. *Bird Study* 2: 2–24.
SNOW, D. W. 1955. The breeding of Blackbird, Song Thrush and Mistle Thrush in Great Britain. Part 2. Clutch size. *Bird Study* 2: 72–84.
SPENCER, R. 1964. Report on bird ringing for 1963. *Brit. Birds* 57: 525–582.

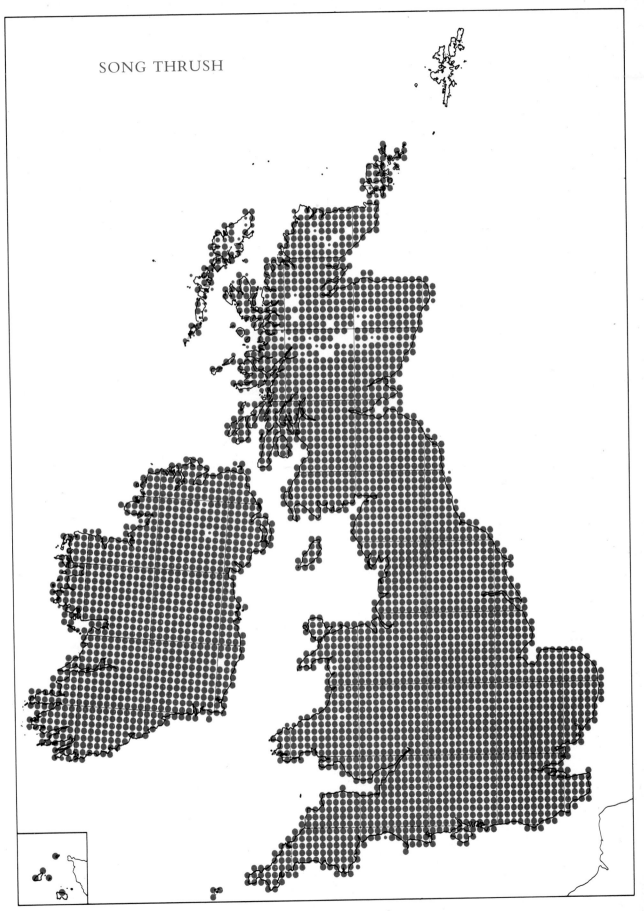

SONG THRUSH

Redwing

Turdus iliacus

Redwings occur in a wide variety of habitats in Scotland. Natural sites in Wester Ross include hillside birch woods, the edges of oak woods, and grassy areas with coppiced alders and gorse, often close to running water; nests have been found under earth banks and among the roots of windblown trees. Elsewhere, the vicinity of large houses with lawns, shrubberies and tall trees is favoured, and there are few in natural birch woodland or pine forest. Breeding has even occurred on treeless Fair Isle (Shetland).

The version of the song heard in Scotland is very distinctive and is often delivered from a high and prominent perch, such as a rock, tree or overhead wire. It consists of a series of four to seven, but most commonly five, descending fluted notes of such tone and volume as to be audible at a considerable distance, particularly in the wide glens which are often frequented. Indeed, it is so distinctive and penetrating that, like the songs of the Cuckoo *Cuculus canorus* and the Chiffchaff *Phylloscopus collybita*, it can be picked out even above the engine noise in a fast travelling car. Thus, although the incidence of singing declines as breeding progresses, initial location of territories is easy early in the season. Nest-finding presents no greater problem with this species than with other thrushes, and the process is made easier by the anxious behaviour and double, chattering alarm notes of the adults when the nest is approached.

The Redwing breeds in the boreal zone from Scandinavia, south of about 70°N, NE Germany and Poland eastwards as far as the Kolyma in NE Siberia. On the Continent, it is an important constituent of the birch forest avifauna, and beyond the tree limit occurs in willow and birch scrub on the tundra. One can deduce that the species has been established for a very long time in Iceland, since the form there, *T. i. coburni*, is larger and darker than the Continental subspecies, *T. i. iliacus*. Since 1928, *coburni* has nested regularly in mixed deciduous and coniferous plantation in the Faeroes; the pair which bred on Fair Isle in 1935 is said to have belonged to this race, which also winters in W Scotland and Ireland.

The Scandinavian population is markedly migratory, vast movements in some years having an eruptive quality, while ringing recoveries show that individuals may winter in widely separated areas in successive years. Colonisation of Scotland may owe something to such invasions, although Williamson (1975) has suggested that the rapid growth in the population in the last decade, as in the case of the Fieldfare *T. pilaris*, is more likely to be due to migrants returning from S Europe and being displaced to the Highlands by easterly winds.

The first known case of nesting in Scotland was in Sutherland in 1925. Breeding was reported in only 17 of the next 41 years, with a total of fewer than 30 records, including an attempt by one pair in Co Kerry in 1951. The location of seven pairs in Scotland in 1967 and the discovery of as many as 20 pairs in Wester Ross alone in 1968 suggested that this species had established a firm foothold. The totals found in Scotland in subsequent years were 21 pairs in 1969, a minimum of six pairs in 1970, some 40–50 holding territory in 1971, and 12 pairs confirmed as breeding (as well as another 30 or so males holding territory) in 1972. Increased observer activity in the *Atlas* years of 1968–72 undoubtedly boosted these totals. Racial identification of Redwings is difficult in the field and the affinities of the Scottish birds are not known, but it has been claimed that most appear to belong to the Continental race.

Though the total discovered in a single year has never exceeded 50 holding territory and 25 pairs confirmed breeding, a calculation based on the number of potential sites and the proportion of those visited at which Redwings were discovered, suggested a 1972 population of about 300 pairs in Scotland.

This species is afforded special protection in Great Britain under Schedule I of the Protection of Birds Act, 1954–67.

Number of 10-km squares in which recorded:
111 (3%)

Possible breeding   32 (29%)
Probable breeding   25 (23%)
Confirmed breeding   54 (49%)

Though some records were originally submitted in confidence, all dots are now shown accurately (as recommended by the Rare Breeding Birds Panel)

References

FERGUSON-LEES, I. J. 1966. Editorial comment on Redwings breeding in Scotland. *Brit. Birds* 59: 500–501.

SHARROCK, J. T. R. 1972. Habitat of Redwings in Scotland. *Scott. Birds* 7: 208–209.

SHARROCK, J. T. R. *et al.* 1975. Rare breeding birds in the United Kingdom in 1973 and 1974. *Brit. Birds* 68: 5–23, 489–506.

WILLIAMSON, K. 1958. Autumn immigration of Redwings into Fair Isle. *Ibis* 100: 582–604.

WILLIAMSON, K. 1973. Habitat of Redwings in Wester Ross. *Scott. Birds* 7: 268–269.

WILLIAMSON, K. 1975. Birds and climatic change. *Bird Study* 22: 143–164.

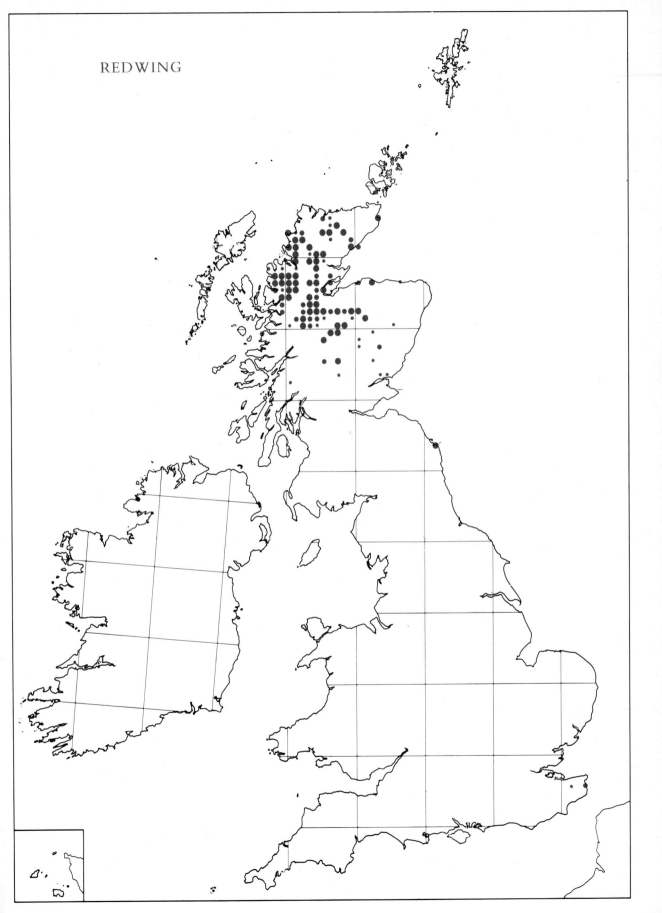

REDWING

Ring Ouzel

Turdus torquatus

The Ring Ouzel is essentially a bird of mountain and moorland, its distribution closely following that of high ground throughout most of Britain and Ireland. A pair's nesting territory nearly always contains a crag, gully, gill or clough, sometimes with a few bushes or stunted trees, and only rarely extends over an area of uniform moorland. In some coastal regions a few pairs may nest on sea-cliffs, but over 90% of nests are higher than 250 m (Flegg and Glue 1975). The highest, often from areas of scree or loose boulder slopes, are over 1,000 m, and individuals have been heard singing at up to 1,200 m in the Cairngorms.

The Ring Ouzel's penetrating whistle and disjointed song carry for long distances over the hill ground, and, provided the observer can get away from the sound of running water and wind, it is by voice that most birds will first be recorded. Search with binoculars will then often reveal the male on a prominent perch. Most spend the winter in S Europe or N Africa, but the earliest returning migrants may arrive in mid-March in the south, though not until April in the north and even early May at the highest sites. Many pairs are double-brooded, and song may continue until the end of June. In late summer, the families often join together to form loose flocks, feeding on various moorland berries.

The nest is frequently on a ledge of rock. Most sites are natural, but a third of nest record cards refer to walls, buildings (usually derelict), quarries, potholes or mine-shafts, including some as much as 5 m below ground level. Most other nests were on grass or heather slopes and less than 2% were in trees (Flegg and Glue 1975). Nests may be very difficult to find and the habitat often affords little chance of watching back, so the best methods of confirming breeding are to watch for adults with food for the young, and noisy family parties shortly after fledging.

The Ring Ouzel has undoubtedly declined in Britain and Ireland during the last 100 years. Baxter and Rintoul (1953), reviewing its fortunes in Scotland, concluded that it had decreased so much during the previous 30 years that it was in danger of being lost as a breeding species. The situation is certainly not as serious as that and, although reports of reductions come from all parts of Scotland, there seem to be few areas from which is has completely gone. Indeed, *Atlas* records from Orkney, Shetland and the Outer Hebrides may indicate a recent spread; this coincides with a considerable increase in the number of spring migrants in recent years. Elsewhere in Britain, there may have been a decrease in S Wales, and breeding may have ceased in Cornwall and the Isle of Man. Up to the end of the 19th century, there were a number of scattered breeding records in lowland England, but such extralimital nesting has not been reported in this century.

In Ireland, the situation has deteriorated even more. Ussher and Warren (1900) considered that the Ring Ouzel bred in all but five of the 32 Irish counties. By 1950, it had disappeared from many, and was probably very thin on the ground even in areas where still present (Kennedy *et al* 1953). Within the next decade it had been lost to five more counties (Ruttledge 1966), and the sad state of its current fortunes in Ireland can be seen from the map, though it must be pointed out that some potential sites were not thoroughly searched during 1968–72.

These changes have been attributed partly to the increase in numbers and range expansion of the Blackbird *T. merula*. The *Atlas* revealed only two 10-km squares on the mainland of Britain and Ireland without either species, and only 3% of those with Ring Ouzels lacked Blackbirds. Interspecific competition may thus have been a cause. Williamson (1975) has, however, linked some changes in distribution with the trends of our climate, and it is probable that the amelioration of the first half of the century caused the Ring Ouzel, a distinctly montane species, to retreat, whilst encouraging the lowland Blackbird to spread to higher altitudes. This may have had a greater effect in Ireland where there is much less high ground on which the Ring Ouzel might be expected to hold its own.

Particularly favoured 10-km squares may regularly hold several dozen pairs, but there will also be many with only one or two. The average is probably about 10–20 pairs and the British and Irish population may number about 8,000–16,000 pairs, at or above the upper end of Parslow's range of 1,000–10,000.

Number of 10-km squares in which recorded:
780 (20%)
Possible breeding   108 (14%)
Probable breeding   155 (20%)
Confirmed breeding   517 (66%)

References

FLEGG, J. J. M. and D. E. GLUE. 1975. The nesting of the Ring Ousel. *Bird Study* 22: 1–8.

SPENCER, R. 1975. Changes in the distribution of recoveries of ringed Blackbirds. *Bird Study* 22: 177–190.

USSHER, R. J. and R. WARREN. 1900. *The Birds of Ireland*. London.

WILLIAMSON, K. 1975. Birds and climatic change. *Bird Study* 22: 143–164.

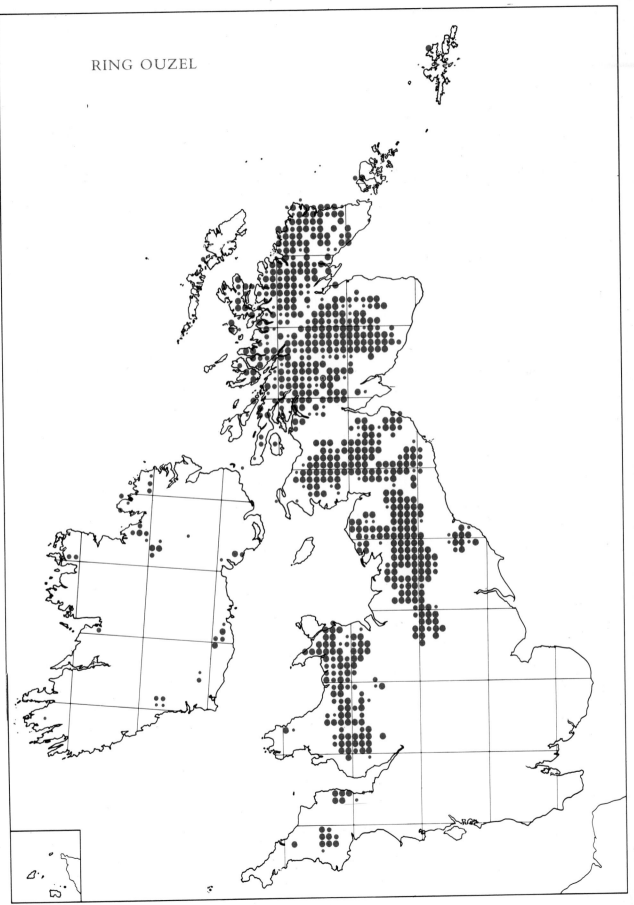

RING OUZEL

Blackbird

Turdus merula

The Blackbird is one of our most familiar birds and is found throughout Britain and Ireland in a variety of habitats. It seems likely that at one time most Blackbirds frequented woodland edge rather than high forest. They were thus able to adapt very successfully to coppice-with-standards management from early mediaeval times, and over the last 150–200 years have ventured out of the woodlands to colonise farmland hedgerows, parks and policies, moorland edge, suburban gardens and even highly urban areas, such as the London squares. Apart from areas consisting of bare moorland and mountain, or containing sparse highland birch woods, the *Atlas* indicates that the Blackbird is ubiquitous.

Studies of the population dynamics of Blackbirds in various habitats have shown that nesting success is higher on farmland and in the suburban environment (particularly gardens) than in woodland. An increased productivity enables London's Blackbirds to maintain their population level despite a higher average annual adult mortality—due largely to traffic, and predation by cats during the breeding season—than occurs in rural populations (Snow and Mayer-Gross 1967, Batten 1973).

Blackbirds are fairly sedentary in the south of their range, but are partial migrants in the north (Snow 1966). They have benefited greatly from the climatic amelioration and during this century the major changes in distribution have involved the colonisation of Shetland, various other Scottish islands and the Faeroes, and a westwards spread in Ireland into Kerry, Mayo and Donegal. This expansion has coincided with an even more extensive colonisation of N Scandinavia (Kalela 1949, Spencer 1975). Nest record card totals show that, since the 1930s, Blackbirds have outstripped Song Thrushes *T. philomelos* in abundance, and are still maintaining this position (Ginn 1969). It has been suggested that hard winters, which affect Blackbirds less severely than Song Thrushes, have contributed to this situation. After the 1962/63 winter, the Common Birds Census population index for the Song Thrush declined by 57%, while that for the Blackbird dropped only 18%.

Throughout most of Britain and Ireland this is such a common bird that discovery and confirmation of breeding is exceedingly easy, even a mid-winter walk along any farm hedgerow providing evidence in the form of an old nest. This is reflected in the high proportion of confirmed breeding records. There is a considerable overlap with Song Thrushes in the sites chosen, though Blackbirds often nest lower down in trees and in banks, or on fairly flat ground under vegetation such as bracken. A very wide range of trees and bushes are used, as well as many man-made structures. The rich, fluted song, which can be heard over long distances, is considered by many to be among the most beautiful of all bird sounds. The breeding season lasts usually from March to July, although warm weather at either end of the normal season can stimulate breeding. Snow (1955) described the abnormal nesting of Blackbirds in the winter of 1953/54: of 13 nests started between November and January, young hatched in at least five and fledged in three.

The Blackbird was rated as abundant (over 1,000,000 pairs) by Parslow. CBC results show presence on virtually all lowland farms, with a mean density in 1972 of 35.7 pairs per km². Woodland densities, though variable, averaged 66.2 pairs per km² in 1972, while 75 pairs per km² has been recorded in fairly dense hawthorn scrub. In suburbia, Blackbirds reach a density of around 250 pairs per km² (Batten 1973). With high densities in towns and suburbs, yet much lower ones where bare mountain and moorland predominate, an average in excess of 2,000 pairs per 10-km square seems probable, in which case there may be over seven million pairs in Britain and Ireland.

Number of 10-km squares in which recorded:
3,718 (96%)
Possible breeding   36 (1%)
Probable breeding   68 (2%)
Confirmed breeding   3,614 (97%)

References

BATTEN, L. A. 1973. Population dynamics of suburban Blackbirds. *Bird Study* 20: 251–258.
GINN, H. B. 1969. The use of annual ringing and nest record card totals as indicators of population levels. *Bird Study* 16: 210–248.
KALELA, O. 1949. Changes in geographical ranges in the avifauna of northern and central Europe in relation to recent changes in climate. *Bird Banding* 20: 77–103.
SNOW, D. W. 1955. The abnormal breeding of birds in the winter of 1953/54. *Brit. Birds* 48: 120–126.
SNOW, D. W. 1958. *A Study of Blackbirds*. London.
SNOW, D. W. 1966. The migration and dispersal of British Blackbirds. *Bird Study* 13: 237–255.
SNOW, D. W. and H. MAYER-GROSS. 1967. Farmland as a nesting habitat. *Bird Study* 14: 43–52.
SPENCER, R. 1975. Changes in the distribution of recoveries of ringed Blackbirds. *Bird Study* 22: 177–190.

BLACKBIRD

Wheatear

Oenanthe oenanthe

The Wheatear is characteristic of the remoter uplands in Britain and Ireland and colonises lowland regions to any extent only where the grazing of sheep or Rabbits maintains a short turf. In S England, some of the remaining heaths and chalk downlands have a few breeding pairs, though with the cessation of grazing and the reduction of Rabbits through myxomatosis many such areas are now too scrub-grown to be attractive. Coastal shingle and cliff-top brows are sometimes tenanted, and ideal conditions are provided by many of the small islands off the west coasts of Ireland, Scotland and Wales. Among the mountains and moorlands of the north and west, dry-stone walls, rocks and screes provide nest sites, and breeding in the Scottish Highlands has been recorded regularly at up to 1,200 m. In Scotland and N England, Wheatears tend to nest along roadsides where the short turf provides a feeding zone and the walls afford nest holes. In some areas, such as SW Ireland, there is a distinct hiatus between the coastal nesting birds near sea-level and those of the loose boulders and scree in the mountains above 250 m, even though these may both be in the same 10-km square.

Wheatears are summer visitors to Britain and Ireland, occasionally arriving in February, but usually in March or early April. Their habit of perching prominently on small eminences makes them conspicuous on grassland and ploughed ground, as well as on walls and rocks, and they have a loud 'chak' call-note and lively though rather unmusical song. They are thus easy to find and, when the adults are feeding young in or out of the nest, it is not difficult to prove breeding. In S Britain, where few now nest, migrants are observed at apparently suitable breeding sites throughout April and May, the later ones often of the large Greenland race *O. o. leucorrhoa*. Most of the possible breeding records in lowland Britain probably refer to such migrants, which quite often explore burrows and holes without staying to breed.

The first clutch may be in mid-April, but most pairs do not nest until May. Lowland nesting Wheatears regularly have two broods, but northern birds and those at high altitudes normally have only one. The nest is often in scree-slopes or under boulders in mountainous areas, but any hole, natural or artificial, may be used. Rabbit burrows are particularly favoured by downland pairs; on the shingle at Dungeness (Kent), sites are provided by old corrugated iron sheets and ammunition boxes sunk into the shingle.

In S England, breeding has been declining for many years. In Sussex, for example, this was a typical species of the South Downs in the 19th century. The local shepherds did a good trade in birds taken for eating until 70 or 80 years ago. This persecution did not diminish the numbers, but the gradual drift away from sheep farming, which had kept the turf short and ideal for Wheatears, began to affect the population, and a gradual decline was detected even in the 1930s. The loss of much marginal land to the plough during the 1939–45 war also accelerated the decline. In East Anglia, the pressures of farming and the decline in Rabbit numbers were combined with a third threat, the planting of conifers, so that only a few of the coastal areas of Suffolk and Norfolk now have breeding Wheatears. Parslow noted that declines took place in almost every county in England south of Lancashire and Yorkshire. In Ireland also, there has been a recent decline in the inland counties, and the map shows few breeding there now. In Scotland, no long-term population trends have been detected.

There are few indications of Wheatear breeding densities in the literature and, since roadsides are attractive to them, impressions gained from motoring through moorland areas may lead to overestimates. Breeding densities from Fair Isle in the northeast, and Cape Clear Island in the southwest, show that such favoured sites may hold 10 or more pairs per km^2, and a similar density has been found in the W Yorkshire Pennines. Conder (1956) showed that territories on Skokholm (Pembrokeshire) ranged from 0.5 to 3.2 ha, but there can be very few parts of the country where Wheatears are as densely packed as that. On a Westmorland farm, about four pairs per km^2 nested annually for ten years. Allowing about one-tenth of this density throughout the 10-km squares where breeding was proved or probable, the total British and Irish population might be about 80,000 pairs, in the upper part of Parslow's suggested range of 10,000–100,000.

Number of 10-km squares in which recorded:
2,408 (62%)
Possible breeding   373 (15%)
Probable breeding   229 (10%)
Confirmed breeding   1,806 (75%)

References

CONDER, P. J. 1956. The territory of the Wheatear *Oenanthe oenanthe*. *Ibis* 98: 453–459.

ROBSON, R. W. and K. WILLIAMSON. 1972. The breeding birds of a Westmorland farm. *Bird Study* 19: 202–214.

WILLIAMSON, K. 1968. Bird communities in the Malham Tarn region of the Pennines. *Field Studies* 2: 651–668.

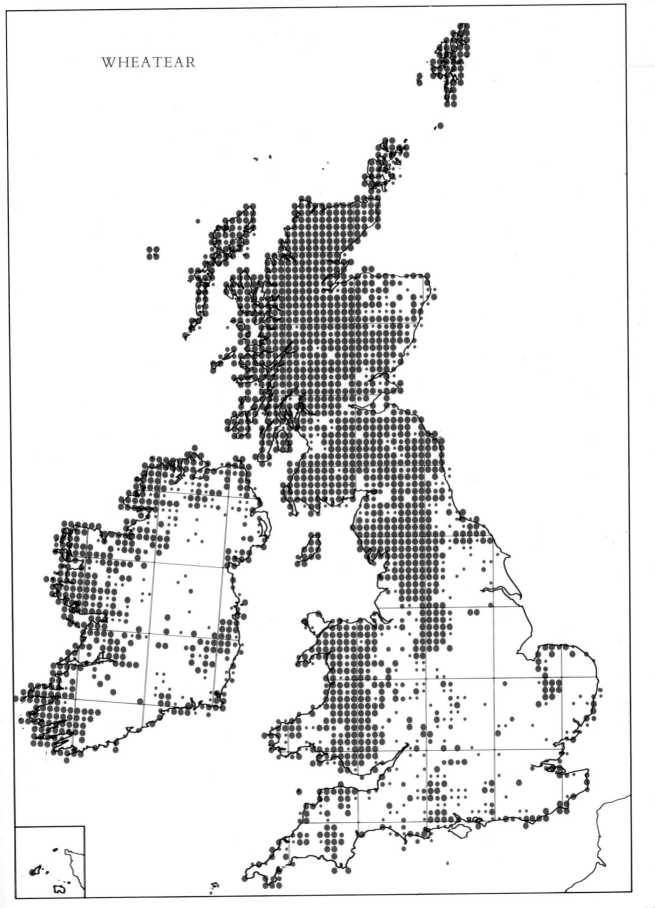

WHEATEAR

Stonechat

Saxicola torquata

In Britain and Ireland, Stonechats are found typically in rough, coastal country with a combination of gorse and heather or bracken with close-cropped grass. When the population level is high there is considerable colonisation of inland heaths and commons, among gorse, heather and even low vegetation such as bramble. Young forestry plantations, with trees less than ten years old, are attractive if the ground cover is heather, but where grass predominates Whinchats *S. rubetra* are more likely to be present. Such areas are becoming an important habitat for these two species in both Britain and Ireland.

Male Stonechats are delightfully extrovert birds, perching prominently on the tops of bushes or posts, 'taccing' noisily, and making hovering flights in full view of the intruder. They are usually not easy to overlook. Many coastal territories are continuously occupied; though the same perches may be used continually for decades, Stonechats may change mates in both spring and autumn and are frequently polygamous. The breeding season is very long, with active nests from mid-March through to the end of August, and in some areas most pairs raise three broods. The nest, often in gorse or dwarf furze, is low down and is frequently entered along a short tunnel.

The nest record cards for Stonechats and Whinchats reveal some of the differences in habitat preference. Rather more Stonechats than Whinchats (45% compared with 29%) nest on heaths and moors, and many more nest on the coast (38% and 7%). The Whinchat is more frequent in agricultural situations (32% compared with 2%). This difference is reflected in nest-site selections, with a third of the Stonechats nesting in gorse but less than 5% of the Whinchats doing so; most Whinchat nests (60%) were in grass. Stonechats are the most characteristic bird of the lowland heaths of Dorset, and in this habitat they are much commoner than Whinchats.

Although ringing has shown that some Stonechats spend the winter abroad, many stay in or move to coastal localities. They are very susceptible to cold winter weather and that of 1916/17 produced a heavy mortality which was gradually made good in succeeding years. The occurrence of seven cold winters in the 24 years 1939–63 brought the numbers down to a very low level. The drastic effect of freezing conditions may be illustrated by the fate of those on Cape Clear Island (Cork), where a thriving breeding population of at least 50 pairs (possibly as many as 150) was cut by the 1961/62 winter to 15–25. The even worse weather of 1962/63 further reduced it to only three pairs in both 1963 and 1964. Yet the resilience of the species is such that there had been an increase to 33 pairs by 1967. The reduction in habitat, as marginal areas are lost to agriculture or urban development, has resulted in fragmentation; isolated pockets of inland-nesting Stonechats may be wiped out in severe weather. The series of mild winters since 1963 has resulted in a recovery in numbers and some recolonisation of inland sites, but it is doubtful if the more widespread distribution of the 19th century will ever be recaptured, despite new forestry plantations. It is the combination of the species' susceptibility to severe weather and man's activities in reducing available habitat that explains the coastal, westerly and southerly bias to the distribution, these being the areas with the mildest winters and least habitat change.

In a survey of Sussex during 1962–73, Hughes and Shrubb (1974) found 54 occupied territories in the best year (1969), an average of about two pairs per occupied 10-km square. Very much higher numbers exist in coastal squares in the west of Britain, and particularly in Ireland. On the basis of an average of 15–30 pairs per occupied 10-km square, there may have been a British and Irish population of 30,000–60,000 pairs in 1972; this is higher than Parslow's 1967 estimate of 1,000–10,000 pairs, made only four years after the severe winters of the early 1960s. Since the end of the *Atlas* survey, more inland areas have been colonised, doubtless an overspill from successful coastal populations.

Number of 10-km squares in which recorded: 2,015 (52%)
Possible breeding   200 (10%)
Probable breeding   208 (10%)
Confirmed breeding   1,607 (80%)

References

DAVIS, P. G. 1975. Observations on the nesting of some heathland birds. *Surrey Bird Rep.* 22: 56–63.

HUGHES, S. W. M. and M. SHRUBB. 1974. The breeding distribution and status of the Stonechat in Sussex 1962–73. *Sussex Bird Rep.* 26: 50–55.

JOHNSON, E. D. H. 1971. Observations on a resident population of Stonechats in Jersey. *Brit. Birds* 64: 201–213, 267–279.

MAGEE, J. D. 1965. The breeding distribution of the Stonechat in Britain and the causes of its decline. *Bird Study* 12: 83–89.

PHILLIPS, J. S. 1970. Interspecific competition in Stonechat and Whinchat. *Bird Study* 17: 320–324.

PHILLIPS, J. S. 1973. Stonechats in young forestry plantations. *Bird Study* 20: 82–84.

SHARROCK, J. T. R. and G. N. BROMFIELD. 1968. Stonechats on Cape Clear Island, 1967. *Cape Clear Bird Obs. Rep.* 9: 49–50.

STONECHAT

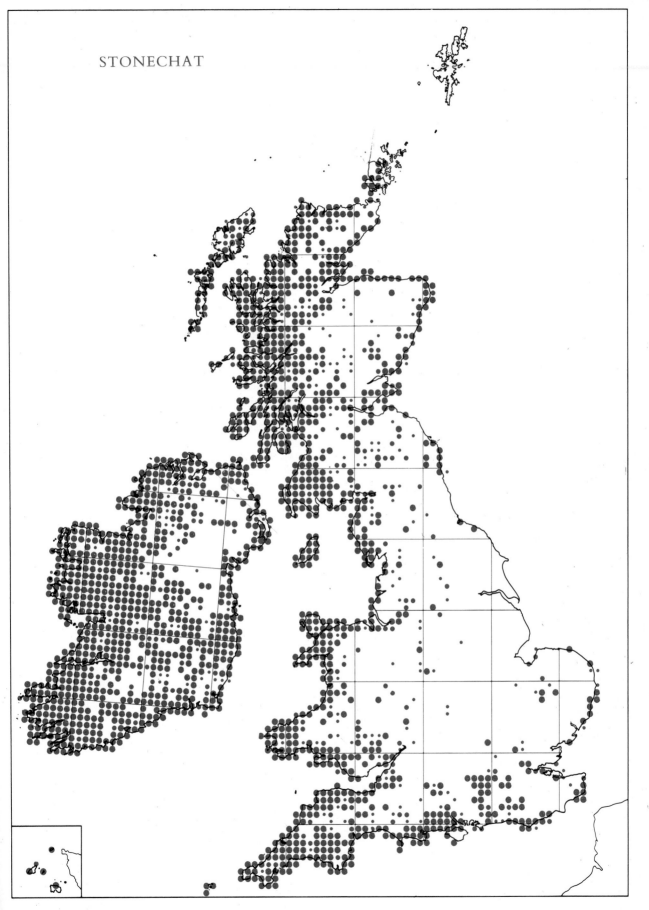

Whinchat

Saxicola rubetra

Though Whinchats nest in a variety of habitats, there is almost invariably a combination of tussocky grass and suitable song and observation posts about 1 m high. Heathland or rough ground with gorse is especially favoured, but all sorts of rough grassland from lowland water-meadows and coastal fresh marsh to the edge of moorland up to 500 m are also occupied, with tall weeds or barbed-wire fences providing suitable perches in the absence of bushes. Bracken-covered hillsides are a favourite habitat in parts of Wales, while young forestry plantations provide an ideal combination of rough grass and perches in both Britain and Ireland. There is a similar association of Whinchats with roadside verges and railway cuttings and embankments, due partly to the fences which border such areas. Provided that the two main requirements are met, almost any small piece of rough ground, even the uncultivated corner of a field in an intensive arable farming area, can support one or two pairs.

The loud and distinctive song and habit of perching prominently make Whinchats easy to locate in areas where they are common, but, since an isolated patch of suitable habitat can hold the only pair in a 10-km square outside the species' main range, birds in such situations may have been missed. Once a pair has been located, however, breeding is usually easy to prove: though the nest may be well concealed, family parties draw attention to themselves, since both the adults and the newly-fledged young 'tac' noisily. Though some of the possible breeding records may represent migrants, the large number of these in the area where the species breeds sparsely (SE of a line from the Humber to Severn) suggests that scattered pairs are probably nesting undetected. In Ireland, and probably in parts of Britain too, pairs or small groups in fringe areas may appear or disappear from one year to the next for no apparent reason.

Whinchats were formerly more widespread and common in southern and eastern England, but have declined over the past 50 or 60 years. At one time, they were numerous on roadside verges and waste ground in this region. The decline has been linked with habitat loss, but the species has disappeared from many areas where suitable habitat still remains: in Surrey, for example, it was a common nesting bird in 1900, but had become one of the rarest by 1972. Part of the reason may be the 'tidier' Britain of today, which demands the mowing of roadside verges: in Ayrshire, Gray (1974) showed that 17% fewer nests were successful on roadside verges than in gorse, but that delaying of the cutting of verges until August removed this difference. Some other factor may also have been operating nationally, however, for there are some signs of a slight recovery since the lowest level in the 1950s and early 1960s. This may have been generated by the increased areas of young forestry plantations, which are attractive to this species. The Irish distribution has changed markedly this century (Kennedy *et al* 1954, Ruttledge 1966): for instance, there was no record from Kildare before 1900, but by the 1960s that county had the greatest density of pairs.

Whinchats are now basically upland birds in Britain, with most in the north and west. Strangely, this is not true of Ireland, where the bulk of the population is in the lowland centre of the country, though Whinchats also occur at up to 300 m in the glens of some mountain areas (*cf* overlay of height of land). This may be partly explained by the Irish lowlands being wilder country than SE England, with rough pasture and old cut-away bog providing suitable habitat, but the reasons for the absence from much of the Irish uplands deserves investigation. It cannot be due to competition with Stonechats *S. torquata*, since even in Ireland the latter are sparsely distributed away from the coastal strip (a bias not shared by Whinchats).

Though the Whinchat may be locally numerous in restricted areas of ideal habitat, it must now be considered an uncommon species over Britain and Ireland as a whole. Some 10-km squares may have 50 or even 100 pairs, but there are probably few holding more than 20 or 30 and the majority have less than half a dozen. On the basis of an average of 10–20 pairs per 10-km square, there would be about 20,000–40,000 pairs, within the lower half of Parslow's range of 10,000–100,000 pairs.

Number of 10-km squares in which recorded:
1,868 (48%)
Possible breeding   224 (12%)
Probable breeding   279 (15%)
Confirmed breeding   1,365 (73%)

References

GRAY, D. B. 1972. Whinchats on a disused railway. *Bird Study* 20: 80–82.

GRAY, D. B. 1974. Breeding behaviour of Whinchats. *Bird Study* 21: 280–282.

PHILLIPS, J. S. 1970. Interspecific competition in Stonechat and Whinchat. *Bird Study* 17: 320–324.

PHILLIPS, J. S. 1973. Stonechats in young forestry plantations. *Bird Study* 20: 82–84.

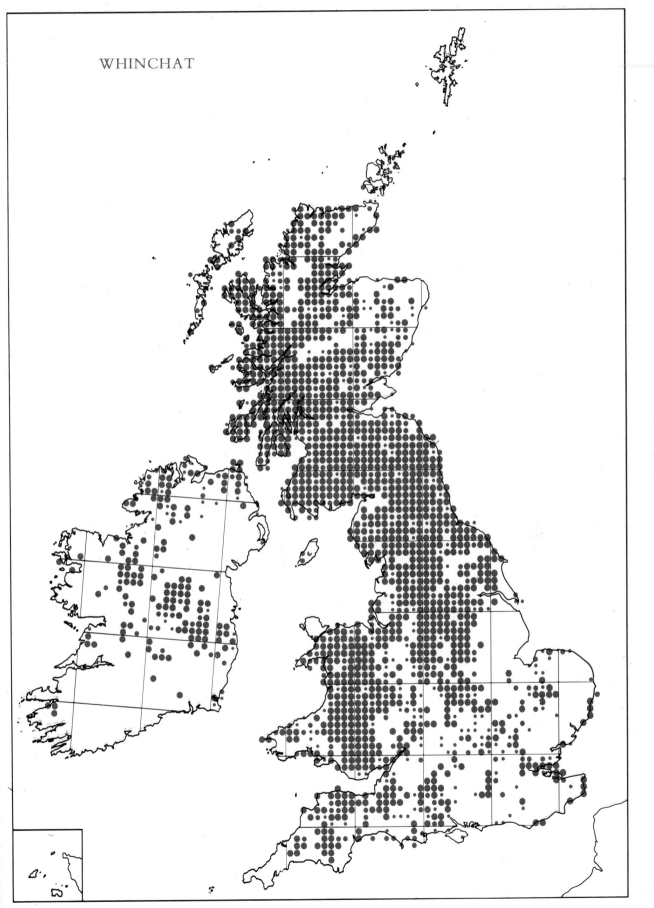

WHINCHAT

Redstart

Phoenicurus phoenicurus

The original habitat of the Redstart was probably pine-clad heath, but in Britain today it has adapted well to a variety of haunts ranging from moorland edge to mature woods in lowland valleys, and including old hedgerow trees, pollarded willows along river banks, well-timbered parks, and even orchards and gardens. In dry areas the nest may be on the ground, often at the end of a short tunnel, but throughout most of Britain the commonest sites are holes in trees or walls. On the Continent, Redstarts often occupy holes in buildings in towns and villages, similar situations to nests of Black Redstarts *P. ochruros*, and may be much commoner there than in the surrounding woodland. As might be expected, Redstarts take readily to nest-boxes, provided these have a large enough entrance hole.

The beautiful display flights of the male, his use of exposed song perches with a wide view and his method of flycatching (the female feeds more on the ground) require plenty of room for manoeuvre. The species is, therefore, more characteristic of open woodland, clearings and woodland edges than of the interior. Courtship chases take place in and out of the scattered trees, the red tails flashing; these chases often indicate the site of the future nest (Buxton 1950). Pairing, nest-building and egg-laying take place in rapid succession after arrival, with the earliest eggs at the end of April, and peak laying in about mid-May. The woodland population is probably limited in some areas by competition for nest sites with other hole-nesters such as tits, Nuthatches *Sitta europaea* and Pied Flycatchers *Ficedula hypoleuca*. Redstarts and Pied Flycatchers frequently occur together in the sessile oakwoods of Wales, the W Midlands and the Lake District.

The Redstart is a summer visitor to Britain, its main winter quarters being in W Africa. Like the Whitethroat *Sylvia communis* and some other species, its numbers have decreased in recent years (see graph) because of the failure of the rains to penetrate to the Sahel zone on the southern fringe of the Sahara desert (Winstanley *et al* 1974). There was a marked decline in much of England before 1940, but

a good recovery by 1967–68. Timber felling may result in local decreases, but much apparently suitable habitat remains, even in parts of E England from which the species is absent. Slight range expansion has recently taken place, to the Isle of Man and E Cornwall. Irish records are very sporadic, but the Redstart's scarcity is not due to any lack of suitable habitat which, there, is usually mature oaks. Two pairs in oakwoods in Kerry in 1973 were the first nesting records for SW Ireland since 1946, and there were more Irish breeding records during 1968–72 than in any comparable period this century.

During BTO census studies in woods in W Scotland, the highest density recorded was 49 pairs per km² in oak/hazel and oak/birch coppice in N Argyll. Open Scots pine, and also alder woods, in Wester Ross held approximately 20 pairs per km², but oak wood in the same region carried twice that density.

While numbers in E England are low, with only a few pairs in each 10-km square, this is a not uncommon species even as far north as the hillside birch woods of Sutherland. Parslow put the Redstart in the range 10,000–100,000; an average of 30–60 pairs per occupied 10-km square suggests a total British and Irish population in the upper half of this range.

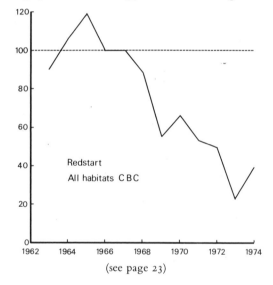

Redstart
All habitats CBC

(see page 23)

Number of 10-km squares in which recorded:
1,671 (43%)
Possible breeding   177 (11%)
Probable breeding   239 (14%)
Confirmed breeding   1,255 (75%)

References
BATTEN, L. A. 1976. Bird communities of some Killarney woodlands. *Proc. Roy. Irish Acad.* 76: 285–313.
BUXTON, J. 1950. *The Redstart.* London.
WILLIAMSON, K. 1974. Breeding birds in the deciduous woodlands of mid-Argyll, Scotland. *Bird Study* 21: 29–44.
WINSTANLEY, D., R. SPENCER and K. WILLIAMSON. 1974. Where have all the Whitethroats gone? *Bird Study* 21: 1–14.

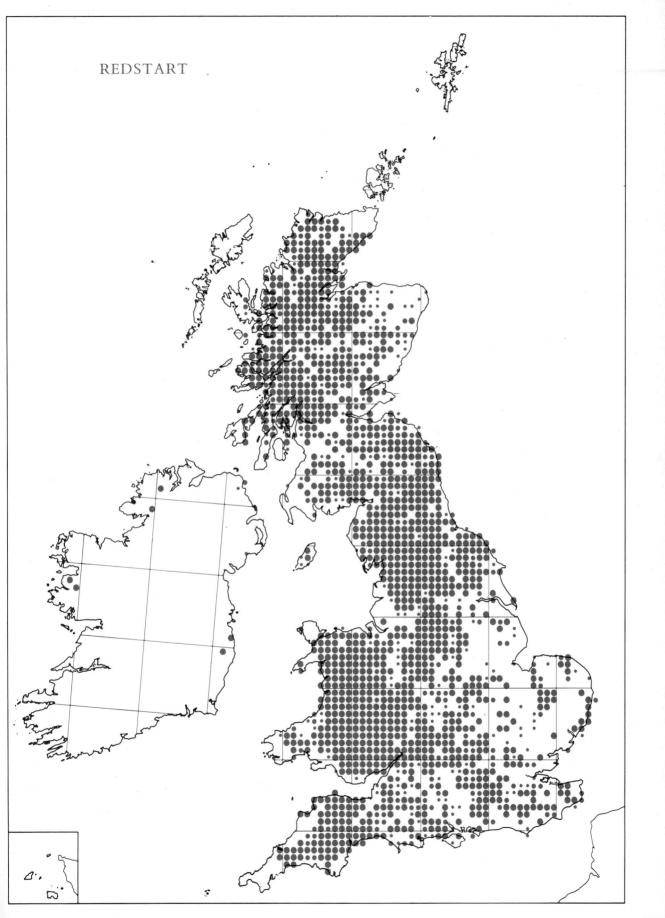

REDSTART

Black Redstart

Phoenicurus ochruros

The Black Redstart is the only rare breeding bird in Britain which is associated with urban areas and industrial buildings. Some breed on sea cliffs, but an important Continental habitat, mountain screes and boulder-strewn slopes, is sparsely represented within the species' restricted range in Britain, and has not yet been used. It should be added, however, that this is also a markedly urban species in some other parts of NW Europe.

The song is loud and distinctive so that initial location should theoretically be easy, but incessant noise from road or rail traffic or industrial plant often drowns it. Many breeding sites are at places which the ornithologist is likely to avoid, unless searching for this particular species, and access to the properties is often difficult to obtain. Some breeding pairs have probably been overlooked, therefore, both near traditional sites and at new ones.

As well as being a summer visitor, or possibly a resident, the Black Redstart is also a winter visitor and passage migrant in Britain. Early spring records, especially on the coast, are not necessarily any indication of nesting. Breeding birds may return early, however, and males are sometimes present by the end of March, females arriving soon afterwards. The nest is usually on a ledge or in a cranny of a cliff or wall (often where a brick is missing), but sometimes within a derelict building or a cave.

The Black Redstart is one of quite a number of species to have colonised Britain in recent times. Apart from one or two isolated records (1845 and possibly 1909), breeding started with two pairs on coastal cliffs in Sussex in 1923 and was then regular for a few years in Cornwall, but sporadic in SE England. The first London colonisation was in 1926, on the derelict site of the previous year's Wembley Exhibition. A few years later, scattered records came from other parts of London, but the Wembley site remained the main centre, with three or four pairs, until increased human activity caused its desertion in 1942. By then, many bombed sites were available in central London and at Dover (Kent) and, for the next decade, seldom less than 15 and sometimes more than 30 singing males or breeding pairs were recorded annually. Colonisation of other urban areas and of coastal cliffs started at this time. The population fluctuated quite widely during 1940–74, with no real evidence of an increase (see graph). Since 1972, breeding has been proved for the first time in Cheshire in 1973 and 1974, and eggs were laid by a female in Orkney in 1973, although no male was seen—the first record of nesting by this species anywhere in Scotland.

In Britain, there are many coastal sites, both natural and man-made, which could be used by Black Redstarts. Inland bombed sites have mostly been redeveloped, but the birds have moved mainly to power stations and gas works (Meadows 1970). Many such places are not occupied by Black Redstarts and there is certainly room for expansion. If the species moved more into urban and suburban areas it could increase in numbers very quickly. At present, however, Britain holds a well established breeding population which has averaged 30 pairs for the last three decades and has probably never exceeded 100 pairs even in the best year.

This species is afforded special protection in Great Britain under Schedule I of the Protection of Birds Act, 1954–67.

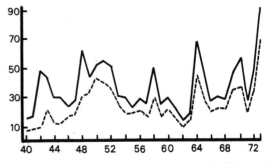

Black Redstarts in Britain, 1940–73: territory-holding males (solid line) and pairs (dotted line) (after Fitter 1976)

Number of 10-km squares in which recorded:
68 (2%)
Possible breeding   16 (24%)
Probable breeding   16 (24%)
Confirmed breeding   36 (53%)

References

FITTER, R. S. R. 1965. The breeding status of the Black Redstart in Britain. *Brit. Birds* 58: 481–492.

FITTER, R. S. R. 1971. Black Redstarts breeding in Britain in 1964–68. *Brit. Birds* 64: 117–124.

FITTER, R. S. R. 1976. Black Redstarts breeding in Britain in 1969–73. *Brit. Birds* 69: 9–15.

MEADOWS, B. S. 1970. Breeding distribution and feeding ecology of the Black Redstart in London. *London Bird Rep.* 34: 72–79.

SHARROCK, J. T. R. *et al.* 1975. Rare breeding birds in the United Kingdom in 1973 and 1974. *Brit. Birds* 68: 5–23, 489–506.

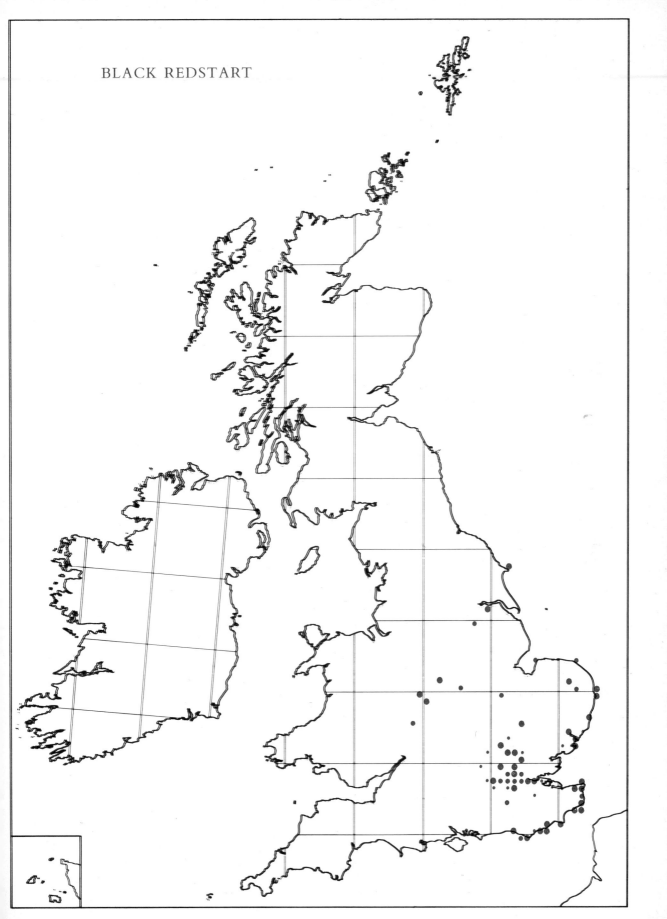

BLACK REDSTART

Nightingale

Luscinia megarhynchos

Nightingales are found in woods and on commons with dense thickets of thorn scrub, especially blackthorn, along overgrown hedgerows, and in coppice-with-standards woods cut on a regular 12–15 years rotation. As they are ground feeders, the light and warmth reaching the woodland floor in the early years of pole-growth is very important, and Stuttard and Williamson (1971) have shown that the highest concentration of nesting pairs is from about the fifth to the eighth year (see graph). The present distribution is largely southeast of a line from the Wash to the River Severn and this is the lowland region where coppice-with-standards management was most intensive in the past. At the edges of and beyond this region, the Nightingale is largely a bird of the river valleys.

The magnificent song can be heard at any time of day or night, but is most frequent at dusk, in the early part of the night and at dawn. Especially when other bird song is sparse and extraneous sounds are few, the song carries far, so that location is easy during nocturnal expeditions into suitable country. The birds themselves are inveterate skulkers, normally perching low down in the cover of the foliage, or foraging amongst the undergrowth. The nest, built close to the ground, is generally regarded as difficult to find; its careful concealment, together with the secretive behaviour of the adults, make proof of breeding hard to obtain. It is, therefore, likely that, whilst the distribution is fairly accurately depicted by the map, most of the records of probable and possible breeding, which make up more than half of the total, refer to unconfirmed breeders rather than migrants.

The distribution during 1968–72 shows little change since the first decade of the century (Ticehurst and Jourdain 1911) or the 1930s (see maps on page 462), there being only a slight contraction south from Yorkshire and S Wales. While the range has not altered greatly, numbers have certainly shown more change, with a widespread marked decline

since a peak in about 1950. Locally, this dearth has been attributed to destruction of suitable habitat, due to scrub clearance, the draining of damp areas, tidier hedgerow management and the decline in rotational cutting of coppiced woods. Former coppice-with-standards, neglected where regular cutting has ceased to be profitable, becomes quickly overgrown and quite unsuited to the species' requirements.

In particularly favoured haunts, there may be high concentrations of Nightingales and it is an unforgettable experience to find, as one still can in some parts of Kent and Sussex, an area with more than a dozen singing at the same time. Such concentrations are now unusual. Common Birds Census information is sparse, though there is one record of 13.8 pairs per km² in the mature yew/oak and associated shrub growth at Kingley Vale NNR (Sussex). Three surveys of singing birds have been organised in Kent, however, and, to give one example, 167 observers heard 977 Nightingales between midnight and dawn on the morning of 24th May 1970, when 98% of all Kentish woodlands were visited. Since Kent accounts for about 5% of all the 10-km squares in which Nightingales were recorded during 1968–72, but is particularly well endowed with them, some 10,000 pairs may breed in England. The BTO organised a national census of this species in summer 1976, but the results are not yet available.

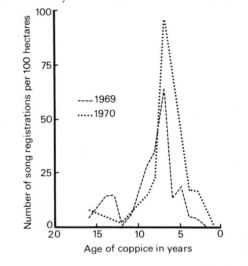

Number of 10-km squares in which recorded:
639 (17%)
Possible breeding   52 (8%)
Probable breeding   287 (45%)
Confirmed breeding   300 (47%)

Though some records were originally submitted in confidence, all dots are now shown accurately (as recommended by the Rare Breeding Birds Panel)

References
STUTTARD, P. and K. WILLIAMSON. 1971. Habitat requirements of the Nightingale. *Bird Study* 18: 9–14.
TICEHURST, N. F. and F. C. R. JOURDAIN. 1911. On the distribution of the Nightingale during the breeding season in Great Britain. *Brit. Birds* 5: 2–21.

Bluethroat *Luscinia svecica*, **see page 450**

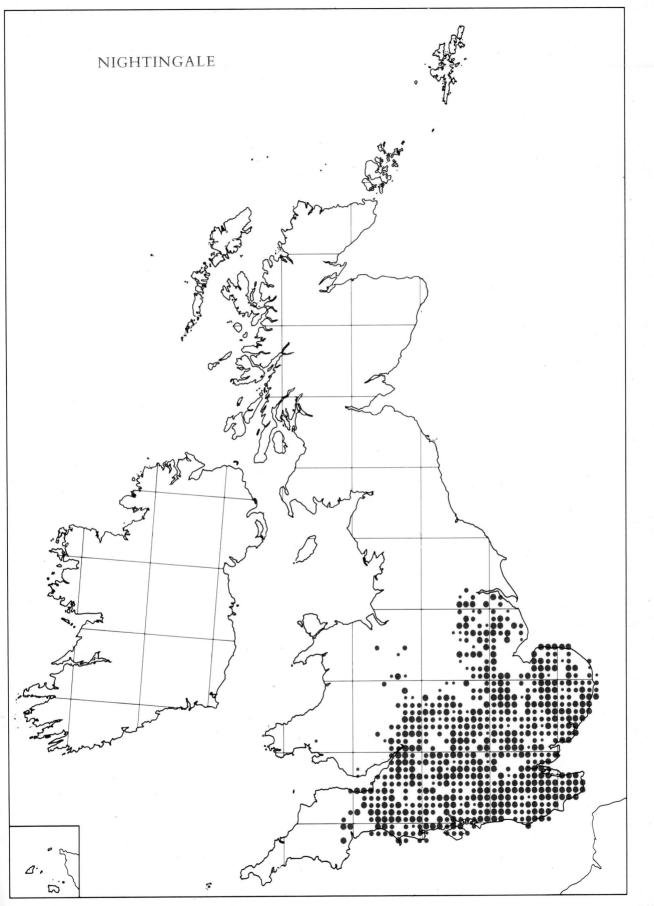

NIGHTINGALE

Robin

Erithacus rubecula

The best known and most loved of all British birds, the Robin is also one of the most widely distributed. Originally an inhabitant of deciduous high forest, it is now abundant and is also often the dominant species in all types of woodland with a history of coppice management in England, though outnumbered by the Chaffinch *Fringilla coelebs* in Scotland. Its friendly familiarity, which has led to its selection as Britain's national bird, may well have arisen through its close association with woodcutters' families at their springtime work in mediaeval coppices. Through successful exploitation of this kind of woodland, the species would have become preadapted to later colonisation of farm hedgerows-with-trees, town parks, churchyards and suburban gardens (Williamson 1974). Even mountain regions are penetrated in the birch woods, and along the bushy gullies of streams.

The plaintive, warbling song, though heard at all seasons, is a feature of the spring woodland chorus at dawn and, especially, dusk. During autumn and winter, the song often dominates the otherwise silent woods. The adults are very secretive when visiting the nest, which is one of the most difficult of our common birds' nests to find. The Robin is notoriously catholic in its choice of site, but most nests are located on or near the ground in the vegetation of an earthbank or hedge. Robins are generally so common, and so confiding near human habitations, however, that confirmation of breeding sets no problem, the most usual means being observation of adults carrying food, or of recently fledged young.

Though present on Orkney since at least the late 18th century, Robins were found in only six (and breeding was confirmed in only three) of the 39 squares there during 1968–72, and the population has been estimated at less than 100 pairs. None is known to have nested in Shetland and, while there has been sporadic breeding on Tiree and Coll in the past, none was found on these islands during *Atlas* fieldwork. Apart from short-term fluctuations, especially decrease and subsequent revival after severe winters (see graph), there is no evidence of any major change in the distribution or numbers of Robins in Britain or Ireland for at least 100 years.

Densities vary widely: some examples from Common Birds Census studies illustrate this (pairs per km^2). Open Scots pine in Wester Ross holds as few as 10, compared with 16–35 in the hillside birch woods, but the planted gardens of English estates and Scottish policies may exceed 300 and the oak/holly woods of Co Kerry have 204–256, equal to good English lowland woods.

Densities fluctuate more widely on farmland. After a severe winter, the surviving Robins fill the woodland niches, as do other birds of coppices, and two or three seasons may elapse before the increasing population spills over into farmland. Since hedgerows are a sub-optimal habitat, the density is dependent upon population level. Over a seven-year period, the average distance between the centres of territories along the tree-filled hedges of a Suffolk farm was just over 1,000 m, but this contracted to 480 m in the best year. The mean density in farmland CBC areas in 1972 was just over 20 pairs per km^2, and almost 60 in woodland. An average of 1,500 pairs per 10-km square would give a British and Irish total of about five million pairs.

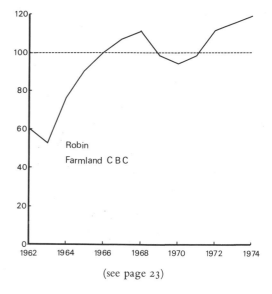

Robin
Farmland CBC

(see page 23)

Number of 10-km squares in which recorded: 3,591 (93%)
Possible breeding   36 (1%)
Probable breeding   52 (1%)
Confirmed breeding   3,503 (98%)

References

BATTEN, L. A. 1976. Bird communities of some Killarney woodlands. *Proc. Roy. Irish Acad.* 76: 285–313.

LACK, D. 1943. *The Life of the Robin.* London.

LEA, D. and W. R. P. BOURNE. 1975. The birds of Orkney. *Brit. Birds* 68: 261–283.

WILLIAMSON, K. 1972. Breeding birds of a mixed farm in Suffolk. *Bird Study* 19: 34–50.

ROBIN

Cetti's Warbler

Cettia cetti

Cetti's Warblers breed usually in areas of low, tangled vegetation in wet or damp situations. Reed-beds, marshes with overgrown hedges and choked ditches, and willow or alder carr all harbour nesting pairs. In some S European countries, where this species is well established, the dependence on moist habitats is not so marked, and territories may be found in dry scrub, although there is usually a stream or wet ditch close at hand. The spread to Britain is very recent and the information gathered during the *Atlas* years concerns only the very first colonists. During the following three breeding seasons, many more were present and the range was extended.

Many birdwatchers might think that this is one of those skulking warblers of thick vegetation which are very difficult to see. Although this is the case in the middle of the day, those who have studied Cetti's Warblers early in the morning, and to a lesser extent at dusk, agree that good views may then be obtained, as they seem to pay little attention to human intruders. Rather dumpy, with mahogany-brown upperparts and grey underparts, looking like large Wrens *Troglodytes troglodytes*, they similarly have an astonishingly loud voice. The explosive song, consisting of a series of staccato notes, and the disyllabic alarm call both carry far over the marshes, and any alert birdwatcher visiting an area which holds a resident male Cetti's Warbler in the spring or summer could hardly overlook it.

Since it is a resident, feeding on insects, the Cetti's Warbler is badly affected by cold weather, and the numbers breeding in parts of the Continent hit by freezing conditions in 1962/63 were much reduced. For example, the Camargue population was devastated, but recovered well over the next few years. The effects of severe weather are, therefore, merely superimposed on the quite spectacular northwards spread, which has been documented by Bonham and Robertson (1975). In Europe at the turn of the century, this warbler was practically confined to the shores of the Mediterranean. By 1927, a gradual northwards progression had taken the species as far as the Loire basin. The Seine river-system was reached in 1932, and the next 20 years saw consolidation in these new areas, although further expansion seems to have been checked to some extent by the colder winters of the 1940s. Ferguson-Lees (1964) noted that breeding had been recorded in several departments across N France and that birds had appeared in West Germany, the Channel Islands, Hampshire and Sussex.

The severe winter of 1962/63 only checked the increase, and more and more breeding sites were occupied in Brittany and elsewhere along the French coast. Belgium was colonised in 1962, but the first record in the Netherlands did not come until late in 1968. Breeding was proved in West Germany during 1975. As illustrations of how difficult it is to do this: Cetti's Warblers had been seen in 28 localities in the Netherlands by the end of 1974, but breeding had not been proved, while proof on Jersey was not forthcoming until 1973, though the first one had been noted in 1960 and they had been annual since 1968.

In Britain, there were four further records in 1967–68, and the first in Ireland, but then none during the next two years. The *Atlas* map shows the situation for 1971–72, including the first case of confirmed breeding, when an adult was seen carrying food in 1972. Since then the increase has been extraordinary. In 1973, Cetti's appeared at six or seven sites in Kent, and others held territories in Suffolk and Norfolk. One found dead in Norwich had been ringed at the main breeding place in Belgium, the only evidence so far which shows the origin of the new colonists. In 1974, there were probably 24 birds in Kent and a further 24 in seven coastal counties from Cornwall eastwards to Norfolk, with breeding proved in S Devon and Norfolk as well as Kent. During 1975, probably three times as many males held territories in the Kent stronghold as during the previous year, including at least 61 singing in the Stour Valley area, and many were reported elsewhere. In the Channel Islands, Jersey had at least four pairs, and breeding was proved on Alderney.

This species is afforded special protection in Great Britain under Schedule I of the Protection of Birds Act, 1954–67.

Number of 10-km squares in which recorded:
  6 (0.2%)
Possible breeding   2 (33%)
Probable breeding   3 (50%)
Confirmed breeding   1 (17%)

Though the records were originally submitted in confidence, all dots are now shown accurately (as recommended by the Rare Breeding Birds Panel)

References

BONHAM, P. F. and J. C. M. ROBERTSON. 1975. The spread of Cetti's Warbler in north-west Europe. *Brit. Birds* 68: 393–408.

FERGUSON-LEES, I. J. 1964. Studies of less familiar birds. 129. Cetti's Warbler. *Brit. Birds* 57: 357–359.

HOLLYER, J. N. 1975. The Cetti's Warbler in Kent. *Kent Bird Rep.* 22: 84–95.

SHARROCK, J. T. R. and E. M. SHARROCK. 1976. *Rare Birds in Britain and Ireland*. Berkhamsted.

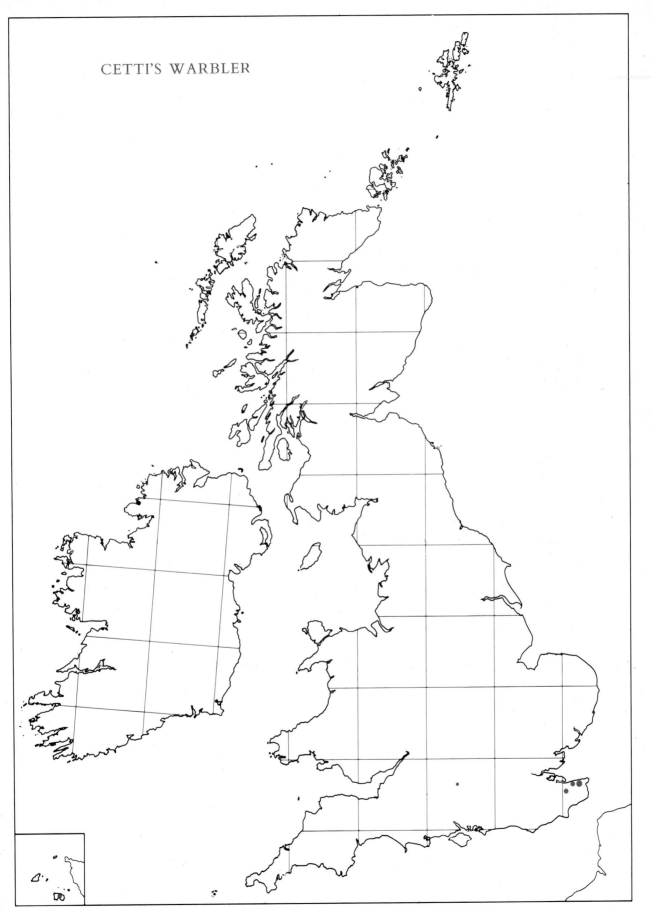

CETTI'S WARBLER

Grasshopper Warbler

Locustella naevia

Grasshopper Warblers used to be thought of as birds of damp, sedgy fields, reed-beds and other marshy places with tangled vegetation. In fact, water is by no means necessary and they have always occurred in the thick, low, tangled growth of downland and heathland as well as of carr and fen. It has been suggested that drier habitats are more frequently used nowadays, as by the Sedge Warbler *Acrocephalus schoenobaenus* and, especially, the Reed Bunting *Emberiza schoeniclus*. Certainly the great increase in conifer afforestation during the last 50 years has provided ideal ground cover of dry, tangled grasses, willowherb and brambles in the early years at each plantation. Afforestation must have amply compensated for the loss of areas of wet habitat through drainage, and allowed the species to spread to regions where no suitable 'natural' sites existed.

The reeling song of the Grasshopper Warbler is far-carrying and distinctive and, provided background noise is at a low level, may be heard at ranges up to one kilometre. Unfortunately, the song has a very high pitch and many older birdwatchers find that it no longer registers. Although birds may sing even in the middle of hot, sunny days, the song is more typical of drizzling, overcast weather and, especially, late evening, night-time and dawn. Returning migrants arrive in S Britain towards the end of April and, from then until mid-May, can sometimes be heard singing in places on the coast, and inland, which are unsuitable for breeding.

The species' skulking behaviour makes nest finding very difficult for all but the most gifted observers. The best chance of proving breeding probably comes when young are being fed and, with luck, the parents may be seen carrying food as they slide furtively through the vegetation. The nestlings leave before they are capable of sustained flight and at this stage it is sometimes possible to see them being fed away from the nest; or parties of recently-fledged young may 'explode' at an observer's feet as he walks through damp grassland. It is certainly no surprise, however, that only one-third of all the *Atlas* records relate to confirmed breeding. Most of the others were of singing birds, many heard in suitable habitat over

several weeks and in each year of the survey, and there is every likelihood that a large majority of the probable breeding records refer to nesting rather than passage.

The numbers of Grasshopper Warblers fluctuate markedly from year to year, due in part to local habitat changes. Wet areas may be drained and so lost to the species, but areas of dense vegetation cleared in one year may be ideal for Grasshopper Warblers again two or three years later. Young forestry plantations quickly develop into perfect nesting sites, and remain attractive for the best part of a decade, until the canopy closes in. Since harvesting followed by replanting is normally on a rotation system, modern forestry offers a succession of usable sites.

The current distribution, with the species absent from much of upland Britain, is not unexpected. The scarcity in the Fens of E England and much of Co Cork is surprising, for both areas contain apparently suitable nesting areas. There seem to have been no major long-term range changes, except for a marked westwards extension in Ireland and perhaps SW England. In N Scotland, where most of the records refer to birds in traditional sites rather than in new plantations, there may have been a recent extension. There was only one instance of confirmed breeding north of the Black Isle during 1968–72, but several of the probable breeding records, including those in the extreme north, refer to small groups of singing birds present throughout the summer.

Parslow placed the Grasshopper Warbler in the range 1,000–10,000 pairs, but the widespread *Atlas* records suggest a population exceeding this. Breeding densities have been noted of 3 pairs in 10 ha of young plantation and up to 5 in 24 ha of chalk grassland scrub. Even assuming, as is probably the case, that each 10-km square from which the species was recorded has only a small area of suitable habitat, it is likely that the average is at least ten pairs. This suggests a total population in Britain and Ireland of about 25,000 pairs, and the true figure could well be higher.

Number of 10-km squares in which recorded:
2,580 (67%)
Possible breeding   134 (5%)
Probable breeding   1,604 (62%)
Confirmed breeding   842 (33%)

References

WILLIAMSON, K. 1974. Habitat changes in a young Forestry Commission plantation. *Bird Study* 21: 215–217.

WILLIAMSON, K. 1975. The breeding bird community of chalk grassland scrub in the Chiltern Hills. *Bird Study* 22: 59–70.

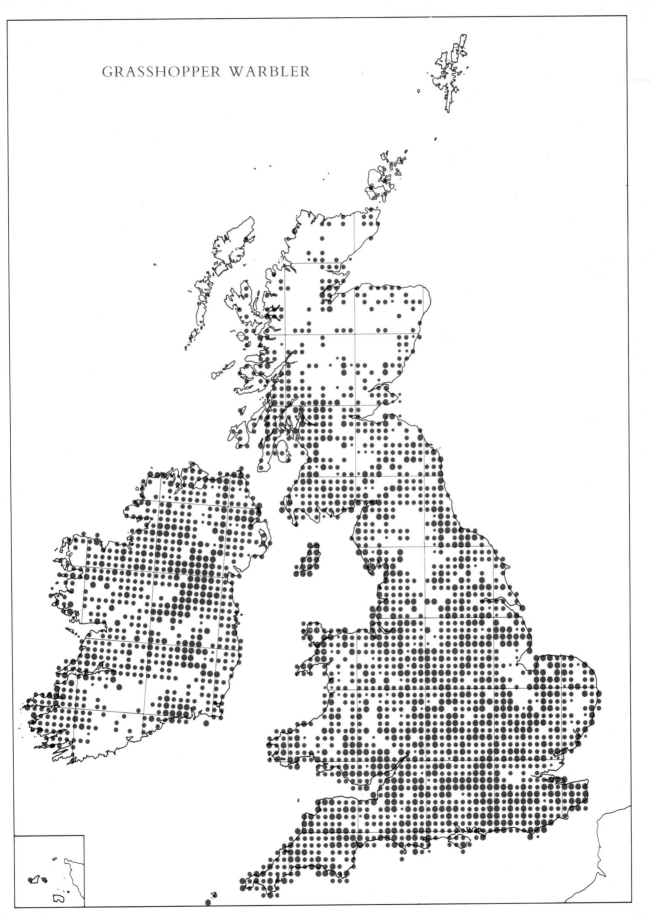

GRASSHOPPER WARBLER

359

Savi's Warbler

Locustella luscinioides

Savi's Warblers usually nest in *Phragmites* reed-beds with a good undergrowth of sedges; in such situations, scattered bushes may be used as song posts. Sedge fields without *Phragmites* may also be used, but the chosen haunt is likely to be very wet, at least in the early part of the summer.

By 1824, when the species was first described, English naturalists were beginning to realise that a 'reed-wren' different from the Reed Warbler *Acrocephalus scirpaceus* was breeding in the marshes of East Anglia. Newton in his revision of Yarrell (1871–74) documented the breeding records from Norfolk, Suffolk, Cambridgeshire and Huntingdonshire, mostly in areas of marsh and fenland which by that time had been drained and ploughed. The sedge-cutters in Cambridgeshire often used to find distinctive nests in the autumn, when they cut the sedge to be bundled and sold as kindling. This once thriving population in the formerly vast marshes of East Anglia seems to have become extinct in 1856. It is tempting to blame the egg-collectors and trophy-hunters of the time, who were always keen to add new species to their hoards, but it seems possible that Savi's Warbler was declining then over much of its peripheral European range.

Savi's is an unstreaked, reed-bed warbler with a rather warmer colour than the much commoner Reed Warbler. It is extremely skulking and an exceptionally difficult bird to see unless a singing male has chosen an open perch. The song is very different from that of the *Acrocephalus* warblers, being a continuous reeling rather like that of its close relative, the Grasshopper Warbler *L. naevia*. The Savi's voice is, however, lower in pitch and rather richer in tone. Almost a hundred years after the last breeding record, a singing male stayed most of the summer of 1954 at Wicken Fen in Cambridgeshire, one of the historic sites of the species. Detailed comparison between its song and that of the Grasshopper Warbler was made by Boston (1956).

Yeatman (1971) documented a recent expansion of Savi's Warblers on the Continent, despite the drainage and reclamation of many suitable areas. Breeding was recorded in Sweden for the first time in 1944, and expansion was noted in Germany at the end of the decade. At the same time, Savi's Warblers were increasing in France. Thus it is not surprising that SE England was again colonised, probably in the 1950s.

The first breeding records were from marshes on a flooded mining subsidence in Kent. Breeding was first proved in 1960, but the small group of birds may have been present for several years. There were 12 singing males in 1965 (Pitt 1967) and three to six were recorded annually during 1968–72. In 1970–71, breeding was proved at two Suffolk sites some 7 km apart (Axell and Jobson 1972).

Searching for nests of so rare a species in such a vulnerable habitat is, of course, out of the question, and proof of breeding is best obtained by watching for the parents feeding young either in or out of the nest. Since there was a distinct lull in the output of song from the first of the Suffolk birds it seems likely that two broods were reared. Any slightly strange-sounding 'Grasshopper Warbler' heard in spring is worthy of close attention and, although all the plotted *Atlas* records fall south and east of a line from the Wash to the Solent, breeding may well have occurred at a marsh farther west. If the range continues to expand, Savi's Warblers are likely to find suitable sites at least throughout the range of Reed Warbler.

During 1973 and 1974, there were records of probable or proved breeding at five sites (including Devon and Norfolk, as well as Kent and Suffolk) and up to 13 singing males may have been involved, perhaps slightly more than there were in any year during 1968–72.

This species is afforded special protection in Great Britain under Schedule I of the Protection of Birds Act, 1954–67.

Number of 10-km squares in which recorded:
  13 (0·3%)
Possible breeding   0
Probable breeding   9 (69%)
Confirmed breeding   4 (31%)

Two dots (probable breeding) have been omitted, but the others have been plotted accurately (as recommended by the Rare Breeding Birds Panel)

References

AXELL, H. E. and G. J. JOBSON. 1972. Savi's Warblers breeding in Suffolk. *Brit. Birds* 65: 229–232.

BOSTON, F. M. 1956. Savi's Warbler in Cambridgeshire. *Brit. Birds* 49: 326–327.

PITT, R. G. 1967. Savi's Warblers breeding in Kent. *Brit. Birds* 60: 349–355.

SHARROCK, J. T. R. *et al.* 1975. Rare breeding birds in the United Kingdom in 1973 and 1974. *Brit. Birds* 68: 5–23, 489–506.

SHARROCK, J. T. R. and E. M. SHARROCK. 1976. *Rare Birds in Britain and Ireland*. Berkhamsted.

YARRELL, W. 1871–74. *A History of British Birds*. 3rd edn, revised by A. NEWTON. London.

YEATMAN, L. J. 1971. *Histoire des Oiseaux d'Europe*. Paris.

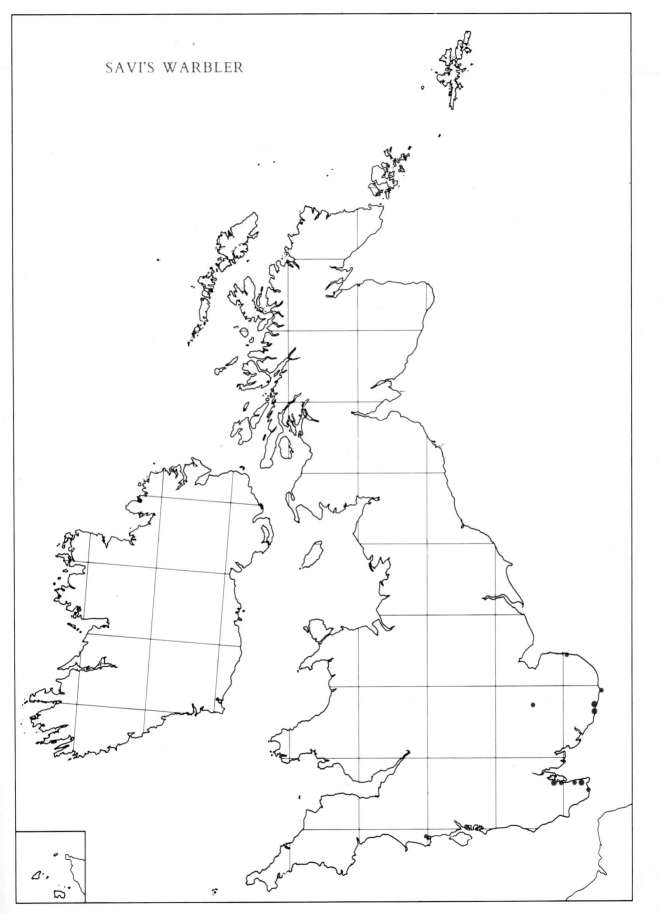

SAVI'S WARBLER

Reed Warbler

Acrocephalus scirpaceus

The Reed Warbler belongs to that small group of birds whose names conjure up a very precise picture of a habitat; indeed, of one particular plant, the common reed. Yet this association of bird and plant is by no means exclusive, and Reed Warblers may be found nesting in many other sorts of vegetation near reed-beds, especially willowherbs, meadowsweet and hawthorn.

When a bird species is closely associated with a particular plant, the obvious starting point in seeking to interpret the pattern of occurrence is the distribution of that plant. The botanical atlas reveals that *Phragmites* is uncommon at altitudes above 200 m and that it occurs most frequently to the south and east of a line from the N Yorkshire coast to Start Point in Devon. The same area, it will be seen, encompasses the great majority of breeding Reed Warblers in Britain. Yet there must be other factors limiting distribution, for *Phragmites* occurs locally in extensive stands as far north as S Shetland, and is widespread in Ireland.

In many northern and western localities, reed growth is markedly inferior to that in typical southern marshes, which might render it less suitable for Reed Warblers. Temperature is perhaps important, since very few Reed Warblers nest north of the 16°C July isotherm; July is the month in which most fledge. Yet another factor may be rainfall, which readily flattens reeds, thereby dislodging nests. With few exceptions, Reed Warbler colonies are in areas receiving less than 1,000 mm of rain a year and less than 75 mm in July.

Most returning migrants probably arrive through SE England and ringing has shown that this is the departure route in autumn. The use of this easterly route may partly explain the failure to colonise Ireland, despite the many extensive reed-beds there.

Though there is the possibility of confusion with the Sedge Warbler, the loud song makes location in waterside habitat an easy matter and reed-bed nests are simple to find. The adults are noisy when the nest is approached and it is not difficult to observe them carrying food to the young, even when nesting outside reed-beds. It is likely, therefore, that the *Atlas* map for this species is very nearly complete, although a few of the blank squares may have had small undetected colonies.

Though drainage, river widening and other forms of habitat destruction have resulted in local reductions or extinctions, the provision of additional habitat by flooded gravel pits and other artificial waters has probably more than compensated for the loss. Apart from an extension of regular breeding into Devon, Cornwall and Scilly, and probably in N Wales and Yorkshire, there has been almost no change since the late 1930s, the map in *The Handbook* closely resembling that shown here. The single instance of probable breeding in Scotland during 1968–72 (display observed in 1970) was closely followed by confirmed breeding on Unst (Shetland) in 1973, when a pair bred in a clump of snowberry. There is every chance that this pair came from the Norwegian population, which has steadily expanded since that country was colonised in 1947 (Voous 1960). Extralimital breeding has been recorded once in Ireland, in Co Down in 1935.

Although no Common Birds Census index has been produced and the species is very difficult to survey using this technique (Bell, Catchpole and Corbett 1968), it seems to have suffered an abrupt decrease between 1968 and 1969 (*cf* Whitethroat *Sylvia communis*). Numbers may have remained rather low since then, but the distribution of breeding birds does not seem to have contracted. Estimation of numbers is particularly difficult with species which may be very uncommon in one 10-km square, yet be present in large numbers at several colonies in an adjacent one. Densities of over 10 pairs per ha are often recorded in well-grown *Phragmites* beds, but suitable habitat is often very limited. An average of 50–100 pairs per 10-km square would give a total population of 40,000–80,000 pairs, within Parslow's range of 10,000–100,000.

Number of 10-km squares in which recorded:
  778 (20%)
Possible breeding   39 (5%)
Probable breeding   147 (19%)
Confirmed breeding   592 (76%)

References

BELL, B. D., C. K. CATCHPOLE and K. J. CORBETT. 1968. Problems of censusing Reed Buntings, Sedge Warblers and Reed Warblers. *Bird Study* 15: 16–21.

BROWN, P. E. and M. G. DAVIES. 1949. *Reed Warblers.* East Molesey.

BUNDY, G. 1975. Reed Warblers breeding in Shetland. *Brit. Birds* 68: 210–211.

CATCHPOLE, C. K. 1972. A comparative study of territory in the Reed Warbler *Acrocephalus scirpaceus* and Sedge Warbler *A. schoenobaenus*. *J. Zool. Lond.* 166: 213–231.

CATCHPOLE, C. K. 1974. Habitat selection and breeding success in the Reed Warbler *Acrocephalus scirpaceus*. *J. Anim. Ecol.* 43: 363–380.

LONG, R. 1975. Mortality of Reed Warblers in Jersey. *Ringing and Migration* 1: 28–32.

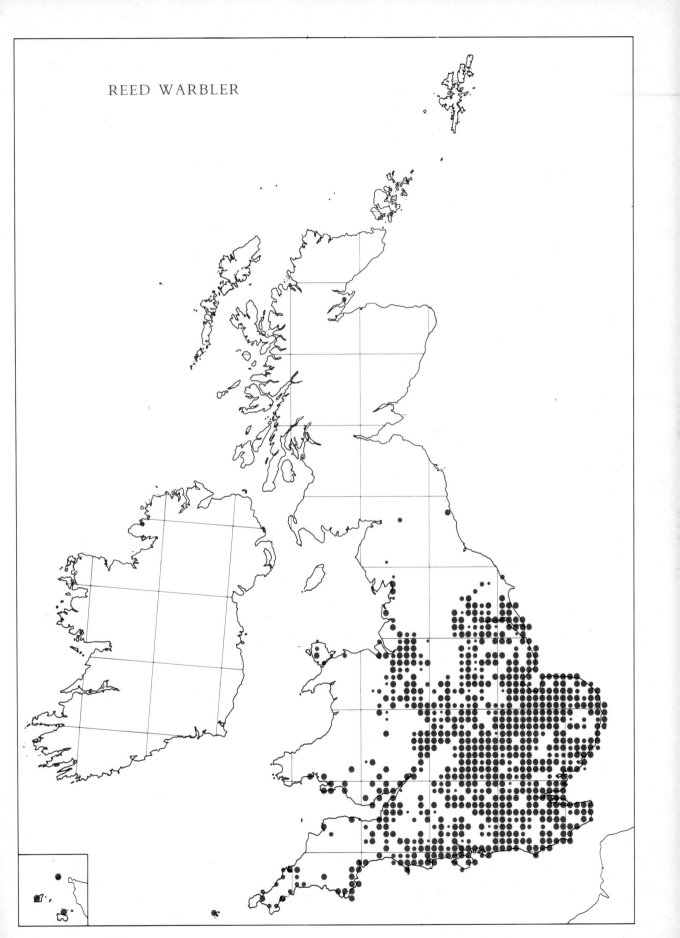

REED WARBLER

Marsh Warbler

Acrocephalus palustris

Although closely related to the Reed Warbler *A. scirpaceus*, the very similar Marsh Warbler is a much rarer species in Britain. It is usually found nesting near water, but in relatively dry areas. Most of the sites now occupied have extensive growth of nettles, meadowsweet or hoary willowherb, with some higher bushes or trees which are used as song posts. In the past, osier-beds, cut on a regular rotation for the basket-making industry in fruit-growing areas, were an important habitat. On the Continent, standing agricultural crops are commonly occupied, as they have been on occasions in Britain: *eg* five pairs in a bean field in the Avon Valley (Harthan 1938). Marsh Warblers are often present in the same haunt as both Reed and Sedge Warblers *A. schoenobaenus*.

Very few nests are built over water. The majority of 144 found by Walpole-Bond (1938), mainly during the 1920s, were supported in whole or in part on meadowsweet or nettle stems, but over 30 were attached to shrubs or bushes. The almond willow, one of the two *Salix* species most commonly found in osier-beds, regularly held nests when managed beds were still an important habitat, the slender stems of two to three years' growth being of an ideal thickness for nest attachment. Much has been written on the structure of the nest and the diagnostic 'basket-handles' which attach it to the supporting vegetation (*eg* Howard 1907–14).

Luckily, few birds are so similar in plumage as Marsh and Reed Warblers. Specific identification of adults may be attempted with some chance of success if the bird is seen well, the rufous lower back distinguishing the Reed from the uniformly olive Marsh Warbler; juveniles, however, present a very real problem, even in the hand. Fortunately, the Marsh Warbler's song is very distinctive, although confusion may arise with mimetic and melodious Reed Warblers (*cf Brit. Birds* 58: 181–188). The range of mimicry in the Marsh Warbler's song is very wide and its quality is truly astonishing: to the human ear, many of the songs and phrases are so like the original that one expects an unlikely mixed flock of birds to fly from the bush where the Marsh Warbler is singing. Over 50 species are listed by Howard (1907–14) and Walpole-Bond (1938) as being imitated, including waders, terns and game-birds. The nest and eggs

are also distinctive but, of course, with such a rare bird, searching for nests was not advocated as a technique for proving breeding for the *Atlas*.

Marsh Warblers are among the latest migrants to return in summer. Arrivals before 20th May are unusual, and some new territories are still being occupied after the first week of June. Song is intense at this stage, but soon diminishes and is very infrequent later in the season. It is thus easy to overlook this species unless the area is visited at the right time, during about three weeks at the end of May and beginning of June. Only one brood is reared, and autumn migration starts early, with the majority leaving by mid-August. Like a few other summer migrants, they are thought to take a southeasterly route to winter quarters in E Africa, but there are no British ringing records to prove this.

Britain is on the western edge of the range and, although breeding has been reported from about 20 counties in S and W England during the last 100 years, the map gives a picture of scattered breeding, and of the one regular pocket, which is probably typical for any five year period since 1940. It is possible that one or two instances of Reed Warblers misidentified as Marsh have been erroneously included, but Marsh Warblers have been identified at some time in the past from all the places where they were recorded in 1968–72. Numbers have undoubtedly decreased during the last 25 years, and the loss of traditional areas through drainage or abandonment of osier-beds (which then grow into unsuitable wet woodland) may have been important factors. With a small population of a migrant species, the loss of traditional areas can lead to the failure of potential pairs to make contact (*cf* Red-backed Shrike *Lanius collurio*).

The present population probably numbers about 50–80 pairs, more than three-quarters of them in Worcestershire.

This species is afforded special protection in Great Britain under Schedule I of the Protection of Birds Act, 1954–67.

Number of 10-km squares in which recorded:
  21 (0·5%)
Possible breeding   3 (14%)
Probable breeding   6 (29%)
Confirmed breeding   12 (57%)

Eight dots have been moved by up to two 10-km squares (the Rare Breeding Birds Panel's recommendation was that two dots be moved by up to two 10-km squares)

References

HARTHAN, A. J. 1938. Some breeding habits of Marsh Warblers in south Worcestershire. *Brit. Birds* 32: 230–232.

HOWARD, H. E. 1907–14. *The British Warblers*. London.

PRICE, M. P. 1969. Nesting habitat of Reed and Marsh Warblers. *Bird Study* 16: 130–131.

WALPOLE-BOND, J. 1938. *A History of Sussex Birds*. London.

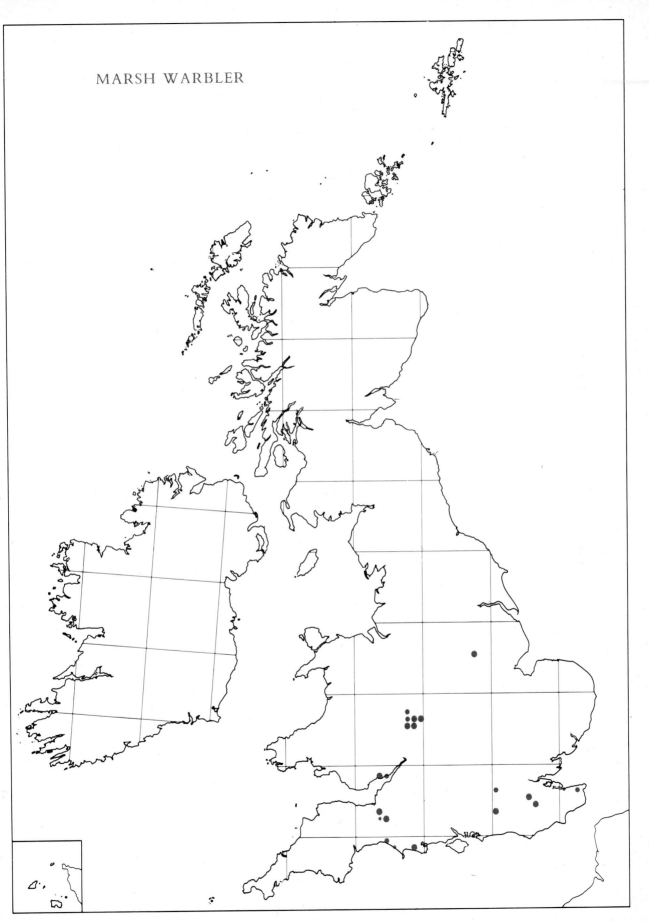

MARSH WARBLER

Sedge Warbler

Acrocephalus schoenobaenus

Sedge Warblers are characteristic of the luxuriant vegetation of many waterside habitats. Although they sometimes encroach on the wetter areas of reedbeds, overlapping with Reed Warblers *A. scirpaceus*, they occupy chiefly the rather drier margins. Indeed, and perhaps with increasing frequency, they also breed in completely dry habitats such as young forestry plantations, and even crops of corn and oilseed rape. In short, though primarily creatures of rather damp, rank vegetation, they are far more catholic than Reed Warblers in their choice of habitat and this versatility is well demonstrated by their colonisation of the sea buckthorn scrub which dominates the coastal dune system at Gibraltar Point (Lincolnshire).

They have a conspicuous song flight, but bushes are regularly used as song posts and may be important to them, for extensive areas of uniform low vegetation tend to have fewer breeding pairs. Whether delivered in flight or from a perch, the song makes location easy, unless it is confused with that of the Reed Warbler. It is far-carrying, and may be heard from early in April until about the middle of July.

The nests, being well hidden, normally low down in dense vegetation, are much more difficult to find than those of the Reed Warbler; when feeding young, however, the adults are rarely secretive, and this behaviour is reflected in the high proportion of proved breeding records on the *Atlas* map.

Arriving a week or two earlier, Sedge Warblers could influence the numbers of Reed Warblers in habitats where they overlap. In a detailed study in Nottinghamshire, however, Catchpole (1972) found that the Reed Warblers were able to insinuate themselves successfully and, indeed, brought about slight shifts and decreases in the Sedge Warbler territories. Both species get the majority of their food outside the defended area, which is five or six times bigger for Sedge Warblers than Reed Warblers, and neither shows sustained aggression on encountering a feeding bird of the other species.

Successful, and well adapted to long distance migration, this species is widely distributed. Of the warblers, only the Willow Warbler *Phylloscopus trochilus* and the Whitethroat *Sylvia communis* occur more extensively in Scotland, while in Ireland, which has fewer species of warblers than Britain, it reaches many of the most northern and western promontories.

The main feature of the map is the species' scarcity in or absence from much of the high ground, particularly in Devon, Wales, the Pennines and the Scottish Highlands. Yet it has been known to breed at altitudes up to 350 m where suitable habitat is available. In Scotland, Orkney was colonised in the mid 19th century and the Outer Hebrides in the 1930s. In both these areas, increases have been noted in the last two decades. There is no record of breeding in Shetland.

No significant changes in distribution have been noted elsewhere in Britain and Ireland. The loss of breeding habitat in some areas may have caused local declines, but elsewhere the provision of new sites associated with gravel and clay pits will have allowed increases. The Common Birds Census results show a marked peak in 1968, followed by a decline coinciding with the crash in Whitethroat numbers (Winstanley *et al* 1974). The population has remained at rather a low level since then.

There are some problems in producing accurate census results for this species, and conventional CBC techniques, on a minimum number of visits, may underestimate the population by a quarter. Rich habitats may easily hold five or six pairs per ha, but such areas do not normally extend over much of a 10-km square. The average density on farmland plots in 1972 was about 1.3 pairs per km². Thus, although some occupied 10-km squares may have only a few pairs, the rich areas elsewhere may hold enough to bring the average to 100 pairs per occupied 10-km square. This gives a total of about 300,000 pairs, which agrees well with Parslow's categorisation of 100,000–1,000,000 pairs.

Number of 10-km squares in which recorded:
2,929 (76%)
Possible breeding   101 (3%)
Probable breeding   784 (27%)
Confirmed breeding   2,044 (70%)

References

BELL, B. D., C. K. CATCHPOLE and K. J. CORBETT. 1968. Problems of censusing Reed Buntings, Sedge Warblers and Reed Warblers. *Bird Study* 15: 16–21.

BONHAM, P. F. and J. T. R. SHARROCK. 1974. Sedge Warblers singing in fields of rape. *Brit. Birds* 67: 389–390.

CATCHPOLE, C. K. 1972. A comparative study in territory in the Reed Warbler *Acrocephalus scirpaceus* and Sedge Warbler *A. schoenobaenus*. *J. Zool. Lond.* 166: 213–231.

WINSTANLEY, D., R. SPENCER and K. WILLIAMSON. 1974. Where have all the Whitethroats gone? *Bird Study* 21: 1–14.

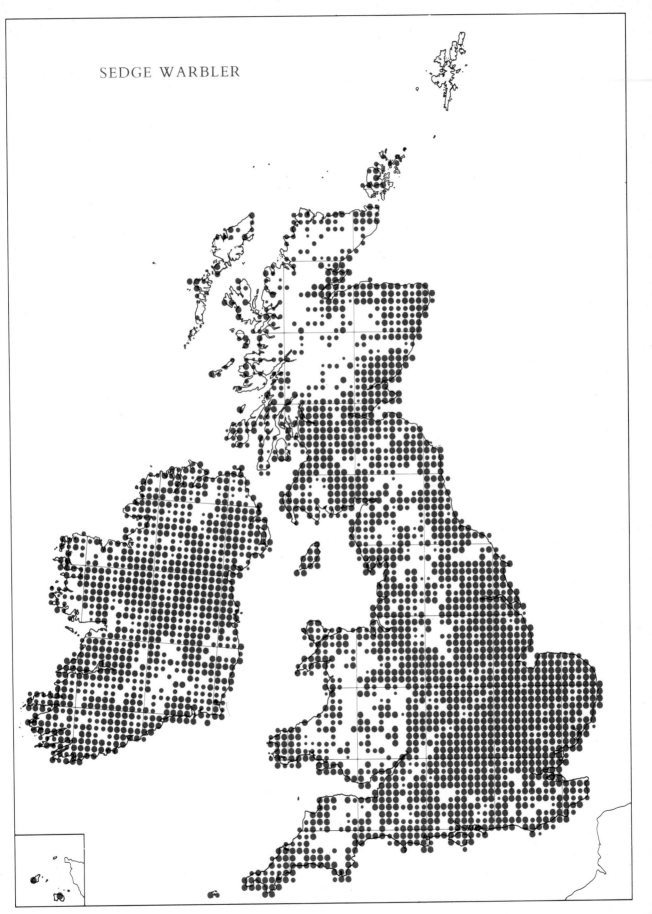

SEDGE WARBLER

Blackcap
Sylvia atricapilla

Blackcaps are most frequently found in mature deciduous or mixed woodland with a good shrub layer. Other habitats include overgrown coppice, tall hedgerows, sallow thickets at gravel-pits, medium-aged forestry plantations, thorn scrub and even garden shrubberies, but there are usually some taller trees available as song posts. When a wood is felled and replanted, Blackcaps remain in the amenity fringe of unfelled, large trees until the new growth reaches a height of 5–6 m after four years or so. In Scotland, and especially in Ireland, there seems to be a very close association with rhododendrons; this may be because so much of the mature deciduous woodland in those countries is in the policies of old estates and demesnes, where ornamental rhododendrons were planted.

Unlike its close relative, the Garden Warbler *S. borin*, the Blackcap is instantly recognisable on sight. The song is loud, rich and beautiful, on occasion rivalling that of Blackbird *Turdus merula* or Nightingale *Luscinia megarhynchos*, and can often be heard over long distances. Nevertheless, great care must be taken to ensure that a Garden Warbler has not been mistaken for a Blackcap, since the songs are quite similar, and *Atlas* workers were urged to locate and see the singing birds of these two species.

There are many records of Blackcaps wintering in Britain and Ireland and this habit seems to be increasing. Song heard in early March probably refers to wintering individuals, although summer migrants start to arrive at the end of March and in early April. This early arrival is possible because the birds feed on berries, such as ivy, if insect food is unavailable during cold weather. Males sing vigorously and will defend their territories by fighting. The females arrive a week or more later and pair almost immediately. Nest-building and egg-laying may follow quickly, but there is normally a pause and most clutches are started in late April or early May. Many males build extra nests within their territories and most pairs are double-brooded. Of almost 1,000 nest record cards analysed by Mason (1976), 70% of nests were below 1 m; while of all the *Sylvia* warblers in Britain, Blackcaps are the most likely to occur in deciduous woodland and the least likely to be found in scrub. The adults are very vocal, making loud 'taccing' alarm calls when the young are in the nest or newly fledged, and this is the best time to obtain proof of breeding.

There are few indications of changes in distribution in the last 100 years other than short-term peripheral ones due to year to year fluctuations. The substantial number of records obtained by *Atlas* workers in Ireland came as a surprise. Previous observer coverage had not been complete enough to permit real comparisons, but there has undoubtedly been a slow increase in recent years, though Mayo and Galway remain outside the normal breeding range. Many of the more northerly records in Scotland were of singing males and some of these may have been unmated. The Common Birds Census index also revealed that there were high population levels in both woodland and, particularly, farmland areas during 1968–72. Recent detailed census work has shown that, whilst Blackcaps and Garden Warblers react to each other's songs, both are able to hold territories and breed successfully in the same area; indeed, on some plots their territories overlap.

Many of the records of occupied 10-km squares in Scotland and Ireland refer to just one or two pairs in the only suitable habitat; only a handful of 10-km squares in Ireland hold more than 20 pairs and the total Irish population may not exceed 1,500 pairs. The Blackcap is a common warbler over much of S and central England, however, and CBC densities in woodland may reach 50 pairs per km^2, while the average was 12.3, nearly treble the Garden Warbler figure; farmland densities in 1972 averaged 2.6 pairs per km^2, almost four times the comparable figure for Garden Warbler. These data suggest an average of about 100 pairs per occupied 10-km square, and a total population in Britain and Ireland of at least 200,000 pairs; it is certainly in the lower part of Parslow's range of 100,000–1,000,000.

Number of 10-km squares in which recorded:
2,185 (57%)
Possible breeding 95 (4%)
Probable breeding 631 (29%)
Confirmed breeding 1,459 (67%)

References

DAVIS, P. E. 1967. Migration season of the *Sylvia* warblers at British bird observatories. *Bird Study* 14: 65–95.

HOWARD, H. E. 1907–14. *The British Warblers*. London.

MASON, C. F. 1976. Breeding biology of the *Sylvia* warblers. *Bird Study* 23: 213–232.

STAFFORD, J. 1956. The wintering of Blackcaps in the British Isles. *Bird Study* 3: 251–257.

WALPOLE-BOND, J. 1938. *A History of Sussex Birds*. London.

WILLIAMSON, K. 1974. Habitat change in a young Forestry Commission plantation. *Bird Study* 21: 215–217.

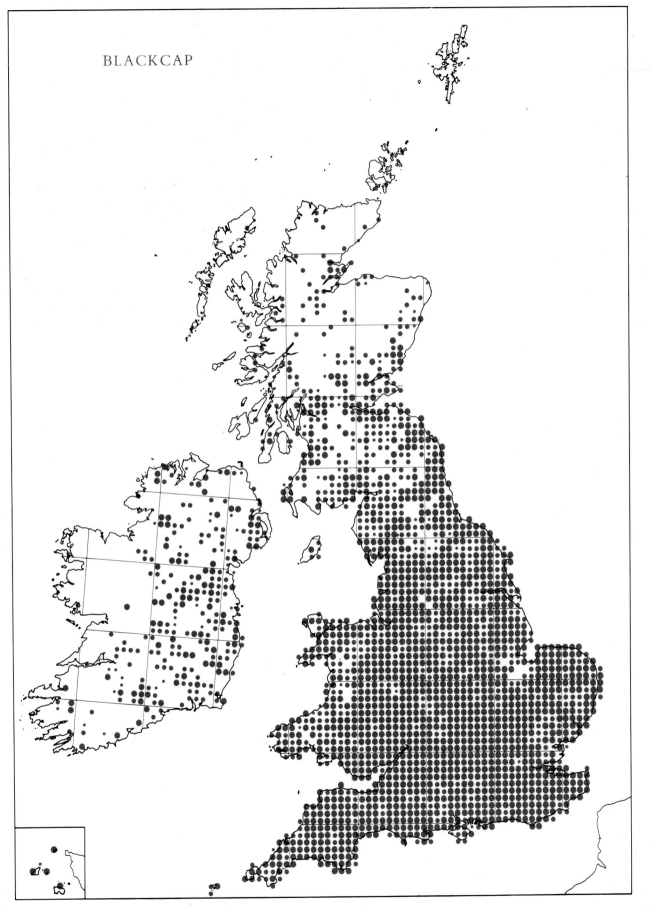

BLACKCAP

Garden Warbler

Sylvia borin

The habitats of the Garden Warbler and Blackcap *S. atricapilla* are very similar in Britain. They frequently nest in close proximity, but the Garden Warbler is more often found away from mature trees, in scrub or in young conifer plantations. In Ireland, there is a wider difference, since Garden Warblers, much rarer there, are usually associated with woods or scrub near loughs, often on islands, and Blackcaps with the woodland of demesnes. The most usual Garden Warbler habitat in Britain is fairly open, deciduous woodland with a dense scrub layer, preferably with tangled brambles. Osier beds, well-grown coppice and even garden shrubberies may be occupied. Both species sometimes use rhododendron thickets, which may provide the only suitable cover in parts of Scotland.

If there are clumps of mature trees, Garden Warblers may breed in young forestry plantations. In a Buckinghamshire wood, where the clear-felled and replanted area was bordered by an amenity fringe of mature trees, Garden Warblers immediately occupied the young plantation, whereas almost all the Blackcaps remained in the amenity fringe (Williamson 1970).

Visually, this is the least distinguished of our *Sylvia* warblers; indeed, it has often been said that it is best recognised by its lack of field characters. Yet when it sings it is immediately obvious that it is closely related to the Blackcap. Location of the singing male is thus not difficult, although identification may be tricky unless the songster is seen. *Atlas* workers were urged to try to see those heard singing, although experienced observers may have felt able to identify correctly the songs of the most typical individuals of each species. Garden Warbler song is generally not so rich, loud or clear as the Blackcap's, though with longer phrases, and often contains rather grating notes reminiscent of the Whitethroat *S. communis*. The alarm calls are also softer and less incisive.

Newly returning migrants generally arrive in late April or May. Males sing immediately they have reached suitable breeding areas, and pairing takes place when the females arrive a week or so later. The frequency and quality of song is depressed after pairing, but it continues throughout the nesting season. Although first clutches are laid on average later than those of the other British *Sylvia* species, some pairs are double-brooded. The nest is generally built low down in quite thick cover: over half of the 585 nests analysed by Mason (1976) were below 60 cm. Identification of the nest and eggs is not always easy but, if an occupied nest is found, an adult can usually be seen. Proof of breeding is best obtained when the parents are feeding young, either in or out of the nest, since at this stage the adults become very agitated when approached. The difference in the proportions of confirmed breeding records for Garden Warbler (62%) and Blackcap (67%) must in part be due to Blackcaps usually being three or four times more common.

Garden Warblers are less widely distributed than Blackcaps (49% of all 10-km squares, compared with 57%). The chief differences in their British distributions are in the Fens of E England and in W Cornwall and SW Lancashire, where the present species is scarce or absent. Their Scottish ranges are quite similar, but there are very many fewer Garden Warblers in Ireland. There, they are almost confined to the Shannon lakes, Lower Lough Erne, Lough Neagh and the Cavan lakes; outside this area, the dots relate almost wholly to sporadic instances of breeding.

Even before the Common Birds Census started in 1962 it was realised that numbers fluctuated from year to year and the CBC results clearly show this. Naturally enough, the populations on farmland are less stable than those in the preferred woodland habitat. Farmland densities seldom reach five pairs per km², and in 1972 averaged 0.66. In woods, however, densities of up to 50 pairs were reached in favoured areas and the 1972 average was 4.5 pairs per km². The mean possibly lies within the range 30–50 pairs per occupied 10-km square, giving a total British and Irish population of between 60,000 and 100,000 pairs. This is rather lower than Parslow's category of 100,000–1,000,000 pairs, which dates from the mid-1960s when the CBC farmland index showed a higher population level than in 1972.

Number of 10-km squares in which recorded:
  1,891 (49%)
Possible breeding   149 (8%)
Probable breeding   574 (30%)
Confirmed breeding   1,168 (62%)

References
HOWARD, H. E. 1907–14. *The British Warblers*. London.
MASON, C. F. 1976. Breeding biology of the *Sylvia* warblers. *Bird Study* 23: 213–232.
WILLIAMSON, K. 1970. Birds and modern forestry. *Bird Study* 17: 167–176.

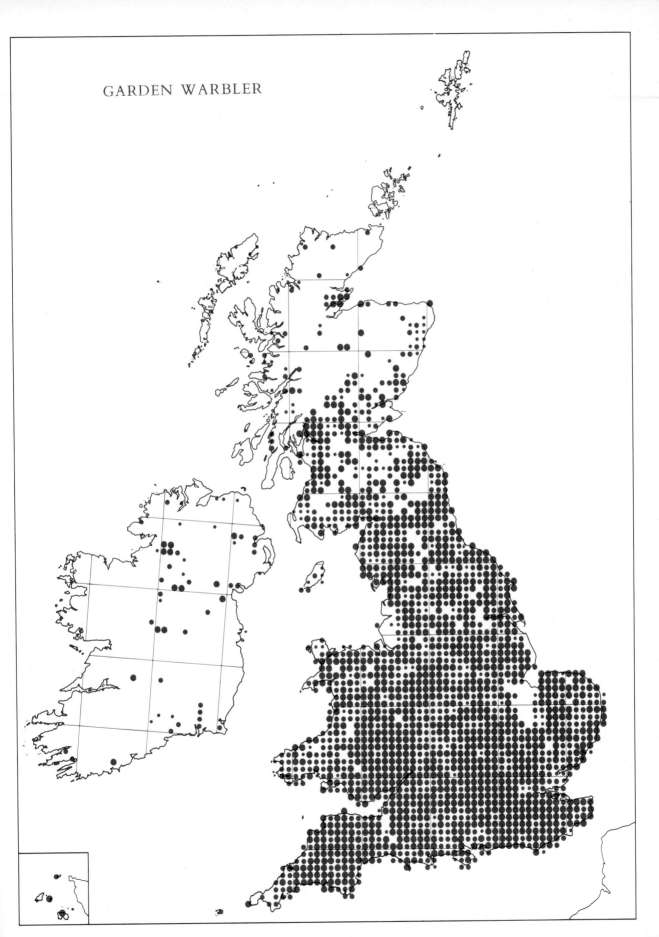

GARDEN WARBLER

Whitethroat

Sylvia communis

The Whitethroat is essentially a bird of scrub-grown situations, such as commons, heaths, waste ground with hawthorn thickets, well-vegetated areas around lakes and marshes, and woodland edges and clearings. It is also characteristic of field and lane hedgerows, though this is a relatively recent environment which has grown up since the enclosures of the 18th century. It is often associated with thick ground cover, like brambles and nettles, in overgrown orchards, untended gardens and uncultivated field corners. Forestry plantations in their young stages are attractive, but become too overgrown after six or seven years. In general, woodland is avoided, unless there is overspill from preferred habitats when the population is high.

Few warblers are as obtrusive as the male Whitethroat on his territory in spring. Frequently he utters his cheerful and ebullient song in flight, demanding an open space for self-advertisement. As two broods are normally reared, this display continues throughout the season. The adults perch openly to chatter at an intruder when the nest is approached, and this also helps in locating territories.

Saunders (1899) wrote: 'Throughout England, Wales and Ireland it is the most generally distributed and plentiful of the warblers'—a view which has been echoed by most ornithological writers of this century. Down to 1968, the first *Atlas* year, this statement held true, the bird being scarce or absent only on high ground. The Common Birds Census results show that 1966 and, especially, 1968 were peak years; but in 1969 some 77% of the previous year's breeding stock failed to reappear. In no season since 1968 has the population reached even a third of that year's level, while in 1974 it fell to one sixth (see graph right). This very dramatic decrease, which was also experienced on the Continent as far east as longitude 15°E (Berthold 1973), has been attributed to mortality in the winter quarters in the Sahel zone of W Africa, between latitudes 12°N and 18°N on the southern fringe of the Sahara, where severe droughts resulted from the failure of the rains (Winstanley *et al* 1974).

In interpreting the *Atlas* map, it must be realised that little fieldwork was done in Scotland and Ireland in 1968, whereas substantial parts of England were covered (see maps on page 24). Even those 10-km squares in England which were not surveyed until

1969–72, however, eventually provided almost 100% proved breeding status. Though the general distribution may not have changed much, especially in the south, the decline probably had the greatest effect in peripheral areas, and before 1969 there would almost certainly have been fewer gaps in Wales, Scotland and, especially, Ireland.

Breeding extends to many islands off the coast of W Scotland, and the only group with none was Orkney, though sporadic nesting has occurred there in the past. On the Scottish mainland, the dots in Caithness and Sutherland may reflect a slight range expansion during the last 25 years.

Flegg (1975) estimated that the crash involved a drop from about 5,000,000 to 1,000,000 pairs. The average for all CBC farmland plots in 1972 was three pairs per km^2, and for scrub and woodland-edge plots six pairs per km^2. Allowing for peripheral squares where it was difficult to find a single pair, these figures probably imply an average of no more than 200 pairs per 10-km square. The British and Irish breeding population since 1969 has, thus, probably been between 500,000 and 700,000 pairs.

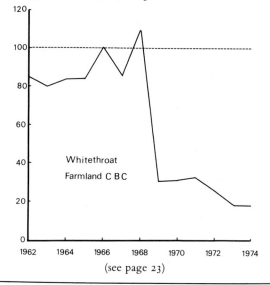

Whitethroat
Farmland C B C

(see page 23)

Number of 10-km squares in which recorded:
3,198 (83%)
Possible breeding   100 (3%)
Probable breeding   722 (23%)
Confirmed breeding   2,376 (74%)

References

BENSON, G. B. G. and K. WILLIAMSON. 1972. Breeding birds of a mixed farm in Suffolk. *Bird Study* 19: 34–50.

BERTHOLD, P. 1973. On the marked decline of the Whitethroat *Sylvia communis* and other species of song-birds in western Europe. *J. Orn.* 114: 348–360.

FLEGG, J. J. M. 1975. Bird population and distribution changes and the impact of man. *Bird Study* 22: 59–70.

SAUNDERS, H. 1899. *Manual of British Birds.* London.

WINSTANLEY, D., R. SPENCER and K. WILLIAMSON. 1974. Where have all the Whitethroats gone? *Bird Study* 21: 1–14.

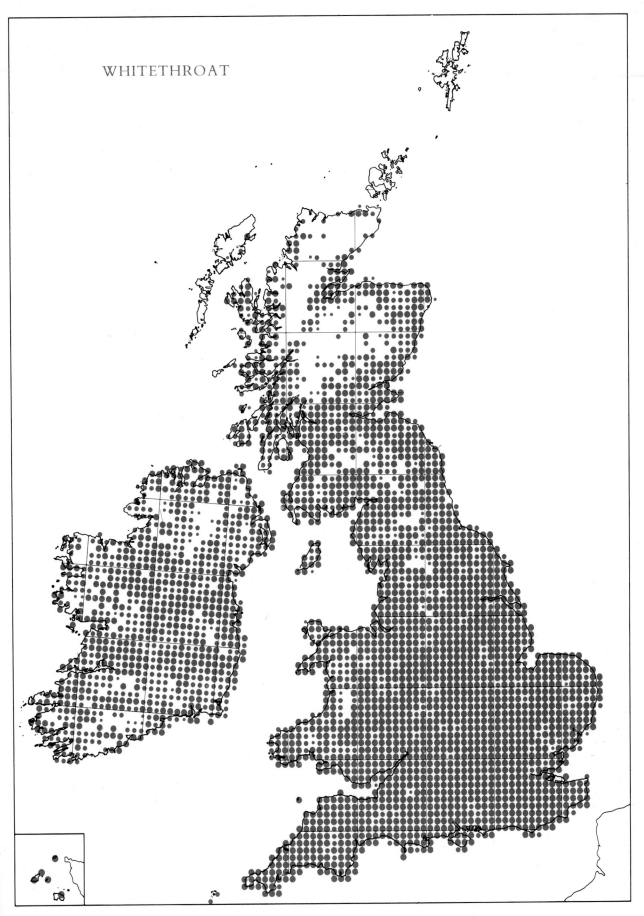

WHITETHROAT

Lesser Whitethroat

Sylvia curruca

The Lesser Whitethroat is typical of tall, dense farmland hedgerows in Britain, but it may breed in other situations more commonly associated with its close relative, the Whitethroat *S. communis*. Unlike the latter, it does not require room for a song-flight, and so tends to skulk in thicker cover. Britain is at the westernmost edge of its breeding range and, unlike the majority of our summer migrants, the Lesser Whitethroat migrates southeastwards to pass round the eastern end of the Mediterranean Sea to its winter quarters.

This species is often very secretive, but when well seen is revealed as one of the most attractively marked of all our warblers, with its dark ear-coverts contrasting with the clean grey upperparts and pink-flushed whitish underparts. Its repetitive, rattling song, usually uttered from dense cover, is somewhat reminiscent of those of the Yellowhammer *Emberiza citrinella* and the Cirl Bunting *E. cirlus*, but is distinctive enough to be identifiable over a long distance amongst the songs of other birds. The males arrive during the second half of April and are followed, about a week later, by the females. Pairing takes place quickly and the eggs are laid early in May. Song diminishes considerably after pair-formation, and persistent songsters in June are likely to be unmated males (Howard 1907–14). Some song may be heard at any stage during the breeding cycle, but much less than the almost continuous outpourings of newly arrived migrants.

The nest is generally built in thick cover, often thorny hedgerow bushes such as hawthorn and blackthorn. About half are at heights above 1 m, with some over 3 m (Mason 1976). As well as in hedgerows, Lesser Whitethroats breed in scrub and heathland situations, bramble patches, overgrown gardens or even young conifer plantations. The presence of some tall trees, whilst not essential, may be advantageous, and newly arrived males often sing from hedgerow standards. The adults usually become very noisy and agitated when there are large young in the nest and confirmation of breeding at this stage, or when the young have recently fledged, may be exceedingly easy.

Suitable breeding habitat is seldom available in Britain above the 200 m contour. Although it seems to be generally accepted that Lesser Whitethroats

have spread farther west and north in the last few decades, there is little firm evidence. Alexander and Lack (1944) stated that Cornwall, Pembroke and Anglesey were first colonised in the 20th century, and Blackett and Ord (1962) recorded nesting in Northumberland. In Scotland, Baxter and Rintoul (1953) mentioned several breeding records, including one as far north as Ross-shire. The situation revealed by the *Atlas* map is thus very similar to that over the previous 40–50 years and there is a suspicion that many of the fringe dots refer to unmated males. There is no suggestion that Lesser Whitethroats have ever bred in Ireland.

The numbers present in Britain have fluctuated over the last 13 years, as shown by the Common Birds Census index. The population of the Lesser Whitethroat did not crash in 1969 as did that of the Whitethroat (see page 372), since the two species have different migration routes and wintering grounds. It is likely that the Lesser Whitethroat is now the commoner of the two in some parts of SE England. The highest densities found during CBC work have come from chalk downland scrub and range from three to six pairs per km². Up to two pairs per km² were found on farmland, but the average, for 1972, was 0.65 pairs per km². Allowing for unsuitable areas and for pockets of high density, a mean value of about 25–50 pairs per occupied 10-km square may be reasonable. This gives a total population of some 25,000–50,000 pairs, in the lower or middle part of Parslow's range of 10,000–100,000 pairs.

Number of 10-km squares in which recorded:
  1,098 (28%)
Possible breeding   124 (11%)
Probable breeding   331 (30%)
Confirmed breeding   643 (59%)

References
BLACKETT, A. and W. ORD. 1962. Lesser Whitethroats breeding in Northumberland. *Brit. Birds* 55: 445.
HOWARD, H. E. 1907–14. *The British Warblers*. London.
MASON, C. F. 1976. Breeding biology of the *Sylvia* warblers. *Bird Study* 23: 213–232.

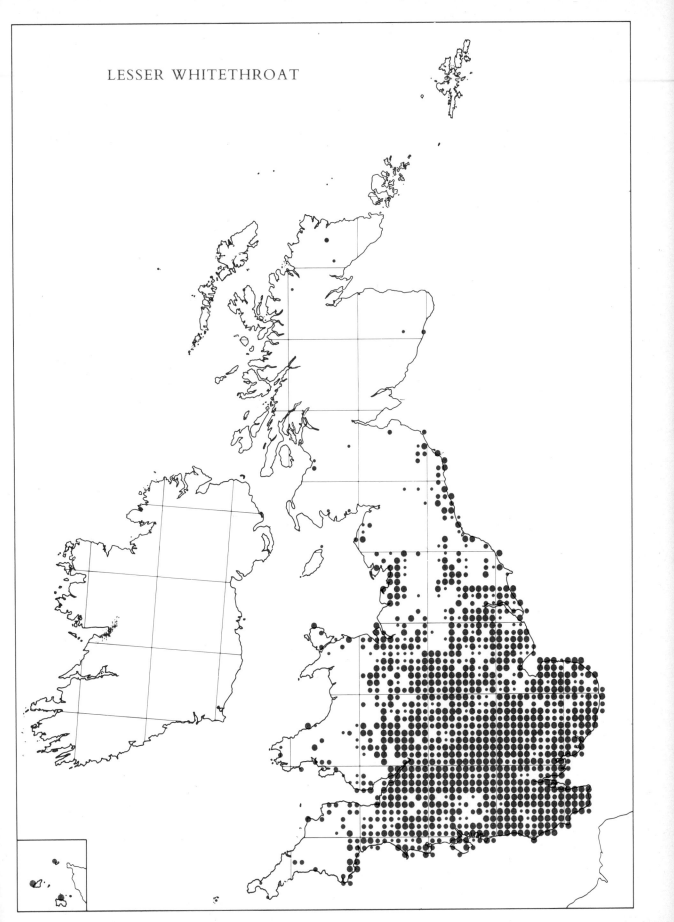

LESSER WHITETHROAT

Dartford Warbler

Sylvia undata

In Britain, Dartford Warblers are almost entirely confined to lowland heath. Areas with mature heather and a generous mixture of gorse are preferred, especially where the latter reaches a height of one to two metres. A few sites on slightly richer soils are used, even when gorse is absent, if the mature heather attains a height of one metre. Territories on heath often include a few trees and shrubs, and up to 15% of the population now nests in pine plantations in which the trees may be as tall as six metres (Bibby and Tubbs 1975). Some, mainly in Sussex, are in gorse/grass situations and, in these circumstances, bramble is an acceptable scrub alternative.

In Dorset, only the Stonechat *Saxicola torquata* has a closer association with lowland heaths than the Dartford Warbler. Moore (1975) found the Stonechat present on 25 out of the 27 heaths he visited and the Dartford Warbler on 19. These are semi-natural habitats which have to be maintained by grazing and periodic burning. They are thus vulnerable to natural colonisation by trees, as well as to commercial afforestation and agricultural development. In addition, many of these heaths are on mineral deposits of sand, gravel and ball-clay which are already being commercially exploited, or may be in the future. The Dartford Warbler is also highly vulnerable to severe weather and may be unable to use some of the lowland heaths beyond its present range because of climatic considerations.

This is one of the most secretive species but it has a characteristic harsh call-note, which may often be heard when the bird itself cannot be seen. At the start of the breeding season, singing and displaying males may occasionally be quite conspicuous. Later, when the young have left the nest, family parties enable breeding to be proved. The restricted habitat and the great interest shown in the species have ensured that the *Atlas* data are complete, with a high proportion of confirmed breeding records.

All the other warblers breeding in Britain (except Cetti's *Cettia cetti*) are predominantly summer visitors, but Dartford Warblers stay in their breeding areas throughout the year, although some, possibly the young birds, wander in the autumn. This means that they are very vulnerable to bad weather, and the severe winters of 1860/61, 1880/81, 1886/87, 1916/17, 1939/40, 1941/42, 1946/47, 1961/62 and 1962/63 were disastrous. The first effect of two in successive years, between 1961 and 1963, was to cut the breeding numbers from the 460 pairs known in 1961 to less than 100 the following year. The Dorset population, however, escaped the worst of the weather, though other groups were wiped out (Tubbs 1963). The next winter's severe cold and snow took its toll and the total breeding in 1963 amounted to no more than a dozen pairs. The usual gradual increase was interrupted by late snow in April 1966 in the New Forest (Tubbs 1967), but the recovery has continued steadily since then.

The breeding distribution was formerly much wider and the population much larger. During the 19th century, nesting was reported west to Cornwall, east to Kent, Essex and Suffolk, and north to Wiltshire, Oxfordshire and Hertfordshire. Isolated pockets of Dartford Warblers also bred in Shropshire and perhaps Staffordshire. The Suffolk population was extinguished about 60 years ago and the last breeding records from Cornwall were in 1940 and Berkshire a few years later; breeding occurred in Essex in 1948. Large areas of suitable habitat had been lost, particularly to agriculture, and that remaining has become severely fragmented in many places, so recolonisation during recovery from climatic setback may have become less easy. Larger areas certainly harbour denser populations than small ones (Bibby and Tubbs 1975). Currently the species is confined to six mainland counties from Devon east to Surrey and Sussex (with the vast majority in Dorset and Hampshire) and the Isle of Wight. By 1974, the population had reached about 560 pairs, but its range had not extended beyond the general areas shown here for 1968–72.

This species is afforded special protection in Great Britain under Schedule I of the Protection of Birds Act, 1954–67.

Number of 10-km squares in which recorded:
31 (0.8%)
Possible breeding   2 (6%)
Probable breeding   6 (19%)
Confirmed breeding   23 (74%)

Nine dots have been moved by up to two 10-km squares (as recommended by the Rare Breeding Birds Panel and R. F. Porter)

References

BIBBY, C. J. and C. R. TUBBS. 1975. Status, habitats and conservation of the Dartford Warbler in England. *Brit. Birds* 68: 177–195.

MOORE, N. W. 1975. Status and habitats of the Dartford Warbler, Whitethroat and Stonechat in Dorset 1959–60. *Brit. Birds* 68: 196–202.

TUBBS, C. R. 1963. The significance of the New Forest to the status of the Dartford Warbler in England. *Brit. Birds* 56: 41–48.

TUBBS, C. R. 1967. Numbers of Dartford Warblers in England during 1962–66. *Brit. Birds* 60: 87–89.

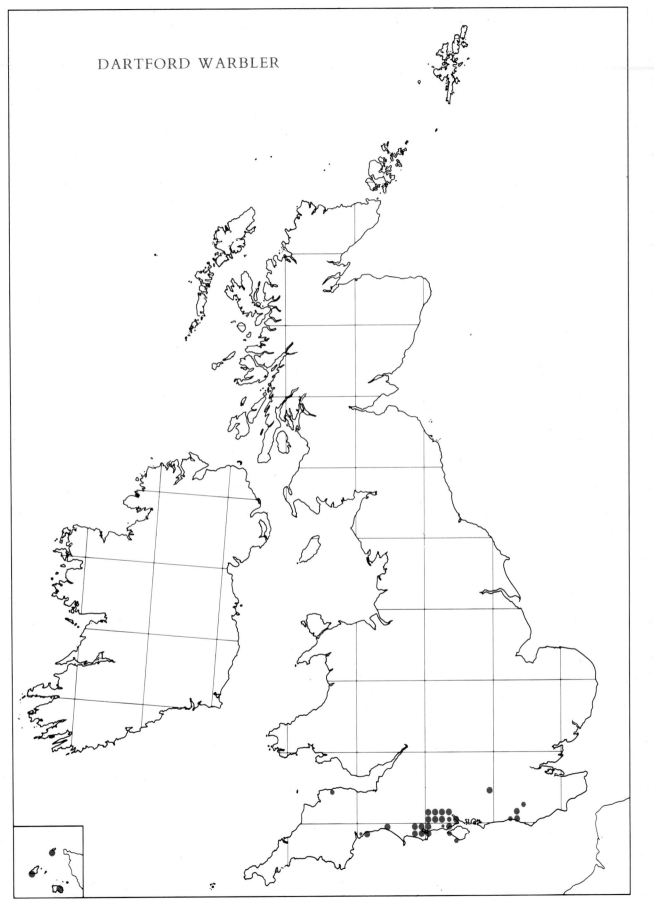

DARTFORD WARBLER

Willow Warbler

Phylloscopus trochilus

Willow Warblers are the commonest and most widely distributed of our summer migrants. They nest amongst almost any kind of pioneer growth of small bushes or trees, but not normally in mature woodland with a closed canopy; though even the smallest glade or clearing, or the narrowest ride, where the canopy is broken and secondary growth flourishes, will have nesting pairs. Hillside birch woods and remnants of the ancient Caledonian forest of birch and Scots pine may hold considerable numbers, and the Willow Warbler forms about one-third of the bird community there, often outnumbering its nearest rival, the Chaffinch *Fringilla coelebs*, by three to one (Yapp 1962). It is a very common species of damp places with alder and sallow. Burnt areas where scrub and trees are regenerating are also favoured, and it quickly becomes the dominant species in the younger stages of conifer afforestation in both lowland and upland regions. Depending on their speed of growth, such plantations may hold Willow Warblers for at least 15 years.

The familiar descending trill attracts attention and breeding can be confirmed by watching for the adults building their nests or feeding their young. The nests are often very well concealed. Migrants sing as they pass through an area in spring, but the map shows that breeding was proved in the majority of squares (91%). Most first clutches are laid during the first half of May, but can be up to a fortnight later in the north (Cramp 1955). Second broods are generally raised. Although there is some territorial overlap with nesting Chiffchaffs *P. collybita*, these usually feed higher in the vegetation than Willow Warblers (Lack 1971). Fieldwork in an upland wood in Wales showed interaction between Willow Warblers and Wood Warblers *P. sibilatrix*, so that their territories were mutually exclusive (Edington and Edington 1972), but this is not true of many lowland woods where the two occur.

The Willow Warbler is dimorphic, with the usual olive-and-yellow form found in Britain being replaced progressively by a brown-and-white one towards the eastern part of its extensive Eurasian range. Some of these brown-and-white birds have been recorded nesting in N Britain (Williamson 1962), and several *Atlas* workers reported breeding birds of this form in Scotland and N England. The altitudinal range is determined by the tree-line, and some in the Highlands of Scotland regularly breed at 700 m or more.

There is little evidence of major changes in distribution in Britain and Ireland. Breeding was first reported in the Outer Hebrides and Orkney in the second half of the 19th century; it may have been overlooked previously, but there, as in many other parts of Britain and Ireland, tree plantings have extended the suitable habitat. Sporadic breeding has been reported from Shetland, but not during 1968–72. There may have been a slight extension westwards in Ireland during the first part of this century. New areas have been occupied in upland regions as forestry has provided acceptable haunts on what was formerly desolate moorland. The conspicuous gap in the fenland of E England presumably reflects the scarcity of suitable breeding sites.

The Common Birds Census farmland and woodland indices both show that the population was at a high level during the first three years of the *Atlas* project. The densities found on individual areas are sometimes very high, often reaching 100–200 pairs per km^2 in wood-edge or scrub. Few data are available from Scottish birch woods, where the density is probably highest, but one in Wester Ross held Willow Warblers at 425 pairs per km^2. The farmland average for CBC plots in 1972 was eight pairs per km^2, and for woodland 41 pairs. Since many of the desolate upland areas are intersected by valleys and flanked by slopes which hold good numbers of Willow Warblers, it is likely that the average breeding density in Britain and Ireland is high, possibly more than 1,000 pairs per occupied 10-km square. Thus, the British and Irish population may exceed 3,000,000 pairs.

Number of 10-km squares in which recorded:
  3,536 (92%)
Possible breeding   26 (1%)
Probable breeding   287 (8%)
Confirmed breeding   3,223 (91%)

References
CRAMP, S. 1955. The breeding of the Willow Warbler. *Bird Study* 2: 121–135.
EDINGTON, J. M. and M. A. EDINGTON. 1972. Spatial patterns and habitat partition in the breeding birds of an upland wood. *J. Anim. Ecol.* 41: 331–357.
LACK, D. 1971. *Ecological Isolation in Birds.* Oxford.
WILLIAMSON, K. 1962. *Identification for Ringers 2. The Genus* Phylloscopus. Oxford.
WILLIAMSON, K. 1969. Bird communities in woodland habitats in Wester Ross, Scotland. *Q. J. Forestry* 53: 305–328.
YAPP, W. B. 1962. *Birds and Woods.* London.

WILLOW WARBLER

Chiffchaff

Phylloscopus collybita

Chiffchaffs are typical of old deciduous or mixed woodland, requiring tall trees as song-posts and rough undergrowth for nesting. Commons, heaths, parks, farm hedgerows with standard trees, coppiced woods and well-grown forestry plantations are the habitats most often frequented.

One result of bird census investigations into the effects of modern forestry techniques was the discovery that Chiffchaffs could be retained when young conifer plantations replaced well-grown deciduous woodland if small islands of trees were left within the plantation or at its edge (Williamson 1972). They are absent from much of the semi-natural woodland in Scotland (and to a lesser extent in W Ireland) except where there is an association with trees underplanted with rhododendrons; hence their preference for large gardens and the policies of old estates.

The reiterated song-notes of Chiffchaffs are at once distinctive and penetrating, audible sometimes even to the motorway driver, and can hardly have been overlooked anywhere during the *Atlas* survey.

The nest is built in low vegetation, usually within 1 m of the ground, but less often on the ground than in the case of the Willow Warbler *P. trochilus*. Confirmation of breeding is not quite so easy as for the Willow Warbler, partly because the habitat makes the birds less easy to watch back, and partly because they are usually scarcer. This is reflected in the considerably lower proportion of confirmed breeding records.

Although most Chiffchaffs leave Britain and Ireland for the winter, many stay late in the autumn and some even throughout the winter. Ringing records show that many remain in the W Mediterranean basin and also farther north in France (Mead 1974), though still sufficiently far south to escape the worst of the cold weather. The Common Birds Census returns (see graph) show that the annual index actually increased from 1962 to 1963, the period of the most severe winter in W Europe during recent history. It increased consistently to 1970, but then halved in four years. There is hardly any other evidence of a long-term change in S Britain, but breeding has become more widespread and frequent in Scotland since about 1950. Chiffchaffs are absent from much of the upland of Snowdonia, the Pennines, the Border hills and the Scottish Highlands and

islands. There is also a scarcity in low-lying, treeless parts of Cambridgeshire and Lincolnshire, and they occurred on only 46% of Midlands farms sending returns to the CBC. In general, this species is less common in E Britain north of the River Tees (Yorkshire).

In Ireland, Chiffchaffs were known in only seven of the 32 counties in 1850, but by 1900 had spread throughout the country, extending into W Kerry in the 1950s. The main areas of absence shown by the *Atlas* fieldwork are in parts of Mayo, Galway and Roscommon in the west. Otherwise, Chiffchaffs are now more widespread in Ireland than in Britain, and there were even some parts of the southwest where *Atlas* fieldwork in 1969–70 suggested that they outnumbered Willow Warblers.

Nevertheless, the species is usually scarcer than the Willow Warbler in woodland. Parslow placed the British and Irish population in the range 100,000 to 1,000,000 pairs. In 1972, the average densities in CBC areas were 2.9 pairs per km^2 on farmland and 12.2 in woodland. Allowing an average of 100 pairs per occupied 10-km square, the total number may be about 300,000 pairs, in the lower part of Parslow's range.

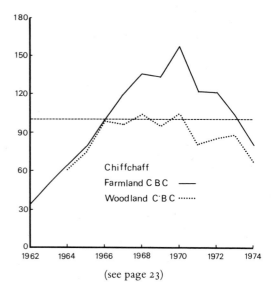

(see page 23)

Number of 10-km squares in which recorded:
2,912 (75%)
Possible breeding   75 (3%)
Probable breeding   792 (27%)
Confirmed breeding   2,045 (70%)

References

MEAD, C. J. 1974. *Bird Ringing*. BTO Guide no. 16. Tring.

MEIKLEJOHN, M. F. M. 1952. Habitat of Chiffchaff in Scotland. *Scott. Nat.* 64: 114–116.

WILLIAMSON, K. 1972. The conservation of bird life in the new coniferous forests. *Forestry* 45: 87–100.

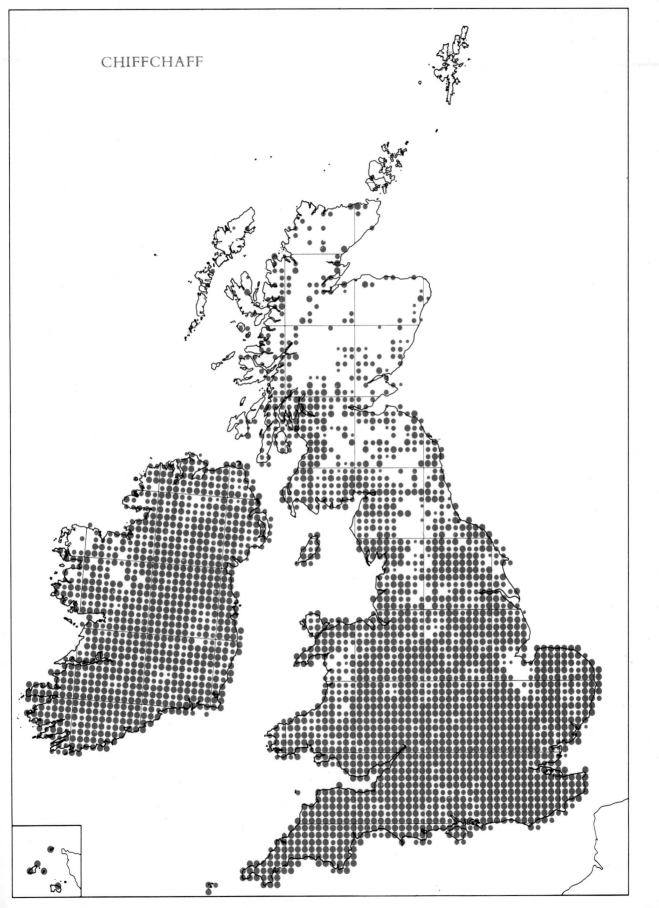

CHIFFCHAFF

Wood Warbler

Phylloscopus sibilatrix

As the vernacular name suggests, Wood Warblers are even more strictly high forest birds than are Chiffchaffs *P. collybita*. The sessile oakwoods of W Britain are their typical haunt, and this is strikingly demonstrated by comparing Wood Warbler distribution with the overlay map of this type of woodland. Even where such woods have been managed as coppice in the past, and few maiden trees remain, the Wood Warbler may flourish (Williamson 1974).

In SE England, oak, beech and chestnut woods are favoured, and to a lesser extent pine and birch, especially if mixed with other tree species. In N England and W Scotland, birch woods are much frequented and Wood Warblers occur in hillside oak scrub in Wales. East of a line from Flamborough Head (Yorkshire) to Portland Bill (Dorset) it is easy to identify on the distribution map the well-wooded New Forest, North and South Downs and Chiltern Hills.

This warbler selects woodland which has a good canopy, little secondary growth, and sparse ground vegetation. The habitat requirements are more exacting than those of the closely related Chiffchaff and Willow Warbler *P. trochilus*, although in certain conditions all three may be found breeding extremely close together. Tiedemann (1971), in a limited study in N Germany, concluded that low branches not more than 2.5 m high should be present for the adults to perch on when bringing food to the nestlings, and that the canopy must give at least 70% shelter from external climatic conditions, such as wind and heat from direct sunlight.

The domed nest of grass, fibres, moss and leaves is built into the woodland floor, where the vegetation is sparse, most commonly among grasses, bracken, bramble and dead leaves. It may most easily be found by watching back, as in the cases of the Willow Warbler and the Chiffchaff.

The song is a very distinctive, shivering trill, often interspersed with a plaintive, piping 'peu, peu, peu'. Since the song is far-carrying possible breeding records are very easy to obtain, but much more effort is required to locate the nest, for the female may sit very close. The adults' anxiety notes, closely resembling calls of Bullfinches *Pyrrhula pyrrhula*, however, will indicate when the nest is approached. There is often an excess of males, and some song records will refer to unmated birds. It is sometimes difficult to determine the territorial relationships within a Wood Warbler population as males will sing from one or more selected areas which may be a fair distance apart, and colour ringing has shown that polygamy occurs.

In Scotland, the Wood Warbler has been extending its range northwards since the mid-19th century, and it had reached N Sutherland by the 1940s, a parallel situation occurring in Norway. The records for Ireland, where breeding has been sporadic in the past, are the first since 1938. The oak woodlands there seem to hold great potential for future expansion if the species can gain a secure foothold, and it is encouraging that one site has now been occupied annually during 1968–75. Decreases have been recorded in many English counties, particularly in the east, since about 1940. Local extinction due to tree-felling in some areas has not been counterbalanced by colonisation of new sites; equally, formerly occupied woods have been deserted despite the fact that there has been no apparent habitat change. Although the Common Birds Census data for the Wood Warbler are insufficient to produce a regular index, the figures indicate that little change in the population has occurred recently.

Parslow placed the Wood Warbler in the range 10,000–100,000 pairs. The densities vary greatly, from just one or two pairs in some areas at the edge of the range, to between 20 and 90 pairs per km² in typical western oakwoods. Taking an average of about 25–50 pairs per 10-km square, the total British and Irish population may be about 30,000–60,000 pairs, in the middle of Parslow's range.

Number of 10-km squares in which recorded: 1,238 (32%)
Possible breeding   128 (10%)
Probable breeding   546 (44%)
Confirmed breeding   564 (46%)

References

TICEHURST, C. B. 1932. *A Systematic Review of the Genus Phylloscopus*. London.

TIEDEMANN, G. 1971. Zur Ökologie und Siedlungsdichte des Waldlaubsängers (*Phylloscopus sibilatrix*). *Vogelwelt* 92: 8–17.

VON HAARTMAN, L. 1969. The nesting habits of Finnish birds. I. Passeriformes. *Commentationes Biologicea* 32: 115–116.

WILLIAMSON, K. 1969. Bird community in woodland habitats in Wester Ross, Scotland. *Q. J. Forestry* 63: 305–328.

WILLIAMSON, K. 1974. Breeding birds in the deciduous woodlands of mid-Argyll, Scotland. *Bird Study* 21: 29–44.

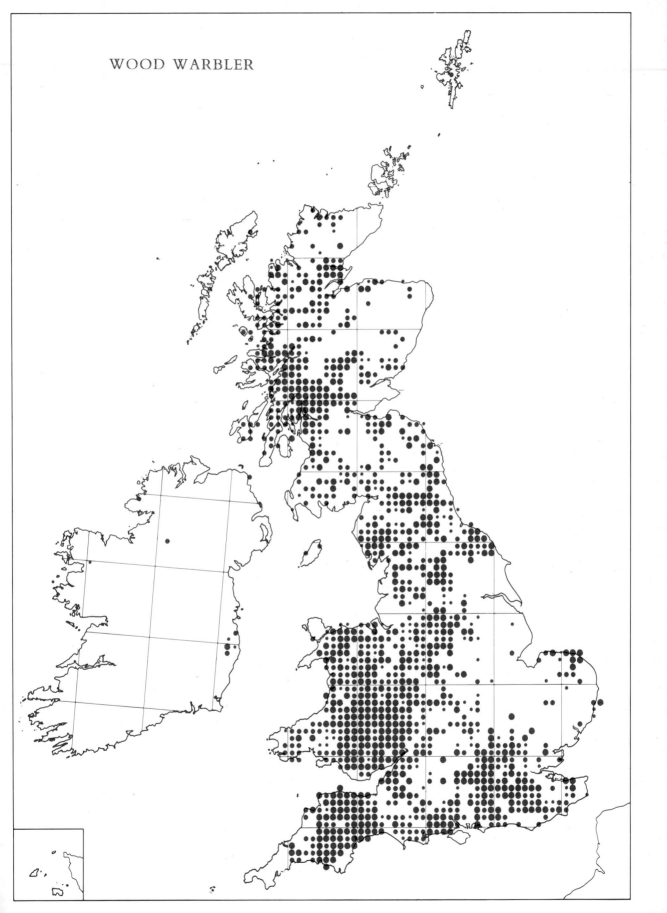

WOOD WARBLER

Goldcrest

Regulus regulus

Goldcrests are typical of coniferous woodland in Britain, and in parts of E England they are sometimes to be found only in the yews and ornamental conifers associated with churchyards and large gardens. The species occurs at low density in sessile oakwoods in W Britain, but is an important constituent of such woods in Ireland, in which it may be the third commonest bird, behind Chaffinch *Fringilla coelebs* and Robin *Erithacus rubecula*. In lowland Britain, the Goldcrest does not usually move into deciduous woods until the population has reached a high level following a succession of mild winters.

The vulnerability of this species to hard weather is well known. There was a population crash in the severe winter of 1962/63, then a steady recovery (see graph), the Common Birds Census showing a tenfold increase by 1975. In the final *Atlas* year, 1972, Goldcrests were to be found in many deciduous woods where there had been none four years earlier. Even in the more maritime climate of Ireland, an occasional hard winter can cause serious depletion.

The high-pitched song has a pulsating quality and a terminal flourish which that of the Firecrest *R. ignicapillus* lacks; like the song of the Grasshopper Warbler *Locustella naevia*, it is one of the first to be lost as a birdwatcher's frequency-range contracts from middle age, so it cannot always be relied upon to reveal the bird's presence. The nest is not very easy to spot, particularly in tall conifers, and searching is usually most productive when the adults are building, or gathering food for the young. Proof of breeding is best obtained by looking and listening for parties of newly-fledged young.

The greatly increased area of conifers which has resulted from afforestation in this century has doubtless benefited the species, providing a wide expanse of optimal habitat during and after hard winters. The recent colonisation of Shetland and the Isles of Scilly is directly attributable to new conifer plantations. The species is still absent from the Fens of E England, where there is little suitable habitat, though one wonders, in view of the rapidly increasing numbers, whether a few may not have spread to this region

since 1972; breeding was suspected at Ely (Cambridgeshire) in 1974.

The greatest densities have been found in Ireland, where perhaps there may be less competition from the fewer species of warblers and tits. In well-grown plantations near Killarney (Co Kerry), Batten (1976) recorded 591 pairs per km^2 in Norway spruce and 387 pairs per km^2 in Sitka spruce; even the yew and oak/holly woods had 160–180 pairs per km^2. In England, the highest figures are from Forestry Commission Norway spruce now 40 years old, where (as at Killarney) Goldcrests were dominant, making 22% of the bird community, with 320 pairs per km^2. The species takes well to exotic conifers, and in 112-years-old coast and sierra redwoods in Montgomeryshire in 1970 the Goldcrest was dominant with 138 pairs per km^2. Deciduous woods in England and Scotland may have up to 25 pairs per km^2, this figure increasing if a few conifers are present.

By 1972, the average density on Common Birds Census woodland plots, many in lowland areas and of broad-leaved species, was 12.9 pairs per km^2. Allowing for the much higher densities in the extensive areas of conifers, an average figure of 500 pairs per occupied 10 km square may even be conservative and this implies a total in Britain and Ireland of over $1\frac{1}{2}$ million pairs. This is above the upper limit of Parslow's (1967) range of 100,000 to 1 million, which was, however, probably correct at that time, not long after the severe winter of 1962/63.

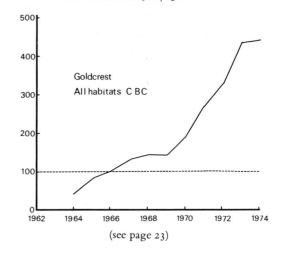

Goldcrest
All habitats C B C

(see page 23)

Number of 10-km squares in which recorded:
  3,259 (84%)
Possible breeding   139 (4%)
Probable breeding   475 (15%)
Confirmed breeding   2,645 (81%)

References

BATTEN, L. A. 1976. Bird communities of some Killarney woodlands. *Proc. Roy. Irish Acad.* 76: 285–313.

WILLIAMSON, K. 1971. The breeding birds of a century-old grove of coast and sierra redwoods in Wales. *Q. J. Forestry* 65: 109–121.

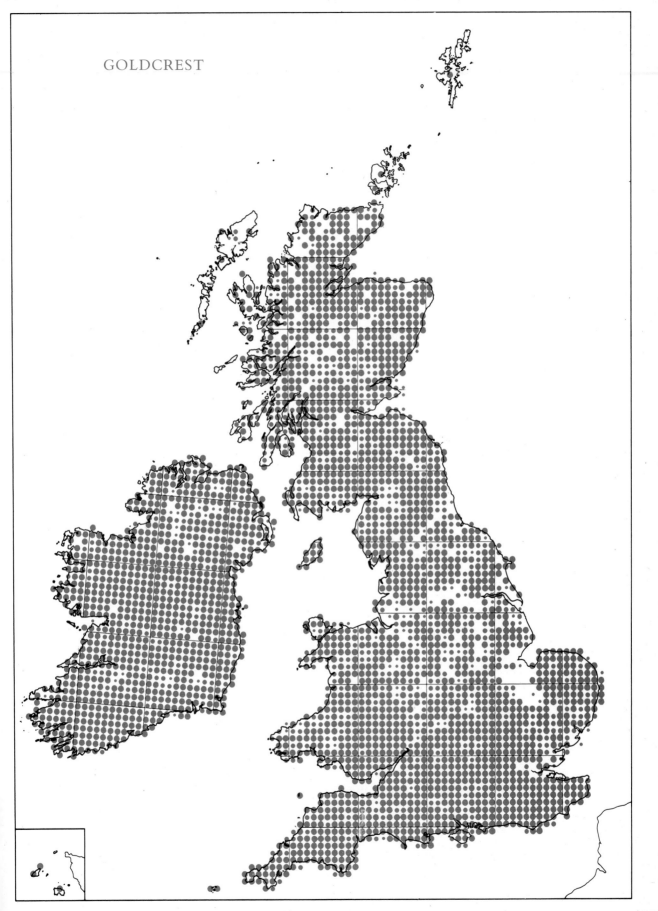

GOLDCREST

Firecrest

Regulus ignicapillus

Norway spruce over nine metres high appears to be the Firecrest's most favoured habitat, but this recently colonising species is now known to occur in a wide range of coniferous and mixed woodland. Individuals holding territory have been recorded from mature Scots pine, Douglas fir and western hemlock underplanted with larch. More recently, males have been found established in yew mixed with beech, and in oak and beech with associated holly (Batten 1973). Firecrests and Goldcrests *R. regulus* often share the same habitat.

There has been a marked expansion of range on the Continent, the species breeding for the first time in the Netherlands in 1930 and in Denmark in 1961. It has spread northwards in France and is known to have increased in N Germany, Belgium and Czechoslovakia.

There were no satisfactory breeding records in England until 1962, when fledged young were seen in the New Forest (Hampshire), following the discovery of three singing males in May–June 1961; a regular population became established there in up to five localities and a nest was found in 1965 (Adams 1966). Singing males were noted in Hertfordshire and Kent in 1968 and in Dorset in 1970, but it was not until 1971 that a more extensive distribution was revealed, as documented by Batten (1971, 1973). By 1972, a Forestry Commission wood in Buckinghamshire held 23 singing males and a total of 43 was known in six counties in that year, including 11 in Hampshire (where a maximum of 27 had been recorded in 1969). By 1975, the main Buckinghamshire area alone had 43 singing males; others were recorded west to Monmouthshire and north to N Yorkshire, and breeding was proved in Worcestershire. The distribution is now known to be more extensive than the *Atlas* map suggests.

Firecrests have increased markedly on passage in both Britain and Ireland in the last two decades. The British breeding population appears to be migratory, arriving at its nesting areas in late April and early May, and departing from late July, though it is not known if the birds actually leave this country.

Nests may be built in a variety of situations. The six British ones for which estimates of height were given varied from 2.5 to 13.5 m: two were in ivy on tree trunks, a third was in a fork of a field maple, two others were in deodar cedars, and the sixth was suspended under a frond of a Norway spruce at 12 m. Conifer fronds are frequently used in Europe.

The best way of locating Firecrests is by learning their song. It is harsher than the Goldcrest's, and lacks its terminal flourish and rhythmic quality. Phonetically, the Firecrest's song could be written as a rapidly repeated succession of 'zit' notes, becoming slightly louder and faster before ending abruptly after 2 to 2½ seconds. The call notes are harsher than the Goldcrest's, sounding more like 'zit-zit' than the 'si-si' of the commoner species. The difference is not so well marked when the first broods of young Goldcrests leave their nests, as their calls are harsher than those of the adults. Young Firecrests develop a white eyestripe whilst they are still in the nest and are, therefore, distinguishable from young Goldcrests at an early age.

The time to find breeding Firecrests is during May and the first half of June, since song becomes less frequent as the summer progresses. Firecrest song often brings a response from Goldcrests, but the reverse has not been noted. The behaviour suggests that there may be some intraspecific competition, though study of the two species in a mature Norway spruce plot shows that their territories overlap to a considerable extent.

With more than half of the known British summering population in a single wood, it is obvious that this species is greatly overlooked and it would be foolhardy to attempt to guess how many Firecrests nest in Britain. Breeding could even be occurring undetected in Ireland.

This species is afforded special protection in Great Britain under Schedule I of the Protection of Birds Act, 1954–67.

Number of 10-km squares in which recorded:
  20 (0.5%)
Possible breeding   7 (35%)
Probable breeding   10 (50%)
Confirmed breeding   3 (15%)

Though some records were originally submitted in confidence, all dots are now shown accurately (as recommended by the Rare Breeding Birds Panel)

References
ADAMS, M. C. 1966. Firecrests breeding in Hampshire. *Brit. Birds* 59: 240–246.
BATTEN, L. A. 1971. Firecrests breeding in Buckinghamshire. *Brit. Birds* 64: 473–475.
BATTEN, L. A. 1973. The colonisation of England by the Firecrest. *Brit. Birds* 66: 159–166.

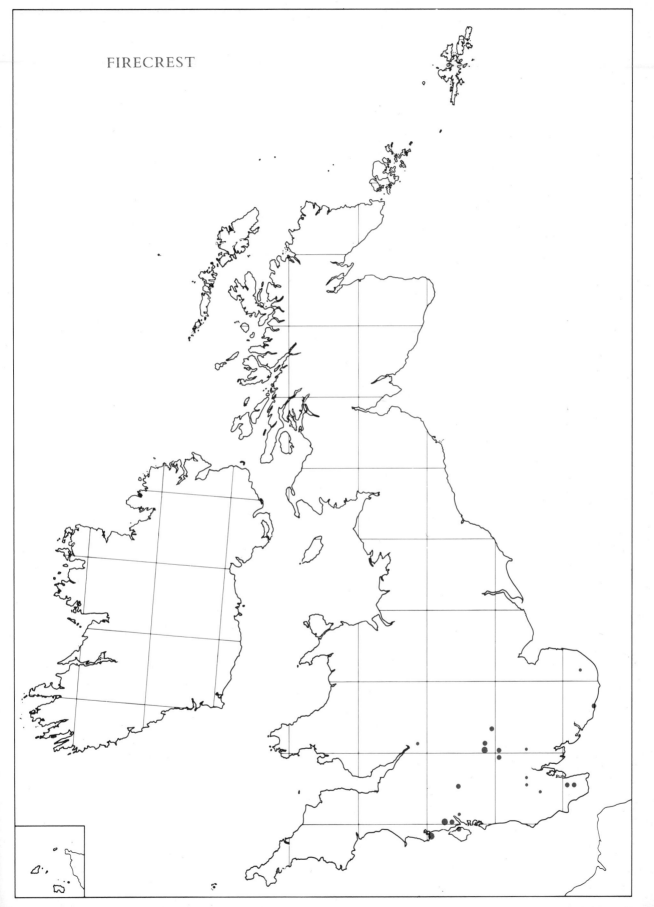

FIRECREST

Spotted Flycatcher

Muscicapa striata

The Spotted Flycatcher is one of the last of our summer migrants to reach us in spring. There are very few records before mid-April and good numbers are not normally present before the second week in May. Such a late arrival is dictated by the availability of the flying insects upon which the birds feed.

In natural habitats, the Spotted Flycatcher is a bird of the woodland edge or forest glade. Wooded streams or trees at the edges of lakes are particularly favoured as insect life is likely to be rich by the water, but high numbers may also be present in open, dry deciduous woodland. Man-modified habitats are often very suitable for this flycatcher. Farmland with copses or spinneys, or mature trees in the hedgerows, will carry scattered breeding pairs almost anywhere in Britain and Ireland. Closer to human habitations, orchards, farmyards (especially where there are cattle or a pond), gardens, churchyards and even public parks are often occupied. Its familiarity as a garden bird in rural situations has given the Spotted Flycatcher a high place in public affection.

The nest is generally built in a shallow niche or opening or against a vertical surface, often within some concealing vegetation. In natural situations, this usually means on a tree or stump, but sometimes on a rock ledge in highland areas and on the coast. In gardens, a position on a wall behind some climbing plant is normal, but open-fronted nest boxes, without any concealment, may be used. Old nests of other species are often used as a base; those of thrushes and Swallows *Hirundo rustica* are the most usual, but over a dozen species have been recorded. The Spotted Flycatcher's nest is neat and delicate and often incorporates spiders' webs. The first clutch is laid at the end of May or early in June and, at least in S Britain, most pairs are double-brooded (Summers-Smith 1952).

The song is thin and squeaky and does not carry far, and the plumage is not at all conspicuous; however, the constant aerobatic forays for food from its perch will quickly reveal the Spotted Flycatcher's presence. *Atlas* fieldworkers very often obtained proof of breeding at farms and country houses when asking for permission to enter private estates, since many owners were delighted to show off 'their' flycatchers' nests. These may be difficult to find early in the nesting cycle, but proof of breeding is very easy by the time the young are being fed, as the high percentage of such records shows. Newly-fledged family parties are also noisy and conspicuous.

Few long-term changes in numbers or distribution have been recorded; although breeding in the Outer Hebrides and Orkney has been spasmodic, the current distribution in N Scotland is possibly more complete than had been supposed (*cf* Baxter and Rintoul 1953) and there may have been an increase in Ireland this century. There are suggestions of a decline in SW Britain, but the species is now breeding in Scilly, from which it was formerly absent (Bannerman 1953). Most of the gaps in the Highlands and N Scotland, Connemara, Mayo and the Fens of E England probably reflect a shortage of suitable habitat, particularly mature trees. The sparse distribution in industrial Yorkshire, coinciding as it does with an area from which the Kingfisher *Alcedo atthis* is also missing (see page 266), may be indicative of a high level of pollution affecting both flying insects and freshwater fish.

In the short term, the results of the Common Birds Census have shown a gradual decrease of about 50% in the last ten years from a peak level in 1965 (when numbers were about 10% higher than in 1962–64). Such fluctuations are not yet understood, but there is no sign of disaster in any particular year, as there was between 1968 and 1969 for the Whitethroat *Sylvia communis* and some other species. Densities on census plots range from ten or more pairs per km^2 in good areas to a general figure of about one pair per km^2 on lowland farms with some tree cover. Since Parslow's population figure of 10,000–100,000 pairs implies, at most, an average of only 30 pairs per occupied 10-km square, it may be rather too low. The current breeding population of Britain and Ireland is probably between 100,000 and 200,000 pairs.

Number of 10-km squares in which recorded:
  3,332 (86%)
Possible breeding   157 (5%)
Probable breeding   172 (5%)
Confirmed breeding   3,003 (90%)

References
BANNERMAN, D. A. 1953. *The Birds of the British Isles*. Vol. 2. Edinburgh and London.
SUMMERS-SMITH, D. 1952. Breeding biology of the Spotted Flycatcher. *Brit. Birds* 45: 153–167.

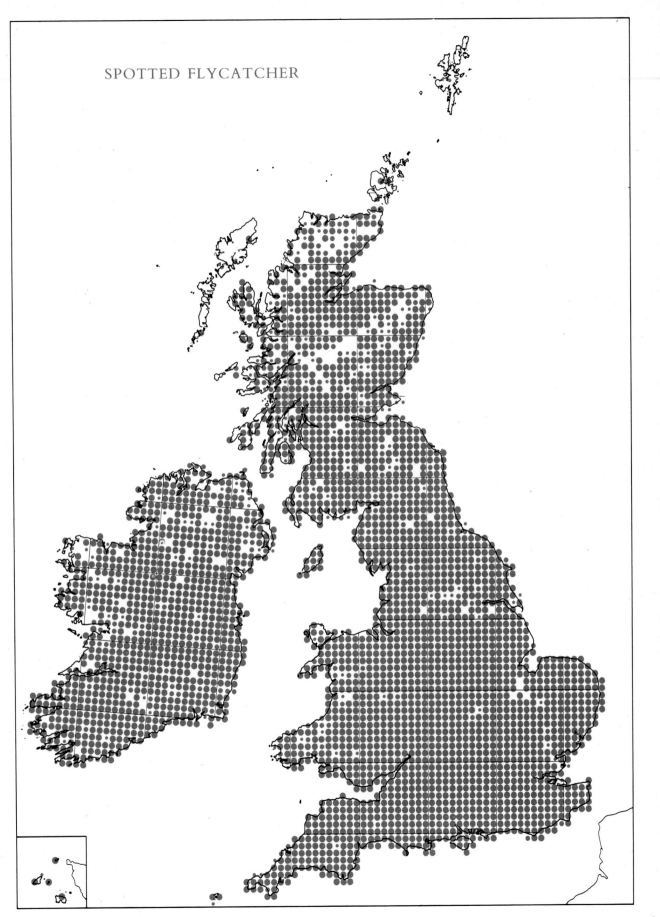

SPOTTED FLYCATCHER

Pied Flycatcher

Ficedula hypoleuca

In Britain, Pied Flycatchers are restricted almost completely to deciduous woodland in upland valleys and foothills to the tree limit, and alder and birch woods alongside rivers, streams and lochs. The western sessile oakwoods, with an abundant food supply of defoliating caterpillars, dead branches for perching, holes for nesting and low ground vegetation, provide the typical habitat (see overlay map). One of the limiting factors may be the availability of nest holes, for unoccupied areas adjacent to existing haunts have been readily colonised following the provision of nest boxes. In one such wood, the Dinas RSPB Reserve (Carmarthenshire), the Pied Flycatcher is the dominant species at double the density (120 pairs per km²) to be found in grazed sessile oak woods without nest boxes.

Nest box schemes to aid the species have been introduced by several county naturalists' trusts. For instance, the Hereford and Radnorshire Trust now has over 1,000 boxes in groups within the varied woodlands of its region. It has established that Pied Flycatchers will use the boxes within their usual oakwood habitat, and in other types of deciduous woodland, as well as in small copses and spinneys (preferably with water of some sort) in the midst of farmland. Since the normal range of the species covers only the western two-thirds of Herefordshire, the boxes in the remainder of the county have enabled a gradual extension and consolidation of breeding to the east. The scheme regularly has over 100 boxes occupied by Pied Flycatchers and is an admirable example of how a group of amateur birdwatchers can, in their spare time, help to enrich the local avifauna.

Pied Flycatchers are summer visitors, staying here from May to August. The habit of several pairs nesting in loose colonies, the loud song and the male's conspicuous black and white plumage make location simple early in the season where the species is common, but isolated pairs away from the main haunts can easily be overlooked. Nest finding is not difficult once there are young, for both parents repeatedly visit them with food. The instances of possible (and even probable) breeding are likely to relate mostly to migrants, or to males which failed to find mates. The fact that unmated males not infrequently occupy holes in trees could mislead the unwary observer.

The distribution apparently changed little between the middle of the 19th and the early 20th centuries, except perhaps for an extension into S Scotland. During 1940–52, however, there was a marked expansion of range, with breeding recorded in 40 counties, compared with 35 during the first part of the century (see maps on page 463).

Between the 1950s and early 1960s, the expansion slowed or even halted, but recently the range has extended farther north in Scotland and (aided by nest box schemes) has been consolidated in SW England and the Lake District. The northwards spread in Scotland may have been helped to some extent by the return of Great Spotted Woodpeckers *Dendrocopos major*, providing nest sites, and it is perhaps worth mentioning that Pied Flycatchers and Green Woodpeckers *Picus viridis* are currently colonising the oakwoods along Loch Lomond together. Sporadic breeding in E England, which was fairly frequent in the 19th century following large spring influxes, has been rare in this century. Nesting has never been reported in Ireland, though apparently suitable habitat exists, especially in Co Wicklow.

Pied Flycatchers can be very common locally, this being emphasised by their semi-colonial nesting habits. Where nest boxes are erected, and where unmanaged woodland with many rotting trees provides the necessary holes, this species may even be dominant. Thus, although many of the 10-km squares with probable or confirmed breeding records away from the centres of distribution hold only a few pairs, the average may be 50 or even more. Parslow's estimate of 1,000–10,000 pairs is too low and 20,000 pairs may be closer to the true figure.

Number of 10-km squares in which recorded:
546 (14%)
Possible breeding   116 (21%)
Probable breeding   94 (17%)
Confirmed breeding   336 (62%)

References
CAMPBELL, B. 1954–55. The breeding distribution and habitats of the Pied Flycatcher (*Muscicapa hypoleuca*) in Britain. *Bird Study* 1: 81–101; 2: 24–32, 179–191.
CAMPBELL, B. 1965. The British breeding distribution of the Pied Flycatcher, 1953–62. *Bird Study* 12: 305–318.
WILLIAMSON, K. 1974. Oak wood breeding bird communities in the Loch Lomond National Nature Reserve. *Q. J. Forestry* 68: 9–28.

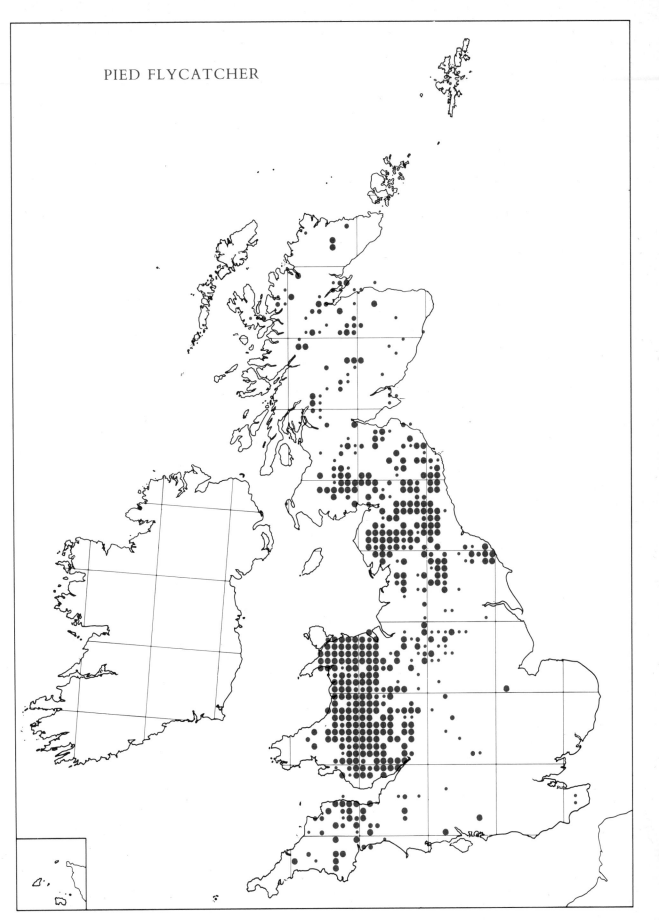

PIED FLYCATCHER

Dunnock

Prunella modularis

The Dunnock is a pioneer species, commonly invading a wide variety of scrub-grown situations. It is infrequent in closed-canopy woodland, except at the edges and in clearings where a good secondary growth of brambles, wild rose and other woody shrubs has developed. Like the Robin *Erithacus rubecula*, it has prospered in England as a result of the coppice management of woodland, where the early pole-growth and vigorous ground vegetation provide optimal habitat. Successful adaptation to coppice prepared the species for a rapid colonisation of the field hedgerow system—a linear coppice-with-standards—which grew up with the enclosures of the 18th and early 19th centuries. As a result, it is today the second commonest bird on English farmland, being outnumbered only by the Blackbird *Turdus merula*.

Williamson (1967) found that Dunnocks occurred on all 28 of a sample of Midlands farms, at a mean density of 28 pairs per km^2. On a farm near Tring (Hertfordshire), a density of 52 pairs per km^2 represented roughly one territory to every 200 m of hedge. The species exceeds the Robin and the Chaffinch *Fringilla coelebs* on lowland farms since it does not require a tall song-post and can make do with low, trimmed hedges. Like these other successful coppice species, and the Blackbird, it has become one of the important birds of the suburban environment, inhabiting gardens, churchyards, parks, industrial waste ground such as the scrub of gravel-pits and disused railway lines; and, similarly, it penetrates to suitable habitats in town and city centres.

In the remoter parts of Scotland, the Dunnock is common only in gardens and policies, but formerly must have been more abundant and widespread. Although it is numerous in birch woods in England, the heavy overgrazing which similar woods have suffered in the Highlands has deprived it of suitable habitat, while in the pine woods it is dominant only in areas where there is vigorous regeneration succeeding felling or fire. This is one of the few relict species of the woodland scrub which spread to the outer islands during the Climatic Optimum (about 5000 BC); the Hebridean race *P. m. hebridium* now occupies exposed moorland, and even offshore islands, where there is a suitable shrubby growth of heather, gorse and bracken, though many of these birds move into the neighbourhood of the crofts in winter time.

The distinctive, thin, reedy, warbling song and the strange wing-flicking display, which is often performed by several Dunnocks together on lawns or in clearings, facilitate the location of breeding pairs. On farmland, 'cold searching' of hedges is productive, but elsewhere the nest may be difficult to find, as it is beautifully camouflaged in thick, low vegetation such as ivy, bramble or nettles. The structure is a fairly substantial, open cup on a foundation of small twigs, containing uniformly deep blue eggs. Though feeding visits to the young are made with stealth, the food is generally quite easily visible in the adult's bill, as also are the white faecal sacs which are carried for a short distance on departure. Such signs, combined with the long breeding season (late March to August), obviate the need to see the actual nest to confirm breeding.

Changes in range and status are obscure, but there is some evidence for a northwards spread in Scotland, with colonisation of Orkney in the late 19th and early 20th centuries; as some range expansion also took place in Scandinavia, the species probably benefited from the climatic amelioration during about 1890–1940. After completion of the *Atlas* survey, an old nest with four eggs, discovered on Fair Isle early in 1974, was the first recorded breeding attempt in Shetland.

It is an interesting commentary on its general abundance and catholic choice of habitat that in Britain the Dunnock is one of the most frequent foster-parents of the young Cuckoo *Cuculus canorus* (Glue and Morgan 1972). Parslow classed the species as 'abundant' (over one million pairs) and Flegg (1975) suggested a total of over eight million birds. In parts of northern Scotland some 10-km squares probably have ten or fewer pairs, but it is a very common species in the south and a conservative guess at an average of 1,500 pairs per 10-km square would indicate a total of over five million pairs in Britain and Ireland.

Number of 10-km squares in which recorded: 3,574 (93%)
Possible breeding   61 (2%)
Probable breeding   192 (5%)
Confirmed breeding   3,321 (93%)

References
FLEGG, J. J. M. 1975. Bird population and distribution changes and the impact of man. *Bird Study* 22: 191–202.
GLUE, D. E. and R. A. MORGAN. 1972. Cuckoo hosts in British habitats. *Bird Study* 19: 187–192.
WILLIAMSON, K. 1967. The bird community of farmland. *Bird Study* 14: 210–226.

DUNNOCK

393

Meadow Pipit

Anthus pratensis

The Meadow Pipit is essentially a bird of open country and has a display flight, as do similar specialists like the Skylark *Alauda arvensis* and Lapwing *Vanellus vanellus*. The rather thin, tinkling sequence, delivered as the male ascends and then 'parachutes' to the ground, is one of the most characteristic sounds of upland Britain and Ireland in spring and early summer. Although it will occasionally take off from or return to a tree, the Meadow Pipit leaves the parkland habitat to the Tree Pipit *Anthus trivialis*, but the two species may overlap in zones of sparse scrub. When silent, and at a distance, these pipits are easily confused, though the Tree Pipit has the brighter plumage and pinker legs, but differences of call-note and song largely prevent this confusion during the breeding season.

The Meadow Pipit's food is almost entirely insect matter and is gathered from the ground layer of vegetation, yet in summer the species is much given to perching on stone walls, fence posts, telegraph wires and similar vantage points. A nervous adult in such a position, with its bill filled with food for nestlings or fledglings, frequently provided *Atlas* fieldworkers with an easy confirmation of breeding.

The species is very widely distributed in summer and has been found breeding from sea level to mountain tops over 1,000 m high. Above 500 m, it is usually by far the commonest breeding passerine and locally is an important item in the diets of Hen Harrier *Circus cyaneus*, Merlin *Falco columbarius* and Kestrel *Falco tinnunculus*. Nest record cards indicate that it is second only to the Dunnock *Prunella modularis* as host to the Cuckoo *Cuculus canorus* (Glue and Morgan 1972), but the picture is perhaps biased by woodlands, and both in Ireland and over much of Britain it is by far the commonest host. Working with a smaller sample than that now available, Coulson (1956) found that roughly one out of every five nest failures by Meadow Pipits was due to parasitism by the Cuckoo. He also noted that clutch size decreased and nesting success increased with a greater altitude.

Although its breeding season habitat is usually regarded as being rough grasslands, heaths, moors and sand-dunes, the Meadow Pipit also breeds in some of the most intensively cultivated districts. Sometimes an unploughed field margin or a river verge provides a foothold. Yet, though it is true that the species tends to avoid active cultivation when nesting, it appears not necessarily to flourish in regions rich in leys or permanent pasture, and indeed was found on only 4% of a sample of Midlands farms examined by the Common Birds Census. Of the areas of thin distribution, the most striking starts in coastal Lancashire and extends in a horseshoe through the S Midlands, before turning north through Northamptonshire and Leicestershire. These are zones of Triassic and Jurassic deposits which include much of the heavier farmland clays of Britain, and it appears that the Meadow Pipit tends to avoid them, as well as the heavier clay soils in parts of East Anglia and Kent. Coincidentally, perhaps, many of these areas where the species is absent or thinly distributed are also those which experience less than 750 mm of rainfall a year.

Parslow found evidence of decreases in parts of S and E England, which he linked with loss of habitat. Afforestation, one of the habitat changes he mentioned, must eventually drive out the species, but census work indicates that in the early years it may lead to a big increase. Thus, on Rhum (Inverness-shire) in 1968, one-year-old ploughed and planted moorland was found to have a density of 52 pairs per km², compared with 18 pairs per km² on adjacent unplanted moorland, and this was still the commonest species in young tree plots aged 15 years (Batten and Pomeroy 1969, Williamson 1973). Of the main habitats for which census densities are available, saltmarshes contain 1–76 pairs per km², chalk hill grasslands 26–55 pairs (though the species may be absent locally), calcareous mires and lings in the Pennines 28–59 pairs and acid moors 18–55 pairs. Impoverished upland areas may have as few as five pairs per km², but the extensive areas with a much greater density must raise the average for each occupied 10-km square to 1,000 or more. The total in Britain and Ireland is probably over 3,000,000 pairs, as estimated by Fisher (1940).

Number of 10-km squares in which recorded: 3,632 (94%)
Possible breeding   132 (4%)
Probable breeding   256 (7%)
Confirmed breeding   3,244 (89%)

References

BATTEN, L. A. and D. E. POMEROY. 1969. Effects of re-afforestation on the birds of Rhum, Scotland. *Bird Study* 16: 13–16.

COULSON, J. C. 1956. Mortality and egg production of the Meadow Pipit with special reference to altitude. *Bird Study* 3: 119–132.

FISHER, J. 1940. *Watching Birds*. London.

GLUE, D. E. and R. A. MORGAN. 1972. Cuckoo hosts in British habitats. *Bird Study* 19: 187–192.

WILLIAMSON, K. 1973. Bird colonisation of new plantations on the moorland of Rhum, Inner Hebrides. *Q. J. Forestry* 59: 157–168.

MEADOW PIPIT

Tree Pipit

Anthus trivialis

Tree Pipits nest in a wide variety of habitats but all are characterised by the presence of tall bushes or trees (or, occasionally, poles or pylons) from which the males can begin their distinctive song-flights. Open woodland, scrub areas, heathland, parkland and pasture with scattered trees may all be used, but song-posts must be present together with open areas of ground where the birds can feed.

Provided that some trees are left, newly felled woodland may be ideal, and the practice of coppicing and leaving standards must have provided this bird with many suitable sites in the past. More recently, newly planted conifers have opened up many areas for the species, but experience in Sussex shows that they may be exploited by the Tree Pipits for a rather short period (Hughes 1972).

Once the distinctive habitat requirements are recognised, suitable areas can be spotted from afar and the loud song and diagnostic song-flight then make location easy. The song can be heard from the time of first arrival in mid-April through to the end of July. The first clutch is generally laid in mid-May and second broods are not uncommon in S England. Confirmation of breeding, as with the other pipits and wagtails, is simple when the young are being fed, since the parents perch conspicuously with their bills full of food, often calling anxiously if the observer is close to the nest.

Tree Pipits have spread northwards in Scotland over the last 100 years. The first proved breeding in Caithness came during 1968–72 and Pennie (1962) observed that this is one of the commonest birds in mature birch woods in Sutherland, where the first county record dates from 1868. This increase took place at the same time as the species' spread northwards in Norway. The hillside birch woods often also hold Meadow Pipits *A. pratensis*, especially in the north, where Tree Pipits are relative newcomers. In the south of Britain, Tree Pipits have declined in traditional sites since the 1930s, but only slightly, and with fluctuations, in recent years (see graph). Whilst this may be attributed at least in part to loss of habitat to forestry and agriculture, there are many apparently unchanged sites where the species is now absent.

In SW England, they have always been scarce in W Devon and E Cornwall; there are no breeding records for W Cornwall, and only one pair has been recorded nesting on the Isles of Scilly (1914). It is very surprising that this summer migrant, common in Wales and Scotland and breeding in the Isle of Man (though this is a recent colonisation), has never even been suspected of nesting in Ireland, where it remains a rare spring and autumn migrant.

Densities on Common Birds Census plots range up to 20–30 pairs per km² in semi-natural habitats, but these are probably exceeded in some upland areas of birch and Scots pine woodland. A newly planted conifer plantation, with taller trees deliberately left standing when it was cleared, had the highest recorded density at 67 pairs per km² (Williamson 1972). A survey covering 70% of Sussex during 1967–70 revealed only 449 occupied territories (Hughes 1972). This corresponds to a density of just over 10 pairs per 10-km square over the whole county (which contains a few blank squares). Since densities in many other areas will be considerably higher, perhaps 25–30 pairs per occupied 10-km square might be a reasonable estimate. Thus, the British population may be between 50,000 and 100,000 pairs, probably just below that suggested by Parslow, who thought it lay within the range 100,000–1,000,000.

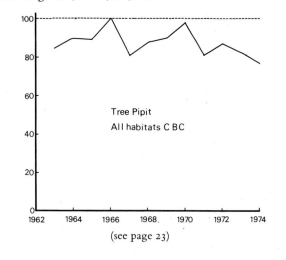

Tree Pipit
All habitats CBC

(see page 23)

Number of 10-km squares in which recorded:
1,793 (46%)
Possible breeding   108 (6%)
Probable breeding   558 (31%)
Confirmed breeding   1,127 (63%)

References

HUGHES, S. W. M. 1972. The breeding distribution and status of the Tree Pipit in Sussex. *Sussex Bird Rep.* 24: 68–79.

HUGHES, S. W. M. 1974. Tree Pipit breeding habitats in Sussex. *Brit. Birds* 67: 390–391.

PENNIE, I. D. 1962. A century of bird-watching in Sutherland. *Scott. Birds* 2: 167–192.

WILLIAMSON, K. 1972. The conservation of bird life in the new coniferous forests. *Forestry* 45: 87–100.

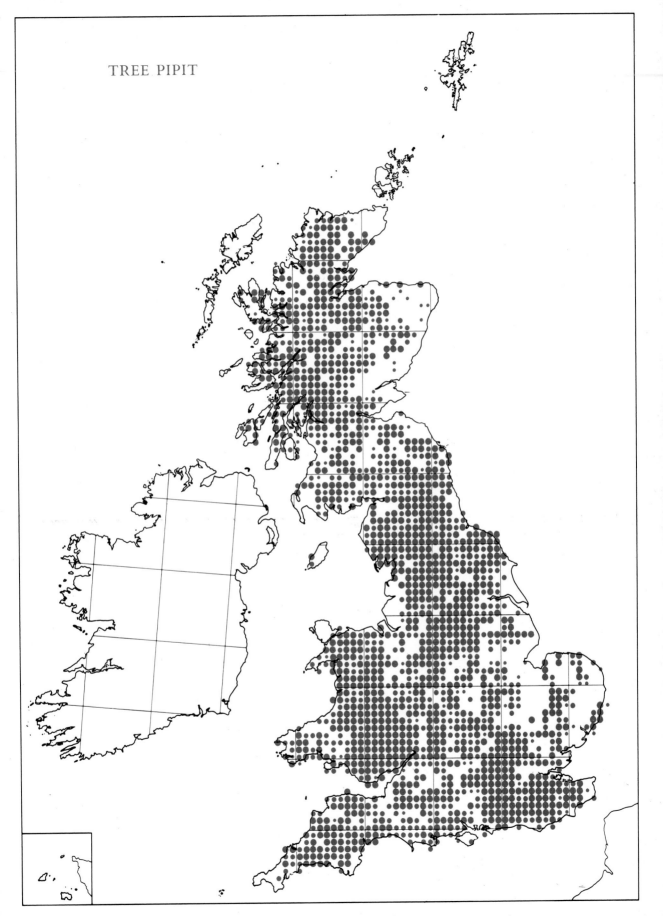

TREE PIPIT

Rock Pipit

Anthus spinoletta

Rock Pipits are characteristic of rocky coastlines. They may nest just above high water mark, or on the cliff-tops, but usually shun totally exposed areas, preferring to centre their territories on such sheltered features as gullies, coves or geos. On a few exposed islands, such as Hirta in the St Kilda group, territories are also situated in the central part of the island, away from the shore and up to 400 m above the sea. Nests farther than 500 m from the shore are very rare, and the only instance of true inland breeding in Britain was in Wales (10-km square SO50) in 1902.

In Britain and Ireland, the Rock Pipit *A. s. petrosus* —with perhaps distinct subspecies in the Outer Hebrides, *A. s. meinertzhageni*, and St Kilda and Shetland, *A. s. kleinschmidti* (Williamson 1965)—lives in a very different habitat from the Water Pipit *A. s. spinoletta* of the mountains of central and S Europe, which overwinters at watercress beds, reservoirs and similar haunts in S England and the Midlands (Johnson 1970). Lack (1971) pointed out that where the Rock Pipit, adapted to salt-blown areas close to the sea, and the Water Pipit, adapted to alpine meadows, are absent from their typical haunts, the less specialised Meadow Pipit *A. pratensis* takes over.

Their restricted habitat, characteristic 'phist' call-note and attractive song-flight make Rock Pipits easy birds for the *Atlas* surveyor to find. In many places, territories are contiguous and anyone walking along the beach is accompanied by a succession of birds. The territories are held during the winter and pairs have usually formed by early March. In the mildest districts, some may have eggs in the nest before the end of the month, but April is more normal. Most pairs are double-brooded and thus afford ample opportunity for breeding to be confirmed; as for many other species, this is best achieved by watching for the parents with food.

The nest is usually well concealed by vegetation on a ledge, or deep in a cleft in the cliff face. In some areas, Rock Pipits are a common host of the Cuckoo *Cuculus canorus*. Food is frequently collected inland, outside the defended territory, when young are being fed, but the seashore provides much of these birds'

food during the winter (Gibb 1956). Since they often feed in the intertidal zone, it is unlikely that they are much affected by severe winters.

The distribution has probably remained unchanged, except in detail, for many decades. The main stretches of coast from which Rock Pipits are absent lack suitable rocky shores. There have been breeding records in Lancashire, but only one instance of probable breeding on the east coast between the Humber and the Thames. Before 1967, only a single nest had been found in Kent, but since then one or two pairs have often bred along the chalk cliffs of the Isle of Thanet. The Sussex population, in similar habitat, was apparently extinct between 1891 and 1932 (except for one pair in 1923), but was then re-established, and a survey in 1965 revealed 45 singing males, including three on the sandstone cliffs in the east of the county.

Any estimation of the number of Rock Pipits must depend very largely on the length of suitable coastline. On the fringe of the British range, in Sussex, there are about 1.5 pairs per km of cliff. Figures for islands are often much higher: Cape Clear Island (Cork), Skokholm (Pembrokeshire), Calf of Man and Isle of May (Fifeshire), all with much more suitable cliffs, range from 3.5 to 15 pairs per km. On the island of Hirta (St Kilda), Williamson (1964) estimated that some 150 pairs bred in an area of about 6 km², about half of them on the cliffs and half 'inland'. Such figures, and the great length of coastline included in many of the 10-km squares where Rock Pipits were found, probably indicates an average of 50 or more pairs per occupied 10-km square. This suggests a British and Irish breeding population of over 50,000 pairs.

Number of 10-km squares in which recorded:
  1,028 (27%)
Possible breeding   102 (10%)
Probable breeding   107 (10%)
Confirmed breeding   819 (80%)

References

GIBB, J. 1956. Food, feeding habits and territory of the Rock Pipit *Anthus spinoletta*. *Ibis* 98: 506–530.

GLUE, D. E. and R. A. MORGAN. 1972. Cuckoo hosts in British habitats. *Bird Study* 19: 187–192.

JOHNSON, I. G. 1970. The Water Pipit as a winter visitor to the British Isles. *Bird Study* 17: 297–319.

LACK, D. 1971. *Ecological Isolation in Birds*. Oxford.

PORTER, R. F. 1966. A breeding survey of the Sussex cliffs in 1965. *Sussex Bird Rep.* 18: 56–57.

SHARROCK, J. T. R. and P. A. WRIGHT. 1968. Census of the cliff-breeding birds of Cape Clear Island. *Cape Clear Bird Obs. Rep.* 9: 33–47.

WILLIAMSON, K. 1964. A census of breeding land birds on Hirta, St Kilda, in summer 1963. *Bird Study* 11: 153–167.

WILLIAMSON, K. 1965. Moult and its relation to taxonomy in Rock and Water Pipits. *Brit. Birds* 58: 493–504.

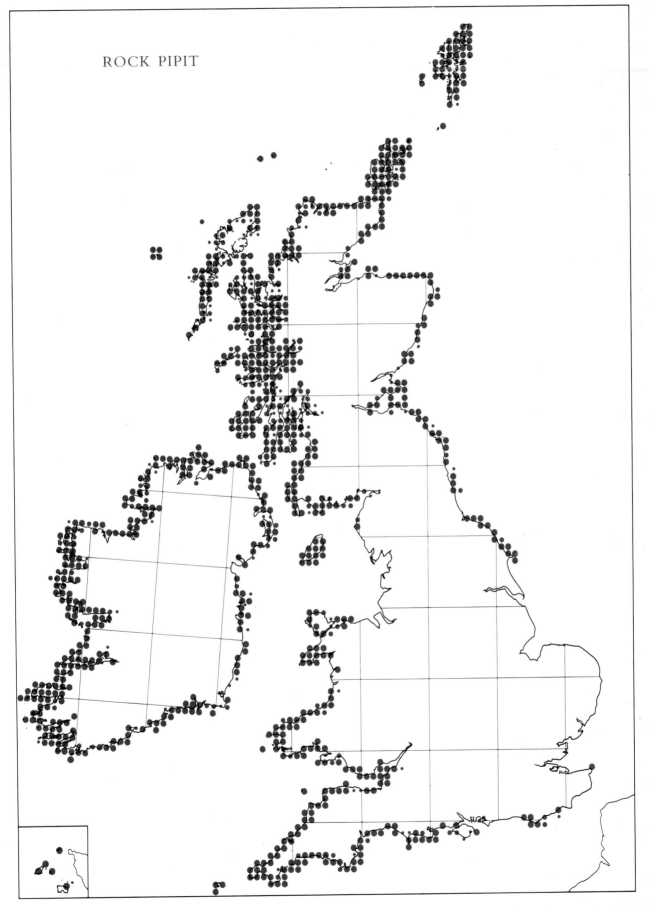

ROCK PIPIT

Pied/White Wagtail

Motacilla alba

Apart from woods and bare mountain and moorland, Pied Wagtails *M. a. yarrellii* breed everywhere in Britain and Ireland. They extend into city centres and to the seashore, including many islands, and even deep into mountainous country, along streams. Though the country name 'water wagtail' is applied to this species, the nest is not always close to water, unlike that of the Grey Wagtail *M. cinerea*.

The sharp 'chisick' flight-call, distinctive bounding flight and obtrusive habits make location of Pied Wagtails relatively easy, but nests may be very hard to find. Though the adults are wary as they approach, the food in their bills is a sure indication of nestlings or fledglings nearby.

There has been little recent change in distribution in Britain; an earlier decline in Orkney may now have been arrested, and the species seems to be more widely distributed in the Hebrides than earlier in the century. In Ireland, there has been a steady increase over the last 50 years and spread in western districts such as Galway and Mayo. *Atlas* workers who ranged extensively over Britain and Ireland gained the impression that this species is now much commoner in Ireland and Scotland than in E England, where, until about 20 years ago, almost every farmyard seemed to have its pair of Pied Wagtails. Though the *Atlas* map's coarse grid does not show it, they are now quite scarce there, and this was sometimes one of the last birds to be found in a 10-km square. The change from mixed to mainly arable farming, with fewer livestock and many farm ponds being filled in, may have contributed to this dearth in lowland Britain. On the other hand, Pied Wagtails are often very common in areas where the roads are lined by dry-stone walls, which must provide innumerable nest-sites, while the roads themselves also make good feeding areas, with insects being easily spotted on the flat surface.

In N Scotland, where they may breed to 600–700 m, Pied Wagtails are largely summer visitors and many ringing recoveries have been reported from S Britain and Europe (Davis 1966), but those in England are less likely to move away during the winter. Following the severe winter of 1962/63, the Common Birds Census showed that numbers in 1963 were only about one-third of the 1962 level, and even by 1974 had not fully recovered. The farmland density in 1972 was 1.4 pairs per km^2, but this figure relates mainly to the areas where numbers are lowest. An average of 150 pairs per occupied 10-km square would give a total British and Irish breeding population of about 500,000 pairs, in the middle of Parslow's range of 100,000–1,000,000.

A few Pied Wagtails breed in adjacent areas of the Continent, but the race in most of Europe and in Iceland is *M. a. alba*, the White Wagtail. This form is the usual one in Shetland, but a few occasionally breed elsewhere in Britain and Ireland. The small map includes White × Pied pairings as well as White × White, since in some cases only one adult White Wagtail was seen. Apart from those in Shetland, these dots represent sporadic breeding of single pairs; since it combines five years' records, the map exaggerates the picture in any one year. No more than a handful of White Wagtails breeds here annually.

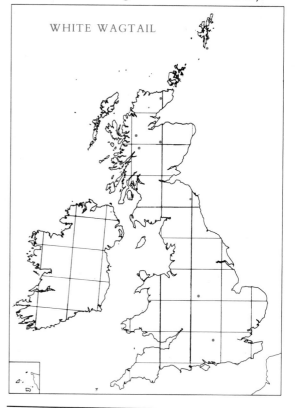

WHITE WAGTAIL

Number of 10-km squares in which recorded:
3,646 (94%)   19 (0.5%)

Possible breeding	90 (2%)	6 (32%)
Probable breeding	70 (2%)	2 (11%)
Confirmed breeding	3,486 (96%)	11 (58%)

The first set of figures refers to Pied *M. a. yarrellii* and the second to White *M. a. alba*.

Reference

DAVIS, P. E. 1966. The movements of Pied Wagtails as shown by ringing. *Bird Study* 13: 147–162.

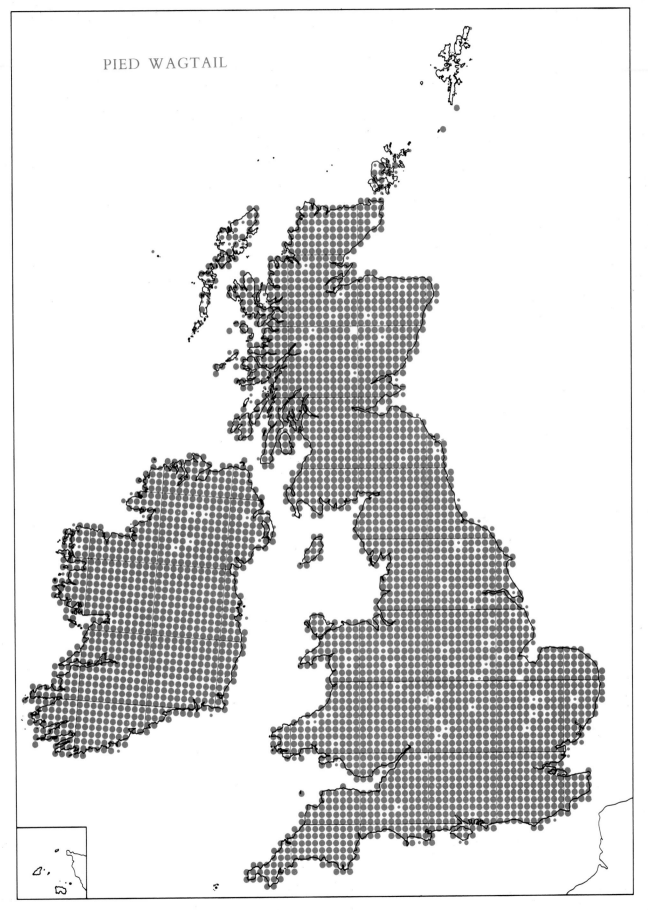

PIED WAGTAIL

Grey Wagtail

Motacilla cinerea

The Grey Wagtail is found primarily along fast-flowing, rocky, upland streams and rivers. It is less restricted to such places, however, than is the Dipper *Cinclus cinclus*. Grey Wagtails also nest beside lowland streams, especially where these have fast-flowing stretches due to weirs or mill-races, at the locks on canals and at the outflows from lakes or reservoirs.

This most elegant of our wagtails is easily located, since the flight call is distinctive and the habitat is so restricted that searches may be concentrated in likely areas. Indeed, in some parts of E England, where only a few breed, the $2\frac{1}{2}$ inch to 1 mile map of a 10-km square can be used to pinpoint the likely spots. First clutches are laid during March or early April, and second and third broods or replacements may still be in the nest during August. The nest is most often built on a rock or masonry ledge, in tree roots over-hanging the bank of a stream, or in ivy on a bridge or tree—generally above flowing water (Tyler 1972). Many nests are situated in culverts or drainage holes, often underneath bridges, and the frequent use of such man-made sites makes finding them very easy. Except when incubating, the adults are noisy and conspicuous when flying to and from the site with material or food, so it is usually also easy to confirm breeding even without finding the nest.

Grey Wagtails suffer badly in severe winters when the streams and rivers are frozen. This leads to fluctuations in the population and may cause peripheral breeding sites to be deserted for several years. Not all individuals are affected, since some are able to feed at sewage plants and water-cress beds where food is very often available when natural waters are frozen over. Others enter towns or go to the coast, and many migrate south to France and Iberia, especially after successful breeding seasons. The cold winter of 1916/17 probably had a particularly bad affect in Ireland, and the two successive hard winters of 1961/62 and 1962/63 took their toll everywhere. Happily, numbers recover quickly, and were at a high level when the *Atlas* period started (Sharrock 1969).

The British and Irish distribution has not altered much during the last century. The impression of those who did *Atlas* fieldwork in both countries is that Grey Wagtails are commoner in Ireland than in comparable habitats in Britain. This may be a function of the milder winters generally enjoyed in Ireland. In Scotland, Baxter and Rintoul (1953) knew of no breeding in the Outer Hebrides, but recorded isolated instances in Orkney and Fair Isle. Although none was reported during 1968–72, the 'first for many years' bred in Orkney and at Stornoway (Outer Hebrides) in 1974.

In England, the areas from which Grey Wagtails are absent mostly lack suitable nesting sites, and the farther one ventures from typical upland breeding haunts the less likely it is that artificial sites, such as weirs, will have breeding pairs. Using the data from coastal passage sites, Sharrock (1964, 1969) calculated that 1959 and 1961, preceding severe winters, were years of high population, and it seems likely that, by the end of the *Atlas* period, these levels had all but been regained.

Such an attractive species has naturally been the subject of several intensive local studies, but these have usually been in lowland areas. Sussex densities (Merritt *et al* 1970) ranged from 3.8 pairs per 10-km square in the Weald to 30.8 on the greensand. Tyler (1970) found 32 pairs in the New Forest, an area equivalent to about four 10-km squares. These densities depend, however, on the number of attractive sites or lengths of suitable streams, which are very much more frequent in upland areas. The BTO Waterways Survey has shown that there are fewer Grey Wagtails along canals (20 pairs per 100 km) than along natural waterways, and that in the latter category there are wide regional differences. The 1974 figures (in pairs per 100 km) were: Midlands and East Anglia 31, N England 37, S England 49, N Ireland 91 and N Wales 114. A reasonably conservative average of all occupied 10-km squares might be 10–20 pairs, which would give a total of 25,000–50,000 pairs in Britain and Ireland. Parslow's 1967 estimate of 1,000–10,000 pairs is clearly low, although the population would then have been only about half that reached by 1972.

Number of 10-km squares in which recorded: 2,740 (71%)
Possible breeding   234 (9%)
Probable breeding   178 (6%)
Confirmed breeding   2,328 (85%)

References

MERRITT, W., R. R. GREENHALF and P. F. BONHAM. 1970. A survey of the Grey Wagtail in Sussex. *Sussex Bird Rep.* 22: 68–80.

SHARROCK, J. T. R. 1964. Grey Wagtail passage in Britain in 1956–60. *Brit. Birds* 57: 10–24.

SHARROCK, J. T. R. 1969. Grey Wagtail passage and population fluctuations in 1956–67. *Bird Study* 16: 17–34.

TYLER, S. J. 1970. Observations on the Grey Wagtail in the New Forest. *Hampshire Bird Rep.* 1969: 37–40.

TYLER, S. J. 1972. Breeding biology of the Grey Wagtail. *Bird Study* 19: 69–80.

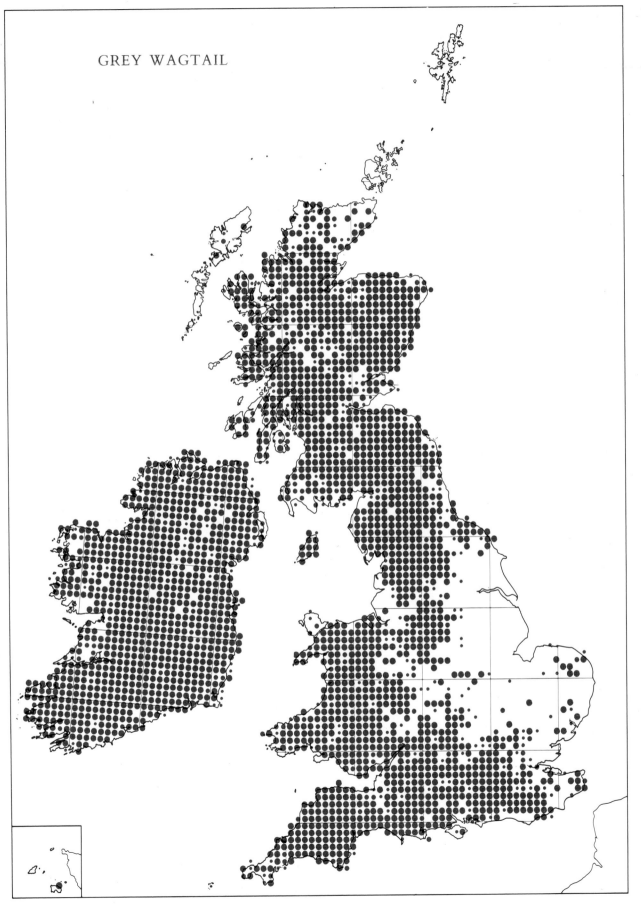

GREY WAGTAIL

Yellow/Blue-headed Wagtail

Motacilla flava

Breeding Yellow Wagtails are almost invariably associated with water—not the rushing upland streams favoured by the Grey Wagtail *M. cinerea*, but damp water meadows and marshy fields along river valleys and freshwater marshes on the coast. Similar conditions provided by sewage purification works, reservoir margins and flooded gravel pits may also have nesting pairs. Market gardens and industrial waste ground in the suburbs provide drier haunts. The Yellow Wagtail's distribution is patchy, however, and it is absent from places which, to the human eye, seem just as suitable as nearby occupied haunts.

The changes in distribution during the 19th and first half of the 20th century have been described in detail by Smith (1950) (see map on page 463). Two former regular colonies in Ireland, one in Galway/Mayo and the other 195 km away around Lough Neagh (Northern Ireland), have both become extinct. The Connacht colonies were on stony or rocky islands in Loughs Corrib and Mask with a few pairs at Lough Carra. A decrease was noticed about 1917 so that very few were breeding by 1922; odd individuals occurred up to 1928. There was a similar contraction at Lough Neagh, starting in about 1922, very noticeable by 1932 and complete by 1942; a few remained at nearby Lough Beg (Antrim) until 1944. Since then, a few isolated pairs have nested, most often in Co Wicklow, where three pairs bred in 1968. In the same year, breeding probably took place at Lough Beg (Derry), but the following years of *Atlas* work produced no further Irish records. In Scotland, the Clyde has always been the species' stronghold, but nesting in the extreme southwest, in Stirlingshire, and along the east coast to Aberdeenshire occurred sporadically until the 1930s.

In England and Wales, there may have been a decline in the south and a slight increase in the north. A few pairs used to nest regularly in Cornwall, and there have been records since 1972 from S Devon. The gaps in the distribution in England coincide with the chalk areas of the Wolds, the Chilterns, N and S Downs and Salisbury Plain. A population index from Common Birds Census work has been available since 1963. The level during 1968, the first year of the *Atlas* (when the only Irish observations were made) was exceptionally high, but otherwise there was rather little variation.

The BTO Waterways Survey data have shown an average of one pair to every 5 km of waterway in England. A special survey of Sussex breeding areas showed that about 200 pairs were present in the county annually during 1965–67 (Shrubb 1968). There are approximately 20 occupied 10-km squares in Sussex, where suitable habitat is restricted to about 180 km². Probably a complement in an average occupied 10-km square would be 25 pairs, giving a total British and Irish population of about 25,000 pairs.

The Yellow Wagtail *M. f. flavissima* is a member of a species complex which shows extensive geographical variation in head-pattern and colour in the males throughout its wide Palearctic range. On rare occasions, birds with the characteristics of extralimital forms have been found breeding here, such as the pair of White-headed *M. f. leucocephala* in Kent in 1908, and two pairs of the Ashy-headed *M. f. cinereocapilla* near Belfast in 1956 (Ennis and Dick 1959). The Blue-headed Wagtail *M. f. flava*, very different in appearance from the British race, but its nearest neighbour on the Continent, is the most regular of these vagrant breeders, with proved or suspected records as far north as Aberdeenshire, and as far west as Cornwall and Ulster. As would be expected, most records are from SE England, and in this region hybridisation with the Yellow Wagtail also takes place.

Walpole-Bond (1938) considered that one in 30 of those nesting in Sussex was a Blue-headed, but none has been recorded recently. During 1968–72 Blue-headed Wagtails were proved to breed in one 10-km square in Kent (TQ94), and may have bred in two others in the north of the county (TR16 and TR26).

Number of 10-km squares in which recorded:
1,161 (30%)
Possible breeding   143 (12%)
Probable breeding   117 (10%)
Confirmed breeding   901 (78%)

References

ENNIS, T. and H. DICK. 1959. Breeding of the Ashy-headed Wagtail and Yellow Wagtail in Northern Ireland. *Brit. Birds* 52: 10–12.

MILNE, B. S. 1959. Variations in a population of Yellow Wagtails. *Brit. Birds* 52: 281–294.

SHRUBB, M. 1968. The status and distribution of Snipe, Redshank and Yellow Wagtail as breeding birds in Sussex. *Sussex Bird Rep.* 20: 53–60.

SMITH, S. 1950. *The Yellow Wagtail*. London.

WALPOLE-BOND, J. 1938. *A History of Sussex Birds*. London.

Waxwing *Bombycilla garrulus*, **see page 450**

YELLOW WAGTAIL

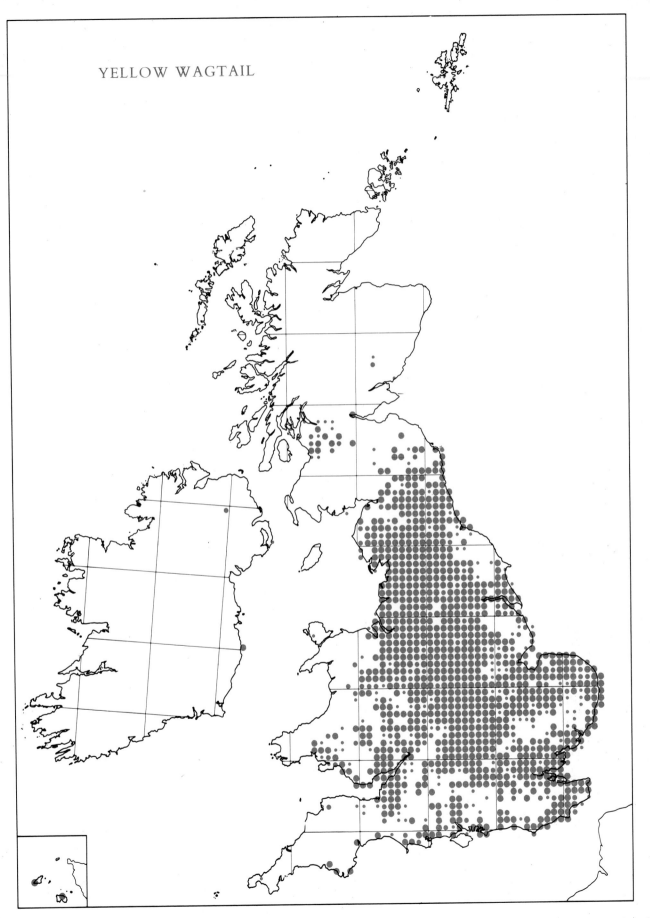

Red-backed Shrike

Lanius collurio

Red-backed Shrikes are found on the Continent in a variety of habitats which provide thorny bushes for their nests—waste ground, heaths, commons, downs, overgrown orchards and gardens, hedgerows and the scrub of railway cuttings and embankments. At one time they occupied such sites in Britain, but are now virtually confined to dry, bushy heathland, particularly where there is a mixture of gorse, heather and small trees. There is a tendency to nest near streams or pools, and this may be linked with the presence of dragonflies and damselflies for food.

Though their use of prominent perches should, in theory, render shrikes conspicuous, they can be remarkably elusive in practice, even when their presence in an area is known or suspected. The ghoulish habit of some individuals in forming 'larders' in which bees and other large insects, and even small mammals and birds, are impaled on thorns is seldom of any help in locating them. They return to traditional areas, however, and sometimes there may be several pairs in close proximity, so that most of the breeding birds were probably found in the course of *Atlas* fieldwork. Although the male will sometimes fly straight to the nest, the easiest method of confirming breeding is by observation of adults with newly-fledged young, for both can be noisy and obvious. The low proportion of proved breeding records may partly reflect the difficulty of nest-finding and observers' laudable reluctance to disturb the birds, as well as the presence of non-breeders at former sites. Ash (1970) thought that, in view of the reduced density, adults might now have difficulty in finding a mate.

Red-backed Shrikes have been declining, and their range contracting, in Britain for over 100 years (see maps on pages 464–465). The same phenomenon has been noted in other parts of W Europe and has been linked with climatic deterioration, the cooler and wetter summers of this century reducing the activity, and perhaps also the total numbers, of the grasshoppers and mantises, dragonflies, bees, moths and butterflies which constitute their main prey (Durango 1950). From more than 300 pairs in 1952 and 250 pairs in 1960, the British population had been re-

duced to about 80–90 pairs by 1971, more than three-quarters of them restricted to the Brecks and coastal heaths of East Anglia (Bibby 1973). An earlier survey by Peakall (1962) had shown the New Forest (Hampshire) to be an important stronghold, but a dramatic crash took place between 1961 and 1966 (Ash 1970), so that by 1972 only 11% of the total British stock remained there, compared with 25% in 1960. The decrease in Britain during this decade was about 10% per annum, and the future of the Red-backed Shrike here is indeed gloomy; there are now probably fewer than 50 pairs.

Although the summers were generally warmer and drier during the 1930s and 1940s, the decline was not checked, and it is unlikely that climate is the sole factor involved. There has been an accelerating loss of habitat, especially in southern counties (Dorset has lost 4,000 ha of heathland in the last 14 years). Egg-collecting has had a serious local effect, eliminating the species from small pockets, but is not the cause of the long-term decline.

It may be that a long-term shift towards the east has been taking place in the centre of gravity of the Red-backed Shrike's range; if so, since it is one of our few southeast-oriented migrants, western peripheral areas such as Britain and France would suffer most. We do not even know, however, whether the species is increasing or decreasing in numbers, taking the whole of its range, nor whether it is spreading eastwards as it contracts in the west. The presence of a pair, which may have nested, in Orkney in 1970 (Balfour 1972) raises the intriguing possibility that, like the Wryneck *Jynx torquilla* (see page 276), the greater influx of Scandinavian spring migrants in recent seasons may lead to new colonisation.

This species is afforded special protection in Great Britain under Schedule I of the Protection of Birds Act, 1954–67.

Number of 10-km squares in which recorded:
111 (3%)
Possible breeding   24 (22%)
Probable breeding   22 (20%)
Confirmed breeding   65 (59%)

Though some records were originally submitted in confidence, all dots are now shown accurately (as recommended by the Rare Breeding Birds Panel)

References

ASH, J. S. 1970. Observations on a decreasing population of Red-backed Shrikes. *Brit. Birds* 63: 185–205, 225–239.

BALFOUR, E. 1972. *Orkney Birds: Status and Guide.* Stromness.

BIBBY, C. 1973. The Red-backed Shrike: a vanishing British species. *Bird Study* 20: 103–110.

DURANGO, S. 1950. Om klimatets inverkan på törnskatans (*Lanius collurio* L.) utbredning och levnadsmöjligheter. *Fauna och Flora* 46: 49–78.

PEAKALL, D. B. 1962. The past and present status of the Red-backed Shrike in Great Britain. *Bird Study* 9: 198–216.

SHARROCK, J. T. R. 1975. Dot-distribution mapping of breeding birds in Europe. *Ardeola* 21: 797–810.

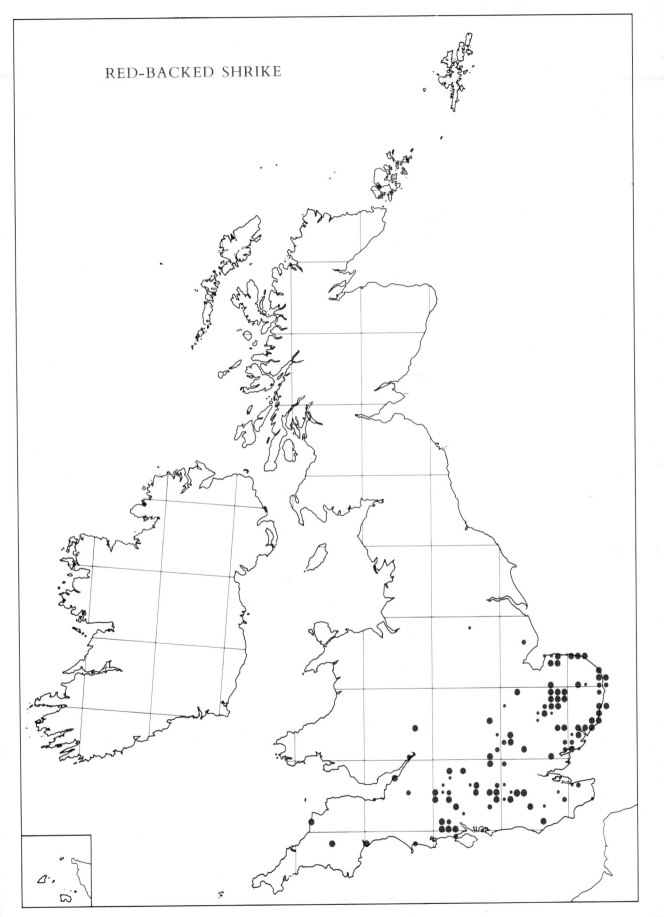

RED-BACKED SHRIKE

Starling

Sturnus vulgaris

Starlings are now very widely established in all kinds of habitat except for the more exposed uplands. They need holes for nesting and can exploit a bewildering variety of cavities, in buildings and mature trees, also cracks and crevices in sea-cliffs, quarries and moorland crags. Spaces under the eaves of houses are the most familiar sites. They also occasionally usurp the holes of Sand Martins *Riparia riparia*, House Sparrows *Passer domesticus* and Swifts *Apus apus*; they will try, sometimes successfully, to dislodge woodpeckers immediately they have completed their work, and competition with Starlings may delay the woodpeckers' breeding season in some areas.

The Starling's song often includes excellent imitations of the calls of other species, including various waders and such rarities as Golden Oriole *Oriolus oriolus* and Quail *Coturnix coturnix*. In urban, suburban and farmland areas, Starlings are thrustful and noisy birds, obvious even to the most casual observer. Proof of breeding is very easy to obtain when the young are being fed in the nest, since they call continuously and are visited frequently by their parents. The used nest hole also acquires a distinctive whitewash of droppings at its entrance. In remote areas, however, a few pairs scattered in thin woodland or nesting in exposed stream banks are easily overlooked. Some of the gaps in Scotland and the few in W Ireland may have contained some nesting Starlings in 1968–72, but the species is only sparsely distributed in similar areas nearby. Despite the gaps in its distribution, the Starling is the fifth most widespread species in Britain and Ireland, and was proved to breed in more squares than any other.

The history of British and Irish Starlings is most interesting. Few birdwatchers today would imagine that this ubiquitous bird apparently declined over the whole of Britain, and retreated from most of Scotland and Ireland, as well as W Wales and SW England, early in the 19th century. At that stage, it seems that some of the western islands, some coastal cliffs and a few inland ruins held the only breeding Starlings in Ireland (Kennedy *et al* 1954). In Scotland they remained common in the Outer Hebrides, Shetland, Orkney and some coastal parts of the north and west, but were absent from the rest of the mainland and most of the Inner Hebrides.

The revival dates from about 1830 and is probably continuing to this day. The parts of N England from which the species had retreated were first recolonised, and it began to spread northwards through Scotland, and westwards in both Britain and Ireland. At the turn of the century, it was still a rather local and scattered breeding bird in many of the new regions. Subsequent changes have included extensions westwards in Wales, SW England and Ireland, and northwards and westwards in Scotland, together with the infilling of areas pioneered much earlier. W Cork, for instance, was reached in the 1930s, but Cape Clear Island in that county and the Dingle peninsula (Kerry) were not colonised until 1955, and the islands of Inishbofin (Galway) and Achill (Mayo) not until the 1960s.

These changes have been linked with agricultural activity, but it seems as likely that, although new methods of husbandry will have had an effect, the main reason is climatic amelioration. The Starling has been an immensely successful bird over most of Europe in this century, and Yeatman (1971) has suggested that the extension of agriculture and decrease in raptors have both had beneficial effects.

Unfortunately it is not possible to survey Starlings accurately during the course of normal Common Birds Census visits. Such figures as are available suggest that 10 pairs per km^2 is a reasonable estimate for farmland in lowland Britain, though much higher densities may be found in some areas. For instance, a mature beech wood in Hertfordshire held over 200 pairs per km^2, utilising nest-holes in old pollarded trees (Williamson 1968). Allowing for high populations in suburban and wooded areas, an average of 1,000–2,000 pairs per occupied 10-km square would give a British and Irish breeding population of some 4,000,000–7,000,000 pairs. This agrees well with the estimate of 7,000,000 nesting birds (3.5 million pairs) for Britain alone, made by Potts (1967).

Number of 10-km squares in which recorded:
3,707 (96%)
Possible breeding   49 (1%)
Probable breeding   19 (1%)
Confirmed breeding   3,639 (98%)

References

BULLOUGH, W. S. 1942. The reproductive cycles of the British and Continental races of the Starling. *Phil. Trans. Roy. Soc. Lond.* (B) 231: 165–246.

DUNNET, G. M. 1955. The breeding of the Starling *Sturnus vulgaris* in relation to its food supply. *Ibis* 97: 619–662.

POTTS, G. R. 1967. Urban Starling roosts in the British Isles. *Bird Study* 14: 25–42.

WILLIAMSON, K. 1968. A breeding bird survey of Queen Wood in the Chilterns, Oxon. *Q. J. Forestry* 42: 118–131.

YEATMAN, L. J. 1971. *Histoire des Oiseaux d'Europe.* Paris.

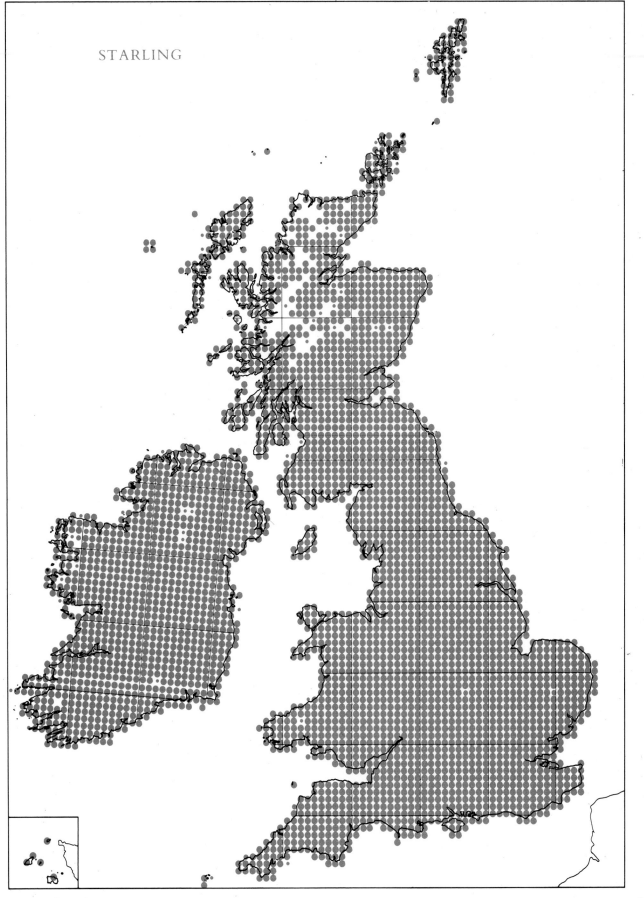

STARLING

Hawfinch

Coccothraustes coccothraustes

Hawfinches occur in deciduous woodland where the large fruits of such trees as wych elm, hornbeam, beech, wild cherry, sycamore and maple are available for much of the year. They also frequent parkland and large gardens where these trees grow, and have taken advantage of the planting of fruit trees, particularly cherries, by settling in orchard country.

This is one of the most elusive of our breeding species. It may be conspicuous, even tame, in some parts of the Continent where it is common, but it is almost invariably shy and unapproachable in Britain. Unless an observer knew the characteristic 'tic' or 'tzik' note, recalling a Robin *Erithacus rubecula* or a Great Spotted Woodpecker *Dendrocopos major*, there was little chance of his finding a Hawfinch during *Atlas* fieldwork. Hearing this call, he might have been lucky enough to catch a glimpse of the distinctive, big-headed silhouette of one in flight, but the *Atlas* map inevitably under-represents the actual distribution.

The most remarkable feature of the Hawfinch is its high, deep bill. It is able to crack open such hard seeds as cherry stones and eat the kernels, and has a specially adapted palate and musculature to make this possible. Such foods are not available to the other finches with their weaker bills. Newton (1967), in a comparative study of the diets of British finches, showed that almost all the Hawfinch's food is obtained by this crushing movement, even when removing peas from pods. Like the Bullfinch *Pyrrhula pyrrhula*, it attacks buds in the spring, and it takes many invertebrates in the summer.

Like most other finches, Hawfinches often breed socially. Groups usually number three to six pairs, although 20 have been found in less than 2 ha, and seven nests along 200 m of hedgerow (Mountfort 1954). Other pairs are solitary, but all feed well away from their territories (Newton 1972). The pairs are formed during March and nests built during April or May. These are platforms of stiff twigs, like those of the Bullfinch with fine roots and grasses in the lining, but the sites chosen are generally high up on horizontal branches or leading shoots. Of 218 listed by Mountfort, only 33 were below 3 m, 150 were at 3–10 m and the highest was 25 m up, at the top of a spruce. Almost one-third of the English nests were in apple or pear trees and about a quarter in oak or sycamore; the former were mostly in groups, and the latter more widely dispersed. The males do sing, but the soft, brief sound does not carry far and is little known. The adults remain secretive and wary throughout the nesting period. The only stage when proof of breeding is easy to obtain is shortly after the young have left the nest; then family parties may be rather noisy and the youngsters are readily identified in silhouette by their shorter tails. Confirmed breeding is unquestionably under-recorded, but, since the species seems to be sedentary in Britain, even the small and medium sized dots on the map are likely to refer to breeding pairs.

The extreme difficulty of detecting the presence of Hawfinches makes the historical record of their distribution in Britain and Ireland a matter of some dispute. The first breeding records came from the early part of the 19th century, but much earlier references—to Hawfinches taking ripe cherries in Norfolk in the 17th century, for example—probably referred to nesting birds. They seem to have been confined to SE England and the Midlands until about 1850, but the next 60–70 years saw a real spread. They became sparsely distributed in all English counties except Cornwall, and in parts of Wales and S Scotland. The only breeding record from Ireland, in Co Kildare, was in 1902 following several years when a few were seen during the summer. There have been a handful of other summer records in Ireland, but none during 1968–72. In Britain, populations have fluctuated erratically over the last 50 years, but a slight expansion of range may have continued.

The distribution shown differs little from that given by Mountfort (see map on page 465). Its most striking feature is the concentration around London and the nearby parts of Kent, Surrey, Berkshire, Buckinghamshire, Hertfordshire and Essex; the high proportion of confirmed breeding records there is strongly suggestive of a greater abundance than elsewhere. Scattered through Britain, there are probably a number of 10-km squares with dozens of breeding pairs. The occasional records of winter flocks of 50 or even 100 Hawfinches in some localities is also indicative of good breeding populations. Allowing for these concentrations, and for 10-km squares where they were missed, an estimate should perhaps be based on an average of 10–20 pairs per 10-km square in which they were recorded. Thus, some 5,000 to 10,000 pairs may be present. This agrees well with Parslow's 1,000–10,000 pairs.

Number of 10-km squares in which recorded:
459 (12%)
Possible breeding   225 (49%)
Probable breeding   81 (18%)
Confirmed breeding   153 (33%)

References
MOUNTFORT, G. 1957. *The Hawfinch*. London.
NEWTON, I. 1967. The adaptive radiation and feeding ecology of some British finches. *Ibis* 109: 33–98.
NEWTON, I. 1972. *Finches*. London.

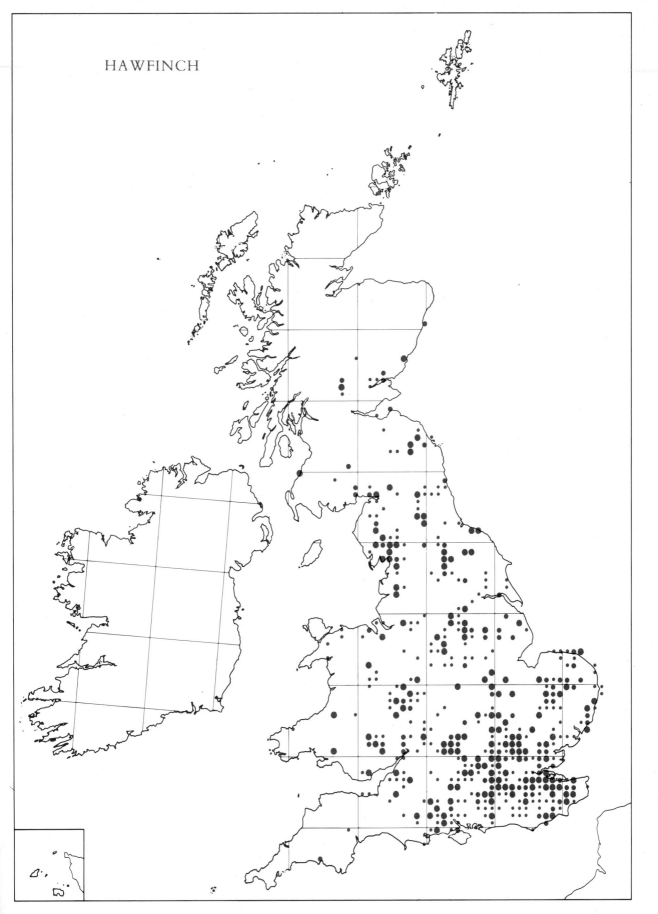

HAWFINCH

Greenfinch

Carduelis chloris

The Greenfinch was originally confined largely to forest edge and even now, in some parts of the Continent, is rarely seen around houses or in cultivated areas. Yet in Britain and Ireland the species now occurs regularly in gardens, especially during the winter. Breeding birds may be found, often in small rather loose colonies of four to six pairs, in city parks, suburban gardens, farmland hedgerows and, particularly, thorn or evergreen scrub areas. In many rural districts, the mature gardens and evergreen shrubs of churchyard, vicarage and manor house provide ideal nesting sites. Early stages of conifer plantations may also hold colonies.

There can be few more familiar species than the Greenfinch, and the characteristic nasal 'dzwee' of the male readily draws an observer's attention. The only other species with a similar note, the Brambling *Fringilla montifringilla*, is so extremely rare in summer that confusion with it cannot have affected the *Atlas* map. Song may start as early as January and pairs are formed mostly in February or early March. Males at breeding sites show a variety of interesting displays, including a weaving song-flight between the tree-tops or across clearings, with exaggerated slow and deep wing-beats. The nest is built during April, mainly by the female. First clutches are laid at the end of that month or during May, and many pairs rear a second brood, so that the breeding season extends into August. The young in the nest are fed on re-gurgitated food, with nothing obvious being carried in the parent's bill. Nevertheless, Greenfinches are not shy and it is often quite easy to watch birds back and confirm breeding by finding the nest. Most nests are between 1.4 and 5 m above ground level and quite bulky, which makes them easy to locate. Since Greenfinches breed in loose colonies, nests are often found close together, affording extra chances of searches being successful. When the young have fledged, their noisy food-begging constitutes a further way in which confirmation of breeding can be obtained.

During this century, Greenfinches have expanded their range in Britain and Ireland and increased in numbers. Several of the W Scottish islands and the Isles of Scilly have been colonised and there have been increases and extensions of range in Cornwall, W Mayo, W Donegal and N Scotland. This range expansion has been assisted by increased planting of commercial woodland, but extensive tracts of countryside without suitable nesting cover still remain, particularly in N and W Scotland, W Wales and small areas in W Ireland. There has been some evidence of a decline in Ireland since about the early 1960s, however, and this appears to be continuing. Greenfinches are rare in the birch woods of N Scotland, and small breeding pockets in remote areas are usually associated with human habitation. The inner suburbs and central urban parts of such large cities as London have been colonised during the 20th century, and this may have been encouraged by increased garden feeding during the winter. The distribution in N Scotland shows a clear association with agricultural land.

The Common Birds Census indicates that the British population was affected by the cold winters of 1961/62 and 1962/63 but recovered quickly, the farmland index remaining remarkably stable since 1966; the woodland index, on the other hand, reached a peak in 1966, but has now declined to about 75% and stabilised. As Newton (1972) pointed out, the colonial nesting of cardueline finches means that there may be large areas between colonies where there are few, if any, nests. CBC data seldom show average densities in excess of 20 pairs per km^2, with the highest being 34. The averages in 1972 were 6.0 pairs per km^2 on farmland and 9.2 in woodland. In suburban situations, densities may be much higher (Batten 1972) and it seems reasonable, therefore, to assume an average of 300–600 pairs per occupied 10-km square. This suggests a total British and Irish population of one or two million pairs, which is higher than Parslow's category of 100,000–1,000,000 pairs.

Number of 10-km squares in which recorded:
  3,318 (86%)
Possible breeding   120 (4%)
Probable breeding   332 (10%)
Confirmed breeding   2,866 (86%)

References

BATTEN, L. A. 1972. The past and present bird life of the Brent Reservoir and its vicinity. *London Nat.* 50: 8–62.

DICKINSON, B. H. B. and H. M. DOBINSON. 1969. A study of a Greenfinch roost. *Bird Study* 16: 135–146.

MONK, J. F. 1954. The breeding biology of the Greenfinch. *Bird Study* 1: 2–14.

NEWTON, I. 1967. The adaptive radiation and feeding ecology of some British finches. *Ibis* 109: 33–98.

NEWTON, I. 1972. *Finches.* London.

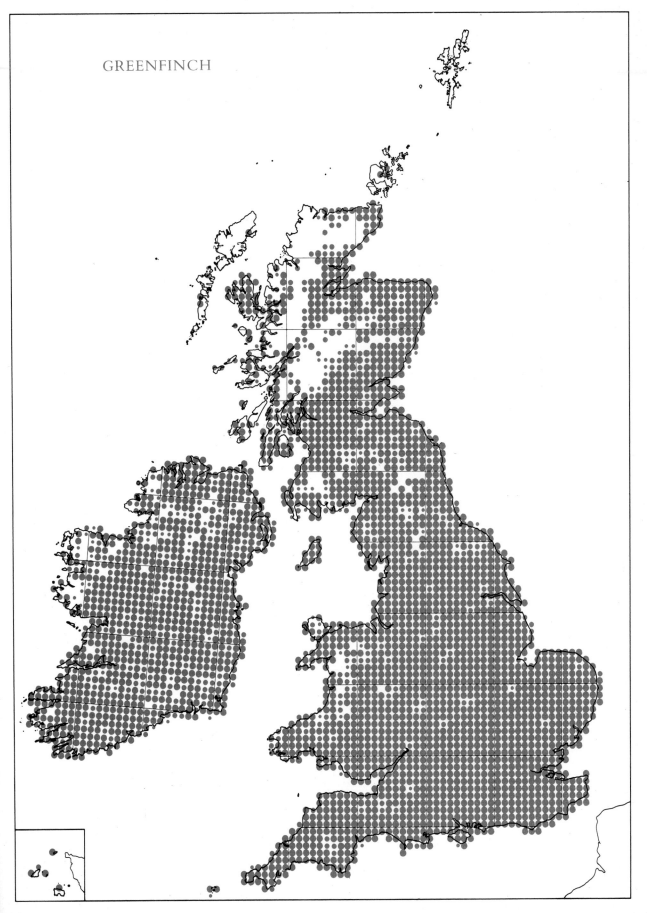

GREENFINCH

413

Goldfinch

Carduelis carduelis

The Goldfinch is found on open ground where there are weeds, especially thistles, and it nests in tall bushes or trees. Farmland, parkland, orchards, gardens, scrub and woodland edges may hold nesting pairs, which will go some distance to feed on whatever seeds are available. Open scrub and waste ground are favoured in inland regions, and coastal dunes and saltmarshes may hold good populations, provided there are suitable bushes or trees for nesting.

The characteristic, twittering flight calls and conspicuous plumage aid location and identification. The pairs are formed by April and early nests may contain eggs before the beginning of May. The nest is generally built higher than those of most other finches, in the fork of a thin branch up to 15 m, but usually 4–10 m from the ground. In such situations, the structure, neat and compact with a deep cup, is likely to sway in the wind, so it is well anchored to the tree, often with spiders' webs. So characteristic is it that breeding may often be proved during the autumn or winter by finding old nests. Both adults may approach the nest together, particularly when building. The territory, defended by the male, is small, and several pairs will generally breed in a loose colony.

The Goldfinch has a particularly long and thin bill which enables it to delve into the heads of such plants as thistles, teasels and knapweeds to extract the seeds, which are generally not available to other finches (Newton 1967). It is most acrobatic in clinging to the plants, although fallen seeds are easier to get, and are preferred, in the autumn.

During the 19th century, a serious and widespread decrease was reported over Britain and Ireland, which has been attributed to the catching of huge numbers for sale as cage-birds. Following the banning of this practice in Britain in 1881 and in Ireland since 1930, marked revivals were recorded, with a return to many former areas at the edge of the range in Scotland and a spread into W Ireland and Scilly. Goldfinches are still caught in some places on the Continent and, indeed, the most usual form of automatic cage-trap for small birds is called a 'chardonneret', the French name for Goldfinch. Despite the recovery, however, the species is now far commoner in Britain south of a line from the Wash to the Dee, and in Ireland, than farther north, as was shown by Norris (1960). This, coupled with the fact that the majority (perhaps 80%) of British Goldfinches emigrate, mostly to the western parts of the Continent from Belgium to Spain, suggests that climatic factors determine the limits of breeding distribution, rather than habitat availability: there is, for example, ample suitable habitat in the agricultural eastern part of Caithness. Numbers fluctuate markedly from year to year, with warm, dry summers being specially favourable. Seed crops are then at their best, allowing more breeding attempts per pair and ensuring greater success; impressive autumn flocks may build up on waste ground in such years and many emigrate (Williamson and Spencer 1960).

The Common Birds Census shows a reasonable population during 1968–72, but recently this has reached record levels (see graph). Few CBC plots hold large numbers, but several rural, coastal scrub and farmland sites have 5–10 pairs per km², while the average for all farmland plots is 2.2. An average of 100 pairs per occupied 10-km square seems a reasonable estimate. This gives a British and Irish population of about 300,000 breeding pairs, considerably more than Parslow's rating of 10,000–100,000 pairs.

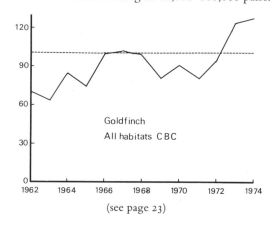

Goldfinch
All habitats CBC

(see page 23)

Number of 10-km squares in which recorded:
  3,018 (78%)
Possible breeding   218 (7%)
Probable breeding   279 (9%)
Confirmed breeding   2,521 (84%)

References

CONDER, P. J. 1948. The breeding biology and behaviour of the Continental Goldfinch *Carduelis carduelis carduelis*. *Ibis* 90: 493–525.

NEWTON, I. 1967. The adaptive radiation and feeding ecology of some British finches. *Ibis* 109: 33–98.

NEWTON, I. 1972. *Finches*. London.

NORRIS, C. A. 1960. The breeding distribution of thirty bird species in 1952. *Bird Study* 7: 129–184.

WILLIAMSON, K. and R. SPENCER. 1960. Ringing recoveries and the interpretation of bird movements. *Bird Migration* 1: 176–181.

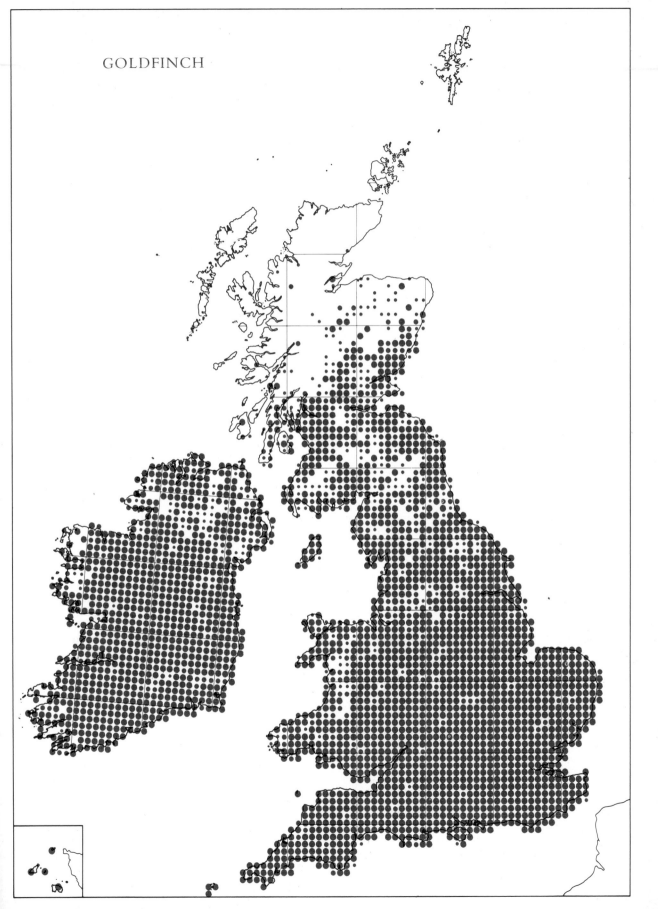

GOLDFINCH

Siskin

Carduelis spinus

Breeding Siskins are always closely associated with conifers, their main food in spring and early summer being seeds of spruces and pines. The traditional British habitat is the Caledonian pine forest of Scotland, but Siskins have now spread to parks, large gardens and policies where conifers (often exotic species) have been introduced. Recent expansion has taken them into new afforestation, and the species has perhaps adapted more rapidly than any to commercial plantings of Sitka spruce from NW Canada.

The musical flight calls and twittering song are distinctive and attract attention so that, where common, they are unlikely to be overlooked. Outside the main range, especially in central England, however, extensive new plantations often hold only a few pairs, and they may be easily missed amongst the masses of Redpolls *Acanthis flammea* which are likely to be nesting in such places. The map may thus underrepresent the situation to some extent, despite publicity given to the possibility of colonisation of new areas. This is reputed to be amongst the most difficult of all native passerine nests to find—the song-bird equivalent of the Greenshank *Tringa nebularia*. Nests in plantations, however, may sometimes be found with ease: in one such place in SW Ireland, where the whole glen echoed with the calls of Siskins, ten nests were found in the course of only a few hours of fieldwork. Confirmation of breeding was more usually achieved by seeing recently fledged young, discovery often being aided by their noisily demanding food from their parents. Some of the possible breeding records, outside the main concentrations, may have referred to late migrants; but, since it is probably through wintering birds staying on in suitable haunts that Siskins colonise new sites, such records may indicate places where breeding will occur in the future.

It is likely that Siskins were confined to the native Scots pine woods of the Scottish Highlands until the middle of the 19th century. Ireland was probably colonised after the introduction of these trees on a large scale, and Siskins then spread and were breeding locally in many counties by 1900. Subsequent expansion was probably from nuclei formed by the demesnes, where ornamental conifers were planted.

There is now a close correlation in Ireland between Siskin distribution and high ground, but this is indirect, the connection being due to the presence of most conifer plantations on the otherwise unproductive land of the valleys, lower slopes and plateau regions of the uplands. In Scotland, the spread from the native woods has similarly been aided by the planting of ornamental conifers and, more recently, by commercial afforestation. Such plantations now form the major habitat and have allowed Siskins to reach parts of the country (*eg* Caithness) where no suitable natural habitat existed. Breeding numbers fluctuate quite violently and the species is to some extent eruptive, but a real increase and extension of range has certainly taken place during the last 30 years, especially since 1960.

Local declines during the later 19th and early 20th centuries were attributed to the activities of birdcatchers and the felling of woods, but these losses have been made good. Early records of nesting in England and Wales were dismissed as coming from escaped captive stock, but small breeding pockets are now established in many places, and there is no doubt that the birds which colonised N Wales, Devon, the New Forest and Norfolk during the 1950s and early 1960s were of wild origin. As the new plantations mature and produce reliable crops of seed, it is reasonable to expect that this attractive species will become really well established in many more areas.

Apart from taking advantage of man's forestry activities, the Siskin is also undergoing an interesting change in behaviour in the winter and spring. First recorded in Surrey in 1963, but now in many counties of England, Wales and Scotland, increasing numbers have been reported feeding on peanuts put out for birds in gardens. Such a change in behaviour, allowing exploitation of a new source of food, may well aid the species in its colonisation.

No accurate census data are available and the Siskin's habit of nesting in loose colonies makes assessment of breeding densities difficult. In some parts of Scotland and Ireland, however, it may be one of the most numerous birds. Within the main body of its range, 10-km squares with extensive areas of suitable habitat may well harbour several hundred pairs, whereas some of the isolated 10-km squares may contain only one or two. There is no doubt that Parslow's classification as 'not scarce', inferring 1,000–10,000 pairs, is now too low, and probably well over 20,000 and possibly twice as many pairs were nesting in Britain and Ireland by the end of the *Atlas* period.

Number of 10-km squares in which recorded:
863 (22%)
Possible breeding   214 (25%)
Probable breeding   230 (27%)
Confirmed breeding   419 (49%)

References
DARE, P. J. 1962. Siskins breeding in Devon. *Brit. Birds* 55: 193–195.
NEWTON, I. 1972. *Finches*. London.
SPENCER, R. and G. H. GUSH. 1973. Siskins feeding in gardens. *Brit. Birds* 66: 91–99.

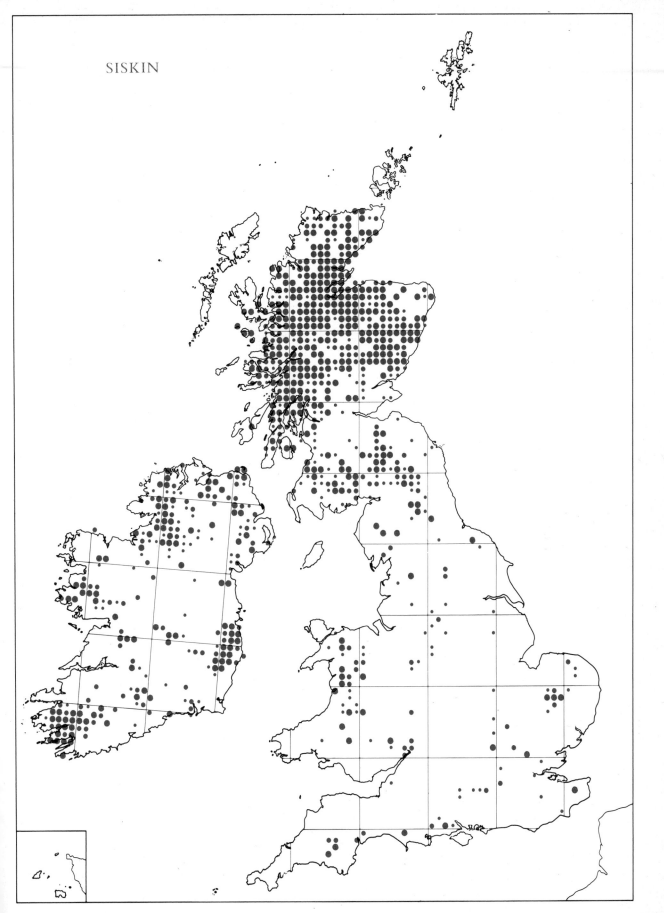

SISKIN

Linnet

Acanthis cannabina

Linnets feed almost exclusively on weed seeds taken from the ground, usually in open country. They nest in small colonies in bushes on heaths, downs and farmland, and can be found in hedges and along the edges of woods. Young conifer plantations and scrub by railways, canals and even motorways may also hold small colonies; and some pairs breed in garden shrubberies. In many coastal regions sea buckthorn, suaeda and other bushes along sand-dunes and sea-cliffs provide suitable sites. In some moorland, salt-marsh and dune habitats, the colonies may be in ground vegetation such as heather, sea purslane and marram.

Colonies usually contain about four to six pairs, although there are instances of up to 40 pairs breeding in a small area. The cheerful, twittering song, the conspicuous display flights, the habit of visiting the nest as a pair, with the male staying on top of a nearby bush, the low nests (seldom higher than 4 m) and the extended breeding season, with eggs laid from April through to August, were all features of assistance to the *Atlas* fieldworker.

Linnets and, to a greater extent, Goldfinches *Carduelis carduelis*, were favourite cage-birds in the 19th century and a widespread decline of both species at that time has been attributed to the activities of bird-catchers. The trade was made illegal in Britain and numbers recovered in the first part of this century. The distribution has not altered much, but recent declines have been reported in some areas. Nesting was established in Shetland in 1934, but none had bred there for several years before 1968–72, although the species remains widely distributed in Orkney. Linnets probably bred in the Outer Hebrides in the 19th century, and certainly did so early in this century; while Parslow (1967) thought they had ceased to nest there, a few did so in 1968–72. In the past, and even during the *Atlas* survey, there may have been some confusion with the very similar Twite *A. flavirostris* in parts of W and NW Scotland.

On the mainland of Scotland, there is a clear association with the farmland areas of the lowlands and east coast, reflecting the species' reliance on the weeds of cultivated land, with few inland squares occupied. Linnets are well distributed in Ireland, although they appear to be rather sparse in central Ulster. It is noticeable that there was a lower propor-

tion of confirmed breeding records in Ireland (81%) than in Britain (86%), which is the reverse of the situation for the Goldfinch (87% and 82%) and suggests that the Linnet is somewhat scarcer in Ireland; this is certainly so in some western parts (*eg* Cork and Kerry), where apparently ideal country is often devoid of Linnets (though a few pairs can be found in most squares). Many of the islands of the far west have breeding colonies, though some (*eg* Cape Clear Island) are evacuated in winter.

Increased cultivation leading to a reduction in marginal land may have affected numbers, but it seems likely that modern farming methods, including the use of herbicides, may have affected the Linnet rather more directly by diminishing the supply of weed seeds available to it as food. Common Bird Census information shows a relatively small adverse effect due to cold weather in 1962/63 and a rapid recovery (see graph).

With a colonial nesting species, densities from individual CBC areas are difficult to interpret, but the mean for all woodland and farmland plots in 1972 was about seven pairs per km². High densities occur in chalk grassland scrub and young conifer plantations; coastal scrub dominated by sea buckthorn at Gibraltar Point (Lincolnshire) held 75 pairs per km². If allowance is made for areas with rather sparse populations, there was perhaps an average of 250–500 pairs per occupied 10-km square, and a British and Irish total of 800,000 to 1.6 million pairs. This is at, or above, the upper limit of Parslow's category of 100,000–1,000,000.

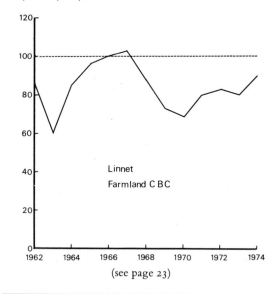

Linnet
Farmland CBC

(see page 23)

Number of 10-km squares in which recorded:
  3,345 (87%)
Possible breeding   195 (6%)
Probable breeding   317 (9%)
Confirmed breeding   2,833 (85%)

References

NEWTON, I. 1967. The adaptive radiation and feeding ecology of some British finches. *Ibis* 109: 33–98.
NEWTON, I. 1972. *Finches*. London.

LINNET

Twite

Acanthis flavirostris

The Twite has the distinction of being the only European bird derived from the Tibetan fauna type. It is supposed that the range formerly extended to the steppe tundra of central Europe and that, with the retreat of the Scandinavian land-ice after the Würm glaciation, a part of the population followed the ice edge westwards, the main stock gradually contracting to Asia. The species now has a disjunct distribution with its main stronghold in the high plateaux and cold steppes of central Asia, and a distant European population restricted to a narrow coastal and montane belt running from N Norway and the Kola Peninsula southwards to Britain and Ireland (Voous 1960).

Even within our area, the distribution is now disjunct, with the main concentration in the coastal regions of N and W Scotland, a small community in the S Pennines, and a third centre in Ireland. The Twites of Scotland and the west coast of Ireland favour the heather moors and coastal cliff-brows, though in Ireland some occur on mountains near the coast. Feeding is usually on short, grassy turf near the sea and in the neighbourhood of crofts. They make their nests in a variety of situations, especially heather on moor or cliff, but also dry-stone walls, small trees and bushes. Those in the Pennines, while still dependent on heather for nesting and the seeds of *Molinia* grass for spring feeding, find most of their summer food at a lower altitude, often up to 2 km from the nest, on the sheep pastures and reseeded fields of upland farms (Orford 1973).

The Twite has been called the 'mountain linnet' and is to some extent the ecological counterpart of *A. cannabina*, replacing it at high altitudes and in northern areas. There is, however, a considerable overlap within Britain and Ireland, and semi-colonial, mixed groups are sometimes found. Such cases seem to be due to Linnets invading typical Twite habitat rather than the reverse, so possibly the mixing is a consequence of the climatic amelioration during the present century. Interspecific competition would be expected, but its extent and effects are unknown.

The twittering calls and pleasant, rambling song have a strong resemblance to those of the Linnet, and the fledged young are hard to distinguish, so there is

a possibility that the map is incomplete, especially in peripheral areas. The habit of finding food a fair distance from the nest, and the continuation of spring movement into June, compound the difficulty of evaluating sightings; but such is the strength of the pair-bond that a pair seen together is a very useful indication of breeding nearby.

The Twites in Europe are adapted to a cool maritime climate and only a fragment of the total number breeds at any distance from the coast. Where they do so, as in the Pennines, the habitat is of recent origin, the zone of hill pastures flanked by heather moor having arisen through clearing and sheep husbandry during the last 1,000 years. As Orford (1973) pointed out, it is difficult to understand the clear dichotomy in habitat preference between the Scottish and Irish maritime populations and the moorland communities of the S Pennines. He thought the latter might have occupied their present ground from the Lancashire and Cheshire mosses, where Twites were formerly widespread. Though there seems now to be growth in the numbers in the S Pennines, this is a long way from compensating for long-term decreases, even disappearances, in other parts of the central and southern range, such as the Cheviots, the Border country, the Pentland Hills and Ireland. Perhaps even more remarkable are the obvious absences from N Yorkshire, the Lake District and the Isle of Man.

In N Scotland and the isles, this is one of the commonest land-birds, and despite local declines in the 1960s, attributed to organochlorine seed-dressings, the population seems to be fairly stable. An abundance of browsing Rabbits which, together with the sheep, keep the turf short, seems to favour the species, while the verges of new roads driven across the moors also make attractive feeding grounds. The decline in the centre and south of the British range (none has nested in Devon since early this century, and nesting in Shropshire and Flintshire is doubtful, or at least sporadic) may be a retreat before the ameliorating climatic conditions which attained their peak in the 1930s. Whether the recent improvement in the carefully explored S Pennines is a pointer to a better future for the species, now that the climate has entered a cooler phase, remains to be seen.

Parslow classed the Twite as 'not scarce', inferring 1,000–10,000 pairs. This seems to be a pessimistic figure since even a conservative average of 25–50 pairs per 10-km square would give a total British and Irish population of 20,000–40,000 pairs.

Number of 10-km squares in which recorded:
785 (20%)
Possible breeding   196 (25%)
Probable breeding   173 (22%)
Confirmed breeding   416 (53%)

References
ORFORD, N. 1973. Breeding distribution of the Twite in central Britain. *Bird Study* 20: 51–62, 121–126.
NEWTON, I. 1972. *Finches*. London.
NUTTALL, J. 1972. The status and distribution of the Twite (*Carduelis flavirostris*) in east Lancashire, with some notes on breeding biology. *Naturalist* no. 923: 140–141.

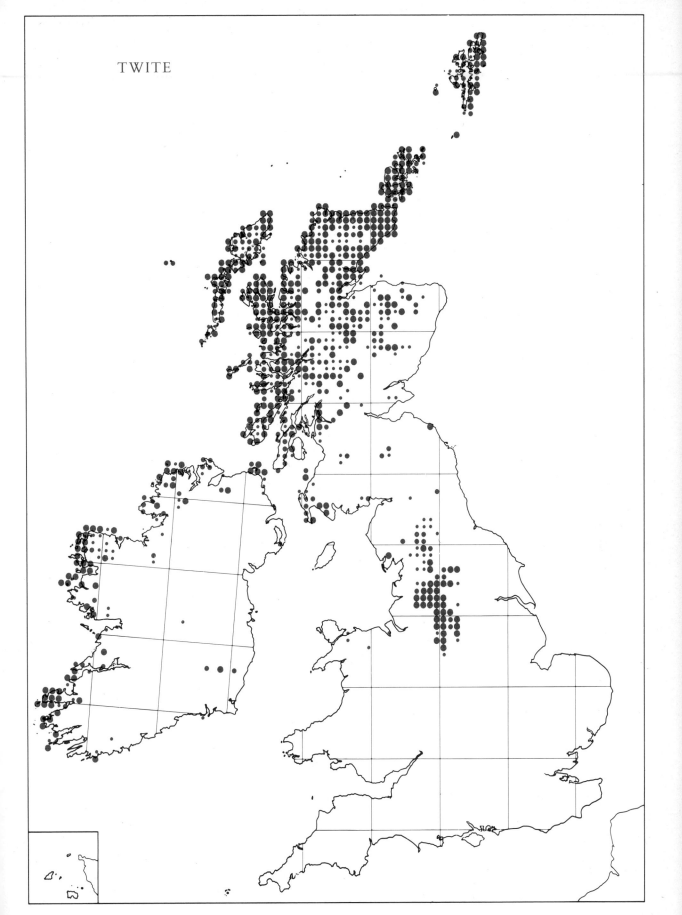

TWITE

Redpoll

Acanthis flammea

The Redpoll has benefited very considerably over the years from the increased planting of upland moors and lowland heaths by commercial forestry interests, and a large part of its recent spread within Britain and Ireland must be due to this creation of new habitat. The hillside birch woods of the north and west, acid heath with silver birches and mixed scrub in England, damp alder woods and carr, tree-fringed streams and the scrub growth invading the dry chalk downs are all attractive haunts. In many districts, Redpolls are beginning to occupy overgrown field hedgerows, and even gardens. In Ireland, this species is more widespread than in Britain; although forestry plantations probably now hold the majority, the more traditional areas, particularly in the callow lands, also have a high density.

Like Linnets *A. cannabina*, Redpolls often tend to breed in small, loose colonies. They have a distinctive flight-call, a rattling 'chi-chi-chi', and indulge in display flights, so will not have been missed by observers familiar with these; some may have been overlooked, however, in the area of scarcity in central S England.

Active nests are most common from May to mid-August. They are generally rather higher in small trees and bushes than Linnets' nests, but some as low as 1 m have been recorded in tree lupins in Suffolk (Campbell and Ferguson-Lees 1972). They are often well concealed, especially where there is ample growth of lichens on the trees. Even during the breeding season, pairs will range widely to exploit food sources, and they may be frustrating subjects to watch back to the nest. Confirmation is thus often difficult to obtain, and watching for family parties with newly fledged young is usually the most profitable method.

An increase and spread in lowland Britain during 1900–10 was followed by a decrease and disappearance from many areas in the 1920s. Since 1950, the Redpoll has embarked on a second phase of expansion, considerably aided by afforestation, and the Common Birds Census index shows a fourfold increase in 1964–74 (see graph). Breeding in Cornwall, Pembrokeshire, Caithness, Orkney and the Outer Hebrides dates from just before, or during, the *Atlas* years of 1968–72, and it may well be that the striking gap in distribution in central S England has been at least partly filled since 1972.

Redpoll numbers are subject to big fluctuations, depending upon the abundance or scarcity of food resources, so that eruptive movements occur from time to time. During its recent expansion, the British stock has invaded and colonised the dune afforestation in the Netherlands (through which British birds pass on migration) and, more recently, coastal plantations in Denmark (Hald-Mortensen 1970).

Densities are not easy to assess, particularly as this species occurs on rather few farm census plots, but several individual sites are known to have 50 pairs per km²; and there are a number of heaths and scrubby areas in SE England, and upland birch woods, where nesting concentrations probably reach or surpass this level. Even taking such a low average as 100 pairs per 10-km square, a total for Britain and Ireland of 300,000 pairs is indicated, and it might be as much as twice that figure. By 1972, Parslow's 1967 estimate of 10,000–100,000 was certainly far too low. In the mid-1970s, Redpolls were undoubtedly commoner than they had been for at least 100 years.

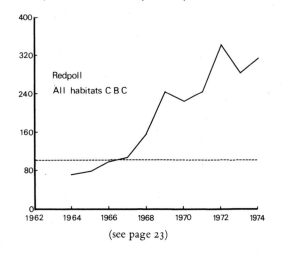

Redpoll
All habitats C B C

(see page 23)

Number of 10-km squares in which recorded:
2,818 (73%)
Possible breeding   279 (10%)
Probable breeding   727 (26%)
Confirmed breeding   1,812 (64%)

References
HALD-MORTENSEN, P. 1970. Lille Gråsisken (*Carduelis flammea cabaret* (Müller)) som ynglefugl i Danmark. *Dansk Orn. Foren. Tidsskr.* 64: 163–193.
NEWTON, I. 1967. The adaptive radiation and feeding ecology of some British finches. *Ibis* 109: 33–98.
NEWTON, I. 1972. *Finches*. London.

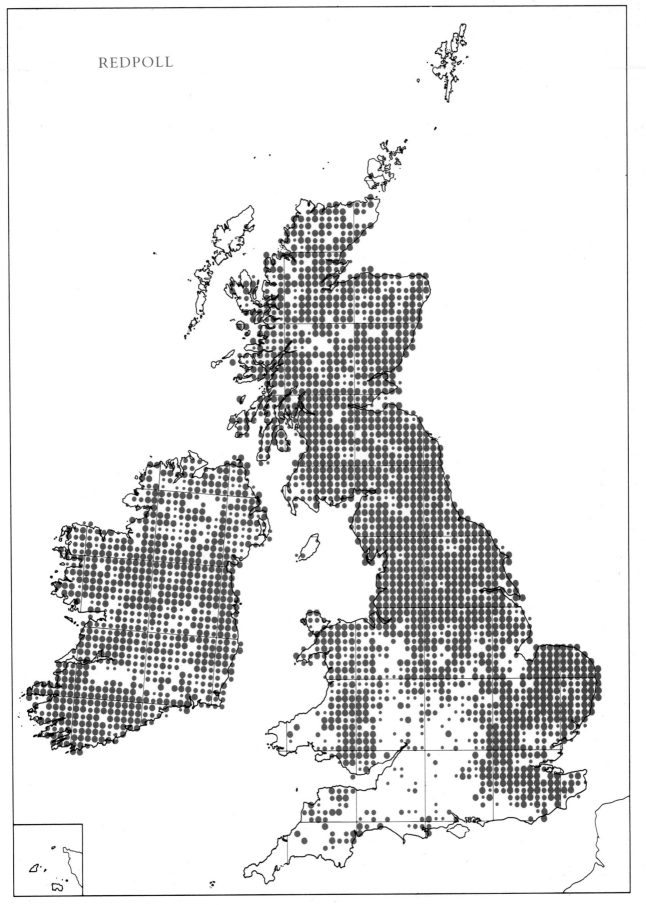

REDPOLL

Serin

Serinus serinus

Though the Serin's natural home was once the fringes of Mediterranean woodland, it is now found in a great variety of habitats, usually in close proximity to man. Some of the commonest haunts on the Continent are parks, orchards, churchyards, tree-lined roadsides, vineyards, town squares and even quite small gardens. With weed-seeds comprising an important part of the diet, feeding birds are encountered on any open waste land, even at harbours and railway yards. It is therefore entirely in keeping with the known habits of the species that British breeding records have come from large, private gardens in rural villages.

Serins conceal their nests in thick foliage, usually over 4 m above ground and well out on a flimsy side-branch. Deciduous trees are most frequently used, but these birds quite often build in isolated evergreens growing among broad-leaved trees, and the first British nest was in an ornamental western red cedar.

The lively tinkling song and twittering call-notes of Serins make them very noticeable in areas where they are common and where flocks occur. In this country, however, the records mostly relate to only one or two birds at a site, and the enormous extent of suitable habitat must make initial location entirely a matter of luck. Confirmation of breeding may come most easily by observation of recently fledged young, though family parties sometimes wander considerable distances from the natal area.

The Serin was first identified in this country in 1852, and until comparatively recent times was only a vagrant; but there was a notable increase after 1960, and by 1974 there had been about 185 occurrences involving some 240 individuals, including two confirmed breeding records (Sharrock and Sharrock 1976). This upsurge was not unexpected, since Serins have been spreading northwards in Europe for as long as records exist—at least 200 years (Olsson 1969, 1971). Their progression is shown on the accompanying map. Formerly a woodland edge species, the Serin has spread into new habitats; but it is not known whether the adaptation to new situations actually triggered the expansion, or whether the spread compelled birds to adopt a more catholic choice of site.

British records, which involve all months, show obvious peaks in April–May and October–November, corresponding with the migration seasons.

The first British breeding record in 1967 (Ferguson-Lees 1968) was subsequently revealed to have been in Dorset. After this, it was expected that 1968–72 would see firm colonisation of S England, with many 10-km squares occupied by the end of the *Atlas* survey. This did not happen, as the map clearly shows, and even in 1976 we are still awaiting the Serin's main assault on our shores.

With only one confirmed breeding record in the five years 1968–72 (Sussex in 1969), and only five other instances of probable breeding (mostly single singing males), Britain could still be without nesting Serins in most years. On the other hand, a few could have been missed in municipal parks or out-of-the-way villages.

This species is afforded special protection in Great Britain under Schedule I of the Protection of Birds Act, 1954–67.

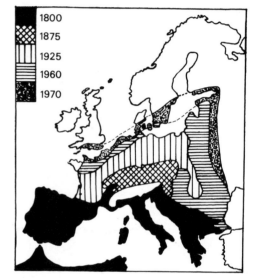

Spread of Serins across Europe, 1800–1970 (after Olsson 1969)

Number of 10-km squares in which recorded:
6 (0.2%)
Possible breeding 0
Probable breeding 5 (83%)
Confirmed breeding 1 (17%)

Five dots have been moved by one 10-km square (as recommended by the Rare Breeding Birds Panel)

References
FERGUSON-LEES, I. J. 1968. Serins breeding in southern England. *Brit. Birds* 61: 87–88.
NEWTON, I. 1972. *Finches*. London.
OLSSON, V. 1969. Die Expansion des Girlitzes (*Serinus serinus*) in Nordeuropa in den letzten Jahrzehnten. *Vogelwarte* 25: 147–156.
OLSSON, V. 1971. Studies of less familiar birds. 165. Serin. *Brit. Birds* 64: 213–223.
SHARROCK, J. T. R. and E. M. SHARROCK. 1976. *Rare birds in Britain and Ireland*. Berkhamsted.

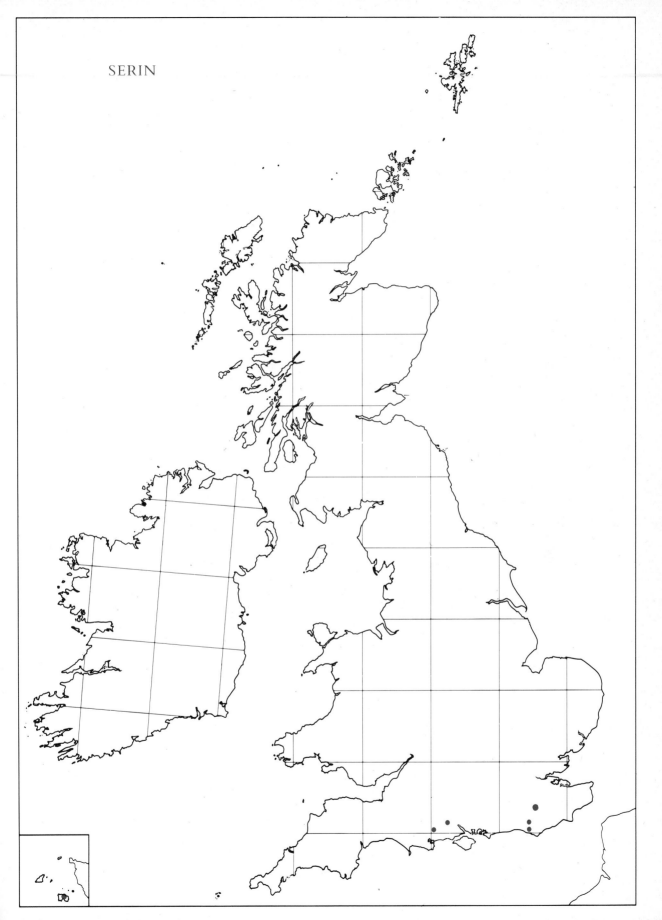

SERIN

Bullfinch

Pyrrhula pyrrhula

Originally a bird of forest edge and scrubland, the Bullfinch can now also be found nesting in overgrown hedgerows, churchyards, town and village gardens, and young forestry plantations—in fact almost any habitat providing bushy tangles for the nest. In fruit-growing areas it is often a pest species, but usually breeds in nearby hedges or spinneys rather than in orchards, since fruit trees seldom provide sufficient cover.

Handsome and easily recognised birds, Bullfinches seldom form flocks and are usually found in pairs or family parties. The thin, piping call-note is distinctive but does not carry very far, and the soft whistling song is so weak that it can be heard only at extremely short range. During the breeding season, however, the pair is usually to be found in company and, although they approach the nest with caution, they can often be seen flying directly away from it. A search should then reveal the characteristic platform of twigs surmounted by a shallow cup of dark rootlets and lighter hair. Nests are generally 1–2 m above ground, and may be found at any time from late April through to August. They are so characteristic that searching outside the breeding season will often enable the identification of old ones.

The species' diet and general ecology have been studied in great detail because of its importance as a pest of commercial orchards. In Britain, damage to commercial fruit trees and bushes may take place at any time from November to April, and can affect apples, cherries, currants, gooseberries, pears and plums. At the same time, flower buds may be removed from ornamental shrubs and trees in gardens. Damage occurs because the species is adapted to taking its food off the growing plant and, as the winter passes, there is progressively less seed or fruit remaining. Bullfinches then turn to flower buds, which are of higher nutritional value than leaf buds, and prefer to take them from fruit trees and bushes because these have been selectively bred by man for a higher yield. Naturally, very heavy losses of flower buds reduce the eventual fruit crop. In seasons when there is a good, lasting supply of natural seed (eg when there is a large crop of ash keys), damage to fruit trees is generally low, for Bullfinches prefer seeds to buds when the former are available. This ability to survive on buds at a time of year when other foods can be in short supply enables the species to survive the crucial, early spring period much better than the less adaptable Greenfinch *Carduelis chloris*. Ringing recoveries of Bullfinches show that few die in April, the month when Greenfinch mortality is highest (Mead 1974).

Over the last 200 years, the Bullfinch has probably extended its range northwards and westwards in Britain and Ireland. None breeds on the Outer Hebrides or Northern Isles nor, strangely, on the Isle of Man, where there is plenty of apparently suitable habitat. Since 1955, there have been reports of increasing numbers, and colonisation of more open habitats, from almost all occupied areas. This has been attributed to the decline of Sparrowhawks *Accipiter nisus*, which was brought about by toxic chemicals. Bullfinches are relatively bold birds, which feed away from thick cover, and it is presumed that their survival is improved by the decrease of their chief predator. (It will be interesting to see if the current revival in Sparrowhawk numbers results in a decline in those of the Bullfinch.) Whatever the reason, the increase led to pressure in Britain for the removal of the Bullfinch from the protected list, and this species is now extensively trapped and destroyed by fruit farmers in many areas. Autumn trapping may result in the natural seed supply lasting longer and a consequent reduction in spring damage to buds, but little or no long-term effect on Bullfinch numbers, even though thousands may be killed on some farms.

The Common Birds Census data show that densities over 20 pairs per km² are rare, although Newton (1972) found up to 50 pairs per km² in favoured areas in Oxfordshire. The mean for all CBC data for 1972 indicates much lower levels of 2.4 pairs per km² on farmland plots and 7.1 in woodland areas. These suggest an average of about 200 pairs per occupied 10-km square and a total British and Irish population of some 600,000 pairs.

Number of 10-km squares in which recorded:
3,202 (83%)
Possible breeding   235 (7%)
Probable breeding   350 (11%)
Confirmed breeding   2,617 (82%)

References

FRYER, J. C. F. 1939. The destruction of buds of trees and shrubs by birds. *Brit. Birds* 33: 90–94.

MEAD, C. J. 1974. *Bird Ringing.* BTO Guide no. 16. Tring.

MURTON, R. K. 1971. *Man and Birds.* London.

NEWTON, I. 1967. The feeding ecology of the Bullfinch (*Pyrrhula pyrrhula* L.) in southern England. *J. Anim. Ecol.* 36: 721–744.

NEWTON, I. 1968. Bullfinches and fruit buds. In MURTON, R. K. and E. N. WRIGHT (eds), *The Problems of Birds as Pests.* Inst. Biol. Symp. no. 17. London.

NEWTON, I. 1972. *Finches.* London.

WRIGHT, E. N. and D. D. B. SUMMERS. 1960. The biology and economic importance of the Bullfinch. *Ann. Appl. Biol.* 48: 415–418.

BULLFINCH

Crossbill

Loxia curvirostra

The Crossbill's specially adapted beak, with the tips of the hooked mandibles overlapping, enables it to snip the seeds from the cones of spruces and pines.

Newton (1970) has pointed out that Crossbills have evolved a one-way migration stratagem which ensures that new areas with good cone crops are exploited. When there is a high Crossbill population level, most leave after the breeding season. They may move only a short distance before finding a suitable area with a good cone crop, but when none is available they continue travelling, and this sometimes results in invasions of Crossbills from the east reaching W Europe, including Britain and Ireland. Such birds often remain to breed in the new areas. The most recent irruptions affecting Britain were in 1953, 1956, 1958, 1959, 1962, 1963, 1966 and 1972. It is fortunate that the first four years of the *Atlas* survey were not complicated in this way.

Different Crossbill populations have the bill-size adapted to the strength of the cones which provide the major part of their food. Those subsisting mainly on Scots pine seeds have larger and deeper bills than those living in the Eurasian belt of spruce forests; they are currently recognised as distinct species, *L. pytyopsittacus* and *L. curvirostra* respectively, though some authors regard them as no more than 'emergent interspecies'. The Scottish Crossbill, which is customarily referred to by the subspecific name *scotica*, has a relict distribution based on the last fragments of the old Caledonian forest. Its taxonomic status is unresolved, the bill being more powerful than that of the common (spruce) Crossbill *L. curvirostra*, yet not so massive as that of the Parrot (pine) Crossbill *L. pytyopsittacus*, and it has been variously regarded as a race of one or other of these, or as a separate species, *L. scotica* (Knox 1975).

Although it is difficult to get a good close-up view, identification of Crossbills is usually not difficult, for they have a characteristic, big-headed silhouette, as well as a frequently uttered, explosive 'chip' which is used as a flight-call and contact note. They sing from prominent perches, such as the top of a conifer, and often drop partially eaten cones, leaving tell-tale traces beneath the trees in which they are feeding. The nesting season may be very early and in Britain females have been found sitting on eggs in December. The majority of English clutches are laid between February and April, and N Scottish ones in March and April; thus, many Crossbills would have finished nesting by the time *Atlas* fieldwork began.

There has been regular breeding of the typical Crossbill in the Brecklands of Norfolk and Suffolk since a vast irruption in 1910, and from about the same time in the New Forest (Hampshire). After other irruptions, nesting has occurred spasmodically in many other counties of England, less widely in Scotland and Wales and least regularly in Ireland. As the vast areas of post-war pine and spruce plantations mature, many new areas in Britain and Ireland will be available for future colonies. The Kielder Forest (Northumberland), where breeding has recently become established, is an example. Conifer forests are not the only habitat in Britain, however, for small clumps, wind-breaks or lines of conifers all provide regular sites, especially in East Anglia.

The majority of the records from the Scottish Highlands probably referred to the native *scotica*, but both this and the common Crossbill are plotted together here, since *Atlas* observers were not asked to attempt to differentiate between them. Nethersole-Thompson estimated *scotica* at about 1,500 adults in the early 1970s, and over 100 pairs of Crossbills were thought to be nesting in the New Forest in 1960, after the 1959 irruption. An average of about 15 pairs per occupied 10-km square would give a total population for Britain and Ireland of about 5,000 pairs. This may be greatly exceeded, of course, in seasons immediately following irruptions.

This species is afforded special protection in Great Britain under Schedule I of the Protection of Birds Act, 1954–67.

Number of 10-km squares in which recorded:
305 (8%)

Possible breeding	131 (43%)
Probable breeding	33 (11%)
Confirmed breeding	141 (46%)

Though some records were originally submitted in confidence, all dots are now shown accurately (as recommended by the Rare Breeding Birds Panel)

References

DAVIS, P. 1963. The Parrot Crossbill irruption at Fair Isle. *Bird Migration* 2: 260–264.

KNOX, A. G. 1975. Crossbill taxonomy. In NETHERSOLE-THOMPSON (1975).

NETHERSOLE-THOMPSON, D. 1975. *Pine Crossbills*. Berkhamsted.

NEWTON, I. 1970. Irruptions of Crossbills in Europe. In WATSON, A. (ed), *Animal Populations in Relation to their Food Resources*. Oxford.

NEWTON, I. 1972. *Finches*. London.

SVÄRDSON, G. 1957. The 'invasion' type of bird migration. *Brit. Birds* 50: 314–343.

Accounts of some recent irruptions have included:
1953, WILLIAMSON, K. (1955), *Scott. Nat.* 66: 155–169; 1953, BARRAUD, E. M. (1956), *Brit. Birds* 49: 289–297; 1956/57, SMITH, F. R. (1959), *Brit. Birds* 52: 1–9; 1962, WILLIAMSON, K. (1963), *Bird Migration* 2: 252–260, 329–340; 1962/63, DAVIS, P. (1964), *Brit. Birds* 57: 477–501.

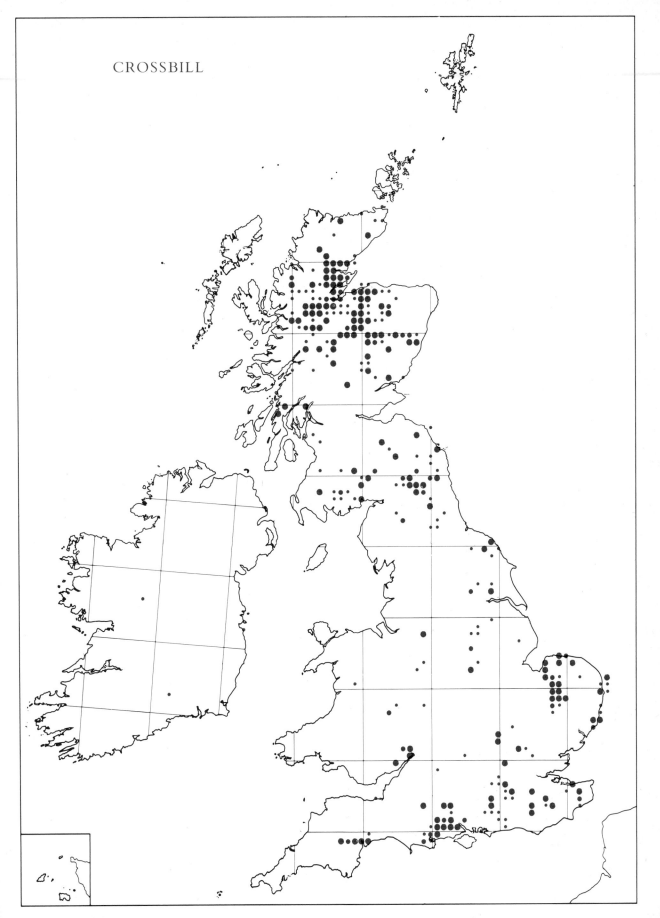

CROSSBILL

429

Chaffinch

Fringilla coelebs

Chaffinches may be found breeding in Britain and Ireland wherever there are trees or bushes. The densest populations occur in mature broad-leaved woodland, but this is a common species in scrub, farmland, parks and gardens. In upland areas, isolated hawthorn bushes on a bracken-covered hillside may be adequate to harbour a pair and, where bushes or small trees, such as alder and birch, grow up a gill, they may be found nesting at 600–700 m.

The loud distinctive song, 'pink' call-note and strong territorial behaviour make location easy, even in marginal habitats where there are only isolated pairs. In the spring, the males start to defend their territories during February, when there are still many Continental winter-visitors present here in flocks. Pairs are formed quite quickly, though nest building, normally by the female alone, does not start until April (Marler 1956). Most clutches are laid in late April or early May; Chaffinches are usually single-brooded. The nests are beautifully made and camouflaged so that they are sometimes rather difficult to find. The structure is characteristic, however, and used nests are readily identifiable. The young are fed in the nest for about a fortnight and breeding is readily proved through seeing parents carrying food.

The range of the Chaffinch has shifted northwards in Europe during the period of climatic amelioration in the past 50 years, at the expense of the Brambling *F. montifringilla*, and this has perhaps been reflected here to a small extent by colonisation of some Hebridean islands and an increase in Orkney, but there has been no case of breeding proved in Shetland yet, and some of the range extensions may be partly, or even wholly, due to the provision of habitat in forestry plantations and gardens in areas which were formerly unsuitable. Tiree and Coll, most of the Outer Hebrides and bare moorland areas on the Caithness/Sutherland border are now the only other large areas uncolonised, but Chaffinches are still only the 13th most widespread species in Britain and Ireland (or the ninth, if only the records of confirmed breeding are considered).

In Britain, the population may have reached a peak in about 1950 and then declined. Few figures are available for this period before the Common Birds Census was started, but Beven (1963), working in Surrey oak woodland, reported minimum numbers in 1959 and a subsequent increase. Mayer-Gross (1965) analysed nest record cards and showed that there was reduced hatching success during the late 1950s. This has been attributed to the effects of toxic agricultural chemicals, particularly seed-dressings, but seems now to have been arrested. From 1962, the first year for which there is a CBC farmland index, the Chaffinch population increased steadily for three years, then stabilised, and has since fluctuated slightly within quite narrow limits. The woodland index, started in 1964, also shows relatively minor fluctuations.

In 1940, James Fisher speculated that the Chaffinch and the Blackbird *Turdus merula* might be the commonest birds in Britain, with five million pairs each. Flegg, in Fisher and Flegg (1974), revised this to four million for Chaffinch and up to $7\frac{1}{2}$ million for Blackbird, with Wren *Troglodytes troglodytes* and Robin *Erithacus rubecula* falling between them. Newton (1972) quoted breeding densities of 49–145 pairs per km² in broad-leaved woodland and 12–102 pairs per km² in conifers. From these figures he estimated a British woodland population of between half a million and two million pairs. CBC data show densities reaching 300 pairs per km² in particularly favoured woods, but the average in 1972 was 36.8 pairs per km² for all woodland, including conifer and scrub with lower densities than deciduous areas, and 19.1 pairs per km² on farmland. Since there are also known to be high Chaffinch densities in the birch and other deciduous woodlands of upland Britain, a general average of 2,000 or more breeding pairs per occupied 10-km square for Britain and Ireland may not be excessive. This would indicate a total of seven million pairs.

Number of 10-km squares in which recorded: 3,553 (92%)
Possible breeding   23 (1%)
Probable breeding   101 (3%)
Confirmed breeding   3,429 (97%)

References
BEVEN, G. 1963. Population changes in a Surrey oakwood during fifteen years. *Brit. Birds* 56: 307–323.
FISHER, J. and J. FLEGG. 1974. *Watching Birds.* Berkhamsted.
MARLER, P. 1956. Behaviour of the Chaffinch *Fringilla coelebs. Behaviour*, suppl. 5: 1–184.
MAYER-GROSS, H. 1965. Hatching success of Blue Tit, Song Thrush and Chaffinch in recent years. *Bird Study* 12: 253–255.
NEWTON, I. 1967. The adaptive radiation and feeding ecology of some British finches. *Ibis* 109: 22–98.
NEWTON, I. 1972. *Finches.* London.

Brambling *Fringilla montifringilla,* **see page 451**

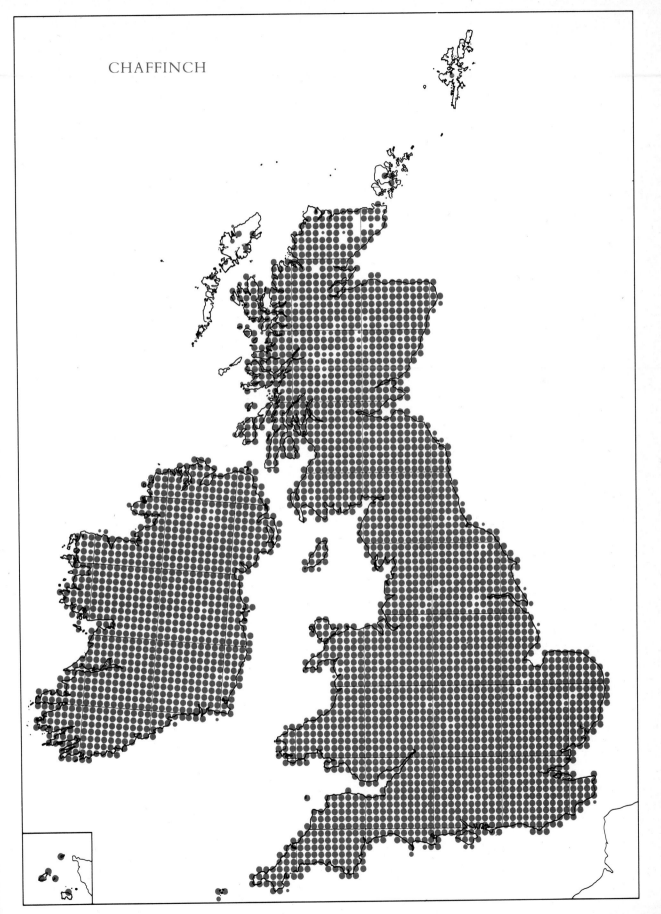

CHAFFINCH

Corn Bunting

Emberiza calandra

HB.

It is doubtful if the Corn Bunting would have reached much of central and W Europe if it had not been for man's influence in creating the agricultural landscape on which it has become so dependent.

In Britain and Ireland, there is a close affinity with arable farms and cornfields with hedges, post-and-wire fences and electricity pylons, which can be used as song-posts. Walpole-Bond (1938) considered uncultivated country to be as important as tilled land in Sussex, where coastal regions are much favoured. There was a thriving population along the Cornish coast, studied by Ryves and Ryves (1934), the birds nesting in low gorse and brambles, though feeding among hay, corn and root crops. In the Outer Hebrides, Corn Buntings breed on the machair and in small cornfields near the coast.

Ryves and Ryves found a great many nests in Cornwall, by far the largest proportion in gorse or bramble. When built in a field of hay or corn, the nest was placed in a depression, most often under a thistle. In their experience, crops were the least favoured site throughout the season, but Walpole-Bond noted early nests in crops and it was only after June that they were built in gorse—either because the crops stood too tall or because they were harvested. In SE Sutherland, Macdonald (1965) found practically all his nests in crops. In Hampshire, Woods (1950) recorded them either close to the ground in young gorse or at up to 1 m in small hawthorns.

The nests of this species are seldom easy to locate, though the persistent and distinctive, jingling songs of the males should mean that it has been overlooked in very few squares. Males may return to the breeding territory as early as January, but females remain in the winter flocks until April or May; nesting normally lasts from June to August with a peak of activity in July.

Corn Buntings may be found breeding almost to the farthest corners of Britain and Ireland, but in places the species has an irregular distribution and presents one of the most fascinating of all *Atlas* maps. Upland areas are avoided, accounting for the absence in much of SW and N England, Wales and large areas of Scotland and Ireland. In Scotland, the distribution follows that of arable farming very closely—the coast of Galloway, across the Forth-Clyde valleys,

then sweeping north to SE Sutherland and the remote croft-lands of Orkney and Shetland. The Hebrides have been reached, but it was in these last three areas that the Corn Bunting suffered its biggest decline in Scotland, between 1930 and 1950. Evans and Flower (1967) considered that the mechanisation of harvesting and, possibly, higher rainfall were contributory factors.

In England, Corn Buntings are most widespread in the east from Yorkshire south to the Wash, and then across country in a wide belt to Dorset. There are peculiar gaps in intensively farmed East Anglia and the Weald of Sussex and Kent. Suffolk has seen a series of fluctuations over the last 30–40 years, with a continuous decline since the 1960s. The Midlands lost Corn Buntings from many places, especially in Shropshire and Worcester, before the 1940s, while in SW England decreases were noted in the Isles of Scilly and Cornwall in the 1930s and after, and in Devon from 1945.

The Welsh distribution used to follow the coastal belt of agricultural land south to Pembrokeshire, and in Anglesey this species was formerly common. Now, following a decline which started in the 1920s, there have been virtually no breeding records (except in E Flintshire) since about 1949. Ireland has also suffered a widespread decline in Corn Bunting numbers. In 1900, this species was known in every county except Leitrim, though it was scarce and local away from the coast, but there are now only a few isolated groups, entirely restricted to the coast. The reasons for the widespread diminution, especially in the west, are not at all clear.

There are areas where Corn Buntings were found in the early years of the *Atlas* survey (1968–69) but had gone by the end (1972). Many 10-km squares are also known to have contained only a handful of pairs. Even if the average density over the whole of the British and Irish range was only one-tenth of the Common Birds Census figure for farmland (2.4 pairs per km^2), however, there would be 30,000 pairs, which is well above Parslow's range of 1,000–10,000.

Number of 10-km squares in which recorded:
1,424 (37%)
Possible breeding   121 (8%)
Probable breeding   600 (42%)
Confirmed breeding   703 (49%)

References

EVANS, P. R. and W. U. FLOWER. 1962. The birds of the Small Isles. *Scott. Birds* 4: 404–445.

MACDONALD, D. 1965. Notes on the Corn Bunting in Sutherland. *Scott. Birds* 3: 235–246.

RYVES, I. N. and B. H. RYVES. 1934. The breeding habits of the Corn Bunting as observed in north Cornwall: with special reference to its polygamous habit. *Brit. Birds* 28: 2–26, 154–164.

WALPOLE-BOND, J. 1938. *A History of Sussex Birds*. London.

WILLIAMSON, K. 1968. Buntings on a barley farm. *Bird Study* 15: 34–37.

WOODS, H. E. 1950. Notes on the breeding habits of the Corn Bunting in Hampshire. *Brit. Birds* 43: 82–83.

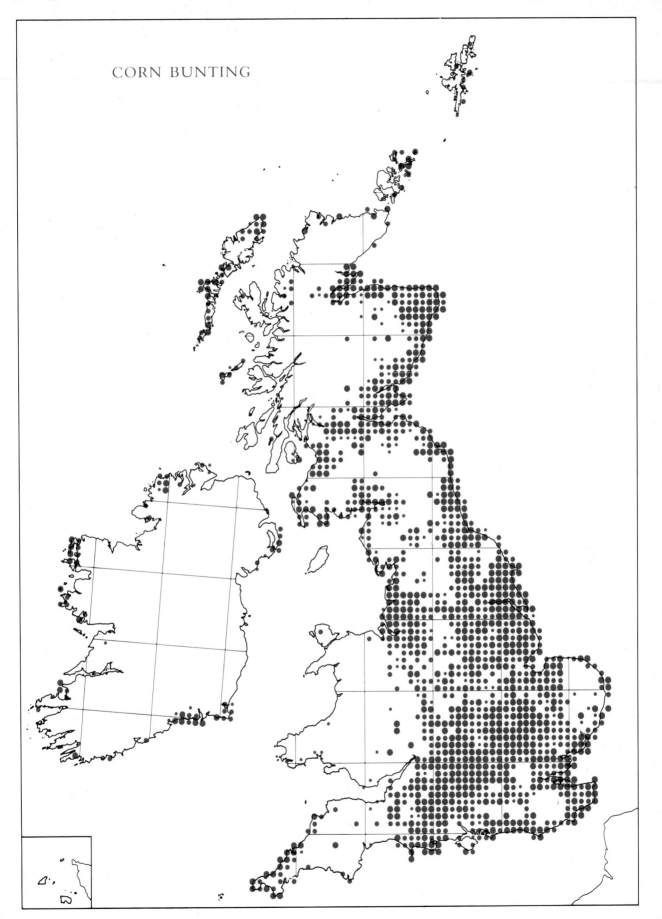

CORN BUNTING

Yellowhammer

Emberiza citrinella

In parts of S Europe, the Cirl Bunting *E. cirlus* ecologically replaces the Yellowhammer, which is then restricted to montane and subalpine regions, but in Britain and Ireland the present species inhabits all types of open country: heaths, commons, young conifer plantations, bracken-covered hillsides, agricultural land and woodland edges. It has adapted well to man's influence on the environment and has become one of the most familiar birds on farms. The linear scrub of hedgerows, as field boundaries, alongside roads and on railway embankments, suits it well. The essential physical components of the habitat seem to be open, dry ground, and bushes, small trees or even telegraph wires for song-posts. The Yellowhammer will not inhabit scrub which becomes too dense, and differs from the Reed Bunting *E. schoeniclus* in requiring these elevated song-posts. The latter species has, however, recently entered dry habitats, such as bushy commons and farm hedgerows, to breed alongside it.

The song is distinctive and is uttered from a prominent perch, making initial location easy. Males start singing during February and defend the song-posts and their immediate neighbourhood. They will attack other males fiercely and also occasionally chase other intruders, including Reed and Corn Buntings *E. calandra*. The territory itself is important for the formation and maintenance of the pair bond. On farmland, Yellowhammers feed a great deal outside their territories in nearby fields, amicably alongside rival pairs. The food consists largely of corn, weed seeds and wild fruits, especially outside the breeding season, and a variety of invertebrates, including small beetles, caterpillars, maggots and millipedes.

The breeding season is extensive and eggs may be found from the end of April until August. The nest is usually sited low down and is well concealed in a bank, base of hedge or small bush, inside a bramble clump or under dead bracken. Early nests are often situated lower, through lack of cover, than later ones, which may occasionally be 2 m or more above ground.

Yellowhammers show virtually no breaks in distribution in the southern half of England and Wales, except for the centres of Manchester and London. In the northern half of Britain, they are absent from higher areas such as the Pennines, the Cheviots and the southern uplands and Highlands of Scotland. In Ireland, they are missing from several upland areas and there are also some interesting lowland gaps, as in Co Cork. In the Inner Hebrides and Orkney, the species is an extremely local breeder, and in Shetland it is known only as a passage migrant. The Outer Hebrides appear to have been colonised only recently, a brood being seen on N Uist in 1970 and flying young on Lewis in 1971.

Apart from a few local increases in parts of Wales and Lancashire, most reports refer to decreases in recent years. In E England, the most marked decreases occurred in the late 1950s. In many cases, no reason for a decline is known, although the destruction of hedgerows, increased urbanisation and use of agricultural chemicals have been mentioned as contributory factors. The Common Birds Census index shows a considerable recovery in the two years following the severe 1962/63 winter which affected so many of our resident bird species. After that, the Yellowhammer population on farmland remained fairly stable, but the woodland index showed a substantial increase between 1968 and 1974.

Andrew (1956) found that Yellowhammer territories varied in size depending on the population density. In a linear farmland hedgerow with a high density, territories had an average length of 60 m, but with half the density the territories doubled in length. Hawthorn scrub in the Chilterns had an average of 42.5 pairs per km^2, while in young Scots pines growing on grassland in Wiltshire there were 60 pairs per km^2. These densities were all from areas particularly suitable for the species, and the average for all farmland CBC areas in 1972 was only 9.5 pairs per km^2. Even taking no more than one-third of this value, however, at just over 300 pairs per 10-km square, the British and Irish population would total one million pairs, equalling the upper limit of Parslow's category of 100,000–1,000,000.

Number of 10-km squares in which recorded:
3,380 (88%)
Possible breeding   71 (2%)
Probable breeding   478 (14%)
Confirmed breeding   2,831 (84%)

References

ANDREW, R. J. 1956. Territorial behaviour of the Yellowhammer *Emberiza citrinella* and Corn Bunting *E. calandra*. *Ibis* 98: 502–505.

MORGAN, R. A. 1975. Breeding bird communities on chalk downland in Wiltshire. *Bird Study* 22: 71–83.

WILLIAMSON, K. 1975. The breeding bird community of chalk grassland scrub in the Chiltern Hills. *Bird Study* 22: 59–70.

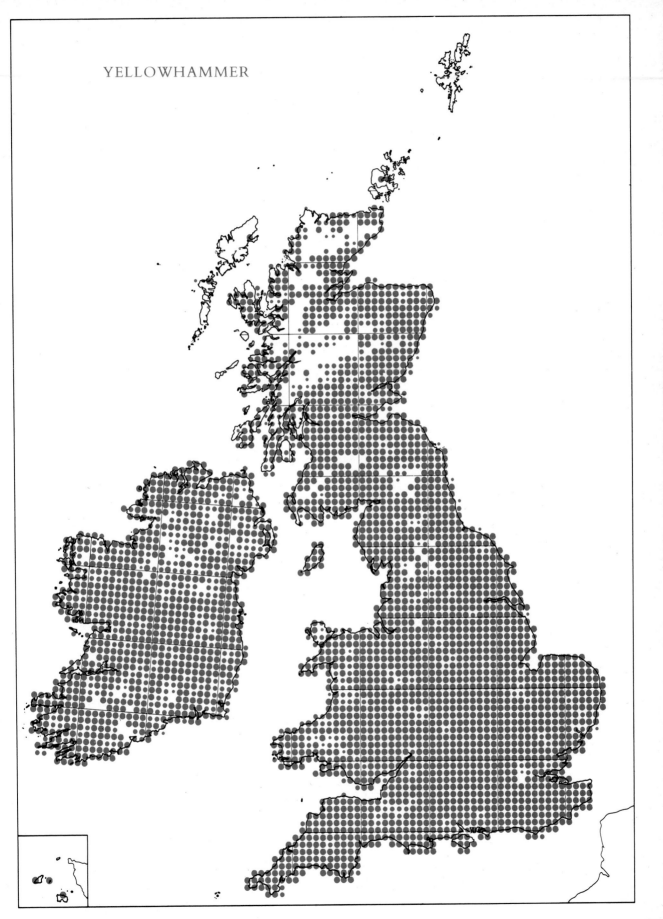

YELLOWHAMMER

Cirl Bunting

Emberiza cirlus

The Cirl Bunting is found mainly in the Mediterranean area, where it favours warm, sheltered valleys, especially among vineyards, citrus fruits and similar cultivation, as well as bushy hillsides. In Britain, where it is at the northern limit of its range, it occurs mostly in farming country with shelter provided by well-grown hedges and tall trees, especially elms. It often occupies sloping ground, such as the lower slopes of the chalk downland escarpments, mostly below 90 m and frequently with a southern aspect. In parts of SW England, it is partial to coastal localities and well-timbered river valleys. Territories are often clustered at the periphery of rural villages and in such situations the nest is frequently in a large garden. Cirl Buntings are also found on heaths with scattered clumps of birch and gorse, and on waste ground such as rubbish tips and the environs of ballast pits.

The rattling song can be heard from late February to September. It recalls that of the Lesser Whitethroat *Sylvia curruca* and might be overlooked as such in areas where the warbler is common but the bunting is not expected; a variant has been likened to the song of the Yellowhammer *E. citrinella* without its final flourish. Cirl Buntings often sing from exposed perches, such as an outer branch of a tall tree or even a television aerial, and so are relatively easy to locate. The three or four eggs are laid in the second half of May, the male feeding the female during incubation. A second brood often follows in July–August. The nest is not so easy to find as that of the Yellowhammer and, at the low density in England, breeding can be difficult to prove. Most instances of confirmed breeding involved observation of adults feeding nestlings or fledged young. The possible and probable records within the main range are likely to have represented unconfirmed breeding rather than transient birds, but those well outside it were probably vagrants.

Montagu first discovered the Cirl Bunting as a British breeding species in Devon in 1800. It was more widespread early in the 20th century than now, extending as a scarce nester north to Yorkshire and Cumberland and flourishing in much of the Midlands and Wales. Breeding was regular in N Wales until the 1930s (see map on page 465), but the range contraction was already under way and, even in its strongholds in S England, numbers were declining. In Sussex, there were 45–50 pairs in the mid-1950s, but only about 20 in the early 1970s; at seven regular sites the number fell from 27–32 in 1963–70 to 17–18 in 1971–73. Being essentially sedentary, the Cirl Bunting is vulnerable to hard winters: the memorable cold of 1962/63 severely depleted the Devon population and a short, severe spell in 1970/71 was locally damaging in Sussex. The range contraction in the last 30–40 years probably results largely from climatic change, the main headquarters of the species now being in that part of Britain with the combination of warm summers and mild winters.

Ticehurst (1909) considered that the Cirl Bunting was commoner than the Yellowhammer, 'which to a large extent it replaces', in many areas of the chalk downs; perhaps, with the rapid development of scrub following the reduction of sheep-grazing and Rabbit activity, the Yellowhammer has become more competitive. Ryves (1948) thought that the Cirl Bunting was highly susceptible to disturbance while nesting. Habitat loss, including hedgerow removal and new building development on the outskirts of rural villages may have contributed to its present weakness.

Today, the most northerly pairs, in the Malvern Hills (Worcestershire), appear to be isolated by the species' absence from the slopes of the Cotswolds. The main distribution can be traced on the areas of chalk from the Chilterns to the N and S Downs, and from the Berkshire Downs to the Hampshire and Dorset coasts. Much of this region has only scattered pairs, however, and there are large gaps such as Salisbury Plain. The southwest peninsula is the most densely occupied region, especially the north to south coastal belt between Exeter and Prawle Point (Devon).

Recent surveys in Devon showed totals of 106 pairs in 1973 and 136 pairs in 1974 (Sitters 1975). Allowing for birds eluding detection, an average of about five pairs per 10-km square is indicated, but Sussex figures suggest a lower density. Therefore, taking an average of 2–4 pairs, the total British population is probably 350–700 pairs, in about the middle of the range of 100–1,000 pairs indicated by Parslow. The fortunes of this attractive southern bunting deserve to be followed carefully in the future.

Number of 10-km squares in which recorded:
174 (5%)
Possible breeding   32 (18%)
Probable breeding   79 (45%)
Confirmed breeding   63 (36%)

References

RYVES, B. H. 1948. *Bird Life in Cornwall*. London.

SITTERS, H. P. 1975. Results of the 1974 Devon breeding status survey. *Devon Birds* 28: 18–27, 35–43.

TICEHURST, N. F. 1909. *A History of the Birds of Kent*. London.

WILSON, P. J. 1974. A survey of the Cirl Bunting in Sussex. *Sussex Bird Rep.* 26: 57–60.

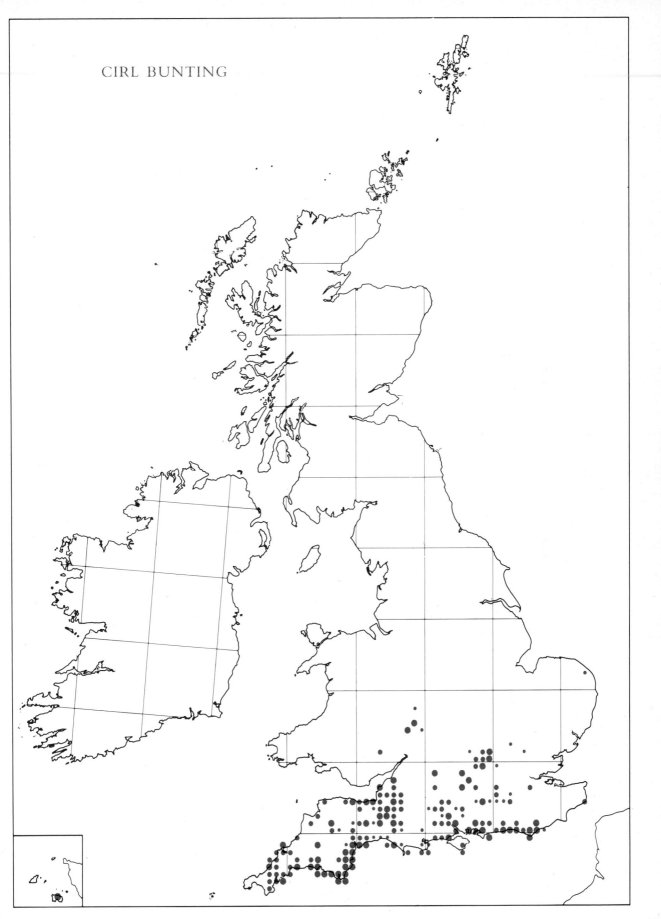

CIRL BUNTING

Reed Bunting

Emberiza schoeniclus

Reed Buntings breed in a wide variety of habitats ranging from reed-beds and marram-covered sand-dunes to marginal land and farm hedgerows. They have aroused much interest in recent years through their ecological expansion from an ancestral wetland habitat into drier situations. They may now be found, for example, in young conifer plantations, and the hawthorn scrub of waterless chalk downland. In a study of Breckland breeding species, Lack (1933) found virtually no overlap between the Reed Bunting and the closely-related Yellowhammer *E. citrinella*, the former occupying marshy districts and the latter occurring along hedgerows and on the edges of heaths. Witherby *et al* (1938–41) stated that the Reed Bunting frequented 'vegetation fringing standing and running water of all sorts', but 'in winter also . . . well away from water'.

A few pairs were reported nesting in dry situations in Hertfordshire even as early as the 1930s, but then Kent (1964) showed that, in Nottinghamshire, a substantial proportion of Reed Buntings was breeding in dry habitats typical of the Yellowhammer. Clearly, Reed Buntings are not now ecologically restricted to wetter haunts. Bell (1969) suggested that an increase in intraspecific competition, due to a contraction of wet habitats, might have occurred, as well as a decline in interspecific competition, associated with a decrease in Yellowhammer numbers.

On her Common Birds Census study plot, Gordon (1972) found that the main move into drier habitats took place in 1968, when the population was high, and suggested that in such conditions an overspill from wetter areas led to settlement in suboptimal sites. The farmland environment has witnessed a widespread reduction of the wetter waste ground as land has been put to maximum productivity, and Reed Buntings, at a time of population growth, have adapted to marginal situations, where continued successful breeding has engendered a wider habitat tolerance in the population. In Hertfordshire, for instance, Williamson (1968) found them holding territory alongside Corn Buntings *E. calandra* in the middle of large barley fields.

Reed Buntings will sing from a thistle, dock stem or reed protruding only a little above the surrounding vegetation. Although nests are usually sited low and often well concealed, singing males are conspicuous, food-carrying adults are easy to observe, and injury-feigning is common when a bird is surprised close to the nest.

The distribution in Britain and Ireland is extremely widespread, as would be expected from the variety of habitats now utilised. The species' clear dislike of upland regions is apparent from the gaps in parts of SW England, the Cotswolds, Snowdonia, the Lake District, Scottish Highlands, Harris (Outer Hebrides) and N Ireland. There are also a few predominantly lowland areas in SW Wales, Monmouthshire and central England where it is missing. The Monmouthshire gap is peculiar because it includes part of the Wye valley, and yet squares farther west in the industrial upland of the S Wales coalfield show very few breaks in distribution. Similarly, part of the gap in Cardiganshire and Carmarthenshire includes the River Teifi valley, and is also flanked by higher ground where the species is recorded. In Scotland, an increase and spread has been recorded in the Inner Hebrides, with breeding in recent years on Eigg, Rhum, Canna and Muck. A continuing increase in Orkney was accompanied by colonisation of Shetland in about 1949, and breeding was known from at least four localities there in 1973.

In typical wetland situations, Reed Buntings occur at a density of 50–70 pairs per km², although at a modern sewage-disposal plant Glue and Bodenham (1974) recorded 208 pairs per km²: if the wet irrigation area was taken alone, the density was as high as 361 pairs per km². The average density on farmland in 1972 was 4.3 pairs per km² and, with high concentrations in some places, the average number in each occupied 10-km square is probably at least 200 pairs. On this basis, the total in Britain and Ireland may exceed 600,000 pairs, a figure which is within the upper half of Parslow's range of 100,000–1,000,000 pairs.

Number of 10-km squares in which recorded:
3,431 (89%)
Possible breeding   129 (4%)
Probable breeding   476 (14%)
Confirmed breeding   2,826 (82%)

References

BELL, B. D. 1969. Some thoughts on the apparent ecological expansion of the Reed Bunting. *Brit. Birds* 62: 209–218.

GLUE, D. E. and D. BODENHAM. 1974. Bird-life at a modern sewage farm. *Bird Study* 21: 229–237.

GORDON, M. 1972. Reed Buntings on an Oxfordshire farm. *Bird Study* 19: 81–90.

KENT, A. K. 1964. The breeding habitats of the Reed Bunting and Yellowhammer in Nottinghamshire. *Bird Study* 11: 123–127.

LACK, D. 1933. Habitat selection in birds, with special reference to the effects of afforestation on the Breckland avifauna. *J. Anim. Ecol.* 2: 239–262.

WILLIAMSON, K. 1968. Buntings on a barley farm. *Bird Study* 15: 34–37.

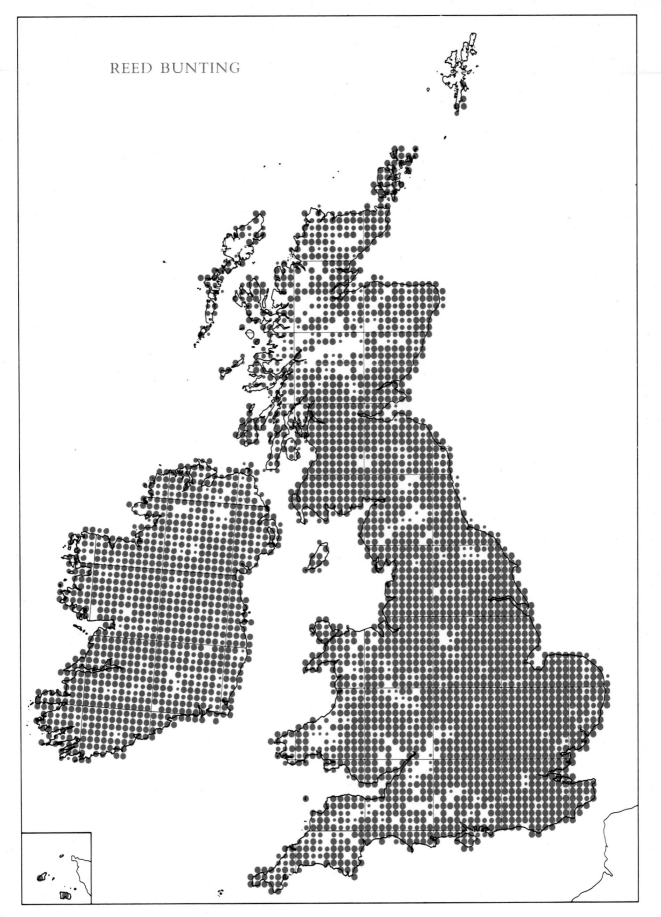

REED BUNTING

Snow Bunting

Plectrophenax nivalis

The Snow Bunting breeds farther north than any other passerine. It is usually an inhabitant of tundra, rocky arctic coasts, barren mountain tops and even nunataks amid extensive ice-fields. In S Greenland and Spitsbergen it has also become a town dweller.

In Britain, it is restricted to remote, mountainous regions in Scotland, such as the Cairngorms, and is one of our rarest breeding species. In the vast expanses of mountain country it is difficult to keep track of the Snow Bunting population, but, ever since the first authenticated nest was discovered in 1886, this species has captured the imagination.

There are two races of Snow Bunting involved in the Scottish breeding stock, *P. n. nivalis* which breeds in Scandinavia and Greenland, and *P. n. insulae* from Iceland. The males of the two are distinguishable in the field by the amount of white on the rump, *nivalis* having a lot of white and *insulae* appearing dark. Over a long period, roughly equal numbers of each have been noted; white-rumped birds predominated in 1955–57 and 1968–70 and dark-rumped birds did so in 1971–72. This suggests periodic alternations in the sources of our unstable Snow Bunting population.

Snow Buntings have a delightful courtship display, the male making good use of his bold, black and white colour pattern (Tinbergen 1951). The flute-like song is delivered both in flight, like a Skylark *Alauda arvensis*, and from the ground. The nest, which may be lined with feathers of the Ptarmigan *Lagopus mutus*, is usually placed deep inside scree or in a crevice below a granite block. Where Snow Buntings are common, in Greenland, Iceland and, formerly, the Faeroe Islands, the males defend territories within small colonies, but in the Cairngorms some pairs travel widely before establishing a territory and unmated males sing and display over large areas of hill country. The breeding season in Scotland is longer than in the Arctic, but later in starting than in Iceland, where eggs are found from mid-May onwards, compared with late May and early June in Scotland. Polyandry leads to many second nests and Nethersole-Thompson recorded 47% of females attempting to rear two broods in a season. In the brief arctic summer, the breeding and moulting seasons overlap and the moult is so rapid in the most northerly part of the range, beyond latitude 75°N, that birds may be rendered flightless for a short time (Green and Summers 1975).

The numbers of Snow Buntings breeding in Scotland fluctuate markedly. In some years only a few unmated males are discovered, while in others five or six pairs are proved to rear young. The history of the species in the Cairngorms is more precisely known than for the rest of Scotland. A small group of five pairs nested in 1909–10, but had died out by 1912. During the milder period of climatic amelioration in 1920–40, few breeding pairs were known, but the 1940s and 1950s were cooler and this apparently led to immigrants settling, and breeding has probably been fairly regular since 1945. In 1947, following a severe winter, at least three pairs nested, and seven or eight singing males were located. The years 1968–69 were good ones, with five singing males and two females, one of which successfully raised a brood and in the next two years at least three pairs reared young. The best season was 1972, with seven or eight singing males and at least five broods reared. Nethersole-Thompson has correlated the fluctuations with climatic changes and suggests that decades with several severe winters in Iceland and Scandinavia have induced more Snow Buntings to settle in Scotland.

Apart from the Cairngorms, the species has bred in the past in Perthshire, Ross-shire, Sutherland and the Ben Nevis area (Inverness-shire), and is reputed to have done so in Shetland and at St Kilda. Breeding took place in Ross-shire during the *Atlas* period, and in Sutherland in 1974. Nethersole-Thompson considers the present range to be comparable with that in the late 19th century.

This species is afforded special protection in Great Britain under Schedule I of the Protection of Birds Act, 1954–67.

Number of 10-km squares in which recorded:
14 (0.4%)
Possible breeding   7 (50%)
Probable breeding   3 (21%)
Confirmed breeding   4 (29%)

Though some records were originally submitted in confidence, all dots are now shown accurately (as recommended by the Rare Breeding Birds Panel)

References

GREEN, H. and R. W. SUMMERS. 1975. Snow Bunting moult in northeast Greenland. *Bird Study* 22: 9–17.

NETHERSOLE-THOMPSON, D. 1966. *The Snow Bunting.* Edinburgh and London.

TINBERGEN, N. 1951. The behavior of the Snow Bunting in spring. *Trans. Linn. Soc. New York* 5: 1–94.

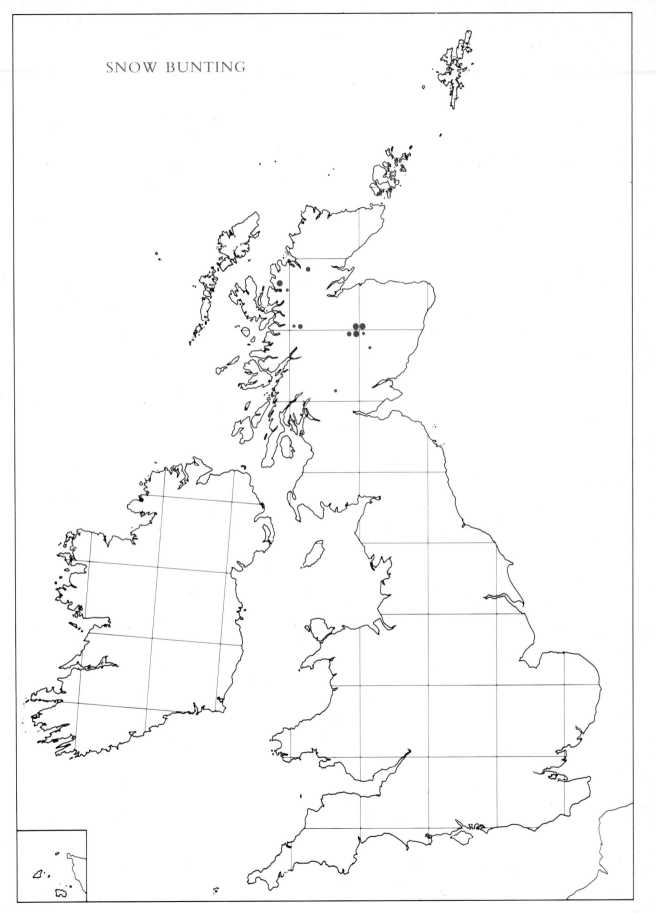

SNOW BUNTING

House Sparrow

Passer domesticus

House Sparrows are commensal with man and rather few breed away from houses, farms, factories and other buildings. The natural colonies often include Tree Sparrows *P. montanus* and are usually where suitable breeding holes are abundant—in mature woodland, on cliffs or rock faces, or at colonies of Sand Martins *Riparia riparia*. The House Sparrows breeding on or in buildings frequently have their nests under the eaves or in roof-spaces, but they will use any convenient nook or cranny. In rural areas, large colonies may occupy farm buildings and stacks of hay and straw; in the absence of suitable buildings, they may make untidy, ball-like, domed nests in trees or bushes.

House Sparrows readily adapt to food sources provided by man and this explains their spread and increase in England two centuries ago, and through Scotland during the 19th century, reaching the north-western parts of the mainland about 80 years ago (Baxter and Rintoul 1953). With the advance of the crop-line in N Europe and Siberia during the climatic amelioration of this century, the species spread northwards via the railway lines and the Norwegian coastal steamer routes.

The House Sparrow seems best equipped to take advantage of changes in the human situation where man's animal associates are involved. The small isolated colony on Hilbre Island in the Dee Estuary was able to survive only because domestic animals were kept and fed; when they were removed, the birds disappeared, but recolonisation began soon after new stock was introduced (Craggs 1967, 1976). When horses provided the normal means of transport in towns and cities, the sparrows were able to forage on corn spilt from nose-bags, and among the litter on stable floors. The advent of mechanical transport may have denied them this food source, just as mechanised farming has reduced the corn available in stubble after harvesting; but they can exploit the increasing quantity of domestic waste, and the steadily growing human penchant for feeding birds in parks and gardens.

Some of the highest villages in Scotland (at 400 or 500 m) lack House Sparrows, probably because of their exposure, but most of the 10-km squares where breeding was not proved are almost uninhabited. In Ireland, there is some evidence of a withdrawal in recent years from parts of the far west, and perhaps also the midlands. This has been attributed to the replacement of thatch by slate roofs, which are far less easily used for nesting (Ruttledge 1966).

Detailed breeding studies by Summers-Smith (1963) have shown that eggs may be laid from March through to August and that two, three and sometimes four broods are reared by each pair. They are pugnacious birds and will dispossess other species of their nest sites. Birdwatchers who put up nest boxes have long recognised this as a problem which may be solved by making the hole too small for House Sparrows, but big enough for tits, the magic diameter being about 2.8 cm. More distressing for the onlooker are the sparrows' attempts, often successful, to dispossess House Martins *Delichon urbica*, and sometimes Swallows *Hirundo rustica*, of their mud nests.

House Sparrows are often destroyed as pests if they infest food factories, and they used to be persecuted as agricultural pests all over the country. There have been reports of epidemic diseases killing large numbers, and this is the species most frequently killed on the roads (Hodson and Snow 1965). Nevertheless, their extended breeding season and indefatigable nesting attempts enable them to maintain a high population in almost all circumstances where there is food available. Summers-Smith (1963) showed that 100 pairs of adults in April would produce about 240 juveniles by the beginning of August, by which time some 50 of the adults would have died. At the start of the next breeding season, adults from the previous year outnumber their progeny.

The House Sparrow is undoubtedly a serious agricultural pest, particularly in standing cereal crops before harvest, at the time of maximum population. Past census attempts were reviewed by Summers-Smith and he estimated just over 9,500,000 individuals for Great Britain. This implied a breeding population of between 2,500,000 and 5,000,000 pairs. Rather few Common Birds Census results are available since the species is difficult to census, but a Suffolk farm typical of many mixed farms in lowland England had a density of about 86 pairs per km². The density in built-up areas will be higher than this. Arbitrarily allowing 10–20 pairs per km² over Britain and half this level over Ireland (since the human population is sparser there), the British and Irish total is probably between 3,500,000 and 7,000,000 pairs.

Number of 10-km squares in which recorded:
  3,643 (94%)
Possible breeding   41 (1%)
Probable breeding   24 (1%)
Confirmed breeding   3,578 (98%)

References
CRAGGS, J. D. 1967. Population studies of an isolated colony of House Sparrows *Passer domesticus*. *Bird Study* 14: 53–60.
CRAGGS, J. D. 1976. The re-establishment of an isolated colony of House Sparrows. *Bird Study* 23: (in press).
HODSON, N. L. and D. W. SNOW. 1965. The Road Deaths Enquiry, 1960–61. *Bird Study* 12: 90–99.
SUMMERS-SMITH, J. D. 1963. *The House Sparrow*. London.

HOUSE SPARROW

443

Tree Sparrow

Passer montanus

Tree Sparrows may often be overlooked, but they are actually quite common and widely distributed over much of England, Wales and lowland Scotland. Most are hole-nesters and are therefore found in wooded areas or where cliffs, quarries or buildings provide suitable sites. In some places, nests are built in ivy on trees or walls. Pollarded willows along lowland waterways are the commonest sites in parts of S England, whereas in Ireland most occur in ruined castles and other buildings, usually near the sea or other water. Old orchards, and trees in parkland and in hedgerows are other favourite places. Within the main range, in E and central England, colonies are often found within dense woodland, the holes of Sand Martins *Riparia riparia* are frequently used and pairs sometimes nest in the open, building untidy round nests among the branches of trees or shrubs. Ordinary nest-boxes, with holes suitable for Blue Tits *Parus caeruleus*, are taken to readily.

This species is not easy to survey, as isolated pairs can be very secretive and wary, and, although their 'chip' and 'teck' calls are characteristic, they may easily be swamped in the noise made by the much more numerous House Sparrows *Passer domesticus* or overlooked in fringe areas where the presence of Tree Sparrows is not expected. Once located, however, it is seldom long before the adults entering or leaving the nest-hole provide evidence of breeding.

Tree Sparrows are renowned for the inexplicable fluctuations that their colonies sometimes undergo. These may build up rapidly over a short period, and then disappear just as quickly. Recent events have been even more dramatic and on a wider scale. For example, the Tree Sparrow was known as a scarce and very scattered breeding species in Ireland from 1852, but none was proved to nest in 1959 and 1960. At that time, the British population was increasing and some migrants were seen in Ireland late in 1960. Breeding started again in 1961 (Ruttledge 1967), and during the next five years over 50 small colonies, almost exclusively coastal (but with rather few in the extreme southwest) were noted.

In Scotland, there were many breeding records,

particularly from islands (including St Kilda), during the 19th century, but most of the colonies had died out by the early 1950s. On the mainland, birds had spread along most of the east coast to Sutherland and were more scattered along the west coast; but, again, many of these colonies had died out 20 years ago. From about 1958–60, the bird's fortunes turned and gradually some of the lost ground was regained. The *Atlas* map shows that in some areas not all its former haunts have yet been reached, but elsewhere there are colonies where none had been noted since ornithological recording began. The last 15 years have seen a gradual spread into areas from which the species had been absent in SW England and W Wales, as well as in Hampshire and Sussex (Hughes and Dougharty 1975). The distribution is still quite like that shown for 1952 by Norris (1960), who suggested that the range was correlated with areas of low rainfall. Outside the main range, there is a clear coastal bias which may result from birds which have wintered in coastal flocks staying to breed during the following summer.

Dense breeding colonies may be found in habitats with a plethora of suitable holes or nest-boxes. A small area of mature deciduous trees in the Chilterns held 62 pairs per km^2 in natural holes (Williamson 1972) and, where nest boxes are provided, colonies of 50 or more pairs may build up in areas as small as 10 ha. The CBC records from farmland give densities up to 27 pairs per km^2, but the national average in 1972 was 6.4 pairs. A detailed survey of Sussex, on the fringe of the species' range, shows that even in 1973, after more than a decade of expansion, it was still no more than local (Hughes and Dougharty 1975). Thus, although there will be many 10-km squares with more than 1,000 breeding pairs, some others on the fringe of its range may hold only a handful. Taking a conservative average of 150 pairs per 10-km square, a total British and Irish population of about 250,000 pairs is indicated, which is much higher than is suggested by Parslow's rating of 'fairly numerous' (10,000–100,000).

Number of 10-km squares in which recorded:
  1,800 (47%)
Possible breeding   161 (9%)
Probable breeding   125 (7%)
Confirmed breeding   1,514 (84%)

References
HUGHES, S. W. M. and F. W. DOUGHARTY. 1975. The recolonisation of Sussex by the Tree Sparrow. *Sussex Bird Rep.* 27: 67–71.
MEAD, C. J. and G. R. M. PEPLER. 1975. Birds and other animals at Sand Martin colonies. *Brit. Birds* 68: 89–99.
NORRIS, C. A. 1960. The breeding distribution of thirty bird species in 1952. *Bird Study* 7: 129–184.
RUTTLEDGE, R. F. 1967. The present breeding distribution of the Tree Sparrow in Ireland. *Irish Bird Rep.* 14: 50–54.
SEEL, D. C. 1964. An analysis of the Nest Record Cards of the Tree Sparrow. *Bird Study* 11: 265–271.
WILLIAMSON, K. 1972. The conservation of bird life in the new coniferous forests. *Forestry* 45: 87–100.

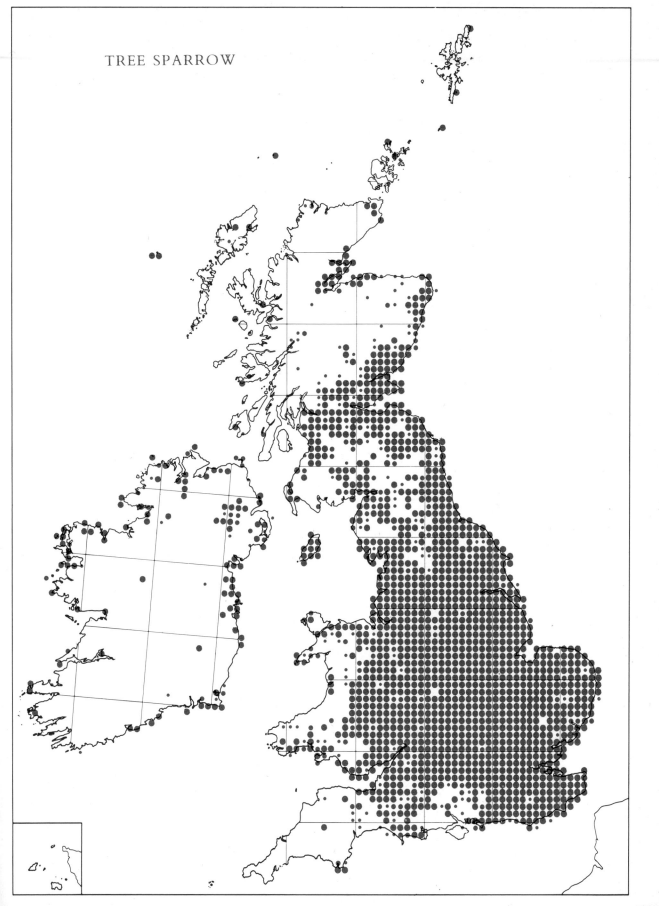

TREE SPARROW

445

Great Northern Diver *Gavia immer*

A few Great Northern Divers regularly spend the summer off the Scottish and Irish coasts, especially in the Minch, and breeding has been suspected on several occasions. Adults were seen with two young in late June 1970 at a loch with wooded islands in Wester Ross. In the following year, a hybrid Great Northern × Black-throated Diver *G. arctica*, paired with a Black-throated Diver, reared one youngster at the same loch.

This species is afforded special protection in Great Britain under Schedule I of the Protection of Birds Act, 1954–67.

Recorded in eight 10-km squares (0.2%): possible breeding in seven and confirmed breeding in one.

Within the two 100-km squares outlined in red, dots are conventionally placed centrally (as recommended by the Rare Breeding Birds Panel)

HUNTER, E. N. 1970. Great Northern Diver breeding in Scotland. *Scott. Birds* 6: 195.

HUNTER, E. N. and R. H. DENNIS. 1972. Hybrid Great Northern Diver × Black-throated Diver in Wester Ross. *Scott. Birds* 7: 89–91.

GREAT NORTHERN DIVER

Purple Heron *Ardea purpurea*

Purple Herons have never been known to breed in Britain or Ireland, but in recent years a number of spring and summer occurrences, including up to five together at Minsmere (Suffolk), have raised hopes that nesting would take place. The necessary habitat of large undisturbed reed-beds (with or without bushes) is scarce, but one record of presence in such habitat (in SE England in 1972) was submitted, though it is considered that breeding probably did not take place. (No map.)

This species is afforded special protection in Great Britain under Schedule I of the Protection of Birds Act, 1954–67.

SHARROCK, J. T. R. and E. M. SHARROCK. 1976. *Rare Birds in Britain and Ireland*. Berkhamsted.

Night Heron *Nycticorax nycticorax*

A feral colony has existed since 1950 in the grounds of Edinburgh Zoo, the birds nesting and roosting in the trees and flying to the Firth of Forth at dusk to feed. There has been no suspicion of nesting by wild Night Herons, despite the regular occurrence of migrants in spring. (No map.)

DORWARD, D. F. 1957. The Night-Heron colony in the Edinburgh Zoo. *Scott. Nat.* 69: 32–36.

Little Bittern *Ixobrychus minutus*

There are many areas suitable for Little Bitterns in Britain and Ireland, including some overgrown flooded gravel pits and natural reed-beds—both large and small areas along rivers and round the edges of lakes. There is no fully documented record, but breeding probably occurred irregularly in East Anglia in the 19th century and on perhaps three or four occasions in S England in the 1940s and 1950s. This species can be very difficult to detect in a large reed-bed: even if summering is proven, confirmation of breeding is likely to depend upon chance sightings of young birds. One case of summering was reported in S England during the *Atlas* period (six weeks in June–July 1970, with the male's thumping song heard), and was considered to represent probable breeding. (No map.)

This species is afforded special protection in Great Britain under Schedule I of the Protection of Birds Act, 1954–67.

Red-crested Pochard *Netta rufina*

Records of nesting in Britain probably all concern escapes from captivity or their progeny, though Continental birds are known to arrive here. A pair nested at St Osyth (Essex) in 1958; and since the mid-1960s breeding has occurred in most years at Frampton-on-Severn, close to the Wildfowl Trust at Slimbridge (Gloucestershire). Two pairs also nested at the

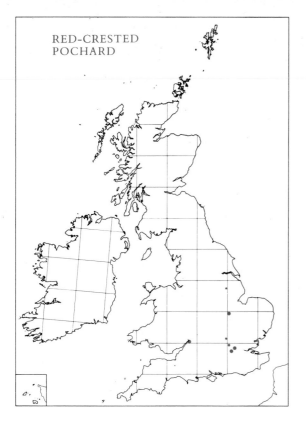

RED-CRESTED
POCHARD

Whooper Swan *Cygnus cygnus*

Nearly every year, a few pairs of Whooper Swans remain for the summer in Scotland and, less often perhaps, in Ireland, frequenting the larger lochs or moorland lochans. In some instances, they have been sick or injured birds. Though Whooper Swans formerly bred in Orkney, perhaps regularly down to the 18th century, nesting has been very sporadic since. Less than half a dozen cases are known in this century, the most recent being on Benbecula (Outer Hebrides) in 1947. A male Whooper Swan was seen displaying to a female Mute Swan *C. olor* on Lough Corrib (Co Galway) in 1972, and hybridisation occurred in 1973: five eggs hatched, but the cygnets died unfledged. There was a similar case at Lough Corrib in 1963.

This species is afforded special protection in Great Britain under Schedule I of the Protection of Birds Act, 1954–67.

Recorded in nine 10-km squares (0·2%): all possible breeding.

Cotswold Water Park (Gloucester/Wiltshire) in 1975, so a feral population may be developing in the west country. In 1971, a free-flying drake joined a captive duck at Apethorpe (Northamptonshire) and their offspring dispersed later, while a pair bred in 1972 in Kew Gardens (Surrey), presumably having come from one of the full-winged groups in the Inner London parks. Probable breeding was reported at Rickmansworth (Hertfordshire), where several Red-crested Pochards were present in 1971.

Recorded in seven 10-km squares (0.2%): possible breeding in two, probable breeding in one and confirmed breeding in four.

PYMAN, G. A. 1959. The status of the Red-crested Pochard in the British Isles. *Brit. Birds* 52: 42–56.

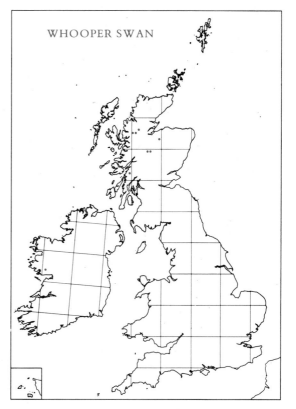

WHOOPER SWAN

Long-tailed Duck *Clangula hyemalis*

Breeding has been claimed on several occasions, including Shetland in 1848 and 1887, and Orkney in 1911. During 1968–72, this species was reported in single 10-km squares in the Outer Hebrides (1969) and in Shetland (1971), and breeding was strongly suspected in the first instance. Single birds and sometimes pairs are not infrequently seen in Scotland in summer. (No map.)

This species is afforded special protection in Great Britain under Schedule I of the Protection of Birds Act, 1954–67.

Kentish Plover *Charadrius alexandrinus*

This plover has the unenviable distinction of being one of the only two breeding species to be lost from Britain during this century, without subsequently re-colonising (the other being the White-tailed Eagle *Haliaeetus albicilla*). The last published nesting record was at Rye Harbour (Sussex) in 1956. A number of pairs still breed in the Channel Islands, however. It is still a regular spring migrant to the English coast from the Humber to the Exe and, in view of the large areas of suitable shore now protected by conservation organisations, it is perhaps surprising that none has remained to breed.

This species is afforded special protection in Great Britain under Schedule I of the Protection of Birds Act, 1954–67.

Recorded in three 10-km squares (0.1%): all confirmed breeding.

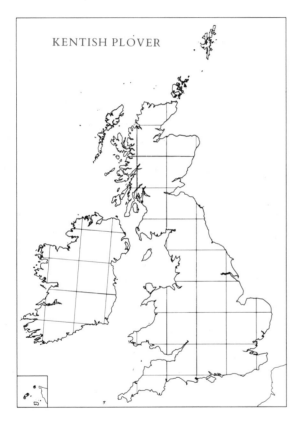

KENTISH PLOVER

Green Sandpiper *Tringa ochropus*

Although its display and song-flights have been noted on many occasions in Scotland (especially in 1933, in 1942 and during 1950–53) there are only two cases of proved breeding: in Westmorland in 1917 and in Inverness-shire in 1959. In view of the intensive *Atlas* coverage of Scotland in 1968–72, the virtual absence of records makes it clear that this is no more than an extremely sporadic breeder in Britain. (No map.)

This species is afforded special protection in Great Britain under Schedule I of the Protection of Birds Act, 1954–67.

Recorded in two 10-km squares (0.1%): both possible breeding.

CLAFTON, F. R. 1959. Green Sandpiper breeding in Inverness-shire. *Brit. Birds* 52: 430–432.
ROBINSON, H. W. 1917. Evidence for the breeding of the Green Sandpiper in Westmorland in 1917. *Brit. Birds* 11: 103–104.

Mediterranean Gull *Larus melanocephalus*

After brief appearances in 1966–67, Mediterranean Gulls nested on an alluvial island at Needs Oar Point (Hampshire) in 1968, among a huge colony of Black-headed Gulls *L. ridibundus* and some terns. A pair raised two young to the flying stage; a second summer male (which had been ringed as a nestling in E Germany) mated with a Black-headed Gull and they raised three young; and an adult female paired with a hybrid Mediterranean × Black-headed and laid eggs which failed to hatch. In subsequent years (to 1975) as many as six males held territory, but only the hybrid male actually nested and the failure of the Mediterranean Gull to consolidate its foothold in this Hampshire gull colony has been attributed to the absence of females. (No map.)

This species is afforded special protection in Great Britain under Schedule I of the Protection of Birds Act, 1954–67.

HUME, R. A. and P. G. LANSDOWN. 1974. Mediterranean Gulls at Blackpill, Glamorgan. *Brit. Birds* 67: 17–24.
SHARROCK, J. T. R. 1974. *Scarce Migrant Birds in Britain and Ireland*. Berkhamsted.
TAVERNER, J. H. 1970. Mediterranean Gulls nesting in Hampshire. *Brit. Birds* 63: 67–79.
TAVERNER, J. H. 1972. Mediterranean Gulls in Hampshire in 1970–71. *Brit. Birds* 65: 185–186.

Little Gull *Larus minutus*

The number of Little Gulls appearing as migrants and summer visitors in Britain and Ireland has increased enormously in recent years. A pair laid three fertile eggs on the Ouse Washes (Cambridgeshire/Norfolk) in summer 1975, but these were destroyed and the incubating sub-adult was killed on the nest, possibly by Brown Rats. Although this was the first proved breeding record, two instances of Little Gulls frequenting suitable habitat during 1968–72 were regarded as possible cases. In another instance (not mapped), a juvenile was seen and the observers considered that it could not have flown across the North Sea, though it might have travelled some distance from its natal area.

This species is afforded special protection in Great Britain under Schedule I of the Protection of Birds Act, 1954–67.

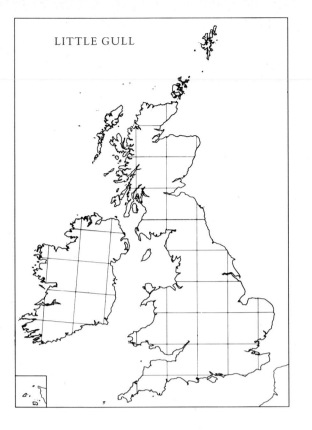

LITTLE GULL

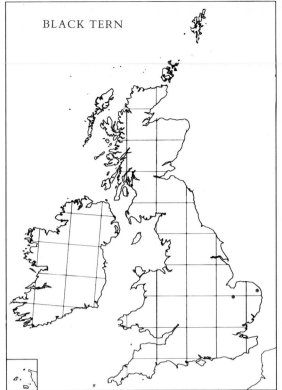

BLACK TERN

One dot has been moved by up to two 10-km squares (as recommended by the Rare Breeding Birds Panel)

COTTIER, E. J. and D. LEA. 1969. Black-tailed Godwits, Ruffs and Black Terns breeding on the Ouse Washes. *Brit. Birds* 62: 259–270.

Black Tern *Chlidonias niger*

Black Terns are common spring migrants in Britain, though rather scarce in Ireland, variable numbers appearing each year. Breeding was formerly regular in parts of E and SE England, but had ceased by the middle of the 19th century, and there are no certain cases between 1858 (on Norfolk floods) and 1966, now that the supposed breeding in Sussex in 1941 and 1942 is discounted. Several pairs built nests on floods on the Ouse Washes (Cambridgeshire/Norfolk) in 1966, two of them laying eggs and rearing a total of three young. Seven nests were found in 1969, probably involving six pairs: young were hatched in five cases, but only one is known to have fledged. A pair was observed taking food to young at the other site shown here in 1970, but to avoid disturbance the nest was not searched for and the outcome is unknown. A further attempt was made on the Ouse Washes in 1975. One pair nested on a rocky islet in an Irish lough in 1967, rearing one young—the only Irish breeding record.

This species is afforded special protection in Great Britain under Schedule 1 of the Protection of Birds Act, 1954–67.

Recorded in two 10-km squares (0.05%): both confirmed breeding.

Shore Lark *Eremophila alpestris*

Following an increase in wintering and passage numbers during the past two decades, a Shore Lark was seen and heard singing in the Scottish Highlands on 6th July 1972. A male was singing about 1 km away from this site on 24th June 1973, and a pair was seen at a third site another 1 km away between 10th July and 16th August, carrying food; cheeping notes, which may have come from small young out of the nest, were heard. None was seen in 1974 or 1975. (No map.)

This species is afforded special protection in Great Britain under Schedule 1 of the Protection of Birds Act, 1954–67.

CAMPBELL, B., A. WATSON SR., A. WATSON and N. PICOZZI. 1974. Proof of breeding of Shore Larks. *Brit. Birds* 67: 127.

SHANNON, G. R. 1974. Studies of less familiar birds. 174. Shore Lark and Temminck's Horned Lark. *Brit. Birds* 67: 502–510.

WATSON, A. 1973. Shore Larks summering and possibly breeding in Scotland. *Brit. Birds* 66: 505–508.

Short-toed Treecreeper
Certhia brachydactyla

Since at least 1969 a few migrant Short-toed Tree-creepers (the typical treecreeper of broadleaved wood-land on the Continent) have been reported at coastal localities in S England. Claims were made that pairs had bred in Dorset in 1971–72, but these were subsequently withdrawn. This is, however, the only treecreeper breeding in the Channel Islands, occupy-ing the woodland of steep valley-sides. Recent re-search has revealed the complexity of identification problems, and detailed investigations will be neces-sary before this bird's status in England can be fully elucidated.

This species is afforded special protection in Great Britain under Schedule I of the Protection of Birds Act, 1954–67.

Recorded in five 10-km squares (0.1%): possible breeding in one and confirmed breeding in four.

MEAD, C. J. 1975. Variation in some characters of three Palaearctic *Certhia* species. *Bull. Brit. Orn. Cl.* 95: 30–39.
MEAD, C. J. and D. I. M. WALLACE. 1976. Identification of European treecreepers. *Brit. Birds* 69: 117–131.

Bluethroat *Luscinia svecica*

The only British nesting record concerns a female which was found incubating six eggs in an acid marsh, with reeds and sedges dominant, in Inverness-shire (NH80) in June 1968. No male was seen and the eggs were unfortunately destroyed by a predator, probably a mouse or a shrew. Numbers of spring migrants have increased in N Scotland in recent years. (No map.)

This species is afforded special protection in Great Britain under Schedule I of the Protection of Birds Act, 1954–67.

GREENWOOD, J. J. D. 1968. Bluethroat breeding in Scotland. *Scott. Birds* 5: 220–222.
GREENWOOD, J. J. D. 1968. Bluethroat nesting in Scotland. *Brit. Birds* 61: 524–525.
SHARROCK, J. T. R. 1974. *Scarce Migrant Birds in Britain and Ireland*. Berkhamsted.

Waxwing *Bombycilla garrulus*

Displaying and singing birds have been seen in late spring after strong autumn/winter irruptions. Though breeding some 35° west of the usual range may seem only a remote possibility, there was at least one in-stance of presence in suitable habitat in Scotland in summer during 1968–72. (No map.)

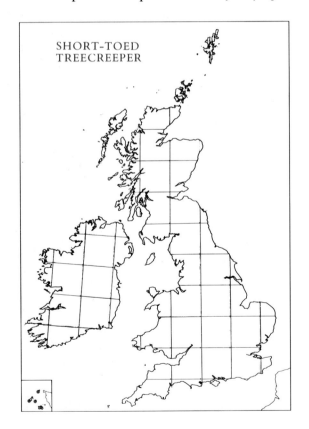

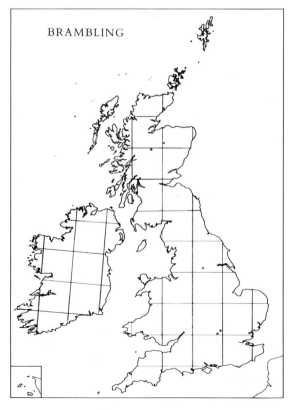

Brambling *Fringilla montifringilla*

While the only record of confirmed breeding in Britain or Ireland was in Sutherland as long ago as 1920, males have been observed uttering their 'dzwee' song (recalling the similar note of the Greenfinch *Carduelis chloris*) in birch and mixed coniferous woodland in England and Scotland in recent years, and breeding may well take place sporadically. One of the instances of probable breeding mapped here relates to a young Brambling × Chaffinch *F. coelebs* hybrid (neither parent was seen) and another to an adult female Brambling trapped with a marked brood-patch; the remaining four relate to singing males.

This species is afforded special protection in Great Britain under Schedule I of the Protection of Birds Act, 1954–67.

Recorded in six 10-km squares (0.2%): possible breeding in two and probable breeding in four.

Though some records were originally submitted in confidence, all dots are now shown accurately (as recommended by the Rare Breeding Birds Panel)

The following four species (and also Wood Duck *Aix sponsa*, see pages 74–75) are not officially admitted to the British and Irish list, but may be in the process of establishing viable feral populations

Bob-white Quail *Colinus virginianus*

Bob-white Quails have been introduced to England (and once to Ireland) from America on a number of occasions since the early 19th century. The most successful case was probably in N Norfolk, where they were established for over 20 years during 1820–45; breeding success is poor in cold, wet springs, but it was severe winters which eventually brought about their extinction. The two main breeding groups in 1968–72 were near Minsmere (Suffolk) and on Tresco (Isles of Scilly). The Minsmere stock probably derives from an introduction of 60 at nearby Dunwich in 1956; from two to eight pairs bred successfully during *Atlas* years, and up to 40 birds were present in winter. The Tresco population originates from six young released in 1964, and a further six in 1965, when two broods were reared in the wild; numbers remained fairly stable throughout *Atlas* years and in 1972 four broods were reared, totalling about 40 young. There have been records (though not breeding) from the nearby island of Bryher. Some have been liberated in Gloucestershire, Herefordshire and Wiltshire, and probably elsewhere. (No map.)

Recorded in four 10-km squares (0.1%): possible breeding in one, probable breeding in one and confirmed breeding in two.

Reeves's Pheasant *Syrmaticus reevesi*

This very attractive pheasant appeals to sportsmen because it frequents hilly, densely-wooded country which other gamebirds usually shun, and because its very fast, high flight provides difficult shooting. It was introduced to at least six Scottish, five English and one Irish county during 1870–90. In 1882, it was stated that at Guisachan in Inverness-shire 'more than 100 had been shot in the course of a single season, and the birds were found to be as hardy as (the young indeed more so than) the commoner varieties of pheasant' and the opinion given that 'it was not too much to expect that in a very few years it would become thoroughly naturalised, and be found in considerable numbers all over the country' (Gray 1882). These introductions all eventually failed, however, perhaps because the males (flying very long distances and lacking the far-carrying calls of other pheasants) became too dispersed for successful pairing. This has not discouraged further introductions, however, and 70 were introduced to Morayshire, over 50 to Inverness-shire and others to Cumberland in 1969. These birds were not recorded by *Atlas* fieldworkers because self-supporting feral populations were not involved and the only *Atlas* records were of mere presence near Woburn, Bedfordshire (where they were introduced during the late 19th century), in Breckland (where a few were introduced at Elveden, Suffolk, in 1950) and in Kinveachy Forest (Inverness-shire), where Reeves's Pheasants were apparently breeding in the wild in 1973–74. Feral populations also existed in Dorset and Ross-shire at least until the mid-1950s, but were not found in 1968–72. (No map.)

Recorded in three 10-km squares (0.1%): all possible breeding.

ANON. 1966. Rearing trials: Reeves Pheasants and Prairie Chickens. *Eley Game Advisory Station Ann. Rev.* 1965/66: 33–37.

BLANK, T. H. 1970. Reeves Pheasant. *Game Conservancy Ann. Rev.* 1969/70: 81–82.

FITTER, R. S. R. 1959. *The Ark in our Midst.* London.

GRAY, R. 1882. On the introduction of Reeves's Pheasant into Scottish game preserves. *Proc. Roy. Physical Soc. Ed.* 70.

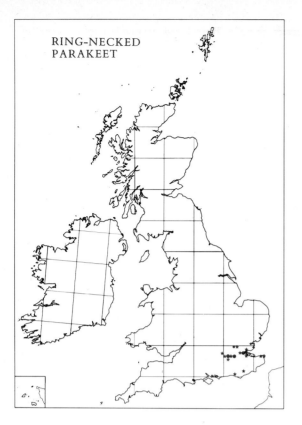

Ring-necked Parakeet *Psittacula krameri*

This attractive, but destructive, African and Indian parrot threatens to become an established feral species. During 1969–71, many (which may have either escaped or been deliberately released) were at liberty in various of London's outer suburbs in Surrey, Kent and Essex, and also the neighbourhood of Gravesend (Kent). Subsequent steady increases show that feral breeding is successful in a few places, no doubt assisted by the recent mild winters. Since 1972–73, the species has bred around Margate (Kent) and is now seen regularly elsewhere in Thanet. It is spreading to the Medway towns from Gravesend. In 1975, two family parties were reported from Herstmonceux (Sussex). Some have been seen at many places in the Thames Valley, where they are derived from a homing flock at an aviary near Marlow (Buckinghamshire). At present, Ring-necked Parakeets occur mainly in suburban parks and large gardens; they nest in holes in trees, and feed readily at bird-tables. The stars on the map show presence in the breeding season during 1973–75, after the end of the *Atlas* survey.

Recorded in four 10-km squares in 1968–72 (0.1%): possible breeding in one, probable breeding in one and confirmed breeding in two.

HUDSON, R. 1974. Feral parakeets near London. *Brit. Birds* 67: 33, 174.

Budgerigar *Melopsittacus undulatus*

Introduced from Australia, Budgerigars are very common cage-birds. They are vulnerable to hard winters, but aviculturists often try to establish free-flying colonies, the birds returning regularly to the aviaries for food. Occasionally such birds nest ferally. Three *Atlas* records in E England refer to a pair which nested in an orchard for two years (SP90), several pairs nesting in 1971–72 after 30 had been released in 1970–71 (TF60), and one pair, increasing to 12–15 birds by 1974 (TL36). A project aiming to establish a feral population on Tresco (Isles of Scilly) started in 1969. Initially in an aviary, then free-flying and then breeding in nest-boxes, these birds were occupying holes in trees in a completely wild state by 1972, and were returning to the aviary for food less and less often. By 1975, there were more than 100 and small flocks (but not breeding) had been noted on the nearby islands of Bryher, St Martins, St Mary's and St Agnes. This seems to be a thriving colony in the mildest part of Britain.

Recorded in four 10-km squares (0.1%): all confirmed breeding.

List of former breeding species

The following species have nested here since 1800, but are not known to have even been present in suitable breeding habitat during 1968–72:

White-tailed Eagle★ *Haliaeetus albicilla*
Baillon's Crake *Porzana pusilla*
Great Bustard★ *Otis tarda*
Black-winged Stilt *Himantopus himantopus*
Gull-billed Tern *Gelochelidon nilotica*
Pallas's Sandgrouse *Syrrhaptes paradoxus*
Bee-eater *Merops apiaster*
Moustached Warbler *Acrocephalus melanopogon*

★ Attempts are currently being made to reintroduce these species to Britain: White-tailed Eagle in the Inner Hebrides and Great Bustard on Salisbury Plain (Wiltshire).

List of additional species

Though not all instances will have been reported, the following species, all escapes from captivity, were entered on *Atlas* cards and the records are filed for future reference:

	Possible	Probable	Confirmed	10-km squares
Muscovy Duck★ *Cairina moschata*	0	0	5	5
Chinese Goose *Anser cygnoides*	1	0	0	1
Barnacle Goose *Branta leucopsis*	0	0	2	2
Barbary Dove *Streptopelia 'risoria'*	0	0	1	1
Canary *Serinus canaria*	0	0	1	1
Java Sparrow *Padda oryzivora*	1	0	0	1
Pin-tailed Whydah *Vidua macroura*	0	1	0	1

★ Records probably very incomplete.

Past distribution maps

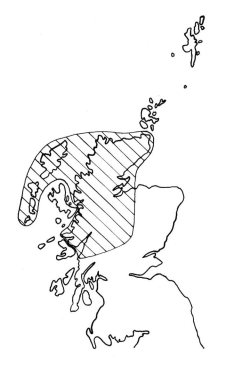

Black-throated Diver *Gavia arctica*. Breeding distribution in Scotland about 1890 (after Harvie-Brown 1895)

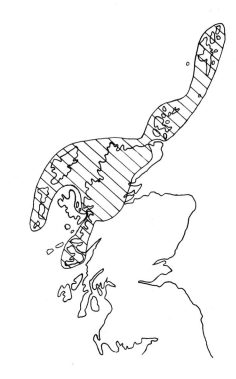

Red-throated Diver *Gavia stellata*. Breeding distribution in Scotland about 1890 (after Harvie-Brown 1895)

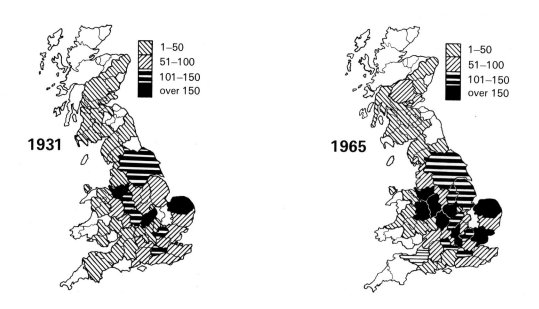

Great Crested Grebe *Podiceps cristatus*. Breeding distribution and density, number of adults per county, 1931 and 1965 (from Prestt and Mills 1966)

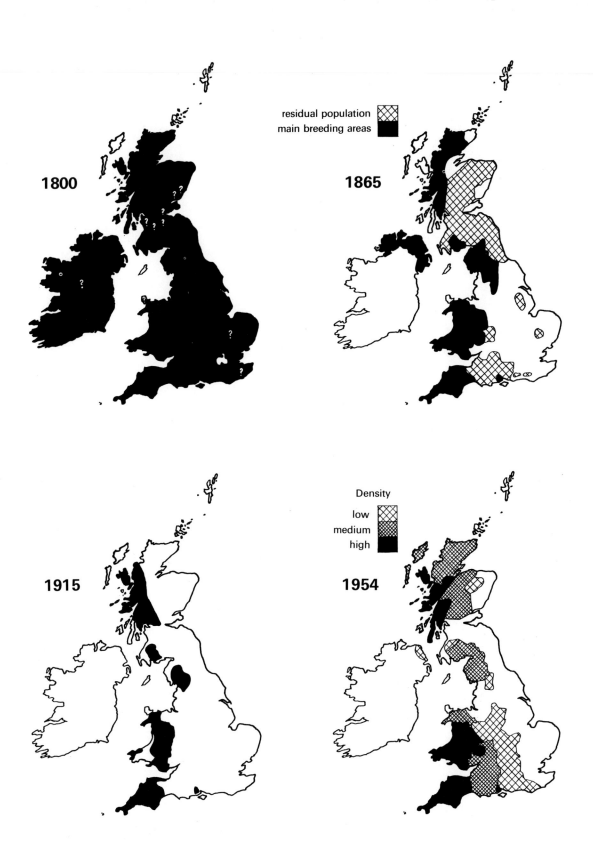

Buzzard *Buteo buteo*. Breeding distribution in 1800, 1865, 1915 and 1954 (from Moore 1957 and Tubbs 1974)

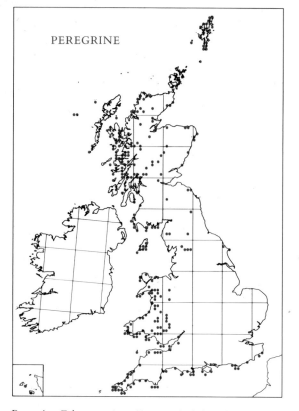

PEREGRINE

Peregrine *Falco peregrinus*. Sites at which breeding regularly occurred during 1900–50, but where breeding was not confirmed during 1968–72; three dots are omitted for security reasons (map by courtesy of Dr D. A. Ratcliffe)

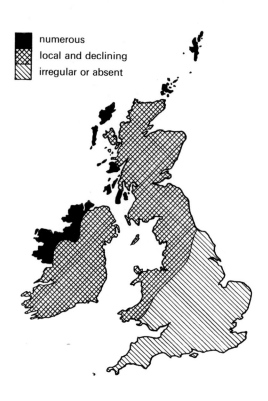

■ numerous
▨ local and declining
⧄ irregular or absent

Corncrake *Crex crex*. Breeding distribution in 1939 (from Norris 1945)

1879

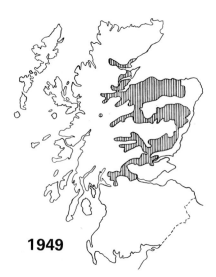

1949

Capercaillie *Tetrao urogallus*. Distribution in 1879 and 1949 (after Pennie 1950–51)

1947

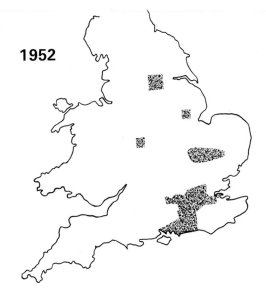

1952

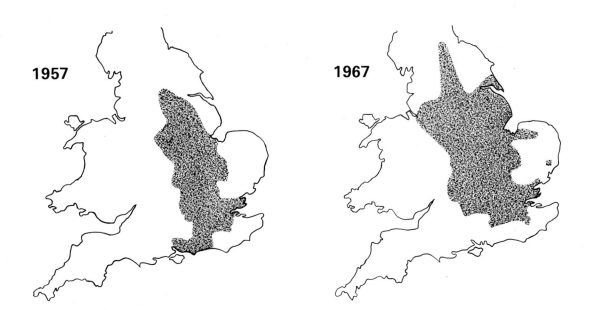

1957

1967

Little Ringed Plover *Charadrius dubius*. Breeding distribution in 1947, 1952, 1957 and 1967 (compiled from the literature)

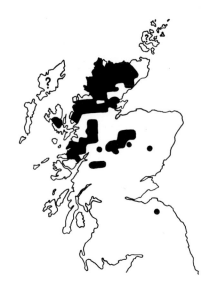

Woodcock *Scolopax rusticola*. Breeding distribution in 1940
(from Witherby *et al* 1938–41)

Greenshank *Tringa nebularia*. Breeding distribution in 1949
(from Nethersole-Thompson 1951)

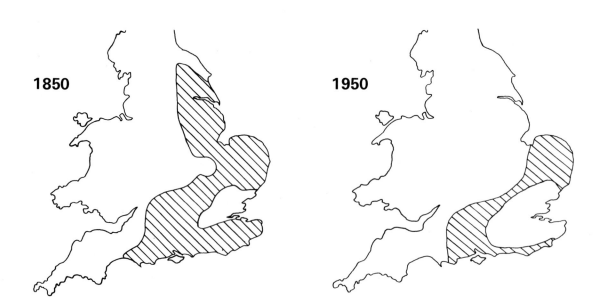

Stone Curlew *Burhinus oedicnemus*. Breeding distribution in 1850 and 1950 (compiled from the literature)

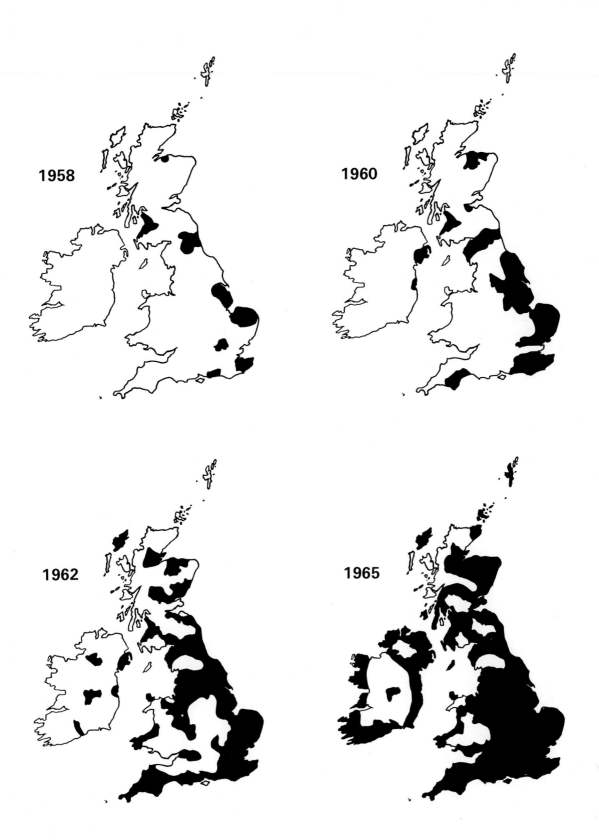

Collared Dove *Streptopelia decaocto*. Breeding distribution in 1958, 1960, 1962 and 1965 (after Hudson 1965, 1972)

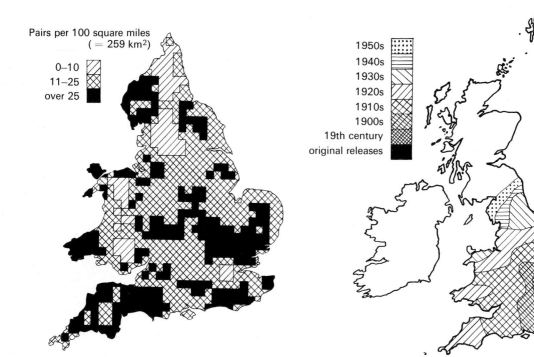

Barn Owl *Tyto alba*. Breeding distribution and density in England and Wales in 1932 (after Blaker 1934)

Little Owl *Athene noctua*. The British spread up to the 1950s (after Witherby *et al* 1938–41, and subsequent literature)

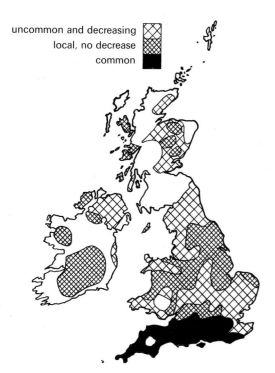

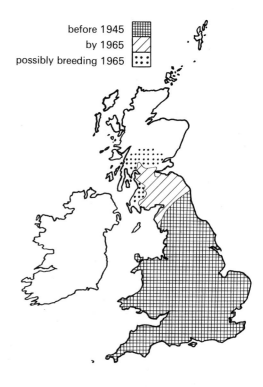

Nightjar *Caprimulgus europaeus*. Breeding status in 1957–58 (from Stafford 1962)

Green Woodpecker *Picus viridis*. Breeding status to 1965 (modified from Parslow 1967)

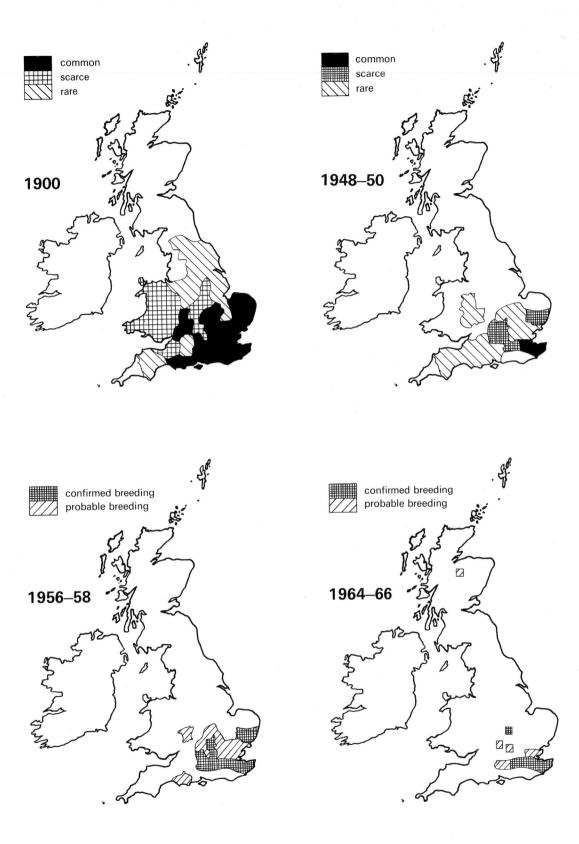

Wryneck *Jynx torquilla*. Breeding distribution in 1900, 1948–50, 1956–58 and 1964–66 (after Monk 1963 and Peal 1968)

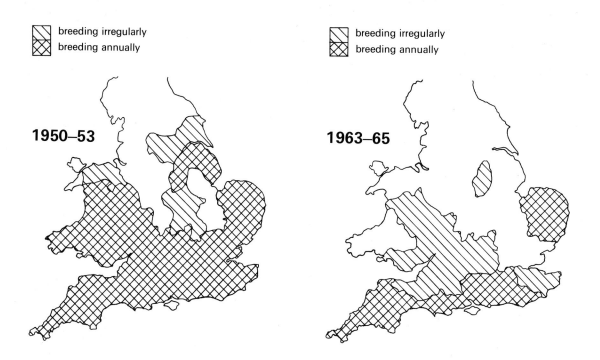

breeding irregularly
breeding annually

breeding irregularly
breeding annually

1950–53

1963–65

Woodlark *Lullula arborea*. Breeding distribution in 1950–53 and 1963–65 (after Parslow 1967)

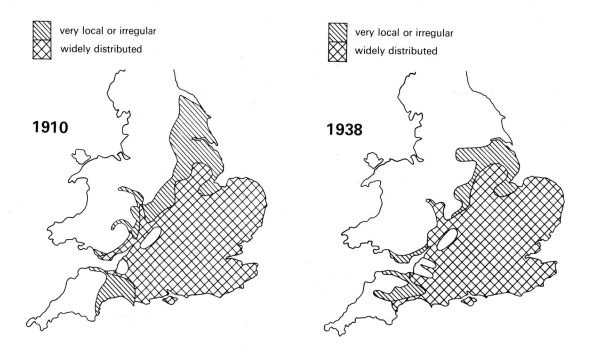

very local or irregular
widely distributed

very local or irregular
widely distributed

1910

1938

Nightingale *Luscinia megarhynchos*. Breeding distribution in 1910 and 1938 (after Ticehurst and Jourdain 1911, and Witherby *et al* 1938–41)

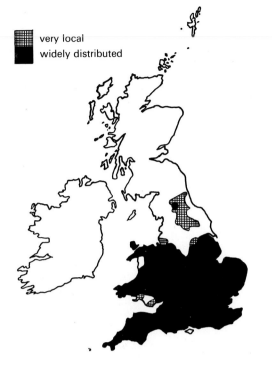

Nuthatch *Sitta europaea*. Breeding distribution in 1938 (after Witherby *et al* 1938–41)

Yellow Wagtail *Motacilla flava*. Breeding distribution in 1950 (after Smith 1950)

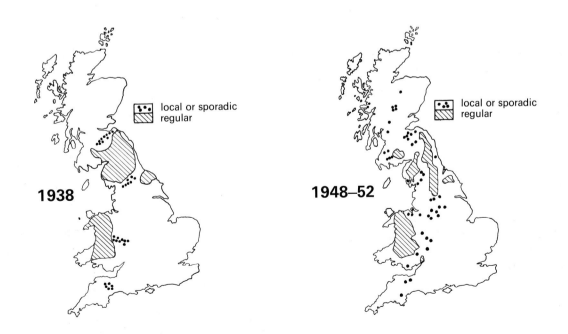

Pied Flycatcher *Ficedula hypoleuca*. Breeding distribution in 1938 and 1948–52 (from Campbell 1954–55)

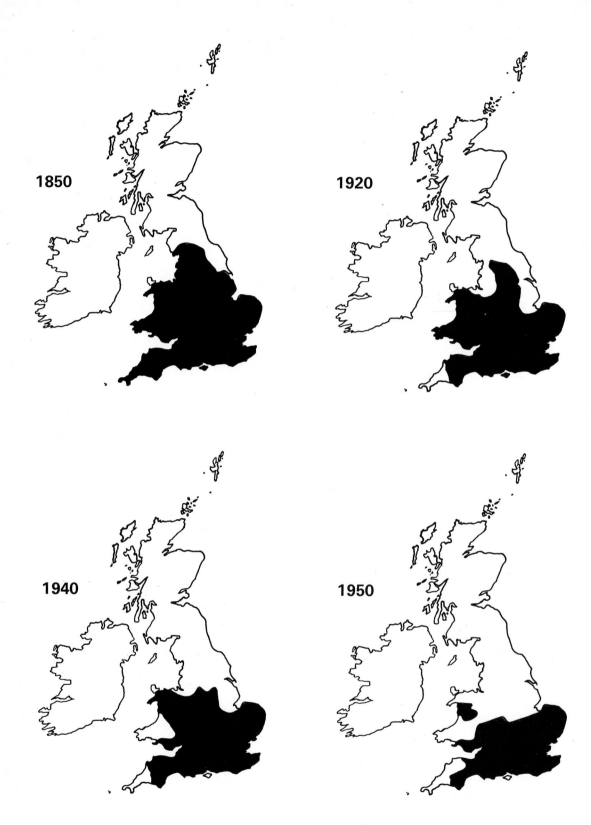

Red-backed Shrike *Lanius collurio*. Breeding distribution in 1850, 1920, 1940 and 1950 (from Peakall 1962)

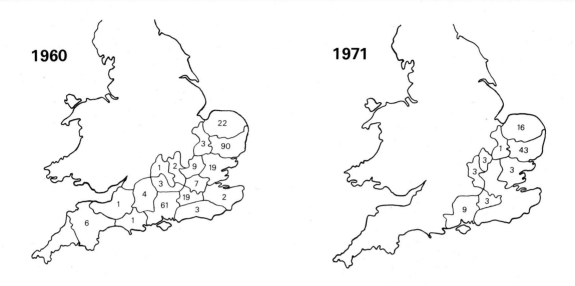

Red-backed Shrike *Lanius collurio*. Numbers of breeding pairs per occupied county in 1960 and 1971 (from Bibby 1973)

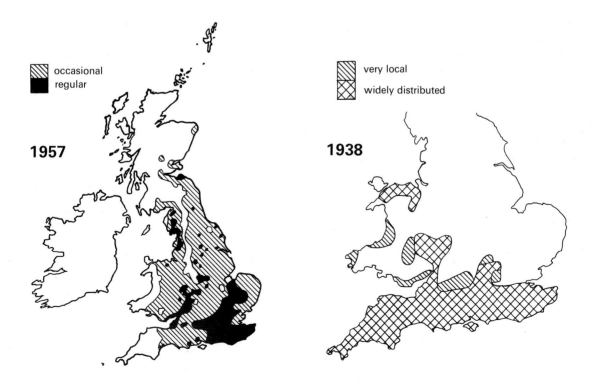

Hawfinch *Coccothraustes coccothraustes*. Breeding distribution in 1957 (after Mountfort 1957)

Cirl Bunting *Emberiza cirlus*. Breeding distribution in 1938 (from Witherby *et al* 1938–41)

Names of plants mentioned in the text

Vernacular names are listed alphabetically. Scientific names follow the nomenclature of DANDY, J. E., *List of British Vascular Plants* (1958); DANDY, J. E., Nomenclatural changes in the 'List of British Vascular Plants' (*Watsonia*, 7 (1969): 159–178); and MITCHELL, A., *A Field Guide to the Trees of Britain and Northern Europe* (1974). With two exceptions used for convenience (dwarf furze and sallow), the vernacular names follow DONY, J. G., F. H. PERRING and C. M. ROB, *English Names of Wild Flowers* (1974).

ALDER *Alnus glutinosa/incana*
APPLE *Malus sylvestris*
ASH *Fraxinus excelsior/ornus*

BAMBOO *Arundinaria/Bambusa/Phyllostachys* spp
BEECH *Fagus sylvatica*
BILBERRY *Vaccinium myrtillus*
BIRCH *Betula pendula/pubescens*
  SILVER *B. pendula*
BLACKBERRY *Rubus fruticosus* agg
BLACKTHORN *Prunus spinosa*
BLUEBELL *Endymion non-scriptus*
BRACKEN *Pteridium aquilinum*
BRAMBLE *Rubus fruticosus* agg
BUCKTHORN, SEA *Hippophae rhamnoides*
BULRUSH *Typha latifolia*
  LESSER *T. angustifolia*

CAMPION, RED *Silene dioica*
  WHITE *S. alba*
CEDAR, DEODAR *Cedrus deodara*
  WESTERN RED *Thuja plicata*
CHERRY *Prunus avium/cerasus/* etc
  WILD *P. avium*
CHESTNUT, SWEET *Castanea sativa*
CLOVER *Trifolium repens/pratense/* etc
CLUB-RUSH *Scirpus lacustris*
COTTON-GRASS *Eriophorum* spp
CROWBERRY *Empetrum nigrum*
CURRANT *Ribes rubrum/nigrum*
CYPRESS *Chamaecyparis/Cupressus* spp

DEODAR *Cedrus deodara*
DOCK *Rumex* spp

ELDER *Sambucus nigra*
ELM *Ulmus glabra/procera/carpinifolia/* × *hollandica*
  WYCH *U. glabra*

FIR, DOUGLAS *Pseudotsuga menziesii*
FUMITORY *Fumaria* spp
  COMMON *F. officinalis*
FURZE, DWARF *Ulex gallii/minor*

GLASSWORT *Salicornia* spp
GOOSEBERRY *Ribes uva-crispa*
GORSE *Ulex europaeus*
  DWARF *U. minor*
  WESTERN *U. gallii*

HAWTHORN *Crataegus monogyna/laevigata*
HAZEL *Corylus avellana*
HEATHER *Calluna vulgaris*
HEMLOCK, WESTERN *Tsuga heterophylla*
HOLLY *Ilex aquifolium*
HONEYSUCKLE *Lonicera periclymenum*
HORNBEAM *Carpinus betulus*

IVY *Hedera helix*

JUNIPER *Juniperus communis*

KALE *Brassica oleracea*
KNAPWEED *Centaurea nigra/scabiosa*

LARCH *Larix decidua/kaempferi*
LUPIN, TREE *Lupinus arboreus*

MAPLE *Acer* spp
  FIELD *A. campestre*
MARRAM *Ammophila arenaria*
MEADOWSWEET *Filipendula ulmaria*
MISTLETOE *Viscum album*
MOORGRASS, PURPLE *Molinia caerulea*
MYRTLE, BOG *Myrica gale*

NETTLE *Urtica dioica/urens*

OAK *Quercus borealis/cerris/ilex/robur/petraea*
  SESSILE *Q. petraea*
OLIVE *Olea europaea*
ORCHID, LIZARD *Himantoglossum hircinum*
OSIER *Salix viminalis*

PEAR *Pyrus communis/salicifolia*
PINE *Pinus* spp
  SCOTS *P. sylvestris*
PLUM *Prunus domestica*
PURSLANE, SEA *Halimione portulacoides*

RAPE *Brassica napus*
RASPBERRY *Rubus idaeus*
REDWOOD, COAST *Sequoia sempervirens*
  SIERRA *Sequoiadendron giganteum*
REED, COMMON *Phragmites australis*
RHODODENDRON *Rhododendron ponticum*

ROWAN *Sorbus aucuparia/discolor/commixta/hupehensis/*
  sargentiana/vilmorinii

SALLOW *Salix cinerea/aurita/caprea*
SEDGE *Carex* spp
SNOWBERRY *Symphoricarpos rivularis*
SORREL *Rumex acetosa/acetosella*
SPRUCE *Picea* spp
  NORWAY *P. abies*
  SITKA *P. sitchensis*
SUAEDA *Suaeda maritima/vera*
SUNFLOWER *Helianthus annuus*
SYCAMORE *Acer pseudoplatanus*

TEASEL *Dipsacus fullonum/pilosus*

THISTLE *Carduus/Cirsium/* etc
THRIFT *Armeria maritima*
TURNIP *Brassica rapa*

WATER-CRESS *Rorippa nasturtium-aquaticum/microphylla*
WILLOW *Salix* spp
  ALMOND *S. triandra*
  GOAT *S. caprea*
  GREY *S. cinerea*
WILLOWHERB *Epilobium* spp
  HOARY *E. parviflorum*
  ROSEBAY *E. angustifolium*

YEW *Taxus baccata*

Names of animals (other than birds) mentioned in the text

Vernacular names are listed alphabetically. Vernacular and scientific names both follow current usage, and have been checked by the staff of the BRC.

ANNELID Annelida
ANT Hymenoptera: Formicidae
  WOOD *Formica rufa*
APHID Hemiptera: Aphidoidea

BEE Hymenoptera: Apidae
BEETLE, DUNG Coleoptera: Scarabaeidae
  ELM-BARK Coleoptera: Scolytidae: *Scolytus scolytus*
BUTTERFISH *Pholis gunnellus*
BUTTERFLY Lepidoptera: Rhopalocera

COYPU *Myocastor coypus*
CRAB Decapoda: Brachyura
CRANEFLY Diptera: Tipulidae
CRICKET Orthoptera

DAMSELFLY Odonata: Zygoptera
DOG *Canis familiaris*
DRAGONFLY Odonata: Anisoptera

EARTHWORM Annelida: Oligochaeta
EEL *Anguilla anguilla*

FOX *Vulpes vulpes*
FROG *Rana temporaria*

GRASSHOPPER Orthoptera

HARE *Lepus capensis/timidus*

LEATHER-JACKET larva of cranefly Diptera: Tipulidae
LEECH Annelida: Hirundinea
LEMMING *Lemmus/Dicrostonyx* spp
  NORWEGIAN *L. lemmus*
LIMPET Mollusca: Prosobranchia
LIZARD *Lacerta* spp

MACKEREL *Scomber scombrus*
MANTIS Dictyoptera: Mantidae

MILLIPEDE Diplopoda
MINK *Mustela vison*
MOTH Lepidoptera: Heterocera
MOUSE *Apodemus/Mus* spp
  HOUSE *M. musculus*
  SHETLAND WOOD *A. sylvaticus granti*
  WOOD *A. sylvaticus*
MUSSEL Lammellibranchia
  ZEBRA *Dreissena polymorpha*

PERCH *Perca fluviatilis*
PIKE *Esox lucius*

RABBIT *Oryctolagus cuniculus*
RAT *Rattus norvegicus/rattus*
  BROWN *R. norvegicus*

SAITHE *Pollachius virens*
SALMON *Salmo salar*
SAND-EEL *Ammodytes/Gymnammodytes/Hyperoplus* spp
SAWFLY Hymenoptera: Symphyta
SHEEP *Ovis* (domestic)
SHREW *Sorex* spp
  COMMON *S. araneus*
  PYGMY *S. minutus*
SHRIMP, FRESHWATER Amphipoda
SLUG Mollusca
SNAIL Mollusca
SPIDER Arachnida
SPRAT *Sprattus sprattus*
SQUIRREL, RED *Sciurus vulgaris*

TROUT, BROWN *Salmo trutta*

VOLE *Arvicola/Clethrionomys/Microtus* spp
  BANK *C. glareolus*
  ORKNEY *M. arvalis orcadensis*
  SHORT-TAILED *M. agrestis*

WASP Hymenoptera: Vespidae
WEEVIL Coleoptera: Curculionidae

Acknowledgements

The BTO/IWC *Atlas* has been a co-operative project in every way. The fieldwork was done by an estimated 10,000 to 15,000 observers. It was originally the intention to acknowledge all these helpers by name in the book, but such a list would have run to several pages, even in small type, and would inevitably have been far from complete. After much discussion, the Atlas Working Group decided that those involved would prefer to be able to buy a cheaper book than to see thousands of names in print. Though they are anonymous, the greatest debt is owed to all those who took part.

The project was funded largely by two grants from the Leverhulme Trust, and otherwise partly by the Department of Lands of the Republic of Ireland and partly by the BTO. Grants towards the travelling expenses of fieldworkers were made by the British Ornithologists' Union, the Scottish Ornithologists' Club and the Royal Irish Academy.

The day-to-day running of the project, the obtaining of even coverage and the checking of results within each region were the responsibility of the regional organisers listed on pages 14–16. Their task extended over nine years, entirely in a spare-time capacity; I owe them all a great deal.

Though it is invidious to single out any one name, this must in fairness be done in the case of David Scott. Unpaid, he quietly and efficiently carried out the same duties for the 860 10-km squares in the Republic of Ireland as I did for the other 3,000-odd squares in a full-time, paid capacity.

Great assistance in obtaining extra data was given by G. L. Atkinson-Willes and Miss Barbara Yarker (Wildfowl Trust), David Saunders (Seabird Group), the Jourdain Society and the British Broadcasting Corporation. The administrative expertise of Major A. D. Peirse-Duncombe helped to ensure that coverage in Scotland was complete and even. Mrs Gwen Bonham efficiently handled the minutes of all Atlas Working Group meetings and supervised the plans for emergency coverage in the final season. Special sets of master cards for the squares still under-covered in 1971 were prepared by the late D. J. and Mrs Munns. Data were extracted from nest record cards by Richard Blindell, C. J. Mead and Miss Valerie Dornan. M. J. Everett readily answered queries relating to reserves of the Royal Society for the Protection of Birds. Many other individuals were unstinting over help within their specialist areas.

The master cards, listing more than a quarter of a million records, were photocopied free of charge by Rank Xerox Ltd.

All stages of map production, from punched tape to the dot-distributions shown here, were carried out by the staff of the Institute of Terrestrial Ecology's Biological Records Centre at Monks Wood Experimental Station, Abbots Ripton, Huntingdon, Cambridgeshire. I wish to thank especially the head of the BRC, Dr F. H. Perring, and Henry Arnold, John Heath and Miss Diana Scott for their efforts, as well as the ITE for their generosity in placing these facilities at our disposal, and the Nature Conservancy Council for financing the production of booklets of provisional maps which enabled a final check of records to be made by the regional *Atlas* organisers.

My fellow members of the Rare Breeding Birds Panel (A. W. Colling, Peter Conder, R. H. Dennis, I. J. Ferguson-Lees and David Lea) were very helpful in suggesting the safest way of displaying records of rare and vulnerable species. Specialist advisers who gave freely of their time were M. J. Everett, R. F. Porter, Dr D. A. Ratcliffe, Major R. F. Ruttledge, David Scott and J. Temple Lang.

The maps displaying past distributions and graphical figures were all drawn by Mrs Brenda Hudson, L. A. Batten drew the graphs of Common Birds Census indices, and Mrs Karen Ferguson-Lees put the special shading on the maps of rare species. The correct positioning of dots in the Northern Isles and Ireland on the main maps was carried out by Miss Stella Woodman.

Some of the final tedious stages of checking, as well as the extraction of data for the inset Quail map, were carried out by David Lawrence.

Although I wrote most of the texts, these were often revised and expanded by other members of BTO staff and 58 were entirely written by them. I wish particularly to thank these ten authors for the speed with which they helped at a crucial time in the production time-table: L. A. Batten, Dr J. J. M. Flegg, H. B. Ginn, D. E. Glue, Robert Hudson, C. J. Mead, R. A. Morgan, A. J. Prater, Robert Spencer and Kenneth Williamson.

Where possible, drafts of texts were read by specialists and the following, as well as BTO staff, helped in this way: J. Alder, the Rev E. A. Armstrong, G. L. Atkinson-Willes, C. J. Bibby, D. S. Bunn, E. J. M. Buxton, Dr C. J. Cadbury, Dr Bruce Campbell, Peter Conder, Dr J. C. Coulson, Dr P. J. Dare, M. Davenport, Peter Walters Davies, P. E. Davis, R. H. Dennis, R. Eastman, M. J. Everett, R. S. R. Fitter, G. H. Green, C. G. Headlam, E. D. H. Johnson, A. Lance, J. Temple Lang, David Lea, Dr N. W. Moore, Dr R. K. Murton, Dr J. B. Nelson, Desmond Nethersole-Thompson, Dr Ian Newton, G. C. Noonan, E. R. Parrinder, R. E. F. Peal, Dr I. D. Pennie, Dr C. M. Perrins, N. Picozzi, Dr G. R. Potts, Ian Prestt, Dr D. A. Ratcliffe, C. M. Reynolds, D. R. Saunders, Dr D. C. Seel, Dr K. E. L. Simmons, Dr D. W. Snow, H. N. Southern, Dr J. Stafford, Dr J. D. Summers-Smith, C. R. Tubbs, R. J. Tulloch, Mrs M. Vizoso (Miss M. Shorten), Dr Adam Watson, Philip Wayre,

J. Wilson, N. A. Wood and Dr W. B. Yapp.

Every text was also read by David Scott, and many of them by G. R. Humphreys and Major R. F. Rutt-ledge, particularly to check all references to Ireland, and, finally, by either I. J. Ferguson-Lees, Robert Spencer or Kenneth Williamson. As well as by my-self, the proofs were checked by I. J. Ferguson-Lees, J. S. Furphy and David Scott.

Densities derived from Common Birds Census data were calculated by L. A. Batten, assisted by C. J. Mead, who generously allowed their work to be in-serted into the relevant texts. C. J. Mead checked all mathematical calculations. Robert Hudson went to endless trouble to supply references from the BTO library, and also checked those listed at the end of each account. Mrs Diana Bertram learnt to decipher my almost-illegible handwriting and typed the first drafts of my 168 texts. Mrs E. Murray and Miss S. Woodman typed many drafts over a three-month period.

Since their work was referred to so frequently and provided the basis for so many texts, the authors of two books, *Breeding Birds of Britain and Ireland* (1973) by John Parslow and *A Field Guide to Birds' Nests* (1972) by Bruce Campbell and James Ferguson-Lees, deserve special acknowledgement. Sir Christo-pher Lever generously loaned the typescript of parts of his forthcoming book on animals introduced by man into Britain.

The production of vignettes of each species by the nine artists was arranged and supervised by Robert Gillmor.

My wife, Erika Sharrock, gave me almost daily assistance throughout eight years with those jobs demanding two people, as well as frequently taking other work off my hands.

All members of the Atlas Working Group were unstinting in their help, and I found it a pleasure to be a part of such a happy team. Kenneth Williamson devoted some three months of work to editing, in-corporating material from numerous sources, in-cluding the comments of specialist referees, and fitting the revised texts into the space available. The work in the final stages also often fell on the shoulders of Robert Spencer and Trevor Poyser.

I wish to give most special thanks to James Ferguson-Lees, Chairman of the Atlas Working Group, for his meticulous and kindly steering of the whole project from conception to conclusion, and for his advice and help given to me personally on many occasions.

J. T. R. SHARROCK

Index of bird names

Vernacular names are indexed under the last word, and scientific nomenclature under the generic name. The principal references to all the main species can easily be identified because they are given adjacent page numbers hyphenated; other references are indexed only where a significant point is stated or mapped.

Acanthis cannabina, 418–419, 420, 422
  flammea, 11, 416, 422–423
  flavirostris, 418, 420–421
Accipiter gentilis, 11, 110–111
  nisus, 20, 108–109, 146, 426
Acrocephalus arundinaceus, 11
  melanopogon, 453
  palustris, 20, 364–365
  schoenobaenus, 358, 362, 364, 366–367
  scirpaceus, 362–363, 364, 366
Aegithalos caudatus, 318–319
Aix galericulata, 72–73, 74
  sponsa, 74–75, 451
Alauda arvensis, 280–281, 324
Alca torda, 230–231, 236
Alcedo atthis, 20, 266–267, 320, 388
Alectoris chukar, 140
  rufa, 140–141, 142
Alopochen aegyptiaca, 96–97
Anas acuta, 68–69
  clypeata, 70–71
  crecca, 60–61
  penelope, 60, 66–67
  platyrhynchos, 58–59, 60, 86
  querquedula, 62–63
  strepera, 64–65
Anser anser, 98–99
  cygnoides, 453
Anthus pratensis, 394–395, 396, 398
  spinoletta, 398–399
  trivialis, 394, 396–397
Apus apus, 264–265
Aquila chrysaetos, 20, 104–105, 290
Ardea cinerea, 20, 21, 54–55, 296
  purpurea, 11, 446
Arenaria interpres, 11
Asio flammeus, 20, 260–261
  otus, 20, 256, 258–259
Athene noctua, 11, 20, 254–255, 256, 460
Avocet, 198–199
Aythya ferina, 78, 80–81
  fuligula, 60, 76, 78–79, 80
  marila, 76–77

Bee-eater, 453
Bittern, 56–57
  Little, 11, 446
Blackbird, 330, 334, 338, 340–341, 392, 430
Blackcap, 368–369, 370
Bluethroat, 450
Bombycilla garrulus, 450
Bonxie, 204–205, 206
Botaurus stellaris, 56–57
Brambling, 430, 450–451
Branta canadensis, 96, 100–101
  leucopsis, 453

Bucephala clangula, 82–83
Budgerigar, 452
Bullfinch, 410, 426–427
Bunting, Cirl, 11, 434, 436–437, 465
  Corn, 432–433, 434, 438
  Ortolan, 11
  Reed, 358, 434, 438–439
  Snow, 440–441
Burhinus oedicnemus, 11, 20, 202–203, 458
Bustard, Great, 453
Buteo buteo, 106–107, 455
Buzzard, 106–107, 455
  Honey, 114–115

Cairina moschata, 453
Calidris alpina, 194–195
  temminckii, 192–193
Canary, 453
Capercaillie, 20, 138–139, 456
Caprimulgus europaeus, 11, 262–263, 460
Carduelis carduelis, 414–415, 418
  chloris, 412–413, 426
  spinus, 11, 416–417
Carpodacus erythrinus, 11
Cepphus grylle, 234–235
Certhia brachydactyla, 322, 450
  familiaris, 322–323
Cettia cetti, 11, 356–357
Chaffinch, 354, 378, 384, 392, 430–431, 451
Charadrius alexandrinus, 448
  dubius, 11, 166, 168–169, 457
  hiaticula, 166–167
Chiffchaff, 378, 380–381, 382
Chlidonias niger, 449
Chough, 298, 304–305
Chrysolophus amherstiae, 20, 148, 150–151
  pictus, 20, 148–149, 150
Chukar, 140
Cinclus cinclus, 326–327, 402
Circus aeruginosus, 116–117
  cyaneus, 11, 118–119
  pygargus, 120–121
Cisticola juncidis, 11
Clangula hyemalis, 447
Coccothraustes coccothraustes, 410–411, 465
Colinus virginianus, 20, 451
Columba livia, 18, 126, 238, 240–241, 242
  oenas, 238–239
  palumbus, 242–243
Coot, 160–161
Cormorant, 21, 50–51, 52
Corncrake, 11, 20, 156–157, 456
Corvus corax, 17, 290–291, 294
  corone, 17, 292–295, 324
  frugilegus, 17, 292, 296–297, 298
  monedula, 17, 292, 298–299, 304

The British Trust for Ornithology

Founded in 1933, the British Trust for Ornithology has throughout its history been deeply committed to the idea of membership participation. Often it is difficult, or even impossible, to evaluate the findings of a single observer, but let 500 or 1,000 pool their results and the broad picture starts to emerge. There could be no more convincing demonstration of this than the maps which form this *Atlas*.

Among its many functions the BTO administers the national Bird Ringing Scheme and organises a Common Birds Census, designed to detect changes in the population levels of our commoner species. For similar reasons, the birds of our estuaries are regularly censused by Trust members, as is the population of our Heronries, while a Nest Records Scheme measures, year by year, the breeding success of our birds.

Thus, the theme common to all BTO studies is that the observations of individual members, guided and co-ordinated by a small research staff, supply information vital to the task of conservation. A measure of this usefulness is that much of the research is done at the request of, and with financial support from, the Nature Conservancy Council.

The members of the Trust come from all walks of life, and the keen beginner is as welcome as the expert. The postal lending library operated by the Trust is unparalleled in any country, while the many conferences it organises are a happy amalgam of information and enthusiasm. For details of membership write to: Assistant Secretary, BTO, Beech Grove, Tring, Herts HP23 5NR.

The Irish Wildbird Conservancy

The Irish Wildbird Conservancy is the largest organisation in Ireland concerned solely with wildlife conservation. The IWC works to improve legislation to conserve wild birds and their habitats; fights environmental pollution; sponsors and carries out surveys to establish a serious basis for conservation and to increase our knowledge of Irish birds. The provisions of the new Wildlife Act in the Republic of Ireland are firmly based on principles proposed by the organisations which amalgamated to form the IWC in 1968. A number of important sanctuaries are maintained, of which the best known are the White-fronted Goose refuge on the Wexford Slobs, owned jointly with the Department of Lands, and Tern Island in Wexford Harbour, the largest European breeding colony of Roseate Terns. Co-operation with the BTO is close and this *Atlas* is only one of three major surveys which have been carried out jointly by both organisations in recent years.

There are branches of the IWC in Cork, Dublin and Wicklow, Galway, North Munster, Waterford and Wexford. New members are put in touch with their local Branch Secretaries and invited to participate in field activities. Members receive a quarterly newsletter and the comprehensive Annual Report and Conservation Review. For details of membership write to: The Irish Wildbird Conservancy, c/o Royal Irish Academy, 19 Dawson Street, Dublin 2, Ireland.